Library of America, a nonprofit organization,
champions our nation's cultural heritage
by publishing America's greatest writing in
authoritative new editions and providing resources
for readers to explore this rich, living legacy.

WAR NO MORE

WAR NO MORE

THREE CENTURIES OF AMERICAN ANTIWAR AND PEACE WRITING

Lawrence Rosenwald, *editor*

THE LIBRARY OF AMERICA

Visit our website at www.loa.org.

Some of the material in this volume is reprinted
by permission of the holders of copyright and publication rights.
Every effort has been made to contact the copyright holders.
If an owner has been unintentionally omitted,
acknowledgment will gladly be made in future printings.
See Sources and Acknowledgments on page 789 for further information.

This paper meets the requirements of
ANSI/NISO Z39.48–1992 (Permanence of Paper).

Distributed to the trade in the United States
by Penguin Random House Inc.
and in Canada by Penguin Random House Canada Ltd.

Library of Congress Control Number: 2015951696
ISBN 978–1–59853–473–3

First Printing
The Library of America—278

Manufactured in the United States of America

War No More:
Three Centuries of American Antiwar and Peace Writing
is published with support from

THE BERKLEY FOUNDATION

and will be kept in print by its gift to
the Guardians of American Letters Fund,
established by The Library of America
to ensure that every volume in the series
will be permanently available.

Contents

Robert Lowell

Bayard Rustin

Leo Szilard

Dorothy Day

Kurt Vonnegut

Edgar L. Jones

Naomi Replansky

Karl Shapiro

William Stafford

Howard Schoenfeld

General Advisory Committee to the U.S. Atomic Energy Commission

Ed McCurdy

Camilo Mejía

Andrew J. Bacevich

Philip Metres

Austin Smith

Nicholson Baker

Anne Montgomery

Mike Kirby

Jane Hirshfield

Illustrations

1. Jane Addams and Emily Greene Balch aboard the *Noordam*, April 1915.
2. Dorothy Day as a young journalist for *The Call*, February 9, 1917.
3. Jeannette Rankin addresses a Union Square rally, September 6, 1924.
4. Bayard Rustin in the Lewisburg Federal Penitentiary, October 12, 1945.
5. Juanita and Wally Nelson in 1946.
6. Albert S. Bigelow beside the *Golden Rule*, 1958.
7. A. J. Muste launches a Committee for Nonviolent Action civil disobedience campaign, July 1, 1959.
8. Thomas Merton and Daniel Berrigan at a Gethsemani Abbey Peacemakers Retreat, August 1962.
9. Grace Paley at an anti-Vietnam War demonstration, March 9, 1965.
10. Burning draft cards with homemade napalm at Catonsville, Maryland, May 17, 1968.
11. Joan Baez at an antiwar rally in London, May 29, 1965.
12. Pete Seeger at the Peace Moratorium in New York, November 13, 1969.
13. Disabled veteran Ron Kovic protesting conditions in VA hospitals, February 28, 1974.
14. Barbara Deming at the Seneca Women's Encampment for a Future of Peace and Justice, summer 1983.
15. Women spelling out PEACE, November 12, 2002.
16. Zack de la Rocha at a protest outside the Democratic National Convention, August 27, 2008.

Foreword

BY JAMES CARROLL

"The essential American soul," D.H. Lawrence observed in writing about James Fenimore Cooper's Leatherstocking tales, "is hard, isolate, stoic, and a killer." That harsh assessment, one must acknowledge, has been borne out across the centuries by a still-unchecked current of war, but through the essential American soul runs a countercurrent of peace, and this volume documents it. Democratic liberalism itself aims at a civics of compromise, while the United States Constitution establishes a structure of amendment that amounts to a politics of self-criticism. Compromise and self-criticism: nonviolence is essential to both.

Wars, though, have defined the nation's narrative, especially once the apocalyptic fratricide of the Civil War set the current running in blood—toward the Jim Crow reenslavement of African Americans, further genocidal assaults against native peoples, imperial adventures abroad, a two-phased World War that permanently militarized the American economy and spawned a bifurcated imagination that so requires an evil enemy that the Cold War morphed seamlessly into the War on Terror. The hard, isolate, and stoic heroes sanctify this dynamic, and are sacrificed to it. Who objects?

Well, Americans sung and unsung do. Henry David Thoreau, repudiating slavery and the U.S. war against Mexico, defined a mode of conscientious objection ("Let your life be a counter friction to stop the machine") that would shape an alternative politics across the globe, across a century, ultimately inspiring Dr. Martin Luther King Jr. and his great cloud of witnesses. But far less celebrated citizens have preached sermons, written letters to presidents, composed statements to juries, penned meditations in prison, and posted manifestos. They are poets ("I shall die," Edna St. Vincent Millay wrote, "but that is all I shall do for death"), pop singers, politicians, common soldiers, activists ("Do you have the guts," Stokely Carmichael asked, "to say 'Hell no!'?"), parents, philosophers, Quakers, physicians, nuns, rabbis, and priests ("Our apologies, good friends," Father Daniel Berrigan declared in court, "for the burning of paper instead of children"). Perhaps the author of the most powerful antiwar statement ever made was the U.S. Army major who, in 1968, told Peter Arnett, "It became necessary to destroy the town to save it."

Conventional wisdom says that the voices of peace are inevitably drowned out by the trumpets of war, but this volume suggests otherwise. The nuclear age itself, by threatening human self-extinction, launched a moral mobilization that still stirs the national conscience, and its testimonies are here. Antiwar protests could not halt the horrors of Vietnam, but they stopped cold the open-ended Pentagon escalation toward absolute destruction. No expert in realpolitik imagined that the millennial conflict between Moscow and Washington could end without mass carnage, but grassroots alarm about nuclear war (sparked, for example, by atomic physicists who denounced "a weapon of genocide") enabled just such an unexpected outcome. Virtue's greatest modern triumph was the nonviolent dismantling of the Berlin Wall. Its lesson must be cherished, and taught.

Because the human future, for the first time in history, is itself imperiled by the ancient impulse to respond to violence with violence, the cry "War no more!" can be heard coming back at us from time ahead, from the as yet unborn men and women—the ultimate voices of peace—who simply will not come into existence if the essential American soul does not change. The voices of this book, a replying chorus of hope, insist that such change is possible.

Introduction

BY LAWRENCE ROSENWALD

COMMITTED pacifists—those for whom "war is wrong—wrong yesterday, wrong today, wrong forever," as Ezra Heywood put it in 1863—will find in *War No More* a means of reaching out and making contact with their traditions, of finding strength and illumination in that contact and shock of recognition. But most prospective readers of the book will not be so committed; what does the anthology offer them?

First, a transformative sense that the writing animated by the antiwar impulse is more distinguished and varied than most portraits of pacifists would suggest it could be. Pacifists and war opponents are often seen as cerebral, pious, humorless, self-righteous, and useless. (Hence the most frequent taunt directed to protesters at peace rallies: "Get a job!") Some of the writers represented here are indeed pious, some are nearly self-righteous, few are funny. But a just characterization of pacifists and their writing requires a richer vocabulary: visionary, sensual, prophetic, outraged, introspective, self-doubting, fantastic, irreverent, witty, obscene, uncertain, heartbroken. All of those traits are on display here.

But the literary rationale has to be supplemented by two others. One is about America. The United States is the only country in the world to have dropped nuclear bombs in wartime. Our current military budget accounts for 37 percent of world military spending, and is roughly equal to the nine next largest military budgets combined. Our heroes, from George Washington to "American Sniper" Chris Kyle, are often soldiers. Which may make it surprising that American antiwar writing is so vital, and has been since the world's first peace societies were established here more than two centuries ago. Or perhaps it makes that fact utterly predictable; the intensity of American warmaking is the context from which the intensity of American antiwar writing emerges. "The United States has more often been teacher than student in the history of the nonviolent idea," wrote Staughton and Alice Lynd, and something similar might be claimed for our contribution to the literature of war resistance. At every turn in American history, from the Revolution to the War on Terror, the writers in this book have begged, prayed, demanded, and in some instances suffered heroically to bring an end to particular wars or war in general. They have seldom succeeded; but gathered together, their words constitute a tradition as exceptional as our military might.

The other rationale is about the moment we are living in. In earlier times, when it was generally conceded that war, however lamentable, was occasionally necessary and just, and as inevitable as the progression of the seasons, a volume of antiwar writing would have been taken to express the idealistic strivings of utopians, admirable but quaint and shallow. For much of that earlier history, supporters of peace movements were indeed utopians, holding on to a vision of universal peace without much of a strategy for winning what William James called "the war against war"; it was enough to fight the good fight, to remain pure in an inevitably fallen world.

With American wars in Afghanistan and Iraq still very present in our consciousness, a War on Terror still ongoing, and an antiwar movement that sometimes seems anemic in comparison with those of generations past, it may be difficult to believe that things have changed—but in recent years they have. The annual editions of the *Human Security Report* suggest a gradual decline in the number and intensity of wars. The Harvard psychologist Steven Pinker traces this development to the growing power of the better angels of our nature. The political scientist Joshua S. Goldstein attributes it to the growing sophistication of those whose business and expertise it is to avert or resolve conflict. The distinguished military historian John Keegan, no supporter of pacifists, writes in *A History of Warfare* that "despite confusion and uncertainty, it seems just possible to glimpse the emerging outline of a world without war." War, he argues, "may well be ceasing to commend itself to human beings as a desirable or productive, let alone rational, means of reconciling their discontents. This is not mere idealism." In that context, this anthology is not only a collection of distinguished texts, not only a document of a vital strain of American thought and feeling, but also a chronicle of the possible emergence of a new way of thinking about the necessities of human life.

So much for the why of the anthology, and now for the how. *War No More* gathers more than three centuries of American antiwar and peace writing, from precolonial Native American traditions and the petitions of the early Quakers all the way to the present moment. "American" is simple; it means "written by people one can plausibly call Americans." The other two terms are surprisingly capacious. Antiwar writing includes work that takes a position against war in general or a particular war. But it also includes work that depicts antiwar action: peace marches, attacks on draft boards, trials of conscientious objectors, the prison experiences that follow them. Such work need not support the action it depicts, only do justice to it.

Establishing the boundaries for the former category was sometimes tricky. Many works commended to me as antiwar writing seemed to me excellent but not oppositional. They were honest accounts of war, realistic and not romantic, but not at odds with supporting the war they depicted, and some were written by people who had in fact supported the war or indeed fought in it. Still, some works of that sort are here—for example, Ambrose Bierce's "Chickamauga," which was written by an unrepentant Civil War soldier and on a strict reading takes no position about war at all, but in which war's horrors are so unsparingly depicted that they seem to become exhibits in a case against war itself.

Peace writing is a less familiar category than antiwar writing, and less easy to define. But some works by their nature call the category into being; they feel closely related to the antiwar texts, but are neither oppositional nor documentary. They are trying to imagine peace not as a cease-fire but as, in Denise Levertov's words, "an energy field more intense than war." The first work in the anthology offers an image of that energy field: the Iroquois Tree of the Great Peace. The last does too, Jane Hirshfield's "I Cast My Hook, I Decide to Make Peace," a homelier image but equally moving: "I put peace in a warm place, towel-covered, to proof, / then into an oven. I wait."

Some who wrote me while I was assembling the anthology pressed me to make it a record of debates about war and wars.

I am grateful for that pressure, but have not yielded to it. None of the work included here is written on behalf of going to war, however alive and engaging such writing has been. That is not to say that the work included here is uniform in viewpoint. The arguments against war are both religious and secular, general and particular, full of love and full of anger, certain and full of doubt. The accounts of antiwar action are sometimes by zealous participants, sometimes by skeptical, sharp-eyed journalists. Conscientious objectors are depicted by themselves, by sympathetic allies, by unsympathetic administrators.

One boundary that was not hard to establish was that of genre; there is none. The anthology includes, in whole or in excerpts, cartoons, essays, interviews, leaflets, letters both private and public, memoirs, novels, parodies, plays, poems, scriptures, sermons, short stories, song lyrics, speeches, and treatises. Anything alive on the page was eligible.

These diversities of genre and viewpoint distinguish the anthology from all other anthologies comparable to it. There are excellent anthologies of antiwar poetry, of antiwar oratory, of antiwar testimony and memoir. There is Staughton and Alice Lynd's wonderful *Nonviolence in America*, full of prose documents by advocates of nonviolent action. There is no other anthology in which dramatists and cartoonists, poets and historians, parodists and visionaries, zealots and skeptics are in conversation together. Some of the writers, like Howard Zinn and Daniel Berrigan, were in actual conversation with one another during their lives. Some of the writers are thoughtfully commenting on the writers who came before them, for example, Barbara Ehrenreich on William James. Sometimes, though, the writers were utterly unaware of one another, however their thoughts and images resembled one another. The anthology both documents a conversation and creates one.

The richness of the conversation going on here is a joy for the anthologist but also a challenge. The antiwar impulse, and the related impulse to imagine peace, have yielded an abundance of distinguished, living work; I had enough material to make several anthologies. The texts included here are those I thought created the best conversation on resistance to war and imagining peace. It is a conversation not yet fully described by historians, nor fully available to activists, but living in these pages.

WAR NO MORE

IROQUOIS TRADITION

"The Tree of the Great Peace"—an excerpt from the prefatory articles to the Constitution of the Iroquois Confederacy—predates the arrival of European colonists in what is now the United States, and has not historically been a part of the tradition of antiwar and peace writing that this anthology documents. Though it remained incompletely transcribed and published until the early twentieth century, this constitution reflects a continuous oral tradition and cultural practices that emerged in precolonial times, c. 1450–1600 by consensus estimates, when the legendary Dekanawideh, the "Great Peacemaker," united five warring Iroquois tribes to begin the *Haudenosaunee*, or Five Nations. (The Five are now Six: Cayuga, Mohawk, Oneida, Onondaga, Seneca, and Tuscarora.)

The peace celebrated here was extended to outsiders only on Iroquois terms, and was sometimes vehemently refused; the Iroquois Constitution also contains rules for war. And yet, across time and great cultural distance, aspects of Dekanawideh's peacemaking seem widely resonant. One is his use of objects from the natural landscape as images of the peace he sought. Another is his concrete emphasis on war's weapons, and on the means by which those weapons can be rendered undangerous—not, as in the biblical image, beaten into plowshares, but here (and later in the passage from the Book of Mormon) simply buried, like so much radioactive waste.

"The Tree of the Great Peace"

I AM Dekanawideh and with the Five Nations' confederate lords I plant the Tree of the Great Peace. I plant it in your territory Adodarhoh and the Onondaga Nation, in the territory of you who are fire keepers.

I name the tree the Tree of the Great Long Leaves. Under the shade of this Tree of the Great Peace we spread the soft, white, feathery down of the globe thistle as seats for you, Adodarhoh and your cousin lords. . . . There shall you sit and watch the council fire of the Confederacy of the Five Nations.

Roots have spread out from the Tree of the Great Peace . . . and the name of these roots is the Great White Roots of Peace. If any man of any nation outside of the Five Nations shall show a desire to obey the laws of the Great Peace . . . they may trace the roots to their source . . . and they shall be welcomed to take shelter beneath the Tree of the Long Leaves.

The smoke of the confederate council fire shall ever ascend and shall pierce the sky so that all nations may discover the central council fire of the Great Peace.

I, Dekanawideh, and the confederate lords now uproot the tallest pine tree and into the cavity thereby made we cast all weapons of war. Into the depths of the earth, down into the deep underearth currents of water flowing into unknown regions, we cast all weapons of strife. We bury them from sight forever and plant again the tree. Thus shall all Great Peace be established and hostilities shall no longer be known between the Five Nations but only peace to a united people.

JOHN WOOLMAN

The Quaker diarist John Woolman (1720–1772) was the most important early American advocate and practitioner of nonviolence. At
twenty-three, having begun his adult life as a tailor and merchant
in Mount Holly, New Jersey, he set out as an itinerant missionary,
hoping to spread the "truth and light" of the Society of Friends.
He would make dozens of similar excursions in subsequent years:
to Virginia, Maryland, and North Carolina, where he met Quaker
slaveholders, persuading many to renounce the practice; to Wyalus-
ing, Pennsylvania, encouraging reconciliation between settlers and
American Indians; and finally to England, where shortly before his
death he convinced the Quakers of London to join him in his opposition to slavery. He was indefatigable, implacable, humorless, and
somehow lovable. Charles Lamb urged young readers to "get the
writings of John Woolman by heart; and love the early Quakers."

Almost two hundred and fifty years after his death, Woolman is still
quoted at antiwar gatherings. He remains most relevant and influential, perhaps, for his principled insistence on the need to discern and
root out the "seeds of war" in the life of the individual: the willingness to pay taxes for wars, the holding of great estates, the wearing of
dyed cloth all among them. For Woolman as for twentieth-century
feminists, the personal is political.

FROM
The Journal of John Woolman

A few years past, money being made current in our province for carrying on wars, and to be sunk by taxes laid on the
inhabitants, my mind was often affected with the thoughts of
paying such taxes, and I believe it right for me to preserve a
memorandum concerning it. I was told that Friends in England
frequently paid taxes when the money was applied to such
purposes. I had conference with several noted Friends on the
subject, who all favoured the payment of such taxes, some of
whom I preferred before myself; and this made me easier for
a time. Yet there was in the deeps of my mind a scruple which
I never could get over, and at certain times I was greatly dis-
tressed on that account.

I all along believed that there were some upright-hearted men who paid such taxes, but could not see that their example was a sufficient reason for me to do so, while I believed that the spirit of Truth required of me as an individual to suffer patiently the distress of goods rather than pay actively.

I have been informed that Thomas à Kempis lived and died in the profession of the Roman Catholic religion, and in reading his writings I have believed him to be a man of a true Christian spirit, as fully so as many who died martyrs because they could not join with some superstitions in that church. All true Christians are of the same spirit but their gifts are diverse, Jesus Christ appointing to each one their peculiar office agreeable to his infinite wisdom.

John Huss contended against the errors crept into the church, in opposition to the Council of Constance, which the historian reports to have consisted of many thousands people. He modestly vindicated the cause which he believed was right, and though his language and conduct toward his judges appear to have been respectful, yet he never could be moved from the principles settled in his mind. To use his own words, "This I most humbly require and desire you all, even for his sake who is the God of us all, that I be not compelled to the thing which my conscience doth repugn or strive against." And again, in his answer to the Emperor, "I refuse nothing, most noble Emperor, whatsoever the Council shall decree or determine upon me, this only one thing I except, that I do not offend God and my conscience."—Foxe's *Acts and Monuments*, p. 233. At length, rather than act contrary to that which he believed the Lord required of him, he chose to suffer death by fire. Thomas à Kempis, without disputing against the articles then generally agreed to, appears to have laboured, by a pious example as well as by preaching and writing, to promote virtue and an inward spiritual religion. And I believe they were both sincere-hearted followers of Christ.

True charity is an excellent virtue, and to sincerely labour for their good whose belief in all points doth not agree with ours is a happy case. To refuse the active payment of a tax which our Society generally paid was exceeding disagreeable, but to do a thing contrary to my conscience appeared yet more dreadful.

When this exercise came upon me, I knew of none under the like difficulty, and in my distress I besought the Lord to enable me to give up all, that so I might follow him wheresoever he was pleased to lead me. And under this exercise I went to our Yearly Meeting at Philadelphia in 1755, at which a committee was appointed, some from each Quarter, to correspond with the Meeting for Sufferings in London, and another to visit our Monthly and Quarterly Meetings. And after their appointment, before the last adjournment of the meeting, it was agreed on in the meeting that these two committees should meet together in Friends' schoolhouse in the city, at a time when the meeting stood adjourned, to consider some things in which the cause of Truth was concerned; and these committees meeting together had a weighty conference in the fear of the Lord, at which time I perceived there were many Friends under a scruple like that before-mentioned.

As scrupling to pay a tax on account of the application hath seldom been heard of heretofore, even amongst men of integrity who have steadily borne their testimony against outward wars in their time, I may here note some things which have occurred to my mind as I have been inwardly exercised on that account.

From the steady opposition which faithful Friends in early times made to wrong things then approved of, they were hated and persecuted by men living in the spirit of this world, and suffering with firmness they were made a blessing to the church, and the work prospered. It equally concerns men in every age to take heed to their own spirit, and in comparing their situation with ours, it looks to me there was less danger of their being infected with the spirit of this world, in paying their taxes, than there is of us now. They had little or no share in civil government, and many of them declared they were through the power of God separated from the spirit in which wars were; and being afflicted by the rulers on account of their testimony, there was less likelihood of uniting in spirit with them in things inconsistent with the purity of Truth. We, from the first settlement of this land, have known little or no troubles of that sort. The profession which for a time was accounted reproachful, at length the uprightness of our predecessors being understood by the rulers and their innocent sufferings moving them, the way of worship was tolerated, and many of our members in these colonies became active in civil government. Being thus tried with favour and prosperity, this world hath appeared inviting. Our minds have been turned to the improvement of our country, to merchandise and sciences, amongst which are many things useful, being followed in pure wisdom; but in our present condition, that a carnal mind is gaining upon us I believe will not be denied.

Some of our members who are officers in civil government are in one case or other called upon in their respective stations to assist in things relative to the wars. Such being in doubt whether to act or crave to be excused from their office, seeing their brethren united in the payment of a tax to carry on the said wars, might think their case not much different and so quench the tender movings of the Holy Spirit in their minds. And thus by small degrees there might be an approach toward that of fighting, till we came so near it as that the distinction would be little else but the name of a peaceable people.

It requires great self-denial and resignation of ourselves to God to attain that state wherein we can freely cease from fighting when wrongfully invaded, if by our fighting there were a probability of overcoming the invaders. Whoever rightly attains to it does in some degree feel that spirit in which our Redeemer gave his life for us, and through divine goodness many of our predecessors and many now living have learned this blessed lesson. But many others, having their religion chiefly by education and not being enough acquainted with that cross which crucifies to the world, do manifest a temper distinguishable from that of an entire trust in God.

In calmly considering these things, it hath not appeared strange to me that an exercise hath now fallen upon some which, as to the outward means of it, is different from what was known to many of those who went before us.

Some time after the Yearly Meeting, a day being appointed and letters wrote to distant members, the said committees met at Philadelphia and by adjournments continued several days. The calamities of war were now increasing. The frontier inhabitants of Pennsylvania were frequently surprised, some slain and many taken captive by the Indians; and while these committees sat, the corpse of one so slain was brought in a wagon and taken through the streets of the city in his bloody garments to alarm the people and rouse them up to war.

Friends thus met were not all of one mind in relation to the tax, which to such who scrupled it made the way more difficult. To refuse an active payment at such a time might be construed an act of disloyalty and appeared likely to displease the rulers, not only here but in England. Still there was a scruple so fastened upon the minds of many Friends that nothing moved it. It was a conference the most weighty that ever I was at, and the hearts of many were bowed in reverence before the Most High. Some Friends of the said committees who appeared easy to pay the tax, after several adjournments withdrew; others of them continued till the last. At length an epistle was drawn by some Friends concerned on that account, and being read several times and corrected, was then signed by such who were free to sign it, which is as follows:

An Epistle of Tender Love and Caution to Friends in Pennsylvania

PHILADELPHIA, 16th day, 12th month, 1755

DEAR AND WELL BELOVED FRIENDS,

We salute you in a fresh and renewed sense of our Heavenly Father's love, which hath graciously overshadowed us in several weighty and solid conferences we have had together with many other Friends upon the present situation of the affairs of the Society in this province; and in that love we find our spirits engaged to acquaint you that under a solid exercise of mind to seek for counsel and direction from the High Priest of our profession, who is the Prince of Peace, we believe he hath renewedly favoured us with strong and lively evidences that in his due and appointed time, the day which hath dawned in these later ages foretold by the prophets, wherein swords should be beaten into plowshares and spears into pruning hooks [Is. 2:4], shall gloriously rise higher and higher, and the spirit of the gospel which teaches to love enemies prevail to that degree that the art of war shall be no more learned, and that it is his determination to exalt this blessed day in this our age, if in the depth of humility we receive his instruction and obey his voice.

And being painfully apprehensive that the large sum granted by the late Act of Assembly for the king's use is principally intended for purposes inconsistent with our peaceable testimony, we therefore think that as we cannot be concerned in wars and fightings, so neither ought we to contribute thereto by paying the tax directed by the said Act, though suffering be the consequence of our refusal, which we hope to be enabled to bear with patience.

And we take this position even though some part of the money to be raised by the said Act is said to be for such benevolent purposes as supporting our friendship with our Indian neighbours and relieving the distresses of our fellow subjects who have suffered in the present calamities, for whom our hearts are deeply pained; and we affectionately and with bowels of tenderness sympathize with them therein. And we could most cheerfully contribute to those purposes if they were not so mixed that we cannot in the manner proposed show our hearty concurrence therewith without at the same time assenting to, or allowing ourselves in, practices which we apprehend contrary to the testimony which the Lord hath given us to bear for his name and Truth's sake. And having the health and prosperity of the Society at heart, we earnestly exhort Friends to wait for the appearing of the true Light and stand in the council of God, that we may know him to be the rock of our salvation and place of our refuge forever. And beware of the spirit of this world, that is unstable and often draws into dark and timorous reasonings, lest the God thereof should be suffered to blind the eye of the mind, and such not knowing the sure foundation, the Rock of Ages, may partake of the terrors and fears that are not known to the inhabitants of that place where the sheep and lambs of Christ ever had a quiet habitation, which a remnant have to say, to the praise of his name, they have been blessed with a measure of in this day of distress.

And as our fidelity to the present government and our willingly paying all taxes for purposes which do not interfere with our consciences may justly exempt us from the imputation of disloyalty, so we earnestly desire that all who by a deep and quiet seeking for direction from the Holy Spirit are, or shall be, convinced that he calls us as a people to this testimony may dwell under the guidance of the same divine Spirit, and manifest by the meekness and humility of their conversation that they are really under that influence, and therein may know true fortitude and patience to bear that and every other testimony committed to them faithfully and uniformly, and that all Friends may know their spirits clothed with true charity, the bond of Christian fellowship, wherein we again salute you and remain your friends and brethren.

Signed by ABRAHAM FARRINGTON, JOHN EVANS, JOHN CHURCHMAN, MORDECAI YARNALL, SAMUEL FOTHERGILL, SAMUEL EASTBURN, WILLIAM BROWN, JOHN SCARBOROUGH, THOMAS CARLETON, JOSHUA ELY, WILLIAM JACKSON, JAMES BARTRAM, THOMAS BROWN, DANIEL STANTON, JOHN WOOL-MAN, ISAAC ZANE, WILLIAM HORNE, BENJAMIN TROTTER, ANTHONY BENEZET, JOHN ARMITT, JOHN PEMBERTON.

FROM

A Plea for the Poor

"Are not two sparrows sold for a farthing, and one of them shall not fall on the ground without your Father"

Mt. 10:29.

THE way of carrying on wars, common in the world, is so far distinguishable from the purity of Christ's religion that many scruple to join in them. Those who are so redeemed from the love of the world as to possess nothing in a selfish spirit, their "life is hid with Christ in God" [Col. 3:3], and these he preserves in resignedness, even in times of commotion. As they possess nothing but what pertains to his family, anxious thoughts about wealth or dominion hath little or nothing in them to work upon, and they learn contentment in being disposed of according to his will who, being omnipotent and always mindful of his children, causeth all things to work for their good. But where that spirit which loves riches works, and in its working gathers wealth and cleaves to customs which have their root in self-pleasing, this spirit, thus separating from universal love, seeks help from that power which stands in the separation; and whatever name it hath, it still desires to defend the treasures thus gotten. This is like a chain where the end of one link encloses the end of another. The rising up of a desire to attain wealth is the beginning. This desire being cherished moves to action, and riches thus gotten please self, and while self hath a life in them it desires to have them defended.

Wealth is attended with power, by which bargains and proceedings contrary to universal righteousness are supported;
and here oppression, carried on with worldly policy and order,
clothes itself with the name of justice and becomes like a seed
of discord in the soil; and as this spirit which wanders from the
pure habitation prevails, so the seed of war swells and sprouts
and grows and becomes strong, till much fruits are ripened.
Thus cometh the harvest spoken of by the prophet, which is
"a heap in the day of grief, and of desperate sorrow" [Is. 17:11].

Oh, that we who declare against wars and acknowledge our
trust to be in God only, may walk in the Light and therein
examine our foundation and motives in holding great estates!
May we look upon our treasures and the furniture of our
houses and the garments in which we array ourselves and try
whether the seeds of war have any nourishment in these our
possessions or not. Holding treasures in the self-pleasing spirit
is a strong plant, the fruit whereof ripens fast. A day of outward
distress is coming and divine love calls to prepare against it!
Harken then, Oh ye children who have known the Light, and
come forth! Leave everything which our Lord Jesus Christ
does not own. Think not his pattern too plain or too coarse
for you. Think not a small portion in this life too little, but let
us live in his spirit and walk as he walked, and he will preserve
us in the greatest troubles.

WARNER MIFFLIN

The Quaker Warner Mifflin (1745–1798) achieved considerable fame as an antislavery activist, and especially for manumitting his own slaves in 1774 and 1775. Hector St. John de Crèvecoeur praised him in the French edition (1784) of *Letters of an American Farmer*, August von Kotzebue's play *Die Quäker* (1812) took him as its subject, and John Greenleaf Whittier praised him as "one of the truest and noblest men of any age or country." He is much less widely known as an opponent of war; but he did travel in 1777 to meet with George Washington and William Howe to present a testimony against war, just before the Battle of Germantown; that testimony was far less popular, even in his supportive community, than his testimony against slavery.

In the following selection from his 1796 memoir *The Defense of Warner Mifflin Against Aspersions Cast on Him on Account of His Endeavours to Promote Righteousness, Mercy, and Peace among Mankind*, he explains his reasons for taking no part in the popular Revolutionary War—even to the extent of avoiding paper money, which seemed to him "one of the Engines of War." His refusals cost him dearly. Being a pacifist between wars, says the movement slogan, is like being a vegetarian between meals. As even Mifflin's restrained, temperate account makes clear, being a pacifist in the middle of one can be a riskier business, given that one is, as Mifflin puts it, "acting so as to be declared an Enemy to [one's] Country."

"I Counted None My Enemy"

THE late Revolution now began to make its appearance and as I was religiously restrained from taking any part therein, I had the epithet of Toryism placed on me by interested holders of Slaves, insinuations were thrown out that my labouring for the freedom of the blacks, was in order to attach them to the British interest, notwithstanding I had liberated mine on the ground of religious conviction, before this revolutionary period arrived—Added to this, on the issue of the Bills of Credit by Congress, I felt restricted from receiving them, lest I might thereby, in some sort defile my hands with one of the Engines of War; from whence I was further dipped into sympathy with the condition of the blacks, in acting so as to be declared an Enemy to my Country, and like them, thrown out from the benefit of its Laws, and this for no other Crime, but yielding to the impulses of divine Grace or Law of God written in my heart, which I ever found the safest ground to move upon—Abundant threats were poured out, that my house should be pulled down over my head, that I should be Shot, Carted &c; this proved a fiery tryal, my soul was almost overwhelmed lest I should bring my family to want, and it might be through a deception. I left my house in the night season and walked into a field in the bitterness of my soul, and without any sensible relief returned back, on stepping into the door I espied a Testament, and opening it in the 13th Chap. of Revelations, found mention there made of a time, when none should buy or sell, but those who received the mark of the Beast in the right Hand or forehead: and it fixed in my mind, that if I took that Money after those impressions, I should receive a mark of the bestial spirit of War in my right hand; and then the penalty which is annexed in the ensuing Chapter must follow—I then resolved through the Lords assistance, which I craved might be afforded, let what would follow, never to deal in any of it, this afforded me some relief, and finding my Wife so far united with me as to refuse it likewise (saying though she did not feel the matter as I did, yet through fear of weakening my hands, she was most easy not to touch it) I became much strengthened and resigned to suffer what might be allotted, feeling at times the prevalence of that power, which delivers from all fear of the malice of Men or infernal spirits, and reduces the soul into perfect subjection to the holy will and ordering.

The War advancing with increasing distress, gloomy prospects opened, and close provings seemed at the door of such who were measurably redeemed from the spirit of party. Not only our Testimony against War, in the support of which our religious Society have been oft brought under tryals; but that against pulling down or setting up of Governments was brought to the Test. As there are those, who from full experience know, that it is not a cunningly devised Fable, but the Truth of God revealed in the heart, through his Light and good Spirit, that shews us we are called to raise the pure Standard of the Prince of Peace, above all party rage, strife, contention, rents and divisions, in the spirit of meekness and wisdom; and in quietness and confidence, patiently to suffer what may arise for the promotion of this peaceable Government of the Shiloh; in and through an innocent life and conversation; wherein the language is felt of "*Glory to God in the highest, on Earth peace and good will to Men*": And this was the experience of many, I am bold to assert it, even during the late cruel War, when thousands of Men were endeavouring in its fierce and voracious spirit to destroy one another—Such have been my own sensations, when at one view I have beheld both parties, and had to risk a passage through them—I counted none my enemy, I felt no fear from any thing on my part in thought, word, or deed; many times concluding, I should have had no objection for the two contending Generals to have known my whole heart and conduct, having at an early period of that Calamity been convinced, it would not do me, even in idea, to wander without the boundaries of my professed principles; or I could not expect to be sustained by the secret aid of the God of the faithful, whose everlasting Arm of help, with humble gratitude I may acknowledge, hath been stretched out for my strengthening and confirmation in a variety of instances.

DAVID LOW DODGE

David Low Dodge (1774–1852) was a merchant, philanthropist, and, after nearly shooting an innkeeper who had entered his room late at night and finding that his "war spirit appeared to be crucified and slain," a busy and useful crusader for peace. In 1812 he published *War Inconsistent with the Religion of Jesus Christ*, and in the summer of 1815 he became the first president of the New York Peace Society—the first peace society in the world. (In 1828 it merged with similar groups in Maine, Massachusetts, and New Hampshire to form the American Peace Society, which organized peace conferences and began publishing the *Advocate of Peace*.)

Dodge's autobiography, printed posthumously in 1854, is of a piece with his public work: respectable, judicious, dignified, pious. Early in the book, however, he becomes a different writer as he recalls a pacifist of a different sort: an opponent of the American Revolution who through his opposition became a sort of wild man, keeping to the forests, in danger from most of his neighbors though supported and fed by others. Dodge's unnamed fugitive anticipates the long history of pacifists subject to oppression: scorned, hunted, jailed.

"An Odd and Singular Man"

I WILL here notice an event, as it illustrates the spirit of the times. There was a respectable farmer who resided in Brooklyn, by the name of John Baker, who was called an odd and singular man, because he openly denounced all kinds of carnal warfare as contrary to the gospel; and, of course, refused to take any part in the revolutionary war. By some he was called a *Tory*, by others a *coward*, while he constantly declared it a matter of conscience. Yet he was drafted for the army, and his neighbors determined he should serve by compulsion. He declared he would die before he would serve as a warrior, and consequently fled to the woods in the fall of 1779. The clergy and the laity urged his compulsion, and the populace turned out and pursued him, as hounds would a fox, and finally they caught and bound him, like Sampson, "with strong cords," placed him in a wagon, and sent two trusty patriots to convey him to Providence, to the troops stationed there. In the course of the night, however, he got hold of a knife, cut himself loose, and escaped to the woods. Subsequently he returned and secreted himself in a large, dense cedar swamp, about half a mile from our house. He made himself as comfortable a shelter as the thick boughs of the double spruce and cedar would permit. There he remained, without fire, during the severe winter of 1780, without the knowledge of any one, except his brother and my parents, to whom he made himself known to save himself from perishing. His brother furnished him, in the night, with some articles of food and clothing from his own house; and my father, by an understanding with him, was absent at certain times, while my mother would supply him with food, blankets, and other conveniences. There was a wall from the woods connected with the swamp, to our garden, forming the back fence. One day, as I was on a snow-bank in the rear of the garden, I looked over the fence and saw a man creeping along the side of the wall; as soon as he saw me he started and ran for the woods. I, with equal speed, made for the house, supposing he was a "wild Indian," of which class of men I had heard many frightful stories, and screamed to my mother that the Indians had come, and fled into the back room and crept under the bed. The term "wild," was applied to Indians on the frontiers at war with Americans, in distinction from a pretty numerous remnant of several tribes who lived quietly in the State. So frightened was I at a glimpse of poor Baker, that for several nights afterwards I dreamed frightful dreams about "wild Indians."

The facts relative to Mr. Baker, I received from my parents, but do not recollect how he was released. Probably the compassion of the community was aroused, as there was reason to suppose that he might have perished by the severity of the winter. In after years, when a young man, I have visited Mr. Baker. He had one of the best cultivated farms in the vicinity, and I never heard a lisp against his character, except his opposition to war.

BENJAMIN RUSH

Benjamin Rush (1746–1813) was a physician and professor of chemistry, a signer of the Declaration of Independence, a surgeon general of the Continental Army, a brilliant observer of the 1793 yellow fever epidemic in Philadelphia, and treasurer of the U.S. Mint from 1797 until his death. He was also a lover of controversy, making enemies as a critic of corruption in military hospitals, a theorist of disease and medical treatment, an advocate of temperance, and an abolitionist.

None of which quite prepares the reader for Rush's 1792 plan for a peace office, first published in the Philadelphia newspaper *Dunlap's American Daily Advertiser.* At its beginning it seems like a vivid but ordinary manifestation of the inventive intellect characteristic of the Founding Fathers, and especially appropriate as the nature of American government was being worked out; the plan anticipates, and indirectly leads to, the legislation that established the United States Institute of Peace in 1984. But then the piece becomes almost hallucinatory, looking forward not to real institutions but to dystopian satires like Dalton Trumbo's *Johnny Got His Gun* (1939) and Kurt Vonnegut's *Slaughterhouse-Five* (1969). No biography of Rush quite manages to explain what set his imagination off in this way, and two of the three on my library's shelves make no mention of it at all.

A Plan of a Peace-Office for the United States

Among the defects which have been pointed out in the federal constitution by its antifederal enemies, it is much to be lamented that no person has taken notice of its total silence upon the subject of an office of the utmost importance to the welfare of the United States, that is, an *office* for promoting and preserving perpetual *peace* in our country.

It is to be hoped that no objection will be made to the establishment of such an office, while we are engaged in a war with the Indians, for as the *War-Office* of the United States was established in the *time of peace*, it is equally reasonable that a *Peace-Office* should be established in the *time of war*.

The plan of this office is as follows:

I. Let a Secretary of the Peace be appointed to preside in this office, who shall be perfectly free from all the present absurd and vulgar European prejudices upon the subject of government; let him be a genuine republican and a sincere Christian, for the principles of republicanism and Christianity are no less friendly to universal and perpetual peace, than they are to universal and equal liberty.

II. Let a power be given to this Secretary to establish and maintain free-schools in every city, village and township of the United States; and let him be made responsible for the talents, principles, and morals, of all his schoolmasters. Let the youth of our country be carefully instructed in reading, writing, arithmetic, and in the doctrines of a religion of some kind: the Christian religion should be preferred to all others; for it belongs to this religion exclusively to teach us not only to cultivate peace with men, but to forgive, nay more—to love our very enemies. It belongs to it further to teach us that the Supreme Being alone possesses a power to take away human life, and that we rebel against his laws, whenever we undertake to execute death in any way whatever upon any of his creatures.

III. Let every family in the United States be furnished at the public expense, by the Secretary of this office, with a copy of an American edition of the BIBLE. This measure has become the more necessary in our country, since the banishment of the bible, as a school-book, from most of the schools in the United States. Unless the price of this book be paid for by the public, there is reason to fear that in a few years it will be met with only in courts of justice or in magistrates' offices; and should the absurd mode of establishing truth by kissing this sacred book fall into disuse, it may probably, in the course of the next generation, be seen only as a curiosity on a shelf in a public museum.

IV. Let the following sentence be inscribed in letters of gold over the doors of every State and Court house in the United States.

THE SON OF MAN CAME INTO THE WORLD, NOT TO DESTROY MEN'S LIVES, BUT TO SAVE THEM.

V. To inspire a veneration for human life, and an horror at the shedding of human blood, let all those laws be repealed which authorise juries, judges, sheriffs, or hangmen to assume the resentments of individuals and to commit murder in cold blood in any case whatever. Until this reformation in our code of penal jurisprudence takes place, it will be in vain to attempt to introduce universal and perpetual peace in our country.

VI.   To subdue that passion for war, which education, added to human depravity, have made universal, a familiarity with the instruments of death, as well as all military shows, should be carefully avoided. For which reason, militia laws should every where be repealed, and military dresses and military titles should be laid aside: reviews tend to lessen the horrors of a battle by connecting them with the charms of order; militia laws generate idleness and vice, and thereby produce the wars they are said to prevent; military dresses fascinate the minds of young men, and lead them from serious and useful professions; were there no *uniforms*, there would probably be no armies; lastly, military titles feed vanity, and keep up ideas in the mind which lessen a sense of the folly and miseries of war.

VII.   In the last place, let a large room, adjoining the federal hall, be appropriated for transacting the business and preserving all the records of this *office*. Over the door of this room let there be a sign, on which the figures of a LAMB, a DOVE and an OLIVE BRANCH should be painted, together with the following inscriptions in letters of gold:

PEACE ON EARTH—GOOD-WILL TO MAN. AH! WHY
WILL MEN FORGET THAT THEY ARE BRETHREN?

Within this apartment let there be a collection of plough-shares and pruning-hooks made out of swords and spears; and on each of the walls of the apartment, the following pictures as large as the life:

1.   A lion eating straw with an ox, and an adder playing upon the lips of a child.

2.   An Indian boiling his venison in the same pot with a citizen of Kentucky.

3.   Lord Cornwallis and Tippoo Saib, under the shade of a sycamore-tree in the East Indies, drinking Madeira wine together out of the same decanter.

4.   A group of French and Austrian soldiers dancing arm and arm, under a bower erected in the neighbourhood of Mons.

5.   A St. Domingo planter, a man of color, and a native of Africa, legislating together in the same colonial assembly.*

To complete the entertainment of this delightful apartment, let a group of young ladies, clad in white robes, assemble every day at a certain hour, in a gallery to be erected for the purpose, and sing odes, and hymns, and anthems in praise of the blessings of peace.

One of these songs should consist of the following lines.

Peace o'er the world her olive wand extends,
And white-rob'd innocence from heaven descends;
All crimes shall cease, and ancient frauds shall fail,
Returning justice lifts aloft her scale.

In order more deeply to affect the minds of the citizens of the United States with the blessings of peace, by *contrasting* them with the evils of war, let the following inscriptions be painted upon the sign, which is placed over the door of the War Office.

1.   An office for butchering the human species.

2.   A Widow and Orphan making office.

3.   A broken bone making office.

4.   A Wooden leg making office.

5.   An office for creating public and private vices.

6.   An office for creating a public debt.

7.   An office for creating speculators, stock Jobbers, and Bankrupts.

8.   An office for creating famine.

9.   An office for creating pestilential diseases.

10.   An office for creating poverty, and the destruction of liberty, and national happiness.

---

*At the time of writing this, there existed wars between the United States and the American Indians, between the British nation and Tippoo Saib, between the planters of St Domingo and their African slaves, and between the French nation and the emperor of Germany.

In the lobby of this office let there be painted representations of all the common military instruments of death, also human skulls, broken bones, unburied and putrifying dead bodies, hospitals crouded with sick and wounded Soldiers, villages on fire, mothers in besieged towns eating the flesh of their children, ships sinking in the ocean, rivers dyed with blood, and extensive plains without a tree or fence, or any other object, but the ruins of deserted farm houses.

Above this group of woeful figures,—let the following words be inserted, in red characters to represent human blood,

"NATIONAL GLORY."

JOSEPH SMITH JR.

Resolved to keep their swords bright, and not to stain them with blood, the anti-Lehi-Nephis go into battle without weapons, refrain from self-defense, and are slaughtered by the Lamanites. But the Lamanites are so moved by the example of their opponents' nonresistance that they are converted by it, "and it came to pass that the people of God were joined that day by more than the number which had been slain."

Joseph Smith Jr. (1805–1844) left no account of his thoughts about this passage as he dictated it in 1827. Few antiwar activists know that the Book of Alma in the Book of Mormon contains this astonishing account of collective nonresistance to war; Mormon scholars who have commented on the passage have argued against taking it as a document of pacifism. No doubt they are right, and certainly the Book of Mormon is no pacifist book. But the passage is there, linked in its imagery, if not by direct influence, to such texts as the Iroquois "Tree of the Great Peace" and the African American spiritual "Down by the River-Side." It is part of the implicit if not the explicit conversation among antiwar writings separated from one another by time, space, and culture: "Brave, setting up signals across vast distances, / considering a nameless way of living, of almost unimagined values," as Muriel Rukeyser put it in "Poem" in 1968.

FROM
The Book of Mormon

(ALMA, CHAPTER 24)

1 And it came to pass that the Amlicites and the
      Amulonites and the Lamanites
  which were in the land of Amulon and also in the
      land of Helam
  and which was in the land of Jerusalem
  —and, in fine, in all the land round about—
  which had not been converted
  and had not taken upon them the name of
      Anti-Nephi-Lehi
  were stirred up by the Amlicites and by the
      Amulonites

to anger against their brethren.

2 And their hatred became exceeding sore against
     them,
even insomuch that they began to rebel against
     their king,
insomuch that they would not that he should be
     their king.
Therefore they took up arms against the people of
     Anti-Nephi-Lehi.

3 Now the king conferred the kingdom upon his son,
and he called his name Anti-Nephi-Lehi.

4 And the king died in that selfsame year
that the Lamanites began to make preparations for
     war against the people of God.

5 Now when Ammon and his brethren and all those
     which had come up with them
saw the preparations of the Lamanites to destroy
     their brethren,
they came forth to the land of Middoni.
And there Ammon met all his brethren;
and from thence they came to the land of Ishmael
that they might hold a council with Lamoni,
and also with his brother Anti-Nephi-Lehi,
what they should do to defend themselves against
     the Lamanites.

6 Now there was not one soul among all the people
which had been converted unto the Lord
that would take up arms against their brethren.
Nay, they would not even make any preparations for
     war;
yea, and also their king commanded them that they
     should not.

7 Now these are the words which he said unto the
     people concerning the matter:
I thank my God, my beloved people,
that our great God has in goodness sent these our
     brethren, the Nephites, unto us,

to preach unto us and to convince us of the
traditions of our wicked fathers.

8 And behold, I thank my great God
that he has given us a portion of his Spirit to soften
our hearts,
that we have opened a correspondence with these
brethren, the Nephites.

9 And behold, I also thank my God that by opening
this correspondence
we have been convinced of our sins
and of the many murders which we have
committed.

10 And I also thank my God, yea, my great God,
that he hath granted unto us that we might repent
of these things,
and also that he hath forgiven us
of these our many sins and murders which we have
committed
and took away the guilt from our hearts through
the merits of his Son.

11 And now behold, my brethren,
since it has been all that we could do,
as we were the most lost of all mankind,
to repent of all our sins and the many murders
which we have committed
and to get God to take them away from our hearts
—for it was all we could do to repent sufficiently
before God
that he would take away our stains—

12 now my best beloved brethren,
since God hath taken away our stains and our
swords have become bright,
then let us stain our swords no more with the blood
of our brethren.

13 Behold, I say unto you:
Nay, let us retain our swords that they be not
stained with the blood of our brethren.
For perhaps if we should stain our swords again,

they can no more be washed bright through the
blood of the Son of our great God,
which shall be shed for the atonement of our sins.

14 And the great God has had mercy on us
and made these things known unto us that we
might not perish.
Yea, and he hath made these things known unto us
beforehand
because he loveth our souls as well as he loveth our
children.
Therefore in his mercy he doth visit us by his
angels,
that the plan of salvation might be made known
unto us
as well as unto future generations.
15 O how merciful is our God!

And now behold, since it has been as much as we
could do
to get our stains taken away from us and our swords
are made bright,
let us hide them away that they may be kept bright
as a testimony to our God at the last day
—or at the day that we shall be brought to stand
before him to be judged—
that we have not stained our swords in the blood of
our brethren
since he imparted his word unto us and has made us
clean thereby.
16 And now my brethren, if our brethren seek to
destroy us,
behold, we will hide away our swords;
yea, even we will bury them deep in the earth,
that they may be kept bright
as a testimony that we have never used them,
at the last day.
And if our brethren destroy us,
behold, we shall go to our God and shall be saved.

17 And now it came to pass that
when the king had made an end of these sayings,
and all the people were assembled together,
they took their swords and all the weapons
which were used for the shedding of man's blood
and they did bury them up deep in the earth.
18 And thus they did,
it being in their view a testimony to God and also
to men
that they never would use weapons again for the
shedding of man's blood.

And this they did, vouching and covenanting with
God that
rather than to shed the blood of their brethren,
they would give up their own lives;
and rather than to take away from a brother,
they would give unto him;
and rather than to spend their days in idleness,
they would labor abundantly with their hands.
19 And thus we see that
when these Lamanites were brought to believe and
to know the truth
that they were firm and would suffer even unto
death rather than to commit sin.
And thus we see that they buried the weapons of
peace—
or they buried the weapons of war for peace.

20 And it came to pass that their brethren the
Lamanites made preparations for war
and came up to the land of Nephi for the purpose
of dethroning the king
and to place another in his stead,
and also of destroying the people of Anti-Nephi-
Lehi out of the land.
21 And it came to pass that when the people saw that
they were coming against them,
they went out to meet them and prostrated
themselves before them to the earth

and began to call on the name of the Lord.
And thus they were in this attitude
when the Lamanites began to fall upon them
and began to slay them with the sword.

22 And thus without meeting any resistance they did
     slay a thousand and five of them.
And we know that they are blessed,
for they have gone to dwell with their God.

23 Now when the Lamanites saw that their brethren
     would not flee from the sword,
neither would they turn aside to the right hand or
     to the left,
but that they would lay down and perish
and praised God even in the very act of perishing
     under the sword—

24 now when the Lamanites saw this,
they did forbear from slaying them.
And there were many whose hearts had swollen in
     them
for those of their brethren who had fallen under the
     sword,
for they repented of the thing which they had done.

25 And it came to pass that they threw down their
     weapons of war
and they would not take them again,
for they were stung for the murders which they had
     committed.
And they came down, even as their brethren,
relying upon the mercies of those whose arms were
     lifted to slay them.

26 And it came to pass that the people of God were
     joined that day
by more than the number which had been slain.
And those which had been slain were righteous
     people;
therefore we have no reason to doubt but what they
     are saved.

27 And there was not a wicked man slain among them,

but there were more than a thousand brought to
the knowledge of the truth.
Thus we see that the Lord worketh in many ways to
the salvation of his people.

28 Now the greatest number of those of the Lamanites
which slew so many of their brethren
were Amlicites and Amulonites,
the greatest number of whom were after the order
of the Nehors.
29 Now among those which joined the people of the
Lord,
there were none which were Amlicites or
Amulonites,
or which were after the order of Nehor,
but they were actual descendants of Laman and
Lemuel.
30 And thus we can plainly discern that
after a people has been once enlightened by the
Spirit of God
and hath had great knowledge of things pertaining
to righteousness
and then have fallen away into sin and transgression,
they become more hardened;
and thus their state becometh worse
than as though they had never known these things.

RALPH WALDO EMERSON

On March 12, 1838, Ralph Waldo Emerson (1803–1882) gave the key-note of a series of lectures sponsored by the nine-year-old American Peace Society, in Boston. Later published under the title "War," it was originally billed as "The Peace Principle." Emerson had made himself a name by the publication of *Nature* in 1836 and the delivery of "The American Scholar" in 1837, but had not yet scandalized religious conservatives with his "Divinity School Address" of July 1838, nor emerged as the dominant literary figure he became after the 1841 publication of *Essays, First Series*.

Two things about "War" are especially salient here. The first is the admiration Emerson has for the martial virtues, and his sense that war can only be overcome if some way can be found for those virtues to be retained and transformed; here he anticipates William James's 1910 essay "The Moral Equivalent of War." The second and perhaps more surprising is how readily Emerson responded to the call of the recently founded peace societies, which must have seemed to many observers like eccentric fringe groups rather than political movements full of promise.

FROM

War

ALL history is the decline of war, though the slow decline. All that society has yet gained is mitigation: the doctrine of the right of war still remains.

For ages (for ideas work in ages, and animate vast societies of men) the human race has gone on under the tyranny—shall I so call it?—of this first brutish form of their effort to be men; that is, for ages they have shared so much of the nature of the lower animals, the tiger and the shark, and the savages of the water-drop. They have nearly exhausted all the good and all the evil of this form: they have held as fast to this degradation as their worst enemy could desire; but all things have an end, and so has this. The eternal germination of the better has unfolded new powers, new instincts, which were really concealed under this rough and base rind. The sublime question has startled one and another happy soul in different quarters of the globe,—Cannot love be, as well as hate? Would

28

not love answer the same end, or even a better? Cannot peace be, as well as war?

This thought is no man's invention, neither St. Pierre's nor Rousseau's, but the rising of the general tide in the human soul,—and rising highest, and first made visible, in the most simple and pure souls, who have therefore announced it to us beforehand; but presently we all see it. It has now become so distinct as to be a social thought: societies can be formed on it. It is expounded, illustrated, defined, with different degrees of clearness; and its actualization, or the measures it should inspire, predicted according to the light of each seer.

The idea itself is the epoch; the fact that it has become so distinct to any small number of persons as to become a subject of prayer and hope, of concert and discussion,—*that* is the commanding fact. This having come, much more will follow. Revolutions go not backward. The star once risen, though only one man in the hemisphere has yet seen its upper limb in the horizon, will mount and mount, until it becomes visible to other men, to multitudes, and climbs the zenith of all eyes. And so it is not a great matter how long men refuse to believe the advent of peace: war is on its last legs; and a universal peace is as sure as is the prevalence of civilization over barbarism, of liberal governments over feudal forms. The question for us is only *How soon?*

That the project of peace should appear visionary to great numbers of sensible men; should appear laughable even, to numbers; should appear to the grave and good-natured to be embarrassed with extreme practical difficulties,—is very natural. "This is a poor, tedious society of yours," they say: "we do not see what good can come of it. Peace! why, we are all at peace now. But if a foreign nation should wantonly insult or plunder our commerce, or, worse yet, should land on our shores to rob and kill, you would not have us sit, and be robbed and killed? You mistake the times; you overestimate the virtue of men. You forget that the quiet which now sleeps in cities and in farms, which lets the wagon go unguarded and the farmhouse unbolted, rests on the perfect understanding of all men that the musket, the halter and the jail stand behind there, ready to punish any disturber of it. All admit that this would be the best policy, if the world were all a church, if all men were the best men, if all would agree to accept this rule. But it is absurd for one nation to attempt it alone."

In the first place, we answer that we never make much account of objections which merely respect the actual state of the world at this moment, but which admit the general expediency and permanent excellence of the project. What is the best must be the true; and what is true,—that is, what is at bottom fit and agreeable to the constitution of man,—must at last prevail over all obstruction and all opposition. There is no good now enjoyed by society that was not once as problematical and visionary as this. It is the tendency of the true interest of man to become his desire and steadfast aim.

But, further, it is a lesson which all history teaches wise men, to put trust in ideas, and not in circumstances. We have all grown up in the sight of frigates and navy yards, of armed forts and islands, of arsenals and militia. The reference to any foreign register will inform us of the number of thousand or million men that are now under arms in the vast colonial system of the British empire, of Russia, Austria and France; and one is scared to find at what a cost the peace of the globe is kept. This vast apparatus of artillery, of fleets, of stone bastions and trenches and embankments; this incessant patrolling of sentinels; this waving of national flags; this reveille and evening gun; this martial music and endless playing of marches and singing of military and naval songs seem to us to constitute an imposing actual, which will not yield in centuries to the feeble, deprecatory voices of a handful of friends of peace.

Thus always we are daunted by the appearances; not seeing that their whole value lies at bottom in the state of mind. It is really a thought that built this portentous war-establishment, and a thought shall also melt it away. Every nation and every man instantly surround themselves with a material apparatus which exactly corresponds to their moral state, or their state of thought. Observe how every truth and every error, each a *thought* of some man's mind, clothes itself with societies, houses, cities, language, ceremonies, newspapers. Observe the ideas of the present day,—orthodoxy, skepticism, missions, popular education, temperance, anti-masonry, anti-slavery; see how each of these abstractions has embodied itself in an imposing apparatus in the community; and how timber, brick, lime and stone have flown into convenient shape, obedient to the master-idea reigning in the minds of many persons.

You shall hear, some day, of a wild fancy which some man has in his brain, of the mischief of secret oaths. Come again one or two years afterwards, and you shall see it has built great houses of solid wood and brick and mortar. You shall see a hundred presses printing a million sheets; you shall see men and horses and wheels made to walk, run and roll for it: this great body of matter thus executing that one man's wild thought. This happens daily, yearly about us, with half thoughts, often with flimsy lies, pieces of policy and speculation. With good nursing they will last three or four years before they will come to nothing. But when a truth appears,—as, for instance, a perception in the wit of one Columbus that there is land in the Western Sea; though he alone of all men has that thought, and they all jeer,—it will build ships; it will build fleets; it will carry over half Spain and half England; it will plant a colony, a state, nations and half a globe full of men.

We surround ourselves always, according to our freedom and ability, with true images of ourselves in things, whether it be ships or books or cannons or churches. The standing army, the arsenal, the camp and the gibbet do not appertain to man. They only serve as an index to show where man is now; what a bad, ungoverned temper he has; what an ugly neighbor he is; how his affections halt; how low his hope lies. He who loves the bristle of bayonets only sees in their glitter what beforehand he feels in his heart. It is avarice and hatred; it is that quivering lip, that cold, hating eye, which built magazines and powder-houses.

It follows of course that the least change in the man will change his circumstances; the least enlargement of his ideas, the least mitigation of his feelings in respect to other men; if, for example, he could be inspired with a tender kindness to the souls of men, and should come to feel that every man was another self with whom he might come to join, as left hand works with right. Every degree of the ascendancy of this feeling would cause the most striking changes of external things: the tents would be struck; the men-of-war would rot ashore; the arms rust; the cannon would become street-posts; the pikes, a fisher's harpoon; the marching regiment would be a caravan of emigrants, *peaceful* pioneers at the fountains of the Wabash and the Missouri. And so it must and will be: bayonet and sword must first retreat a little from their ostentatious prominence; then quite hide themselves, as the sheriff's halter does now, inviting the attendance only of relations and friends; and then, lastly, will be transferred to the museums of the curious, as poisoning and torturing tools are at this day.

War and peace thus resolve themselves into a mercury of the state of cultivation. At a certain stage of his progress, the man fights, if he be of a sound body and mind. At a certain higher stage, he makes no offensive demonstration, but is alert to repel injury, and of an unconquerable heart. At a still higher stage, he comes into the region of holiness; passion has passed away from him; his warlike nature is all converted into an active medicinal principle; he sacrifices himself, and accepts with alacrity wearisome tasks of denial and charity; but, being attacked, he bears it and turns the other cheek, as one engaged, throughout his being, no longer to the service of an individual but to the common soul of all men.

Since the peace question has been before the public mind, those who affirm its right and expediency have naturally been met with objections more or less weighty. There are cases frequently put by the curious,—moral problems, like those problems in arithmetic which in long winter evenings the rustics try the hardness of their heads in ciphering out. And chiefly it is said,—Either accept this principle for better, for worse, carry it out to the end, and meet its absurd consequences; or else, if you pretend to set an arbitrary limit, a "Thus far, no farther," then give up the principle, and take that limit which the common-sense of all mankind has set, and which distinguishes offensive war as criminal, defensive war as just. Otherwise, if you go for no war, then be consistent, and give up self-defence in the highway, in your own house. Will you push it thus far? Will you stick to your principle of non-resistance when your strong-box is broken open, when your wife and babes are insulted and slaughtered in your sight? If you say yes, you only invite the robber and assassin; and a few bloody-minded desperadoes would soon butcher the good.

In reply to this charge of absurdity on the extreme peace doctrine, as shown in the supposed consequences, I wish to say that such deductions consider only one half of the fact. They look only at the passive side of the friend of peace, only at his passivity; they quite omit to consider his activity. But no man, it may be presumed, ever embraced the cause of peace and philanthropy for the sole end and satisfaction of being plundered and slain. A man does not come the length of the spirit of martyrdom without some active purpose, some equal motive, some flaming love. If you have a nation of men who have risen to that height of moral cultivation that they will not declare war or carry arms, for they have not so much madness left in their brains, you have a nation of lovers, of benefactors, of true, great and able men. Let me know more of that nation; I shall not find them defenceless, with idle hands springing at their sides. I shall find them men of love, honor and truth; men of an immense industry; men whose influence is felt to the end of the earth; men whose very look and voice carry the sentence of honor and shame; and all forces yield to their energy and persuasion. Whenever we see the doctrine of peace embraced by a nation, we may be assured it will not be one that invites injury; but one, on the contrary, which has a friend in the bottom of the heart of every man, even of the violent and the base; one against which no weapon can prosper; one which is looked upon as the asylum of the human race and has the tears and the blessings of mankind.

In the second place, as far as it respects individual action in difficult and extreme cases, I will say, such cases seldom or never occur to the good and just man; nor are we careful to say, or even to know, what in such crises is to be done. A wise man will never impawn his future being and action, and decide beforehand what he shall do in a given extreme event. Nature and God will instruct him in that hour.

The question naturally arises, How is this new aspiration of the human mind to be made visible and real? How is it to pass out of thoughts into things?

Not, certainly, in the first place, *in the way of routine and mere forms,*—the universal specific of modern politics; not by organizing a society, and going through a course of resolutions and public manifestoes, and being thus formally accredited to the public and to the civility of the newspapers. We have played this game to tediousness. In some of our cities they choose

noted duellists as presidents and officers of anti-duelling societies. Men who love that bloated vanity called public opinion
think all is well if they have once got their bantling through
a sufficient course of speeches and cheerings, of one, two, or
three public meetings; as if *they* could do anything: they vote
and vote, cry hurrah on both sides, no man responsible, no man
caring a pin. The next season, an Indian war, or an aggression
on our commerce by Malays; or the party this man votes with
have an appropriation to carry through Congress: instantly he
wags his head the other way, and cries, Havoc and war!

This is not to be carried by public opinion, but by private
opinion, by private conviction, by private, dear and earnest
love. For the only hope of this cause is in the increased insight,
and it is to be accomplished by the spontaneous teaching, of
the cultivated soul, in its secret experience and meditation,—
that it is now time that it should pass out of the state of beast
into the state of man; it is to hear the voice of God, which bids
the devils that have rended and torn him come out of him and
let him now be clothed and walk forth in his right mind.

Nor, in the next place, is the peace principle to be carried
into effect by fear. It can never be defended, it can never be
executed, by cowards. Everything great must be done in the
spirit of greatness. The manhood that has been in war must be
transferred to the cause of peace, before war can lose its charm,
and peace be venerable to men.

The attractiveness of war shows one thing through all the
throats of artillery, the thunders of so many sieges, the sack of
towns, the jousts of chivalry, the shock of hosts,—this namely,
the conviction of man universally, that a man should be himself
responsible, with goods, health and life, for his behavior; that
he should not ask of the State protection; should ask nothing
of the State; should be himself a kingdom and a state; fearing
no man; quite willing to use the opportunities and advantages
that good government throw in his way, but nothing daunted,
and not really the poorer if government, law and order went by
the board; because in himself reside infinite resources; because
he is sure of himself, and never needs to ask another what in
any crisis it behooves him to do.

What makes to us the attractiveness of the Greek heroes? of
the Roman? What makes the attractiveness of that romantic

style of living which is the material of ten thousand plays and romances, from Shakspeare to Scott; the feudal baron, the French, the English nobility, the Warwicks, Plantagenets? It is their absolute self-dependence. I do not wonder at the dislike some of the friends of peace have expressed at Shakspeare. The veriest churl and Jacobin cannot resist the influence of the style and manners of these haughty lords. We are affected, as boys and barbarians are, by the appearance of a few rich and wilful gentlemen who take their honor into their own keeping, defy the world, so confident are they of their courage and strength, and whose appearance is the arrival of so much life and virtue. In dangerous times they are presently tried, and therefore their name is a flourish of trumpets. They, at least, affect us as a reality. They are not shams, but the substance of which that age and world is made. They are true heroes for their time. They make what is in their minds the greatest sacrifice. They will, for an injurious word, peril all their state and wealth, and go to the field. Take away that principle of responsibleness, and they become pirates and ruffians.

This self-subsistency is the charm of war; for this self-subsistency is essential to our idea of man. But another age comes, a truer religion and ethics open, and a man puts himself under the dominion of principles. I see him to be the servant of truth, of love and of freedom, and immoveable in the waves of the crowd. The man of principle, that is, the man who, without any flourish of trumpets, titles of lordship or train of guards, without any notice of his action abroad, expecting none, takes in solitude the right step uniformly, on his private choice and disdaining consequences,—does not yield, in my imagination, to any man. He is willing to be hanged at his own gate, rather than consent to any compromise of his freedom or the suppression of his conviction. I regard no longer those names that so tingled in my ear. This is a baron of a better nobility and a stouter stomach.

The cause of peace is not the cause of cowardice. If peace is sought to be defended or preserved for the safety of the luxurious and the timid, it is a sham, and the peace will be base. War is better, and the peace will be broken. If peace is to be maintained, it must be by brave men, who have come up to the same height as the hero, namely, the will to carry their life in their hand, and stake it at any instant for their principle, but who have gone one step beyond the hero, and will not seek another man's life;—men who have, by their intellectual insight or else by their moral elevation, attained such a perception of their own intrinsic worth, that they do not think property or their own body a sufficient good to be saved by such dereliction of principle as treating a man like a sheep.

If the universal cry for reform of so many inveterate abuses, with which society rings,—if the desire of a large class of young men for a faith and hope, intellectual and religious, such as they have not yet found, be an omen to be trusted; if the disposition to rely more in study and in action on the unexplored riches of the human constitution,—if the search of the sublime laws of morals and the sources of hope and trust, in man, and not in books, in the present, and not in the past, proceed; if the rising generation can be provoked to think it unworthy to nestle into every abomination of the past, and shall feel the generous darings of austerity and virtue, then war has a short day, and human blood will cease to flow.

It is of little consequence in what manner, through what organs, this purpose of mercy and holiness is effected. The proposition of the Congress of Nations is undoubtedly that at which the present fabric of our society and the present course of events do point. But the mind, once prepared for the reign of principles, will easily find modes of expressing its will. There is the highest fitness in the place and time in which this enterprise is begun. Not in an obscure corner, not in a feudal Europe, not in an antiquated appanage where no onward step can be taken without rebellion, is this seed of benevolence laid in the furrow, with tears of hope; but in this broad America of God and man, where the forest is only now falling, or yet to fall, and the green earth opened to the inundation of emigrant men from all quarters of oppression and guilt; here, where not a family, not a few men, but mankind, shall say what shall be; here, we ask, Shall it be War, or shall it be Peace?

WILLIAM LLOYD GARRISON

William Lloyd Garrison (1805–1879) is most widely known as an abolitionist, a "soul on fire" for that cause in the phrase of his late biographer Henry Mayer; he is less well-known as a nonresistant, namely an opponent of all war and violence. But he was that too, opposing not only war but capital punishment and indeed all engagement with political activity that required even implicit consent to the use of violence. His hatred of slavery and his hatred of violence, he felt, were one.

The force of Garrison's opposition to violence led him and some like-minded friends to break off from the American Peace Society in 1838 and found the New England Non-Resistance Society; the present "Declaration of Sentiments" is the latter group's statement of principles, which Garrison drafted. As a statement of principles it has much in common with the principles of John Woolman; as an exercise in rhetoric it is a world away, conducted with an unbridled military vigor that casts its own long shadow on the antiwar tradition.

Garrison himself gave up his pacifist commitments to support the Civil War, finding abolitionism the more compelling cause when the two causes came into conflict. But his nonresistance writings retained their force, influencing Tolstoy generations later and, through him, Mohandas Gandhi.

Declaration of Sentiments Adopted by the Peace Convention, Held in Boston, September 18, 19, & 20, 1838

ASSEMBLED in Convention, from various sections of the American Union, for the promotion of peace on earth, and good will among men, we, the undersigned, regard it as due to ourselves, to the cause which we love, to the country in which we live, and to the world, to publish a DECLARATION, expressive of the principles we cherish, the purposes we aim to accomplish, and the measures we shall adopt to carry forward the work of peaceful, universal reformation.

We cannot acknowledge allegiance to any human government; neither can we oppose any such government, by a resort to physical force. We recognize but one KING and LAWGIVER, one JUDGE and RULER of mankind. We are bound by the laws of a kingdom which is not of this world; the subjects of which are forbidden to fight; in which MERCY and TRUTH are met together, and RIGHTEOUSNESS and PEACE have kissed each other; which has no state lines, no national partitions, no geographical boundaries; in which there is no distinction of rank, or division of caste, or inequality of sex; the officers of which are PEACE, its exactors RIGHTEOUSNESS, its walls SALVATION, and its gates PRAISE; and which is destined to break in pieces and consume all other kingdoms.

Our country is the world, our countrymen are all mankind. We love the land of our nativity, only as we love all other lands. The interests, rights, liberties of American citizens are no more dear to us, than are those of the whole human race. Hence, we can allow no appeal to patriotism, to revenge any national insult or injury. The PRINCE OF PEACE, under whose stainless banner we rally, came not to destroy, but to save, even the worst of enemies. He has left us an example, that we should follow his steps. GOD COMMANDETH HIS LOVE TOWARD US, IN THAT WHILE WE WERE YET SINNERS, CHRIST DIED FOR US.

We conceive, that if a nation has no right to defend itself against foreign enemies, or to punish its invaders, no individual possesses that right in his own case. The unit cannot be of greater importance than the aggregate. If one man may take life, to obtain or defend his rights, the same license must necessarily be granted to communities, states, and nations. If *he* may use a dagger or a pistol, *they* may employ cannon, bomb-shells, land and naval forces. The means of self-preservation must be in proportion to the magnitude of interests at stake, and the number of lives exposed to destruction. But if a rapacious and blood-thirsty soldiery, thronging these shores from abroad, with intent to commit rapine and destroy life, may not be resisted by the people or magistracy, then ought no resistance to be offered to domestic troublers of the public peace, or of private security. No obligation can rest upon Americans to regard foreigners as more sacred in their persons than themselves, or to give them a monopoly of wrong-doing with impunity.

The dogma, that all the governments of the world are approvingly ordained of God, and that THE POWERS THAT BE in the United States, in Russia, in Turkey, are in accordance with his will, is not less absurd than impious. It makes the impartial Author of human freedom and equality, unequal and tyrannical. It cannot be affirmed, that THE POWERS THAT BE, in any nation, are actuated by the spirit, or guided by the example of Christ, in the treatment of enemies; therefore, they cannot be agreeable to the will of God; and, therefore, their overthrow, by a spiritual regeneration of their subjects, is inevitable.

We register our testimony, not only against all wars, whether offensive or defensive, but all prepations for war; against every naval ship, every arsenal, every fortification; against the militia system and a standing army; against all military chieftains and soldiers; against all monuments commemorative of victory over a foreign foe, all trophies won in battle, all celebrations in honor of military or naval exploits; against all appropriations for the defence of a nation by force and arms, on the part of any legislative body; against every edict of government, requiring of its subjects military service. Hence, we deem it unlawful to bear arms, or to hold a military office.

As every human government is upheld by physical strength, and its laws are enforced virtually at the point of the bayonet, we cannot hold any office which imposes upon its incumbent the obligation to compel men to do right, on pain of imprisonment or death. We therefore voluntarily exclude ourselves from every legislative and judicial body, and repudiate all human politics, worldly honors, and stations of authority. If *we* cannot occupy a seat in the legislature, or on the bench, neither can we elect *others* to act as our substitutes in any such capacity.

It follows, that we cannot sue any man at law, to compel him by force to restore any thing which he may have wrongfully taken from us or others; but if he has seized our coat, we shall surrender up our cloak, rather than subject him to punishment.

We believe that the penal code of the old covenant, AN EYE FOR AN EYE, AND A TOOTH FOR A TOOTH, has been abrogated by JESUS CHRIST; and that, under the new covenant, the forgiveness, instead of the punishment of enemies, has been enjoined upon all his disciples, in all cases whatsoever. To extort money from enemies, or set them upon a pillory, or cast them into prison, or hang them upon a gallows, is obviously not to forgive, but to take retribution. VENGEANCE IS MINE—I WILL REPAY, SAITH THE LORD.

The history of mankind is crowded with evidences, proving that physical coercion is not adapted to moral regeneration; that the sinful dispositions of man can be subdued only by love; that evil can be exterminated from the earth only by goodness; that it is not safe to rely upon an arm of flesh, upon man whose breath is in his nostrils, to preserve us from harm; that there is great security in being gentle, harmless, long-suffering, and abundant in mercy; that it is only the meek who shall inherit the earth, for the violent who resort to the sword are destined to perish with the sword. Hence, as a measure of sound policy,—of safety to property, life and liberty,—of public quietude and private enjoyment,—as well as on the ground of allegiance to HIM who is KING OF KINGS, and LORD OF LORDS,—we cordially adopt the non-resistance principle; being confident that it provides for all possible consequences, will ensure all things needful to us, is armed with omnipotent power, and must ultimately triumph over every assailing force.

We advocate no jacobinical doctrines. The spirit of jacobinism is the spirit of retaliation, violence, and murder. It neither fears God, nor regards man. *We* would be filled with the spirit of CHRIST. If we abide by our principles, it is impossible for us to be disorderly, or plot treason, or participate in any evil work; we shall submit to every ordinance of man, FOR THE LORD'S SAKE; obey all the requirements of government, except such as we deem contrary to the commands of the gospel; and in no case resist the operation of law, except by meekly submitting to the penalty of disobedience.

But, while we shall adhere to the doctrine of non-resistance and passive submission to enemies, we purpose, in a moral and spiritual sense, to speak and act boldly in the cause of GOD; to assail iniquity, in high places and in low places; to apply our principles to all existing civil, political, legal, and ecclesiastical institutions; and to hasten the time, when the kingdoms of this world will have become the kingdoms of our LORD and of his CHRIST, and he shall reign for ever.

It appears to us a self-evident truth, that, whatever the gospel is designed to destroy at any period of the world, being contrary to it, ought now to be abandoned. If, then, the time is predicted, when swords shall be beaten into ploughshares, and spears into pruning-hooks, and men shall not learn the art of war any more, it follows that all who manufacture, sell, or wield these deadly weapons, do thus array themselves against the peaceful dominion of the SON OF GOD on earth.

Having thus briefly, but frankly, stated our principles and purposes, we proceed to specify the measures we propose to adopt, in carrying our object into effect.

We expect to prevail, through THE FOOLISHNESS OF PREACHING—striving to commend ourselves unto every man's conscience, in the sight of GOD. From the press, we shall promulgate our sentiments as widely as practicable. We shall endeavor to secure the co-operation of all persons, of whatever name or sect. The triumphant progress of the cause of TEMPERANCE and of ABOLITION in our land, through the instrumentality of benevolent and voluntary associations, encourages us to combine our own means and efforts for the promotion of a still greater cause. Hence, we shall employ lecturers, circulate tracts and publications, form societies, and petition our state and national governments, in relation to the subject of UNIVERSAL PEACE. It will be our leading object to devise ways and means for effecting a radical change in the views, feelings and practices of society, respecting the sinfulness of war, and the treatment of enemies.

In entering upon the great work before us, we are not unmindful that, in its prosecution we may be called to test our sincerity, even as in a fiery ordeal. It may subject us to insult, outrage, suffering, yea, even death itself. We anticipate no small amount of misconception, misrepresentation, calumny. Tumults may arise against us. The ungodly and violent, the proud and pharisaical, the ambitious and tyrannical, principalities and powers, and spiritual wickedness in high places, may combine to crush us. So they treated the MESSIAH, whose example we are humbly striving to imitate. If we suffer with him, we know that we shall reign with him. We shall not be afraid of their terror, neither be troubled. Our confidence is in the LORD ALMIGHTY, not in man. Having withdrawn from human protection, what can sustain us but that faith which overcomes the world? We shall not think it strange concerning the fiery trial which is to try us, as though some strange thing had happened unto us; but rejoice, inasmuch as we are partakers of CHRIST's sufferings. Wherefore, we commit the keeping of our souls to GOD, in well-doing, as unto a faithful Creator. FOR EVERY ONE THAT FORSAKES HOUSES, OR BRETHREN, OR SISTERS, OR FATHER, OR MOTHER, OR WIFE, OR CHILDREN, OR LANDS, FOR CHRIST'S SAKE, SHALL RECEIVE A HUNDRED FOLD, AND SHALL INHERIT EVERLASTING LIFE.

Firmly relying upon the certain and universal triumph of the sentiments contained in this DECLARATION, however formidable may be the opposition arrayed against them,— in solemn testimony of our faith in their divine origin—we hereby affix our signatures to it; commending it to the reason and conscience of mankind, giving ourselves no anxiety as to what may befall us, and resolving in the strength of the LORD GOD calmly and meekly to abide the issue.

HENRY WADSWORTH LONGFELLOW

Henry Wadsworth Longfellow (1807–1882) was once among America's most admired poets, though his stock has fallen considerably. "The Arsenal at Springfield," first published in 1845, is an uncharacteristically political poem for him, and seems to have been a collaborative effort; his second wife Fanny was with him when he visited the arsenal the poem describes, and she afterwards wrote that she urged him to write a peace poem about it. Longfellow himself said the poem was inspired by an antiwar speech by Charles Sumner. Whatever its sources, the poem remains alive not because of its political analysis but because of its evocative account of war as manifested in its weapons, the arsenal gun barrels that ironically, cruelly resemble the pipes of a great organ.

The Arsenal at Springfield

This is the Arsenal. From floor to ceiling,
    Like a huge organ, rise the burnished arms;
But from their silent pipes no anthem pealing
    Startles the villages with strange alarms.

Ah! what a sound will rise, how wild and dreary,
    When the death-angel touches those swift keys!
What loud lament and dismal Miserere
    Will mingle with their awful symphonies!

I hear even now the infinite fierce chorus,
    The cries of agony, the endless groan,
Which, through the ages that have gone before us,
    In long reverberations reach our own.

On helm and harness rings the Saxon hammer,
    Through Cimbric forest roars the Norseman's song,
And loud, amid the universal clamor,
    O'er distant deserts sounds the Tartar gong.

I hear the Florentine, who from his palace
  Wheels out his battle-bell with dreadful din,
And Aztec priests upon their teocallis
  Beat the wild war-drums made of serpent's skin;

The tumult of each sacked and burning village;
  The shout that every prayer for mercy drowns;
The soldiers' revels in the midst of pillage;
  The wail of famine in beleaguered towns;

The bursting shell, the gateway wrenched asunder,
  The rattling musketry, the clashing blade;
And ever and anon, in tones of thunder,
  The diapason of the cannonade.

Is it, O man, with such discordant noises,
  With such accursed instruments as these,
Thou drownest Nature's sweet and kindly voices,
  And jarrest the celestial harmonies?

Were half the power, that fills the world with terror,
  Were half the wealth, bestowed on camps and courts,
Given to redeem the human mind from error,
  There were no need of arsenals nor forts:

The warrior's name would be a name abhorred!
  And every nation, that should lift again
Its hand against a brother, on its forehead
  Would wear forevermore the curse of Cain!

Down the dark future, through long generations,
  The echoing sounds grow fainter and then cease;
And like a bell, with solemn, sweet vibrations,
  I hear once more the voice of Christ say, "Peace!"

Peace! and no longer from its brazen portals
  The blast of War's great organ shakes the skies!
But beautiful as songs of the immortals,
  The holy melodies of love arise.

ADIN BALLOU

If William Lloyd Garrison is the fiery orator of nonresistance, Adin Ballou (1803–1890) is its temperate theoretician, setting out the doctrine with almost mathematical precision. Like Garrison, he appears on Tolstoy's list of pacifist influences (Tolstoy once told a journalist he considered Ballou to be America's most important writer, and the two corresponded just before Ballou's death). Also like Garrison, his commitment to nonresistance emerged from his reading of the New Testament, and in particular the Sermon on the Mount (in 1841, he and other "practical Christians" founded Hopedale, a utopian community near Milford, Massachusetts). Unlike Garrison, however, he held fast to his first principles, choosing nonresistance over violent abolitionism even as the Civil War approached, and never yielding; the issue strained the pair's previous friendship. Both writers continue to matter to opponents of war and violence, Christian and otherwise: after Tolstoy, both Gandhi and Martin Luther King Jr. acknowledged their indebtedness to these forbears.

The Term Non-Resistance

THE term non-resistance itself next demands attention. It requires very considerable qualifications. I use it as applicable *only* to the conduct of human beings towards human beings—not towards the inferior animals, inanimate things or satanic influences. If an opponent, willing to make me appear ridiculous, should say—"You are a non-resistant, and therefore must be *passive* to all assailing beings, things and influences, to satan, man, beast, bird, serpent, insect, rocks, timbers, fires, floods, heat, cold and storm,"—I should answer, *not so*; my non-resistance relates solely to conduct between human beings. This is an important limitation of the term. But I go further, and disclaim using the term to express *absolute passivity*, even towards human beings. I claim the right to offer the utmost *moral* resistance, not sinful, of which God has made me capable, to every manifestation of evil among mankind. Nay, I hold it my *duty* to offer such moral resistance. In this sense my very non-resistance becomes the highest kind of *resistance* to evil. This is another important qualification of the term. But I do not stop here. There is an uninjurious, benevolent *physical* force. There are cases in which it would not only be allowable, but in the highest degree commendable, to *restrain* human beings by this kind of force. Thus, maniacs, the insane, the delirious sick, ill natured children, the intellectually or *morally* non-compos mentis, the intoxicated and the violently passionate, are frequently disposed to perpetrate outrages and inflict injuries, either on themselves or others, which ought to be kindly and uninjuriously prevented by the muscular energy of their friends. And in cases where deadly violence is inflicted with deliberation and malice aforethought, one may nobly throw his body as a temporary barrier between the destroyer and his helpless victim, choosing to die in that position, rather than be a passive spectator. Thus another most important qualification is given to the term non-resistance. It is not non-resistance to animals and inanimate things, nor to satan, but only to human beings. Nor is it *moral* non-resistance to human beings, but chiefly physical. Nor is it physical non-resistance to all human beings, under all circumstances, but only so far as to abstain totally from the infliction of personal injury, as a means of resistance. It is simply non-resistance of injury with injury—evil with evil.

Will the opposer exclaim—"This is no non-resistance at all; the term is mischosen!" I answer. So said the old opposers of the Temperance Reformation, respecting the term "*total abstinence*." They began by insisting that the term *must* be taken unqualifiedly, and pronounced total abstinence an *absurdity*. It was replied—"we limit its application to the use of ardent spirits and intoxicating liquours." "Then you exclude these substances from the arts and from external applications, do you?" rejoined the opposers. "No," replied the advocates of the cause, "we mean *total abstinence* from the *internal* use—the *drinking* of those liquors." "But are they not sometimes necessary for medical purposes?" said the opposers, "and *then* may they not be taken internally?" "Certainly, with proper precautions," was the reply; "we mean by *total abstinence*, precisely *this* and no more, ☞ the entire disuse of all ardent spirits and intoxicating liquors, *as a beverage*." "That," exclaimed the objectors, (despairing of a reductio ad absurdam,) "is *no total* abstinence *at all*; the term is mischosen!" Nevertheless, it was a most significant term. It had in it an almost talismanic power. It expressed better than any other just what was meant, and wrought a prodigious change in public opinion and practice. The term *non-resistance* is equally significant and talismanic. It signifies total abstinence from all resistance of injury with injury. It is thus far *non-resistance*—no farther.

The almost universal opinion and practice of mankind has been on the side of resistance of injury *with* injury. It has been held justifiable and *necessary*, for individuals and nations to inflict any amount of *injury* which would effectually resist a supposed greater injury. The consequence has been universal suspicion, defiance, armament, violence, torture and blood-shed. The earth has been rendered a vast slaughter-field—a the-atre of reciprocal cruelty and vengeance—strewn with human skulls, reeking with human blood, resounding with human groans, and steeped with human tears. Men have become drunk with mutual revenge; and they who could inflict the greatest amount of injury, in pretended defence of life, honor, rights, property, institutions and laws, have been idolized as the heroes and rightful sovereigns of the world. Non-resistance explodes this horrible delusion; announces the impossibility of overcoming evil with evil; and, making its appeal directly to all the *injured* of the human race, enjoins on them, in the name of God, never more to *resist injury with injury*; assuring them that by adhering to the law of love under all provocations, and scrupulously suffering wrong, rather than inflicting it, they shall gloriously "overcome evil with good," and exterminate all their enemies by turning them into faithful friends.

THEODORE PARKER

The prestige of oratory has declined since the days of Theodore Parker (1810–1860); to call something "oratorical" is to insult it. But oratory in the nineteenth century had and often deserved a high regard. Parker's 1847 speech against the Mexican War, which for him as for others was a war to advance the cause of slavery, is among the great blunt orations of the period; not the high-flown oratory of Edward Everett that Emerson loved so much, but the kind that leads in this volume to Eugene Debs and Shirley Chisholm. (Toward the end of his short life Parker made his living by his oratory, delivering some 100 lectures a year in all the northern states east of the Mississippi, and reaching some 100,000 listeners annually.)

Parker was largely self-taught and far on the religious left. His chief theological cause was the notion that genuine religion manifested itself in moral action; his chief political cause was abolitionism, and Julia Ward Howe was among his converts. He spoke and acted against the Fugitive Slave Law, he was one of those who supported John Brown, and he surely would have supported the Civil War had he lived to see it. But he died in Florence of tuberculosis in 1860.

Speech Delivered at the Anti-War Meeting, in Faneuil Hall, February 4, 1847

Mr. Chairman,—We have come here to consult for the honor of our country. The honor and dignity of the United States are in danger. I love my country; I love her honor. It is dear to me almost as my own. I have seen stormy meetings in Faneuil Hall before now, and am not easily disturbed by a popular tumult. But never before did I see a body of armed soldiers attempting to overawe the majesty of the people, when met to deliberate on the people's affairs. Yet the meetings of the people of Boston have been disturbed by soldiers before now, by British bayonets; but never since the Boston massacre on the 5th of March, 1770! Our fathers hated a standing army. This is a new one, but behold the effect! Here are soldiers with bayonets, to overawe the majesty of the people! They went to our meeting last Monday night, the hireling soldiers of President Polk, to overawe and disturb the meetings of honest men. Here they are now, and in arms!

We are in a war; the signs of war are seen here in Boston. Men, needed to hew wood and honestly serve society, are marching about your streets; they are learning to kill men, men who never harmed us, nor them; learning to kill their brothers. It is a mean and infamous war we are fighting. It is a great boy fighting a little one, and that little one feeble and sick. What makes it worse is, the little boy is in the right, and the big boy is in the wrong, and tells solemn lies to make his side seem right. He wants, besides, to make the small boy pay the expenses of the quarrel.

The friends of the war say "Mexico has invaded our territory!" When it is shown that it is we who have invaded hers, then it is said, "Ay, but she owes us money." Better say outright, "Mexico has land, and we want to steal it!"

This war is waged for a mean and infamous purpose, for the extension of slavery. It is not enough that there are fifteen Slave States, and 3,000,000 men here who have no legal rights—not so much as the horse and the ox have in Boston: it is not enough that the slaveholders annexed Texas, and made slavery perpetual therein, extending even north of Mason and Dixon's line, covering a territory forty-five times as large as the State of Massachusetts. Oh, no; we must have yet more land to whip negroes in!

The war had a mean and infamous beginning. It began illegally, unconstitutionally. The Whigs say, "the President made the war." Mr. Webster says so! It went on meanly and infamously. Your Congress lied about it. Do not lay the blame on the democrats; the whigs lied just as badly. Your Congress has seldom been so single-mouthed before. Why, only sixteen voted against the war, or the lie. I say this war is mean and infamous all the more, because waged by a people calling itself democratic and Christian. I know but one war so bad in modern times, between civilized nations, and that was the war for the partition of Poland. Even for that there was more excuse.

We have come to Faneuil Hall to talk about the war; to work against the war. It is rather late, but "better late than never." We have let two opportunities for work pass unemployed. One came while the annexation of Texas was pending. Then was the time to push and be active. Then was the time for

Massachusetts and all the North, to protest as one man against the extension of slavery. Everybody knew all about the matter, the democrats and the whigs. But how few worked against that gross mischief! One noble man lifted up his warning voice;* a man noble in his father,—and there he stands in marble; noble in himself—and there he stands yet higher up—and I hope time will show him yet nobler in his son, and there he stands, not in marble, but in man! He talked against it, worked against it, fought against it. But Massachusetts did little. Her tonguey men said little; her handy-men did little. Too little could not be done or said. True, we came here to Faneuil Hall and passed resolutions; good resolutions they were, too. Daniel Webster wrote them, it is said. They did the same in the State House; but nothing came of them. They say "Hell is paved with resolutions;" these were of that sort of resolutions; which resolve nothing because they are of words, not works!

Well, we passed the resolutions; you know who opposed them; who hung back and did nothing, nothing good I mean; quite enough not good. Then we thought all the danger was over; that the resolutions settled the matter. But then was the time to confound at once the enemies of your country; to show an even front hostile to slavery.

But the chosen time passed over, and nothing was done. Do not lay the blame on the democrats; a whig Senate annexed Texas, and so annexed a war. We ought to have told our delegation in Congress, if Texas were annexed, to come home, and we would breathe upon it and sleep upon it, and then see what to do next. Had our resolutions, taken so warmly here in Faneuil Hall in 1845, been but as warmly worked out, we had now been as terrible to the slave power as the slave power, since extended, now is to us!

Why was it that we did nothing? That is a public secret. Perhaps I ought not to tell it to the people. (Cries of "Tell it.")

The annexation of Texas, a slave territory big as the kingdom of France, would not furl a sail on the ocean; would not stop a mill-wheel at Lowell! Men thought so.

*John Quincy Adams.

That time passed by, and there came another. The Government had made war; the Congress voted the dollars, voted the men, voted a lie. Your representative, men of Boston, voted for all three; the lie, the dollars, and the men; all three, in obedience to the slave power! Let him excuse that to the conscience of his party; it is an easy matter. I do not believe he can excuse it to his own conscience. To the conscience of the world it admits of no excuse. Your President called for volunteers, 50,000 of them. Then came an opportunity such as offers not once in one hundred years, an opportunity to speak for freedom and the rights of mankind! Then was the time for Massachusetts to stand up in the spirit of '76, and say, "We won't send a man, from Cape Ann to Williamstown—not one Yankee man, for this wicked war." Then was the time for your Governor to say, "Not a volunteer for this wicked war." Then was the time for your merchants to say, "Not a ship, not a dollar for this wicked war;" for your manufacturers to say, "We will not make you a cannon, nor a sword, nor a kernel of powder, nor a soldier's shirt, for this wicked war." Then was the time for all good men to say, "This is a war for slavery, a mean and infamous war; an aristocratic war, a war against the best interests of mankind. If God please, we will die a thousand times, but never draw blade in this wicked war." (Cries of "Throw him over," &c.) Throw him over, what good would that do? What would you do next, after you have thrown him over? ("Drag you out of the hall!") What good would that do? It would not wipe off the infamy of this war! would not make it less wicked!

That is what a democratic nation, a Christian people ought to have said, ought to have done. But we did not say so; the Bay State did not say so, nor your Governor, nor your merchants, nor your manufacturers, nor your good men; the Governor accepted the President's decree, issued his proclamation calling for soldiers, recommended men to enlist, appealing to their "patriotism" and "humanity."

Governor Briggs is a good man, and so far I honor him. He is a temperance man, strong and consistent; I honor him for that. He is a friend of education; a friend of the people. I wish there were more such. Like many other New England men, he started from humble beginnings; but unlike many such successful men of New England, he is not ashamed of the lowest round he ever trod on. I honor him for all this. But that was a time which tried men's souls, and his soul could not stand the rack. I am sorry for him. He did as the President told him.

What was the reason for all this? Massachusetts did not like the war, even then; yet she gave her consent to it. Why so? There are two words which can drive the blood out of the cheeks of cowardly men in Massachusetts any time. They are "Federalism" and "Hartford Convention!" The fear of those words palsied the conscience of Massachusetts, and so her Governor did as he was told. I feel no fear of either. The Federalists did not see all things; who ever did? They had not the ideas which were destined to rule this nation; they looked back when the age looked forward. But to their own ideas they were true; and if ever a nobler body of men held state in any nation, I have yet to learn when or where. If we had had the shadow of Caleb Strong in the Governor's chair, not a volunteer for this war had gone out of Massachusetts.

I have not told quite all the reasons why Massachusetts did nothing. Men knew the war would cost money; that the dollars would in the end be raised, not by a direct tax, of which the poor man paid according to his little, and the rich man in proportion to his much, but by a tariff which presses light on property, and hard on the person; by a tax on the backs and mouths of the people. Some of the whigs were glad last Spring, when the war came, for they hoped thereby to save the child of their old age, the tariff of '42. There are always some rich men, who say "No matter what sort of a Government we have, so long as we get our dividends;" always some poor men, who say "No matter how much the nation suffers, if we fill our hungry purses thereby." Well, they lost their virtue, lost their tariff, and gained just nothing; what they deserved to gain.

Now a third opportunity has come; no, it has not come; we have brought it. The President wants a war tax on tea and coffee. Is that democratic, to tax every man's breakfast and supper, for the sake of getting more territory to whip negroes in? (Numerous cries of "Yes.") Then what do you think despotism would be? He asks a loan of $28,000,000 for this war. He wants $3,000,000 to spend privately for this war. In eight months past, he has asked I am told for $74,000,000. Seventy-four millions of dollars to conquer slave territory! Is that democratic too? He wants to increase the standing army, to have ten regiments more! A pretty business that. Ten regiments to gag the people in Faneuil Hall. Do you think that is democratic? Some men have just asked Massachusetts for $20,000 for the volunteers! It is time for the people to rebuke all this wickedness.

I think there is a good deal to excuse the volunteers. I blame them, for some of them know what they are about. Yet I pity them more, for most of them, I am told, are low, ignorant men; some of them drunken and brutal. From the uproar they make here to-night, arms in their hands, I think what was told me is true! I say I pity them! They are my brothers; not the less brothers because low and misguided. If they are so needy that they are forced to enlist by poverty, surely I pity them. If they are of good families, and know better, I pity them still more! I blame most the men that have duped the rank and file! I blame the captains and colonels, who will have least of the hardships, most of the pay, and all of the "glory." I blame the men that made the war; the men that make money of it. I blame the great party men of the land. Did not Mr. Clay say he hoped he could slay a Mexican? (Cries, "No, he didn't.") Yes, he did; said it on Forefather's day! Did not Mr. Webster, in the streets of Philadelphia, bid the volunteers, misguided young men, go and uphold the stars of their country? (Voices, "He did right!") No, he should have said the stripes of his country, for every volunteer to this wicked war is a stripe on the nation's back! Did not he declare this war unconstitutional, and threaten to impeach the President who made it, and then go and invest a son in it? Has it not been said here, "Our country, howsoever bounded," bounded by robbery or bounded by right lines! Has it not been said, all round, "Our country, right or wrong!"

I say I blame not so much the volunteers as the famous men who deceive the nation! (Cries of "Throw him over, kill him, kill him," and a flourish of bayonets.) Throw him over! you will not throw him over. Kill him! I shall walk home unarmed and unattended, and not a man of you will hurt one hair of my head.

I say again, it is time for the people to take up this matter. Your Congress will do nothing till you tell them what and how! Your 29th Congress can do little good. Its sands are nearly run, God be thanked! It is the most infamous Congress we ever had. We began with the Congress that declared Independence, and swore by the Eternal Justice of God. We have come down to the 29th Congress, which declared war existed by the act of Mexico, declared a lie; the Congress that swore by the Baltimore Convention! We began with George Washington, and have got down to James K. Polk.

It is time for the people of Massachusetts to instruct their servants in Congress to oppose this war; to refuse all supplies for it; to ask for the recall of the army into our own land. It is time for us to tell them that not an inch of slave territory shall ever be added to the realm. Let us remonstrate; let us petition; let us command. If any class of men have hitherto been remiss, let them come forward now and give us their names—the merchants, the manufacturers, the whigs and the democrats. If men love their country better than their party or their purse, now let them show it.

Let us ask the General Court of Massachusetts to cancel every commission which the Governor has given to the officers of the volunteers. Let us ask them to disband the companies not yet mustered into actual service; and then, if you like that, ask them to call a convention of the people of Massachusetts, to see what we shall do in reference to the war; in reference to the annexation of more territory; in reference to the violation of the Constitution! (Loud groans from crowds of rude fellows in several parts of the hall.) That was a tory groan; they never dared groan so in Faneuil Hall before; not even the British tories, when they had no bayonets to back them up! I say, let us ask for these things!

Your President tells us it is treason to talk so! Treason is it? treason to discuss a war which the government made, and which the people are made to pay for? If it be treason to speak against the war, what was it to make the war, to ask for 50,000 men and $74,000,000 for the war? Why, if the people cannot discuss the war they have got to fight and to pay for, who under heaven can? Whose business is it, if it is not yours and mine? If my country is in the wrong, and I know it, and hold my peace, then I am guilty of treason, moral treason. Why, a wrong,—it is only the threshold of ruin. I would not have my country take the next step. Treason is it, to show that this war is wrong and wicked! Why, what if George III., any time from '75 to '83, had gone down to Parliament and told them it was treason to discuss the war then waging against these colonies! What do you think the Commons would have said? What would the Lords say? Why, that King, foolish as he was, would have been lucky, if he had not learned there was a joint in his neck, and; stiff as he bore him, that the people knew how to find it.

I do not believe in killing kings, or any other men; but I do say, in a time when the nation was not in danger, that no British king, for two hundred years past, would have dared call it treason to discuss the war—its cause, its progress, or its termination!

Now is the time to act! Twice we have let the occasion slip; beware of the third time! Let it be infamous for a New-England man to enlist; for a New-England merchant to loan his dollars, or to let his ships in aid of this wicked war; let it be infamous for a manufacturer to make a cannon, a sword, or a kernel of powder, to kill our brothers with, while we all know that they are in the right, and we in the wrong.

I know my voice is a feeble one in Massachusetts. I have no mountainous position from whence to look down and overawe the multitude; I have no back-ground of political reputation to echo my words; I am but a plain humble man; but I have a back-ground of Truth to sustain me, and the Justice of Heaven arches over my head! For your sakes, I wish I had that oceanic eloquence whose tidal flow should bear on its bosom the drift-weed which politicians have piled together, and sap and sweep away the sand hillocks of soldiery blown together by the idle wind; that oceanic eloquence which sweeps all before it, and leaves the shore hard, smooth and clean! But feeble as I am, let me beg of you, fellow-citizens of Boston, men and brothers, to come forward and protest against this wicked war, and the end for which it is waged. I call on the whigs, who love their country better than they love the tariff of '42; I call on the democrats, who think Justice is greater than the

Baltimore Convention,—I call on the whigs and democrats to come forward and join with me, in opposing this wicked war! I call on the men of Boston, on the men of the old Bay State, to act worthy of their fathers, worthy of their country, worthy of themselves! Men and brothers, I call on you all to protest against this most infamous war, in the name of the State, in the name of the country, in the name of man, yes, in the name of God! Leave not your children saddled with a war debt, to cripple the nation's commerce for years to come. Leave not your land cursed with slavery, extended and extending, palsying the nation's arm and corrupting the nation's heart. Leave not your memory infamous among the nations, because you feared men, feared the Government; because you loved money got by crime, land plundered in war, loved land unjustly bounded; because you debased your country by defending the wrong she dared to do; because you loved slavery; loved war, but loved not the Eternal Justice of all-judging God. If my counsel is weak and poor, follow one stronger and more manly. I am speaking to men; think of these things, and then act like men.

THOMAS CORWIN

Thomas Corwin (1794–1865) and Theodore Parker both gave notable speeches against the Mexican War, but Corwin delivered his in the thick of things, on the floor of the Senate, where he represented Ohio as a Whig, and where his flowery, indefatigable polemical style had already won him admirers (John Quincy Adams, for one, once referred to one of Corwin's vanquished oratorical antagonists as "the late Mr. Crary of Michigan"). But the February 11, 1847, speech was Corwin's one great moment. Afterwards he shied away from such strident opposition, stressing party unity over principle and disappointing those who had seen in him the great hope of the antislavery campaign and a possible candidate for national office.

FROM
Speech of Mr. Corwin, of Ohio, on the Mexican War

Mr. President, this uneasy desire to augment our territory, has depraved the moral sense, and blunted the otherwise keen sagacity of our people. What has been the fate of all nations who have acted upon the idea, that they must advance! Our young orators cherish this notion with a fervid, but fatally mistaken zeal. They call it by the mysterious name of "destiny." "Our destiny," they say, is onward, and hence they argue, with ready sophistry, the propriety of seizing upon any territory and any people, that may lay in the way of our "fated" advance. Recently these Progressives have grown classical; some assiduous student of antiquities has helped them to a patron saint. They have wandered back into the desolated Pantheon, and there, amongst the Polytheistic relics of that "pale mother of dead empires," they have found a God whom these Romans, centuries gone by, baptized "Terminus."

Sir, I have heard much and read somewhat of this gentleman Terminus. Alexander, of whom I have spoken, was a devotee of this divinity. We have seen the end of him and his empire. It was said to be an attribute of this God that he must *always* advance, and never recede. So both republican and imperial Rome believed. It was, as they said, their destiny. And for a while it did seem to be even so. Roman Terminus did advance.

Under the eagles of Rome he was carried from his home on the Tiber, to the furthest East on one hand, and to the far West, amongst the then barbarous tribes of western Europe, on the other. But at length the time came, when retributive justice had become "a destiny." The despised Gaul calls out to the contemned Goth, and Attilla with his Huns, answers back the battle shout to both. The "blue-eyed nations of the North," in succession or united, pour forth their countless hosts of warriors upon Rome and Rome's always-advancing God Terminus. And now the battle-axe of the barbarian strikes down the conquering eagle of Rome. Terminus at last recedes, slowly at first, but finally he is driven to Rome, and from Rome to Byzantium. Whoever would know the further fate of this Roman Deity, so recently taken under the patronage of American Democracy, may find ample gratification of his curiosity, in the luminous pages of Gibbon's "Decline and Fall." Such will find, that Rome thought as you now think, that it was her destiny to conquer provinces and nations, and no doubt she sometimes said as you say, "I will conquer a peace." And where now is she, the Mistress of the World? The spider weaves his web in her palaces, the owl sings his watch-song in her towers. Teutonic power now lords it over the servile remnant, the miserable memento of old and once omnipotent Rome. Sad, very sad, are the lessons which time has written for us. Through and in them all, I see nothing but the inflexible execution of that old law, which ordains as eternal, that cardinal rule, "Thou shalt not covet thy neighbor's goods, nor *any thing* which is his." Since I have lately heard so much about the dismemberment of Mexico, I have looked back to see how, in the course of events, which some call "Providence," it has fared with other nations, who engaged in this work of dismemberment. I see that in the latter half of the eighteenth century, three powerful nations, Russia, Austria and Prussia, united in the dismemberment of Poland. They said, too, as you say, "it is our destiny." They "wanted room." Doubtless each of these thought, with his share of Poland, his power was too strong ever to fear invasion, or even insult. One had his California, another his New Mexico, and the third his Vera Cruz. Did they remain untouched and incapable of harm? Alas! No—far, very far, from it. Retributive justice must fulfil its destiny too. A very few years pass off, and we hear of a new man, a Corsican lieutenant, the self-named "armed soldier of Democracy," Napoleon. He ravages Austria, covers her land with blood, drives the Northern Cæsar from his capital, and sleeps in his palace. Austria may now remember how her power trampled upon Poland. Did she not pay dear, very dear, for her California?

But has Prussia no atonement to make? You see this same Napoleon, the blind instrument of Providence, at work there. The thunders of his cannon at Jena proclaim the work of retribution for Poland's wrongs; and the successors of the Great Frederick, the drill-sergeant of Europe, are seen flying across the sandy plain that surrounds their capitol, right glad if they may escape captivity or death. But how fares it with the Autocrat of Russia? Is he secure in his share of the spoils of Poland? No. Suddenly we see, sir, six hundred thousand armed men marching to Moscow. Does his Vera Cruz protect him now? Far from it. Blood, slaughter, desolation spread abroad over the land, and finally the conflagration of the old commercial metropolis of Russia, closes the retribution, she must pay for her share in the dismemberment of her weak and impotent neighbor. Mr. President, a mind more prone to look for the judgments of Heaven in the doings of men than mine, cannot fail in this to see the Providence of God. When Moscow burned it seemed as if the earth was lighted up, that the Nations might behold the scene. As that mighty sea of fire gathered and heaved and rolled upwards, and yet higher, till its flames licked the stars, and fired the whole Heavens, it did seem as though the God of the Nations was writing in characters of flame on the front of his throne, that doom that shall fall upon the strong nation, which tramples in scorn upon the weak. And what fortune awaits Him, the appointed executor of this work, when it was all done? He, too, conceived the notion that his destiny pointed onward to universal dominion. France was too small—Europe, he thought, should bow down before him. But as soon as this idea took possession of his soul, he too becomes powerless. His Terminus must recede too. Right there, while he witnessed the humiliation, and doubtless meditated the subjugation of Russia, He who holds the winds in his fist, gathered the snows of the north and blew them upon his six hundred thousand men; they fled—they froze—they perished. And now the mighty Napoleon, who had resolved on universal dominion, *he* too is summoned to answer for the violation of that ancient law, "thou shalt not covet any thing which is thy neighbors." How is the mighty fallen. He, beneath whose proud footstep Europe trembled, he is now an exile at Elba, and now finally a prisoner on the rock of St. Helena, and there on a barren island, in an unfrequented sea, in the crater of an extinguished volcano, *there* is the death-bed of the mighty conqueror. All his *annexations* have come to that! His last hour is now come, and he, the man of *destiny*, he who had rocked the world as with the throes of an earthquake, is now powerless, still—even as the beggar, so he died. On the wings of a tempest that raged with unwonted fury, up to the throne of the only Power that controlled him while he lived, went the fiery soul of that wonderful warrior, another witness to the existence of that eternal decree, that they who do not rule in righteousness, shall perish from the earth. He has found "room" at last. And France, *she* too has found "room." Her "eagles" now no longer scream along the banks of the Danube, the Po, and the Borysthenes. They have returned home; to their old eyre, between the Alps, the Rhine, and the Pyrinees; so shall it be with yours. You may carry them to the loftiest peaks of the Cordilleras, they may wave with insolent triumph in the Halls of the Montezumas, the armed men of Mexico may quail before them, but the weakest hand in Mexico, uplifted in prayer to the God of Justice, may call down against you a Power, in the presence of which, the iron hearts of your warriors shall be turned into ashes.

Mr. President, if the history of our race has established any truth, it is but a confirmation of what is written, "the way of the transgresssor is hard." Inordinate ambition, wantoning in power, and spurning the humble maxims of justice has—ever has—and ever shall end in ruin. Strength cannot always trample upon weakness—the humble shall be exalted—the bowed down will at length be lifted up. It is by faith in the law of strict justice, and the practice of its precepts, that nations alone can be saved. All the annals of the human race, sacred and profane, are written over with this great truth, in characters of living light. It is my fear, my fixed belief, that in this invasion, this war with Mexico, we have forgotten this vital truth. Why is it, that we have been drawn into this whirlpool of war? How clear and strong was the light that shone upon the path of duty a year ago! The last disturbing question with England was settled—our power extended its peaceful sway from the Atlantic to the Pacific; from the Alleghanies we looked out upon Europe, and from the tops of the Stony Mountains we could descry the shores of Asia; a rich commerce with all the nations of Europe poured wealth and abundance into our lap on the Atlantic side, while an unoccupied commerce of three hundred millions of Asiatics waited on the Pacific for our enterprise to come and possess it. One hundred millions of dollars will be wasted in this fruitless war. Had this money of the people been expended in making a railroad from your Northern Lakes to the Pacific, as one of your citizens has begged of you in vain, you would have made a highway for the world between Asia and Europe. Your capitol then would be within thirty or forty days travel of any and every point on the map of the civilized world. Through this great artery of trade, you would have carried through the heart of your own country, the teas of China, and the spices of India, to the markets of England and France. Why, why, Mr. President, did we abandon the enterprises of peace, and betake ourselves to the barbarous achievements of war? Why did we "forsake *this* fair and fertile field to batten on that moor."

But, Mr. President, if further acquisition of territory is to be the result either of conquest or treaty, then I scarcely know which should be preferred, eternal war with Mexico, or the hazards of internal commotion at home, which last I fear *may* come if another province is to be added to our territory. There is one topic connected with this subject which I tremble when I approach, and yet I cannot forbear to notice it. It meets you in every step you take, it threatens you which way soever you go in the prosecution of this war. I allude to the question of slavery. Opposition to its further extension, it must be obvious to every one, is a deeply-rooted determination with men of all parties in what we call the non-slave-holding States. New York, Pennsylvania, and Ohio, three of the most powerful, have already sent their legislative instructions here—so it will be, I doubt not, in all the rest. It is vain now to speculate about the reasons for this. Gentlemen of the South may call it prejudice, passion, hypocrisy, fanaticism. I shall not dispute with them now on that point. The great fact that it is so, and not otherwise, is

what it concerns us to know. You nor I cannot alter or change
this opinion if we would. These people only say, we will not,
cannot consent that you shall carry slavery where it does not
already exist. They do not seek to disturb you in that institution, as it exists in your States. Enjoy it if you will, and as you
will. This is their language, this their determination. How is
it in the South? Can it be expected that they should expend in
common, their blood and their treasure, in the acquisition of
immense territory, and then willingly forego the right to carry
thither their slaves, and inhabit the conquered country if they
please to do so? Sir, I know the feelings and opinions of the
South too well to calculate on this. Nay, I believe they would
even contend to any extremity for the mere *right*, had they no
wish to exert it. I believe (and I confess I tremble when the
conviction presses upon me) that there is equal obstinacy on
both sides of this fearful question. If then, we persist in war,
which if it terminate in any thing short of a mere wanton waste
of blood as well as money, must end (as this bill proposes) in
the acquisition of territory, to which at once this controversy
must attach—this bill would seem to be nothing less than a
bill to produce internal commotion. Should we prosecute this
war another moment, or expend one dollar in the purchase or
conquest of a single acre of Mexican land, the North and the
South are brought into collision on a point where neither will
yield. Who can forsee or foretell the result! Who so bold or
reckless as to look such a conflict in the face unmoved! I do not
envy the heart of him who can realize the possibility of such
a conflict without emotions too painful to be endured. Why
then shall we, the representatives of the Sovereign States of this
Union—the chosen guardians of this confederated Republic,
why should we precipitate this fearful struggle, by continuing a
war the results of which must be to force us at once upon it? Sir,
rightly considered, *this* is treason, treason to the Union, treason to the dearest interests, the loftiest aspirations, the most
cherished hopes of our constituents. It is a crime to risk the
possibility of such a contest. It is a crime of such infernal hue,
that every other in the catalogue of iniquity, when compared
with it, whitens into virtue. Oh, Mr. President, it does seem
to me, if Hell itself could yawn and vomit up the fiends that
inhabit its penal abodes, commissioned to disturb the harmony

of this world, and dash the fairest prospect of happiness that ever allured the hopes of men, the first step in the consummation of this diabolical purpose would be, to light up the fires of internal war, and plunge the sister States of this Union into the bottomless gulf of civil strife. We stand this day on the crumbling brink of that gulf—we see its bloody eddies wheeling and boiling before us—shall we not pause before it be too late? How plain again is here the path, I may add the only way of duty, of prudence, of true patriotism. Let us abandon all idea of acquiring further territory, and by consequence cease at once to prosecute this war. Let us call home our armies, and bring them at once within our own acknowledged limits. Show Mexico that you are sincere when you say you desire nothing by conquest. She has learned that she cannot encounter you in war, and if she had not, she is too weak to disturb you here. Tender her peace, and my life on it, she will then accept it. But whether she shall or not, you will have peace without her consent. It is your invasion that has made war, your retreat will restore peace. Let us then close forever the approaches of internal feud, and so return to the ancient concord and the old ways of national prosperity and permanent glory. Let us here, in this temple consecrated to the Union, perform a solemn lustration; let us wash Mexican blood from our hands, and on these altars, in the presence of that image of the Father of his Country that looks down upon us, swear to preserve honorable peace with all the world, and eternal brotherhood with each other.

HENRY DAVID THOREAU

Thoreau's "Civil Disobedience," originally titled "Resistance to Civil Government," is among the early texts of this anthology by far the most influential in contemporary antiwar movements, and the most alive. (I remember hearing the war tax resister Bob Bady quote it at a meeting in 1989: "Let your life be a friction to stop the machine," said Bob, like Thoreau a skilled carpenter and lover of good machinery.)

The fact of its influence is surprising. Thoreau himself (1817–1862) sought solitude as much as he sought influence, and would have hated being at the meetings where people quote him; "I love Henry dearly," said a friend, "but as for taking his arm, I should as soon take the arm of an elm tree." And he was no pacifist: though he had opposed the Mexican War as a war for slavery, he later ardently supported John Brown and militant abolitionism.

What makes the essay so influential? Like Woolman, Thoreau brilliantly identifies the moments at which opposition to war should, if war opponents are consistent, result in radical individual choices. Unlike Woolman, however, Thoreau finds a secular vocabulary for making that argument. Like Garrison, Thoreau exalts the individual over the state; unlike Garrison, indeed directly countering Garrisonian nonresistance by calling the essay "*Resistance* to Civil Government," he sees the opponent of war as having a crucial patriotic duty, as being in fact more of a patriot than the person who passively supports the war. ("Dissent is patriotic," as contemporary antiwar protest signs so often say.) He has no patience with those who have only an attitude; he galvanizes them to action, and all who feel impatient with deliberation are inspired by him.

In particular, *men* are inspired by him; again unlike Woolman, but strikingly like William James some sixty years later, Thoreau suggests that courageous war resistance is as courageous, as manly, as anything else, and perhaps that manliness is essential to it.

Civil Disobedience

I HEARTILY accept the motto,—"That government is best which governs least"; and I should like to see it acted up to more rapidly and systematically. Carried out, it finally amounts to this, which also I believe,—"That government is best which governs not at all"; and when men are prepared for it, that will be the kind of government which they will have. Government is at best but an expedient; but most governments are usually, and all governments are sometimes, inexpedient. The objections which have been brought against a standing army, and they are many and weighty, and deserve to prevail, may also at last be brought against a standing government. The standing army is only an arm of the standing government. The government itself, which is only the mode which the people have chosen to execute their will, is equally liable to be abused and perverted before the people can act through it. Witness the present Mexican war, the work of comparatively a few individuals using the standing government as their tool; for, in the outset, the people would not have consented to this measure.

This American government,—what is it but a tradition, though a recent one, endeavoring to transmit itself unimpaired to posterity, but each instant losing some of its integrity? It has not the vitality and force of a single living man; for a single man can bend it to his will. It is a sort of wooden gun to the people themselves. But it is not the less necessary for this; for the people must have some complicated machinery or other, and hear its din, to satisfy that idea of government which they have. Governments show thus how successfully men can be imposed on, even impose on themselves, for their own advantage. It is excellent, we must all allow. Yet this government never of itself furthered any enterprise, but by the alacrity with which it got out of its way. *It* does not keep the country free. *It* does not settle the West. *It* does not educate. The character inherent in the American people has done all that has been accomplished; and it would have done somewhat more, if the government had not sometimes got in its way. For government is an expedient by which men would fain succeed in letting one another alone; and, as has been said, when it is most expedient, the governed are most let alone by it. Trade and commerce, if they were not made of India-rubber, would never manage to bounce over the obstacles which legislators are continually putting in their way; and, if one were to judge these men wholly by the effects of their actions and not partly by their intentions, they would deserve to be classed and punished with those mischievous persons who put obstructions on the railroads.

But, to speak practically and as a citizen, unlike those who call themselves no-government men, I ask for, not at once no government, but *at once* a better government. Let every man make known what kind of government would command his respect, and that will be one step toward obtaining it.

After all, the practical reason why, when the power is once in the hands of the people, a majority are permitted, and for a long period continue, to rule, is not because they are most likely to be in the right, nor because this seems fairest to the minority, but because they are physically the strongest. But a government in which the majority rule in all cases cannot be based on justice, even as far as men understand it. Can there not be a government in which majorities do not virtually decide right and wrong, but conscience?—in which majorities decide only those questions to which the rule of expediency is applicable? Must the citizen ever for a moment, or in the least degree, resign his conscience to the legislator? Why has every man a conscience, then? I think that we should be men first, and subjects afterward. It is not desirable to cultivate a respect for the law, so much as for the right. The only obligation which I have a right to assume, is to do at any time what I think right. It is truly enough said, that a corporation has no conscience; but a corporation of conscientious men is a corporation *with* a conscience. Law never made men a whit more just; and, by means of their respect for it, even the well-disposed are daily made the agents of injustice. A common and natural result of an undue respect for law is, that you may see a file of soldiers, colonel, captain, corporal, privates, powder-monkeys, and all, marching in admirable order over hill and dale to the wars, against their wills, ay, against their common sense and consciences, which makes it very steep marching indeed, and produces a palpitation of the heart. They have no doubt that it is a damnable business in which they are concerned; they are all peaceably inclined. Now, what are they? Men at all? or small movable forts and magazines, at the service of some unscrupulous man in power? Visit the Navy-Yard, and behold a marine, such a man as an American government can make, or such as it can make a man with its black arts,—a mere shadow and reminiscence of humanity, a man laid out alive and standing, and already, as one may say, buried under arms with funeral accompaniments, though it may be,—

> "Not a drum was heard, not a funeral note,
>   As his corse to the rampart we hurried;
> Not a soldier discharged his farewell shot
>   O'er the grave where our hero we buried."

The mass of men serve the state thus, not as men mainly, but as machines, with their bodies. They are the standing army, and the militia, jailers, constables, posse comitatus, &c. In most cases there is no free exercise whatever of the judgment or of the moral sense; but they put themselves on a level with wood and earth and stones; and wooden men can perhaps be manufactured that will serve the purpose as well. Such command no more respect than men of straw or a lump of dirt. They have the same sort of worth only as horses and dogs. Yet such as these even are commonly esteemed good citizens. Others,—as most legislators, politicians, lawyers, ministers, and office-holders,—serve the state chiefly with their heads; and, as they rarely make any moral distinctions, they are as likely to serve the Devil, without *intending* it, as God. A very few, as heroes, patriots, martyrs, reformers in the great sense, and *men*, serve the state with their consciences also, and so necessarily resist it for the most part; and they are commonly treated as enemies by it. A wise man will only be useful as a man, and will not submit to be "clay," and "stop a hole to keep the wind away," but leave that office to his dust at least:—

> "I am too high-born to be propertied
> To be a secondary at control,
> Or useful serving-man and instrument
> To any sovereign state throughout the world."

He who gives himself entirely to his fellow-men appears to them useless and selfish; but he who gives himself partially to them is pronounced a benefactor and philanthropist.

How does it become a man to behave toward this American government to-day? I answer, that he cannot without disgrace be associated with it. I cannot for an instant recognize that political organization as *my* government which is the *slave's* government also.

All men recognize the right of revolution; that is, the right to refuse allegiance to, and to resist, the government, when its tyranny or its inefficiency are great and unendurable. But almost all say that such is not the case now. But such was the case, they think, in the Revolution of '75. If one were to tell me that this was a bad government because it taxed certain foreign commodities brought to its ports, it is most probable that I should not make an ado about it, for I can do without them. All machines have their friction; and possibly this does enough good to counterbalance the evil. At any rate, it is a great evil to make a stir about it. But when the friction comes to have its machine, and oppression and robbery are organized, I say, let us not have such a machine any longer. In other words, when a sixth of the population of a nation which has undertaken to be the refuge of liberty are slaves, and a whole country is unjustly overrun and conquered by a foreign army, and subjected to military law, I think that it is not too soon for honest men to rebel and revolutionize. What makes this duty the more urgent is the fact, that the country so overrun is not our own, but ours is the invading army.

Paley, a common authority with many on moral questions, in his chapter on the "Duty of Submission to Civil Government," resolves all civil obligation into expediency; and he proceeds to say, "that so long as the interest of the whole society requires it, that is, so long as the established government cannot be resisted or changed without public inconveniency, it is the will of God that the established government be obeyed, and no longer. . . . This principle being admitted, the justice of every particular case of resistance is reduced to a computation of the quantity of the danger and grievance on the one side, and of the probability and expense of redressing it on the other." Of this, he says, every man shall judge for himself. But Paley appears never to have contemplated those cases to which the rule of expediency does not apply, in which a people, as well as an individual, must do justice, cost what it may. If I have unjustly wrested a plank from a drowning man, I must restore it to him though I drown myself. This, according to Paley, would be inconvenient. But he that would save his life, in such a case, shall lose it. This people must cease to hold slaves, and to make war on Mexico, though it cost them their existence as a people.

In their practice, nations agree with Paley; but does any one think that Massachusetts does exactly what is right at the present crisis?

"A drab of state, a cloth-o'-silver slut,
To have her train borne up, and her soul trail in the dirt."

Practically speaking, the opponents to a reform in Massachusetts are not a hundred thousand politicians at the South, but a hundred thousand merchants and farmers here, who are more interested in commerce and agriculture than they are in humanity, and are not prepared to do justice to the slave and to Mexico, *cost what it may.* I quarrel not with far-off foes, but with those who, near at home, co-operate with, and do the bidding of, those far away, and without whom the latter would be harmless. We are accustomed to say, that the mass of men are unprepared; but improvement is slow, because the few are not materially wiser or better than the many. It is not so important that many should be as good as you, as that there be some absolute goodness somewhere; for that will leaven the whole lump. There are thousands who are *in opinion* opposed to slavery and to the war, who yet in effect do nothing to put an end to them; who, esteeming themselves children of Washington and Franklin, sit down with their hands in their pockets, and say that they know not what to do, and do nothing; who even postpone the question of freedom to the question of free-trade, and quietly read the prices-current along with the latest advices from Mexico, after dinner, and, it may be, fall asleep over them both. What is the price-current of an honest man and patriot to-day? They hesitate, and they regret, and sometimes they petition; but they do nothing in earnest and with effect. They will wait, well disposed, for others to remedy the evil, that they may no longer have it to regret. At most, they give only a cheap vote, and a feeble countenance and God-speed, to the right, as it goes by them. There are nine hundred and ninety-nine patrons of virtue to one virtuous man. But it is easier to deal with the real possessor of a thing than with the temporary guardian of it.

All voting is a sort of gaming, like checkers or backgammon, with a slight moral tinge to it, a playing with right and wrong, with moral questions; and betting naturally accompanies it. The character of the voters is not staked. I cast my vote, perchance, as I think right; but I am not vitally concerned that that right should prevail. I am willing to leave it to the majority. Its obligation, therefore, never exceeds that of expediency. Even voting *for the right* is *doing* nothing for it. It is only expressing to men feebly your desire that it should prevail. A wise man will not leave the right to the mercy of chance, nor wish it to prevail through the power of the majority. There is but little virtue in the action of masses of men. When the majority shall at length vote for the abolition of slavery, it will be because they are indifferent to slavery, or because there is but little slavery left to be abolished by their vote. *They* will then be the only slaves. Only *his* vote can hasten the abolition of slavery who asserts his own freedom by his vote.

I hear of a convention to be held at Baltimore, or elsewhere, for the selection of a candidate for the Presidency, made up chiefly of editors, and men who are politicians by profession; but I think, what is it to any independent, intelligent, and respectable man what decision they may come to? Shall we not have the advantage of his wisdom and honesty, nevertheless? Can we not count upon some independent votes? Are there not many individuals in the country who do not attend conventions? But no: I find that the respectable man, so called, has immediately drifted from his position, and despairs of his country, when his country has more reason to despair of him. He forthwith adopts one of the candidates thus selected as the only *available* one, thus proving that he is himself *available* for any purposes of the demagogue. His vote is of no more worth than that of any unprincipled foreigner or hireling native, who may have been bought. O for a man who is a *man*, and, as my neighbor says, has a bone in his back which you cannot pass your hand through! Our statistics are at fault: the population has been returned too large. How many *men* are there to a square thousand miles in this country? Hardly one. Does not America offer any inducement for men to settle here? The American has dwindled into an Odd Fellow,—one who may be known by the development of his organ of gregariousness, and a manifest lack of intellect and cheerful self-reliance; whose first and chief concern, on coming into the world, is to see that the Almshouses are in good repair; and, before yet he has lawfully donned the virile garb, to collect a fund for the support of the widows and orphans that may be; who, in short, ventures to live only by the aid of the Mutual Insurance company, which has promised to bury him decently.

It is not a man's duty, as a matter of course, to devote himself to the eradication of any, even the most enormous wrong; he may still properly have other concerns to engage him; but it is his duty, at least, to wash his hands of it, and, if he gives it no thought longer, not to give it practically his support. If I devote myself to other pursuits and contemplations, I must first see, at least, that I do not pursue them sitting upon another man's shoulders. I must get off him first, that he may pursue his contemplations too. See what gross inconsistency is tolerated. I have heard some of my townsmen say, "I should like to have them order me out to help put down an insurrection of the slaves, or to march to Mexico;—see if I would go"; and yet these very men have each, directly by their allegiance, and so indirectly, at least, by their money, furnished a substitute. The soldier is applauded who refuses to serve in an unjust war by those who do not refuse to sustain the unjust government which makes the war; is applauded by those whose own act and authority he disregards and sets at naught; as if the State were penitent to that degree that it hired one to scourge it while it sinned, but not to that degree that it left off sinning for a moment. Thus, under the name of Order and Civil Government, we are all made at last to pay homage to and support our own meanness. After the first blush of sin comes its indifference; and from immoral it becomes, as it were, *un*moral, and not quite unnecessary to that life which we have made.

The broadest and most prevalent error requires the most disinterested virtue to sustain it. The slight reproach to which the virtue of patriotism is commonly liable, the noble are most likely to incur. Those who, while they disapprove of the character and measures of a government, yield to it their allegiance and support, are undoubtedly its most conscientious supporters, and so frequently the most serious obstacles to reform. Some are petitioning the State to dissolve the Union, to disregard the requisitions of the President. Why do they not dissolve it themselves,—the union between themselves and the State,—and refuse to pay their quota into its treasury? Do not they stand in the same relation to the State, that the State does to the Union? And have not the same reasons prevented the State from resisting the Union, which have prevented them from resisting the State?

How can a man be satisfied to entertain an opinion merely, and enjoy *it*? Is there any enjoyment in it, if his opinion is that he is aggrieved? If you are cheated out of a single dollar by your neighbor, you do not rest satisfied with knowing that you are cheated, or with saying that you are cheated, or even with petitioning him to pay you your due; but you take effectual steps at once to obtain the full amount, and see that you are never cheated again. Action from principle, the perception and the performance of right, changes things and relations; it is essentially revolutionary, and does not consist wholly with anything which was. It not only divides states and churches, it divides families; ay, it divides the *individual*, separating the diabolical in him from the divine.

Unjust laws exist: shall we be content to obey them, or shall we endeavor to amend them, and obey them until we have succeeded, or shall we transgress them at once? Men generally, under such a government as this, think that they ought to wait until they have persuaded the majority to alter them. They think that, if they should resist, the remedy would be worse than the evil. But it is the fault of the government itself that the remedy *is* worse than the evil. *It* makes it worse. Why is it not more apt to anticipate and provide for reform? Why does it not cherish its wise minority? Why does it cry and resist before it is hurt? Why does it not encourage its citizens to be on the alert to point out its faults, and *do* better than it would have them? Why does it always crucify Christ, and excommunicate Copernicus and Luther, and pronounce Washington and Franklin rebels?

One would think, that a deliberate and practical denial of its authority was the only offence never contemplated by government; else, why has it not assigned its definite, its suitable and proportionate penalty? If a man who has no property refuses but once to earn nine shillings for the State, he is put in prison for a period unlimited by any law that I know, and determined only by the discretion of those who placed him there; but if he should steal ninety times nine shillings from the State, he is soon permitted to go at large again.

If the injustice is part of the necessary friction of the machine of government, let it go, let it go: perchance it will wear smooth,—certainly the machine will wear out. If the injustice has a spring, or a pulley, or a rope, or a crank, exclusively for itself, then perhaps you may consider whether the remedy will not be worse than the evil; but if it is of such a nature that it requires you to be the agent of injustice to another, then, I say, break the law. Let your life be a counter friction to stop the machine. What I have to do is to see, at any rate, that I do not lend myself to the wrong which I condemn.

As for adopting the ways which the State has provided for remedying the evil, I know not of such ways. They take too much time, and a man's life will be gone. I have other affairs to attend to. I came into this world, not chiefly to make this a good place to live in, but to live in it, be it good or bad. A man has not everything to do, but something; and because he cannot do *everything*, it is not necessary that he should do *something* wrong. It is not my business to be petitioning the Governor or the Legislature any more than it is theirs to petition me; and, if they should not hear my petition, what should I do then? But in this case the State has provided no way: its very Constitution is the evil. This may seem to be harsh and stubborn and unconciliatory; but it is to treat with the utmost kindness and consideration the only spirit that can appreciate or deserves it. So is all change for the better, like birth and death, which convulse the body.

I do not hesitate to say, that those who call themselves Abolitionists should at once effectually withdraw their support, both in person and property, from the government of Massachusetts, and not wait till they constitute a majority of one, before they suffer the right to prevail through them. I think that it is enough if they have God on their side, without waiting for that other one. Moreover, any man more right than his neighbors constitutes a majority of one already.

I meet this American government, or its representative, the State government, directly, and face to face, once a year—no more—in the person of its tax-gatherer; this is the only mode in which a man situated as I am necessarily meets it; and it then says distinctly, Recognize me; and the simplest, the most effectual, and, in the present posture of affairs, the indispens-ablest mode of treating with it on this head, of expressing your little satisfaction with and love for it, is to deny it then. My civil neighbor, the tax-gatherer, is the very man I have to deal with,—for it is, after all, with men and not with parchment that I quarrel,—and he has voluntarily chosen to be an agent of the government. How shall he ever know well what he is and does as an officer of the government, or as a man, until he is obliged to consider whether he shall treat me, his neighbor, for whom he has respect, as a neighbor and well-disposed man, or as a maniac and disturber of the peace, and see if he can get over this obstruction to his neighborliness without a ruder and more impetuous thought or speech corresponding with his action. I know this well, that if one thousand, if one hundred, if ten men whom I could name,—if ten *honest* men only,—ay, if *one* HONEST man, in this State of Massachusetts, *ceasing to hold slaves*, were actually to withdraw from this copartnership, and be locked up in the county jail therefor, it would be the abolition of slavery in America. For it matters not how small the beginning may seem to be: what is once well done is done forever. But we love better to talk about it: that we say is our mission. Reform keeps many scores of newspapers in its ser-vice, but not one man. If my esteemed neighbor, the State's ambassador, who will devote his days to the settlement of the question of human rights in the Council Chamber, instead of being threatened with the prisons of Carolina, were to sit down the prisoner of Massachusetts, that State which is so anxious to foist the sin of slavery upon her sister,—though at present she can discover only an act of inhospitality to be the ground of a quarrel with her,—the Legislature would not wholly waive the subject the following winter.

Under a government which imprisons any unjustly, the true place for a just man is also a prison. The proper place to-day, the only place which Massachusetts has provided for her freer and less desponding spirits, is in her prisons, to be put out and locked out of the State by her own act, as they have already put themselves out by their principles. It is there that the fugitive slave, and the Mexican prisoner on parole, and the Indian come to plead the wrongs of his race, should find them; on that separate, but more free and honorable ground, where the State places those who are not *with* her, but *against* her,—the only house in a slave State in which a free man can abide with honor. If any think that their influence would be lost there, and their voices no longer afflict the ear of the State, that they would not be as an enemy within its walls, they do not know by how much truth is stronger than error, nor how much more eloquently and effectively he can combat injustice who has experienced a little in his own person. Cast your whole vote, not a strip of paper merely, but your whole influence. A minority is power-less while it conforms to the majority; it is not even a minority then; but it is irresistible when it clogs by its whole weight. If the alternative is to keep all just men in prison, or give up war and slavery, the State will not hesitate which to choose. If a thousand men were not to pay their tax-bills this year, that would not be a violent and bloody measure, as it would be to pay them, and enable the State to commit violence and shed innocent blood. This is, in fact, the definition of a peaceable revolution, if any such is possible. If the tax-gatherer, or any other public officer, asks me, as one has done, "But what shall I do?" my answer is, "If you really wish to do anything, resign your office." When the subject has refused allegiance, and the officer has resigned his office, then the revolution is accom-plished. But even suppose blood should flow. Is there not a sort of blood shed when the conscience is wounded? Through this wound a man's real manhood and immortality flow out, and he bleeds to an everlasting death. I see this blood flowing now.

I have contemplated the imprisonment of the offender, rather than the seizure of his goods,—though both will serve the same purpose,—because they who assert the purest right, and consequently are most dangerous to a corrupt State, commonly have not spent much time in accumulating property. To such the State renders comparatively small service, and a slight tax is wont to appear exorbitant, particularly if they are obliged to earn it by special labor with their hands. If there were one who lived wholly without the use of money, the State itself would hesitate to demand it of him. But the rich man,—not to make any invidious comparison,—is always sold to the institution which makes him rich. Absolutely speaking, the more money, the less virtue; for money comes between a man and his objects; and obtains them for him; and it was certainly no great virtue to obtain it. It puts to rest many questions which he would otherwise be taxed to answer; while the only new question which it puts is the hard but superfluous one, how to spend it. Thus his moral ground is taken from under his feet. The opportunities of living are diminished in proportion as what are called the "means" are increased. The best thing a man can do for his culture when he is rich is to endeavor to carry out those schemes which he entertained when he was poor. Christ answered the Herodians according to their condition. "Show me the tribute-money," said he;—and one took a penny out of his pocket;—if you use money which has the image of Cæsar on it, and which he has made current and valuable, that is, *if you are men of the State*, and gladly enjoy the advantages of Cæsar's government, then pay him back some of his own when he demands it; "Render therefore to Cæsar that which is Cæsar's, and to God those things which are God's,"—leaving them no wiser than before as to which was which; for they did not wish to know.

When I converse with the freest of my neighbors, I perceive that, whatever they may say about the magnitude and serious-ness of the question, and their regard for the public tranquillity, the long and the short of the matter is, that they cannot spare the protection of the existing government, and they dread the consequences to their property and families of disobedience to it. For my own part, I should not like to think that I ever rely on the protection of the State. But, if I deny the authority of the State when it presents its tax-bill, it will soon take and waste all my property, and so harass me and my children without end. This is hard. This makes it impossible for a man to live hon-estly, and at the same time comfortably, in outward respects. It will not be worth the while to accumulate property; that would be sure to go again. You must hire or squat somewhere, and raise but a small crop, and eat that soon. You must live within yourself, and depend upon yourself always tucked up and ready for a start, and not have many affairs. A man may grow rich in Turkey even, if he will be in all respects a good subject of the Turkish government. Confucius said: "If a state is governed by the principles of reason, poverty and misery are subjects of shame; if a state is not governed by the principles of reason, riches and honors are the subjects of shame." No: until I want the protection of Massachusetts to be extended to me in some distant Southern port, where my liberty is endangered, or until I am bent solely on building up an estate at home by peaceful enterprise, I can afford to refuse allegiance to Massachusetts, and her right to my property and life. It costs me less in every sense to incur the penalty of disobedience to the State, than it would to obey. I should feel as if I were worth less in that case.

Some years ago, the State met me in behalf of the Church, and commanded me to pay a certain sum toward the support of a clergyman whose preaching my father attended, but never I myself. "Pay," it said, "or be locked up in the jail." I declined to pay. But, unfortunately, another man saw fit to pay it. I did not see why the schoolmaster should be taxed to support the priest, and not the priest the schoolmaster; for I was not the State's schoolmaster, but I supported myself by voluntary subscription. I did not see why the lyceum should not present its tax-bill, and have the State to back its demand, as well as the Church. However, at the request of the selectmen, I condescended to make some such statement as this in writing:—"Know all men by these presents, that I, Henry Thoreau, do not wish to be regarded as a member of any incorporated society which I have not joined." This I gave to the town clerk; and he has it. The State, having thus learned that I did not wish to be regarded as a member of that church, has never made a like demand on me since; though it said that it must adhere to its original presumption that time. If I had known how to name them, I should then have signed off in detail from all the societies which I never signed on to; but I did not know where to find a complete list.

I have paid no poll-tax for six years. I was put into a jail once on this account, for one night; and, as I stood considering the walls of solid stone, two or three feet thick, the door of wood and iron, a foot thick, and the iron grating which strained the light, I could not help being struck with the foolishness of that institution which treated me as if I were mere flesh and blood and bones, to be locked up. I wondered that it should have concluded at length that this was the best use it could put me to, and had never thought to avail itself of my services in some way. I saw that, if there was a wall of stone between me and my townsmen, there was a still more difficult one to climb or break through, before they could get to be as free as I was. I did not for a moment feel confined, and the walls seemed a great waste of stone and mortar. I felt as if I alone of all my townsmen had paid my tax. They plainly did not know how to treat me, but behaved like persons who are underbred. In every threat and in every compliment there was a blunder; for they thought that my chief desire was to stand the other side of that stone wall. I could not but smile to see how industriously they locked the door on my meditations, which followed them out again without let or hindrance, and *they* were really all that was dangerous. As they could not reach me, they had resolved to punish my body; just as boys, if they cannot come at some person against whom they have a spite, will abuse his dog. I saw that the State was half-witted, that it was timid as a lone woman with her silver spoons, and that it did not know its friends from its foes, and I lost all my remaining respect for it, and pitied it.

Thus the State never intentionally confronts a man's sense, intellectual or moral, but only his body, his senses. It is not armed with superior wit or honesty, but with superior physical strength. I was not born to be forced. I will breathe after my own fashion. Let us see who is the strongest. What force has a multitude? They only can force me who obey a higher law than I. They force me to become like themselves. I do not hear of *men* being *forced* to live this way or that by masses of men. What sort of life were that to live? When I meet a government which says to me, "Your money or your life," why should I be in haste to give it my money? It may be in a great strait, and not know what to do: I cannot help that. It must help itself; do as I do. It is not worth the while to snivel about it. I am not responsible for the successful working of the machinery of society. I am not the son of the engineer. I perceive that, when an acorn and a chestnut fall side by side, the one does not remain inert to make way for the other, but both obey their own laws, and spring and grow and flourish as best they can, till one, perchance, overshadows and destroys the other. If a plant cannot live according to its nature, it dies; and so a man.

The night in prison was novel and interesting enough. The prisoners in their shirt-sleeves were enjoying a chat and the evening air in the doorway, when I entered. But the jailer said, "Come, boys, it is time to lock up"; and so they dispersed, and I heard the sound of their steps returning into the hollow apartments. My room-mate was introduced to me by the jailer, as "a first-rate fellow and a clever man." When the door was locked, he showed me where to hang my hat, and how he managed matters there. The rooms were whitewashed once a month; and this one, at least, was the whitest, most simply furnished, and probably the neatest apartment in the town. He naturally wanted to know where I came from, and what brought me there; and, when I had told him, I asked him in my turn how he came there, presuming him to be an honest man, of course; and, as the world goes, I believe he was. "Why," said he, "they accuse me of burning a barn; but I never did it." As near as I could discover, he had probably gone to bed in a barn when drunk, and smoked his pipe there; and so a barn was burnt. He had the reputation of being a clever man, had been there some three months waiting for his trial to come on, and would have to wait as much longer; but he was quite domesticated and contented, since he got his board for nothing, and thought that he was well treated.

He occupied one window, and I the other; and I saw, that, if one stayed there long, his principal business would be to look out the window. I had soon read all the tracts that were left there, and examined where former prisoners had broken out, and where a grate had been sawed off, and heard the history of the various occupants of that room; for I found that even here there was a history and a gossip which never circulated beyond the walls of the jail. Probably this is the only house in the town where verses are composed, which are afterward printed in a circular form, but not published. I was shown quite a long list of verses which were composed by some young men who had been detected in an attempt to escape, who avenged themselves by singing them.

I pumped my fellow-prisoner as dry as I could, for fear I should never see him again; but at length he showed me which was my bed, and left me to blow out the lamp.

It was like travelling into a far country, such as I had never expected to behold, to lie there for one night. It seemed to me that I never had heard the town-clock strike before, nor the evening sounds of the village; for we slept with the windows open, which were inside the grating. It was to see my native village in the light of the Middle Ages, and our Concord was turned into a Rhine stream, and visions of knights and castles passed before me. They were the voices of old burghers that I heard in the streets. I was an involuntary spectator and auditor of whatever was done and said in the kitchen of the adjacent village-inn,—a wholly new and rare experience to me. It was a closer view of my native town. I was fairly inside of it. I never had seen its institutions before. This is one of its peculiar institutions; for it is a shire town. I began to comprehend what its inhabitants were about.

In the morning, our breakfasts were put through the hole in the door, in small oblong-square tin pans, made to fit, and holding a pint of chocolate, with brown bread, and an iron spoon. When they called for the vessels again, I was green enough to return what bread I had left; but my comrade seized it, and said that I should lay that up for lunch or dinner. Soon after he was let out to work at haying in a neighboring field, whither he went every day, and would not be back till noon; so he bade me good-day, saying that he doubted if he should see me again.

When I came out of prison,—for some one interfered, and paid that tax,—I did not perceive that great changes had taken place on the common, such as he observed who went in a youth, and emerged a tottering and gray-headed man; and yet a change had to my eyes come over the scene,—the town, and State, and country,—greater than any that mere time could effect. I saw yet more distinctly the State in which I lived. I saw to what extent the people among whom I lived could be trusted as good neighbors and friends; that their friendship was for summer weather only; that they did not greatly propose to do right; that they were a distinct race from me by their prejudices and superstitions, as the Chinamen and Malays are; that, in their sacrifices to humanity, they ran no risks, not even to their property; that, after all, they were not so noble but they treated the thief as he had treated them, and hoped, by a certain outward observance and a few prayers, and by walking in a particular straight though useless path from time to time, to save their souls. This may be to judge my neighbors harshly; for I believe that many of them are not aware that they have such an institution as the jail in their village.

It was formerly the custom in our village, when a poor debtor came out of jail, for his acquaintances to salute him, looking through their fingers, which were crossed to represent the grating of a jail window, "How do ye do?" My neighbors did not thus salute me, but first looked at me, and then at one another, as if I had returned from a long journey. I was put into jail as I was going to the shoemaker's to get a shoe which was mended. When I was let out the next morning, I proceeded to finish my errand, and having put on my mended shoe, joined a huckleberry party, who were impatient to put themselves under my conduct; and in half an hour,—for the horse was soon tackled,—was in the midst of a huckleberry field, on one of our highest hills, two miles off, and then the State was nowhere to be seen.

This is the whole history of "My Prisons."

I have never declined paying the highway tax, because I am as desirous of being a good neighbor as I am of being a bad subject; and, as for supporting schools, I am doing my part to educate my fellow-countrymen now. It is for no particular item in the tax-bill that I refuse to pay it. I simply wish to refuse allegiance to the State, to withdraw and stand aloof from it effectually. I do not care to trace the course of my dollar, if I could, till it buys a man or a musket to shoot one with,—the dollar is innocent,—but I am concerned to trace the effects of my allegiance. In fact, I quietly declare war with the State, after my fashion, though I will still make what use and get what advantage of her I can, as is usual in such cases.

If others pay the tax which is demanded of me, from a sympathy with the State, they do but what they have already done in their own case, or rather they abet injustice to a greater extent than the State requires. If they pay the tax from a mistaken interest in the individual taxed, to save his property, or prevent his going to jail, it is because they have not considered wisely how far they let their private feelings interfere with the public good.

This, then, is my position at present. But one cannot be too much on his guard in such a case, lest his action be biassed by obstinacy, or an undue regard for the opinions of men. Let him see that he does only what belongs to himself and to the hour.

I think sometimes, Why, this people mean well; they are only ignorant; they would do better if they knew how: why give your neighbors this pain to treat you as they are not inclined to? But I think again, this is no reason why I should do as they do, or permit others to suffer much greater pain of a different kind. Again, I sometimes say to myself, When many millions of men, without heat, without ill will, without personal feeling of any kind, demand of you a few shillings only, without the possibility, such is their constitution, of retracting or altering their present demand, and without the possibility, on your side, of appeal to any other millions, why expose yourself to this overwhelming brute force? You do not resist cold and hunger, the winds and the waves, thus obstinately; you quietly submit to a thousand similar necessities. You do not put your head into the fire. But just in proportion as I regard this as not wholly a brute force, but partly a human force, and consider that I have relations to those millions as to so many millions of men, and not of mere brute or inanimate things, I see that appeal is possible, first and instantaneously, from them to the Maker of them, and, secondly, from them to themselves. But, if I put my head deliberately into the fire, there is no appeal to fire or to the Maker of fire, and I have only myself to blame. If I could convince myself that I have any right to be satisfied with men as they are, and to treat them accordingly, and not according, in some respects, to my requisitions and expectations of what they and I ought to be, then, like a good Mussulman and fatalist, I should endeavor to be satisfied with things as they are, and say it is the will of God. And, above all, there is this difference between resisting this and a purely brute or natural force, that I can resist this with some effect; but I cannot expect, like Orpheus, to change the nature of the rocks and trees and beasts.

I do not wish to quarrel with any man or nation. I do not wish to split hairs, to make fine distinctions, or set myself up as better than my neighbors. I seek rather, I may say, even an excuse for conforming to the laws of the land. I am but too ready to conform to them. Indeed, I have reason to suspect myself on this head; and each year, as the tax-gatherer comes round, I find myself disposed to review the acts and position of the general and State governments, and the spirit of the people, to discover a pretext for conformity.

> "We must affect our country as our parents;
> And if at any time we alienate
> Our love or industry from doing it honor,
> We must respect effects and teach the soul
> Matter of conscience and religion,
> And not desire of rule or benefit."

I believe that the State will soon be able to take all my work of this sort out of my hands, and then I shall be no better a patriot than my fellow-countrymen. Seen from a lower point of view, the Constitution, with all its faults, is very good; the law and the courts are very respectable; even this State and this American government are, in many respects, very admirable and rare things, to be thankful for, such as a great many have described them; but seen from a point of view a little higher, they are what I have described them; seen from a higher still, and the highest, who shall say what they are, or that they are worth looking at or thinking of at all?

However, the government does not concern me much, and I shall bestow the fewest possible thoughts on it. It is not many moments that I live under a government, even in this world. If a man is thought-free, fancy-free, imagination-free, that which *is not* never for a long time appearing *to be* to him, unwise rulers or reformers cannot fatally interrupt him.

I know that most men think differently from myself; but those whose lives are by profession devoted to the study of these or kindred subjects, content me as little as any. Statesmen and legislators, standing so completely within the institution, never distinctly and nakedly behold it. They speak of moving society, but have no resting-place without it. They may be men of a certain experience and discrimination, and have no doubt invented ingenious and even useful systems, for which we sincerely thank them; but all their wit and usefulness lie within certain not very wide limits. They are wont to forget that the world is not governed by policy and expediency. Webster never goes behind government, and so cannot speak with authority about it. His words are wisdom to those legislators who contemplate no essential reform in the existing government; but for thinkers, and those who legislate for all time, he never once glances at the subject. I know of those whose serene and wise speculations on this theme would soon reveal the limits of his mind's range and hospitality. Yet, compared with the cheap professions of most reformers, and the still cheaper wisdom and eloquence of politicians in general, his are almost the only sensible and valuable words, and we thank Heaven for him. Comparatively, he is always strong, original, and, above all, practical. Still his quality is not wisdom, but prudence. The lawyer's truth is not Truth, but consistency, or a consistent expediency. Truth is always in harmony with herself, and is not concerned chiefly to reveal the justice that may consist with wrong-doing. He well deserves to be called, as he has been called, the Defender of the Constitution. There are really no blows to be given by him but defensive ones. He is not a leader, but a follower. His leaders are the men of '87. "I have never made an effort," he says, "and never propose to make an effort; I have never countenanced an effort, and never mean to countenance an effort, to disturb the arrangement as originally made, by which the various States came into the Union." Still thinking of the sanction which the Constitution gives to slavery, he says, "Because it was a part of the original compact,—let it stand." Notwithstanding his special acuteness and ability, he is unable to take a fact out of its merely political relations, and behold it as it lies absolutely to be disposed of by the intellect,—what, for instance, it behooves a man to do here in America to-day with regard to slavery,—but ventures, or is driven, to make some such desperate answer as the following, while professing to speak absolutely, and as a private man,—from which what new and singular code of social duties might be inferred? "The manner," says he, "in which the governments of those States where slavery exists are to regulate it, is for their own consideration, under their responsibility to their constituents, to the general laws of propriety, humanity, and justice, and to God. Associations formed elsewhere, springing from a feeling of humanity, or any other cause, have nothing whatever to do with it. They have never received any encouragement from me, and they never will."*

They who know of no purer sources of truth, who have traced up its stream no higher, stand, and wisely stand, by the Bible and the Constitution, and drink at it there with reverence and humility; but they who behold where it comes trickling into this lake or that pool, gird up their loins once more, and continue their pilgrimage toward its fountain-head.

No man with a genius for legislation has appeared in America. They are rare in the history of the world. There are orators, politicians, and eloquent men, by the thousand; but the speaker has not yet opened his mouth to speak, who is capable of settling the much-vexed questions of the day. We love eloquence for its own sake, and not for any truth which it may utter, or any heroism it may inspire. Our legislators have not yet learned the comparative value of free-trade and of freedom, of union, and of rectitude, to a nation. They have no genius or talent for comparatively humble questions of taxation and finance, commerce and manufactures and agriculture. If we were left solely to the wordy wit of legislators in Congress for our guidance, uncorrected by the seasonable experience and the effectual complaints of the people, America would not long retain her rank among the nations. For eighteen hundred years, though perchance I have no right to say it, the New Testament has been written; yet where is the legislator who has wisdom and practical talent enough to avail himself of the light which it sheds on the science of legislation?

The authority of government, even such as I am willing to submit to,—for I will cheerfully obey those who know and can do better than I, and in many things even those who neither know nor can do so well,—is still an impure one: to be strictly just, it must have the sanction and consent of the governed. It can have no pure right over my person and property but what I concede to it. The progress from an absolute to a limited monarchy, from a limited monarchy to a democracy, is a progress toward a true respect for the individual. Even the Chinese

*These extracts have been inserted since the Lecture was read.

philosopher was wise enough to regard the individual as the basis of the empire. Is a democracy, such as we know it, the last improvement possible in government? Is it not possible to take a step further towards recognizing and organizing the rights of man? There will never be a really free and enlightened State, until the State comes to recognize the individual as a higher and independent power, from which all its own power and authority are derived, and treats him accordingly. I please myself with imagining a State at last which can afford to be just to all men, and to treat the individual with respect as a neighbor; which even would not think it inconsistent with its own repose, if a few were to live aloof from it, not meddling with it, nor embraced by it, who fulfilled all the duties of neighbors and fellow-men. A State which bore this kind of fruit, and suffered it to drop off as fast as it ripened, would prepare the way for a still more perfect and glorious State, which also I have imagined, but not yet anywhere seen.

OBADIAH ETHELBERT BAKER

Obadiah Ethelbert Baker (1838–1923) was neither a great poet nor a public one; he wrote mainly for his wife Melissa Dalton, with whom he often exchanged journals during the Civil War years, she at home in Iowa and he a common soldier in the 2nd Iowa Cavalry Volunteers. His poem to her of November 30, 1862—written in camp in Mississippi not long after the Battle of Corinth, in which he fought—remained unpublished in the pages of one of these journals until 2005. The two were safely reunited after his honorable discharge in April 1865, and moved to California. But his private lament is still resonant: "When will we learn to war no more?"

Nov. 30th To an absent Wife

Wish I was sitting by thy side,
   My dear beloved wife;
Far from the cannon's awful roar,
   Far from this awful strife.

My thoughts are of thee through the day,
   I dream of thee at night;
I long to kiss thy lips once more,
   And see thy face so bright

O God! When will this strife be o'er?
   When will we learn to war no more?

CYRUS PRINGLE

The Quaker nurseryman Cyrus Pringle (1838–1911) was an opponent of war on principle and without doubt when he was drafted into the Union Army in July 1863. Though an uncle offered to pay the $300 that could legally have kept him a civilian, he refused, unable to condone the hiring of a substitute. He comes across in his private diary during the war years somewhat as John Woolman does in his, as a person of conscience without irony. The diary is therefore at its most vivid when Pringle is describing not his own certainties but the alternately gentlemanly and horrific ways in which conscientious objectors to war—then a legal category in the making, and clearly a troubling one—were treated by their superior officers: inveigled, ordered, threatened, and finally tortured.

Pringle was discharged from service by the direct order of President Lincoln, which probably saved his life. After the war he became one of the nation's leading botanical fieldworkers, surveying the flora of Mexico for over two decades and describing over 1,000 new plant species. His diary was published posthumously at the beginning of 1918, his suffering and his moral example newly relevant in a country once again at war.

FROM

The Record of a Quaker Conscience: Cyrus Pringle's Diary

10*th* mo., 3*d*.—Today dawned fair and our Camp is dry again. I was asked to clean the gun I brought, and declining, was tied some two hours upon the ground.

6*th*. AT WASHINGTON.—At first, after being informed of our declining to serve in his hospital, Colonel Foster did not appear altered in his kind regard for us. But his spleen soon became evident. At the time we asked for a trial by court-martial, and it was his duty to place us under arrest and proceed with the preferring of his charges against us. For a while he seemed to hesitate and consult his inferior officers, and among them his Chaplain. The result of the conference was our being ordered into our companies, that, separated, and with the force of the officers of a company bearing upon us, we might the more likely be subdued. Yet the Colonel assured L. M. M., interceding in my behalf, when the lieutenant commanding my company threatened force upon me, that he should not allow any personal injury. When we marched next day I was compelled to bear a gun and equipments. My associates were more fortunate, for, being asked if they would carry their guns, declined and saw no more trouble from them. The captain of the company in which P. D. was placed told him he did not believe he was ugly about it, and that he could only put him under arrest and prefer charges against him. He accordingly was taken under guard, where he lay till we left for here.

The next morning the men were busy in burnishing their arms. When I looked toward the one I had borne, yellow with rust, I trembled in the weakness of the flesh at the trial I felt impending over me. Before the Colonel was up I knocked at his tent, but was told he was asleep, though, through the opening, I saw him lying gazing at me. Although I felt I should gain no relief from him, I applied again soon after. He admitted me and, lying on his bed, inquired with cold heartlessness what I wanted. I stated to him, that I could never consent to serve, and, being under the war-power, was resigned to suffer instead all the just penalties of the law. I begged of him release from the attempts by violence to compel my obedience and service, and a trial, though likely to be made by those having no sympathy with me, yet probably in a manner conformable to law.

He replied that he had shown us all the favour he should; that he had, now, turned us over to the military power and was going to let that take its course; that is, henceforth we were to be at the mercy of the inferior officers, without appeal to law, justice, or mercy. He said he had placed us in a pleasant position, against which we could have no reasonable objection, and that we had failed to perform our agreement. He wished to deny that our consent was only temporary and conditional. He declared, furthermore, his belief, that a man who would not fight for his country did not deserve to live. I was glad to withdraw from his presence as soon as I could.

I went back to my tent and lay down for a season of retirement, endeavouring to gain resignation to any event. I dreaded torture and desired strength of flesh and spirit. My trial soon came. The lieutenant called me out, and pointing to the gun that lay near by, asked if I was going to clean it. I replied to him, that I could not comply with military requisitions, and felt resigned to the consequences. "I do not ask about your feelings; I want to know if you are going to clean that gun?" "I cannot do it," was my answer. He went away, saying, "Very well," and I crawled into the tent again. Two sergeants soon called for me, and taking me a little aside, bid me lie down on my back, and stretching my limbs apart tied cords to my wrists and ankles and these to four stakes driven in the ground somewhat in the form of an X.

I was very quiet in my mind as I lay there on the ground [soaked] with the rain of the previous day, exposed to the heat of the sun, and suffering keenly from the cords binding my wrists and straining my muscles. And, if I dared the presumption, I should say that I caught a glimpse of heavenly pity. I wept, not so much from my own suffering as from sorrow that such things should be in our own country, where Justice and Freedom and Liberty of Conscience have been the annual boast of Fourth-of-July orators so many years. It seemed that our forefathers in the faith had wrought and suffered in vain, when the privileges they so dearly bought were so soon set aside. And I was sad, that one endeavouring to follow our dear Master should be so generally regarded as a despicable and stubborn culprit.

After something like an hour had passed, the lieutenant came with his orderly to ask me if I was ready to clean the gun. I replied to the orderly asking the question, that it could but give me pain to be asked or required to do anything I believed wrong. He repeated it to the lieutenant just behind him, who advanced and addressed me. I was favoured to improve the opportunity to say to him a few things I wished. He said little; and, when I had finished, he withdrew with the others who had gathered around. About the end of another hour his orderly came and released me.

I arose and sat on the ground. I did not rise to go away. I had nowhere to go, nothing to do. As I sat there my heart swelled with joy from above. The consolation and sweet fruit of tribulation patiently endured. But I also grieved, that the world was so far gone astray, so cruel and blind. It seemed as if the gospel of Christ had never been preached upon earth, and the beautiful example of his life had been utterly lost sight of.

Some of the men came about me, advising me to yield, and among them one of those who had tied me down, telling me what I had already suffered was nothing to what I must yet suffer unless I yielded; that human flesh could not endure what they would put upon me. I wondered if it could be that they could force me to obedience by torture, and examined myself closely to see if they had advanced as yet one step toward the accomplishment of their purposes. Though weaker in body, I believed I found myself, through divine strength, as firm in my resolution to maintain my allegiance to my Master.

HERMAN MELVILLE

By the time Herman Melville (1819–1891) wrote "Shiloh," probably in 1864 or early 1865, he was an ex-celebrity, his recent literary career a succession of failures. The greatest American novelist of the nineteenth century had turned exclusively to poetry, which was as little read as his later prose had been; his *Battle-Pieces and Other Aspects of the War*, published in 1866, sold fewer than 500 copies.

The Civil War gave rise to a new kind of antiwar writing, not to be seen again to any significant extent until World War II. Many of the writers commenting on it here supported the war, for the sake of the Union or hatred of slavery; some, like Ambrose Bierce, fought in it, and did not repent their service. What they opposed were the traits common to all wars, even the good ones: the empty distinctions between friend and foe, and the insufficiency of even the highest rhetoric—"fame or country least their care"—to justify the slaughter of one army of human beings by another.

Shiloh

A Requiem

(APRIL, 1862)

Skimming lightly, wheeling still,
   The swallows fly low
Over the field in clouded days,
   The forest-field of Shiloh—
Over the field where April rain
Solaced the parched ones stretched in pain
Through the pause of night
That followed the Sunday fight
   Around the church of Shiloh—
The church so lone, the log-built one,
That echoed to many a parting groan
    And natural prayer
  Of dying foemen mingled there—
Foemen at morn, but friends at eve—
  Fame or country least their care:

(What like a bullet can undeceive!)
   But now they lie low,
While over them the swallows skim,
   And all is hushed at Shiloh.

WALT WHITMAN

Walt Whitman (1819–1892) wrote abundantly and often very movingly about the Civil War: poems in *Drum-Taps* (1865), prose reminiscences in *Specimen Days* (1882), letters to his family and especially to his mother Louisa Van Velsor Whitman. His experience as a volunteer hospital nurse for wounded Union soldiers exposed him to some of the war's most harrowing and excruciating consequences. He never finally *opposed* the war, however, even as he witnessed and lamented its human costs. An ardent supporter of the war president Abraham Lincoln, he even occasionally wished that more violent force could be brought to bear more quickly against the Confederacy, to hasten a victory he felt was essential, at any price.

"Reconciliation," however, published in *Drum-Taps* in 1865, beautifully states one of the principles central to much opposition to war: "my enemy is dead, a man divine as myself is dead." (The British war poet Wilfred Owen will echo that line in 1918, in "Strange Meeting": "I am the enemy you killed, my friend.")

Reconciliation

Word over all, beautiful as the sky,
Beautiful that war and all its deeds of carnage must in
    time be utterly lost,
That the hands of the sisters Death and Night
    incessantly softly wash again, and ever again, this
    soil'd world;
For my enemy is dead, a man divine as myself is dead,
I look where he lies white-faced and still in the coffin—I
    draw near,
Bend down and touch lightly with my lips the white face
    in the coffin.

TIMOTHY H. O'SULLIVAN AND ALEXANDER GARDNER

What like a photograph can undeceive us—to adapt a phrase from Melville's "Shiloh"—about war? This is the "useful moral" Alexander Gardner (1821–1882) finds in *A Harvest of Death*, taken by Timothy H. O'Sullivan (1840–1882) on the battlefield at Gettysburg, on July 4, 1863, and gathered in *Gardner's Photographic Sketch Book of the War* (1866) in the same year that "Shiloh" was published.

A Harvest of Death

SLOWLY, over the misty fields of Gettysburg—as all reluctant to expose their ghastly horrors to the light—came the sunless morn, after the retreat by Lee's broken army. Through the shadowy vapors, it was, indeed, a "harvest of death" that was presented; hundreds and thousands of torn Union and rebel soldiers—although many of the former were already interred—strewed the now quiet fighting ground, soaked by the rain, which for two days had drenched the country with its fitful showers.

A battle has been often the subject of elaborate description; but it can be described in one simple word, *devilish*! and the distorted dead recall the ancient legends of men torn in pieces by the savage wantonness of fiends. Swept down without preparation, the shattered bodies fall in all conceivable positions. The rebels represented in the photograph are without shoes. These were always removed from the feet of the dead on account of the pressing need of the survivors. The pockets turned inside out also show that appropriation did not cease with the coverings of the feet. Around is scattered the litter of the battle-field, accoutrements, ammunition, rags, cups and canteens, crackers, haversacks, &c., and letters that may tell the name of the owner, although the majority will surely be buried unknown by strangers, and in a strange land. Killed in the frantic efforts to break the steady lines of an army of patriots, whose heroism only excelled theirs in motive, they paid with life the price of their treason, and when the wicked strife was finished, found nameless graves, far from home and kindred.

95

Such a picture conveys a useful moral: It shows the blank horror and reality of war, in opposition to its pageantry. Here are the dreadful details! Let them aid in preventing such another calamity falling upon the nation.

JULIA WARD HOWE

Julia Ward Howe (1819–1910) wrote her "Battle Hymn of the Republic" in 1861, and her "Appeal to Womanhood throughout the World" in 1870: first the most famous American war song (later parodied to antiwar purposes by Mark Twain), then one of the most famous American peace manifestos, read even today by war opponents on Mother's Day. Howe is both the first woman writer represented in this anthology and the first writer represented to associate women with peacemaking, an association that though contested remains important.

Howe was a poet, author, and activist of extraordinary energy and productivity in spite of her husband Samuel Gridley Howe's long opposition to such public work. (Her published writing sometimes comments on the oppressions of marriage.) After her husband gave up his opposition, yielding at last to his wife's irresistible force, Howe became still more active: as suffragette and peace campaigner, as traveler and lecturer, and as president of the Association for the Advancement of Women.

Appeal to Womanhood Throughout the World

AGAIN, in the sight of the Christian world, have the skill and power of two great nations exhausted themselves in mutual murder. Again have the sacred questions of international justice been committed to the fatal mediation of military weapons. In this day of progress, in this century of light, the ambition of rulers has been allowed to batter the dear interests of domestic life for the bloody exchanges of the battle field. Thus men have done. Thus men will do. But women need no longer be made a party to proceedings which fill the globe with grief and horror. Despite the assumptions of physical force, the mother has a sacred and commanding word to say to the sons who owe their life to her suffering. That word should now be heard, and answered to as never before.

Arise, then, Christian women of this day! Arise, all women who have hearts, whether your baptism be that of water or of tears! Say firmly: We will not have great questions decided by irrelevant agencies. Our husbands shall not come to us, reeking with carnage, for carresses and applause. Our sons shall not be taken from us to unlearn all that we have been able to teach them of charity, mercy and patience. We, women of one country, will be too tender of those of another country, to allow our sons to be trained to injure theirs. From the bosom of the devastated earth a voice goes up with our own. It says: Disarm, disarm! The sword of murder is not the balance of justice. Blood does not wipe out dishonor, nor violence vindicate possession. As men have often forsaken the plough and the anvil at the summons of war, let women now leave all that may be left of home for a great and earnest day of council.

Let them meet first, as women, to bewail and commemorate the dead. Let them then solemnly take council with each other as to the means whereby the great human family can live in peace, man as the brother of man, each bearing after his own kind the sacred impress, not of Cæsar, but of God.

In the name of womanhood and of humanity, I earnestly ask that a general congress of women, without limit of nationality, may be appointed and held at some place deemed most convenient, and at the earliest period consistent with its objects, to promote the alliance of the different nationalities, the amicable settlement of international questions, the great and general interests of peace.

AMBROSE BIERCE

Ambrose Bierce (1842–1914) enlisted in the Union Army in 1861 and served in it until January 1865, when he was released from active duty because of wounds sustained in battle. Among the battles he fought in was that at Chickamauga in 1863, which is the subject of the story included here. He was no pacifist; defining *war* in his *Devil's Dictionary* (1911), he explained: "war loves to come like a thief in the night; professions of eternal amity provide the night." But few literary accounts of war make it seem so meaningless or so cruel.

After the war, Bierce became a journalist and writer of fiction, living mostly in or around San Francisco. He published "Chickamauga" in 1889. In 1898, though employed by war-boosting William Randolph Hearst, he warned against the impending Spanish-American War. In 1913 he went to Mexico, apparently to observe Pancho Villa's revolution, then disappeared.

Chickamauga

ONE sunny autumn afternoon a child strayed away from its rude home in a small field and entered a forest unobserved. It was happy in a new sense of freedom from control, happy in the opportunity of exploration and adventure; for this child's spirit, in bodies of its ancestors, had for thousands of years been trained to memorable feats of discovery and conquest—victories in battles whose critical moments were centuries, whose victors' camps were cities of hewn stone. From the cradle of its race it had conquered its way through two continents and passing a great sea had penetrated a third, there to be born to war and dominion as a heritage.

The child was a boy aged about six years, the son of a poor planter. In his younger manhood the father had been a soldier, had fought against naked savages and followed the flag of his country into the capital of a civilized race to the far South. In the peaceful life of a planter the warrior-fire survived; once kindled, it is never extinguished. The man loved military books and pictures and the boy had understood enough to make himself a wooden sword, though even the eye of his father would hardly have known it for what it was. This weapon he now bore bravely, as became the son of an heroic race, and pausing now

99

and again in the sunny space of the forest assumed, with some exaggeration, the postures of aggression and defense that he had been taught by the engraver's art. Made reckless by the ease with which he overcame invisible foes attempting to stay his advance, he committed the common enough military error of pushing the pursuit to a dangerous extreme, until he found himself upon the margin of a wide but shallow brook, whose rapid waters barred his direct advance against the flying foe that had crossed with illogical ease. But the intrepid victor was not to be baffled; the spirit of the race which had passed the great sea burned unconquerable in that small breast and would not be denied. Finding a place where some bowlders in the bed of the stream lay but a step or a leap apart, he made his way across and fell again upon the rear-guard of his imaginary foe, putting all to the sword.

Now that the battle had been won, prudence required that he withdraw to his base of operations. Alas; like many a mightier conqueror, and like one, the mightiest, he could not

curb the lust for war,
Nor learn that tempted Fate will leave the loftiest star.

Advancing from the bank of the creek he suddenly found himself confronted with a new and more formidable enemy: in the path that he was following, sat, bolt upright, with ears erect and paws suspended before it, a rabbit! With a startled cry the child turned and fled, he knew not in what direction, calling with inarticulate cries for his mother, weeping, stumbling, his tender skin cruelly torn by brambles, his little heart beating hard with terror—breathless, blind with tears—lost in the forest! Then, for more than an hour, he wandered with erring feet through the tangled undergrowth, till at last, overcome by fatigue, he lay down in a narrow space between two rocks, within a few yards of the stream and still grasping his toy sword, no longer a weapon but a companion, sobbed himself to sleep. The wood birds sang merrily above his head; the squirrels, whisking their bravery of tail, ran barking from tree to tree, unconscious of the pity of it, and somewhere far away was a strange, muffled thunder, as if the partridges were drumming in celebration of nature's victory over the son of her immemorial enslavers. And back at the little plantation, where white men and black were hastily searching the fields and hedges in alarm, a mother's heart was breaking for her missing child.

Hours passed, and then the little sleeper rose to his feet. The chill of the evening was in his limbs, the fear of the gloom in his heart. But he had rested, and he no longer wept. With some blind instinct which impelled to action he struggled through the undergrowth about him and came to a more open ground—on his right the brook, to the left a gentle acclivity studded with infrequent trees; over all, the gathering gloom of twilight. A thin, ghostly mist rose along the water. It frightened and repelled him; instead of recrossing, in the direction whence he had come, he turned his back upon it, and went forward toward the dark inclosing wood. Suddenly he saw before him a strange moving object which he took to be some large animal—a dog, a pig—he could not name it; perhaps it was a bear. He had seen pictures of bears, but knew of nothing to their discredit and had vaguely wished to meet one. But something in form or movement of this object—something in the awkwardness of its approach—told him that it was not a bear, and curiosity was stayed by fear. He stood still and as it came slowly on gained courage every moment, for he saw that at least it had not the long menacing ears of the rabbit. Possibly his impressionable mind was half conscious of something familiar in its shambling, awkward gait. Before it had approached near enough to resolve his doubts he saw that it was followed by another and another. To right and to left were many more; the whole open space about him were alive with them—all moving toward the brook.

They were men. They crept upon their hands and knees. They used their hands only, dragging their legs. They used their knees only, their arms hanging idle at their sides. They strove to rise to their feet, but fell prone in the attempt. They did nothing naturally, and nothing alike, save only to advance foot by foot in the same direction. Singly, in pairs and in little groups, they came on through the gloom, some halting now and again while others crept slowly past them, then resuming their movement. They came by dozens and by hundreds; as far on either hand as one could see in the deepening gloom they extended and the black wood behind them appeared to be inexhaustible. The very ground seemed in motion toward the creek. Occasionally one who had paused did not again go on, but lay motionless. He was dead. Some, pausing, made strange gestures with their hands, erected their arms and lowered them again, clasped their heads; spread their palms upward, as men are sometimes seen to do in public prayer.

Not all of this did the child note; it is what would have been noted by an elder observer; he saw little but that these were men, yet crept like babes. Being men, they were not terrible, though unfamiliarly clad. He moved among them freely, going from one to another and peering into their faces with childish curiosity. All their faces were singularly white and many were streaked and gouted with red. Something in this—something too, perhaps, in their grotesque attitudes and movements— reminded him of the painted clown whom he had seen last summer in the circus, and he laughed as he watched them. But on and ever on they crept, these maimed and bleeding men, as heedless as he of the dramatic contrast between his laughter and their own ghastly gravity. To him it was a merry spectacle. He had seen his father's negroes creep upon their hands and knees for his amusement—had ridden them so, "making believe" they were his horses. He now approached one of these crawling figures from behind and with an agile movement mounted it astride. The man sank upon his breast, recovered, flung the small boy fiercely to the ground as an unbroken colt might have done, then turned upon him a face that lacked a lower jaw—from the upper teeth to the throat was a great red gap fringed with hanging shreds of flesh and splinters of bone. The unnatural prominence of nose, the absence of chin, the fierce eyes, gave this man the appearance of a great bird of prey crimsoned in throat and breast by the blood of its quarry. The man rose to his knees, the child to his feet. The man shook his fist at the child; the child, terrified at last, ran to a tree near by, got upon the farther side of it and took a more serious view of the situation. And so the clumsy multitude dragged itself slowly and painfully along in hideous pantomime—moved forward down the slope like a swarm of great black beetles, with never a sound of going—in silence profound, absolute.

Instead of darkening, the haunted landscape began to brighten. Through the belt of trees beyond the brook shone a strange red light, the trunks and branches of the trees making a black lacework against it. It struck the creeping figures and gave them monstrous shadows, which caricatured their movements on the lit grass. It fell upon their faces, touching their whiteness with a ruddy tinge, accentuating the stains with which so many of them were freaked and maculated. It sparkled on buttons and bits of metal in their clothing. Instinctively the child turned toward the growing splendor and moved down the slope with his horrible companions; in a few moments had passed the foremost of the throng—not much of a feat, considering his advantages. He placed himself in the lead, his wooden sword still in hand, and solemnly directed the march, conforming his pace to theirs and occasionally turning as if to see that his forces did not straggle. Surely such a leader never before had such a following.

Scattered about upon the ground now slowly narrowing by the encroachment of this awful march to water, were certain articles to which, in the leader's mind, were coupled no significant associations: an occasional blanket, tightly rolled lengthwise, doubled and the ends bound together with a string; a heavy knapsack here, and there a broken rifle—such things, in short, as are found in the rear of retreating troops, the "spoor" of men flying from their hunters. Everywhere near the creek, which here had a margin of lowland, the earth was trodden into mud by the feet of men and horses. An observer of better experience in the use of his eyes would have noticed that these footprints pointed in both directions; the ground had been twice passed over—in advance and in retreat. A few hours before, these desperate, stricken men, with their more fortunate and now distant comrades, had penetrated the forest in thousands. Their successive battalions, breaking into swarms and re-forming in lines, had passed the child on every side— had almost trodden on him as he slept. The rustle and murmur of their march had not awakened him. Almost within a stone's throw of where he lay they had fought a battle; but all unheard by him were the roar of the musketry, the shock of the cannon, "the thunder of the captains and the shouting." He had slept through it all, grasping his little wooden sword with perhaps a tighter clutch in unconscious sympathy with his martial environment, but as heedless of the grandeur of the struggle as the dead who had died to make the glory.

The fire beyond the belt of woods on the farther side of the creek, reflected to earth from the canopy of its own smoke, was now suffusing the whole landscape. It transformed the sinuous line of mist to the vapor of gold. The water gleamed with dashes of red, and red, too, were many of the stones protruding above the surface. But that was blood; the less desperately wounded had stained them in crossing. On them, too, the child now crossed with eager steps; he was going to the fire. As he stood upon the farther bank he turned about to look at the companions of his march. The advance was arriving at the creek. The stronger had already drawn themselves to the brink and plunged their faces into the flood. Three or four who lay without motion appeared to have no heads. At this the child's eyes expanded with wonder; even his hospitable understanding could not accept a phenomenon implying such vitality as that. After slaking their thirst these men had not had the strength to back away from the water, nor to keep their heads above it. They were drowned. In rear of these, the open spaces of the forest showed the leader as many formless figures of his grim command as at first; but not nearly so many were in motion. He waved his cap for their encouragement and smilingly pointed with his weapon in the direction of the guiding light—a pillar of fire to this strange exodus.

Confident of the fidelity of his forces, he now entered the belt of woods, passed through it easily in the red illumination, climbed a fence, ran across a field, turning now and again to coquet with his responsive shadow, and so approached the blazing ruin of a dwelling. Desolation everywhere! In all the wide glare not a living thing was visible. He cared nothing for that; the spectacle pleased, and he danced with glee in imitation of the wavering flames. He ran about, collecting fuel, but every object that he found was too heavy for him to cast in from the distance to which the heat limited his approach. In despair he flung in his sword—a surrender to the superior forces of nature. His military career was at an end.

Shifting his position, his eyes fell upon some outbuildings which had an oddly familiar appearance, as if he had dreamed of them. He stood considering them with wonder, when suddenly the entire plantation, with its inclosing forest, seemed to turn as if upon a pivot. His little world swung half around; the points of the compass were reversed. He recognized the blazing building as his own home!

For a moment he stood stupefied by the power of the revelation, then ran with stumbling feet, making a half-circuit of the ruin. There, conspicuous in the light of the conflagration, lay the dead body of a woman—the white face turned upward, the hands thrown out and clutched full of grass, the clothing deranged, the long dark hair in tangles and full of clotted blood. The greater part of the forehead was torn away, and from the jagged hole the brain protruded, overflowing the temple, a frothy mass of gray, crowned with clusters of crimson bubbles—the work of a shell.

The child moved his little hands, making wild, uncertain gestures. He uttered a series of inarticulate and indescribable cries—something between the chattering of an ape and the gobbling of a turkey—a startling, soulless, unholy sound, the language of a devil. The child was a deaf mute.

Then he stood motionless, with quivering lips, looking down upon the wreck.

STEPHEN CRANE

Like Ambrose Bierce, Stephen Crane (1871–1900) saw war at first hand, reporting as a journalist on the Greco-Turkish War in 1897 and the Spanish-American War in 1898. Like Bierce he was no pacifist, seeking to enlist in the latter war after the sinking of the *Maine*. Unlike Bierce he never served as a soldier; his application to enlist was rejected on medical grounds.

Most of Crane's war writing, from *The Red Badge of Courage* (1895) on, takes no position for or against war in general or wars in particular, his aim and great success being simply the realistic depiction of war as it is. "War Is Kind" is the anomaly, regularly turning up in antiwar literature anthologies since its publication. Its opposition is not so much to war as to wartime rhetoric, its target the comforting lie, "war is kind," which in the poem is repeatedly juxtaposed to uncomforting accounts of soldiers' mass deaths. It is, in the critic and memoirist Paul Fussell's wonderful phrase, not so much an antiwar poem as an "anti-home-front poem."

War Is Kind

Do not weep, maiden, for war is kind.
Because your lover threw wild hands toward the sky
And the affrighted steed ran on alone,
Do not weep.
War is kind.

    Hoarse, booming drums of the regiment,
    Little souls who thirst for fight,
    These men were born to drill and die.
    The unexplained glory flies above them,
    Great is the battle-god, great, and his kingdom—
    A field where a thousand corpses lie.

Do not weep, babe, for war is kind.
Because your father tumbled in the yellow trenches,
Raged at his breast, gulped and died,
Do not weep.
War is kind.

Swift blazing flag of the regiment,
Eagle with crest of red and gold,
These men were born to drill and die.
Point for them the virtue of slaughter,
Make plain to them the excellence of killing
And a field where a thousand corpses lie.

Mother whose heart hung humble as a button
On the bright splendid shroud of your son,
Do not weep.
War is kind.

MARK TWAIN

Much of the later work of Mark Twain (1843–1910) is marked by a lacerating contempt for human nature, quite different from his more nuanced and humorous earlier portraits of flawed individual characters. He found especially good material for his misanthropy in the human appetite for war in general ("The War Prayer") and in the American appetite for the Spanish-American War in particular ("Battle Hymn of the Republic [Brought Down to Date]"). Financial troubles, rheumatism, and the death of his daughter Susy at twenty-four may all have contributed to the deepening pessimism of his last decade. Neither "The War Prayer" nor his "Battle Hymn" appeared in print during his lifetime; when *Harper's Bazaar* rejected the latter in 1905, he wrote a friend that he expected as much, because "[n]one but the dead are permitted to tell the truth."

Twain is the earliest author in this anthology to dramatize antiwar feeling through parody, brilliantly choosing as his parody-text Julia Ward Howe's "The Battle Hymn of the Republic." That strategy of parody through inversion becomes increasingly important to antiwar writers, perhaps most poignantly in Dalton Trumbo's *Johnny Got His Gun* (1939), its title playing on the familiar lyrics of George M. Cohan's anti-German propaganda song "Over There" (1917).

Battle Hymn of the Republic
(Brought Down to Date)

Mine eyes have seen the orgy of the launching of the
      Sword;
He is searching out the hoardings where the stranger's
      wealth is stored;
He hath loosed his fateful lightnings, and with woe and
      death has scored;
  His lust is marching on.

I have seen him in the watch-fires of a hundred circling
      camps,
They have builded him an altar in the Eastern dews and
      damps;

I have read his doomful mission by the dim and flaring
      lamps—
  His night is marching on.

I have read his bandit gospel writ in burnished rows of
      steel:
"As ye deal with my pretensions, so with you my wrath
      shall deal;
Let the faithless son of Freedom crush the patriot with
      his heel;
  Lo, Greed is marching on!"

We have legalized the strumpet and are guarding her
      retreat;*
Greed is seeking out commercial souls before his
      judgment seat;
O, be swift, ye clods, to answer him! be jubilant my feet!
  Our god is marching on!

In a sordid slime harmonious, Greed was born in yonder
      ditch,
With a longing in his bosom—and for others' goods an
      itch—
As Christ died to make men holy, let men die to make us
      rich—
  Our god is marching on.

*In Manila the government has placed a certain industry under the protection
of our flag.

The War Prayer

IT WAS a time of great and exalting excitement. The country was up in arms, the war was on, in every breast burned the holy fire of patriotism; the drums were beating, the bands playing, the toy pistols popping, the bunched firecrackers hissing and spluttering; on every hand and far down the receding and fading spread of roofs and balconies a fluttering wilderness of flags flashed in the sun; daily the young volunteers marched down the wide avenue gay and fine in their new uniforms, the proud fathers and mothers and sisters and sweethearts cheering them with voices choked with happy emotion as they swung by; nightly the packed mass meetings listened, panting, to patriot oratory which stirred the deepest deeps of their hearts, and which they interrupted at briefest intervals with cyclones of applause, the tears running down their cheeks the while; in the churches the pastors preached devotion to flag and country, and invoked the God of Battles, beseeching His aid in our good cause in outpouring of fervid eloquence which moved every listener. It was indeed a glad and gracious time, and the half dozen rash spirits that ventured to disapprove of the war and cast a doubt upon its righteousness straightway got such a stern and angry warning that for their personal safety's sake they quickly shrank out of sight and offended no more in that way.

Sunday morning came—next day the battalions would leave for the front; the church was filled; the volunteers were there, their young faces alight with martial dreams—visions of the stern advance, the gathering momentum, the rushing charge, the flashing sabers, the flight of the foe, the tumult, the enveloping smoke, the fierce pursuit, the surrender!—then home from the war, bronzed heroes, welcomed, adored, submerged in golden seas of glory! With the volunteers sat their dear ones, proud, happy, and envied by the neighbors and friends who had no sons and brothers to send forth to the field of honor, there to win for the flag, or, failing, die the noblest of noble deaths. The service proceeded; a war chapter from the Old Testament was read; the first prayer was said; it was followed by an organ burst that shook the building, and with one impulse the house rose, with glowing eyes and beating hearts, and poured out that tremendous invocation—

"God the all-terrible! Thou who ordainest,
Thunder thy clarion and lightning thy sword!"

Then came the "long" prayer. None could remember the like of
it for passionate pleading and moving and beautiful language.
The burden of its supplication was, that an ever-merciful and
benignant Father of us all would watch over our noble young
soldiers, and aid, comfort, and encourage them in their patriotic work; bless them, shield them in the day of battle and
the hour of peril, bear them in His mighty hand, make them
strong and confident, invincible in the bloody onset; help them
to crush the foe, grant to them and to their flag and country
imperishable honor and glory—

An aged stranger entered and moved with slow and noiseless
step up the main aisle, his eyes fixed upon the minister, his long
body clothed in a robe that reached to his feet, his head bare,
his white hair descending in a frothy cataract to his shoulders,
his seamy face unnaturally pale, pale even to ghastliness. With
all eyes following him and wondering, he made his silent way;
without pausing, he ascended to the preacher's side and stood
there, waiting. With shut lids the preacher, unconscious of his
presence, continued his moving prayer, and at last finished it
with the words, uttered in fervent appeal, "Bless our arms,
grant us the victory, O Lord our God, Father and Protector of
our land and flag!"

The stranger touched his arm, motioned him to step aside—
which the startled minister did—and took his place. During
some moments he surveyed the spellbound audience with
solemn eyes, in which burned an uncanny light; then in a deep
voice he said:

"I come from the Throne—bearing a message from
Almighty God!" The words smote the house with a shock; if
the stranger perceived it he gave no attention. "He has heard
the prayer of His servant your shepherd, and will grant it if such
shall be your desire after I, His messenger, shall have explained
to you its import—that is to say, its full import. For it is like
unto many of the prayers of men, in that it asks for more than
he who utters it is aware of—except he pause and think.

"God's servant and yours has prayed his prayer. Has he
paused and taken thought? Is it one prayer? No, it is two—one

uttered, the other not. Both have reached the ear of Him Who heareth all supplications, the spoken and the unspoken. Ponder this—keep it in mind. If you would beseech a blessing upon yourself, beware! lest without intent you invoke a curse upon a neighbor at the same time. If you pray for the blessing of rain upon your crop which needs it, by that act you are possibly praying for a curse upon some neighbor's crop which may not need rain and can be injured by it.

"You have heard your servant's prayer—the uttered part of it. I am commissioned of God to put into words the other part of it—that part which the pastor—and also you in your hearts—fervently prayed silently. And ignorantly and unthinkingly? God grant that it was so! You heard these words: 'Grant us the victory, O Lord our God!' That is sufficient. The *whole* of the uttered prayer is compact into those pregnant words. Elaborations were not necessary. When you have prayed for victory you have prayed for many unmentioned results which follow victory—*must* follow it, cannot help but follow it. Upon the listening spirit of God the Father fell also the unspoken part of the prayer. He commandeth me to put it into words. Listen!

"O Lord our Father, our young patriots, idols of our hearts, go forth to battle—be Thou near them! With them—in spirit—we also go forth from the sweet peace of our beloved firesides to smite the foe. O Lord our God, help us to tear their soldiers to bloody shreds with our shells; help us to cover their smiling fields with the pale forms of their patriot dead; help us to drown the thunder of the guns with the shrieks of their wounded, writhing in pain; help us to lay waste their humble homes with a hurricane of fire; help us to wring the hearts of their unoffending widows with unavailing grief; help us to turn them out roofless with their little children to wander unfriended the wastes of their desolated land in rags and hunger and thirst, sports of the sun flames of summer and the icy winds of winter, broken in spirit, worn with travail, imploring Thee for the refuge of the grave and denied it—for our sakes who adore Thee, Lord, blast their hopes, blight their lives, protract their bitter pilgrimage, make heavy their steps, water their way with their tears, stain the white snow with the blood of their wounded feet! We ask it, in the spirit of love, of

Him Who is the Source of Love, and Who is the ever-faithful refuge and friend of all that are sore beset and seek His aid with humble and contrite hearts. Amen."

(*After a pause.*) "Ye have prayed it; if ye still desire it, speak! The messenger of the Most High waits."

It was believed afterward that the man was a lunatic, because there was no sense in what he said.

WILLIAM JAMES

"Next to Thoreau's essay on civil disobedience," write Alice and Staughton Lynd in their documentary history *Nonviolence in America* (1995), "'The Moral Equivalent of War' . . . is probably the most influential statement in the history of American nonviolence." They are no doubt right; but James's essay is vastly less likely to be quoted at antiwar rallies. The reason is connected with the essay's innovation: its attempt to retain, for those opposing war, the most admirable energies animating those who support it, "the higher aspects of militarist sentiment." James works so hard setting out those aspects, and is clearly so drawn to them, that one can almost forget that the essay is in the end intended as oppositional.

From that same trait, however, comes much of the essay's influence; as the Lynds go on to note, "the American Friends Service Committee, the Civil Conservation Corps, and the Peace Corps all derive from . . . James' argument." Anyone wanting to engage in "the war against war," namely, to bring martial virtues to bear against military activities, can draw sustenance from James's essay.

James's life was an apt preparation for the writing of this essay at the end of it. He grew up in one of the most intense of all American families, his father being the eccentric, visionary philosopher Henry James the elder, his brother the great novelist Henry James, his sister the great diarist Alice James. His education was largely informal, he was to some extent an autodidact, and he moved from field to field, from physiology to psychology to philosophy. He was arguably the founder of American psychology; his *Principles of Psychology* (1890) remains a classic, as does his *Varieties of Religious Experience* (1902), with its emphasis on experience and its indifference to religious doctrine. He was among the founders of that peculiarly American school of philosophy called pragmatism, with its insistence on testing philosophical principles by the standard of "[whether] they pay." And he was an early example of the engaged academic intellectual, taking stands on American intervention in Venezuela and later, with Mark Twain and others, in Cuba and the Philippines; on lynching; on the needs of African Americans; and on the conditions at mental hospitals.

The Moral Equivalent of War

THE war against war is going to be no holiday excursion or camping party. The military feelings are too deeply grounded to abdicate their place among our ideals until better substitutes are offered than the glory and shame that come to nations as well as to individuals from the ups and downs of politics and the vicissitudes of trade. There is something highly paradoxical in the modern man's relation to war. Ask all our millions, north and south, whether they would vote now (were such a thing possible) to have our war for the Union expunged from history, and the record of a peaceful transition to the present time substituted for that of its marches and battles, and probably hardly a handful of eccentrics would say yes. Those ancestors, those efforts, those memories and legends, are the most ideal part of what we now own together, a sacred spiritual possession worth more than all the blood poured out. Yet ask those same people whether they would be willing in cold blood to start another civil war now to gain another similar possession, and not one man or woman would vote for the proposition. In modern eyes, precious though wars may be, they must not be waged solely for the sake of the ideal harvest. Only when forced upon one, only when an enemy's injustice leaves us no alternative, is a war now thought permissible.

It was not thus in ancient times. The earlier men were hunting men, and to hunt a neighboring tribe, kill the males, loot the village and possess the females, was the most profitable, as well as the most exciting, way of living. Thus were the more martial tribes selected, and in chiefs and peoples a pure pugnacity and love of glory came to mingle with the more fundamental appetite for plunder.

Modern war is so expensive that we feel trade to be a better avenue to plunder; but modern man inherits all the innate pugnacity and all the love of glory of his ancestors. Showing war's irrationality and horror is of no effect upon him. The horrors make the fascination. War is the *strong* life; it is life *in extremis*; war-taxes are the only ones men never hesitate to pay, as the budgets of all nations show us.

History is a bath of blood. The Iliad is one long recital of how Diomedes and Ajax, Sarpedon and Hector *killed*. No detail of the wounds they made is spared us, and the Greek mind fed upon the story. Greek history is a panorama of jingoism and imperialism—war for war's sake, all the citizens being warriors. It is horrible reading, because of the irrationality of it all—save for the purpose of making "history"—and the history is that of the utter ruin of a civilization in intellectual respects perhaps the highest the earth has ever seen.

Those wars were purely piratical. Pride, gold, women, slaves, excitement, were their only motives. In the Peloponnesian war, for example, the Athenians ask the inhabitants of Melos (the island where the "Venus of Milo" was found), hitherto neutral, to own their lordship. The envoys meet, and hold a debate which Thucydides gives in full, and which, for sweet reasonableness of form, would have satisfied Matthew Arnold. "The powerful exact what they can," said the Athenians, "and the weak grant what they must." When the Meleans say that sooner than be slaves they will appeal to the gods, the Athenians reply: "Of the gods we believe and of men we know that, by a law of their nature, wherever they can rule they will. This law was not made by us, and we are not the first to have acted upon it; we did but inherit it, and we know that you and all mankind, if you were as strong as we are, would do as we do. So much for the gods; we have told you why we expect to stand as high in their good opinion as you." Well, the Me-leans still refused, and their town was taken. "The Athenians," Thucydides quietly says, "thereupon put to death all who were of military age and made slaves of the women and children. They then colonized the island, sending thither five hundred settlers of their own."

Alexander's career was piracy pure and simple, nothing but an orgy of power and plunder, made romantic by the character of the hero. There was no rational principle in it, and the moment he died his generals and governors attacked one another. The cruelty of those times is incredible. When Rome finally conquered Greece, Paulus Aemilius was told by the Roman Senate to reward his soldiers for their toil by "giving" them the old kingdom of Epirus. They sacked seventy cities and carried off a hundred and fifty thousand inhabitants as slaves. How many they killed I know not; but in Etolia they killed all the senators, five hundred and fifty in number. Brutus was "the noblest Roman of them all," but to reanimate his soldiers on the eve of Philippi he similarly promises to give them the cities of Sparta and Thessalonica to ravage, if they win the fight.

Such was the gory nurse that trained societies to cohesiveness. We inherit the warlike type; and for most of the capacities of heroism that the human race is full of we have to thank this cruel history. Dead men tell no tales, and if there were any tribes of other type than this they have left no survivors. Our ancestors have bred pugnacity into our bone and marrow, and thousands of years of peace won't breed it out of us. The popular imagination fairly fattens on the thought of wars. Let public opinion once reach a certain fighting pitch, and no ruler can withstand it. In the Boer war both governments began with bluff, but couldn't stay there, the military tension was too much for them. In r898 our people had read the word WAR in letters three inches high for three months in every newspaper. The pliant politician McKinley was swept away by their eagerness, and our squalid war with Spain became a necessity.

At the present day, civilized opinion is a curious mental mixture. The military instincts and ideals are as strong as ever, but are confronted by reflective criticisms which sorely curb their ancient freedom. Innumerable writers are showing up the bestial side of military service. Pure loot and mastery seem no longer morally avowable motives, and pretexts must be found for attributing them solely to the enemy. England and we, our army and navy authorities repeat without ceasing, arm solely for "peace," Germany and Japan it is who are bent on loot and glory. "Peace" in military mouths to-day is a synonym for "war expected." The word has become a pure provocative, and no government wishing peace sincerely should allow it ever to be printed in a newspaper. Every up-to-date Dictionary should say that "peace" and "war" mean the same thing, now *in posse*, now *in actu*. It may even reasonably be said that the intensely sharp competitive *preparation* for war by the nations *is the real war*, permanent, unceasing; and that the battles are only a sort of public verification of the mastery gained during the "peace"-interval.

It is plain that on this subject civilized man has developed a sort of double personality. If we take European nations, no legitimate interest of any one of them would seem to justify the tremendous destructions which a war to compass it would necessarily entail. It would seem as though common sense and reason ought to find a way to reach agreement in every conflict of honest interests. I myself think it our bounden duty to believe in such international rationality as possible. But, as things stand, I see how desperately hard it is to bring the peace-party and the war-party together, and I believe that the difficulty is due to certain deficiencies in the program of pacificism which set the militarist imagination strongly, and to a certain extent justifiably, against it. In the whole discussion both sides are on imaginative and sentimental ground. It is but one utopia against another, and everything one says must be abstract and hypothetical. Subject to this criticism and caution, I will try to characterize in abstract strokes the opposite imaginative forces, and point out what to my own very fallible mind seems the best utopian hypothesis, the promising line of conciliation.

In my remarks, pacificist tho' I am, I will refuse to speak of the bestial side of the war-régime (already done justice to by many writers) and consider only the higher aspects of militaristic sentiment. Patriotism no one thinks discreditable; nor does any one deny that war is the romance of history. But inordinate ambitions are the soul of every patriotism, and the possibility of violent death the soul of all romance. The militarily patriotic and romantic-minded everywhere, and especially the professional military class, refuse to admit for a moment that war may be a transitory phenomenon in social evolution. The notion of a sheep's paradise like that revolts, they say, our higher imagination. Where then would be the steeps of life? If war had ever stopped, we should have to reinvent it, on this view, to redeem life from flat degeneration.

Reflective apologists for war at the present day all take it religiously. It is a sort of sacrament. Its profits are to the vanquished as well as to the victor; and quite apart from any question of profit, it is an absolute good, we are told, for it is human nature at its highest dynamic. Its "horrors" are a cheap price to pay for rescue from the only alternative supposed, of a world of clerks and teachers, of co-education and zoophily, of "consumer's leagues" and "associated charities," of industrialism unlimited, and feminism unabashed. No scorn, no hardness, no valor any more! Fie upon such a cattleyard of a planet!

So far as the central essence of this feeling goes, no healthy minded person, it seems to me, can help to some degree partaking of it. Militarism is the great preserver of our ideals of hardihood, and human life with no use for hardihood would be contemptible. Without risks or prizes for the darer, history would be insipid indeed; and there is a type of military character which every one feels that the race should never cease to breed, for every one is sensitive to its superiority. The duty is incumbent on mankind, of keeping military characters in stock—of keeping them, if not for use, then as ends in themselves and as pure pieces of perfection,—so that Roosevelt's weaklings and mollycoddles may not end by making everything else disappear from the face of nature.

This natural sort of feeling forms, I think, the innermost soul of army-writings. Without any exception known to me, militarist authors take a highly mystical view of their subject, and regard war as a biological or sociological necessity, uncontrolled by ordinary psychological checks and motives. When the time of development is ripe the war must come, reason or no reason, for the justifications pleaded are invariably fictitious. War is, in short, a permanent human *obligation*. General Homer Lea, in his recent book "the Valor of Ignorance," plants himself squarely on this ground. Readiness for war is for him the essence of nationality, and ability in it the supreme measure of the health of nations.

Nations, General Lea says, are never stationary—they must necessarily expand or shrink, according to their vitality or decrepitude. Japan now is culminating; and by the fatal law in question it is impossible that her statesmen should not long since have entered, with extraordinary foresight, upon a vast policy of conquest—the game in which the first moves were her wars with China and Russia and her treaty with England, and of which the final objective is the capture of the Philippines, the Hawaiian Islands, Alaska, and the whole of our Coast west of the Sierra Passes. This will give Japan what her ineluctable vocation as a state absolutely forces her to claim, the possession of the entire Pacific Ocean; and to oppose these deep designs we Americans have, according to our author, nothing but our conceit, our ignorance, our commercialism, our corruption, and our feminism. General Lea makes a minute technical comparison of the military strength which we at present could oppose to the strength of Japan, and concludes that the islands, Alaska, Oregon, and Southern California, would fall almost without resistance, that San Francisco must surrender in a fortnight to a Japanese investment, that in three or four months the war would be over, and our republic, unable to regain what it had heedlessly neglected to protect sufficiently, would then "disintegrate," until perhaps some Caesar should arise to weld us again into a nation.

A dismal forecast indeed! Yet not unplausible, if the mentality of Japan's statesmen be of the Caesarian type of which history shows so many examples, and which is all that General Lea seems able to imagine. But there is no reason to think that women can no longer be the mothers of Napoleonic or Alexandrian characters; and if these come in Japan and find their opportunity, just such surprises as "the Valor of Ignorance" paints may lurk in ambush for us. Ignorant as we still are of the innermost recesses of Japanese mentality, we may be foolhardy to disregard such possibilities.

Other militarists are more complex and more moral in their considerations. The "Philosophie des Krieges," by S. R. Steinmetz is a good example. War, according to this author, is an ordeal instituted by God, who weighs the nations in its balance. It is the essential form of the State, and the only function in which peoples can employ all their powers at once and convergently. No victory is possible save as the resultant of a totality of virtues, no defeat for which some vice or weakness is not responsible. Fidelity, cohesiveness, tenacity, heroism, conscience, education, inventiveness, economy, wealth physical health and vigor—there isn't a moral or intellectual point of superiority that doesn't tell, when God holds his assizes and hurls the peoples upon one another. *Die Weltgeschichte ist das Weltgericht*; and Dr. Steinmetz does not believe that in the long run chance and luck play any part in apportioning the issues.

The virtues that prevail, it must be noted, are virtues anyhow, superiorities that count in peaceful as well as in military competition; but the strain on them, being infinitely intenser in the latter case, makes war infinitely more searching as a trial. No ordeal is comparable to its winnowings. Its dread hammer is the welder of men into cohesive states, and nowhere but in such states can human nature adequately develop its capacity. The only alternative is "degeneration."

Dr. Steinmetz is a conscientious thinker, and his book, short as it is, takes much into account. Its upshot can, it seems to me, be summed up in Simon Patten's word, that mankind was nursed in pain and fear, and that the transition to a "pleasure-economy" may be fatal to a being wielding no powers of defense against its disintegrative influences. If we speak of the *fear of emancipation from the fear-regime*, we put the whole situation into a single phrase; fear regarding ourselves now taking the place of the ancient fear of the enemy.

Turn the fear over as I will in my mind, it all seems to lead back to two unwillingnesses of the imagination, one aesthetic, and the other moral: unwillingness, first to envisage a future in which army-life, with its many elements of charm, shall be forever impossible, and in which the destinies of peoples shall nevermore be decided quickly, thrillingly, and tragically, by force, but only gradually and insipidly by "evolution"; and, secondly, unwillingness to see the supreme theatre of human strenuousness closed, and the splendid military aptitudes of men doomed to keep always in a state of latency and never show themselves in action. These insistent unwillingnesses, no less than other esthetic and ethical insistencies have, it seems to me, to be listened to and respected. One cannot meet them effectively by mere counter-insistency on war's expensiveness and horror. The horror makes the thrill; and when the question is of getting the extremest and supremest out of human nature, talk of expense sounds ignominious. The weakness of so much merely negative criticism is evident—pacificism makes no converts from the military party. The military party denies neither the bestiality nor the horror, nor the expense; it only says that these things tell but half the story. It only says that war is *worth* them; that, taking human nature as a whole, its wars are its best protection against its weaker and more cowardly self, and that mankind cannot *afford* to adopt a peace-economy.

Pacificists ought to enter more deeply into the esthetical and ethical point of view of their opponents. Do that first in any controversy, says J. J. Chapman, *then move the point*, and your opponent will follow. So long as anti-militarists propose no substitute for war's disciplinary function, no *moral equivalent* of war, analogous, as one might say, to the mechanical equivalent of heat, so long they fail to realize the full inwardness of the situation. And as a rule they do fail. The duties, penalties, and sanctions pictured in the utopias they paint are all too weak and tame to touch the military-minded. Tolstoy's pacifism is the only exception to this rule, for it is profoundly pessimistic as regards all this world's values, and makes the fear of the Lord furnish the moral spur provided elsewhere by the fear of the enemy. But our socialistic peace-advocates all believe absolutely in this world's values; and instead of the fear of the Lord and the fear of the enemy, the only fear they reckon with is the fear of poverty if one be lazy. This weakness pervades all the socialistic literature with which I am acquainted. Even in Lowes Dickinson's exquisite dialogue,* high wages and short hours are the only forces invoked for overcoming man's distaste for repulsive kinds of labor. Meanwhile men at large still live as they always have lived, under a pain-and-fear economy—for those of us who live in an ease-economy are but an island in the stormy ocean—and the whole atmosphere of present-day utopian literature tastes mawkish and dishwatery to people who still keep a sense for life's more bitter flavors. It suggests, in truth, ubiquitous inferiority.

Inferiority is always with us, and merciless scorn of it is the keynote of the military temper. "Dogs, would you live forever?" shouted Frederick the Great. "Yes," say our utopians, "let us live forever, and raise our level gradually." The best thing about our "inferiors" to-day is that they are as tough as nails, and physically and morally almost as insensitive. Utopianism would see them soft and squeamish, while militarism would keep their callousness, but transfigure it into a meritorious characteristic, needed by "the service," and redeemed by that from the suspicion of inferiority. All the qualities of a man acquire dignity when he knows that the service of the collectivity that owns him needs them. If proud of the collectivity, his own pride rises in proportion. No collectivity is like an army for nourishing such pride; but it has to be confessed that the only sentiment which the image of pacific cosmopolitan industrialism is capable of arousing in countless worthy breasts is shame at the idea of belonging to *such* a collectivity. It is obvious that the United States of America as they exist to-day impress a mind like General Lea's as so much human blubber. Where is the sharpness and precipitousness, the contempt for

*Justice and Liberty, N. Y., 1909

life, whether one's own, or another's? Where is the savage "yes" and "no," the unconditional duty? Where is the conscription? Where is the blood-tax? Where is anything that one feels honored by belonging to?

Having said thus much in preparation, I will now confess my own utopia. I devoutly believe in the reign of peace and in the gradual advent of some sort of a socialistic equilibrium. The fatalistic view of the war-function is to me nonsense, for I know that war-making is due to definite motives and subject to prudential checks and reasonable criticisms, just like any other form of enterprise. And when whole nations are the armies, and the science of destruction vies in intellectual refinement with the sciences of production, I see that war becomes absurd and impossible from its own monstrosity. Extravagant ambitions will have to be replaced by reasonable claims, and nations must make common cause against them. I see no reason why all this should not apply to yellow as well as to white countries, and I look forward to a future when acts of war shall be formally outlawed as between civilized peoples.

All these beliefs of mine put me squarely into the anti-militarist party. But I do not believe that peace either ought to be or will be permanent on this globe, unless the states pacifically organized preserve some of the old elements of army-discipline. A permanently successful peace-economy cannot be a simple pleasure-economy. In the more or less socialistic future towards which mankind seems drifting we must still subject ourselves collectively to those severities which answer to our real position upon this only partly hospitable globe. We must make new energies and hardihoods continue the manliness to which the military mind so faithfully clings. Martial virtues must be the enduring cement; intrepidity, contempt of softness, surrender of private interest, obedience to command, must still remain the rock upon which states are built—unless, indeed, we wish for dangerous reactions against commonwealths fit only for contempt, and liable to invite attack whenever a centre of crystallization for military-minded enterprise gets formed anywhere in their neighborhood.

The war-party is assuredly right in affirming and reaffirming that the martial virtues, although originally gained by the race through war, are absolute and permanent human goods.

Patriotic pride and ambition in their military form are, after all, only specifications of a more general competitive passion. They are its first form, but that is no reason for supposing them to be its last form. Men now are proud of belonging to a conquering nation, and without a murmur they lay down their persons and their wealth, if by so doing they may fend off subjection. But who can be sure that *other aspects of one's country* may not, with time and education and suggestion enough, come to be regarded with similarly effective feelings of pride and shame? Why should men not some day feel that it is worth a blood-tax to belong to a collectivity superior in *any* ideal respect? Why should they not blush with indignant shame if the community that owns them is vile in any way whatsoever? Individuals, daily more numerous, now feel this civic passion. It is only a question of blowing on the spark till the whole population gets incandescent, and on the ruins of the old morals of military honour, a stable system of morals of civic honour builds itself up. What the whole community comes to believe in grasps the individual as in a vise. The war-function has graspt us so far; but constructive interests may some day seem no less imperative, and impose on the individual a hardly lighter burden.

Let me illustrate my idea more concretely. There is nothing to make one indignant in the mere fact that life is hard, that men should toil and suffer pain. The planetary conditions once for all are such, and we can stand it. But that so many men, by mere accidents of birth and opportunity, should have a life of *nothing else* but toil and pain and hardness and inferiority imposed upon them, should have *no* vacation, while others natively no more deserving never get any taste of this campaigning life at all,—*this* is capable of arousing indignation in reflective minds. It may end by seeming shameful to all of us that some of us have nothing but campaigning, and others nothing but unmanly ease. If now—and this is my idea—there were, instead of military conscription a conscription of the whole youthful population to form for a certain number of years a part of the army enlisted against *Nature*, the injustice would tend to be evened out, and numerous other goods to the commonwealth would follow. The military ideals of hardihood and discipline would be wrought into the growing fibre of the people; no one would remain blind as the luxurious classes now are blind, to man's real relations to the globe he lives on, and to the permanently sour and hard foundations of his higher life. To coal and iron mines, to freight trains, to fishing fleets in December, to dish-washing, clothes-washing, and window-washing, to road-building and tunnel-making, to foundries and stoke-holes, and to the frames of skyscrapers, would our gilded youths be drafted off, according to their choice, to get the childishness knocked out of them, and to come back into society with healthier sympathies and soberer ideas. They would have paid their blood-tax, done their own part in the immemorial human warfare against nature, they would tread the earth more proudly, the women would value them more highly, they would be better fathers and teachers of the following generation.

Such a conscription, with the state of public opinion that would have required it, and the many moral fruits it would bear, would preserve in the midst of a pacific civilization the manly virtues which the military party is so afraid of seeing disappear in peace. We should get toughness without callousness, authority with as little criminal cruelty as possible, and painful work done cheerily because the duty is temporary, and threatens not, as now, to degrade the whole remainder of one's life. I spoke of the "moral equivalent" of war. So far, war has been the only force that can discipline a whole community, and until an equivalent discipline is organized, I believe that war must have its way. But I have no serious doubt that the ordinary prides and shames of social man, once developed to a certain intensity, are capable of organizing such a moral equivalent as I have sketched, or some other just as effective for preserving manliness of type. It is but a question of time, of skillful propagandism, and of opinion-making men seizing historic opportunities.

The martial type of character can be bred without war. Strenuous honour and disinterestedness abound elsewhere. Priests and medical men are in a fashion educated to it, and we should all feel some degree of it imperative if we were conscious of our work as an obligatory service to the state. We should be *owned*, as soldiers are by the army, and our pride would rise accordingly. We could be poor, then, without humiliation, as army officers now are. The only thing needed henceforward is to inflame the civic temper as past history has inflamed the military temper. H. G. Wells, as usual, sees the centre of the situation. "In many ways," he says, "military organization is the most peaceful of activities. When the contemporary man steps from the street, of clamorous insincere advertisement, push, adulteration, underselling and intermittent employment, into the barrack-yard, he steps on to a higher social plane, into an atmosphere of service and co-operation and of infinitely more honourable emulations. Here at least men are not flung out of employment to degenerate because there is no immediate work for them to do. They are fed and drilled and trained for better services. Here at least a man is supposed to win promotion by self-forgetfulness and not by self-seeking. And beside the feeble and irregular endowment of research by commercialism, its little short-sighted snatches at profit by innovation and scientific economy, see how remarkable is the steady and rapid development of method and appliances in naval and military affairs! Nothing is more striking than to compare the progress of civil conveniences which has been left almost entirely to the trader, to the progress in military apparatus during the last few decades. The house-appliances of to-day for example, are little better than they were fifty years ago. A house of to-day is still almost as ill-ventilated, badly heated by wasteful fires, clumsily arranged and furnished as the house of 1858. Houses a couple of hundred years old are still satisfactory places of residence, so little have our standards risen. But the rifle or battleship of fifty years ago was beyond all comparison inferior to those we possess; in power, in speed, in convenience alike. No one has a use now for such superannuated things."*

Wells adds† that he thinks that the conceptions of order and discipline, the tradition of service and devotion, of physical fitness, unstinted exertion, and universal responsibility, which universal military duty is now teaching European nations, will remain a permanent acquisition, when the last ammunition has been used in the fireworks that celebrate the final peace. I believe as he does. It would be simply preposterous if the only force that could work ideals of honour and standards of

*First and Last Things, 1908, p.215.
†Ibid., p. 226.

efficiency into English or American natures should be the fear of being killed by the Germans or the Japanese. Great indeed is Fear; but it is not, as our military enthusiasts believe and try to make us believe, the only stimulus known for awakening the higher ranges of men's spiritual energy. The amount of alteration in public opinion which my utopia postulates is vastly less than the difference between the mentality of those black warriors who pursued Stanley's party on the Congo with their cannibal war-cry of "Meat! Meat" and that of the "general-staff" of any civilized nation. History has seen the latter interval bridged over: the former one can be bridged over much more easily.

JOHN F. KENDRICK

The English battle hymn "Onward, Christian Soldiers" (1865) was often parodied during World War I, on both sides of the Atlantic. In "Joe Soap's Army" (c. 1915), it was made to express the gallows humor of the trenches ("marching without fear" rhymed with "our old commander, safely in the rear"). In "Christians at War"—the most controversial American example—its original assertion that Christ "leads against the foe" is ridiculed as hypocrisy. Should "gentle Jesus" really bless our dynamite?

First published in *Solidarity*, the official organ of the Industrial Workers of the World, on December 4, 1915, "Christians at War" was widely reprinted and was subsequently used against the union in court on several occasions as evidence of its anti-American extremism. Its author, John F. Kendrick of Chicago, remains relatively obscure, but his experience as a veteran of the Spanish-American War surely shaped his attitudes; he later wrote a wartime memoir, "The Mid-Summer Picnic of '98," intended as a "slap against those who don't understand that a short campaign in a short war can be deadly."

Christians at War

Onward, Christian soldiers!
Duty's way is plain:
Slay your Christian neighbors,
Or by them be slain,
Pulpiteers are spouting
Effervescent swill.
God above is calling you
To rob and rape and kill.
All your acts are sanctified
By The Lamb on high;
If you love The Holy Ghost,
Go murder, pray and die.

Onward, Christian soldiers,
Rip and tear and smite!
Let the gentle Jesus
Bless your dynamite.
Splinter skulls with shrapnel,

Fertilize the sod:
Folks who do not speak your tongue
Deserve the curse of God.
Smash the doors of every home,
Pretty maidens seize;
Use your might and sacred right
To treat them as you please.

Onward, Christian soldiers!
Eat and drink your fill;
Rob with bloody fingers,
Christ O.K.'s the bill,
Steal the farmers' savings,
Take their grain and meat;
Even though the children starve,
The Saviour's bums must eat.
Burn the peasants' cottages,
Orphans leave bereft;
In Jehovah's holy name
Wreak ruin right and left.

Onward, Christian soldiers!
Drench the land with gore;
Mercy is a weakness
All the gods abhor.
Bayonet the babies,
Jab the mothers, too;
Hoist The Cross of Calvary
To hallow all you do.
File your bullets' noses flat,
Poison every well;
God decrees your "enemies"
Must all go plumb to hell.

Onward, Christian soldiers!
Blighting all you meet,
Trampling human freedom
Under pious feet.
Praise The Lord whose dollar-sign
Dupes his favored race!

Make the foreign trash respect
Your bullion brand of grace.
Trust in mock salvation,
Serve as pirates' tools;
History will say of you:
"That pack of g— d— fools."

EMMA GOLDMAN

Emma Goldman (1869–1940) would seem unlikely to turn up in an anthology of antiwar writing; her friend Margaret Anderson once referred to her as "an exponent of free love and bombs," and in her later years she confessed to having assisted Alexander Berkman in his failed 1892 attempt to assassinate the industrialist Henry Clay Frick. But the failure of that attempt changed her; she retained a commitment to direct action, but turned away from supporting individual acts of violence. In any case, her argument in the excerpt that follows—that "preparedness" tends to lead toward war—requires no rejection of individual violence, or for that matter of war generally, and in fact makes Goldman an ally in advance of Republican president Dwight Eisenhower in his critique of the military-industrial complex.

Goldman was born in Lithuania, studied in German and Russian schools, came to the United States in 1885, was inspired by the trial and execution of the Haymarket anarchists in 1886, and became a legendarily charismatic anarchist orator. (My mother heard her once, and said she was spellbinding.) After Berkman's release from prison, she and he edited *Mother Earth*, where the present text was first published. She was imprisoned in 1916 for explaining birth control from the podium and in 1917 for opposing the draft. On her release from prison she was deported to the Soviet Union, but was as opposed to Bolshevism as to capitalism; she found allies in the 1930s among the Spanish anarcho-syndicalists, and after their defeat worked on behalf of European refugees from fascism.

FROM
Preparedness, the Road to Universal Slaughter

Ever since the beginning of the European conflagration, the whole human race almost has fallen into the deathly grip of the war anesthesis, overcome by the mad teeming fumes of a blood soaked chloroform, which has obscured its vision and paralyzed its heart. Indeed, with the exception of some savage tribes, who know nothing of Christian religion or of brotherly love, and who also know nothing of dreadnaughts, submarines, munition manufacture and war loans, the rest of the race is under this terrible narcosis. The human mind seems to be conscious of but one thing, murderous speculation. Our whole civilization, our entire culture is concentrated in the mad demand for the most perfected weapons of slaughter.

Ammunition! Ammunition! O, Lord, thou who rulest heaven and earth, thou God of love, of mercy and of justice, provide us with enough ammunition to destroy our enemy. Such is the prayer which is ascending daily to the Christian heaven. Just like cattle, panic-stricken in the face of fire, throw themselves into the very flames, so all of the European people have fallen over each other into the devouring flames of the furies of war, and America, pushed to the very brink by unscrupulous politicians, by ranting demagogues, and by military sharks, is preparing for the same terrible feat.

In the face of this approaching disaster, it behooves men and women not yet overcome by the war madness to raise their voice of protest, to call the attention of the people to the crime and outrage which are about to be perpetrated upon them.

America is essentially the melting pot. No national unit composing it, is in a position to boast of superior race purity, particular historic mission, or higher culture. Yet the jingoes and war speculators are filling the air with the sentimental slogan of hypocritical nationalism, "America for Americans," "America first, last, and all the time." This cry has caught the popular fancy from one end of the country to another. In order to maintain America, military preparedness must be engaged in at once. A billion dollars of the people's sweat and blood is to be expended for dreadnaughts and submarines for the army and the navy, all to protect this precious America.

The pathos of it all is that the America which is to be protected by a huge military force is not the America of the people, but that of the privileged class; the class which robs and exploits the masses, and controls their lives from the cradle to the grave. No less pathetic is it that so few people realize that preparedness never leads to peace, but that it is indeed the road to universal slaughter.

With the cunning methods used by the scheming diplomats and military cliques of Germany to saddle the masses with Prussian militarism, the American military ring with its Roosevelts, its Garrisons, its Daniels, and lastly its Wilsons, are moving the very heavens to place the militaristic heel upon the necks of the American people, and, if successful, will hurl

America into the storm of blood and tears now devastating the countries of Europe.

Forty years ago Germany proclaimed the slogan: "Germany above everything. Germany for the Germans, first, last and always. We want peace; therefore we must prepare for war. Only a well armed and thoroughly prepared nation can maintain peace, can command respect, can be sure of its national integrity." And Germany continued to prepare, thereby forcing the other nations to do the same. The terrible European war is only the culminating fruition of the hydra-headed gospel, military preparedness.

Since the war began, miles of paper and oceans of ink have been used to prove the barbarity, the cruelty, the oppression of Prussian militarism. Conservatives and radicals alike are giving their support to the Allies for no other reason than to help crush that militarism, in the presence of which, they say, there can be no peace or progress in Europe. But though America grows fat on the manufacture of munitions and war loans to the Allies to help crush Prussians the same cry is now being raised in America which, if carried into national action, would build up an American militarism far more terrible than German or Prussian militarism could ever be, and that because nowhere in the world has capitalism become so brazen in its greed and nowhere is the state so ready to kneel at the feet of capital.

Like a plague, the mad spirit is sweeping the country, infesting the clearest heads and staunchest hearts with the deathly germ of militarism. National security leagues, with cannon as their emblem of protection, naval leagues with women in their lead have sprung up all over the country, women who boast of representing the gentler sex, women who in pain and danger bring forth life and yet are ready to dedicate it to the Moloch War. Americanization societies with well known liberals as members, they who but yesterday decried the patriotic clap-trap of to-day, are now lending themselves to befog the minds of the people and to help build up the same destructive institutions in America which they are directly and indirectly helping to pull down in Germany—militarism, the destroyer of youth, the raper of women, the annihilator of the best in the race, the very mower of life.

Even Woodrow Wilson, who not so long ago indulged in the phrase "A nation too proud to fight," who in the beginning of the war ordered prayers for peace, who in his proclamations spoke of the necessity of watchful waiting, even he has been whipped into line. He has now joined his worthy colleagues in the jingo movement, echoing their clamor for preparedness and their howl of "America for Americans." The difference between Wilson and Roosevelt is this: Roosevelt, a born bully, uses the club; Wilson, the historian, the college professor, wears the smooth polished university mask, but underneath it he, like Roosevelt, has but one aim, to serve the big interests, to add to those who are growing phenomenally rich by the manufacture of military supplies.

Woodrow Wilson, in his address before the Daughters of the American Revolution, gave his case away when he said, "I would rather be beaten than ostracized." To stand out against the Bethlehem, du Pont, Baldwin, Remington, Winchester metallic cartridges and the rest of the armament ring means political ostracism and death. Wilson knows that; therefore he betrays his original position, goes back on the bombast of "too proud to fight" and howls as loudly as any other cheap politician for preparedness and national glory, the silly pledge the navy league women intend to impose upon every school child: "I pledge myself to do all in my power to further the interests of my country, to uphold its institutions and to maintain the honor of its name and its flag. As I owe everything in life to my country, I consecrate my heart, mind and body to its service and promise to work for its advancement and security in times of peace and to shrink from no sacrifices or privation in its cause should I be called upon to act in its defence for the freedom, peace and happiness of our people."

To uphold the institutions of our country—that's it—the institutions which protect and sustain a handful of people in the robbery and plunder of the masses, the institutions which drain the blood of the native as well as of the foreigner, and turn it into wealth and power; the institutions which rob the alien of whatever originality he brings with him and in return gives him cheap Americanism, whose glory consists in mediocrity and arrogance.

The very proclaimers of "America first" have long before this betrayed the fundamental principles of real Americanism, of the kind of Americanism that Jefferson had in mind when he said that the best government is that which governs least; the kind of America that David Thoreau worked for when he proclaimed that the best government is the one that doesn't govern at all; or the other truly great Americans who aimed to make of this country a haven of refuge, who hoped that all the disinherited and oppressed people in coming to these shores would give character, quality and meaning to the country. That is not the America of the politician and munition speculators. Their America is powerfully portrayed in the idea of a young New York Sculptor; a hard cruel hand with long, lean, merciless fingers, crushing in over the heart of the immigrant, squeezing out its blood in order to coin dollars out of it and give the foreigner instead blighted hopes and stunted aspirations.

No doubt Woodrow Wilson has reason to defend these institutions. But what an ideal to hold out to the young generation! How is a military drilled and trained people to defend freedom, peace and happiness? This is what Major General O'Ryan has to say of an efficiently trained generation: "The soldier must be so trained that he becomes a mere automaton; he must be so trained that it will destroy his initiative; he must be so trained that he is turned into a machine. The soldier must be forced into the military noose; he must be jacked up; he must be ruled by his superiors with pistol in hand."

This was not said by a Prussian Junker; not by a German barbarian; not by Treitschke or Bernhardi, but by an American Major General. And he is right. You cannot conduct war with equals; you cannot have militarism with free born men; you must have slaves, automatons, machines, obedient disciplined creatures, who will move, act, shoot and kill at the command of their superiors. That is preparedness, and nothing else.

ELLEN N. LA MOTTE

"Ellen La Motte, who was an ex Johns Hopkins nurse, wanted to nurse near the front. She was still gun shy but she did want to nurse at the front, and [she] met Mary Borden-Turner who was running a hospital at the front and Ellen La Motte did for a few months nurse at the front." Thus Gertrude Stein remembers Ellen N. La Motte (1873–1961) in her *Autobiography of Alice B. Toklas* (1933); the two had met around the turn of the century in Baltimore, where La Motte would become a supervising nurse and expert in the treatment of tuberculosis (and where Stein was flunking out of medical school). La Motte was also active in women's suffrage campaigns, and reported on militant suffragettes in England for the *Baltimore Sun*.

The two were reacquainted in Paris in 1915, where La Motte finished her first book, *The Tuberculosis Nurse: Her Function and Her Qualifications*, published that year. Her second, *The Backwash of War* (1916), is drawn from her "few months" experiences in a military field hospital that Mary Borden had donated to the French government, located about six miles behind the lines, near Ypres. "Heroes" and its companion sketches in Borden's remarkable collection do not overtly oppose the war. But their unflinching depiction of the war's casualties and absurdities seemed to the U.S. government sufficiently dangerous to warrant action, and the book was censored in 1918, not to appear again until 1934. La Motte devoted much of her work after the war to opposing the opium trade, publishing three book-length studies and two books of short stories.

Heroes

WHEN he could stand it no longer, he fired a revolver up through the roof of his mouth, but he made a mess of it. The ball tore out his left eye, and then lodged somewhere under his skull, so they bundled him into an ambulance and carried him, cursing and screaming, to the nearest field hospital. The journey was made in double-quick time, over rough Belgian roads. To save his life, he must reach the hospital without delay, and if he was bounced to death jolting along at breakneck speed, it did not matter. That was understood. He was a deserter, and discipline must be maintained. Since he had failed in the job, his life must be saved, he must be nursed back to health, until he was well enough to be stood up against a wall and shot. This is War. Things like this also happen in peace time, but not so obviously.

At the hospital, he behaved abominably. The ambulance men declared that he had tried to throw himself out of the back of the ambulance, that he had yelled and hurled himself about, and spat blood all over the floor and blankets—in short, he was very disagreeable. Upon the operating table, he was no more reasonable. He shouted and screamed and threw himself from side to side, and it took a dozen leather straps and four or five orderlies to hold him in position, so that the surgeon could examine him. During this commotion, his left eye rolled about loosely upon his cheek, and from his bleeding mouth he shot great clots of stagnant blood, caring not where they fell. One fell upon the immaculate white uniform of the Directrice, and stained her, from breast to shoes. It was disgusting. They told him it was *La Directrice*, and that he must be careful. For an instant he stopped his raving, and regarded her fixedly with his remaining eye, then took aim afresh, and again covered her with his coward blood. Truly it was disgusting.

To the *Médecin Major* it was incomprehensible, and he said so. To attempt to kill oneself, when, in these days, it was so easy to die with honour upon the battlefield, was something he could not understand. So the *Médecin Major* stood patiently aside, his arms crossed, his supple fingers pulling the long black hairs on his bare arms, waiting. He had long to wait, for it was difficult to get the man under the anæsthetic. Many cans of ether were used, which went to prove that the patient was a drinking man. Whether he had acquired the habit of hard drink before or since the war could not be ascertained; the war had lasted a year now, and in that time many habits may be formed. As the *Médecin Major* stood there, patiently fingering the hairs on his hairy arms, he calculated the amount of ether that was expended—five cans of ether, at so many francs a can—however, the ether was a donation from America, so it did not matter. Even so, it was wasteful.

At last they said he was ready. He was quiet. During his struggles, they had broken out two big teeth with the mouth gag, and that added a little more blood to the blood already choking him. Then the *Médecin Major* did a very skilful operation. He trephined the skull, extracted the bullet that had lodged beneath it, and bound back in place that erratic eye. After which the man was sent over to the ward, while the surgeon returned hungrily to his dinner, long overdue.

In the ward, the man was a bad patient. He insisted upon tearing off his bandages, although they told him that this meant bleeding to death. His mind seemed fixed on death. He seemed to want to die, and was thoroughly unreasonable, although quite conscious. All of which meant that he required constant watching and was a perfect nuisance. He was so different from the other patients, who wanted to live. It was a joy to nurse them. This was the *Salle* of the *Grands Blessés*, those most seriously wounded. By expert surgery, by expert nursing, some of these were to be returned to their homes again, *réformés*, mutilated for life, a burden to themselves and to society; others were to be nursed back to health, to a point at which they could again shoulder eighty pounds of marching kit, and be torn to pieces again on the firing line. It was a pleasure to nurse such as these. It called forth all one's skill, all one's humanity. But to nurse back to health a man who was to be court-martialled and shot, truly that seemed a dead-end occupation.

They dressed his wounds every day. Very many yards of gauze were required, with gauze at so many francs a bolt. Very much ether, very much iodoform, very many bandages—it was an expensive business, considering. All this waste for a man who was to be shot, as soon as he was well enough. How much better to expend this upon the hopeless cripples, or those who were to face death again in the trenches.

The night nurse was given to reflection. One night, about midnight, she took her candle and went down the ward, reflecting. Ten beds on the right hand side, ten beds on the left hand side, all full. How pitiful they were, these little soldiers, asleep. How irritating they were, these little soldiers, awake. Yet how sternly they contrasted with the man who had attempted suicide. Yet did they contrast, after all? Were they finer, nobler, than he? The night nurse, given to reflection, continued her rounds.

In bed number two, on the right, lay Alexandre, asleep. He had received the *Médaille Militaire* for bravery. He was better now, and that day had asked the *Médecin Major* for permission to smoke. The *Médecin Major* had refused, saying that it would disturb the other patients. Yet after the doctor had gone, Alexandre had produced a cigarette and lighted it, defying them all from behind his *Médaille Militaire*. The patient in the next bed had become violently nauseated in consequence, yet Alexandre had smoked on, secure in his *Médaille Militaire*. How much honour lay in that?

Here lay Félix, asleep. Poor, querulous, feeble-minded Félix, with a foul fistula, which filled the whole ward with its odour. In one sleeping hand lay his little round mirror, in the other, he clutched his comb. With daylight, he would trim and comb his moustache, his poor, little drooping moustache, and twirl the ends of it.

Beyond lay Alphonse, drugged with morphia, after an intolerable day. That morning he had received a package from home, a dozen pears. He had eaten them all, one after the other, though his companions in the beds adjacent looked on with hungry, longing eyes. He offered not one, to either side of him. After his gorge, he had become violently ill, and demanded the basin in which to unload his surcharged stomach.

Here lay Hippolyte, who for eight months had jerked on the bar of a captive balloon, until appendicitis had sent him into hospital. He was not ill, and his dirty jokes filled the ward, provoking laughter, even from dying Marius. How filthy had been his jokes—how they had been matched and beaten by the jokes of others. How filthy they all were, when they talked with each other, shouting down the length of the ward.

Wherein lay the difference? Was it not all a dead-end occupation, nursing back to health men to be patched up and returned to the trenches, or a man to be patched up, court-martialled and shot? The difference lay in the Ideal.

One had no ideals. The others had ideals, and fought for them. Yet had they? Poor selfish Alexandre, poor vain Félix, poor gluttonous Alphonse, poor filthy Hippolyte—was it possible that each cherished ideals, hidden beneath? Courageous dreams of freedom and patriotism? Yet if so, how could such beliefs fail to influence their daily lives? Could one cherish standards so noble, yet be himself so ignoble, so petty, so commonplace?

At this point her candle burned out, so the night nurse took another one, and passed from bed to bed. It was very incomprehensible. Poor, whining Félix, poor whining Alphonse, poor whining Hippolyte, poor whining Alexandre—all fighting for *La Patrie*. And against them the man who had tried to desert *La Patrie*.

So the night nurse continued her rounds, up and down the ward, reflecting. And suddenly she saw that these ideals were imposed from without—that they were compulsory. That left to themselves, Félix, and Hippolyte, and Alexandre, and Alphonse would have had no ideals. Somewhere, higher up, a handful of men had been able to impose upon Alphonse, and Hippolyte, and Félix, and Alexandre, and thousands like them, a state of mind which was not in them, of themselves. Base metal, gilded. And they were all harnessed to a great car, a Juggernaut, ponderous and crushing, upon which was enthroned Mammon, or the Goddess of Liberty, or Reason, as you like. Nothing further was demanded of them than their collective physical strength—just to tug the car forward, to cut a wide swath, to leave behind a broad path along which could follow, at some later date, the hordes of Progress and Civilization. Individual nobility was superfluous. All the Idealists demanded was physical endurance from the mass.

Dawn filtered in through the little square windows of the ward. Two of the patients rolled on their sides, that they might talk to one another. In the silence of early morning their voices rang clear.

"Dost thou know, *mon ami*, that when we captured that German battery a few days ago, we found the gunners chained to their guns?"

Paris,
18 December, 1915

RANDOLPH BOURNE

Randolph Bourne (1886–1918) was born in Bloomfield, New Jersey. His face was congenitally deformed, and he came down with spinal tuberculosis at the age of four, which left him short of stature and with a misshapen back. He blossomed as a student at Columbia, becoming a cosmopolitan intellectual, a pragmatist, and a productive writer. After graduation and a year of travel he wrote for the *New Republic* and *Seven Arts*, on modern culture and progressive education; he was at that point what Van Wyck Brooks called "the flying wedge of the younger generation," a valued younger member of a company of intellectuals.

World War I split him from that company, most members of which supported the war. "The War and the Intellectuals" rejects the war itself almost in passing, and directs its fury instead against the war's intellectual rationalizers, notably Bourne's former teacher and colleague John Dewey, and against the suppression of antiwar speech that those rationalizers supported. That makes it the first text in this anthology, though not the last, to express its opposition to war through a critique of the arguments and character of those who support it.

"Below the Battle" is quite different, not an argument against war but a portrait of an unnamed war opponent, or rather of someone who might become one: Bourne as novelist, one might say, rather than Bourne as polemicist, an innovation in the history of war resistance, pointing forward to such works as William Stafford's *Down in My Heart* (1947) and Paul Goodman's "A Young Pacifist" (1967).

Bourne died in 1918, in the influenza epidemic that marked that horrific year; at the time of his death he was engaged to the actress Esther Cornell.

The War and the Intellectuals

To those of us who still retain an irreconcilable animus against war, it has been a bitter experience to see the unanimity with which the American intellectuals have thrown their support to the use of war-technique in the crisis in which America found herself. Socialists, college professors, publicists, new-republicans, practitioners of literature, have vied with each other in confirming with their intellectual faith the collapse of neutrality and the riveting of the war-mind on a hundred million more of the world's people. And the intellectuals are not content with confirming our belligerent gesture. They are now complacently asserting that it was they who effectively willed it, against the hesitation and dim perceptions of the American democratic masses. A war made deliberately by the intellectuals! A calm moral verdict, arrived at after a penetrating study of inexorable facts! Sluggish masses, too remote from the world-conflict to be stirred, too lacking in intellect to perceive their danger! An alert intellectual class, saving the people in spite of themselves, biding their time with Fabian strategy until the nation could be moved into war without serious resistance! An intellectual class, gently guiding a nation through sheer force of ideas into what the other nations entered only through predatory craft or popular hysteria or militarist madness! A war free from any taint of self-seeking, a war that will secure the triumph of democracy and internationalize the world! This is the picture which the more self-conscious intellectuals have formed of themselves, and which they are slowly impressing upon a population which is being led no man knows whither by an indubitably intellectualized President. And they are right, in that the war certainly did not spring from either the ideals or the prejudices, from the national ambitions or hysterias, of the American people, however acquiescent the masses prove to be, and however clearly the intellectuals prove their putative intuition.

Those intellectuals who have felt themselves totally out of sympathy with this drag toward war will seek some explanation for this joyful leadership. They will want to understand this willingness of the American intellect to open the sluices and flood us with the sewage of the war spirit. We cannot forget the virtuous horror and stupefaction which filled our college professors when they read the famous manifesto of their ninety-three German colleagues in defence of their war. To the American academic mind of 1914 defence of war was inconceivable. From Bernhardi it recoiled as from a blasphemy, little dreaming that two years later would find it creating its own cleanly reasons for imposing military service on the country and for talking of the rough rude currents of health and regeneration that war would send through the American body politic. They would have thought anyone mad who talked of shipping American men by the hundreds of thousands—conscripts—to die on the fields of France. Such a spiritual change seems catastrophic when we shoot our minds back to those days when neutrality was a proud thing. But the intellectual progress has been so gradual that the country retains little sense of the irony. The war sentiment, begun so gradually but so perseveringly by the preparedness advocates who came from the ranks of big business, caught hold of one after another of the intellectual groups. With the aid of Roosevelt, the murmurs became a monotonous chant, and finally a chorus so mighty that to be out of it was at first to be disreputable and finally almost obscene. And slowly a strident rant was worked up against Germany which compared very creditably with the German fulminations against the greedy power of England. The nerve of the war-feeling centred, of course, in the richer and older classes of the Atlantic seaboard, and was keenest where there were French or English business and particularly social connections. The sentiment then spread over the country as a class-phenomenon, touching everywhere those upper-class elements in each section who identified themselves with this Eastern ruling group. It must never be forgotten that in every community it was the least liberal and least democratic elements among whom the preparedness and later the war sentiment was found. The farmers were apathetic, the small business men and workingmen are still apathetic towards the war. The election was a vote of confidence of these latter classes in a President who would keep the faith of neutrality. The intellectuals, in other words, have identified themselves with the least democratic forces in American life. They have assumed the leadership for war of those very classes whom the American democracy has been immemorially fighting. Only in a world where irony was dead could an intellectual class enter war at the head of such illiberal cohorts in the avowed cause of world-liberalism and world-democracy. No one is left to point out the undemocratic nature of this war-liberalism. In a time of faith, skepticism is the most intolerable of all insults.

Our intellectual class might have been occupied, during the last two years of war, in studying and clarifying the ideals and aspirations of the American democracy, in discovering a true Americanism which would not have been merely nebulous but might have federated the different ethnic groups and traditions.

They might have spent the time in endeavoring to clear the public mind of the cant of war, to get rid of old mystical notions that clog our thinking. We might have used the time for a great wave of education, for setting our house in spiritual order. We could at least have set the problem before ourselves. If our intellectuals were going to lead the administration, they might conceivably have tried to find some way of securing peace by making neutrality effective. They might have turned their intellectual energy not to the problem of jockeying the nation into war, but to the problem of using our vast neutral power to attain democratic ends for the rest of the world and ourselves without the use of the malevolent technique of war. They might have failed. The point is that they scarcely tried. The time was spent not in clarification and education, but in a mulling over of nebulous ideals of democracy and liberalism and civilization which had never meant anything fruitful to those ruling classes who now so glibly used them, and in giving free rein to the elementary instinct of self-defence. The whole era has been spiritually wasted. The outstanding feature has been not its Americanism but its intense colonialism. The offence of our intellectuals was not so much that they were colonial—for what could we expect of a nation composed of so many national elements?—but that it was so one-sidedly and partisanly colonial. The official, reputable expression of the intellectual class has been that of the English colonial. Certain portions of it have been even more loyalist than the King, more British even than Australia. Other colonial attitudes have been vulgar. The colonialism of the other American stocks was denied a hearing from the start. America might have been made a meeting-ground for the different national attitudes. An intellectual class, cultural colonists of the different European nations, might have threshed out the issues here as they could not be threshed out in Europe. Instead of this, the English colonials in university and press took command at the start, and we became an intellectual Hungary where thought was subject to an effective process of Magyarization. The reputable opinion of the American intellectuals became more and more either what could be read pleasantly in London, or what was written in an earnest effort to put Englishmen straight on their war-aims and war-technique. This Magyarization of thought produced as a counter-reaction a peculiarly offensive and inept German apologetic, and the two partisans divided the field between them. The great masses, the other ethnic groups, were inarticulate. American public opinion was almost as little prepared for war in 1917 as it was in 1914.

The sterile results of such an intellectual policy are inevitable. During the war the American intellectual class has produced almost nothing in the way of original and illuminating interpretation. Veblen's "Imperial Germany;" Patten's "Culture and War," and addresses; Dewey's "German Philosophy and Politics;" a chapter or two in Weyl's "American Foreign Policies;"—is there much else of creative value in the intellectual repercussion of the war? It is true that the shock of war put the American intellectual to an unusual strain. He had to sit idle and think as spectator not as actor. There was no government to which he could docilely and loyally tender his mind as did the Oxford professors to justify England in her own eyes. The American's training was such as to make the fact of war almost incredible. Both in his reading of history and in his lack of economic perspective he was badly prepared for it. He had to explain to himself something which was too colossal for the modern mind, which outran any language or terms which we had to interpret it in. He had to expand his sympathies to the breaking-point, while pulling the past and present into some sort of interpretative order. The intellectuals in the fighting countries had only to rationalize and justify what their country was already doing. Their task was easy. A neutral, however, had really to search out the truth. Perhaps perspective was too much to ask of any mind. Certainly the older colonials among our college professors let their prejudices at once dictate their thought. They have been comfortable ever since. The war has taught them nothing and will teach them nothing. And they have had the satisfaction, under the rigor of events, of seeing prejudice submerge the intellects of their younger colleagues. And they have lived to see almost their entire class, pacifists and democrats too, join them as apologists for the "gigantic irrelevance" of war.

We have had to watch, therefore, in this country the same process which so shocked us abroad,—the coalescence of the intellectual classes in support of the military programme. In this country, indeed, the socialist intellectuals did not even have the grace of their German brothers and wait for the declaration of war before they broke for cover. And when they declared for war they showed how thin was the intellectual veneer of their socialism. For they called us in terms that might have emanated from any bourgeois journal to defend democracy and civilization, just as if it was not exactly against those very bourgeois democracies and capitalist civilizations that socialists had been fighting for decades. But so subtle is the spiritual chemistry of the "inside" that all this intellectual cohesion—herd-instinct become herd-intellect—which seemed abroad so hysterical and so servile, comes to us here in highly rational terms. We go to war to save the world from subjugation! But the German intellectuals went to war to save their culture from barbarization! And the French went to war to save their beautiful France! And the English to save international honor! And Russia, most altruistic and self-sacrificing of all, to save a small State from destruction! Whence is our miraculous intuition of our moral spotlessness? Whence our confidence that history will not unravel huge economic and imperialist forces upon which our rationalizations float like bubbles? The Jew often marvels that his race alone should have been chosen as the true people of the cosmic God. Are not our intellectuals equally fatuous when they tell us that our war of all wars is stainless and thrillingly achieving for good?

An intellectual class that was wholly rational would have called insistently for peace and not for war. For months the crying need has been for a negotiated peace, in order to avoid the ruin of a deadlock. Would not the same amount of resolute statesmanship thrown into intervention have secured a peace that would have been a subjugation for neither side? Was the terrific bargaining power of a great neutral ever really used? Our war followed, as all wars follow, a monstrous failure of diplomacy. Shamefacedness should now be our intellectuals' attitude, because the American play for peace was made so little more than a polite play. The intellectuals have still to explain why, willing as they now are to use force to continue the war to absolute exhaustion, they were not willing to use force to coerce the world to a speedy peace.

Their forward vision is no more convincing than their past rationality. We go to war now to internationalize the world! But surely their League to Enforce Peace is only a palpable apocalyptic myth, like the syndicalists' myth of the "general strike." It is not a rational programme so much as a glowing symbol for the purpose of focusing belief, of setting enthusiasm on fire for international order. As far as it does this it has pragmatic value, but as far as it provides a certain radiant mirage of idealism for this war and for a world-order founded on mutual fear, it is dangerous and obnoxious. Idealism should be kept for what is ideal. It is depressing to think that the prospect of a world so strong that none dare challenge it should be the immediate ideal of the American intellectual. If the League is only a makeshift, a coalition into which we enter to restore order, then it is only a description of existing fact, and the idea should be treated as such. But if it is an actually prospective outcome of the settlement, the keystone of American policy, it is neither realizable nor desirable. For the programme of such a League contains no provision for dynamic national growth or for international economic justice. In a world which requires recognition of economic internationalism far more than of political internationalism, an idea is reactionary which proposes to petrify and federate the nations as political and economic units. Such a scheme for international order is a dubious justification for American policy. And if American policy had been sincere in its belief that our participation would achieve international beatitude, would we not have made our entrance into the war conditional upon a solemn general agreement to respect in the final settlement these principles of international order? Could we have afforded, if our war was to end war by the establishment of a league of honor, to risk the defeat of our vision and our betrayal in the settlement? Yet we are in the war, and no such solemn agreement was made, nor has it even been suggested.

The case of the intellectuals seems, therefore, only very speciously rational. They could have used their energy to force a just peace or at least to devise other means than war for carrying through American policy. They could have used their intellectual energy to ensure that our participation in the war meant the international order which they wish. Intellect was not so used. It was used to lead an apathetic nation into an irresponsible war, without guarantees from those belligerents whose cause we were saving. The American intellectual, therefore, has been rational neither in his hindsight nor his foresight. To explain him we must look beneath the intellectual reasons to the emotional disposition. It is not so much what they thought as how they felt that explains our intellectual class. Allowing for colonial sympathy, there was still the personal shock in a world-war which outraged all our preconceived notions of the way the world was tending. It reduced to rubbish most of the humanitarian internationalism and democratic nationalism which had been the emotional thread of our intellectuals' life. We had suddenly to make a new orientation. There were mental conflicts. Our latent colonialism strove with our longing for American unity. Our desire for peace strove with our desire for national responsibility in the world. That first lofty and remote and not altogether unsound feeling of our spiritual isolation from the conflict could not last. There was the itch to be in the great experience which the rest of the world was having. Numbers of intelligent people who had never been stirred by the horrors of capitalistic peace at home were shaken out of their slumber by the horrors of war in Belgium. Never having felt responsibility for labor wars and oppressed masses and excluded races at home, they had a large fund of idle emotional capital to invest in the oppressed nationalities and ravaged villages of Europe. Hearts that had felt only ugly contempt for democratic strivings at home beat in tune with the struggle for freedom abroad. All this was natural, but it tended to over-emphasize our responsibility. And it threw our thinking out of gear. The task of making our own country detailedly fit for peace was abandoned in favor of a feverish concern for the management of the war, advice to the fighting governments on all matters, military, social and political, and a gradual working up of the conviction that we were ordained as a nation to lead all erring brothers towards the light of liberty and democracy. The failure of the American intellectual class to erect a creative attitude toward the war can be explained by these sterile mental conflicts which the shock to our ideals sent raging through us.

Mental conflicts end either in a new and higher synthesis or adjustment, or else in a reversion to more primitive ideas which have been outgrown but to which we drop when jolted out of our attained position. The war caused in America a recrudescence of nebulous ideals which a younger generation was fast outgrowing because it had passed the wistful stage and was discovering concrete ways of getting them incarnated in actual institutions. The shock of the war threw us back from this pragmatic work into an emotional bath of these old ideals. There was even a somewhat rarefied revival of our primitive Yankee boastfulness, the reversion of senility to that republican childhood when we expected the whole world to copy our republican institutions. We amusingly ignored the fact that it was just that Imperial German regime, to whom we are to teach the art of self-government, which our own Federal structure, with its executive irresponsible in foreign policy and with its absence of parliamentary control, most resembles. And we are missing the exquisite irony of the unaffected homage paid by the American democratic intellectuals to the last and most detested of Britain's tory premiers as the representative of a "liberal" ally, as well as the irony of the selection of the best hated of America's bourbon "old guard" as the missionary of American democracy to Russia.

The intellectual state that could produce such things is one where reversion has taken place to more primitive ways of thinking. Simple syllogisms are substituted for analysis, things are known by their labels, our heart's desire dictates what we shall see. The American intellectual class, having failed to make the higher syntheses, regresses to ideas that can issue in quick, simplified action. Thought becomes any easy rationalization of what is actually going on or what is to happen inevitably tomorrow. It is true that certain groups did rationalize their colonialism and attach the doctrine of the inviolability of British sea-power to the doctrine of a League of Peace. But this agile resolution of the mental conflict did not become a higher synthesis, to be creatively developed. It gradually merged into a justification for our going to war. It petrified into a dogma to be propagated. Criticism flagged and emotional propaganda began. Most of the socialists, the college professors and the practitioners of literature, however, have not even reached this high-water mark of synthesis. Their mental conflicts have been resolved much more simply. War in the interests of democracy! This was almost the sum of their philosophy. The primitive idea to which they regressed became almost insensibly translated into a craving for action. War was seen as the crowning relief of their indecision. At last action, irresponsibility, the end of anxious and torturing attempts to reconcile peace-ideals with the drag of the world towards Hell. An end to the pain of trying to adjust the facts to what they ought to be! Let us consecrate the facts as ideal! Let us join the greased slide towards war! The momentum increased. Hesitations, ironies, consciences, considerations,—all were drowned in the elemental blare of doing something aggressive, colossal. The new-found Sabbath "peacefulness of being at war"! The thankfulness with which so many intellectuals lay down and floated with the current betrays the hesitation and suspense through which they had been. The American university is a brisk and happy place these days. Simple, unquestioning action has superseded the knots of thought. The thinker dances with reality.

With how many of the acceptors of war has it been mostly a dread of intellectual suspense? It is a mistake to suppose that intellectuality necessarily makes for suspended judgments. The intellect craves certitude. It takes effort to keep it supple and pliable. In a time of danger and disaster we jump desperately for some dogma to cling to. The time comes, if we try to hold out, when our nerves are sick with fatigue, and we seize in a great healing wave of release some doctrine that can be immediately translated into action. Neutrality meant suspense, and so it became the object of loathing to frayed nerves. The vital myth of the League of Peace provides a dogma to jump to. With war the world becomes motor again and speculation is brushed aside like cobwebs. The blessed emotion of self-defence intervenes too, which focused millions in Europe. A few keep up a critical pose after war is begun, but since they usually advise action which is in one-to-one correspondence with what the mass is already doing, their criticism is little more than a rationalization of the common emotional drive.

The results of war on the intellectual class are already apparent. Their thought becomes little more than a description and justification of what is going on. They turn upon any rash one who continues idly to speculate. Once the war is on, the conviction spreads that individual thought is helpless, that the only way one can count is as a cog in the great wheel. There is no good holding back. We are told to dry our unnoticed and ineffective tears and plunge into the great work. Not only is everyone forced into line, but the new certitude becomes idealized. It is a noble realism which opposes itself to futile obstruction and the cowardly refusal to face facts. This realistic boast is so loud and sonorous that one wonders whether realism is always a stern and intelligent grappling with realities. May it not be sometimes a mere surrender to the actual, an abdication of the ideal through a sheer fatigue from intellectual suspense? The pacifist is roundly scolded for refusing to face the facts, and for retiring into his own world of sentimental desire. But is the realist, who refuses to challenge or criticise facts, entitled to any more credit than that which comes from following the line of least resistance? The realist thinks he at least can control events by linking himself to the forces that are moving. Perhaps he can. But if it is a question of controlling war, it is difficult to see how the child on the back of a mad elephant is to be any more effective in stopping the beast than is the child who tries to stop him from the ground. The ex-humanitarian, turned realist, sneers at the snobbish neutrality, colossal conceit, crooked thinking, dazed sensibilities, of those who are still unable to find any balm of consolation for this war. We manufacture consolations here in America while there are probably not a dozen men fighting in Europe who did not long ago give up every reason for their being there except that nobody knew how to get them away.

But the intellectuals whom the crisis has crystallized into an acceptance of war have put themselves into a terrifyingly strategic position. It is only on the craft, in the stream, they say, that one has any chance of controlling the current forces for liberal purposes. If we obstruct, we surrender all power for influence. If we responsibly approve, we then retain our power for guiding. We will be listened to as responsible thinkers, while those who obstructed the coming of war have committed intellectual suicide and shall be cast into outer darkness. Criticism by the ruling powers will only be accepted from those intellectuals who are in sympathy with the general tendency of the war.

Well, it is true that they may guide, but if their stream leads to disaster and the frustration of national life, is their guiding any more than a preference whether they shall go over the right-hand or the left-hand side of the precipice? Meanwhile, however, there is comfort on board. Be with us, they call, or be negligible, irrelevant. Dissenters are already excommunicated. Irreconcilable radicals, wringing their hands among the debris, become the most despicable and impotent of men. There seems no choice for the intellectual but to join the mass of acceptance. But again the terrible dilemma arises,—either support what is going on, in which case you count for nothing because you are swallowed in the mass and great incalculable forces bear you on; or remain aloof, passively resistant, in which case you count for nothing because you are outside the machinery of reality.

Is there no place left, then, for the intellectual who cannot yet crystallize, who does not dread suspense, and is not yet drugged with fatigue? The American intellectuals, in their pre-occupation with reality, seem to have forgotten that the real enemy is War rather than imperial Germany. There is work to be done to prevent this war of ours from passing into popular mythology as a holy crusade. What shall we do with leaders who tell us that we go to war in moral spotlessness, or who make "democracy" synonymous with a republican form of government? There is work to be done in still shouting that all the revolutionary by-products will not justify the war, or make war anything else than the most noxious complex of all the evils that afflict men. There must be some to find no consolation whatever, and some to sneer at those who buy the cheap emotion of sacrifice. There must be some irreconcilables left who will not even accept the war with walrus tears. There must be some to call unceasingly for peace, and some to insist that the terms of settlement shall be not only liberal but demo-cratic. There must be some intellectuals who are not willing to use the old discredited counters again and to support a peace which would leave all the old inflammable materials of arma-ment lying about the world. There must still be opposition to any contemplated "liberal" world-order founded on military coalitions. The "irreconcilable" need not be disloyal. He need not even be "impossibilist." His apathy towards war should take the form of a heightened energy and enthusiasm for the education, the art, the interpretation that make for life in the midst of the world of death. The intellectual who retains his animus against war will push out more boldly than ever to make his case solid against it. The old ideals crumble; new ideals must be forged. His mind will continue to roam widely and ceaselessly. The thing he will fear most is premature crystallization. If the American intellectual class rivets itself to a "liberal" philosophy that perpetuates the old errors, there will then be need for "democrats" whose task will be to divide, confuse, disturb, keep the intellectual waters constantly in motion to prevent any such ice from ever forming.

Below the Battle

HE is one of those young men who, because his parents happened to mate during a certain ten years of the world's history, has had now to put his name on a wheel of fate, thereby submitting himself to be drawn into a brief sharp course of military training before being shipped across the sea to kill Germans or be killed by them. He does not like this fate that menaces him, and he dislikes it because he seems to find nothing in the programme marked out for him which touches remotely his aspirations, his impulses, or even his desires. My friend is not a happy young man, but even the unsatisfactory life he is living seems supplemented at no single point by the life of the drill-ground or the camp or the stinking trench. He visualizes the obscenity of the battlefield and turns away in nausea. He thinks of the weary regimentation of young men, and is filled with disgust. His mind has turned sour on war and all that it involves. He is poor material for the military proclamation and the drill-sergeant.

I want to understand this friend of mine, for he seems rather typical of a scattered race of young Americans of to-day. He does not fall easily into the categories of patriot and coward which the papers are making popular. He feels neither patriotism nor fear, only an apathy toward the war, faintly warmed into a smouldering resentment at the men who have clamped down the war-pattern upon him and that vague mass of people and ideas and workaday living around him that he thinks of as his country. Now that resentment has knotted itself into a tortured tangle of what he should do, how he can best be true to his creative self? I should say that his apathy cannot be imputed to cowardly ease. My friend earns about fifteen hundred dollars a year as an architect's assistant, and he lives alone in a little room over a fruitshop. He worked his way through college, and he has never known even a leisurely month. There is nothing Phæacian about his life. It is scarcely to save his skin for riotous living that he is reluctant about war. Since he left college he has been trying to find his world. He is often seriously depressed and irritated with himself for not having hewed out a more glorious career for himself. His work is just interesting enough to save it from drudgery, and yet not nearly independent and exacting enough to give him a confident professional sense. Outside his work, life is deprived and limited rather than luxurious. He is fond of music and goes to cheap concerts. He likes radical meetings, but never could get in touch with the agitators. His friends are seeking souls just like himself. He likes midnight talks in cafés and studios, but he is not especially amenable to drink. His heart of course is hungry and turbid, but his two or three love-affairs have not clarified anything for him. He eats three rather poor restaurant meals a day. When he reads, it is philosophy—Nietzsche, James, Bergson—or the novels about youth—Rolland, Nexö, Cannan, Frenssen, Beresford. He has a rather constant mood of futility, though he is in unimpeachable health. There are moments when life seems quite without sense or purpose. He has enough friends, however, to be not quite lonely, and yet they are so various as to leave him always with an ache for some more cohesive, purposeful circle. His contacts with people irritate him without rendering him quite unhopeful. He is always expecting he doesn't know quite what, and always being frustrated of he doesn't quite know what would have pleased him. Perhaps he never had a moment of real external or internal ease in his life.

Obviously a creature of low vitality, with neither the broad vision to be stirred by the President's war message, nor the red blood to itch for the dummy bayonet-charge. Yet somehow he does not seem exactly weak, and there is a consistency about his attitude which intrigues me. Since he left college eight years ago, he has been through most of the intellectual and emotional fads of the day. He has always cursed himself for being so superficial and unrooted, and he has tried to write a little of the thoughts that stirred him. What he got down on paper was, of course, the usual large vague feeling of a new time that all of us feel. With the outbreak of the Great War, most of his socialist and pacifist theories were knocked flat. The world turned out to be an entirely different place from what he had thought it. Progress and uplift seemed to be indefinitely suspended, though it was a long time before he realized how much he had been corroded by the impact of news and the endless discussions he heard. I think he gradually worked himself into a truly neutral indifference. The reputable people and the comfortable classes who were having all the conventional emotions rather disgusted him. The neurotic fury about self-defence seemed to come from types and classes that he instinctively detested. He was not scared, and somehow he could not get enthusiastic about defending himself with "preparedness" unless he were badly scared. Things got worse. All that he valued seemed frozen until the horrible mess came to a close. He had gone to an unusually intelligent American college, and he had gotten a feeling for a humane civilization that had not left him. The war, it is true, bit away piece by piece every ideal that made this feeling seem plausible. Most of the big men—intellectuals—whom he thought he respected had had so much of their idealism hacked away and got their nerves so frayed that they became at last, in their panic, willing and even eager to adopt the war-technique in aid of their government's notions of the way to impose democracy on the world.

My poor young friend can best be understood as too naive and too young to effect this metamorphosis. Older men might mix a marvellous intellectual brew of personal anger, fear, a sense of "dishonor," fervor for a League of Peace, and set going a machinery that crushed everything intelligent, humane and civilized. My friend was less flexible. War simply did not mix with anything that he had learned to feel was desirable. Something in his mind spewed it out whenever it was suggested as a cure for our grievous American neutrality. As I got all this from our talks, he did not seem weak. He merely had no notion of the patriotism that meant the springing of a nation to arms. He read conscientiously *The New Republic*'s feast of eloquent idealism, with its appealing harbingers of a cosmically efficacious and well-bred war. He would often say, This is all perfectly convincing; why, then, are we not all convinced? He seemed to understand the argument for American participation. We both stood in awe at the superb intellectual structure that was built up. But my friend is one of those unfortunate youths whose heart has to apprehend as well as his intellect, and it was his heart that inexorably balked. So he was in no mood to feel the worth of American participation, in spite of the infinite tact and Fabian strategy of the Executive and his intellectualist backers. He felt apart from it all. He had not the imagination to see a healed world-order built out of the rotten materials of armaments, diplomacy and "liberal" statesmanship. And he wasn't affected by the psychic complex of panic, hatred, rage, class-arrogance and patriotic swagger that was creating in newspaper editors and in the "jeunesse dorée" around us the authentic élan for war.

My friend is thus somehow in the nation but not of the nation. The war has as yet got no conceivable clutch on his soul. He knows that theoretically he is united with a hundred million in purpose, sentiment and deed for an idealistic war to defend democracy and civilization against predatory autocracy. Yet somehow, in spite of all the excitement, nobody has as yet been able to make this real to him. He is healthy, intelligent, idealistic. The irony is that the demand which his country now makes on him is one to which not one single cell or nerve of idealism or desire responds. The cheap and silly blare of martial life leaves him cold. The easy inflation of their will-to-power which is coming to so many people from their participation in volunteer or government service, or, better still, from their urging others to farm, enlist, invest, retrench, organize,—none of this allures him. His life is uninteresting and unadventurous, but it is not quite dull enough to make this activity or anything he knows about war seem a release into lustier expression. He has ideals but he cannot see their realization through a desperate struggle to the uttermost. He doubts the "saving" of an America which can only be achieved through world-suicide. He wants democracy, but he does not want the kind of democracy we will get by this war enough to pay the suicidal cost of getting it in the way we set about it.

Dulce et decorum est pro patria mori, sweet and becoming is it to die for one's country. This is the young man who is suddenly asked to die for his country. My friend was much concerned about registration. He felt coercive forces closing in upon him. He did not want to register for the purposes of being liable to conscription. It would be doing something positive when he felt only apathy. Furthermore, if he was to resist, was it not better to take a stand now than to wait to be drafted? On the other hand, was it not too much of a concession to rebel at a formality? He did not really wish to be a martyr. Going to prison for a year for merely refusing to register was rather a grotesque and futile gesture. He did not see himself as a hero, shedding inspiration by his example to his fellows. He did not care what others did. His objection to prison was not so much fear perhaps as contempt for a silly sacrifice. He could not keep up his pose of complete aliency from the war-enterprise, now that registration was upon him. Better submit stoically, he thought, to the physical pressure, mentally reserving his sense of spiritual aliency from the enterprise into which he was being remorselessly moulded. Yet my friend is no arrant prig. He does not pretend to be a "world-patriot," or a servant of some higher law than his country's. Nor does he feel blatantly patriotic. With his groping philosophy of life, patriotism has merely died as a concept of significance for him. It is to him merely the emotion that fills the herd when it imagines itself engaged in massed defence or massed attack. Having no such images, he has no feeling of patriotism. He still feels himself inextricably a part of this blundering, wistful, crass civilization we call America. All he asks is not to be identified with it for warlike ends. He does not feel pro-German. He tells me there is not a drop of any but British blood in his veins. He does not love the Kaiser. He is quite willing to believe that it is the German government and not the German people whom he is asked to fight, although it may be the latter whom he is obliged to kill. But he cannot forget that it is the American government rather than the American people who got up the animus to fight the German government. He does not forget that the American government, having through tragic failure slipped into the war-technique, is now trying to manipulate him into that war-technique. And my friend's idea of *patria* does not include the duty of warlike animus, even when the government decides such animus is necessary to carry out its theories of democracy and the future organization of the world. There are ways in which my friend would probably be willing to die for his country. If his death now meant the restoration of those ravaged lands and the bringing back of the dead, that would be a cause to die for. But he knows that dead cannot be brought back or the brotherly currents restored. The work of madness will not be undone. Only a desperate war will be prolonged. Everything seems to him so mad that there is nothing left worth dying for. *Pro patria mori*, to my friend, means something different from lying gaunt as a conscript on a foreign battlefield, fallen in the last desperate fling of an interminable world-war.

Does this mean that if he is drafted he will refuse to serve? I do not know. It will not be any plea of "conscientious objection" that keeps him back. That phrase to him has already an archaic flavor which implies a ruling norm, a stiff familiar whom he must obey in the matter. It implies that one would be delighted to work up one's blood-lust for the business, except that this unaccountable conscience, like a godly grandmother, absolutely forbids. In the case of my friend, it will not be any objective "conscience." It will be something that is woven into his whole modern philosophic feel for life. This is what paralyzes him against taking one step toward the war-machine. If he were merely afraid of death, he would seek some alternative service. But he does not. He remains passive and apathetic, waiting for the knife to fall. There is a growing cynicism in him about the brisk and inept bustle of war-organization. His attitude suggests that if he is worked into war-service, he will have to be coerced every step of the way.

Yet he may not even rebel. He may go silently into the ranks in a mood of cold contempt. His horror of useless sacrifice may make even the bludgeoning of himself seem futile. He may go in the mood of so many young men in the other countries, without enthusiasm, without idealism, without hope and without belief, victims of a tragically blind force behind them. No other government, however, has had to face from the very start quite this appalling skepticism of youth. My friend is significant because all the shafts of panic, patriotism and national honor have been discharged at him without avail. All the seductions of "liberal" idealism leave him cold. He is to be susceptible to nothing but the use of crude, rough, indefeasible violence. Nothing could be more awkward for a "democratic" President than to be faced with this cold, staring skepticism of youth, in the prosecution of his war. The attitude of my friend suggests that there is a personal and social idealism in America which is out of reach of the most skilful and ardent appeals of the older order, an idealism that cannot be hurt by the taunts of cowardice and slacking or kindled by the slogans of capitalistic democracy. This is the cardinal fact of our war—the non-mobilization of the younger intelligentsia.

What will they do to my friend? If the war goes on they will need him. Pressure will change skepticism into bitterness. That bitterness will well and grow. If the country submissively pours month after month its wealth of life and resources into the work of annihilation, that bitterness will spread out like a stain over the younger American generation. If the enterprise goes on endlessly, the work, so blithely undertaken for the defence of democracy, will have crushed out the only genuinely precious thing in a nation, the hope and ardent idealism of its youth.

TRADITIONAL (GOSPEL)

"Down by the River-Side" was first published in 1918 but was being sung long before that, probably as early as the Civil War. It is and is not an antiwar song. Its opposition to war is found only in its refrain line, and even that is as personal as it is political. Most of its text is focused on a utopian vision of a final time, when the singer will wear a starry crown and golden shoes and a long white robe, and many recorded performances express that utopian vision and energy rather than war resistance.

Still, the maker or makers of the song chose "ain't gonna study war no more" as their refrain line, and imagined, in that final time, a conversation with the "Prince of Peace." The antiwar energies of the song were latent even when not expressed, and later in the twentieth century, notably at protests against the Vietnam War, those energies were activated, and the song became a canonical song of opposition.

Down by the River-Side

SOLO.   CHORUS.

1. Goin't' lay down my bur-den, Down by the river-side, Down by the river-side,
2. Goin't' lay down my sword and shield, Down by the river-side, Down by the river-side,
3. Goin't' try on my long white robe, Down by the river-side, Down by the river-side,
4. Goin't' try on my star-ry crown, Down by the river-side, Down by the river-side,

SOLO.

Down by the riv-er-side, Goin't' lay down my bur-den, Down by the river-side,
Down by the riv-er-side, Goin't' lay down my sword and shield, Down by the river-side,
Down by the riv-er-side, Goin't' try on my long white robe, Down by the river-side,
Down by the riv-er-side, Goin't' try on my star-ry crown, Down by the river-side,

CHORUS.

Goin' to stud-y war no more. Ain't goin't' stud-y war no more, Ain't goin't'

stud-y war no more, Ain't goin't' study war no more, ... Ain't goin't' war no more.
goin't' study war no more,

5. Goin't' meet my dear old mother.   7. Goin't' meet dem Hebrew children.
6. Goin't' meet my dear old father.   8. Goin't' meet my loving Jesus.

EMILY GREENE BALCH

Emily Greene Balch (1867–1961) went to Bryn Mawr, studied poverty in France, came back to Boston, and with some faculty members at Wellesley College founded Boston's first settlement house, which led to her meeting Jane Addams. She began teaching at Wellesley in 1896, and by 1913 was chair of both economics and sociology. She joined with Addams and other women to oppose World War I; her opposition to the war led to her being refused reappointment by Wellesley in 1918. Afterwards, she joined the staff of *The Nation*, collaborated with Addams to help found the Women's International League for Peace and Freedom, and devoted much of the rest of her life to the work of that organization. Though she supported American involvement in World War II, her activity during the war focused on assisting refugees and defending the rights of conscientious objectors. She won the Nobel Peace Prize in 1946.

Her 1918 letter to Wellesley College president Ellen Pendleton is perhaps the most courteous and deferential statement of unbendable opposition to war ever written; her Nobel Prize speech is unusual in its spaciousness of vision, and is surely among the most scholarly speeches ever given by a Peace laureate, the only one ever to prophesy large-scale war tax resistance.

Her memory is honored at Wellesley College, where I direct the Program in Peace & Justice Studies, by an internship named for her.

To the President of Wellesley College

110 Morningside Drive, N.Y.C.
April third, 1918

Dear Miss Pendleton,

I should like to state to you, as well as I am able, my fundamental position in these tragic and heroic days through which our country and all the world is passing.

In the first place I am entirely in sympathy with the purposes of our country in the war as expressed for us by the President. I rejoice in his international leadership and am thankful that such a leader has been raised up to us. I feel moreover that we can never adequately appreciate the heroism and self-sacrifice that are being poured out so unstintedly in the war day by day. I could desire nothing more than also to give myself wholly in trying to bring about a better world.

In such a time when love of country is conscious as never before, and when patriotism has such special claims upon us all, it is a very painful thing to be obliged to forego, in any degree, full inner cooperation with the methods by which the ends for which we all are working are being sought. Nevertheless I believe so deeply that the way of war is not the way of Christianity, I find it so impossible to reconcile war with the truth of Jesus' teachings, that even now I am obliged to give up the happiness of full and unquestioning cooperation where the choice is mine to make.

On the other hand any effort to obstruct the war, to work against enlistment or anything of the sort, would seem to me not only inexpedient and silly, as well as unlawful, but also morally wrong. It is, I suppose hardly necessary to add that Junkerism and militarism and all their manifestations, from faithlessness and fraud to atrocities and annexations, are abhorrent to me.

In all such activities as food conservation and relief reconstruction work of all kinds I can of course take part gladly to the limit of my ability.

I fully realize that wiser as well as infinitely more spiritual disciples of Christ believe that they are following him in taking part in the war according to their respective functions. This does not excuse me however from doing what seems to me right as I see it. I may have a larger vision some day, then I can follow the new leading. Meanwhile one of the hardest things about holding the position that I do is that it is so hard to keep it clear of Pharisaism.

Now as to the practical side of all this. It means that I have no temptation to dampen patriotism even in forms that I could not personally adopt nor to carry on any propaganda for my own peculiar views in connection, direct or indirect, with my teaching. It means that at Wellesley or elsewhere I desire to do all that in me lies toward making the world safe for democracy by whatever phrase we may choose to express our national purpose at its purest, to work for honest and vigorous thinking, self-control and above all for service.

(Signed)
Emily G. Balch

FROM
Toward Human Unity or Beyond Nationalism

Nobel Lecture, delivered at Oslo, April 7th, 1948

Another thing—men are everywhere becoming less "private-minded." There is a growing community sense. It is as though the urge which found expression in monasteries and nunneries in the middle ages were finding new expression. In the political field this consciousness of the common interest and of the rich possibilities of common action has embodied itself in part in the great movements toward economic democracy, co-operation, democratic socialism and communism. I am sure we make a great mistake if we underrate the element of unselfish idealism in these historic movements which are today writing history at such a rate.

A dark and terrible side of this sense of community of interests is the fear of a horrible common destiny which in these days of atomic weapons darkens men's minds all around the globe. Men have a sense of being subject to the same fate, of being all in the same boat. But fear is a poor motive to which to appeal and I am sure that "peace people" are on a wrong path when they expatiate on the horrors of a new world war. Fear weakens the nerves and distorts the judgment. It is not by fear that mankind must exorcise the demon of destruction and cruelty, but by motives more reasonable, more humane and more heroic.

The peace movement or the movement to end war has been fed by many springs and has taken many forms. It has been carried on mainly by private unofficial organizations, local, national and international. I would say that peace workers or pacifists have dealt mainly with two types of issue, the moral or individual, and the political or institutional. As a type of the former we may take those who are now generally known specifically as pacifists. Largely on religious or ethical grounds they repudiate violence and strive to put friendly and constructive activity in its place.

There has been personal refusal of war service on grounds of conscience on a large scale and at great personal cost by thousands of young men called up for military service. While many people fail to understand and certainly do not approve their position, I believe that it has been an invaluable witness to the supremacy of conscience over all other considerations and a very great service to a public too much affected by the conception that might makes right. It is interesting that at the Nuremberg war-guilt trials the court refused to accept the principle that a man is absolved from responsibility for an act by the fact that it was ordered by his superiors or his government. This is a legal affirmation of a principle that conscientious objectors maintain in action.

It is to me surprising that the repudiation of the entire theory and practice of conscription has not found expression in a wider and more powerful movement drawing strength from the widespread concern for individual liberty. We are horrified at many slighter infringements of individual freedom, far less terrible than this. But we are so accustomed to conscription that we take it for granted. A practical and political form of opposition to conscription is the proposal, first put forward, so far as I know, by an American woman, DOROTHY DETZER, long secretary of the United States Section of the Women's International League for Peace and Freedom. She urged something that suggests the Kellogg Pact but is quite specific, namely a multilateral treaty between governments to renounce the use of conscription. A bill to this effect is now in the United States Congress but attracts little attention.

I feel it rather surprising also that refusal of war has never taken the form, on any large scale, of refusal to pay taxes for military use, a refusal which would have involved not only young men but (and mainly) older men and women holders, of property.

Peace work of this first type relies mainly on education. The work done and now being done to educate men's minds against war and for peace is colossal, and can only be referred to.

Perhaps it is under this head that the Nobel Foundation and the work of BERTHA VON SUTTNER should be listed, for this the world, and not alone the beneficiaries must be grateful.

The other type of "peace" activity is political, specifically aiming to affect governmental or other action on concrete issues. For instance peace organizations criticized the terms of the Peace Treaties made at Versailles and (in America at least) opposed the demand for unconditional surrender in the second world war.

The Women's International League for Peace and Freedom (with which I have long been connected) has worked both as an international body and in its national sections from 1915 till now and I trust will long do so, in the political field of policies affecting peace, though not alone on the political level. Among its strongest supporters have always been Scandinavian women. I am presenting to the Nobel library, if I may, a brief history of this organization "A Venture in Internationalism" a pamphlet now out of print and consequently rare.

The form of work for peace which has most obviously made history is the long continued effort to create some form of world organization which should both prevent wars and foster international co-operation.

The efforts to secure peace by creating a comprehensive organ have been many and varied. One of the most curious was the confederation of certain tribes of Iroquois Indians in America known as "The Six Nations." One of the earliest was the ancient Amphyctyonic Council in Greece. There has been a long series of schemes, each more or less premature and Utopian, but each making its own contribution, from those of SULLY and WILLIAM PENN and KANT to WOODROW WILSON and his co-workers and successors. WILSON did not live to see the League of Nations established nor did his own country ever join it. At present there is tendency to underrate its importance. I, for one, would not for a great deal lose out of my life my years in Geneva during the first spring-time of the hopes and activities of the League of Nations.

As we know only too well, the League of Nations, lacking Russia and the United States, was not sufficiently inclusive. Also when the pinch came, different governments proved unready to make the sacrifices or face the risks involved in effective opposition to imperialism in Japan, reaction in Spain, fascism in Italy or nazism in Germany.

The new institution, the United Nations, has some marked advantages over its predecessors. Its origin was the work, not of a small group of statesmen mainly preoccupied with elaborating the treaties of Versailles and the rest, but was worked out in careful preliminary discussion, first at Dumbarton Oaks, then at San Francisco, by a comprehensive group of countries which included, this time, the United States and Russia, though not the Axis powers, and which owes an immense debt to President FRANKLIN ROOSEVELT. It has the experience of the League of Nations to draw upon and the second world war offers it useful warnings. With less of a flush of idealism, hopefulness and confidence than the League of Nations enjoyed in its early days, it is soberer, and Norway has given it in TRYGVE LIE a Secretary General who inspires confidence and hope.

———————

In such a world all war would be civil war and we must hope that it will grow increasingly inconceivable. It has already become capable of such unlimited destruction and such fearful possibilities of uncontrollable and little understood "chain reactions" of all sorts that it would seem that no one not literally insane could decide to start an atomic war.

I have spoken against fear as a basis for peace. What we ought to fear, especially we Americans, is not that someone may drop atomic bombs on us but that we may allow a world situation to develop in which ordinarily reasonable and humane men, acting as our representatives, may use such weapons in our name. We ought to be resolved beforehand that no provocation, no temptation shall induce us to resort to the last dreadful alternative of war.

May no young man ever again be faced with the choice between violating his conscience by co-operating in competitive mass-slaughter or separating himself from those who, endeavouring to serve liberty, democracy, humanity can find no better way than to conscript young men to kill.

As the world community develops in peace, it will open up great untapped reservoirs in human nature. Like a spring released from pressure would be the response of a generation of young men and women growing up in an atmosphere of friendliness and security, in a world demanding their service, offering them comradeship, calling to all adventurous and forward-reaching natures.

We are not asked to subscribe to any Utopia or to believe in a perfect world just around the corner. We are asked to be patient with necessarily slow and groping advance on the road forward, and to be ready for each step ahead as it becomes practicable. We are asked to equip ourselves with courage, hope, readiness for hard work, and to cherish large and generous ideals.

EUGENE V. DEBS

On June 16, 1918, at a rally in Canton, Ohio, socialist presidential candidate Eugene V. Debs (1855–1926) made a speech that crossed a line. "They have always taught and trained you to believe it to be your patriotic duty to go to war and to have yourselves slaughtered at their command," he told the crowd; "[b]ut in all the history of the world you, the people, have never had a voice in declaring war . . . If war is right let it be declared by the people. You who have your lives to lose, you certainly above all others have the right to decide the momentous issue of war and peace." Such words amounted to sedition under the wartime Espionage Act, and the sixty-two-year-old Debs was promptly arrested.

The dignified eloquence of Debs's statements to the court and to the jury during his September trial was widely noted, even by those opposed to his views. It did him little immediate good: the following April, he arrived at a federal penitentiary in Atlanta to begin serving out a ten-year prison sentence. He continued his campaign for president from his cell, receiving nearly a million votes.

Debs grew up in Indiana, worked on the railroads, cautiously participated in his first strike in 1877, became a railroad union official, and was elected city clerk of Terre Haute in 1879. What made him a socialist was the Pullman strike of 1894; "in the gleam of every bayonet and in the flash of every rifle *the class struggle was revealed*," he wrote later, though he was critical of the Industrial Workers of the World and retained some faith in electoral politics, running for president five times and winning as much as 6 percent of the vote. He was released from prison early, on December 23, 1921, by President Harding, who said he wanted him to be able to eat his Christmas dinner with his family.

Address to the Jury

MAY it please the Court, and Gentlemen of the Jury:

For the first time in my life I appear before a jury in a court of law to answer to an indictment for crime. I am not a lawyer. I know little about court procedure, about the rules of evidence or legal practice. I know only that you gentlemen are to hear the evidence brought against me, that the Court is to instruct you in the law, and that you are then to determine by your

169

verdict whether I shall be branded with criminal guilt and be
consigned, perhaps to the end of my life, in a felon's cell.

Gentlemen, I do not fear to face you in this hour of accusation, nor do I shrink from the consequences of my utterances
or my acts. Standing before you, charged as I am with crime, I
can yet look the Court in the face, I can look you in the face,
I can look the world in the face, for in my conscience, in my
soul, there is festering no accusation of guilt.

Permit me to say in the first place that I am entirely satisfied
with the Court's ruling. I have no fault to find with the district
attorney or with the counsel for the prosecution.

I wish to admit the truth of all that has been testified to in
this proceeding. I have no disposition to deny anything that
is true. I would not, if I could, escape the results of an adverse
verdict. I would not retract a word that I have uttered that I
believe to be true to save myself from going to the penitentiary
for the rest of my days.

I am charged in the indictment, first, that I did willfully
cause and attempt to cause or incite, insubordination, mutiny,
disloyalty and refusal of duty within the military forces of the
United States; that I did obstruct and attempt to obstruct the
recruiting and enlistment service of the United States. I am
charged also with uttering words intended to bring into contempt and disrepute the form of government of the United
States, the Constitution of the United States, the military
forces of the United States, the flag of the United States, and
the uniform of the army and navy.

THE COURT: Mr. Debs, permit me to say that the last
charge which you have read to the jury has been withdrawn
from their consideration by the Court.

DEBS: Pardon me. I was not aware of that.

THE COURT: I have directed a verdict of "not guilty" as
to that charge.

DEBS: I am accused further of uttering words intended to
procure and incite resistance to the United States and to promote the cause of the Imperial German Government.

Gentlemen, you have heard the report of my speech at
Canton on June 16, and I submit that there is not a word in
that speech to warrant these charges. I admit having delivered
the speech. I admit the accuracy of the speech in all of its main

features as reported in this proceeding. There were two distinct reports. They vary somewhat, but they are agreed upon all the material statements embodied in that speech.

In what I had to say there my purpose was to educate the people to understand something about the social system in which we live and to prepare them to change this system by perfectly peaceable and orderly means into what I, as a Socialist, conceive to be a real democracy.

From what you heard in the address of counsel for the prosecution, you might naturally infer that I am an advocate of force and violence. It is not true. I have never advocated violence in any form. I always believed in education, in intelligence, in enlightenment, and I have always made my appeal to the reason and to the conscience of the people.

I admit being opposed to the present form of government. I admit being opposed to the present social system. I am doing what little I can, and have been for many years, to bring about a change that shall do away with the rule of the great body of the people by a relatively small class and establish in this country an industrial and social democracy.

In the course of the speech that resulted in this indictment, I am charged with having expressed sympathy for Kate Richards O'Hare, for Rose Pastor Stokes, for Ruthenberg, Wagenknecht and Baker. I did express my perfect sympathy with these comrades of mine. I have known them for many years. I have every reason to believe in their integrity, every reason to look upon them with respect, with confidence and with approval.

Kate Richards O'Hare never uttered the words imputed to her in the report. The words are perfectly brutal. She is not capable of using such language. I know that through all of the years of her life she has been working in the interests of the suffering, struggling poor, that she has consecrated all of her energies, all of her abilities, to their betterment. The same is true of Rose Pastor Stokes. Through all her life she has been on the side of the oppressed and downtrodden. If she were so inclined she might occupy a place of ease. She might enjoy all of the comforts and leisures of life. Instead of this, she has renounced them all. She has taken her place among the poor, and there she has worked with all of her ability, all of her energy, to make it possible for them to enjoy a little more of the comforts of life.

I said that if these women whom I have known all of these years—that if they were criminals, if they ought to go to the penitentiary, then I, too, am a criminal, and I ought to be sent to prison. I have not a word to retract—not one. I uttered the truth. I made no statement in that speech that I am not prepared to prove. If there is a single falsehood in it, it has not been exposed. If there is a single statement in it that will not bear the light of truth, I will retract it. I will make all of the reparation in my power. But if what I said is true, and I believe it is, then whatever fate or fortune may have in store for me I shall preserve inviolate the integrity of my soul and stand by it to the end.

When I said what I did about the three comrades of mine who are in the workhouse at Canton, I had in mind what they had been ever since I have known them in the service of the working class. I had in mind the fact that these three working men had just a little while before had their hands cuffed and were strung up in that prison house for eight hours at a time until they fell to the floor fainting from exhaustion. And this because they had refused to do some menial, filthy services that were an insult to their dignity and their manhood.

I have been accused of expressing sympathy for the Bolsheviki of Russia. I plead guilty to the charge. I have read a great deal about the Bolsheviki of Russia that is not true. I happen to know of my own knowledge that they have been grossly misrepresented by the press of this country. Who are these much-maligned revolutionists of Russia? For years they had been the victims of a brutal Czar. They and their antecedents were sent to Siberia, lashed with a knout, if they even dreamed of freedom. At last the hour struck for a great change. The revolution came. The Czar was overthrown and his infamous regime ended. What followed? The common people of Russia came into power—the peasants, the toilers, the soldiers—and they proceeded as best they could to establish a government of the people.

DISTRICT ATTORNEY WERTZ: If the Court please, I would like to ask the Court to instruct the defendant that his arguments are to be confined to the evidence in the case. There isn't any evidence in this case about the Bolsheviki at all or the Russian revolution.

THE COURT: I think I will permit the defendant to proceed in his own way. Of course, you are not a lawyer, Mr. Debs. The usual rule is that the remarks of counsel should be confined to the testimony in the case, but it does not forbid counsel from making references to facts or matters of general public history or notoriety by way of illustrating your arguments and comments upon the testimony in the case. So I will permit you to proceed in your own way.

DEBS: Thank you. It may be that the much-despised Bolsheviki may fail at last, but let me say to you that they have written a chapter of glorious history. It will stand to their eternal credit. The leaders are now denounced as criminals and outlaws. Let me remind you that there was a time when George Washington, who is now revered as the father of his country, was denounced as a disloyalist; when Sam Adams, who is known to us as the father of the American Revolution, was condemned as an incendiary, and Patrick Henry, who delivered that inspired and inspiring oration, that aroused the Colonists, was condemned as a traitor. They were misunderstood at the time. They stood true to themselves, and they won an immortality of gratitude and glory.

When great changes occur in history, when great principles are involved, as a rule the majority are wrong. The minority are right. In every age there have been a few heroic souls who have been in advance of their time who have been misunderstood, maligned, persecuted, sometimes put to death. Long after their martyrdom monuments were erected to them and garlands were woven for their graves.

I have been accused of having obstructed the war. I admit it. Gentlemen, I abhor war. I would oppose the war if I stood alone. When I think of a cold, glittering steel bayonet being plunged in the white, quivering flesh of a human being, I recoil with horror. I have often wondered if I could take the life of my fellow man, even to save my own.

Men talk about holy wars. There are none. Let me remind you that it was Benjamin Franklin who said, "There never was a good war or a bad peace."

Napoleon Bonaparte was a high authority upon the subject of war. And when in his last days he was chained to the rock at St. Helena, when he felt the skeleton hand of death reaching for him, he cried out in horror, "War is the trade of savages and barbarians."

I have read some history. I know that it is ruling classes that make war upon one another, and not the people. In all of the history of this world the people have never yet declared a war. Not one. I do not believe that really civilized nations would murder one another. I would refuse to kill a human being on my own account. Why should I at the command of any one else, or at the command of any power on earth?

Twenty centuries ago there was one appeared upon earth we know as the Prince of Peace. He issued a command in which I believe. He said, "Love one another." He did not say, "Kill one another," but "love one another." He espoused the cause of the suffering poor—just as Rose Pastor Stokes did, just as Kate Richards O'Hare did—and the poor heard him gladly. It was not long before he aroused the ill will and hatred of the usurers, the money changers, the profiteers, the high priests, the lawyers, the judges, the merchants, the bankers—in a word, the ruling class. They said of him just what the ruling class says of the Socialist to-day, "He is preaching dangerous doctrine. He is inciting the common rabble. He is a menace to peace and order." And they had him arraigned, tried, convicted, condemned, and they had his quivering body spiked to the gates of Jerusalem.

This has been the tragic history of the race. In the ancient world Socrates sought to teach some new truths to the people, and they made him drink the fatal hemlock. It has been true all along the track of the ages. The men and women who have been in advance, who have had new ideas, new ideals, who have had the courage to attack the established order of things, have all had to pay the same penalty.

A century and a half ago, when the American colonists were still foreign subjects, and when there were a few men who had faith in the common people and believed that they could rule themselves without a king, in that day to speak against the king was treason. If you read Bancroft or any other standard historian, you will find that a great majority of the colonists believed in the king and actually believed that he had a divine right to rule over them. They had been taught to believe that to say a word against the king, to question his so-called divine right, was sinful. There were ministers who opened their Bibles to prove that it was the patriotic duty of the people to loyally serve and support the king. But there were a few men in that day who said, "We don't need a king. We can govern ourselves." And they began an agitation that has been immortalized in history.

Washington, Adams, Paine—these were the rebels of their day. At first they were opposed by the people and denounced by the press. You can remember that it was Franklin who said to his compeers, "We have now to hang together or we'll hang separately by and by." And if the Revolution had failed, the revolutionary fathers would have been executed as felons. But it did not fail. Revolutions have a habit of succeeding when the time comes for them. The revolutionary forefathers were opposed to the form of government in their day. They were opposed to the social system of their time. They were denounced, they were condemned. But they had the moral courage to stand erect and defy all the storms of detraction; and that is why they are in history, and that is why the great respectable majority of their day sleep in forgotten graves. The world does not know they ever lived.

At a later time there began another mighty agitation in this country. It was against an institution that was deemed a very respectable one in its time, the institution of chattel slavery, that became all-powerful, that controlled the President, both branches of Congress, the Supreme Court, the press, to a very large extent the pulpit. All of the organized forces of society, all the powers of government, upheld chattel slavery in that day. And again there were a few lovers of liberty who appeared. One of them was Elijah Lovejoy. Elijah Lovejoy was as much despised in his day as are the leaders of the I.W.W. in our day. Elijah Lovejoy was murdered in cold blood in Alton, Illinois, in 1837 simply because he was opposed to chattel slavery— just as I am opposed to wage slavery. When you go down the Mississippi River and look up at Alton, you see a magnificent white shaft erected there in memory of a man who was true to himself and his convictions of right and duty unto death.

It was my good fortune to personally know Wendell Phillips. I heard the story of his persecution in part, at least, from his own eloquent lips just a little while before they were silenced in death.

William Lloyd Garrison, Garret Smith, Thaddeus Stevens—
these leaders of the abolition movement, who were regarded
as monsters of depravity, were true to the faith and stood their
ground. They are all in history. You are teaching your children
to revere their memories, while all of their detractors are in
oblivion.

Chattel slavery disappeared. We are not yet free. We are
engaged in another mighty agitation to-day. It is as wide as the
world. It is the rise of the toiling and producing masses who are
gradually becoming conscious of their interest, their power, as
a class, who are organizing industrially and politically, who are
slowly but surely developing the economic and political power
that is to set them free. They are still in the minority, but they
have learned how to wait, and to bide their time.

It is because I happen to be in this minority that I stand
in your presence to-day, charged with crime. It is because I
believe, as the revolutionary fathers believed in their day, that a
change was due in the interests of the people, that the time had
come for a better form of government, an improved system, a
higher social order, a nobler humanity and a grander civilization. This minority that is so much misunderstood and so bitterly maligned is in alliance with the forces of evolution, and as
certain as I stand before you this afternoon, it is but a question
of time until this minority will become the conquering majority and inaugurate the greatest change in all of the history of
the world. You may hasten the change; you may retard it; you
can no more prevent it than you can prevent the coming of the
sunrise on the morrow.

My friend, the assistant prosecutor, doesn't like what I had to
say in my speech about internationalism. What is there objec-
tionable to internationalism? If we had internationalism there
would be no war. I believe in patriotism. I have never uttered
a word against the flag. I love the flag as a symbol of freedom.
I object only when that flag is prostituted to base purposes, to
sordid ends, by those who, in the name of patriotism, would
keep the people in subjection.

I believe, however, in a wider patriotism. Thomas Paine
said, "My country is the world. To do good is my religion."
Garrison said, "My country is the world and all mankind are
my countrymen." That is the essence of internationalism. I

believe in it with all of my heart. I believe that nations have been pitted against nations long enough in hatred, in strife, in warfare. I believe there ought to be a bond of unity between all of these nations. I believe that the human race consists of one great family. I love the people of this country, but I don't hate the people of any country on earth—not even the Germans. I refuse to hate a human being because he happens to be born in some other country. Why should I? To me it does not make any difference where he was born or what the color of his skin may be. Like myself, he is the image of his creator. He is a human being endowed with the same faculties, he has the same aspirations, he is entitled to the same rights, and I would infinitely rather serve him and love him than to hate him and kill him.

We hear a great deal about human brotherhood—a beautiful and inspiring theme. It is preached from a countless number of pulpits. It is vain for us to preach of human brotherhood while we tolerate this social system in which we are a mass of warring units, in which millions of workers have to fight one another for jobs, and millions of business men and professional men have to fight one another for trade, for practice—in which we have individual interests and each is striving to care for himself alone without reference to his fellow men. Human brotherhood is yet to be realized in this world. It can never be under the capitalist-competitive system in which we live.

Yes, I was opposed to the war. I am perfectly willing, on that count, to be branded as a disloyalist, and if it is a crime under the American law, punishable by imprisonment, for being opposed to human bloodshed, I am perfectly willing to be clothed in the stripes of a convict and to end my days in a prison cell.

If my friends, the attorneys, had known me a little better they might have saved themselves some trouble in procuring evidence to prove certain things against me which I have not the slightest inclination to deny, but rather, upon the other hand, I have a very considerable pride in.

You have heard a great deal about the St. Louis platform. I wasn't at the convention when that platform was adopted, but I don't ask to be excused from my responsibility on that account. I voted for its adoption. I believe in its essential principles. There was some of its phrasing that I would have otherwise. I afterwards advocated a restatement. The testimony to the effect that I had refused to repudiate it was true.

At the time that platform was adopted the nation had just entered upon the war and there were millions of people who were not Socialists who were opposed to the United States being precipitated into that war. Time passed; conditions changed. There were certain new developments and I believed there should be a restatement. I have been asked why I did not favor a repudiation of what was said a year before. For the reason that I believed then, as I believe now, that the statement correctly defined the attitude of the Socialist Party toward war. That statement, bear in mind, did not apply to the people of this country alone, but to the people of the world. It said, in effect, to the people, especially to the workers, of all countries, "Quit going to war. Stop murdering one another for the profit and glory of the ruling classes. Cultivate the arts of peace. Humanize humanity. Civilize civilization." That is the essential spirit and the appeal of the much-hated, condemned St. Louis platform.

Now, the Republican and Democratic parties hold their conventions from time to time. They revise their platforms and their declarations. They do not repudiate previous platforms. Nor is it necessary. With the change of conditions these platforms are outgrown and others take their places. I was not in the convention, but I believed in that platform. I do to-day. But from the beginning of the war to this day, I have never, by word or act, been guilty of the charges that are embraced in this indictment. If I have criticized, if I ever condemned, it is because I have believed myself justified in doing so under the laws of the land. I have had precedents for my attitude. This country has been engaged in a number of wars, and every one of them has been opposed, every one of them has been condemned by some of the most eminent men in the country. The war of the Revolution was opposed. The Tory press denounced its leaders as criminals and outlaws. And that was when they were under the "divine right" of a king to rule men.

The War of 1812 was opposed and condemned; the Mexican war was bitterly condemned by Abraham Lincoln, by Charles Sumner, by Daniel Webster and by Henry Clay. That war took place under the Polk administration. These men denounced the President; they condemned his administration; and they said that the war was a crime against humanity. They were not indicted; they were not tried for crime. They are honored to-day by all of their countrymen. The War of the Rebellion was opposed and condemned. In 1864 the Democratic Party met in convention at Chicago and passed a resolution condemning the war as a failure. What would you say if the Socialist Party were to meet in convention to-day and condemn the present war as a failure? You charge us with being disloyalists and traitors. Were the Democrats of 1864 disloyalists and traitors because they condemned the war as a failure?

I believe in the Constitution of the United States. Isn't it strange that we Socialists stand almost alone to-day in defending the Constitution of the United States? The revolutionary fathers who had been oppressed under king rule understood that free speech and free press and the right of free assemblage by the people were the fundamental principles of democratic government. The very first amendment to the Constitution reads: "Congress shall make no law respecting an establishment of religion, or prohibiting the free exercise thereof; or abridging the freedom of speech, or of the press; or the right of the people peaceably to assemble, and to petition the government for a redress of grievances." That is perfectly plain English. It can be understood by a child. I believe that the revolutionary fathers meant just what is here stated—that Congress shall make no law abridging the freedom of speech or of the press, or of the right of the people to peaceably assemble, and to petition the government for a redress of grievances.

That is the right that I exercised at Canton on the 16th day of last June; and for the exercise of that right I now have to answer to this indictment. I believe in the right of free speech in war as well as in peace. I would not, under any circumstances, gag the lips of my biggest enemy. I would under no circumstances suppress free speech. It is far more dangerous to attempt to gag the people than to allow them to speak freely of what is in their hearts. I do not go as far as Wendell Phillips did. Wendell Phillips said that the glory of free men is that they trample unjust laws under their feet. That is how they repealed them. If a human being submits to having his lips sealed, to be in silence reduced to vassalage, he may have all else, but he is still lacking in all that dignifies and glorifies real manhood.

Now, notwithstanding this fundamental provision in the national law, Socialists' meetings have been broken up all over this country. Socialist speakers have been arrested by hundreds and flung into jail, where many of them are lying now. In some cases not even a charge was lodged against them, guilty of absolutely no crime except the crime of attempting to exercise the right guaranteed to them by the Constitution of the United States.

I have told you that I am no lawyer, but it seems to me that I know enough to know that if Congress enacts any law that conflicts with this provision in the Constitution, that law is void. If the Espionage Law finally stands, then the Constitution of the United States is dead. If that law is not the negation of every fundamental principle established by the Constitution, then certainly I am unable to read or to understand the English language.

To the Court: Your Honor, I don't know whether I would be in order to quote from a book I hold in my hand, called "The New Freedom," by Woodrow Wilson, President of the United States.

The Court: I will grant you that permission.

Debs: I want to show the gentlemen of the jury, if I can, that every statement I made in my Canton speech is borne out in this book by Woodrow Wilson, called "The New Freedom." It consists of his campaign speeches while a candidate for the presidency. Of course, he uses different language than I did, for he is a college professor. He is an educated gentleman. I never had a chance to get an education. I had to go to work in my childhood. I want to show you that the statement made by Rose Pastor Stokes, for which she has been convicted, and the approval of which has brought condemnation upon me, is substantially the same statement made by Mr. Wilson when he was a candidate for the presidency of the United States:

"To-day, when our government has so far passed into the hands of special interests; to-day, when the doctrine is implicitly avowed that only select classes have the equipment necessary for carrying on government; to-day, when so many conscientious citizens, smitten with the scene of social wrong and suffering, have fallen victims to the fallacy that benevolent government can be meted out to the people by kind-hearted trustees of prosperity and guardians of the welfare of dutiful employees—to-day, supremely does it behoove this nation to remember that a people shall be saved by the power that sleeps in its own deep bosom, or by none; shall be renewed in hope, in conscience, in strength, by waters welling up from its own sweet, perennial springs."

So this government has passed into the hands of special interests. Rose Pastor Stokes' language is somewhat different. Instead of "special interests" she said "profiteers." She said that a government that was for the profiteers could not be for the people, and that as long as the government was for the profiteers, she was for the people. That is the statement that I indorsed, approved and believed in with all my heart. The President of the United States tells us that our government has passed into the control of special interests. When we Socialists make the same contention, we are branded as disloyalists, and we are indicted as criminals. But that is not all, nor nearly all:

"There are, of course, Americans who have not yet heard that anything is going on. The circus might come to town, have the big parade and go, without their catching a sight of the camels or a note of the calliope. There are people, even Americans, who never move themselves or know that anything else is moving."

Just one other quotation: "For a long time this country of ours has lacked one of the institutions which free men have always and everywhere held fundamental. For a long time there has been no sufficient opportunity of counsel among the people; no place and method of talk, of exchange of opinion, of parley. Communities have outgrown the folk-moot and the town meeting. Congress, in accordance with the genius of the land, which asks for action and is impatient of words— Congress has become an institution which does its work in the privacy of committee rooms and not on the floor of the Chamber; a body that makes laws, a legislature; not a body that debates, not a parliament. Party conventions afford little or no opportunity for discussion; platforms are privately manufac- tured and adopted with a whoop. It is partly because citizens have foregone the taking of counsel together that the unholy alliances of bosses and Big Business have been able to assume to govern for us.

"I conceive it to be one of the needs of the hour to restore the processes of common counsel, and to substitute them for the processes of private arrangement which now determine the policies of cities, states and nation. We must learn, we freemen, to meet, as our fathers did, somehow, somewhere, for consultation. There must be discussion and debate, in which all freely participate."

Well, there has been something said in connection with this about profiteering—in connection with this indictment.

To THE COURT: Would it be in order for me to read a brief statement, showing to what extent profiteering has been carried on during the last three years?

THE COURT: No. There would be no concensus of opinion or agreement upon that statement. It is a matter that is not really in the case, and when you go to compile a statement, you are then undertaking to assume something without producing evidence to substantiate it.

DEBS: Now, in the course of this proceeding you, gentlemen, have perhaps drawn the inference that I am pro-German, in the sense that I have any sympathy with the Imperial Government of Germany. My father and mother were born in Alsace. They loved France with a passion that is holy. They understood the meaning of Prussianism, and they hated it with all their hearts. I did not need to be taught to hate Prussian militarism. I knew from them what a hateful, what an oppressive, what a brutalizing thing it was and is. I cannot imagine how any one could suspect that for one moment I could have the slightest sympathy with such a monstrous thing. I have been speaking and writing against it practically all of my life. I know that the Kaiser incarnates all there is of brute force and of murder. And yet I would not, if I had the power, kill the Kaiser. I would do to him what Thomas Paine wanted to do to the king of England. He said, "Destroy the king, but save the man."

The thing that the Kaiser incarnates and embodies, called militarism, I would, if I could, wipe from the face of the earth,—not only the militarism of Germany, but the militarism of the whole world. I am quite well aware of the fact that the war now deluging the world with blood was precipitated there. Not by the German people, but by the class that rules, oppresses, robs and degrades the German people. President Wilson has repeatedly said that we were not making war on the German people, and yet in war it is the people who are slain, and not the rulers who are responsible for the war.

With every drop in my veins I despise kaiserism, and all that kaiserism expresses and implies. I have sympathy with the suffering, struggling people everywhere. It does not make any difference under what flag they were born, or where they live, I have sympathy with them all. I would, if I could, establish a social system that would embrace them all. It is precisely at this point that we come to realize that there is a reason why the peoples of the various nations are pitted against each other in brutal warfare instead of being united in one all-embracing brotherhood.

War does not come by chance. War is not the result of accident. There is a definite cause for war, especially a modern war. The war that began in Europe can readily be accounted for. For the last forty years, under this international capitalist system, this exploiting system, these various nations of Europe have been preparing for the inevitable. And why? In all these nations the great industries are owned by a relatively small class. They are operated for the profit of that class. And great abundance is produced by the workers; but their wages will only buy back a small part of their product. What is the result? They have a vast surplus on hand; they have got to export it; they have got to find a foreign market for it. As a result of this these nations are pitted against each other. They are industrial rivals—competitors. They begin to arm themselves to open, to maintain the market and quickly dispose of their surplus. There is but the one market. All these nations are competitors for it, and sooner or later every war of trade becomes a war of blood.

Now, where there is exploitation there must be some form of militarism to support it. Wherever you find exploitation you find some form of military force. In a smaller way you find it in this country. It was there long before war was declared. For instance, when the miners out in Colorado entered upon a strike about four years ago, the state militia, that is under the control of the Standard Oil Company, marched upon a camp,

where the miners and their wives and children were in tents,—
and, by the way, a report of this strike was issued by the United
States Commission on Industrial Relations. When the soldiers
approached the camp at Ludlow, where these miners, with
their wives and children, were, the miners, to prove that they
were patriotic, placed flags above their tents, and when the state
militia, that is paid by Rockefeller and controlled by Rockefeller, swooped down upon that camp, the first thing they did
was to shoot these United States flags into tatters. Not one of
them was indicted or tried because he was a traitor to his country. Pregnant women were killed, and a number of innocent
children slain. This in the United States of America,—the fruit
of exploitation. The miners wanted a little more of what they
had been producing. But the Standard Oil Company wasn't
rich enough. It insisted that all they were entitled to was just
enough to keep them in working order. There is slavery for you.
And when at last they protested, when they were tormented by
hunger, when they saw their children in tatters, they were shot
down as if they had been so many vagabond dogs.

And while I am upon this point let me say just another word.
Workingmen who organize, and who sometimes commit overt
acts, are very often times condemned by those who have no
conception of the conditions under which they live. How many
men are there, for instance, who know anything of their own
knowledge about how men work in a lumber camp—a logging
camp, a turpentine camp? In this report of the United States
Commission on Industrial Relations you will find the statement proved that peonage existed in the state of Texas. Out
of these conditions springs such a thing as the I.W.W.—When
men receive a pittance for their pay, when they work like galley
slaves for a wage that barely suffices to keep their protesting
souls within their tattered bodies. When they can endure the
conditions no longer, and they make some sort of a demonstration, or perhaps commit acts of violence, how quickly are they
condemned by those who do not know anything about the
conditions under which they work!

Five gentlemen of distinction, among them Professor John
Graham Brooks, of Harvard University, said that a word that
so fills the world as the I.W.W. must have something in it. It
must be investigated. And they did investigate it, each along

his own lines, and I wish it were possible for every man and woman in this country to read the result of their investigation. They tell you why and how the I.W.W. was instituted. They tell you, moreover, that the great corporations, such as the Standard Oil Company, such as the Coal Trust, and the Lumber Trust, have, through their agents, committed more crimes against the I.W.W. than the I.W.W. have ever committed against them.

I was asked not long ago if I was in favor of shooting our soldiers in the back. I said, "No, I would not shoot them in the back. I wouldn't shoot them at all. I would not have them shot." Much has been made of a statement that I declared that men were fit for something better than slavery and cannon fodder. I made the statement. I make no attempt to deny it. I meant exactly what I said. Men *are* fit for something better than slavery and cannon fodder; and the time will come, though I shall not live to see it, when slavery will be wiped from the earth, and when men will marvel that there ever was a time when men who called themselves civilized rushed upon each other like wild beasts and murdered one another, by methods so cruel and barbarous that they defy the power of man to describe. I can hear the shrieks of the soldiers of Europe in my dreams. I have imagination enough to see a battlefield. I can see it strewn with the legs of human beings, who but yesterday were in the flush and glory of their young manhood. I can see them at eventide, scattered about in remnants, their limbs torn from their bodies, their eyes gouged out. Yes, I can see them, and I can hear them. I have looked above and beyond this frightful scene. I think of the mothers who are bowed in the shadow of their last great grief—whose hearts are breaking. And I say to myself, "I am going to do the little that lies in my power to wipe from this earth that terrible scourge of war."

If I believed in war I could not be kept out of the first line trenches. I would not be patriotic at long range. I would be honest enough, if I believed in bloodshed, to shed my own. But I do not believe that the shedding of blood bears any actual testimony to patriotism, to lead a country to civilization. On the contrary, I believe that warfare, in all of its forms, is an impeachment of our social order, and a rebuke to our much vaunted Christian civilization.

And now, Gentlemen of the Jury, I am not going to detain you too long. I wish to admit everything that has been said respecting me from this witness chair. I wish to admit everything that has been charged against me except what is embraced in the indictment which I have read to you. I cannot take back a word. I can't repudiate a sentence. I stand before you guilty of having made this speech. I stand before you prepared to accept the consequences of what there is embraced in that speech. I do not know, I cannot tell, what your verdict may be; nor does it matter much, so far as I am concerned.

Gentlemen, I am the smallest part of this trial. I have lived long enough to appreciate my own personal insignificance in relation to a great issue that involves the welfare of the whole people. What you may choose to do to me will be of small consequence after all. I am not on trial here. There is an infinitely greater issue that is being tried in this court, though you may not be conscious of it. American institutions are on trial here before a court of American citizens. The future will tell.

And now, Your Honor, permit me to return my hearty thanks for your patient consideration. And to you, Gentlemen of the Jury, for the kindness with which you have listened to me.

My fate is in your hands. I am prepared for the verdict.

M. C. OTTO

World War I was more than a year over when M. C. Otto (1876–1968),
a German-American philosophy professor at the University of Wisconsin, called attention to the wartime ordeal of his former student
Carl Haessler, then imprisoned in Alcatraz for his refusal to fight. An
"uncompromising" young man, Haessler had neither faith-based nor
any other principled opposition to war in general to offer as justification for his unwillingness to cooperate with military authorities.
He considered himself a "patriotic political objector"—a radical,
willing to face a court-martial to advance the struggle against "the
big machine" of American capitalism. Otto both admires and seems
slightly daunted by his old pupil's convictions.

Haessler would be released in August 1920, by presidential pardon.
(Eager to "return to normalcy," Warren G. Harding eventually par-
doned or commuted the sentences of many such objectors and dissidents, among them Eugene V. Debs.) After a career in the labor
movement, he fought against another war in his mid-seventies, coun-
seling conscientious objectors to Vietnam.

An Experiment in Conscience

It was a snatch of an exasperated father's outburst, overheard
by chance, that precipitated the problem in my mind. "Do you
hear me?" the irate sire scolded into the back of his disheveled,
shuffling offspring, as he pushed him into the house. "How
many times have I told you to do what you know to be right,
no matter what the other boys do?" And the door which the
father slammed behind him seemed symbolic of the finality of
his moral creed. A neighbor tells me that I stopped in front of
the house and stared at the door. Very likely. But my mind had
jumped over miles and years and I was really gazing into the
frankest, steadiest, most self-possessed brown eyes I have ever
met. And as I walked on I was thinking not of what I had just
heard but of the possessor of those eyes, a youth who had tried
to apply this father's philosophy to life—with very unhappy
consequences.

How distinctly I recall my first clear awareness of him! It
happened in a university class room. He came into my life at

the other end of an acute question, leveled at me like a spear. I remember noting his red hair, his intelligent, sensitive face, his cleanliness and health. But what impelled me to go below a ready-to-hand answer was the way he looked at me. It was a man looking at a man, not a pupil looking at a professor. In time I did something to analyze that look; discovered the subdued fire in the calm eyes, the suggestion of irony about the expressive mouth, the strength of the finely formed chin. I discovered, too, that he owed much to those capable looking shoulders. At this first encounter I simply felt instinctively the advisability of caution; that what I said would not be the end but the beginning of discussion. So it proved—then, and many another time. Nor will I say that I always enjoyed it. He was too keenly analytical of one's theories and one's facts, too nimble-minded in attack and defense, too persistent in following up logical implications, to be an unfailing comfort in a class room. Besides I suspected him of finding secret delight in professor baiting! Little by little, however, the central impulse of his being penetrated through his gestures—an uncompromising, at times almost quixotic intellectual honesty. He wanted to know the truth about life, and consequently was impatient of shams, of sentimentalism, of mental quackery. And his insistence upon intellectualizing life was not always controlled by a nice sense of proportion nor by a sweet reasonableness toward the cherished beliefs of his opponent. His very objectivity, his natural tendency to treat problems impersonally, resulted in his everlasting stepping on the toes of some prejudice or other. And while I reassured myself—for I came to like the fellow— that he would outgrow his rashness as he would his youth, I could not but wonder, even in those days, what end he would make if he carried this uncompromising allegiance to facts into the world.

COLLEGE DAYS

His record in college was a brilliant one. He completed the four years' course in three, with a break of twelve months at the end of his sophomore year, during which he was engaged as an editorial assistant on a well-known philosophical monthly. He was elected to Phi Beta Kappa, and at the conclusion of his course was chosen Rhodes Scholar to represent his Alma Mater, the University of Wisconsin, at Oxford. His undergraduate days had been characterized by alert and ardent leadership in the more serious and progressive student enterprises. He was not the kind that the rah rah boys would slap on the back and ask for the makings, for although totally without moral or religious dogmatism, he was almost austere in his personal habits. Moreover, he was too iconoclastic and outspoken, and too disdainful of popularity to be anything like a general favorite. But he was in no sense friendless or alone.

The three years at Balliol, Oxford, were thriving, formative years. His letters were full of the joy of new friendships, of sunny afternoons on the river, of hospitable weekends at English country houses or by the sea in Ireland, of the beauty of the Scotch Highlands, of the charm of Irish maidens, of intimate gossip about authors and statesmen. It was all very like the testimony of another who was not far from him in time or space: "Exquisite peace and quiet, long days of rich pleasure and sweet nights of rest, kindliness and laughter and the friendly word of casual acquaintances . . . and over all the enduring beauty of the world." Below it all, the educational methods and customs of Balliol, indeed the very stones themselves, brought him into intimate touch with the rich past of English life. Vacations spent in France, Germany, Switzerland, and Italy enlarged and clarified his outlook. But the most deepgoing effect of these years was naturally one very closely related to the central motive of his life; he got a living appreciation of man's long struggle for freedom. Nay, more; he became identified with that struggle. The first sign of his dedication was a change in the tone and content of his letters. There was less of laughter and adventure, more of problems and discussions. Gradually, deep mental agitation crept into them, until in time, his letters became little else than records of his religious, moral and social unrest. It was a period of doubt and perplexity common enough to many lives, but one to which he had been a stranger. Could a man believe in any form of vital social idealism and maintain his intellectual integrity? Was not all hope of moral improvement a form of self-deception; in other words, sentimentalism? "I must find an answer to this question," he wrote. "I must get out of this apologetic attitude

in the matter of living a good life, or one of these days some
stronger temptation will send me sprawling in filth."

Then followed, with all the omens of spiritual dawn, the
enthusiastic avowal of Fabian socialism. He had been mildly
interested in socialistic ideas while still at Wisconsin, but his
conversion was now due to some of his Oxford tutors, to his
reading of Shaw, the Webbs, and others, and to his residence
at a college settlement in the London slums. After that his
buoyancy returned with a rush, and to the end of his stay
abroad he was full of tales of his experiences as a propagandist
of the new faith, and of keen, witty criticisms of emotional
schemes of social amelioration. It was no accident that the one
memento of his Oxford days that he brought home for himself
was a magnificent portrait of George Meredith—arch foe of
sentimentalism and friend of a new social order. That was in
the autumn of 1914.

Meanwhile the war had broken out. For a brief time he was
on the verge of volunteering in the English army. His Balliol
classmates were going—comrades of the three biggest years
he had known. It was a hard tug, and there was genuine anxiety on this side. He fought it out alone, and on intellectual
grounds. In his view the contest did not concern the people
of any of the contending nations. He regarded it as a struggle
between the Anglo-French-Russian imperialistic orbit and the
Austro-German-Turkish orbit, and he condemned both. He
came home opposed to the war.

BACK IN AMERICA

He came home—though he did not then know it—to give
his philosophy crucial trial. For a year he was at work preparing for his doctorate and winning his spurs as a teacher at the
University of Illinois. Happy, expansive days! It was Balliol
adapted to the Middle West. Merry voices on the tennis courts
at sunrise; cross-country runs in the mellow afternoons; lively
teas with students and younger instructors, at which age-worn
perplexities were neatly pigeon-holed.

It was not to be expected that those responsible for the
preservation of institutional respectability would look with
approval or even complacency upon a group of young men and

women who, however artless and high-minded, approached the institutions and customs of society in a spirit of free inquiry rather than of reverence. It must be admitted, moreover, that the leader of the group appeared to take mischievous delight in irritating those in authority. His friends were therefore not surprised to learn that his tenure in the university was uncertain. "The conditions of retaining my instructorship," he wrote to one of his friends, "have been made clear to me: no stirring up discussions in student publications, softer pedal on my social ideas, less cocky in challenging opinions of reverend signiors." If he agreed to this he was to have an advance in salary and the privilege of giving a course of his own. "At the same time," the letter went on, "I am offered the post of western organizer for the Intercollegiate Socialist Society at a better salary. If I had not lost my heart to the comrade with whom I have talked of marriage, and if you were not so certain that much can be accomplished for fundamental social reconstruction by my staying in philosophy, I believe I'd give the Intercollegiate a trial."

But with 1917 the war moved nearer to America—and nearer to him. Little by little he became the animating spirit of a group of radicals who opposed America's entrance into the conflict. They engaged anti-war speakers, they circulated anti-war literature, they organized themselves as a speakers' bureau—nine instructors, representing economics, history, sociology, English, and philosophy, and two ministers, a presbyterian and a unitarian—and answered the calls that came pouring in. No great imagination is required to picture the consternation this aroused. But that is a story in itself—of enthusiastic audiences, of petty persecution, of honest but vain endeavors to win these hot youths from their errors. To this little group those busy and dedicated months will always remain (to adapt one of President Wilson's noble phrases), among the great memories of their lives. It all slithered out when America joined forces with the Allies.

WAR AND THE DRAFT

Not, however, for the youth with the intelligent, sensitive face, and the steady brown eyes with a touch of fire in them like light at the bottom of a pool. Many times he had quoted with full approval words which he had discovered before he was twenty in an essay by William James: "In point of fact the *highest* ethical life—however few may be called to bear its burdens—consists at all times in the breaking of rules which have grown too narrow for the actual case. There is but one unconditional commandment, which is that we should seek incessantly, with fear and trembling, so to vote and to act as to bring about the very largest total universe of good which we can see." Here was the chance to stand by his conception of morality. Here was his chance to support a cause he thought to be right "with good humored inflexibility then most when the whole cry was on the other side," as Emerson puts it. Most of us do not feel called upon to translate our moral thrills into social fact. He did. He was subject to the first draft, and when the time came he wrote on his registration blank, "If drafted, I can not serve, as I cannot patriotically support this war."

For some reason the Draft Board, as a rule very jealous of its secrets and very efficient in keeping them, lost this one to the public. And from then on Carl Haessler's name began to figure in the newspapers as a conscientious or political objector.

Still, the academic year ended quietly enough. He was granted his Ph.D by the university, and left for the summer vacation, with friendly good-byes to his colleagues, quite unaware that his connection with the university had already been terminated. The news reached him, however, by mail almost as soon as he arrived at his home. "I understand," wrote the head of his department, himself plainly facing a moral issue and attempting to face it squarely, "I understand that you will not accept service if drafted under the registration; that is a question of conscience for you. Now I am firmly convinced that your attitude in this matter puts the question of your appointment in a new light. You have raised a question of conscience for me. I would not say or do anything that would seem to infringe upon your freedom of thought or action. But I do wish to make clear my position and to say that I cannot recommend anyone for a position in the department who holds that view."

What to do now? He had spent years preparing himself for the academic field, and here at the very beginning the door seemed to have shut. For, of course, his dismissal from Illinois, for the time at least, closed every other university to him. But he wanted still to keep his academic connections, and so carried out his design of applying for membership in the Western Philosophical Association.

The executive committee of this organization refused him admission. His "reported declaration of intention to resist the draft," which the committee "on the basis of the available information" felt obliged to construe as "rebellion against the government," constituted "an insuperable obstacle to membership in the organization."

Meanwhile he had turned, at first with regret, but later with growing satisfaction and zeal, to work on a metropolitan socialist daily. His ability, his devotion, his good will, quickly won him a place in the respect and affections of his new associates. Now, too, his bride, a graduate of Vassar, came to join in his labors. But while there was much in his many activities to give life zest, he lived constantly under an ominous shadow. His brother went to the front in France, his parents were unable to sympathize with what seemed to them his wrongheadedness, and he knew that he would soon have to face the call of the government. The day came. It was a cheery but somewhat leaner young man who responded.

IN CAMP

The local press, with which he had had many a bout, was quick to announce the result. Confronted by the reality, ran the report, Carl Haessler had, as predicted, collapsed in his defiance and had entered the service He had, so to speak, decided to "pluck up drowned honor by the locks." The facts, however, were far different. His status had not been officially determined. And while he was doing the most menial and dirty camp work, his sense of humor triumphed in notes like this:

"Do you remember Samuel Butler's caution to teachers in 'The Way of all Flesh,' to be careful lest their lives be some day written by some pupil of theirs who had not been too high in their grades? What has befallen me would tickle old Butler's heart into an alarming fit of humorous moralizing. My captain is a man whom I flunked in logic at Illinois, and who had to drop out of the university in consequence. At least that is what he told his brother officers when he asked to have me put in his company. I just faintly remembered him. He issued orders to 'ride' me, but a curious undercurrent of rough indignation among the regulars made them take me under their wing instead."

The issue was put squarely up to him perhaps a month after he had left for camp, and news of it came in a letter to his wife:

> M. G. Co., 46 Inf., Camp Sheridan, Ala.
> Friday, June 21, 1918, 8 p.m.

Dearest:

After being put in quarters under guard, I was first released from guard and then told that all restrictions were removed but that a uniform would be issued to me and I would be expected to do military service. If I refused that would mean being put into the camp stockade, courtmartialed and sentenced, possibly to 25 years. The uniform is on my cot now and when I get up tomorrow morning I shall have to make my choice.

Darling lover, you know now what my decision will be but I want you to have the reasons as they now appeal to me before you on paper.

(1) I regard this war as tragically unnecessary and motivated originally by commercial and imperialistic considerations. From the patriotic point of view, no citizen looking at this war in this way can do his best by the country unless he refuses to assist in such a war in any way and unless he does what he can to make such wars impossible in the future by moral and intellectual leadership.

(2) From the socialist point of view, this war is largely unjustified and an aspiring socialist leader must stand by his colors and must not hesitate to do himself what he would like the rank and file to do. If radicalism is to crumble at the first bellow of the war drum, radicalism is worthless and a fraud.

(3) From the preaching-teaching point of view, how can I ever talk to my followers again if I now recede from fear of the consequences? I shall have muzzled myself forever and more thoroughly than any prison term could do. I might almost as well die as voluntarily stop myself from teaching and preaching.

(4) There remains a dross of personal feeling, of resentment at being sanctimoniously ordered to help in an unholy war, of pride

in keeping to my convictions while they are mine, of hope even perhaps (to tell the whole truth) of capitalizing martyrdom, and a "Siberian record," of resolve not to disappoint those who have come through me to believe in radicalism, of determination not to give aid and comfort to the capitalist enemy by surrendering, and so on.

But on the other side . . . there is a terrific pull at my heart. What could we not do together after the war! I would be sure to come back since both Lieut. —— and Lieut. —— have already offered me safety-first jobs.

But dearest, how can I commit soul-suicide while in good health and good spirits and with a clear perception of the situation? If my opinion of the war had changed I would have put on the uniform long ago, but I will not do it while I have the strength to resist and still believe the war a crime on the part of our country.

So now, beloved wife, I must close this letter. I hope the courtmartial may come soon and my fate be decided and settled without delay. I have been well treated so far, with courtesy and respect beyond my expectation. . . .

Carl.

COURTMARTIAL

The courtmartial took place in August. The following statement, which was Exhibit A in the courtmartial, is copied from the official report of the proceedings:

"I, Carl Haessler, Recruit, Machine Gun Company, 46th Infantry, respectfully submit the following statement in extenuation in connection with my proposed plea of guilty to the charge of violation of the 64th Article of War, the offense having been committed June 22, 1918, in Camp Sheridan, Ala.

The offense was not committed from private, secret, personal, impulsive, religious, pacifist or pro-German grounds. An admixture of quasi personal motives is admitted, but they were in no sense the guiding or controlling factors. I have evidence for each of these assertions, should it be required.

The wilful disobedience of my Captain's and of my Lieutenant-Colonel's orders to report in military uniform arose from a conviction which I hesitate to express before my country's military officers but which I nevertheless am at present unable to shake off, namely, that America's participation in the World War was unnecessary, of doubtful benefit (if any) to the country and to humanity, and accomplished largely, though not exclusively, through the pressure of the allied and American commercial imperialists.

Holding this conviction, I conceived my part as a citizen to be opposition to the war before it was declared, active efforts for a peace without victory after the declaration, and a determination so far as possible to do nothing in aid of the war while its character seemed to remain what I thought it was. I hoped in this way to help bring the war to an earlier close and to help make similar future wars less probable in this country.

I further believe that I am and shall be rendering the country a service by helping to set an example for other citizens to follow in the matter of fearlessly acting on unpopular convictions instead of forgetting them in time of stress. The crumbling of American radicalism under pressure in 1917 has only been equalled by that of the majority of German Socialist leaders in August, 1914.

Looking at my case from the point of view of the administration and of this court, I readily admit the necessity of exemplary punishment. I regret that I have been forced to make myself a nuisance, and I grant that this war could not be carried on if objections like mine were recognized by those conducting the war. My respect for the administration has been greatly increased by the courteous and forbearing treatment accorded me since having been drafted, but my view of international politics and diplomacy, acquired during my three years of graduate study in England, has not altered since June, 1917, when I formally declared that I could not accept service if drafted. Although officers have on three occasions offered me noncombatant service if I would put on the uniform, I have regretfully refused each time on the ground that "bomb proof" service on my part would give the lie to my sincerity (which was freely granted by Judge Julian Mack when he and his colleagues examined me at Camp Gordon). If I am to render any war services, I shall not ask for special privileges.

I wish to conclude this long statement by reiterating that I am not a pacifist or pro-German, not a religious or private objector, but regard myself as a patriotic political objector, acting largely from public and social grounds.

I regret that, while my present view of this war continues, I cannot freely render any service in aid of the war. I shall not complain about the punishment that this court may see fit to mete out to me."

Signed: CARL HAESSLER.

A true copy.
Captain, Inf. R. C. 46 Inf. Judge Advocate.

The result of the trial was unknown until late in September, when the prisoner communicated the news to his wife. "Miracle Woman," he wrote, "I am sure your brave spirit will need all the strength you can summon . . . The prison officers read out to me that I am to be 'dishonorably discharged, to forfeit all pay and allowances due and to be confined as the reviewing authority may direct for a period of twelve years at hard labor.' The sentence has been approved in Washington and is to be served in the Disciplinary Barracks Ft. Leavenworth, Kans., where I go within the next month. The sentence began July 18, and with good behavior will expire Oct. 18, 1926. Eight years sacrificed of our common life for the sake of our common ideal. I would not murmur at giving more, but I doubt the wisdom of social arrangements that make such stupid sacrifices inevitable . . . I have no word against the army as such. It is the cause the army is made to fight for that I reject, more emphatically now than in June of last year when I resolved that I would not lend myself to such an undertaking."

In October, 1918, then, Carl Haessler was imprisoned in Fort Leavenworth. Last June—the reason can only be guessed at—he was transferred to Alcatraz. His spirit, however, was not broken by his imprisonment. It glows with something rich and eloquent in a letter not intended for the public eye. "If you have a philosophy that can sustain you through this ordeal," he had been asked by one very dear to him, "do pass it on to us." Let his reply be our parting word:

"You and I are not mere creatures who wish to live at any cost. We would invest our lives for rich social returns. Both of us groped and fumbled about in the world for many years before we came to a realization of the direction in which our enterprise had to be prosecuted. We began to see that the vast capitalist structure of modern civilization, by which the favored rich became still richer by waiting for interest and dividends to come in, had to be sapped and undermined. This we began valiantly and persistently to do until the big machine turned on us and on a million others, and we were separated. But the work goes doggedly on. Even now our great investment looks sound to me, of a long-time soundness."

WALTER GUEST KELLOGG

Conscientious objection to war has been part of the American experience since the colonial era, if not before. By World War I, though, it had been found necessary to establish some rules to determine and define who counted as a conscientious objector and who did not, and generally to shape how the government should deal with young men refusing to fight. Walter Guest Kellogg (1877–1956) was put in charge of this operation in 1917, being then a major in the Judge Advocate General's office; he had a Columbia law degree and as an undergraduate senior at the same school had been the class poet. *The Conscientious Objector* (1919) is his account of his work, and became a West Point textbook. Kellogg finds conscientious objectors repellent on the whole, but nevertheless describes their stories with vivid precision. The case of Richard L. Stierheim—a private from Ingomar, Pennsylvania—seems to him "like a page of romance" rather than a legal problem. Stierheim refused to fight and deserted his unit; but his bravery was so conspicuous that military authorities had to bend their own rules, suspending what otherwise might have been his death sentence.

The Stierheim Case

THE story of Richard L. Stierheim reads like a page of romance. Stierheim, although an objector, had probably never received the offer of noncombatant service provided for by the Executive Order; on the other hand, it seemingly nowhere appears that he had advised his commanding officer that he claimed to be an objector. He was sent overseas in Company D, 315th Infantry. Finding himself in a combatant unit and his company about to go into action against the enemy, he left his organization and remained absent until apprehended on the Spanish border some days later.

When tried by court-martial for his desertion he testified that he had left his company because he didn't believe in war. He said: "By going up to the front and being killed I didn't see how I could stand up on Judgment Day and say I died fighting for God Almighty." He admitted that his object in deserting was to avoid the necessity of going into battle.

The following facts are shown by letters from his Commanding General and others:

> "On the night of November 3, 1918, during an attack of his
> company and organization against Hill 378, north of Verdun,
> Stierheim volunteered to go out into 'No-Man's Land' at night
> to rescue wounded men. He rescued six wounded men unas-
> sisted, while a great number of machine guns were firing at him.
> One wounded man who had been shot six times was behind a
> tree from which he could not move; Stierheim walked over and
> brought him in. After his company had been relieved and was
> in the rear under cover from shell fire, he volunteered to go
> forward again with the regimental chaplain to help bury the
> dead. Thereafter he volunteered to be one of a litter party to
> carry wounded to a Battalion Aid Post, maintained by Captain
> Bulford in a dugout in a valley below a farm house; and thence
> to the Regimental Aid Post. This valley was under considerable
> shell fire during most of the time, and it was often quite difficult
> to get patients to the Aid Post, and also to evacuate them to
> the Regimental Post, because of the shell fire, and also because
> of mud, shell holes and steep grades; but during the following
> eight or nine days, and until the declaration of the armistice on
> November 11, 1918, Stierheim conducted many patients through
> the valley, and showed an absolute indifference to danger.
> He also made many trips to the farm house for water for the
> wounded men, under heavy fire."

Lieutenant Gallagher, his company commander, in writing
of Stierheim's conduct, says: "I have never seen such bravery,
and feel that a man of his caliber deserves some consideration,"
and recommends clemency "for his conspicuous gallantry,
unselfish and untiring efforts."

Captain Bulford writes of him: "This man showed courage
and devotion to duty far above the average and it is desired
that the Commanding Officer be informed of his courageous
work."

Stierheim deserved "some consideration" and he got it. General Pershing, Commander-in-Chief of the American Expedi-
tionary Forces, forwarded the record of Steirheim's trial to the
Judge Advocate General with this statement:

> "I have not confirmed the sentence because, while the evidence
> clearly shows that the accused was guilty of desertion as charged,

and the sentence was therefore warranted, his subsequent voluntary and meritorious service in action, as more particularly referred to in the above mentioned letter of the Commanding General of the 79th Division, and the recommendation of the accused's company commander, prompt me to recommend that the entire sentence be remitted, and that he be restored to duty and assigned to noncombatant service. With this recommendation I transmit the record for the action of the President."

ARTURO GIOVANNITTI

Scott Nearing is best known for *Living the Good Life* (1954), which he wrote with his wife Helen Nearing and which became an almost sacred text for many in the counterculture. But before he "dropped out" to find simplicity on a Vermont farm, he had a long history of activist work for progressive causes; his views on economic inequality, and on child labor in particular, got him fired from the Wharton School in 1915. His views on World War I got him fired again, this time from the University of Toledo, 1917; later, like Eugene V. Debs, he was indicted under the Espionage Act, not for a speech but for a pamphlet titled *The Great Madness: A Victory for American Plutocracy* (1917). He was tried in February 1919 and acquitted.

Nearing's own antiwar writing is turgid and preachy; this lively account of his Espionage Act trial by the Italian-American poet, journalist, and self-described "militant revolutionist" Arturo Giovannitti (1884–1959) does him better justice. (Giovannitti had himself been acquitted of murder charges after a textile strike in 1912; he published *Arrows in the Gale*, a book of poems, in 1914, and his antiwar play *Come era nel principio* was performed in New York in 1916.)

Scott Nearing Reprieves Democracy

ON the 15th day of February, 1919—so will the People's Commissary of Historical Research write a few years hence—the city of New York began to proclaim its moral and intellectual independence from the dictatorship of Woodrow Wilson and struck the first blow at the judicial terror inaugurated by his Fouquier-Tinville, Thomas W. Gregory. On that day twelve respectable citizens, none of whom had invested anything, not even sympathy, in the ventures and fortunes of Socialism, acquitted Scott Nearing of a charge of sedition and by that act granted a temporary respite to the execution of Democracy on the part of the bourgeois Bolshevism of the Democratic Party.

The facts in the case are well known. Nearing wrote a pamphlet entitled The Great Madness, in which, among various things, he stated that the reasons that prompted America to join the war were purely commercial, if not altogether mercenary, and that the desire to save democracy and to establish international amity had as much to do with it as a prize-fight in

Nevada has to do with the physical improvement of the white race, or a cock fight in New Mexico with the future welfare of our gallinaceous posterity.

So long as Nearing merely confined himself to believing this, he was perfectly safe, neither Hudson Maxim nor the National Security League having yet invented a seismograph applicable to the human cranium to detect and record seditious vibrations—but when he said it, and wrote it down and allowed it to be printed and circulated, then the trouble began. Mr. Gregory himself has repeatedly stated that nobody was ever prosecuted for holding an opinion—indeed, it is when the opinion is no longer *held*, but allowed to run at large that the law must get busy to bottle it up again. In other words, to further quote our ineffable Attorney General, anybody is absolutely free to think whatever he pleases, provided he keeps his mouth shut—a sound and wise principle of great antiquity which was never interfered with, save by the Dominican torture of the Inquisition and our own Liberty Bond solicitors, the only two great institutions that insisted on prying all lips open, to the greater glory of God and democracy. So there is no telling when your mouth is open, shut or just ajar. The only way one can find out is to wait till one is indicted.

Now, Scott Nearing had no intention whatever of undermining the morale of the army and inciting to resistance against the government. His intention was that of thinking about the war, and being a professor, and therefore much addicted to thinking aloud, he recorded his own meditations in writing, feeling wisely apprehensive of the accuracy of police stenographers. Very likely he naively assumed that he was in the privileged position of a scientist trying to get at the causes of social phenomena, and as such phenomena had already taken place, and his findings could neither change nor modify their effects, he also assumed that he was immune from prosecution. Of course he was right, and also was wrong.

That he was against the war for the horrors that it entails was no more accountable against him than if he had been against a Texas cyclone, and his privilege to so feel was cheerfully recognized even by the District Attorney. But when he set out to discover the causes of the war and the cyclone, and attributed them to the rapacity of American capitalism and the inclemencies of the Texan climate, then he deliberately interfered with the rights of other citizens to carry on their legitimate business and sell real estate, and maliciously and feloniously libelled the government of the United States and the sweet meteorological disposition of the State of Texas.

Had he undertaken to study a volcanic eruption in Italy or a cloudburst in the South Sea Islands, and arrived at the conclusion that they were not an act of God, as our insurance policies claim, but a dastardly deed of the Devil, nobody would have quarreled with him and no ecclesiastical tribunal in the world would have burned him alive. Theologians differ on such subjects, and as a matter of fact they rather incline to attribute those pranks to the Evil One, especially when it is the righteous and the godly that perish. Infernal forces and motives are always sought out by divines and prosecutors whose sole business is to discover sins and crimes rather than virtues and saintly purposes—but when it comes to wars, famines, unemployment, poverty, social injustice, then it is the inscrutable will of God that is at work. The reason is that the Devil could be defeated, but God must not be resisted.

But let us get back to Nearing. The first time I ever heard him speak in public was in the courtroom, at his own trial. The reason why I never went to any of his lectures was because he was a professor, and I always had a double grudge against professors, both as a student in the palmy days of my college life when they examined me, and as a militant revolutionist when I began to examine them. The only professor who ever won my esteem and admiration was the director of a school of cutting, who insisted on making me a suit of clothes for nothing on the chance that I might advertise his sartorial atheneum during a tailors' strike. I am sorry to say that he went bankrupt before the suit was delivered.

So when Scott Nearing joined the Socialist movement, I decided that it was chiefly due to the fact that no other movement wanted him, and I kept disdainfully away from his meetings. I scornfully disposed of him as a pampered intellectual trying to rap for silence in the epic din of a proletarian mob in order to make a little squeak of his own. I refused to believe that he was a Socialist. I didn't give a hang for his economics. I held in supercilious contempt all his social cataplasms: child labor laws, old age pensions, income taxes, government ownership and the rest of the indecent farrago of petty bourgeois reforms. In a word, I concluded that he was the academic correlative of that pious and sanctimonious demi-monde in the Socialist Party that had given us a lot of spirituality with John Spargo and Alexander Irvine, a quagmire of muckraking bunk with Charlie Russell, a gush of romantic glucose with Ernest Poole and Upton Sinclair and a flood of saccharine sentimentality over the cardial affairs of those two elongated Puritans, Walling and Stokes. Ah me! Ou sont-ils les jours d'Antan? Gone, gone, all of them are gone! Putrescant in pace!

Well, I most contritely make humble and honorable amends for having judged Scott Nearing according to precedent. I take back whatever I thought of him. I regret and kick myself for having missed his speeches and lectures for over a year, and I promise that from now on I shall dog his steps like the most devoted socialette that ever embellished a pew of the Rand School. But again, on second thought, it was just as good that I never heard him before, for in that case I should have missed the real big thrill of his trial. Let us call it a trial, but really it was no trial at all. The government never had a chance—it was just Scott Nearing taking the platform by a skilful coup d'etat brilliantly staged by his attorney, Seymour Stedman, and lecturing judge, jury, audience and court attendants on the weighty questions of the day. It was fine. It was thrilling. It was a big and manful job. It felt so good to see it done, that I almost got reconciled with professors, the Lord forbid!

The prosecution must have felt like a Meyer London resolution in the committee room of Congress. It confined itself to reading The Great Madness to the jury, and to proving its authorship and publication, which were cheerfully admitted by all witnesses, chiefly officials of the Rand School of Social Science. Then it rested its case, and from that moment on it was Scott Nearing who took charge of the proceedings, who held court, who answered questions and asked them, who argued, debated, lectured, read, scolded and cracked jokes. For two whole days he turned the courtroom into a classroom, the witness stand into a chair of revolutionary economics, the judge into an invited guest of the faculty and the jury into a bunch of still unhazed freshmen. With a debonair smile on his wholesome young face, with his legs crossed and a pile of books, mostly his own, on his lap, he talked hour after hour with a clear resonant voice that carried to every corner of the hall, unhaltingly, directly, aggressively, never stopping a single second to select his words or to qualify his statements.

He was not an accused on trial before his judges, not a thinker defending a new unorthodox theory before a synod of academicians, nor was he even the usual agitator haranguing a hostile crowd—he was just the scientific investigator who had arrived at the true diagnosis of a social sore and was telling it to his patients. Indeed I had the distinct impression that that crowd felt as if they were in the waiting room of a clinic listening to a famous doctor prescribing plain remedies to them, and marveling that it was all so true and so simple.

Lawyer Stedman, a fine, sagacious male Portia whose head bears a striking likeness to that of Cicero, and whose overbrimming sense of humor would cheer up even a bone-dry State, was soon reduced to asking a question every hour or so, the rest of the time being filled with the ready and driving answer. Even Mr. Barnes, the Government's Attorney, soon found no room to wedge in an objection, or perhaps was too deeply engrossed in the arguments of the defendant to think of objecting. Only the judge tried now and then to dam the flood of sparkling eloquence with a few inconsequential questions; but that was just to save the floundering decorum of the court and to remind the public that it was still a trial that was going on.

But Nearing did not care about the trial. He answered everything directly, without hesitation, almost belligerently, and the more involved and captious the question, the more straightforward and pugnacious was the answer. He tore through all the barbed wire entanglements of the procedure like a tank in full blast, unmindful of the pitfalls and hidden mines of the cross-examination, splendidly and joyously unconcerned about whatever subtle and cavilling interpretation might be put on his words. So much so that Mr. Stedman had to stop him on several occasions and once had to invoke the authority of the court in order to keep his own client with the bounds of the interrogatory. And all the time Nearing kept on smiling his strange unhumorous smile that was neither meant to disarm nor to provoke his opponent, but, so at least I felt, was a necessary part of his martial accoutrement, a sort of pleasant war paint that could not be dispensed with.

What he said—for the whole trial consisted of what he said—I hope will soon be published in book form, it being impossible to quote him in full and inadequate to quote him in part. Besides I am a very poor reporter. Suffice it to say, however, that he stood by everything he wrote, that he took nothing back, apologized for nothing, palliated nothing, and reiterated everything he had written with added emphasis, from his uncompromising opposition to the war to his determination to fight till human exploitation, the fountainhead of all wars, has been forever blotted out of the earth.

When he got through all felt that he had made his point, and that he had tried from the very beginning to carry his point rather than to win his case. That he was finally acquitted after thirty hours of deliberation on the part of the jury was an insignificant incident. The jury simply couldn't help it. They must have felt in the seclusion of their room, after such a long session of lessons, that they were there not to write a verdict, but to write their examination papers on a major subject of which two weeks before they knew nothing about. And they made the only answer pupils can make on moot academic questions—they agreed with the personal theory of their professor.

But really it did not matter at all whether he was acquitted or not. He himself did not care, nor did anyone else. It wasn't important. Personally I am almost sorry that he was acquitted. I resent it as a great injustice. Why should such a man be denied the great distinction of serving twenty years in the Revolutionary Parliament of Fort Leavenworth when a man like Victor Berger is granted that privilege?

I could not help drawing a parallel between the two: one defending himself with all weapons, the other accusing; one trying to wriggle out of a mess by crying: "I did not do it; it's my enemy Bill Haywood that done it," and the other superbly shouting across the storm: "Yes, I did it, and I will do it again, and more."

I wonder whether we couldn't swap Nearing for Victor Berger. Truly the latter belongs to Congress, among the respectables. Truly Nearing belongs to the penitentiary among the outcasts.

SARA TEASDALE

Oppositional is one of the last terms likely to be applied to Sara Teasdale (1884–1933), a once widely acclaimed and popular poet whose works, in the wake of modernism, have sometimes been disparaged as sentimental or merely genteel. In fact she did oppose war in general and America's entry into World War I in particular, privately lamenting the "war-madness" and "lunacy" she saw all around her in New York, and the idea that, after "four thousand years of so-called civilization . . . disputes between peoples are still settled by killing." But political protest and poetry did not sit easily together, for her; when she published *Love Songs*, six months or so after the U.S. ended its neutrality, she left out her few explicitly antiwar lyrics, like "Spring in the Naugatuck Valley" (1915), about a Connecticut munitions plant, and never later collected them.

Her poem "'There Will Come Soft Rains'"—published after the war had ended, in *Flame and Shadow* (1920)—hauntingly envisions a world from which humankind has "perished utterly," twenty-five years before the dropping of the atomic bomb made such imaginings common. (Years later, Ray Bradbury would appropriate the poem in his postapocalyptic science fiction story borrowing her title.) In its way, it is surely an antiwar poem, and yet it almost seems to take comfort in the disappearance of the human, and of human pain.

"There Will Come Soft Rains"

(War Time)

There will come soft rains and the smell of the ground,
And swallows circling with their shimmering sound;

And frogs in the pools singing at night,
And wild plum-trees in tremulous white;

Robins will wear their feathery fire
Whistling their whims on a low fence-wire;

And not one will know of the war, not one
Will care at last when it is done.

Not one would mind, neither bird nor tree
If mankind perished utterly;

And Spring herself, when she woke at dawn,
Would scarcely know that we were gone.

JANE ADDAMS

Jane Addams (1860–1935) grew up in Freeport, Illinois, in a wealthy Republican family; her father helped found the party, and was an associate of Abraham Lincoln's. She went to college at Rockford Female Seminary, receiving the school's first bachelor's degree, and after college traveled in Europe. In association with her friend Ellen Gates Starr she founded Hull House in 1889, and became important in the settlement house movement and in civic reform generally, by force of intellect and will and by what Floyd Dell called her "passion of conciliation."

That passion did not keep her from opposing World War I, or from suffering the consequences of that opposition. Many of her contemporaries—even some of those with whom she had made common cause in earlier struggles—denounced her for her efforts. It is in fact that sudden loss of community that she explores here, in an excerpt from her memoir *Peace and Bread in Time of War* (1922), rather than the reasons for her opposition to the war in the first place. She patiently, rigorously, insightfully, unsparingly sets out what it cost her as an opponent of war to become, in Hawthorne's phrase, an "outcast of society."

She persisted in spite of such ostracism, and in 1919 helped found the Women's International League for Peace and Freedom, becoming its first president and winning the Nobel Peace Prize in 1931 in part for her work with that organization, the first American woman to win the prize. (The second was her WILPF colleague Emily Greene Balch in 1946, she too an opponent of the war, she too suffering the consequences of that opposition, in being denied reappointment to her teaching position at Wellesley College in 1918.)

Personal Reactions During War

AFTER the United States had entered the war there began to appear great divergence among the many types of pacifists, from the extreme left, composed of non-resistants, through the middle-of-the-road groups, to the extreme right, who could barely be distinguished from mild militarists. There were those people, also, who although they felt keenly both the horror and the futility of war, yet hoped for certain beneficent results from the opportunities afforded by the administration of war; they were much pleased when the government took over the management of the railroads, insisting that governmental ownership had thus been pushed forward by decades; they were also sure that the War Labor Policies Board, the Coal Commission and similar war institutions would make an enormous difference in the development of the country, in short, that militarism might be used as an instrument for advanced social ends. Such justifications had their lure and one found old pacifist friends on all the war boards and even in the war department itself. Certainly we were all eager to accept whatever progressive social changes came from the quick reorganization demanded by war, and doubtless prohibition was one of these, as the granting of woman suffrage in the majority of the belligerent nations, was another. But some of us had suspected that social advance depends as much upon the process through which it is secured as upon the result itself; if railroads are nationalized solely in order to secure rapid transit of ammunition and men to points of departure for Europe, when that governmental need no longer exists what more natural than that the railroads should no longer be managed by the government?

My temperament and habit had always kept me rather in the middle of the road; in politics as well as in social reform I had been for "the best possible." But now I was pushed far toward the left on the subject of the war and I became gradually convinced that in order to make the position of the pacifist clear it was perhaps necessary that at least a small number of us should be forced into an unequivocal position. If I sometimes regretted having gone to the Woman's Congress at The Hague in 1915, or having written a book on Newer Ideals of Peace in 1911 which had made my position so conspicuously clear, certainly far oftener I was devoutly grateful that I had used such unmistakable means of expression before the time came when any spoken or written word in the interests of Peace was forbidden.

It was on my return from The Hague Congress in July, 1915, that I had my first experience of the determination on the part of the press to make pacifist activity or propaganda so absurd that it would be absolutely without influence and its authors so discredited that nothing they might say or do would be regarded as worthy of attention. I had been accustomed to newspaper men for many years and had come to regard them as a good natured fraternity, sometimes ignorant of the subject on which they asked an interview, but usually quite ready to report faithfully albeit somewhat sensationally. Hull-House had several times been the subject of sustained and inspired newspaper attacks, one, the indirect result of an exposure of the inefficient sanitary service in the Chicago Health Department had lasted for many months; I had of course known what it was to serve unpopular causes and throughout a period of campaigning for the Progressive Party I had naturally encountered the "opposition press" in various parts of the country, but this concerted and deliberate attempt at misrepresentation on the part of newspapers of all shades of opinion was quite new in my experience. After the United States entered the war, the press throughout the country systematically undertook to misrepresent and malign pacifists as a recognized part of propaganda and as a patriotic duty. We came to regard this misrepresentation as part of the war technique and in fact an inevitable consequence of war itself, but we were slow in the very beginning to recognize the situation, and I found my first experience which came long before the United States entered the war rather overwhelming.

Upon our return from the Woman's International Congress at The Hague in 1915, our local organization in New York City with others, notably a group of enthusiastic college men, had arranged a large public meeting in Carnegie Hall. Dr. Anna Howard Shaw presided and the United States delegates made a public report of our impressions in "war stricken Europe" and of the moral resources in the various countries we visited that might possibly be brought to bear against a continuation of the war. We had been much impressed with the fact that it was an old man's war, that the various forms of doubt and opposition to war had no method of public expression and that many of the soldiers themselves were far from enthusiastic in regard to actual fighting as a method of settling international difficulties. War was to many of them much more anachronistic than to the elderly statesmen who were primarily responsible for the soldiers' presence in the trenches.

It was the latter statement which was my undoing, for in illustration of it I said that in practically every country we had visited, we had heard a certain type of young soldier say that it had been difficult for him to make the bayonet charge (enter into actual hand to hand fighting) unless he had been stimulated; that the English soldiers had been given rum before such a charge, the Germans ether and that the French were said to use absinthe. To those who heard the address it was quite clear that it was not because the young men flinched at the risk of death but because they had to be inflamed to do the brutal work of the bayonet, such as disembowelling, and were obliged to overcome all the inhibitions of civilization.

Dr. Hamilton and I had notes for each of these statements with the dates and names of the men who had made them, and it did not occur to me that the information was new or startling. I was, however, reported to have said that no soldier could go into a bayonet charge until he was made half drunk, and this in turn was immediately commented upon, notably in a scathing letter written to the New York Times by Richard Harding Davis, as a most choice specimen of a woman's sentimental nonsense. Mr. Davis himself had recently returned from Europe and at once became the defender of the heroic soldiers who were being traduced and belittled. He lent the weight of his name and his very able pen to the cause, but it really needed neither, for the misstatement was repeated, usually with scathing comment, from one end of the country to the other.

I was conscious, of course, that the story had struck athwart the popular and long-cherished conception of the nobility and heroism of the soldier as such, and it seemed to me at the time that there was no possibility of making any explanation, at least until the sensation should have somewhat subsided. I might have repeated my more sober statements with the explanation that whomsoever the pacifist held responsible for war, it was certainly not the young soldiers themselves who were, in a sense, its most touching victims, "the heroic youth of the world whom a common ideal tragically pitted against each other." Youth's response to the appeal made to their self-sacrifice, to their patriotism, to their sense of duty, to their high-hearted hopes for the future, could only stir one's admiration, and we should have been dull indeed had we failed to be moved by this most moving spectacle in the world. That they had so responded to the higher appeals only confirms Ruskin's statement that "we admire the soldier not because he goes forth to slay but to be slain." The fact that many of them were obliged to make a great effort to bear themselves gallantly in the final tests of "war's brutalities" had nothing whatever to do with their courage and sense of devotion. All this, of course, we had realized during our months in Europe.

After the meeting in Carnegie Hall and after an interview with President Wilson in Washington, I returned to Chicago to a public meeting arranged in the Auditorium; I was met at the train by a committee of aldermen appointed as a result of a resolution in the City Council. There was an indefinite feeling that the meeting at The Hague might turn out to be of significance, and that in such an event its chairman should have been honored by her fellow citizens. But the bayonet story had preceded me and every one was filled with great uneasiness. To be sure, a few war correspondents had come to my rescue—writing of the overpowering smell of ether preceding certain German attacks; the fact that English soldiers knew when a bayonet charge was about to be ordered because rations of rum were distributed along the trenches. Some people began to suspect that the story, exaggerated and grotesque as it had become, indicated not cowardice but merely an added sensitiveness which the modern soldier was obliged to overcome. Among the many letters on the subject which filled my mail for weeks, the bitter and abusive were from civilians or from the old men to whom war experiences had become a reminiscence, the larger number and the most understanding ones came from soldiers in active service.

Only once did I try a public explanation. After an address in Chautauqua, New York, in which I had not mentioned bayonets, I tried to remake my original statement to a young man of the associated press only to find it once more so garbled that I gave up in despair, quite unmoved by the young man's letter of apology which followed hard upon the published report of his interview.

I will confess that the mass psychology of the situation interested me even then and continued to do so until I fell ill with a serious attack of pleuro-pneumonia, which was the beginning of three years of semi-invalidism. During weeks of feverish discomfort I experienced a bald sense of social opprobrium and wide-spread misunderstanding which brought me very near to self pity, perhaps the lowest pit into which human nature can sink. Indeed the pacifist in war time, with his precious cause in the keeping of those who control the sources of publicity and consider it a patriotic duty to make all types of peace propaganda obnoxious, constantly faces two dangers. Strangely enough he finds it possible to travel from the mire of self pity straight to the barren hills of self-righteousness and to hate himself equally in both places.

From the very beginning of the great war, as the members of our group gradually became defined from the rest of the community, each one felt increasingly the sense of isolation which rapidly developed after the United States entered the war into that destroying effect of "aloneness," if I may so describe the opposite of mass consciousness. We never ceased to miss the unquestioning comradeship experienced by our fellow citizens during the war, nor to feel curiously outside the enchantment given to any human emotion when it is shared by millions of others. The force of the majority was so overwhelming that it seemed not only impossible to hold one's own against it, but at moments absolutely unnatural, and one secretly yearned to participate in "the folly of all mankind." Our modern democratic teaching has brought us to regard popular impulses as possessing in their general tendency a valuable capacity for evolutionary development. In the hours of doubt and self-distrust the question again and again arises, has the individual or a very small group, the right to stand out against millions of his fellow countrymen? Is there not a great value in mass judgment and in instinctive mass enthusiasm, and even if one were right a thousand times over in conviction, was he not absolutely wrong in abstaining from this communion with his fellows? The misunderstanding on the part of old friends and associates and the charge of lack of patriotism was far easier to bear than those dark periods of faint-heartedness. We gradually ceased to state our position as we became convinced that it served no practical purpose and, worse than that, often found that the immediate result was provocative.

We could not, however, lose the conviction that as all other forms of growth begin with a variation from the mass, so the moral changes in human affairs may also begin with a differing group or individual, sometimes with the one who at best is designated as a crank and a freak and in sterner moments is imprisoned as an atheist or a traitor. Just when the differing individual becomes the centro-egotist, the insane man, who must be thrown out by society for its own protection, it is impossible to state. The pacifist was constantly brought sharply up against a genuine human trait with its biological basis, a trait founded upon the instinct to dislike, to distrust and finally to destroy the individual who differs from the mass in time of danger. Regarding this trait as the basis of self-preservation it becomes perfectly natural for the mass to call such an individual a traitor and to insist that if he is not for the nation he is against it. To this an estimated nine million people can bear witness who have been burned as witches and heretics, not by mobs, for of the people who have been "lynched" no record has been kept, but by order of ecclesiastical and civil courts.

There were moments when the pacifist yielded to the suggestion that keeping himself out of war, refusing to take part in its enthusiasms, was but pure quietism, an acute failure to adjust himself to the moral world. Certainly nothing was clearer than that the individual will was helpless and irrelevant. We were constantly told by our friends that to stand aside from the war mood of the country was to surrender all possibility of future influence, that we were committing intellectual suicide, and would never again be trusted as responsible people or judicious advisers. Who were we to differ with able statesmen, with men of sensitive conscience who also absolutely abhorred war, but were convinced that this war for the preservation of democracy would make all future wars impossible, that the priceless values of civilization which were at stake could at this moment be saved only by war? But these very dogmatic statements spurred one to alarm. Was not war in the interest of democracy for the salvation of civilization a contradiction of terms, whoever said it or however often it was repeated?

Then, too, we were always afraid of fanaticism, of preferring a consistency of theory to the conscientious recognition of the social situation, of a failure to meet life in the temper of a practical person. Every student of our time had become more or less a disciple of pragmatism and its great teachers in the United States had come out for the war and defended their positions with skill and philosophic acumen. There were moments when one longed desperately for reconciliation with one's friends and fellow citizens; in the words of Amiel, "Not to remain at variance with existence but to reach that understanding of life which enables us at least to obtain forgiveness." Solitude has always had its demons, harder to withstand than the snares of the world, and the unnatural desert into which the pacifist was summarily cast out seemed to be peopled with them. We sorely missed the contagion of mental activity, for we are all much more dependent upon our social environment and daily newspaper than perhaps any of us realize. We also doubtless encountered, although subconsciously, the temptations described by John Stuart Mill: "In respect to the persons and affairs of their own day, men insensibly adopt the modes of feeling and judgment in which they can hope for sympathy from the company they keep."

The consciousness of spiritual alienation was lost only in moments of comradeship with the like minded, which may explain the tendency of the pacifist in war time to seek his intellectual kin, his spiritual friends, wherever they might be found in his own country or abroad.

It was inevitable that in many respects the peace cause should suffer in public opinion from the efforts of groups of people who, early in the war, were convinced that the country as a whole was for peace and who tried again and again to discover a method for arousing and formulating the sentiment against war. I was ill and out of Chicago when the People's Council held a national convention there, which was protected by the city police but threatened with dispersion by the state troops, who, however, arrived from the capital several hours after the meeting had adjourned. The incident was most sensational and no one was more surprised than many of the members of the People's Council who thus early in the war had supposed that they were conducting a perfectly legitimate convention. The incident gave tremendous "copy" in a city needing rationalizing rather than sensationalizing at that moment. There is no doubt that the shock and terror of the "anarchist riots" occurring in Chicago years ago have left their traces upon the nervous system of the city somewhat as a nervous shock experienced in youth will long afterwards determine the action of a mature man under widely different circumstances.

On the whole, the New York groups were much more active and throughout the war were allowed much more freedom both of assembly and press, although later a severe reaction followed expressed through the Lusk Committee and other agencies. Certainly neither city approximated the freedom of London and nothing surprised me more in 1915 and again in 1919 than the freedom of speech permitted there.

We also read with a curious eagerness the steadily increasing number of books published from time to time during the war, which brought a renewal of one's faith or at least a touch of comfort. These books broke through that twisting and suppressing of awkward truths, which was encouraged and at times even ordered by the censorship. Such manipulation of news and motives was doubtless necessary in the interest of war propaganda if the people were to be kept in a fighting mood. Perhaps the most vivid books came from France, early from Romain Rolland, later from Barbusse, although it was interesting to see how many people took the latter's burning indictment of war merely as a further incitement against the enemy. On the scientific side were the frequent writings of David Starr Jordan and the remarkable book of Nicolai on "The Biology of War." The latter enabled one, at least in one's own mind, to refute the pseudo-scientific statement that war was valuable in securing the survival of the fittest. Nicolai insisted that primitive man must necessarily have been a peaceful and social animal and that he developed his intelligence through the use of the tool, not through the use of the weapon; it was the primeval community which made the evolution of man possible, and coöperation among men is older and more primitive than mass combat which is an outgrowth of the much later property instinct. No other species save ants, who also possess property, fights in masses against other masses of its own kind. War is in fact not a natural process and not a struggle for existence in the evolutionary sense. He illustrated the evolutionary survival of the fittest by two tigers inhabiting the same jungle or feeding ground, the one who has the greater skill and strength as a hunter survives and the other starves, but the strong one does not go out to kill the weak one, as the war propagandist implied; or by two varieties of mice living in the same field or barn; in the biological struggle, the variety which grows a thicker coat survives the winter while the other variety freezes to extinction, but if one variety of mice should go forth to kill the other, it would be absolutely abnormal and quite outside the evolutionary survival which is based on the adjustment of the organism to its environment. George Nasmyth's book on Darwinism and the Social Order was another clear statement of the mental confusion responsible for the insistence that even a biological progress is secured through war. Mr. Brailsford wrote constantly on the economic results of the war and we got much comfort from John Hobson's "Toward International Government," which gave an authoritative account of the enormous amount of human activity actually carried on through international organizations of all sorts, many of them under governmental control. Lowes Dickenson's books, especially the spirited challenge in "The Choice Before Us," left his readers with the distinct impression that "war is not inevitable but proceeds from definite and removable causes." From every such book the pacifist was forced to the conclusion that none save those interested in the realization of an idea are in a position to bring it about and that if one found himself the unhappy possessor of an unpopular conviction, there was nothing for it but to think as clearly as he was able and be in a position to serve his country as soon as it was possible for him to do so.

But with or without the help of good books a hideous sensitiveness remained, for the pacifist, like the rest of the world, has developed a high degree of suggestibility, sharing that consciousness of the feelings, the opinions and the customs of his own social group which is said to be an inheritance from an almost pre-human past. An instinct which once enabled the man-pack to survive when it was a question of keeping together or of perishing off the face of the earth, is perhaps not underdeveloped in any of us. There is a distinct physical as well as moral strain when this instinct is steadily suppressed or at least ignored.

The large number of deaths among the older pacifists in all the warring nations can probably be traced in some measure to the peculiar strain which such maladjustment implies. More than the normal amount of nervous energy must be consumed in holding one's own in a hostile world. These older men, Kier

Hardie and Lord Courtney in England, Jenkin Lloyd Jones, Rauchenbusch, Washington Gladden in the United States, Lammasch and Fried in Austria, had been honored by their fellow citizens because of marked ability to interpret and understand them. Suddenly to find every public utterance wilfully misconstrued, every attempt at normal relationship repudiated, must react in a baffled suppression which is health-destroying even if we do not accept the mechanistic explanation of the human system. Certainly by the end of the war we were able to understand, although our group certainly did not endorse the statement of Cobden, one of the most convinced of all internationalists: "I made up my mind during the Crimean War that if ever I lived in the time of another great war of a similar kind between England and another power, I would not as a public man open my mouth on the subject, so convinced am I that appeals to reason, conscience or interest have no force whatever on parties engaged in war, and that exhaustion on one or both sides can alone bring a contest of physical force to an end."

On the other hand there were many times when we stubbornly asked ourselves, what after all, has maintained the human race on this old globe despite all the calamities of nature and all the tragic failings of mankind, if not faith in new possibilities, and courage to advocate them. Doubtless many times these new possibilities were declared by a man who, quite unconscious of courage, bore the "sense of being an exile, a condemned criminal, a fugitive from mankind." Did every one so feel who, in order to travel on his own proper path had been obliged to leave the traditional highway? The pacifist, during the period of the war could answer none of these questions but he was sick at heart from causes which to him were hidden and impossible to analyze. He was at times devoured by a veritable dissatisfaction with life. Was he thus bearing his share of blood-guiltiness, the morbid sense of contradiction and inexplicable suicide which modern war implies? We certainly had none of the internal contentment of the doctrinaire, the ineffable solace of the self-righteous which was imputed to us. No one knew better than we how feeble and futile we were against the impregnable weight of public opinion, the appalling imperviousness, the coagulation of motives, the universal confusion of a world at war. There was scant solace to be found in this type of statement: "The worth of every conviction consists precisely in the steadfastness with which it is held," perhaps because we suffered from the fact that we were no longer living in a period of dogma and were therefore in no position to announce our sense of security! We were well aware that the modern liberal having come to conceive truth of a kind which must vindicate itself in practice, finds it hard to hold even a sincere and mature opinion which from the very nature of things can have no justification in works. The pacifist in war time is literally starved of any gratification of that natural desire to have his own decisions justified by his fellows.

That, perhaps, was the crux of the situation. We slowly became aware that our affirmation was regarded as pure dogma. We were thrust into the position of the doctrinaire, and although, had we been permitted, we might have cited both historic and scientific tests of our so-called doctrine of Peace, for the moment any sanction even by way of illustration was impossible.

It therefore came about that ability to hold out against mass suggestion, to honestly differ from the convictions and enthusiasms of one's best friends did in moments of crisis come to depend upon the categorical belief that a man's primary allegiance is to his vision of the truth and that he is under obligation to affirm it.

REINHOLD NIEBUHR

The noted theologian and social critic Reinhold Niebuhr (1892–1971) makes an odd appearance in this anthology, given his famous critique of Gandhian nonviolence in *Moral Man and Immoral Society* (1932) and his condoning of obliteration bombing during World War II; he was, as James Loeb of Americans for Democratic Action said in 1948, "the leading liberal opponent of pacifism." But as a young man traveling in Europe after World War I he was seeing firsthand, and with fresh eyes, the consequences of war on the ground, and rejected them and their cause: "I am done," he wrote, "with the war business."

1923

In Europe

I HAVE been spending a few days with S—— and P—— in the Ruhr district. Flew back to London from Cologne by aeroplane. The Ruhr cities are the closest thing to hell I have ever seen. I never knew that you could see hatred with the naked eye, but in the Ruhr one is under the illusion that this is possible. The atmosphere is charged with it. The streets are filled with French soldiers in their grey-blue uniforms. Schools have been turned into barracks. Germans turn anxious and furtive glances upon every stranger. French officers race their automobiles wildly through the streets with sirens blowing shrilly. If you can gain the confidence of Germans so that they will talk they will tell you horrible tales of atrocities, deportations, sex crimes, etc. Imagination fired by fear and hatred undoubtedly tends to elaborate upon the sober facts. But the facts are bad enough.

When we arrived at Cologne after spending days in the French zone of occupation we felt as if we had come into a different world. The obvious reluctance of the British to make common cause with the French in the Ruhr adventure has accentuated the good will between the British troops and the native population. But a day in Cologne cannot erase the memory of Essen and Duesseldorf. It rests upon the mind like a horrible nightmare. One would like to send every sentimental spellbinder of war days into the Ruhr. This, then, is the glorious issue for which the war was fought! I didn't know Europe in 1914, but I can't imagine that the hatred between peoples could have been worse than it is now.

This is as good a time as any to make up my mind that I am done with the war business. Of course, I wasn't really in the last war. Would that I had been! Every soldier, fighting for his country in simplicity of heart without asking many questions, was superior to those of us who served no better purpose than to increase or perpetuate the moral obfuscation of nations. Of course, we really couldn't know everything we know now. But now we know. The times of man's ignorance God may wink at, but now he calls us all to repent. I am done with this business. I hope I can make that resolution stick.

Talking about the possibility of the church renouncing war, as we came over on the boat, one of the cynics suggested that the present temper of the church against war was prompted by nausea rather than idealism. He insisted that the church would not be able to prove for some time that it is really sincere in this matter. I suppose he is right; though I do not know that one ought to be contemptuous of any experience which leads to the truth. A pain in the stomach may sometimes serve an ultimate purpose quite as well as an idea in the head. Yet it is probably true that nausea finally wears off and the question will then be whether there is a more fundamental force which will maintain a conviction in defiance of popular hysteria.

For my own part I am not going to let my decision in regard to war stand alone. I am going to try to be a disciple of Christ, rather than a mere Christian, in all human relations and experiment with the potency of trust and love much more than I have in the past.

OLIVER WENDELL HOLMES JR.

It is common enough to find war resisters in the courtroom; many of the writers in this anthology have ended up there, sometimes pleading their case with memorable eloquence. But few have had the opportunity to be heard in the Supreme Court, largely because the government's power to wage war is broadly understood as unquestionable. What brought Rosika Schwimmer before the Court in 1929 was not the war power itself but a question of citizenship; Schwimmer had applied to become an American, but stated on her application that "she would not bear arms to defend the Constitution." A majority of the Supreme Court Justices affirmed a lower court decision that such a reservation was sufficient grounds to disqualify her. The younger Oliver Wendell Holmes (1841–1935), however, wrote a lively, unpretentious, and funny dissent in her favor, concluding with the reflection, "I had not supposed hitherto that we regretted our inability to expel [our citizens] because they believed more than some of us do in teachings of the Sermon on the Mount."

Holmes was eighty-eight when he wrote this dissent, with a distinguished career behind him: as soldier, scholar, lawyer, teacher of law, judge in Massachusetts (he wrote more than 1,400 opinions for the Massachusetts court), and from 1902 till 1932 as Justice of the Supreme Court. He supported the imprisonment of Eugene Debs for urging men to refuse the draft, but perhaps his experiences as a soldier in the Civil War gave him a sense of why a rational person might oppose warmaking generally, and be nonetheless a valued citizen of her community and nation.

(A longtime advocate of pacifist and feminist causes, Schwimmer lived to see the decision against her overturned, in *Girouard v. United States* in 1946. She nevertheless died a stateless person two years later, in New York City.)

Dissent in United States v. Schwimmer

THE applicant seems to be a woman of superior character and intelligence, obviously more than ordinarily desirable as a citizen of the United States. It is agreed that she is qualified for citizenship except so far as the views set forth in a statement of facts "may show that the applicant is not attached to the principles of the Constitution of the United States and well disposed to the good order and happiness of the same, and except in so far as the same may show that she cannot take the oath of allegiance without a mental reservation." The views referred to are an extreme opinion in favor of pacifism and a statement that she would not bear arms to defend the Constitution. So far as the adequacy of her oath is concerned I hardly can see how that is affected by the statement, inasmuch as she is a woman over fifty years of age, and would not be allowed to bear arms if she wanted to. And as to the opinion, the whole examination of the applicant shows that she holds none of the now-dreaded creeds but thoroughly believes in organized government and prefers that of the United States to any other in the world. Surely it cannot show lack of attachment to the principles of the Constitution that she thinks that it can be improved. I suppose that most intelligent people think that it might be. Her particular improvement looking to the abolition of war seems to me not materially different in its bearing on this case from a wish to establish cabinet government as in England, or a single house, or one term of seven years for the President. To touch a more burning question, only a judge mad with partisanship would exclude because the applicant thought that the Eighteenth Amendment should be repealed.

Of course the fear is that if a war came the applicant would exert activities such as were dealt with in *Schenck* v. *United States*, 249 U. S. 47. But that seems to me unfounded. Her position and motives are wholly different from those of Schenck. She is an optimist and states in strong and, I do not doubt, sincere words her belief that war will disappear and that the impending destiny of mankind is to unite in peaceful leagues. I do not share that optimism nor do I think that a philosophic view of the world would regard war as absurd. But most people who have known it regard it with horror, as a last resort, and even if not yet ready for cosmopolitan efforts, would welcome any practicable combinations that would increase the power on the side of peace. The notion that the applicant's optimistic anticipations would make her a worse citizen is sufficiently answered by her examination, which seems to me a better argument for her admission than any that I can offer. Some of her answers might excite popular prejudice, but if there is any principle of the Constitution that more imperatively calls for attachment than any other it is the principle of free thought—not free thought for those who agree with us but freedom for the thought that we hate. I think that we should adhere to that principle with regard to admission into, as well as to life within this country. And recurring to the opinion that bars this applicant's way, I would suggest that the Quakers have done their share to make the country what it is, that many citizens agree with the applicant's belief and that I had not supposed hitherto that we regretted our inability to expel them because they believe more than some of us do in the teachings of the Sermon on the Mount.

E. E. CUMMINGS

E. E. Cummings (1894–1962) is best known as a playfully, radically innovative poet, which he was. But he was also a politically engaged one. His first big published work was *The Enormous Room* (1922), an autobiographical novel about his imprisonment in a French World War I concentration camp; Cummings served in an ambulance corps, but then he and a friend also serving were accused of sedition because the friend's letters expressed pacifist views. Eventually he was released and sent home.

"i sing of Olaf" was first published in his collection *ViVa* in 1931, the same year in which Cummings made a six-week visit to the Soviet Union. It is the first obscene poem in the anthology, and the first avant-garde one, suggesting that the large modernist changes in form and decorum mattered even for politically engaged writing. The poem is also the first in the anthology to depict a war resister beaten to death and not just threatened with it.

"i sing of Olaf glad and big"

i sing of Olaf glad and big
whose warmest heart recoiled at war:
a conscientious object-or

his wellbelovéd colonel(trig
westpointer most succinctly bred)
took erring Olaf soon in hand;
but—though an host of overjoyed
noncoms(first knocking on the head
him)do through icy waters roll
that helplessness which others stroke
with brushes recently employed
anent this muddy toiletbowl,
while kindred intellects evoke
allegiance per blunt instruments—
Olaf(being to all intents
a corpse and wanting any rag
upon what God unto him gave)
responds, without getting annoyed
"I will not kiss your fucking flag"

straightway the silver bird looked grave
(departing hurriedly to shave)

but—though all kinds of officers
(a yearning nation's blueeyed pride)
their passive prey did kick and curse
until for wear their clarion
voices and boots were much the worse,
and egged the firstclassprivates on
his rectum wickedly to tease
by means of skilfully applied
bayonets roasted hot with heat—
Olaf(upon what were once knees)
does almost ceaselessly repeat
"there is some shit I will not eat"

our president,being of which
assertions duly notified
threw the yellowsonofabitch
into a dungeon,where he died

Christ(of His mercy infinite)
i pray to see;and Olaf,too

preponderatingly because
unless statistics lie he was
more brave than me:more blond than you.

FLOYD DELL

Unlike other war resisters brought to trial during World War I for conspiracy to obstruct the draft, Floyd Dell (1887–1969) was his own best chronicler; the present excerpt from his 1933 autobiography *Homecoming* shows him at his best as a writer, the account being full of texture and Dell having a precise, ironic, and ungrandiose sense of himself. No doubt he was like that in the courtroom as well, so it is no surprise that the charges against him and his codefendants were dropped after two successive trials resulted in hung juries.

Dell himself came from poverty and Illinois, became a journalist and man of letters in Chicago, moved to New York and helped edit *The Masses*, championed modernist literature though rejecting the experimentalists, worked with the Provincetown Players, wrote prolifically, and was a great success for a while. Later, as writers moved toward Marxism and the avant-garde, his successes were fewer. Appropriately enough, he found a job in 1935 writing for the Works Progress Administration; of the work he did for the WPA he later wrote, "I am still as proud of my governmental reports as of anything I have ever written."

On Trial

AT ten-thirty in the morning of April fifteenth, five of us—Max Eastman, Merrill Rogers, who was the business manager of the Masses, Art Young, Josephine Bell, a girl poet, and I—filed into one of the courtrooms on the third floor of the old Postoffice Building, which was used as a Federal Court, and took our places about a large table in the front enclosure. Ahead was a table at which sat three smiling men from the district attorney's office; up on the dais, behind a desk, sat a black-gowned judge, busy with some papers; to the right was a jury box with twelve empty chairs; and behind us, filling the room, was a venire of a hundred and fifty men, from whom a jury was presently to be selected, to try us on the charge of "conspiring to promote insubordination and mutiny in the military and naval forces of the United States, and to obstruct recruiting and enlistment to the injury of the service."

We rose to answer to our names, sat down, and the trial had begun. Our liberties to the extent of twenty years apiece, and our hypothetical fortunes to the extent of ten thousand dollars apiece, were now at stake. On the bench was Judge Augustus N. Hand, a rather slender and slightly grizzled man of reassuringly judicious and patient demeanor. In charge of the prosecution was Assistant District Attorney Earl B. Barnes, a thin and angular man with a perpetual sharp smile; it was apparent that he would send us to prison, if he could, in the most good-humored way possible, as a matter of duty, and with no personal grudge. He was assisted by two affable young men, Mr. Cobb and Mr. Rothwell. We were, after all, in New York City, where there were some elements of civilization left—not in the South, or in California. But ranged against us were the newspapers with their screaming headlines of Allied defeat, and the militant tunes of a Liberty Bond band in the park beneath the windows. On our side were certain constitutional rights of the press—which were being deliberately violated every day by the government. Our attorneys were Morris Hillquit, recently Socialist candidate for mayor of New York City, and Dudley Field Malone, who had resigned his position as Collector of the Port of New York as a protest against President Wilson's refusal to fulfill the Democratic party's pledge to give the vote to women.

The jury box filled up, and after questioning by defense and prosecution one man after another was excused. In the panel were real-estate agents, retired capitalists, bankers, managers, foremen and salesmen—never a wage-worker. It was composed almost entirely of old men. The prospective jurors frankly admitted extreme prejudice against Socialists, pacifists and conscientious objectors, though it was usually ready to assent cheerfully to the prosecuting attorney's suggestion that these prejudices were not such as would stand in the way of an impartial consideration of the evidence.

It is hard to tell what a man is like from a few brief answers to a few questions. It was a species of lightning guess-work to decide what kind of mind and heart and conscience a prospective juror had—what malevolent prejudices, what weak susceptibilities to popular emotions, what impenetrable stupidities might lurk behind those unrevealing, brief replies. "Are you prejudiced?" "Yes." "Can you set aside that prejudice?" "Yes." These might be the replies of a fool or a coward or a liar; or they might be the replies of an honest man, open to conviction of the truth, and steadfast as a rock in maintaining that truth against all opposition. We had to gamble on our impressions of character, and choose irrevocably.

The jury was finally selected in the course of two days. The judge quashed one count of the indictment, leaving us now charged only with conspiracy to obstruct recruiting or enlisting; but we could still be given twenty years in prison for that. And the girl-poet, Josephine Bell, was let go.

The case thereupon went to the jury, and somewhat to our surprise a great deal of time was taken up in establishing beyond the peradventure of a doubt, by the testimony of office boys and printers, that such a magazine as ours really existed. Then, much more interesting, there was presented to the jury the evidence against us, in the form of editorials, jokes, pictures, and poems which we had printed. It took a long time to read everything we had written—a whole day. I felt a certain pride as an author in having my own writings, among others, thus treated as matters of social and political importance; and I reflected that even if during the rest of my literary career my work should receive no other public testimonial, I should never complain that it had been permitted to languish neglected. There are different ways in which the State may encourage its young writers; if this present ceremonial was open to criticism from some points of view, yet it could not be said that it was lacking in impressiveness. And if this were not exactly a wreath of laurel that had been handed me, yet I wore it as proudly.

Among my writings, one particular paragraph had been cited in the indictment as an "overt act" in violation of the Espionage law. This passage, constituting an introduction to a brief account of the tortures inflicted on British conscientious objectors, was read to the jury: "There are some laws that the individual feels he cannot obey, and he will suffer any punishment, even that of death, rather than recognize them as having authority over him. This fundamental stubbornness of the free soul, against which all the powers of the State are helpless, constitutes a conscientious objection, whatever its sources may be in political or social opinion."

So it was, I reflected, a tribute to courage which had brought me into court! I had not ceased, at the proper moment, to admire a certain "stubbornness of the free soul." Or, admiring it if I must, I had not duly reflected that the time was inopportune for utterance of the disturbing truth that against such heroic stubbornness all the powers of the State are helpless! A fault of taste, perhaps; but I had observed that all times are inopportune for the utterance of truth. Truth is always in bad taste. . . . Meanwhile, our legal defenders addressed the jury, pointing out that these "overt acts" constituted simply a lawful exercise of the constitutional right of free expression of opinion.

In turn, then, we the defendants took the stand and explained our views. And I felt that the jurors, who looked and listened so intently hour after hour while we were testifying, were having a spiritual adventure as gratifying as it was doubtless unique in their experience. Busy men all their lives, too tired perhaps at the end of the day's getting and spending ever to explore for themselves the realms of economic and social thought, they were now given by an odd chance an opportunity to view some fascinating landscapes of thought. And though they might in the end, reminded of their duty by a tune outside the window, decide that we were dangerous men and send us off to prison, still this would be a thing to remember. . . .

I did not fail to recognize why it was that we were thus permitted to entertain the jury with reasoned and eloquent discourse. I had observed in certain other war-time trials that the defendants were not treated with such courteous consideration. No, for in these war-time trials the defendants were often both poor and of foreign origin—and as such not entitled by American custom to the civilities which we reserve for our peers. These "foreigners" were here to do our dirty work and take our orders, with no right to criticize. But we, as it appeared, were American-born and bred, obviously well-educated, belonging by prescriptive right among those who give rather than among those who take orders; and if we were found on the "wrong" side of such a controversy, along with discontented foreign-born workers, it would naturally be inquired how the devil we came to be there, and our reply would meet with a respectful, if puzzled, hearing. In our case, the mention of constitutional rights could not be met with the judicial sneer which is accorded to those who mention such rights with a foreign accent; it was "our" constitution, and we had a right to talk about it. We did not wave our hands when we started to explain ourselves, nor were we shabby; and so we were not interrupted by an impatient judge.

Art Young had been busy all through the trial drawing humorous pictures of the judge, the jury, the witnesses, the court attendants. But once he fell asleep. "For heaven's sake, wake him up and give him a pencil," whispered one of our attorneys. For there is an etiquette of the court-room. It is discourteous to show weariness or boredom while being tried. One may not smoke, or read, or whisper much, or laugh at all. And this, to such as have not yet got used to it, is one of the serious hardships of being on trial.

I was told to take the stand, and I did so with pleasure. It was not only an agreeable break in the routine, but a chance to speak after an enforced silence that had lasted for days. Moreover, here was a perfect audience. The government does not do things by halves: it had provided a carefully selected group of men for me to talk to; others might tire and go away, but they had to sit there and listen to me. Under such circumstances, it was easy to explain what I thought about war, militarism, conscientious objectors, and other related subjects.

Also, I found in cross-examination the distinct excitement of a primitive sort of game of wits. The method of conducting a discussion in a court-room is faintly suggestive of a Socratic dialogue. And though your questioner stands twenty feet away, and you are speaking up so the jury can hear, you lose all sense of any presence save that of your interlocutor. You are surprised when, at some interruption from outside that magic circle of question and answer, you discover yourself in a court-room full of people. It is a strange, stimulating, and—or so I found it—an agreeable experience.

All this discussion of our various opinions on almost every conceivable political topic had extended the trial into its second week. On the ninth day, the attorneys for both sides summed up. The district attorney most surprisingly paid us all compliments in asking the jury to convict us. "These men," he said, "are men of extraordinary intelligence." And me in particular he characterized thus: "Dell, a trained journalist, a writer of exquisite English, keenly ironical, bitingly sarcastic." Thank you, Mr. Barnes! "And so, gentlemen of the jury," he concluded, "I confidently expect you to bring in a verdict of guilty against each and every one of the defendants."

The jury, being duly charged, retired late that afternoon. And we awaited the verdict. We thought a good deal about those jurors as we walked up and down the corridors, smoking and talking with our friends, through the long hours that passed so slowly thereafter. A defendant cannot sit for days in the same room with twelve jurymen without getting to some extent acquainted with them, and feeling that they are for or against him. . . .

But that, after all, was mere guessing. How could we be sure that the man we thought most hostile might not turn out to be our best friend?—perhaps our only friend! And of those who were for us, how could we be certain that they had the courage to hold out? Some friend experienced in the ways of juries would take our arm and whisper: "Expect anything." From behind the heavy door of the jury-room came sounds of excited argument. . . .

Art Young took me aside and asked me quietly: "Floyd, when you were a little boy did you ever read any books about the Nihilists?" "Yes," I said. "And did you think that maybe some day you might have to go to prison for something you believed?" "Yes," I said. "Then it's all right," said Art Young, "no matter what happens." And I was glad to know that Art Young was spiritually ready to go to prison.

I realized that I had never been more serene and at ease in my whole life than during the nine days of this trial. I had been curiously happy. It might be unreasonable, but it was so. And one who is being psychoanalyzed is not surprised to find his emotions unreasonable.

While we waited, I began to ponder for myself the question which the jury had retired to decide. Were we innocent or guilty? We certainly hadn't "conspired" to do anything. But what had we tried to do? Defiantly tell the truth. For what purpose? To keep some truth alive in a world full of lies. And what was the good of that? I didn't know. But I was glad I had taken part in that act of defiant truth-telling.

The jury could be heard noisily arguing about us—or about something.

After dinner we returned, with a few friends, and bivouacked in the dim corridor, waiting. Late that night the judge was sent for, and we went eagerly into the court-room. The jury filed in. Had they brought in a verdict? No; they desired further instructions.

The judge then repeated a definition of "conspiracy" which no one but a lawyer would pretend to understand, and the jury went back. And already the inevitable rumors began to percolate. "Six to six."

Six to six! The struggle of contending views of life had ceased in the court-room, and been taken up by the jury. Other protagonists and antagonists, whose exact identity was unknown to us, were fighting the thing out in that little room. The debate had not ended, it had merely changed its place and personnel. . . . And then we remembered that our fate was involved in that debate; and we felt a warm rush of emotion, of gratitude toward these unknown defenders who had made our cause their own.

Next morning the debate in the jury-room grew fiercer, noisier. At noon the jury came in, hot, weary, angry, limp, and exhausted. They had fought the case amongst themselves for eleven vehement hours. And they could not agree upon a verdict.

But the judge refused to discharge them; and they went back, after further instructions, with grim determination on their faces.

And again we wandered about the corridors—all day; and returned in the evening to camp outside the court-room. . . . Then, in the unlighted windows of the skyscraper opposite, we discovered a dim and ghostly reflection of the interior of the jury-room. Men were standing up and sitting down, four and five at a time. A vote? Someone raised his arm. Someone strode across the room. Someone took off his coat. I stood at our window and watched . . . and then went away. I had waited for twenty-nine hours. I could wonder no more. The whole thing seemed as dim and unreal as that ghostly reflection in the window. I thought about stars and flowers and ideas and my sweetheart. . . .

At eleven o'clock the jurors reported continued disagreement, but were sent back.

The next noon, hopelessly deadlocked, the jury was discharged, with all our thanks. And so we were free.

EDNA ST. VINCENT MILLAY

Edna St. Vincent Millay (1892–1950), often read as a timelessly grace-ful lyric poet, was also drawn to political themes: injustice, violence, human depravity, principled resistance. In 1920 she published *Aria Da Capo*, one of the few distinguished antiwar plays; she was engaged as citizen and writer in the movement in the 1920s to free the Italian anarchists Nicola Sacco and Bartolomeo Vanzetti. "Conscientious Objector," published in 1934 and still read aloud at gatherings of the antiwar left, is a poem in praise of war resistance, though not of a single resister (even an invented one, like Cummings's Olaf). Instead, it celebrates the refusal to aid and abet violence of many sorts, linking the cause of the wartime CO with other causes.

Millay grew up in Maine, went to Vassar, came to New York, met everyone, flourished, won the Pulitzer Prize in 1923. Like Dell and Dorothy Day she worked with the Provincetown Players. Like a good many others, she found herself turning away, as World War II loomed and began and continued, from her earlier leftist and pacifist com-mitments, and became a passionate if not always poetically successful supporter of the Allied war effort.

Conscientious Objector

I shall die, but that is all that I shall do for Death.

I hear him leading his horse out of the stall; I hear the
    clatter on the barn-floor.
He is in haste; he has business in Cuba, business in the
    Balkans, many calls to make this morning.
But I will not hold the bridle while he cinches the girth.
And he may mount by himself: I will not give him a leg
    up.

Though he flick my shoulders with his whip, I will not
    tell him which way the fox ran.
With his hoof on my breast, I will not tell him where the
    black boy hides in the swamp.
I shall die, but that is all that I shall do for Death; I am
    not on his pay-roll.

I will not tell him the whereabouts of my friends nor of
    my enemies either.
Though he promise me much, I will not map him the
    route to any man's door.
Am I a spy in the land of the living, that I should deliver
    men to Death?
Brother, the password and the plans of our city are safe
    with me; never through me
Shall you be overcome.

DALTON TRUMBO

Dalton Trumbo (1905–1976) is usually remembered as a screen-writer, and above all as one of the Hollywood Ten, those who in 1947 were blacklisted in Hollywood for their refusal to cooperate with the House Un-American Activities Committee's investigation of Communist influence in the motion picture industry. *Johnny Got His Gun* (1939) was written earlier, when Trumbo was as much a novel-ist as anything else; it won him a National Book Award. The novel begins as antiwar parody—"Johnny Get Your Gun" is a phrase sung unironically in George M. Cohan's "Over There," an exhortation to young American men to join the army and fight in World War I. It is World War I that Trumbo's narrator and protagonist Joe Bonham goes to fight in, and there in battle he loses arms, legs, eyes, ears, and tongue. (Trumbo had read of a visit paid by Edward, Prince of Wales, to a soldier in a similar condition.) The novel tells us what we cannot know, i.e., Joe's thoughts—from the moment of his waking to realize his condition till the book's end. Much of it looks back on Joe's childhood, beautifully based on Trumbo's own, and it is rarely dogmatic in its opposition to war. But sometimes Joe's thoughts rise to anger and opposition, as in the passage included here.

Trumbo himself was working on screenplays for war movies at the same time as he was writing the novel. After Pearl Harbor he arranged with his publisher to keep the novel out of circulation until after the war had ended. When isolationist, often anti-Semitic readers wrote him to praise the novel's antiwar message, he reported them to the FBI. In 1971, just five years before his death and in the middle of another war, Trumbo made a film of the novel, less pure in form than the novel itself and surprisingly ungraphic but still emotionally harrowing.

FROM

Johnny Got His Gun

LYING on your back without anything to do and anywhere to go was kind of like being on a high hill far away from noise and people. It was like being on a camping trip all by yourself. You had plenty of time to think. You had time to figure things out. Things you'd never thought of before. Things like for example going to war. You were so completely alone on your hill that noise and people didn't enter into your figuring of things at all.

You figured only for yourself without considering a single little thing outside yourself. It seemed that you thought clearer and that your answers made more sense. And even if they didn't make sense it didn't matter because you weren't ever going to be able to do anything about them anyhow.

He thought here you are Joe Bonham lying like a side of beef all the rest of your life and for what? Somebody tapped you on the shoulder and said come along son we're going to war. So you went. But why? In any other deal even like buying a car or running an errand you had the right to say what's there in it for me? Otherwise you'd be buying bad cars for too much money or running errands for fools and starving to death. It was a kind of duty you owed yourself that when anybody said come on son do this or do that you should stand up and say look mister why should I do this for who am I doing it and what am I going to get out of it in the end? But when a guy comes along and says here come with me and risk your life and maybe die or be crippled why then you've got no rights. You haven't even the right to say yes or no or I'll think it over. There are plenty of laws to protect guys' money even in war time but there's nothing on the books says a man's life's his own.

Of course a lot of guys were ashamed. Somebody said let's go out and fight for liberty and so they went and got killed without ever once thinking about liberty. And what kind of liberty were they fighting for anyway? How much liberty and whose idea of liberty? Were they fighting for the liberty of eating free ice cream cones all their lives or for the liberty of robbing anybody they pleased whenever they wanted to or what? You tell a man he can't rob and you take away some of his liberty. You've got to. What the hell does liberty mean anyhow? It's just a word like house or table or any other word. Only it's a special kind of word. A guy says house and he can point to a house to prove it. But a guy says come on let's fight for liberty and he can't show you liberty. He can't prove the thing he's talking about so how in the hell can he be telling you to fight for it?

No sir anybody who went out and got into the front line trenches to fight for liberty was a goddam fool and the guy who got him there was a liar. Next time anybody came gabbling to him about liberty—what did he mean next time? There wasn't going to be any next time for him. But the hell with that. If there could be a next time and somebody said let's fight for liberty he would say mister my life is important. I'm not a fool and when I swap my life for liberty I've got to know in advance what liberty is and whose idea of liberty we're talking about and just how much of that liberty we're going to have. And what's more mister are you as much interested in this liberty as you want me to be? And maybe too much liberty will be as bad as too little liberty and I think you're a goddam fourflusher talking through your hat and I've already decided that I like the liberty I've got right here the liberty to walk and see and hear and talk and eat and sleep with my girl. I think I like that liberty better than fighting for a lot of things we won't get and ending up without any liberty at all. Ending up dead and rotting before my life is even begun good or ending up like a side of beef. Thank you mister. You fight for liberty. Me I don't care for some.

Hell's fire guys had always been fighting for liberty. America fought a war for liberty in 1776. Lots of guys died. And in the end does America have any more liberty than Canada or Australia who didn't fight at all? Maybe so I'm not arguing I'm just asking. Can you look at a guy and say he's an American who fought for his liberty and anybody can see he's a very different guy from a Canadian who didn't? No by god you can't and that's that. So maybe a lot of guys with wives and kids died in 1776 when they didn't need to die at all. They're dead now anyway. Sure but that doesn't do any good. A guy can think of being dead a hundred years from now and he doesn't mind it. But to think of being dead tomorrow morning and to be dead forever to be nothing but dust and stink in the earth is that liberty?

They were always fighting for something the bastards and if anyone dared say the hell with fighting it's all the same each war is like the other and nobody gets any good out of it why they hollered coward. If they weren't fighting for liberty they were fighting for independence or democracy or freedom or decency or honor or their native land or something else that didn't mean anything. The war was to make the world safe for democracy for the little countries for everybody. If the war was over now then the world must be all safe for democracy. Was it? And what kind of democracy? And how much? And whose?

Then there was this freedom the little guys were always getting killed for. Was it freedom from another country? Freedom from work or disease or death? Freedom from your mother-in-law? Please mister give us a bill of sale on this freedom before we go out and get killed. Give us a bill of sale drawn up plainly so we know in advance what we're getting killed for and give us also a first mortgage on something as security so we can be sure after we've won your war that we've got the same kind of freedom we bargained for.

And take decency. Everybody said America was fighting a war for the triumph of decency. But whose idea of decency? And decency for who? Speak up and tell us what decency is. Tell us how much better a decent dead man feels than an indecent live one. Make a comparison there in facts like houses and tables. Make it in words we can understand. And don't talk about honor. The honor of a Chinese or an Englishman or an African negro or an American or a Mexican? Please all you guys who want to fight to preserve our honor let us know what the hell honor is. Is it American honor for the whole world we're fighting for? Maybe the world doesn't like it. Maybe the South Sea Islanders like their honor better.

For Christ sake give us things to fight for we can see and feel and pin down and understand. No more highfalutin words that mean nothing like native land. Motherland fatherland homeland native land. It's all the same. What the hell good to you is your native land after you're dead? Whose native land is it after you're dead? If you get killed fighting for your native land you've bought a pig in a poke. You've paid for something you'll never collect.

And when they couldn't hook the little guys into fighting for liberty or freedom or democracy or independence or decency or honor they tried the women. Look at the dirty Huns they would say look at them how they rape the beautiful French and Belgian girls. Somebody's got to stop all that raping. So come on little guy join the army and save the beautiful French and Belgian girls. So the little guy got bewildered and he signed up and in a little while a shell hit him and his life spattered out of him in red meat pulp and he was dead. Dead for another word and all the fierce old bats of the D.A.R. get out and hurrah themselves hoarse over his grave because he died for womanhood.

Now it might be that a guy would risk getting killed if his women were being raped. But if he did why he was only striking a bargain. He was simply saying that according to the way he felt at the time the safety of his women was worth more than his own life. But there wasn't anything particularly noble or heroic about it. It was a straight deal his life for something he valued more. It was more or less like any other deal a man might make. But when you change your women to all the women in the world why you begin to defend women in the bulk. To do that you have to fight in the bulk. And by that time you're fighting for a word again.

When armies begin to move and flags wave and slogans pop up watch out little guy because it's somebody else's chestnuts in the fire not yours. It's words you're fighting for and you're not making an honest deal your life for something better. You're being noble and after you're killed the thing you traded your life for won't do you any good and chances are it won't do anybody else any good either.

Maybe that's a bad way to think. There are lots of idealists around who will say have we got so low that nothing is more precious than life? Surely there are ideals worth fighting for even dying for. If not then we are worse than the beasts of the field and have sunk into barbarity. Then you say that's all right let's be barbarous just so long as we don't have war. You keep your ideals just as long as they don't cost me my life. And they say but surely life isn't as important as principle. Then you say oh no? Maybe not yours but mine is. What the hell is principle? Name it and you can have it.

You can always hear the people who are willing to sacrifice somebody else's life. They're plenty loud and they talk all the time. You can find them in churches and schools and newspapers and legislatures and congresses. That's their business. They sound wonderful. Death before dishonor. This ground sanctified by blood. These men who died so gloriously. They shall not have died in vain. Our noble dead.

Hmmmm.

But what do the dead say?

Did anybody ever come back from the dead any single one of the millions who got killed did any one of them ever come back and say by god I'm glad I'm dead because death is always better than dishonor? Did they say I'm glad I died to make the world safe for democracy? Did they say I like death better than losing liberty? Did any of them ever say it's good to think I got my guts blown out for the honor of my country? Did any of them ever say look at me I'm dead but I died for decency and that's better than being alive? Did any of them ever say here I am I've been rotting for two years in a foreign grave but it's wonderful to die for your native land? Did any of them say hurray I died for womanhood and I'm happy see how I sing even though my mouth is choked with worms?

Nobody but the dead know whether all these things people talk about are worth dying for or not. And the dead can't talk. So the words about noble deaths and sacred blood and honor and such are all put into dead lips by grave robbers and fakes who have no right to speak for the dead. If a man says death before dishonor he is either a fool or a liar because he doesn't know what death is. He isn't able to judge. He only knows about living. He doesn't know anything about dying. If he is a fool and believes in death before dishonor let him go ahead and die. But all the little guys who are too busy to fight should be left alone. And all the guys who say death before dishonor is pure bull the important thing is life before death they should be left alone too. Because the guys who say life isn't worth living without some principle so important you're willing to die for it they are all nuts. And the guys who say you'll see there'll come a time you can't escape you're going to have to fight and die because it'll mean your very life why they are also nuts. They are talking like fools. They are saying that two and two make nothing. They are saying that a man will have to die in order to protect his life. If you agree to fight you agree to die. Now if you die to protect your life you aren't alive anyhow so how is there any sense in a thing like that? A man doesn't say I will starve myself to death to keep from starving. He doesn't say I will spend all my money in order to save my money. He doesn't say I will burn my house down in order to keep it from burning. Why then should he be willing to die for the privilege of living? There ought to be at least as much common sense about living and dying as there is about going to the grocery store and buying a loaf of bread.

And all the guys who died all the five million or seven million or ten million who went out and died to make the world safe for democracy to make the world safe for words without meaning how did they feel about it just before they died? How did they feel as they watched their blood pump out into the mud? How did they feel when the gas hit their lungs and began eating them all away? How did they feel as they lay crazed in hospitals and looked death straight in the face and saw him come and take them? If the thing they were fighting for was important enough to die for then it was also important enough for them to be thinking about it in the last minutes of their lives. That stood to reason. Life is awfully important so if you've given it away you'd ought to think with all your mind in the last moments of your life about the thing you traded it for. So did all those kids die thinking of democracy and freedom and liberty and honor and the safety of the home and the stars and stripes forever?

You're goddam right they didn't.

They died crying in their minds like little babies. They forgot the thing they were fighting for the thing they were dying for. They thought about things a man can understand. They died yearning for the face of a friend. They died whimpering for the voice of a mother a father a wife a child. They died with their hearts sick for one more look at the place where they were born please god just one more look. They died moaning and sighing for life. They knew what was important. They knew that life was everything and they died with screams and sobs. They died with only one thought in their minds and that was I want to live I want to live I want to live.

He ought to know.

He was the nearest thing to a dead man on earth.

He was a dead man with a mind that could still think. He knew all the answers that the dead knew and couldn't think about. He could speak for the dead because he was one of them. He was the first of all the soldiers who had died since the beginning of time who still had a brain left to think with. Nobody could dispute with him. Nobody could prove him wrong. Because nobody knew but he.

He could tell all these high-talking murdering sonsofbitches who screamed for blood just how wrong they were. He could tell them mister there's nothing worth dying for I know because I'm dead. There's no word worth your life. I would rather work in a coal mine deep under the earth and never see sunlight and eat crusts and water and work twenty hours a day. I would rather do that than be dead. I would trade democracy for life. I would trade independence and honor and freedom and decency for life. I will give you all these things and you give me the power to walk and see and hear and breathe the air and taste my food. You take the words. Give me back my life. I'm not asking for a happy life now. I'm not asking for a decent life or an honorable life or a free life. I'm beyond that. I'm dead so I'm simply asking for life. To live. To feel. To be something that moves over the ground and isn't dead. I know what death is and all you people who talk about dying for words don't even know what life is.

There's nothing noble about dying. Not even if you die for honor. Not even if you die the greatest hero the world ever saw. Not even if you're so great your name will never be forgotten and who's that great? The most important thing is your life little guys. You're worth nothing dead except for speeches. Don't let them kid you any more. Pay no attention when they tap you on the shoulder and say come along we've got to fight for liberty or whatever their word is there's always a word.

Just say mister I'm sorry I got no time to die I'm too busy and then turn and run like hell. If they say coward why don't pay any attention because it's your job to live not to die. If they talk about dying for principles that are bigger than life you say mister you're a liar. Nothing is bigger than life. There's nothing noble in death. What's noble about lying in the ground and rotting? What's noble about never seeing the sunshine again? What's noble about having your legs and arms blown off? What's noble about being an idiot? What's noble about being blind and deaf and dumb? What's noble about being dead? Because when you're dead mister it's all over. It's the end. You're less than a dog less than a rat less than a bee or an ant less than a little white maggot crawling around on a dungheap. You're dead mister and you died for nothing.

You're dead mister.

Dead.

WILLIAM EVERSON

World War II was so broadly supported, so broadly perceived as just and necessary, that it is easy to forget those who said no to it: jailed COs like David Dellinger, Lowell Naeve, Robert Lowell, and Bayard Rustin, and those like William Stafford and William Everson (1912–1994) who did alternative service in civilian camps. How strange the experiences of these last must have been, not fighting, not resisting, doing useful but somehow irrelevant ordinary work in the woods! Everson's elegy gives us a glimpse of that life in the community of Camp Angel, a community both contingent and intentional.

Everson was born in Sacramento to Christian Scientist parents, both printers. He was led to become a poet by reading Robinson Jeffers; "Jeffers showed me God," he later wrote. He was sent to Camp Angel, on the coast of Oregon, in 1943, and in his free time—after the day's hard labor—he printed *Ten War Elegies* on the camp's makeshift press and ran a fine arts program. After the war he migrated to San Francisco and the circle of Kenneth Rexroth. In 1951 he became Catholic, worked at the Catholic Worker House in Oakland, and joined the Dominican Order, taking the name Brother Antoninus (and the nickname "the Beat Friar"). He left that order in 1969, marrying a week later and becoming poet-in-residence at the University of California, Santa Cruz.

War Elegy X

(THE INTERNMENT, WALDPORT, OREGON; JANUARY 1943)

To sunder the rock—that is our day.
In the weak light,
Under high fractured cliffs
We turn with our hands the raw granite,
We break it with iron.
Under that edge it suffers reduction.
Harsh, dense and resistant,
The obdurate portions
Flaw and divide.

From the road in the dawns we behold the sea,
In its prone slumber,

Holding the west with heavy ease.
The rock closes it out,
Narrows our sky,
In the morning thaws lets fall its sparse rubble.
We wait, suspended in time;
Locked out of our lives
We abide, we endure,
Our temporal grievance diminished and slight
In the total awareness of what obtains,
Outside, in the bone-broken world.
Confronting encroachment the mind toughens and grows.
From this exigence
Both purpose and faith achieve coherence:
Such is our gain.
We perceive our place in the terrible pattern,
And temper with pity the fierce gall,
Hearing the sadness,
The loss and the utter desolation,
Howl at the heart of the world.

LOWELL NAEVE

Raised in Sioux City, Iowa, Lowell Naeve (1917–2014) left home a year or so after high school, traveling to Los Angeles, Mexico City, and finally New York, and picking up odd jobs along the way to pay for art classes. In New York he met his future wife Virginia Paccassi, also an aspiring artist, and ran into trouble with his draft board. A free spirit prompted by personal conscience rather than any particular faith or ideology, he was deeply opposed to military conscription, and so spent most of 1941–46 behind bars: first in New York's West Street Detention Center, then in Danbury Federal Penitentiary, then back again in both prisons. *A Field of Broken Stones* (1950), his illustrated memoir of these years, was smuggled out of the latter institution in a hollow picture frame.

In the short excerpt reprinted below, Naeve describes a typical day in West Street—where one fellow prisoner was the gangster Louis "Lepke" Buchalter—around June 1941. The small act of resistance to authority it describes was the first of many. (It was probably Naeve—and not the "fire-breathing Catholic C.O." Robert Lowell, as has usually been reported—who responded to Lepke's question "I'm in for killing. What are you in for?" with a line now legendary in the antiwar community: "Oh, I'm in for refusing to kill.")

After his release, Naeve worked as a woodcut artist, art teacher, and filmmaker, and owned a dog kennel; he published a collection of drawings, *Phantasies of a Prisoner*, in 1958. In 1965 he emigrated to Canada with his family, encouraging Vietnam-era "draft dodgers" to follow him rather than suffer in prison as he had. He died in Creston, British Columbia, at the age of ninety-seven.

FROM

A Field of Broken Stones

THE day in West Street began, it seemed to me, when I came up from work in the officers' mess. It would be about ten in the morning. I'd see Hymie Weiss, one of Lepke's partners in Murder, Inc., enter the elevator with an escort of four guards. There was a desperateness about the way they would get the elevator all ready, take him out of his cage, put him on the elevator, and take him to the roof for exercise.

Weiss would be up on the roof for an hour, then they'd bring him back. After they had locked him up, they'd get the elevator ready again, escort the big boss Lepke out, take him to the roof for an hour. And so it went every day. . . .

The rest of us were given an hour and a half of exercise together. The "roof" of West Street was very small, about seventy-five by twenty-five feet. It was caged up on the sides and top with heavy steel mesh. Inside of the cage we took our exercise. Beside the exercise enclosure was an open part of the roof. On this stood a short guard-tower with steps leading up to it. Between the tower and the cage was a wooden boardwalk. When not in the tower, the guard sometimes stood on the boardwalk. He carried a machine-gun.

Inside the cage there were two ping-pong tables, a shuffle-board court, etc., but there was little room to do anything. Most of the men just sat, lifted their faces to the sun, and talked; some paced up and down, worried about their coming trials.

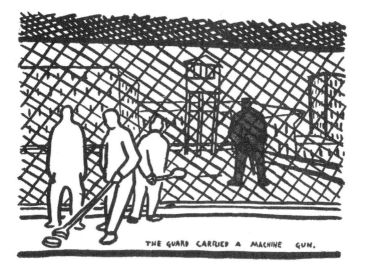

THE GUARD CARRIED A MACHINE GUN.

After exercise period I had to go to work in the officers' mess again.

. . . While working in the officers' mess, waiting on the warden, the captain, and the guards, I became disgusted with myself for submitting to being ordered around. I did not like the idea of being forced to do things I didn't want to do. But I said nothing, I only did like everyone else, kept still, grumbled to myself.

On the fourth day, to bolster my sinking morale, I decided to practice a little "equality." I picked up a piece of Officer Pie, took a glass of Officer Milk, and just outside the officers' mess, in full view, began to drink the milk and eat the pie.

The night captain, a large surly-tongued individual about to receive his pension, was standing nearby. He watched me raise the pie to my mouth. He looked at the pie, looked a little more—Christ, what a big piece! He was about to yell. He couldn't accuse me of stealing. I turned slowly to look at him, then returned to eating the pie. He paused, half turned, hesitated again, then strode down the passageway.

After supper, when work was over in the officers' mess, I would go up to my cell block and talk with some of the other prisoners, or draw on some typing paper I had managed to obtain.

After the guards took the ten o'clock count and turned out the lights, I would frequently stay up, talk to the other prisoners. It being June, the jail was usually so hot we couldn't get to sleep till after midnight.

The conversations in our cell block centered around a fellow named Bard—he was a shakedown artist, broad-shouldered—a short Charles Atlas. In the cell block were two or three others who had made a living off of "this dame" and "that dame."

"I was in Atlantic City," one would say, "and I met this rich broad. . . . I'm telling you, man, this woman was a bitch, really a bitch." And then he'd tell his story. . . . After he had finished, another would tell about a "broad" in St. Louis. He would, so he'd say, do this and that to her—"What a lay!" . . . Bard hardly ever spoke, but it all centered around him. The lesser shakedown artists looked up to him; it was rumored he was married to a burlesque queen. The others thought he knew all the tricks. All hung around, hoping he would let them in on some new secret.

There was talk till the place cooled off a little, then we went to our bunks.

At night, the bars were most impressive. By day West Street Jail was, more than anything else, a pressing din, a place of perpetual noise. The sounds of the place were dominated by the loudspeakers above us. They all blatted out the same tunes. Occasionally a microphone announcement from the "front desk" broke into the barrage of music.

Within the din could be heard the swishing of mops, the sliding of mop buckets, the sound of steel gates slamming shut, the sound of keys turning locks. We could hear guards barking out orders, their many keys going clink clink clink as they walked along.

But above it all—grind-ing-ly blar-ing-ly—the loudspeakers droned on. They dominated the place, smothered to a hum all other sounds.

ROBERT LOWELL

Robert Lowell (1917–1977) was already a prominent poet when he wrote to President Roosevelt in September 1943 to announce his refusal to serve in World War II. (That he wrote directly to the president, rather than to his draft board, reflects his other prominence as well, that of the descendant of a family of Boston aristocrats.) Like David Dellinger, Lowell Naeve, and others he was put in prison for his action, in the same prisons in fact. Unlike them, however, he held back from entanglements with the prison pacifist community. "Memories of West Street and Lepke" (1959), his later poetic reflection on his prison time, is critical of his earlier "manic" self and of the other pacifists in the jail, whom he clearly finds less interesting than the murderous gangster Louis "Lepke" Buchalter.

Along the way to becoming America's leading public poet Lowell had a number of other encounters with antiwar communities and actions; in October 1967, for instance, he read "Waking Early Sunday Morning" at a rally before the March on the Pentagon. But he was always ambivalent about the peace movement, and sought no fellowship with other objectors, even as he personally opposed the proliferation of nuclear weapons and the war in Vietnam.

Letter to President Roosevelt

September 7, 1943

DEAR Mr. President:

I very much regret that I must refuse the opportunity you offer me in your communication of August 6, 1943, for service in the Armed Forces.

I am enclosing with this letter a copy of the declaration which, in accordance with military regulations, I am presenting on September 7 to Federal District Attorney in New York, Mr. Matthias F. Correa. Of this declaration I am sending copies also to my parents, to a select number of friends and relatives, to the heads of the Washington press bureaus, and to a few responsible citizens who, no more than yourself, can be suspected of subversive activities.

You will understand how painful such a decision is for an American whose family traditions, like your own, have always

252

found their fulfillment in maintaining, through responsible participation in both the civil and the military services, our country's freedom and honor.

> I have the honor, Sir, to inscribe myself,
> with sincerest loyalty and respect,
> your fellow-citizen,

Robert Traill Spence Lowell, Jr.

DECLARATION OF
PERSONAL RESPONSIBILITY

Orders for my induction into the armed forces on September eighth 1943 have just arrived. Because we glory in the conviction that our wars are won not by irrational valor but through the exercise of moral responsibility, it is fitting for me to make the following declaration which is also a decision.

Like the majority of our people I watched the approach of this war with foreboding. Modern wars had proved subversive to the Democracies and history had shown them to be the iron gates to totalitarian slavery. On the other hand, members of my family had served in all our wars since the Declaration of Independence: I thought—our tradition of service is sensible and noble; if its occasional exploitation by Money, Politics and Imperialism is allowed to seriously discredit it, we are doomed.

When Pearl Harbor was attacked, I imagined that my country was in intense peril and come what might, unprecedented sacrifices were necessary for our national survival. In March and August of 1942 I volunteered, first for the Navy and then for the Army. And when I heard reports of what would formerly have been termed atrocities, I was not disturbed: for I judged that savagery was unavoidable in our nation's struggle for its life against diabolic adversaries.

Today these adversaries are being rolled back on all fronts and the crisis of war is past. But there are no indications of peace. In June we heard rumors of the staggering civilian casualties that had resulted from the mining of the Ruhr Dams. Three weeks ago we read of the razing of Hamburg, where

200,000 non-combatants are reported dead, after an almost apocalyptic series of all-out air-raids.

This, in a world still nominally Christian, is *news*. And now the Quebec Conference confirms our growing suspicions that the bombings of the Dams and of Hamburg were not mere isolated acts of military expediency, but marked the inauguration of a new long-term strategy, indorsed and co-ordinated by our Chief Executive.

The war has entered on an unforeseen phase: one that can by no possible extension of the meaning of the words be called defensive. By demanding unconditional surrender we reveal our complete confidence in the outcome, and declare that we are prepared to wage a war without quarter or principles, to the permanent destruction of Germany and Japan.

Americans cannot plead ignorance of the lasting consequences of a war carried through to unconditional surrender—our Southern states, three-quarters of a century after their terrible battering down and occupation, are still far from having recovered even their material prosperity.

It is a fundamental principle of our American Democracy, one that distinguishes it from the demagoguery and herd hypnosis of the totalitarian tyrannies, that with us each individual citizen is called upon to make voluntary and responsible decisions on issues which concern the national welfare. I therefore realize that I am under the heavy obligation of assenting to the prudence and justice of our present objectives before I have the right to accept service in our armed forces. No matter how expedient I might find it to entrust my moral responsibility to the State, I realize that it is not permissible under a form of government which derives its sanctions from the rational assent of the governed.

Our rulers have promised us unlimited bombings of Germany and Japan. Let us be honest: we intend the permanent destruction of Germany and Japan. If this program is carried out, it will demonstrate to the world our Machiavellian contempt for the laws of justice and charity between nations; it will destroy any possibility of a European or Asiatic national autonomy; it will leave China and Europe, the two natural power centers of the future, to the mercy of the USSR, a totalitarian tyranny committed to world revolution and total global domination through propaganda and violence.

In 1941 we undertook a patriotic war to preserve *our lives, our fortunes, and our sacred honor* against the lawless aggressions of a totalitarian league: in 1943 we are collaborating with the most unscrupulous and powerful of totalitarian dictators to destroy law, freedom, democracy, and above all, our continued national sovereignty.

With the greatest reluctance, with every wish that I may be proved in error, and after long deliberation on my responsibilities to myself, my country, and my ancestors who played responsible parts in its making, I have come to the conclusion that I cannot honorably participate in a war whose prosecution, as far as I can judge, constitutes a betrayal of my country.

BAYARD RUSTIN

If one had to list the greatest accomplishment of Bayard Rustin's career, it would probably be the 1963 March on Washington. He was called in as official organizer less than two months in advance—and against the private objections of some civil rights leaders, who worried that his sexual orientation, an open secret, would detract from their aims. Against the odds, Rustin (1912–1987) brought a fractious movement together and helped to orchestrate an event that changed history.

Rustin's life as an activist spanned many decades and embraced more than a single cause, however; he was at once intensely principled and politically savvy, a rare combination. In the late 1930s, as a student at City College, he joined the Young Communist League, working by day to coordinate the league's Committee against Discrimination in the Armed Forces, and by night singing the blues in a Greenwich Village nightclub. He broke with the party in 1941 after it called for American intervention in the war against Germany—his Pennsylvania Quaker upbringing and deeply held pacifist convictions trumping shallower affiliations—and became A. J. Muste's youth secretary and protégé at the Fellowship of Reconciliation. In 1942 he joined other fellowship members in nonviolent protests—among the first "Freedom Rides"—on segregated buses in the South.

Rustin continued to protest segregation during the war, as a prisoner of conscience in federal correctional facilities in Ashland, Kentucky, and Lewisburg, Pennsylvania, where he spent twenty-eight months, all told. (His letter to his draft board opposing conscription is reprinted below.) Prison authorities isolated and then transferred Rustin not only for his civil disobedience but for his "psychopathic personality"—his too overt sexual relations with other prisoners. Even the charitable Muste chided him for such behavior.

Following his release in 1947, Rustin resumed his civil rights work. Gandhi personally invited him to India to attend a pacifist conference scheduled for 1949; after Gandhi's assassination, he met with members of his circle. In 1956 he arrived in Montgomery, Alabama, to advise the young Martin Luther King Jr. on both strategy and Gandhian thought; he helped to organize the Southern Christian Leadership Conference to aid King, and mentored young activists in the Student Nonviolent Coordinating Committee and the Congress on Racial Equality.

Rustin was a risky colleague to have in those days, both because of his history with communism and because of his homosexuality, so he was sometimes kept out of sight; the dimensions of his role in the peace and civil rights movements have become clearer only since his death. In 2013, President Obama posthumously awarded him the Presidential Medal of Freedom, presenting it to his longtime partner Walter Naegle.

To Local Board No. 63

November 16, 1943

Gentlemen:

For eight years I have believed war to be impractical and a denial of our Hebrew-Christian tradition. The social teachings of Jesus are: (1) respect for personality; (2) service the "sumum bonum"; (3) overcoming evil with good; and (4) the brotherhood of man. Those principles as I see it are violated by participation in war.

Believing this, and having before me Jesus' continued resistance to that which he considered evil, I was compelled to resist war by registering as a conscientious objector in October 1940.

However, a year later, September 1941, I became convinced that conscription as well as war equally is inconsistent with the teachings of Jesus. I must resist conscription also.

On Saturday, November 13, 1943, I received from you an order to report for a physical examination to be taken Tuesday, November 16, at eight o'clock in the evening. I wish to inform you that I cannot voluntarily submit to an order springing from the Selective Service and Training Act for War.

There are several reasons for this decision, all stemming from the basic spiritual truth that men are brothers in the sight of God:

1. War is wrong. Conscription is a concomitant of modern war. Thus conscription for so vast an evil as war is wrong.

2. Conscription for war is inconsistent with freedom of conscience, which is not merely the right to believe, but to act on the degree of truth that one receives, to follow a vocation which is God-inspired and God-directed.

Today I feel that God motivates me to use my whole being to combat by nonviolent means the ever-growing racial tension in the United States; at the same time the state directs that I shall do its will; which of these dictates can I follow—that of God or that of the state? Surely, I must at all times attempt to obey the law of the state. But when the will of God and the will of the state conflict, I am compelled to follow the will of God. If I cannot continue in my present vocation, I must resist.

   3. The Conscription Act denies brotherhood—the most basic New Testament teaching. Its design and purpose is to set men apart—German against American, American against Japanese. Its aim springs from a moral impossibility—that ends justify means, that from unfriendly acts a new and friendly world can emerge.

In practice further, it separates black from white—those supposedly struggling for a common freedom. Such a separation also is based on the moral error that racism can overcome racism, that evil can produce good, that men virtually in slavery can struggle for a freedom they are denied. This means that I must protest racial discrimination in the armed forces, which is not only morally indefensible but also in clear violation of the Act. This does not, however, imply that I could have a part in conforming to the Act if discrimination were eliminated.

Segregation, separation, according to Jesus, is the basis of continuous violence. It was such an observation which encouraged him to teach, "It has been said to you in olden times that thou shalt not kill, but I say unto you, do not call a man a fool"—and he might have added: "for if you call him such, you automatically separate yourself from him and violence begins." That which separates man from his brother is evil and must be resisted.

I admit my share of guilt for having participated in the institutions and ways of life which helped bring fascism and war. Nevertheless, guilty as I am, I now see as did the Prodigal Son that it is never too late to refuse longer to remain in a non-creative situation. It is always timely and virtuous to change—to take in all humility a new path.

Though joyfully following the will of God, I regret that I must break the law of the state. I am prepared for whatever may follow.

I herewith return the material you have sent me, for conscientiously I cannot hold a card in connection with an Act I no longer feel able to accept and abide by.

Today I am notifying the Federal District Attorney of my decision and am forwarding him a copy of this letter.

I appreciate now as in the past your advice and consideration, and trust that I shall cause you no anxiety in the future. I want you to know I deeply respect you for executing your duty to God and country in these difficult times in the way you feel you must. I remain

Sincerely yours,
Bayard Rustin

P.S. I am enclosing samples of the material which from time to time I have sent out to hundreds of persons, Negro and white, throughout our nation. This indicates one type of the creative work to which God has called me.

LEO SZILARD

Among the many things changed by the advent of nuclear weapons was the nature of war resistance. Some who had no quarrel with the war against Germany and Japan took a stand against the use of such weapons, which seemed to alter war itself, threatening utter annihilation. Among the first of these antinuclear activists were some of the scientists who had conceived of nuclear weapons in the first place and participated in their development. Better able than most military and civilian leaders to imagine the destruction these weapons were capable of, and to foresee the consequences of nuclear conflict, they sought to prevent the first use of the terrible power they had helped to unleash.

Leo Szilard (1898–1964) was a leader of these scientists. Born in Budapest, he emigrated to Germany in 1919, studying physics at the University of Berlin; among his teachers was Albert Einstein, with whom he developed and patented the "Einstein-Szilard refrigerator." In 1933 he fled Nazi Germany and went to England, where he first realized the military potential of a multiplying neutron chain reaction. He came to the United States in 1938—collaborating with Einstein on an August 1939 letter warning President Roosevelt of the potential of "extremely powerful bombs of a new type"—and became a citizen in 1943. He played a significant role in the development of the first nuclear reactors, though he often found himself at odds with the military men who took over his research work.

In early July 1945—just over a month before the atomic bomb was dropped on Hiroshima—Szilard circulated the letter and petition reprinted below among his colleagues on the Manhattan Project. Slightly revised, it went to President Truman bearing seventy signatures, but it did not make it up the chain of command in time for Truman to see it before the destruction of Hiroshima and Nagasaki.

After the war Szilard turned his research from nuclear physics to molecular biology. He persisted in his opposition to the proliferation of nuclear weapons, publicly opposing the development of the hydrogen bomb and founding the Council for Abolishing War (now the Council for a Livable World) in 1962.

A Petition to the President of the United States

July 4, 1945

Dear

Inclosed is the text of a petition which will be submitted to the President of the United States. As you will see, this petition is based on purely moral considerations.

It may very well be that the decision of the President whether or not to use atomic bombs in the war against Japan will largely be based on considerations of expediency. On the basis of expediency, many arguments could be put forward both for and against our use of atomic bombs against Japan. Such arguments could be considered only within the framework of a thorough analysis of the situation which will face the United States after this war and it was felt that no useful purpose would be served by considering arguments of expediency in a short petition.

However small the chance might be that our petition may influence the course of events, I personally feel that it would be a matter of importance if a large number of scientists who have worked in this field went clearly and unmistakably on record as to their opposition on moral grounds to the use of these bombs in the present phase of the war.

Many of us are inclined to say that individual Germans share the guilt for the acts which Germany committed during this war because they did not raise their voices in protest against those acts. Their defense that their protest would have been of no avail hardly seems acceptable even though these Germans could not have protests without running risks to life and liberty. We are in a position to raise our voices without incurring any such risks even though we might incur the displeasure of some of those who are at present in charge of controlling the work on "atomic power."

The fact that the people of the United States are unaware of the choice which faces us increases our responsibility in this matter since those who have worked on "atomic power" represent a sample of the population and they alone are in a position to form an opinion and declare their stand.

Anyone who might wish to go on record by signing the petition ought to have an opportunity to do so and, therefore, it would be appreciated if you could give every member of your group an opportunity for signing.

Leo Szilard

P.S.—Anyone who wants to sign the petition ought to sign both attached copies and ought to read not only the petition but also this covering letter.

July 3, 1945

A PETITION TO THE PRESIDENT OF
THE UNITED STATES

Discoveries of which the people of the United States are not aware may affect the welfare of this nation in the near future. The liberation of atomic power which has been achieved places atomic bombs in the hands of the Army. It places in your hands, as Commander-in-Chief, the fateful decision whether or not to sanction the use of such bombs in the present phase of the war against Japan.

We, the undersigned scientists, have been working in the field of atomic power for a number of years. Until recently we have had to reckon with the possibility that the United States might be attacked by atomic bombs during this war and that her only defense might lie in a counterattack by the same means. Today with this danger averted we feel impelled to say what follows:

The war has to be brought speedily to a successful conclusion and the destruction of Japanese cities by means of atomic bombs may very well be an effective method of warfare. We feel, however, that such an attack on Japan could not be justified in the present circumstances. We believe that the United States ought not to resort to the use of atomic bombs in the present phase of the war, at least not unless the terms which will be imposed upon Japan after the war are publicly announced and subsequently Japan is given an opportunity to surrender.

If such public announcement gave assurance to the Japanese that they could look forward to a life devoted to peaceful pursuits in their homeland and if Japan still refused to surrender, our nation would then be faced with a situation which might require a re-examination of her position with respect to the use of atomic bombs in the war.

Atomic bombs are primarily a means for the ruthless annihilation of cities. Once they were introduced as an instrument of war it would be difficult to resist for long the temptation of putting them to such use.

The last few years show a marked tendency toward increasing ruthlessness. At present our Air Forces, striking at the Japanese cities, are using the same methods of warfare which were condemned by American public opinion only a few years ago when applied by the Germans to the cities of England. Our use of atomic bombs in this war would carry the world a long way further on this path of ruthlessness.

Atomic power will provide the nations with new means of destruction. The atomic bombs at our disposal represent only the first step in this direction and there is almost no limit to the destructive power which will become available in the course of this development. Thus a nation which sets the precedent of using these newly liberated forces of nature for purposes of destruction may have to bear the responsibility of opening the door to an era of devastation on an unimaginable scale.

In view of the foregoing, we, the undersigned, respectfully petition that you exercise your power as Commander-in-Chief to rule that the United States shall not, in the present phase of the war, resort to the use of atomic bombs.

DOROTHY DAY

For all of her unswerving commitment to nonviolence, Dorothy Day (1897–1980) fiercely and almost bitterly denounced President Truman in *The Catholic Worker*, in September 1945, for his "jubilance" over the dropping of the atomic bombs. Like Leo Szilard and many subsequent antinuclear writers, Day sensed that with the atomic bomb something new had come into the world, and that some new language was needed to oppose it.

Day was born in Brooklyn and studied at the University of Illinois for two years, then returned to New York to become a journalist; she worked with Floyd Dell at *The Masses*, and like Dell and Edna St. Vincent Millay was involved with the Provincetown Players. She became a Catholic the year after the birth of her daughter Tamar in 1926; in 1933, partly under the influence of the French personalist Peter Maurin (though Day was too much her own person ever to be very much under anyone's influence), she founded *The Catholic Worker* newspaper—still published today, and with a circulation in the late 1930s of 100,000—and the first Catholic Worker house of hospitality. Her pacifism cost the newspaper readers during World War II; horror at the consequences of the bombings in Hiroshima and Nagasaki won some of them back.

I met Dorothy Day when I was in my twenties; my friend Chuck Matthei, a noted draft resister and community organizer, was staying at the Catholic Worker house in New York, and invited me to meet him there. I had no idea who she was, but Chuck was a magical person to me, so Dorothy became one too; I can still see her, though by now my memory of her is overlaid with my memories of all the photographs I've seen of her.

We Go on Record—

Mr. Truman was jubilant. President Truman. True man. What a strange name, come to think of it. We refer to Jesus Christ as true God and true Man. Truman is a true man of his time in that he was jubilant. He was not a son of God, brother of Christ, brother of the Japanese, jubilating as he did. He went from table to table on the cruiser which was bringing him home from the Big Three conference, telling the great news, "jubilant," the newspaper said. *Jubilate Deo*. We have killed 318,000 Japanese.

That is, we hope we have killed them, the Associated Press, page one, column one, of the Herald Tribune says. The effect is hoped for, not known. It is to be hoped they are vaporized, our Japanese brothers, scattered, men, women and babies, to the four winds, over the seven seas. Perhaps we will breathe their dust into our nostrils, feel them in the fog of New York on our faces, feel them in the rain on the hills of Easton.

Jubilate Deo. President Truman was jubilant. We have created. We have created destruction. We have created a new element, called Pluto. Nature had nothing to do with it.

"A cavern below Columbia was bomb's cradle"; born not that men might live, but that men might be killed. Brought into being in a cavern, and then tried in a desert place, in the midst of tempest and lightning, tried out, and then again on the eve of the Feast of the Transfiguration of our Lord Jesus Christ, on a far off island in the eastern hemisphere, tried out again, this "new weapon which conceivably might wipe out mankind, and perhaps the planet itself."

"Dropped on a town, one bomb would be equivalent to a severe earthquake and would utterly destroy the place. A scientific brain trust has solved the problem of how to confine and release almost unlimited energy. It is impossible yet to measure its effects."

"We have spent two billion on the greatest scientific gamble in history and won," said President Truman jubilantly.

("UNRRA meets today facing a crisis on funds. It is close to scraping the bottom of its financial barrel, will open its third council session tomorrow, hoping to get enough new funds to carry it through the winter.")

(Germany is told of Hard Winter by Eisenhower.)

(Pall of Apathy Shrouds Bitter, Hungry Vienna.)

The papers list the scientists (the murderers) who are credited with perfecting this new weapon. One outstanding authority "who earlier had developed a powerful electrical bombardment machine called the cyclotron, was Professor O. E. Lawrence, a Nobel prize winner of the University of California. In the heat of the race to unlock the atom, he built the world's most powerful atom smashing gun, a machine whose electrical projectiles carried charges equivalent to 25,000,000 volts. But such machines were found in the end to be unnecessary. The atom of Uranium 235 was smashed with surprising ease. Science discovered that not sledgehammer blows, but subtle taps from slow travelling neutrons managed more on a tuning technique were all that were needed to disintegrate the Uranium 235 atom."

(Remember the tales we used to hear, that one note of a violin, if that one note could be discovered, could collapse the Empire State building. Remember too, that God's voice was heard not in the great and strong wind, not in the earthquake, not in the fire, but "in the whistling of a gentle air.")

Scientists, army officers, great universities (Notre Dame included) and captains of industry,—all are given credit lines in the press for their work of preparing the bomb,—and other bombs, the President assures us are in production now.

Great Britain controls the supply of uranium ore, in Canada and Rhodesia. We are making the bombs. This new great force will be used for good, the scientists assured us. And then they wiped out a city of 318,000. This was good. The President was jubilant.

Today's paper with its columns of description of the new era, the atomic era, which this colossal slaughter of the innocents has ushered in, is filled with stories covering every conceivable phase of the new discovery. Pictures of the towns and the industrial plants where the parts are made are spread across the pages. In the forefront of the town of Oak Ridge, Tennessee, is a chapel, a large comfortable looking chapel benignly settled beside the plant. And the scientists making the first tests in the desert, prayed, one newspaper account said.

Yes. God is still in the picture. God is not mocked. Today, the day of this so great news, God made a madman dance and talk, who had not spoken for twenty years. God sent a typhoon to damage the Carrier Hornet. God permitted a fog to obscure vision and a bomber crashed into the Empire State building. God permits these things. We have to remember it. We are held in God's hands, all of us, and President Truman too, and these scientists who have created death, but will use it for good. He, God, holds our life and our happiness, our sanity and our health; our lives are in his hands.

He is our Creator. Creator.

. . . And I think, as I think on these things, that while here in the western hemisphere, we went in for precision bombing (what chance of *precision* bombing now?) while we went in for obliteration bombing, Russia was very careful not to bomb cities, to wipe out civilian populations. Perhaps she was thinking of the poor, of the workers, as brothers.

I remember, too, that many stories have come out of Russia of her pride in scientific discoveries and of how eagerly and pridefully they were trying to discover the secret of life—how to create life (not death).

Exalted pride, yes, but I wonder which will be easier to forgive?

And as I write, Pigsie, who works at Secaucus, New Jersey, feeding hogs, and cleaning out the excrement of hogs, who comes in once a month to find beauty and surcease and glamour and glory in the drink of the Bowery, trying to drive the hell and the smell out of his nostrils and his life, sleeps on our doorstep, in this best, and most advanced and progressive of all possible worlds. And as I write, our cat, Rainbow, slinks by with a shrill rat in her jaws, out of the kitchen closet, here at Mott street. Here in this greatest of cities which covered the cavern where this stupendous discovery was made, which institutes an era of unbelievable richness and power and glory for man . . .

Everyone says, "I wonder what the Pope thinks of it?" How everyone turns to the Vatican for judgment, even though they do not seem to listen to the voice there! But our Lord Himself has already pronounced judgment on the atomic bomb. When James and John, (John the beloved) wished to call down fire from heaven on their enemies, Jesus said,

"You know not of what spirit you are. The Son of man came not to destroy souls but to save." He said also, "What you do unto the least of these my brethren, you do unto me."

KURT VONNEGUT

In 1969 Kurt Vonnegut (1922–2007) published *Slaughterhouse-Five*, the *other* famous American antiwar novel, the first being Dalton Trumbo's *Johnny Got His Gun* (1939). He knew full well, before he started the book, that he had set himself a preposterous task—a character in *Slaughterhouse-Five* compares writing an antiwar novel to writing an "anti-glacier novel." But his story was personal, and he persisted: during the Battle of the Bulge in World War II, as a private with the 106th Infantry Division, he had been captured by the Germans and imprisoned in a basement slaughterhouse in Dresden, where he and other POWs survived the apocalyptic firebombing of February 1945. (The best recent historical study has established that as many as 25,000 people were killed by the bombing; Vonnegut believed the number to have been higher than 100,000.) The scenes he witnessed in the aftermath of the bombing ripened in him for decades before they found expression in print.

"Wailing Shall Be in All Streets," written sometime between the fall of 1945 and the summer of 1947, was his first attempt to put his horrific experiences into words. He submitted the memoir to *Harper's*, *The Atlantic*, *The American Mercury*, and *The Yale Review*, none of whom were interested—perhaps because he was a still-unpublished writer, perhaps because he lamented the "obscene brutality" of Allied conduct at a moment when no one wanted to hear about it. The novel is funny, fantastic, and complex; "Wailing" is earnest and concrete and straightforward. Like other writing directed against World War II, it supports the war's rationale; it was, writes Vonnegut, fought from "near-Holy motives." But it is unsparingly opposed to the conduct of that war: "the killing of children—'Jerry' children or 'Jap' children, or whatever enemies the future may hold for us—can never be justified."

Wailing Shall Be in All Streets

Iᴛ was a routine speech we got during our first day of basic training, delivered by a wiry little lieutenant: "Men, up to now you've been good, clean, American boys with an American's love for sportsmanship and fair play. We're here to change that. Our job is to make you the meanest, dirtiest bunch of scrappers in the history of the World. From now on you can forget the Marquess of Queensberry Rules and every other set of rules.

Anything and everything goes. Never hit a man above the belt when you can kick him below it. Make the bastard scream. Kill him any way you can. Kill, kill, kill, do you understand?"

His talk was greeted with nervous laughter and general agreement that he was right. "Didn't Hitler and Tojo say the Americans were a bunch of softies? Ha! They'll find out." And of course, Germany and Japan did find out: a toughened-up democracy poured forth a scalding fury that could not be stopped. It was a war of reason against barbarism, supposedly, with the issues at stake on such a high plane that most of our feverish fighters had no idea why they were fighting—other than that the enemy was a bunch of bastards. A new kind of war, with all destruction, all killing approved. Germans would ask, "Why are you Americans fighting us?" "I don't know, but we're sure beating the hell out of you," was a stock answer.

A lot of people relished the idea of total war: it had a modern ring to it, in keeping with our spectacular technology. To them it was like a football game: "Give 'em the axe, the axe, the axe . . ." Three small-town merchants' wives, middle-aged and plump, gave me a ride when I was hitch-hiking home from Camp Atterbury. "Did you kill a lot of them Germans?" asked the driver, making cheerful small-talk. I told her I didn't know. This was taken for modesty. As I was getting out of the car, one of the ladies patted me on the shoulder in motherly fashion: "I'll bet you'd like to get over and kill some of them dirty Japs now, wouldn't you?" We exchanged knowing winks. I didn't tell those simple souls that I had been captured after a week at the front; and more to the point, what I knew and thought about killing dirty Germans, about total war. The reason for my being sick at heart then and now has to do with an incident that received cursory treatment in the American newspapers. In February, 1945, Dresden, Germany, was destroyed, and with it over one hundred thousand human beings. I was there. Not many know how tough America got.

I was among a group of one hundred and fifty infantry privates, captured in the Bulge breakthrough and put to work in Dresden. Dresden, we were told, was the only major German city to have escaped bombing so far. That was in January, 1945. She owed her good fortune to her unwarlike countenance:

hospitals, breweries, food-processing plants, surgical supply houses, ceramics, musical instrument factories, and the like. Since the war, hospitals had become her prime concern. Every day hundreds of wounded came into the tranquil sanctuary from the east and west. At night we would hear the dull rumble of distant air raids. "Chemnitz is getting it tonight," we used to say, and speculated what it might be like to be under the yawning bomb-bays and the bright young men with their dials and cross-hairs. "Thank heaven we're in an 'open city,'" we thought, and so thought the thousands of refugees—women, children, and old men—who came in a forlorn stream from the smouldering wreckage of Berlin, Leipzig, Breslau, Munich. . . . They flooded the city to twice its normal population.

There was no war in Dresden. True, planes came over nearly every day and the sirens wailed, but the planes were always en route elsewhere. The alarms furnished a relief period in a tedious work day, a social event, a chance to gossip in the shelters. The shelters, in fact, were not much more than a gesture, casual recognition of the national emergency: wine cellars and basements with benches in them and sand bags blocking the windows, for the most part. There were a few more adequate bunkers in the center of the city, close to the government offices, but nothing like the staunch subterranean fortress that rendered Berlin impervious to her daily pounding. Dresden had no reason to prepare for attack—and thereby hangs a beastly tale.

Dresden was surely among the World's most lovely cities. Her streets were broad, lined with shade-trees. She was sprinkled with countless little parks and statuary. She had marvelous old churches, libraries, museums, theaters, art galleries, beer gardens, a zoo, and a renowned university. It was at one time a tourist's paradise. They would be far better informed on the city's delights than am I. But the impression I have is that in Dresden—in the physical city—were the symbols of the good life; pleasant, honest, intelligent. In the Swastika's shadow those symbols of the dignity and hope of mankind stood waiting, monuments to truth. The accumulated treasure of hundreds of years, Dresden spoke eloquently of those things excellent in European civilization wherein our debt lies deep. I was a prisoner, hungry, dirty, and full of hate for our captors, but I loved that city and saw the blessed wonder of her past and the rich promise of her future.

In February, 1945, American bombers reduced this treasure to crushed stone and embers; disemboweled her with high-explosives and cremated her with incendiaries. The atom bomb may represent a fabulous advance, but it is interesting to note that primitive TNT and thermite managed to exterminate in one bloody night more people than died in the whole London blitz. Fortress Dresden fired a dozen shots at our airmen. Once back at their bases and sipping hot coffee, they probably remarked, "Flak unusually light tonight. Well, guess it's time to turn in." Captured British pilots from tactical fighter units (covering front-line troops) used to chide those who had flown heavy bombers on city raids with, "How on Earth did you stand the stink of boiling urine and burning perambulators?"

A perfectly routine piece of news: "Last night our planes attacked Dresden. All planes returned safely." The only good German is a dead one: over one hundred thousand evil men, women, and children (the able-bodied were at the fronts) forever purged of their sins against humanity. By chance I met a bombardier who had taken part in the attack. "We hated to do it," he told me.

The night they came over we spent in an underground meat locker in a slaughterhouse. We were lucky, for it was the best shelter in town. Giants stalked the Earth above us. First came the soft murmur of their dancing on the outskirts, then the grumbling of their plodding toward us, and finally the ear-splitting crashes of their heels upon us—and thence to the outskirts again. Back and forth they swept: saturation bombing.

"I screamed and I wept and I clawed the walls of our shelter," an old lady told me. "I prayed to God to 'please, please, please, dear God, stop them.' But he didn't hear me. No power could stop them. On they came, wave after wave. There was no way we could surrender; no way to tell them we couldn't stand it anymore. There was nothing anyone could do but sit and wait for morning." Her daughter and grandson were killed.

Our little prison was burned to the ground. We were to be evacuated to an outlying camp occupied by the South African prisoners. Our guards were a melancholy lot, aged Volkssturmers and disabled veterans. Most of them were Dresden residents and had friends and families somewhere in the holocaust. A corporal, who had lost an eye after two years on the Russian front, ascertained before we marched that his wife, his two children, and both of his parents had been killed. He had one cigarette. He shared it with me.

Our march to new quarters took us on the city's edge. It was impossible to believe that anyone survived in its heart. Ordinarily the day would have been cold, but occasional gusts from the colossal inferno made us sweat. And ordinarily the day would have been clear and bright, but an opaque and towering cloud turned noon to twilight. A grim procession clogged the outbound highways; people with blackened faces streaked with tears, some bearing wounded, some bearing dead. They gathered in the fields. None spoke. A few with Red Cross armbands did what they could for the casualties.

Settled with the South Africans, we enjoyed a week without work. At the end of it communications were reestablished with higher headquarters and we were ordered to hike seven miles to the area hardest hit. Nothing in the district had escaped the fury. A city of jagged building shells, of splintered statuary and shattered trees; every vehicle stopped, gnarled and burned, left to rust or rot in the path of the frenzied might. The only sounds other than our own were those of falling plaster and their echoes. I cannot describe the desolation properly, but I can give an idea of how it made us feel, in the words of a delirious British soldier in a makeshift P.W. hospital: "It's frightenin', I tell you. I would walk down one of them bloody streets and feel a thousand eyes on the back of me 'ead. I would 'ear 'em whisperin' behind me. I would turn around to look at 'em and there wouldn't be a bloomin' soul in sight. You can feel 'em and you can 'ear 'em but there's never anybody there." We knew what he said was so.

For "salvage" work we were divided into small crews, each under a guard. Our ghoulish mission was to search for bodies. It was rich hunting that day and the many thereafter. We started on a small scale—here a leg, there an arm, and an occasional baby—but struck a mother lode before noon. We cut our way through a basement wall to discover a reeking hash of over one hundred human beings. Flame must have swept through before the building's collapse sealed the exits, because the flesh of those within resembled the texture of prunes. Our job, it was explained, was to wade into the shambles and bring forth the remains. Encouraged by cuffing and guttural abuse, wade in we did. We did exactly that, for the floor was covered with an unsavory broth from burst water mains and viscera. A number of victims, not killed outright, had attempted to escape through a narrow emergency exit. At any rate, there were several bodies packed tightly into the passageway. Their leader had made it halfway up the steps before he was buried up to his neck in falling brick and plaster. He was about fifteen, I think.

It is with some regret that I here besmirch the nobility of our airmen, but boys, you killed an appalling lot of women and children. The shelter I have described and innumerable others like it were filled with them. We had to exhume their bodies and carry them to mass funeral pyres in the parks—so I know. The funeral pyre technique was abandoned when it became apparent how great was the toll. There was not enough labor to do it nicely, so a man with a flame-thrower was sent down instead, and he cremated them where they lay. Burned alive, suffocated, crushed—men, women, and children indiscriminately killed. For all the sublimity of the cause for which we fought, we surely created a Belsen of our own. The method was impersonal, but the result was equally cruel and heartless. That, I am afraid, is a sickening truth.

When we had become used to the darkness, the odor, and the carnage, we began musing as to what each of the corpses had been in life. It was a sordid game: "Rich man, poor man, beggar man, thief . . ." Some had fat purses and jewelry, others had precious foodstuffs. A boy had his dog still leashed to him. Renegade Ukrainians in German uniform were in charge of our operations in the shelters proper. They were roaring drunk from adjacent wine cellars and seemed to enjoy their job hugely. It was a profitable one, for they stripped each body of valuables before we carried it to the street. Death became so commonplace that we could joke about our dismal burdens and cast them about like so much garbage. Not so with the first of them, especially the young: we had lifted them onto the stretchers with care, laying them out with some semblance of funeral dignity in their last resting place before the pyre. But our awed and sorrowful propriety gave way, as I said, to rank callousness. At the end of a grisly day we would smoke and survey the impressive heap of dead accumulated. One of us flipped his cigarette butt into the pile: "Hell's bells," he said, "I'm ready for Death anytime he wants to come after me."

A few days after the raid the sirens screamed again. The listless and heartsick survivors were showered this time with leaflets. I lost my copy of the epic, but remember that it ran something like this: "To the people of Dresden: We were forced to bomb your city because of the heavy military traffic your railroad facilities have been carrying. We realize that we haven't always hit our objectives. Destruction of anything other than military objectives was unintentional, unavoidable fortunes of war." That explained the slaughter to everyone's satisfaction, I am sure, but it aroused no little contempt for the American bomb-sight. It is a fact that forty-eight hours after the last B-17 had droned west for a well-earned rest, labor battalions had swarmed over the damaged rail yards and restored them to nearly normal service. None of the rail bridges over the Elbe was knocked out of commission. Bomb-sight manufacturers should blush to know that their marvelous devices laid bombs down as much as three miles wide of what the military claimed to be aiming for. The leaflet should have said, "We hit every blessed church, hospital, school, museum, theater, your university, the zoo, and every apartment building in town, but we honestly weren't trying hard to do it. C'est la guerre. So sorry. Besides, saturation bombing is all the rage these days, you know."

There was tactical significance: stop the railroads. An excellent maneuver, no doubt, but the technique was horrible. The planes started kicking high-explosives and incendiaries through their bomb-bays at the city limits, and for all the pattern their hits presented, they must have been briefed by a Ouija board. Tabulate the loss against the gain. Over one hundred thousand non-combatants and a magnificent city destroyed by bombs dropped wide of the stated objectives: the railroads were knocked out for roughly two days. The Germans counted it the greatest loss of life suffered in any single raid. The death of Dresden was a bitter tragedy, needlessly and willfully executed. The killing of children—"Jerry" children or "Jap" children, or whatever enemies the future may hold for us—can never be justified.

The facile reply to great groans such as mine is the most hateful of all clichés, "fortunes of war," and another, "They asked for it. All they understand is force." *Who* asked for it? The only thing *who* understands is force? Believe me, it is not easy to rationalize the stamping out of vineyards where the grapes of wrath are stored when gathering up babies in bushel baskets or helping a man dig where he thinks his wife may be buried. Certainly enemy military and industrial installations should have been blown flat, and woe unto those foolish enough to seek shelter near them. But the "Get Tough America" policy, the spirit of *revenge*, the approbation of all destruction and killing, has earned us a name for obscene brutality, and cost the World the possibility of Germany's becoming a peaceful and intellectually fruitful nation in anything but the most remote future.

Our leaders had a carte blanche as to what they might or might not destroy. Their mission was to win the war as quickly as possible, and, while they were admirably trained to do just that, their decisions as to the fate of certain priceless World heirlooms—in one case Dresden—were not always judicious. When, late in the war, with the Wehrmacht breaking up on all fronts, our planes were sent to destroy this last major city, I doubt if the question was asked, "How will this tragedy benefit us, and how will that benefit compare with the ill-effects in the long run?" Dresden, a beautiful city, built in the art spirit, symbol of an admirable heritage, so anti-Nazi that Hitler visited it but twice during his whole reign, food and hospital center so bitterly needed now—plowed under and salt strewn in the furrows.

There can be no doubt that the Allies fought on the side of right and the Germans and Japanese on the side of wrong. World War II was fought for near-Holy motives. But I stand convinced that the brand of justice in which we dealt, wholesale bombings of civilian populations, was blasphemous. That the enemy did it first has nothing to do with the moral problem. What I saw of our air war, as the European conflict neared an end, had the earmarks of being an irrational war for war's sake.

Soft citizens of the American democracy learned to kick a man below the belt and make the bastard scream.

The occupying Russians, when they discovered that we were Americans, embraced us and congratulated us on the complete desolation our planes had wrought. We accepted their congratulations with good grace and proper modesty, but I felt then as I feel now, that I would have given my life to save Dresden for the World's generations to come. That is how everyone should feel about every city on Earth.

EDGAR L. JONES

Edgar L. Jones (1915–2001) was an ambulance driver and journalist during World War II, then for most of his life a reporter and editorialist for the *Baltimore Sun*. His *Atlantic* piece from February 1946 does two things, one familiar and one new. The familiar thing is that like Hemingway and others, he deromanticizes war, even "the good war," describing soldiers' actions and attitudes unsparingly and fully, thus making unreflective support of war more difficult. The new thing is how this knowledge is deployed: not against the home front or the commanders, but toward a political goal. The war was over, and the question before the United States was whether to continue the draft in peacetime. In the end, the answer was yes, and the draft was reinstated in 1948; but in the years intervening, the question was open, and a means for thinking about war and peace generally.

In opposing a peacetime draft Jones is not opposing war; rather he is asking, in relation to his knowledge of what war actually is, that everything possible be done to give peace "a fair trial": an anticipation of John Lennon's 1969 protest rally favorite, "Give Peace a Chance."

FROM

One War Is Enough

I

PROBABLY I shall be tagged as a psychoneurotic veteran of too much bloodshed when I say that I get alternately fighting mad and cold sick inside whenever I hear people talk about the next war. I cannot understand how they can be resigned to the prospects of another global conflict, so casual in their assumption that wars are inevitable, so damnably unaware of the consequences of their current complacency.

Has everyone in this country lost faith in peace? Here we stand at the threshold of what could be a new and better world, and our fainthearted citizenry insists upon looking backward and muttering that what has always been must be. Maybe the United Nations Organization will succeed in preventing further global conflicts, but the men from Missouri and forty-seven other states have to be shown. World peace, according to our self-acclaimed realists, is at best a heart-warming dream:

common sense demands that we put our trust in bombs and battleships. So let us teach our youths, along with the new generations in Germany and Japan, that wars are wrong, but at the same time let us be practical and bring up our children to be good soldiers, just in case.

Cynical as most of us overseas were, I doubt if many of us seriously believed that people at home would start planning for the next war before we could get home and talk without censorship about this one. Although our hopes and fears for the future were varied, our common goal was most assuredly more than the elimination of a few world powers so that the remaining nations could square off for yet another war. Nor did we endure the half-life of a regimented military existence just to have people tell us that it is inevitable that our children will have to suffer similar bitter experiences.

We had a right, I think, to expect that in return for our services the global home front would give peace a fair trial. We made our various sacrifices to give our own and younger generations a chance to improve on the past, not to have the unchanging Old Guard take our victory from us and rebuild the world along their deadly pre-war pattern of distrust, secrecy, and intrigue. We wanted peace, not a world divided into armed camps; permanent peace, not a short wait between wars. Many of us had to bomb, burn, and blast into oblivion an untold number of helpless victims of total war. Only a few of us are so unaware of our own war crimes that we can let it be said that we fought only to preserve the old way of life.

Surely the entire home front could not have suffered through four years of anguished waiting, dreading each incoming telegram, shuddering at each new invasion headline, and still consider war to be the only dependable solution to international controversies. Instead of viewing the rest of the world with suspicion and singling out the next enemy, there must be some Americans willing to rely upon the fact that millions of global citizens are as peace-loving as ourselves. Certainly we do not all believe that we can successfully talk peace at the point of a gun or bring up our children as conscientious civilians by first exposing them to military indoctrination, the very antithesis of education for democracy.

But if there are some Americans who want peace badly enough to give up their right to wage war, they are being out-voiced by our militant Old Guard, whose idea of a foreign policy is to keep the United States armed to the teeth and ever ready to challenge any country which disputes our world leadership. Regardless of the existence of personal misgivings, we, as a nation, are placing our reliance not on international coöperation but upon the atomic bomb and the willingness of "our boys" to back our decisions with their lives. If it takes two to make a war, we are making certain that we are one of them.

I do not pretend to speak for all veterans. In the course of forty months of war duty and five major battles I was only an ambulance driver, a merchant seaman, an Army historian, and a war correspondent, never a downright GI. Possibly the men who were subjected much more completely than I to the whims of militarism are now satisfied with their hollow victory, but I doubt it. I never met that fabulous character, Typical GI Joe, whose every thought and post-war desire was so well known to politicians and the writers of advertising copy. But I met a lot of other Joes, and my guess is that before long—and the sooner the better—the veteran serviceman is going to wake from his deep dreams of peace, a job, and a home and realize that his country has let him down, and badly.

Being a GI was a point of view, not a military classification, and the more thoroughly one was exposed to the waste, unfair-ness, senselessness, and horror of war, the more completely one substituted the serviceman's perspective for an anachronistic civilian way of thinking. The man in uniform stood apart from society and judged it, often too harshly, in the light of his own insecurity, the sacrifices which were demanded of him, and the possibility that he was being played for a sucker. In varying degrees, depending upon a man's length of service, the GI perspective included bitter contempt for the home front's abysmal lack of understanding, its pleasures and comforts, and its nauseating capacity to talk in patriotic platitudes.

The fighting man was not a deep-thinking man, despite all the lofty sentiments attributed to him. He left the peace talk to the civilians who had the time and place for it. Having been maneuvered into a position where he had to kill or be killed, he did not trouble himself with pretenses that he was a crusader. He fought because his people at home expected him to fight, and he let them seek the necessary justification for his own ruthlessness. The most he wanted was to end the war, and all wars, as soon as possible, so that he could live in peace and let others, including his own children, live in peace. He expected the home front to share his aversion for war and to figure out a better way to settle future disputes.

Civilian Joe is too concerned at present with his personal problems of readjustment to get mad at what he habitually blasphemed in his uniformed days as home-front stupidity. He is still too dazed from being home and free again to be bluntly vocal. When the veteran does start talking back, this country is going to have its wartime illusions badly shattered.

Observers not subjected for long periods to the serviceman's barren existence were in no position to interpret accurately a GI's life, because they lacked the necessary perspective. Congressmen on fly-by-night overseas tours did not understand the men doing the fighting, nor did press representatives, with one notable exception. To a greater extent than any other civilian, Ernie Pyle saw the war from the GI point of view, and he hated it with GI thoroughness. But even Ernie found it difficult to sympathize with States-side soldiers and shore-based sailors who complained as bitterly as the dirtiest dogface about their lot in life while enjoying all the physical comforts which the infantrymen lacked.

The plain, unpublicized fact of the matter was that nine out of ten servicemen wanted nothing more to do with wars after their first week of basic training. Whether stationed in Washington or on a scrap of coral sand, the average GI considered himself to be the purposeless victim of malignant justice. As he so often remarked, "From where I stand, this whole thing stinks!" He hated everyone conceivably responsible for his misfortune, cursing out the home front as vehemently as the Japanese and the Germans. His special gripes, however, were reserved for the undemocratic, stupefying, favor-ridden totalitarian nature of military life itself. He had no use for a system in which one class got the best of everything, and the other class got less than what was left.

2

WE Americans have the dangerous tendency in our international thinking to take a holier-than-thou attitude toward other nations. We consider ourselves to be more noble and decent than other peoples, and consequently in a better position to decide what is right and wrong in the world. What kind of war do civilians suppose we fought, anyway? We shot prisoners in cold blood, wiped out hospitals, strafed lifeboats, killed or mistreated enemy civilians, finished off the enemy wounded, tossed the dying into a hole with the dead, and in the Pacific boiled the flesh off enemy skulls to make table ornaments for sweethearts, or carved their bones into letter openers. We topped off our saturation bombing and burning of enemy civilians by dropping atomic bombs on two nearly defenseless cities, thereby setting an all-time record for instantaneous mass slaughter.

As victors we are privileged to try our defeated opponents for their crimes against humanity; but we should be realistic enough to appreciate that if we were on trial for breaking international laws, we should be found guilty on a dozen counts. We fought a dishonorable war, because morality had a low priority in battle. The tougher the fighting, the less room for decency; and in Pacific contests we saw mankind reach the blackest depths of bestiality.

Not every American soldier, or even one per cent of our troops, deliberately committed unwarranted atrocities, and the same might be said for the Germans and Japanese. The exigencies of war necessitated many so-called crimes, and the bulk of the rest could be blamed on the mental distortion which war produced. But we publicized every inhuman act of our opponents and censored any recognition of our own moral frailty in moments of desperation.

I have asked fighting men, for instance, why they—or actually, why *we*—regulated flame-throwers in such a way that enemy soldiers were set afire, to die slowly and painfully, rather than killed outright with a full blast of burning oil. Was it because they hated the enemy so thoroughly? The answer was invariably, "No, we don't hate those poor bastards particularly; we just hate the whole goddam mess and have to take it out on somebody." Possibly for the same reason, we mutilated the bodies of enemy dead, cutting off their ears and kicking out their gold teeth for souvenirs, and buried them with their testicles in their mouths, but such flagrant violations of all moral codes reach into still-unexplored realms of battle psychology.

It is not my intention either to excuse our late opponents or to discredit our own fighting men. I do, however, believe that all of us, not just the battle-enlightened GI's, should fully understand the horror and degradation of war before talking so casually of another one. War does horrible things to men, our own sons included. It demands the worst of a person and pays off in brutality and maladjustment. It has become so mechanical, inhuman, and crassly destructive that men lose all sense of personal responsibility for their actions. They fight without compassion, because that is the only way to fight a total war. To give just one illustration, I asked an infantry colonel whether he gave his battalion a pre-battle lecture. The colonel replied approximately as follows:—

"You can damn well bet I put 'em straight ahead of time, and they were the best damn outfit in the Philippines. I taught 'em ethics, fighting ethics. I taught 'em there were two kinds of ethics, one for us and one for the yellowbellies across the line. I taught 'em that the best way to kill a man was when he was lying down with his back up; the next best way was when he was sitting with his back towards ya, and the third best was when he was standing with his back towards ya. . . . Always shoot 'em in the back if possible; that's what I taught 'em, and there wasn't another battalion could touch 'em!"

Among other things about modern warfare, I think the home front should also comprehend the full significance of the fact that a front-line soldier had a good chance of being killed in this war by his own side as well as by his opponents. Battle positions changed so rapidly that American soldiers were shelled by American artillery and warships, bombed and strafed by American planes, and machine-gunned by American tanks—not occasionally, but often. We also sank our own ships and shot down numbers of our own planes—how many no one knows, but the ship I was on in the invasion of Sicily knocked out four German planes and three of our own, which was considered a good average.

Peter Bowman summed up our victory to date in *Beach Red* when he wrote, "Battle doesn't determine who is right. Only who is left." We destroyed fascists, not fascism; men, not ideas. Our triumphs did not serve as evidence that democracy is best for the world, any more than Russian victories proved that communism is an ideal system for all mankind. Only through our peacetime efforts to abolish war and bring a larger measure of freedom and security to all peoples can we reveal to others that we are any better than our defeated opponents.

Today we stand on trial—we are either for peace or for war, and the rest of the world is prepared to move with us or against us. The burden of proof is on us; and our willingness to make peace, not our capacity to wage war, is the true measure of our good-neighborliness.

NAOMI REPLANSKY

Naomi Replansky (b. 1918) was born into a family of Russian-Jewish immigrants in the Bronx and now lives in Manhattan with her long-time companion, the writer Eva Kollisch. In 1946, however, she found herself in Santa Monica, a little-published twenty-eight-year-old poet charged with the remarkable task of helping Bertolt Brecht translate some of his poems into English. Brecht had clipped a collection of wartime photographs from magazines and newspapers, and had written pithy quatrains about each. Later published as *Kriegsfibel* [*War Primer*] (1955), his still-evocative text-image poems inspired her equally evocative "Epitaph: 1945." Collected in her first book, *Ring Song*, in 1952, the poem has a nursery-rhyme simplicity of form that contrasts uncannily with the suffering it registers: it is a haunting marvel of compression.

Replansky worked on an assembly line during the war and afterward earned her living as a computer programmer, in the era of the punched card. She has continued her interest in translation (working on poems and plays by Brecht and other German writers, and also on Yiddish writers including Itzik Manger). In 2012 her *Collected Poems* was published; it won the 2013 William Carlos Williams Award of the Poetry Society of America.

Epitaph: 1945

My spoon was lifted when the bomb came down
That left no face, no hand, no spoon to hold.
One hundred thousand died in my hometown.
This came to pass before my soup was cold.

KARL SHAPIRO

"The Conscientious Objector" is a poem written by a soldier trying to imagine and do justice to his philosophical antagonist. It accordingly dramatizes both the soldier's anger at the resister and the civic necessity of having the resister be there in the first place: "Your conscience is / What we come back to in the armistice."

Born in Baltimore and educated at the University of Virginia, Karl Shapiro (1913–2000) was an established poet before he was drafted as a soldier in March 1941. He managed to write numerous poems during his three years' service in Australia and New Guinea, characterizing himself as "a poet in a Battle Zone, which he had seen almost nothing of, who was serenely writing good poetry." He received a special Guggenheim in 1944 and the Pulitzer Prize in poetry for his book *V-Letter and Other Poems* (1944). ("The Conscientious Objector" was published in his volume *The Trial of a Poet*, in 1947.) He went on to have a distinguished poetic career, but chiefly as a poet of "hendecasyllables and the conversational," committed to formal rigor and to a full representation of ordinary life.

Many of the traditions of American war resistance are profoundly Christian in origin, and many antiwar writers are also Christians. That preponderance becomes less pronounced around this moment, as the community of war resistance begins to diversify; the presence of American-born Jewish writers like Replansky and Shapiro hints at that enlargement.

The Conscientious Objector

The gates clanged and they walked you into jail
More tense than felons but relieved to find
The hostile world shut out, the flags that dripped
From every mother's windowpane, obscene
The bloodlust sweating from the public heart,
The dog authority slavering at your throat.
A sense of quiet, of pulling down the blind
Possessed you. Punishment you felt was clean.

The decks, the catwalks, and the narrow light
Composed a ship. This was a mutinous crew
Troubling the captains for plain decencies,

A *Mayflower* brim with pilgrims headed out
To establish new theocracies to west,
A Noah's ark coasting the topmost seas
Ten miles above the sodomites and fish.
These inmates loved the only living doves.

Like all men hunted from the world you made
A good community, voyaging the storm
To no safe Plymouth or green Ararat;
Trouble or calm, the men with Bibles prayed,
The gaunt politicals construed our hate.
The opposite of all armies, you were best
Opposing uniformity and yourselves;
Prison and personality were your fate.

You suffered not so physically but knew
Maltreatment, hunger, ennui of the mind.
Well might the soldier kissing the hot beach
Erupting in his face damn all your kind.
Yet you who saved neither yourselves nor us
Are equally with those who shed the blood
The heroes of our cause. Your conscience is
What we come back to in the armistice.

WILLIAM STAFFORD

William Stafford's commitments to poetry and to nonviolence were both lifelong and often came together memorably; he could easily have been represented here with a poem against war (perhaps "At the Un-National Monument along the Canadian Border," or "For the Unknown Enemy"), or with some of the many aphorisms and reflections on conflict he jotted in his journals (collected posthumously by his son Kim in 2003, in *Every War Has Two Losers*).

Stafford's 1947 memoir *Down in My Heart* recounts the four years he spent in "alternative service" in Civilian Public Service Camps in Arkansas, California, and Illinois. "To Meet a Friend"—a chapter from the memoir—dramatizes one of the difficult choices that faced conscientious objectors in World War II. Some, like Stafford, conformed to the rules set up to accommodate them, performing "work of national importance" instead of fighting, in Stafford's case forestry work. Others, pushed more severely by their principles, protested even this nonviolent alternative, and faced severer consequences. Stafford's portrait of his friend George is a study in the kind of mixed emotions that must have made such choices, like many wartime choices, so difficult.

After his release, Stafford (1914–1993) took a teaching job at Lewis & Clark College, remaining there for most of the rest of his life. He won the National Book Award in 1963 for his collection *Traveling Through the Dark* and was named Consultant in Poetry to the Library of Congress in 1970.

To Meet a Friend

I do not want to live here.
The water is good, and the soil grows corn.
The people like each other.

I do not want to live here.
The land slopes right,
   and the sun likes it here.
There is incredible white snow in winter.

But every day a native of the world falls down.
Many are hurt in the mills and in the fields.
Some day everyone will be blind.

I do not want to just live here.

IT was dark all over camp that night when George called
from Los Angeles. Our few lights over the paths were still
shaded and dimmed because of the Coast dim-out; and the
cabins where the rows of men were sleeping were all dark—just
one light, down in the library barracks; George used to sit there
late. It was the only place like home in all the camp.

I took the call in the little Forest Service office, while the
night watchman leaned against the door in the shadow behind
me; and as I listened to George I watched the shaded light over
the desk swing its cone back and forth over the board for truck
keys and the Monday assignment sheet and the old metal filing
case where we kept the work records of each man—the record
of his service, his AWOLs, his refusals to work: the record that
saved him or sent him to prison.

George was on bail, awaiting trial, and he suggested that I
get leave and meet him for a day in town.

I met him at the Paseo, and we walked around the square.
He was thinner than ever, a skinny college boy, with a mobile
face that could turn suddenly still and inexpressive. I remember
exactly how it was that day, talking to my friend, out on bail
and due to go to prison in a week. When you are a CO and near
the prison stage yourself, you notice certain things:

*Along State Street after the rain the people go, smiling. They
stop to look at the store windows. On a newspaper rack someone
has hung up a girl's glove, picked up and saved for an unknown
person. In a room of the library where you go the students kneel
to get books from the lower shelves. Often they remain kneeling to
leaf through, to follow, to wonder. Then they sit down, legs drawn
up, feet out beside them, and forget all else.*

*Two girls come in and wait. A few minutes later the parents of
one of them come in, the mother crippled, hobbling forward, arms
outstretched to greet one of the girls. The father waits.*

The girl at the desk in the library is waiting. She tosses out the cards without looking up. Her suit is all right angles, and her walk is on a marked line. Someone is watching her.

No one is watching you. You are the person beside the aisle. People who wave are waving at another person, someone behind you. On the street no one calls your name; but in spite of not talking to anyone you are learning everyone's language—more than ever before. You are going to a big school, with halls that go everywhere. It costs everything you have to attend it. Its books are all over the world.

That is the way it was in town that Sunday afternoon being a CO with George. He was a criminal—not, like others so punished, because he lacked a sense of social responsibility, but because of an oversupply; and his experiences during the month since he had gone over the hill from camp had made him see a complex of ideas, a kind of picture, which he tried to express to me as we walked around the town and then down to the beach where we sat on the sand and looked out at the Pacific and the blue islands across the channel.

After leaving camp George had worked a few days for a church in Los Angeles and then had started toward Chicago, where a job in a social settlement house awaited him. He was standing under a street light in Amarillo waiting for a ride when the police car swerved up beside him. In the big room at the jail where the officers first took him were men being held for investigation, and the policemen had said to them:

"Here's a dirty yellow bastard who wouldn't fight for his country. Anyone who wants to bust him—go ahead." No one swung, though many talked, in phrases like the policeman's.

"I've never felt so far from home as on that night," George told me, as he lifted sand and let it sift through his fingers; "but I've had worse nights since. They put me in the tank that night and issued the bust-him invitation to the others there, but they were more sore at the cops than they were at me."

I thought of George in camp—his singing, his fiery speeches at camp meetings, his long discussions in the barracks while we lay around resting after work and waiting for supper. The tension in the barracks had actually become worse since the formal end of the war, and it was during one of those discussions that George had said, "As long as we grant the state the right to conscript, it is futile to hope for peace." He stood there in the barracks by the oil-drum stove and dragged a match across the top when he said that, and he looked up and down the long barracks, shot with the late sunlight as he talked. He was headed for jail; we all knew it. The flies were buzzing along the small windows; Lennie was arguing with Dan down by the magazine rack; the roomful of conscripted men were listening, or reading, or just sprawling there to wait—and all, maybe, headed for prison.

George had sat down at his typewriter, looked at the wall in that straight way of his, and rapidly typed out a letter to the Attorney General outlining his reasons for leaving Civilian Public Service: a precedent for slave labor, not a place for constructive service in crucial times, a dictatorial program administered, in spite of the wording of the law, by military men. George signed his name and the address he expected to have in Los Angeles. He got together some essentials—Gregg's Power of Non-Violence, a Pocket Songster, some changes of clothing, and a shirt Bob had given him. He gave Henry his ball glove, Phil his blue jacket with the hole in the elbow, and the camp co-op store his work gloves and boots. We stood and waved to him when he left, in the camp truck, before work call the next day.

That departure had been just a month ago, and now George and I were already strangers.

"How can you stay up there in camp doing Forest Service work when there are people starving abroad, and children in the cities all around here falling into delinquency? Why do you consent to waste your time up there? You know you're just being kept out of the way."

"I don't consent," I said. "I want to do something better. If I leave to do it, as you have, we both know it will mean prison. And what good can you do in prison? I can do more good where I am."

"You can make your protest plain. You can do your best to perform the chores that need to be done; if you are kept from them, it is at least not your fault."

"I don't believe that I can take a stand and do something without regard to the effect of my action on others; I want to change others, not alienate them."

"If you want to get on the good side of others, why don't you join their army?" George would end up by saying. "No. You've got to draw the line against conscription—complete refusal to take orders."

George had already found that there was no rest, no stopping place, no parole; and he had found the exhilaration of making a complete decision that ended uncertainty and the need of making other decisions.

"Why," he said, "when I finally realized that the die was cast, that my fortune was all out there ahead of me, I was nearly too happy to just walk. I smiled so broadly that everyone I passed thought he knew me, and many smiled or said hello. I have felt so right about leaving ever since I left, that there is no doubt in my mind that I have done what I should have done."

Everything that had happened to George in punishment for his attempt to do constructive work had strengthened his conviction that he was right to rebel.

"One night I was put in a cell by myself, Bill—in an empty block. There was only one light, and it was out in the corridor, a dim connection between me and the world, between me and light and life. And that night the bulb burned out; I was sitting there, and suddenly it was dark. Just stones and iron around me and no light, no noise. Do you know how it would be?"

I looked at George and tried to imagine; I try to imagine it sometimes now.

"I suddenly realized where I was, what might happen—how far I was from any kind of life I had ever dreamed of living. I thought of my mother, of my friends. What if no one ever got me out of there? What if it stayed dark—with bars around and me screaming—forever?"

George put his hands carefully on his knees and sat without moving, his eyes turned toward the islands.

"I think *that* was the worst night.

"In the Los Angeles county jail," he went on, "the food was bad; everyone was hungry. You could buy some more if you had money, but it was expensive.

"Have you ever seen the kind of place where visitors can talk to prisoners, Bill?" he asked, breaking off and beginning on a new subject with a kind of inhale and exhale, as if freeing himself of something. "The metal screen you talk through is made of such heavy wire, and the holes between are so small, that you can hardly see unless you get only three or four inches from the wire—and that's all you can do. There is a little corridorlike place where the visitors stand. A policeman is there to listen. . . ."

George talked for hours about the ordinary occurrences and surroundings of his life—a life that now repelled, now fascinated, me, a life that was no longer tied to considerations of policy, personal prestige, or the endless decisions, diplomacies, and hopes of ordinary social living. During that talk I learned the exhilarations of the outlaw, his personal freedoms, and his constant living with rebellion.

While George was talking, we watched a maidservant escorting two little children along the edge of the surf. One of the children could barely toddle, and he stumbled and rolled over when a reaching breaker rolled over his feet. We watched, but with no alarm, and the next wave confused and frightened him so much that when he got up he ran the wrong direction and was knocked flat by the next roller. He didn't know any way to go but farther out. George dashed down and picked him up, while the servant wrung her hands and cried out. George came running up the sloping beach, with the child kicking and crying, and gave him to the frantic nurse. By the time George had wrung the water from his baggy trouser legs and pranced around to dry, he judged it time for him to go to the highway to catch a ride down to Los Angeles. He didn't want to be away from the city of his parole overnight.

There wasn't anything more to say. George was going back to be sentenced to prison; we both knew it. And I left him there by that road. He laughed and waved when he got a ride, and climbed into a car that went away fast beneath the palm trees by the open water. I walked back up State Street, looking at the society I lived in.

I got a letter from George after he was sentenced to Tucson Prison Camp. He wrote:

"I am sitting on a large white rock which separates us from the free world. Below in the valley are the straight red roofs of camp. The formidable rock houses of our supervisors blend quietly into the rocks. The blue smoke and gray steam from the powerhouse drift protectingly over the scene. Now faint, now clear, the steady hum of the dynamo comes on the breeze, and occasionally the happy cries of children at play. How I would like to play with them and romp and roll in the yard. But that would never be allowed. Still in the deepening twilight may be seen the uneven row of white rocks so coldly severing our part of camp from that of the officers. . . ."

Later I heard from him again—he was allowed seven correspondents, with a limited number of letters. He had been sent, because of nonco-operation, to a more strict prison. This time he had gone with a committee to try to get the warden to end racial segregation in the prison. The warden had said: "Yes, it's all right for CO's and your friends to try to make these reforms while you're here; but you won't be here forever, and when you leave I'll be left with the job of administering a nonsegregated prison with prisoners who want segregation. . . ."

And the last time I heard of George I read about him on the front page of a paper in San Francisco. He and about ten others were on the fifteenth day of a hunger strike, protesting the continued imprisonment of men who would not kill and the continued drafting of men for the purpose of killing. George had been in solitary confinement for several months. The warden was ready to begin force-feeding—when the men's health made it necessary.

As I read that paper about George, he was in prison—to stay, evidently, for some time. The war had been over for a year, and I had been free for six months. I sat there in my home, with the newspaper in my hand, and thought about George and our talk on the beach and his question, "Can you imagine how it is?" And I thought about him that night, or any night, sitting in a cell, with one bulb burning in the corridor to light the stone between him and his friends and work and the islands off across the channel.

HOWARD SCHOENFELD

It is one of the iconic episodes in the history of American war resistance, a sensation when it happened and recounted many times since in memoirs and oral histories: from his solitary cell in the penitentiary at Danbury, Connecticut, the conscientious objector Don Benedict refused the warden's demands that he pitch in the prison's softball championship unless all of those similarly confined were released. At the eleventh hour, the warden relented; Benedict "pitched batter after batter out" and won the series; and the prisoners walked free.

The version of these events that follows comes from Howard Schoenfeld's "The Danbury Story," first published in shortened form in *The Nation* in 1947 and then more completely in the CO anthology *Prison Etiquette: The Convict's Compendium to Useful Information* (1950). Schoenfeld (1915–2004) served eleven months in Danbury and seven more after that in a Quaker work camp. Born in Pittsburgh and raised in Hot Springs, Arkansas, he spent most of his life, from his twenties onward, in Greenwich Village; after his release he wrote science fiction, fantasy, and mystery stories, scripts for the TV show *Atom Squad* (1953), and the crime novel *Let Them Eat Bullets* (1954).

Some of Benedict's own recollections of his prison time appear later in this book, and are considerably less joyous. On the softball field, athletic and victorious, he seemed every inch the conventional hero; heroism of conscience may be harder to see and harder to celebrate, but the stakes were surely higher, as Benedict and Schoenfeld both understood.

FROM
The Danbury Story

WEEKS PASSED.

One day a guard entered the cell block, walked down the corridor and opened the door to Benedict's cell. Benedict, like most of the pacifists in our group, was a fine athlete. Outside, his physical prowess was a legend in amateur athletic circles, and, in particular, he excelled as a soft ball pitcher. Big muscled, strong and agile, his speed ball was so swift only one man in the prison could catch him. The prison team, built around his pitching, was tied for first place in its league, and his ability to hold the opposition scoreless had placed it there. The inmates, probably for the first time in the history of prison ball, were solidly behind their team, which originally entered the league expecting to serve as a scrub practise team for the other amateurs in that area.

The Warden, a sports lover, was delighted with the unusual situation, and it did not surprise us to hear the guard offer Benedict his freedom if he would pitch the championship play-off games, which were scheduled for that day. Benedict pointed out he was in no condition to pitch after his long confinement, and wasn't sure he could make it. The guard explained he would be given time to limber up and mentioned how disappointed the inmates would be if the championship was lost. Benedict thereupon said he would do it. He added, however, only on condition that all the men in solitary, including the inmates not in the pacifist group, were released. The guard said he would speak to the Warden about it, and we heard him trudge down the corridor.

We waited in silence till he came back. The Warden could not agree to Benedict's terms, but he offered a compromise. He would release all the conscientious objectors for the game, and Benedict permanently. Benedict refused. The guard disappeared, returning shortly thereafter with another offer. The Warden would release everyone for the game, and Benedict permanently. Benedict refused. The guard disappeared.

About a half hour later a Lieutenant of guards entered and told Benedict the men were warming up for the first game. The inmates, he said, were aware of his refusal to pitch, and were resentful towards him and the rest of us. He then said he thought he could prevail on the Warden to release all the conscientious objectors permanently, and the other men in solitary for the game, if Benedict would do it. Benedict refused.

Fully an hour passed before the Captain of guards entered and released us. The prison team had lost the first game of the series, and the Warden, unable to endure further losses, had agreed to Benedict's terms.

Grinning hugely, we left our cells, and laughing at each other's pasty complexions, bearded faces, and unkempt hair, hurried out into the prison yard. A wave of applause went through the inmate stands as Benedict rushed down the field and began warming up.

Benedict, in true Frank Merriwell fashion, summoned his strength after the long weeks of demoralized living, and, in a superhuman and prodigious performance, pitched batter after batter out, enabling the prison team to rally and score, and win the series.

Word of the remarkable feat reached the neighboring cities through the sports pages of their newspapers, and later, when Benedict was released, over 20,000 people paid fancy admission prices to see him in action at a benefit game.

Morale broke down completely in the prison after the games, when we were rounded up, including Benedict, and thrown back into solitary. The guard on duty was so disgusted he did not even bother to lock our cells.

The next day at noon the Warden reversed his stand and released us. The midday whistle had blown and the men were already in the mess hall, eating. We straggled across the empty yard, basking in the sun, enjoying our freedom. A spontaneous wave of applause broke out among the men as the first of our group entered the hall. Surging across the hall the wave became a crescendo. Six hundred pairs of hands joined in and the crescendo became pandemonium. Guards ran up and down the aisles; they were ignored. The pandemonium increased when Benedict entered the hall, maintaining itself at an incredible pitch. A volcano of thunderous and deafening applause burst out when Arle Brooks entered, but when the so-called criminals who had been in solitary came in, the convicts literally went wild, beating their metal cups on the tables, and stamping their feet.

We stood in the center of the hall, astounded at the demonstration. It became clear to me that although they were applauding Benedict, Brooks, and all of us who had been in solitary, they were doing something more. A mass catharsis of human misery was taking place before our eyes. Some of the men were weeping, others were laughing like madmen. It was like nothing I had ever seen before, and nothing I ever expect to see again.

GENERAL ADVISORY COMMITTEE TO THE U.S. ATOMIC ENERGY COMMISSION

In August 1949 the Soviet Union exploded its first atomic bomb, ending the American monopoly on nuclear weapons. Their test triggered a secret debate within the U.S. government over whether to undertake an "all-out" effort to build a "super bomb" that would use the immense heat of a fission (atomic) bomb to ignite fusion reactions in isotopes of hydrogen. Although scientists had known since 1942 that a hydrogen bomb was theoretically possible, after seven years it was still unclear whether building one was technically feasible. At the end of October 1949 the General Advisory Committee of the Atomic Energy Commission met in Washington to debate "the super" over the course of a three-day meeting. Led by J. Robert Oppenheimer, the GAC was made up of leading scientists and scientific administrators, many of whom had played major roles in the wartime atomic bomb project. (Oppenheimer had watched the first detonation of an atomic bomb, on July 16, 1945, in New Mexico; thinking back on the experience later, he said that on seeing the detonation he recalled Lord Krishna's declaration in the Bhagavad Gita, "Now I am become Death, the destroyer of worlds.")

After three days of deliberations, the committee unanimously recommended against pursuing the hydrogen bomb for reasons both technical—set forth in the main committee report—and moral, as expressed in the report's majority and minority annexes. The protests of the GAC scientists fell on deaf ears, and in January 1950 President Truman ordered work on the hydrogen bomb to proceed. A series of theoretical breakthroughs in 1951 made the bomb feasible, and the initial test of the new design concept in November 1952 released almost 700 times the energy of the weapon dropped on Hiroshima. Soviet scientists raced to catch up, and in November 1955 successfully exploded their own hydrogen super bomb.

Annexes to the General Advisory Committee Report of October 30, 1949

October 30, 1949

WE have been asked by the Commission whether or not they should immediately initiate an "all-out" effort to develop a weapon whose energy release is 100 to 1000 times greater and whose destructive power in terms of area of damage is 20 to 100 times greater than those of the present atomic bomb. We recommend strongly against such action.

We base our recommendation on our belief that the extreme dangers to mankind inherent in the proposal wholly outweigh any military advantage that could come from this development. Let it be clearly realized that this is a super weapon; it is in a totally different category from an atomic bomb. The reason for developing such super bombs would be to have the capacity to devastate a vast area with a single bomb. Its use would involve a decision to slaughter a vast number of civilians. We are alarmed as to the possible global effects of the radioactivity generated by the explosion of a few super bombs of conceivable magnitude. If super bombs will work at all, there is no inherent limit in the destructive power that may be attained with them. Therefore, a super bomb might become a weapon of genocide.

The existence of such a weapon in our armory would have far-reaching effects on world opinion: reasonable people the world over would realize that the existence of a weapon of this type whose power of destruction is essentially unlimited represents a threat to the future of the human race which is intolerable. Thus we believe that the psychological effect of the weapon in our hands would be adverse to our interest.

We believe a super bomb should never be produced. Mankind would be far better off not to have a demonstration of the feasibility of such a weapon until the present climate of world opinion changes.

It is by no means certain that the weapon can be developed at all and by no means certain that the Russians will produce one within a decade. To the argument that the Russians may succeed in developing this weapon, we would reply that our undertaking it will not prove a deterrent to them. Should they use the weapon against us, reprisals by our large stock of atomic bombs would be comparably effective to the use of a super.

In determining not to proceed to develop the super bomb, we see a unique opportunity of providing by example some limitations on the totality of war and thus of limiting the fear and arousing the hopes of mankind.

James B. Conant
Hartley Rowe
Cyril Stanley Smith
L. A. DuBridge
Oliver E. Buckley
J. R. Oppenheimer

October 30, 1949

AN OPINION ON THE DEVELOPMENT
OF THE "SUPER"

A decision on the proposal that an all-out effort be undertaken for the development of the "Super" cannot in our opinion be separated from considerations of broad national policy. A weapon like the "Super" is only an advantage when its energy release is from 100–1000 times greater than that of ordinary atomic bombs. The area of destruction therefore would run from 150 to approximately 1000 square miles or more.

Necessarily such a weapon goes far beyond any military objective and enters the range of very great natural catastrophes. By its very nature it cannot be confined to a military objective but becomes a weapon which in practical effect is almost one of genocide.

It is clear that the use of such a weapon cannot be justified on any ethical ground which gives a human being a certain individuality and dignity even if he happens to be a resident of an enemy country. It is evident to us that this would be the view of peoples in other countries. Its use would put the United States in a bad moral position relative to the peoples of the world.

Any postwar situation resulting from such a weapon would leave unresolvable enmities for generations. A desirable peace cannot come from such an inhuman application of force. The postwar problems would dwarf the problems which confront us at present.

The application of this weapon with the consequent great release of radioactivity would have results unforeseeable at present, but would certainly render large areas unfit for habitation for long periods of time.

The fact that no limits exist to the destructiveness of this weapon makes its very existence and the knowledge of its construction a danger to humanity as a whole. It is necessarily an evil thing considered in any light.

For these reasons we believe it important for the President of the United States to tell the American public, and the world, that we think it wrong on fundamental ethical principles to initiate a program of development of such a weapon. At the same time it would be appropriate to invite the nations of the world to join us in a solemn pledge not to proceed in the development or construction of weapons of this category. If such a pledge were accepted even without control machinery, it appears highly probable that an advanced stage of development leading to a test by another power could be detected by available physical means. Furthermore, we have in our possession, in our stockpile of atomic bombs, the means for adequate "military" retaliation for the production or use of a "super."

E. FERMI
I. I. RABI

ED McCURDY

I grew up in the 1950s listening to "Last Night I Had the Strangest Dream," responding to it as the devout respond to hymns in church. I had no idea that the song had an author; it seemed as eternal and authorless as "Happy Birthday."

But it did have an author, the singer and songwriter and actor Ed McCurdy (1919–2000). He grew up in Pennsylvania, then after high school became a nightclub singer and vaudeville performer (serenading the fan-dancer Sally Rand while pushing her on her swing). Later he hosted a show on Canadian radio, met a lot of American folksingers there, and became a folksinger himself and also a television and advertising personality. He retired as a vocal performer in the late 1960s for health reasons and had a second career as a character actor on Canadian television.

He wrote "Strangest Dream" in the spring of 1950. It has been recorded by performers including The Weavers and Simon & Garfunkel, and in seventy-six languages; is the theme song of the Peace Corps; and was sung by East German schoolchildren as they watched the dismantling of the Berlin Wall. Its lyrics are disarmingly simple, offering straightforward utopian vision: "I dreamed the world had all agreed / To put an end to war." Nothing about how or when, nothing oppositional or analytic, just the vision, candidly identified as the speaker's "strangest dream."

Last Night I Had the Strangest Dream

Last night I had the strangest dream,
I'd ever dreamed before,
I dreamed the world had all agreed
To put an end to war.

I dreamed I saw a mighty room,
The room was full of men
And the Paper they were signing said
They'd never fight again.

And when the Paper was all signed,
And a million copies made,

They all joined hands and bowed their heads
And grateful prayers were prayed.

And the people in the streets below
Were dancing 'round and 'round,
While swords and guns and uniforms
Were scattered on the ground.

Last night I had the strangest dream,
I'd ever dreamed before,
I dreamed the world had all agreed
To put an end to war.

Last night I had the strangest dream,
I'd ever dreamed before,
I dreamed the world had all agreed
To put an end to war.

RAY BRADBURY

"August 2026: There Will Come Soft Rains," first published in *Collier's* when Ray Bradbury (1920–2012) was twenty-nine, borrows its title from Sara Teasdale's gently apocalyptic poem, quotes that poem, and has much in common with it. But Teasdale, writing in 1920, was imagining the end of the human race at a distance; nothing in her world threatened immediate annihilation. Bradbury, writing in 1950, five years after the dropping of the atomic bomb and one year after the news that the Soviet Union had produced atomic bombs of its own, has all too clear an idea of what annihilation might look like and when it might come, and depicts it vividly.

Bradbury was among the most famous American science fiction writers during his lifetime, and probably the one most respected outside the science fiction community; it is no accident that his story appeared in *Collier's* rather than in *Astounding Science Fiction*. His best works are in fact uncategorizable, notable among them *The Martian Chronicles* (the loosely linked collection into which the present story was fitted) and the anti-book-burning fantasy *Fahrenheit 451*, later made into a movie by François Truffaut. (Bradbury asked that his epitaph contain only his name, his dates, and the words "author of *Fahrenheit 451*.")

The science fiction community itself sometimes looked askance at him, finding his work scientifically imprecise and impressionistic; his general distrust of technology, insightfully manifested in the present story, may have seemed a suspicious trait in a science fiction writer.

August 2026: There Will Come Soft Rains

In the living room the voice-clock sang, *Tick-tock, seven o'clock, time to get up, time to get up, seven o'clock!* as if it were afraid that nobody would. The morning house lay empty. The clock ticked on, repeating and repeating its sounds into the emptiness. *Seven-nine, breakfast time, seven-nine!*

In the kitchen the breakfast stove gave a hissing sigh and ejected from its warm interior eight pieces of perfectly browned toast, eight eggs sunnyside up, sixteen slices of bacon, two coffees, and two cool glasses of milk.

"Today is August 4, 2026," said a second voice from the kitchen ceiling, "in the city of Allendale, California." It repeated the date three times for memory's sake. "Today is Mr. Featherstone's birthday. Today is the anniversary of Tilita's marriage. Insurance is payable, as are the water, gas, and light bills."

Somewhere in the walls, relays clicked, memory tapes glided under electric eyes.

Eight-one, tick-tock, eight-one o'clock, off to school, off to work, run, run, eight-one! But no doors slammed, no carpets took the soft tread of rubber heels. It was raining outside. The weather box on the front door sang quietly: "Rain, rain, go away; rubbers, raincoats for today . . ." And the rain tapped on the empty house, echoing.

Outside, the garage chimed and lifted its door to reveal the waiting car. After a long wait the door swung down again.

At eight-thirty the eggs were shriveled and the toast was like stone. An aluminum wedge scraped them into the sink, where hot water whirled them down a metal throat which digested and flushed them away to the distant sea. The dirty dishes were dropped into a hot washer and emerged twinkling dry.

Nine-fifteen, sang the clock, *time to clean.*

Out of warrens in the wall, tiny robot mice darted. The rooms were acrawl with the small cleaning animals, all rubber and metal. They thudded against chairs, whirling their mustached runners, kneading the rug nap, sucking gently at hidden dust. Then, like mysterious invaders, they popped into their burrows. Their pink electric eyes faded. The house was clean.

Ten o'clock. The sun came out from behind the rain. The house stood alone in a city of rubble and ashes. This was the one house left standing. At night the ruined city gave off a radioactive glow which could be seen for miles.

Ten-fifteen. The garden sprinklers whirled up in golden founts, filling the soft morning air with scatterings of brightness. The water pelted windowpanes, running down the charred west side where the house had been burned evenly free of its white paint. The entire west face of the house was black, save for five places. Here the silhouette in paint of a man mowing a lawn. Here, as in a photograph, a woman bent to pick flowers. Still farther over, their images burned on wood in one titanic instant, a small boy, hands flung into the air; higher up, the image of a thrown ball, and opposite him a girl, hands raised to catch a ball which never came down.

The five spots of paint—the man, the woman, the children, the ball—remained. The rest was a thin charcoaled layer.

The gentle sprinkler rain filled the garden with falling light.

Until this day, how well the house had kept its peace. How carefully it had inquired, "Who goes there? What's the password?" and, getting no answer from lonely foxes and whining cats, it had shut up its windows and drawn shades in an old-maidenly preoccupation with self-protection which bordered on a mechanical paranoia.

It quivered at each sound, the house did. If a sparrow brushed a window, the shade snapped up. The bird, startled, flew off! No, not even a bird must touch the house!

The house was an altar with ten thousand attendants, big, small, servicing, attending, in choirs. But the gods had gone away, and the ritual of the religion continued senselessly, uselessly.

Twelve noon.

A dog whined, shivering, on the front porch.

The front door recognized the dog voice and opened. The dog, once huge and fleshy, but now gone to bone and covered with sores, moved in and through the house, tracking mud. Behind it whirred angry mice, angry at having to pick up mud, angry at inconvenience.

For not a leaf fragment blew under the door but what the wall panels flipped open and the copper scrap rats flashed swiftly out. The offending dust, hair, or paper, seized in miniature steel jaws, was raced back to the burrows. There, down tubes which fed into the cellar, it was dropped into the sighing vent of an incinerator which sat like evil Baal in a dark corner.

The dog ran upstairs, hysterically yelping to each door, at last realizing, as the house realized, that only silence was here.

It sniffed the air and scratched the kitchen door. Behind the door, the stove was making pancakes which filled the house with a rich baked odor and the scent of maple syrup.

The dog frothed at the mouth, lying at the door, sniffing, its eyes turned to fire. It ran wildly in circles, biting at its tail, spun in a frenzy, and died. It lay in the parlor for an hour.

Two o'clock, sang a voice.

Delicately sensing decay at last, the regiments of mice hummed out as softly as blown gray leaves in an electrical wind.

Two-fifteen.

The dog was gone.

In the cellar, the incinerator glowed suddenly and a whirl of sparks leaped up the chimney.

Two thirty-five.

Bridge tables sprouted from patio walls. Playing cards fluttered onto pads in a shower of pips. Martinis manifested on an oaken bench with egg-salad sandwiches. Music played.

But the tables were silent and the cards untouched.

At four o'clock the tables folded like great butterflies back through the paneled walls.

Four-thirty.

The nursery walls glowed.

Animals took shape: yellow giraffes, blue lions, pink antelopes, lilac panthers cavorting in crystal substance. The walls were glass. They looked out upon color and fantasy. Hidden films clocked through well-oiled sprockets, and the walls lived. The nursery floor was woven to resemble a crisp, cereal meadow. Over this ran aluminum roaches and iron crickets, and in the hot still air butterflies of delicate red tissue wavered among the sharp aroma of animal spoors! There was the sound like a great matted yellow hive of bees within a dark bellows, the lazy bumble of a purring lion. And there was the patter of okapi feet and the murmur of a fresh jungle rain, like other hoofs, falling upon the summer-starched grass. Now the walls dissolved into distances of parched weed, mile on mile, and warm endless sky. The animals drew away into thorn brakes and water holes.

It was the children's hour.

Five o'clock. The bath filled with clear hot water.

Six, seven, eight o'clock. The dinner dishes manipulated like magic tricks, and in the study a click. In the metal stand opposite the hearth where a fire now blazed up warmly, a cigar popped out, half an inch of soft gray ash on it, smoking, waiting.

Nine o'clock. The beds warmed their hidden circuits, for nights were cool here.

Nine-five. A voice spoke from the study ceiling:

"Mrs. McClellan, which poem would you like this evening?" The house was silent.

The voice said at last, "Since you express no preference, I shall select a poem at random." Quiet music rose to back the voice. "Sara Teasdale. As I recall, your favorite. . . .

> *"There will come soft rains and the smell of the ground,*
> *And swallows circling with their shimmering sound;*
>
> *And frogs in the pools singing at night,*
> *And wild plum trees in tremulous white;*
>
> *Robins will wear their feathery fire,*
> *Whistling their whims on a low fence-wire;*
>
> *And not one will know of the war, not one*
> *Will care at last when it is done.*
>
> *Not one would mind, neither bird nor tree,*
> *If mankind perished utterly;*
>
> *And Spring herself, when she woke at dawn*
> *Would scarcely know that we were gone."*

The fire burned on the stone hearth and the cigar fell away into a mound of quiet ash on its tray. The empty chairs faced each other between the silent walls, and the music played.

At ten o'clock the house began to die.

The wind blew. A falling tree bough crashed through the kitchen window. Cleaning solvent, bottled, shattered over the stove. The room was ablaze in an instant!

"Fire!" screamed a voice. The house lights flashed, water pumps shot water from the ceilings. But the solvent spread on the linoleum, licking, eating, under the kitchen door, while the voices took it up in chorus: "Fire, fire, fire!"

The house tried to save itself. Doors sprang tightly shut, but the windows were broken by the heat and the wind blew and sucked upon the fire.

The house gave ground as the fire in ten billion angry sparks moved with flaming ease from room to room and then up the stairs. While scurrying water rats squeaked from the walls, pistoled their water, and ran for more. And the wall sprays let down showers of mechanical rain.

But too late. Somewhere, sighing, a pump shrugged to a stop. The quenching rain ceased. The reserve water supply which had filled baths and washed dishes for many quiet days was gone.

The fire crackled up the stairs. It fed upon Picassos and Matisses in the upper halls, like delicacies, baking off the oily flesh, tenderly crisping the canvases into black shavings.

Now the fire lay in beds, stood in windows, changed the colors of drapes!

And then, reinforcements.

From attic trapdoors, blind robot faces peered down with faucet mouths gushing green chemical.

The fire backed off, as even an elephant must at the sight of a dead snake. Now there were twenty snakes whipping over the floor, killing the fire with a clear cold venom of green froth.

But the fire was clever. It had sent flame outside the house, up through the attic to the pumps there. An explosion! The attic brain which directed the pumps was shattered into bronze shrapnel on the beams.

The fire rushed back into every closet and felt of the clothes hung there.

The house shuddered, oak bone on bone, its bared skeleton cringing from the heat, its wire, its nerves revealed as if a surgeon had torn the skin off to let the red veins and capillaries quiver in the scalded air. Help, help! Fire! Run, run! Heat snapped mirrors like the first brittle winter ice. And the voices wailed Fire, fire, run, run, like a tragic nursery rhyme, a dozen voices, high, low, like children dying in a forest, alone, alone. And the voices fading as the wires popped their sheathings like hot chestnuts. One, two, three, four, five voices died.

In the nursery the jungle burned. Blue lions roared, purple giraffes bounded off. The panthers ran in circles, changing color, and ten million animals, running before the fire, vanished off toward a distant steaming river. . . .

Ten more voices died. In the last instant under the fire avalanche, other choruses, oblivious, could be heard announcing the time, playing music, cutting the lawn by remote-control mower, or setting an umbrella frantically out and in the slamming and opening front door, a thousand things happening, like a clock shop when each clock strikes the hour insanely before or after the other, a scene of maniac confusion, yet unity; singing, screaming, a few last cleaning mice darting bravely out to carry the horrid ashes away! And one voice, with sublime disregard for the situation, read poetry aloud in the fiery study, until all the film spools burned, until all the wires withered and the circuits cracked.

The fire burst the house and let it slam flat down, puffing out skirts of spark and smoke.

In the kitchen, an instant before the rain of fire and timber, the stove could be seen making breakfasts at a psychopathic rate, ten dozen eggs, six loaves of toast, twenty dozen bacon strips, which, eaten by fire, started the stove working again, hysterically hissing!

The crash. The attic smashing into kitchen and parlor. The parlor into cellar, cellar into sub-cellar. Deep freeze, armchair, film tapes, circuits, beds, and all like skeletons thrown in a cluttered mound deep under.

Smoke and silence. A great quantity of smoke.

Dawn showed faintly in the east. Among the ruins, one wall stood alone. Within the wall, a last voice said, over and over again and again, even as the sun rose to shine upon the heaped rubble and steam:

"Today is August 5, 2026, today is August 5, 2026, today is . . ."

OMAR N. BRADLEY

Born in a Missouri log cabin, Omar N. Bradley (1893–1981) graduated from West Point in 1915, a classmate of Dwight Eisenhower. Like Eisenhower, Bradley never served overseas during World War I and spent much of the conflict guarding copper mines in Montana. During the interwar years he held a series of command and teaching assignments, including a tour as an instructor at the Infantry School under George Marshall. Bradley received his first combat command in 1943, successfully leading a corps in Tunisia and Sicily, and then went to England to help Eisenhower plan the invasion of Normandy. Afterward he led American ground forces in northwest Europe from D-day until the German surrender. From 1949 to 1953 he served as the first chairman of the Joint Chiefs of Staff, during which time he supported building the hydrogen bomb and endorsed Truman's decision to fight a limited war in Korea.

Not the life story one would expect in a writer figuring in this book. But the 1958 piece included here is entirely consistent with his career and sensibility; he saw as a military man that a nuclear war was unwinnable and catastrophic, and turned his intelligence to solving the problem posed by nuclear weapons with the same trust in human rationality and precision of calculation that had distinguished his military career. So far, at least as regards nuclear weapons, his trust in human rationality has not been falsified.

A Decent Respect for Human Intelligence

THE central problem of our time—as I view it—is how to employ human intelligence for the salvation of mankind. It is a problem we have put upon ourselves. For we have defiled our intellect by the creation of such scientific instruments of destruction that we are now in desperate danger of destroying ourselves.

As a result, we are now speeding inexorably toward a day when even the ingenuity of our scientists may be unable to save us from the consequences of a single rash act or a lone reckless hand upon the switch of an uninterceptable missile. For twelve years now we've fought to stave off this ultimate threat of disaster by devising arms which would be both ultimate and disastrous.

This irony can probably be compounded a few more years, or perhaps even a few decades. Missiles will bring anti-missiles, and anti-missiles will bring anti-anti-missiles. But inevitably, this whole electronic house of cards will reach a point where it can be constructed no higher.

At that point we shall have come to the peak of this whole incredible dilemma into which the world is shoving itself. And when that time comes there will be little we can do other than to settle down uneasily, smother our fears, and attempt to live in the shadow of death.

Should this situation come to pass, we would have but one single and thin thread to cling to. We call it reason. We reason that no government, no single group of men—indeed, not even one wilful individual—would be so foolhardy, so reckless, as to precipitate a war which would most surely end in mutual destruction.

This reasoning may have the benefit of logic. But even logic sometimes goes awry. How can we assume that reason will prevail in a crisis when there is ordinarily so little reason among men? Reason has failed before, it can fail again.

Have we already gone too far in this search for peace through the accumulation of peril? Is there any way to halt this trend? I believe there is a way out. And I believe it because I have acquired a decent respect for human intelligence.

It may be that the problems of accommodation in a world split by rival ideologies are more difficult than those with which we have struggled in the construction of ballistics missiles. But I believe, too, that if we apply to these human problems, the energy, creativity, and the perseverance we have devoted to science, even problems of accommodation will yield to reason. Admittedly, the problem of peaceful accommodation in the world is infinitely more complex than a trip to the moon. But if we will only come to the realization that it must be worked out—whatever it may mean even to such sacred traditions as absolute national sovereignty—I believe that we can find a workable solution.

I confess that this is as much an article of faith as it is an expression of reason. But this, my friends, is what we need, faith in our ability to do what must be done. Without that faith we shall never get started. And until we get started, we shall never know what can be done.

If I am sometimes discouraged, it is not by the magnitude of the problem, but by our colossal indifference to it. I am unable to understand why we do not make greater, more diligent and more imaginative use of reason and human intelligence in seeking an accord and compromise which will make it possible for mankind to control the atom and banish it as an instrument of war.

This is the real and—indeed—the most strenuous challenge to man's intellect today. By comparison with it, the conquest of space is of small significance. For until we learn how to live together, until we rid ourselves of the strife that mocks our pretensions of civilization, our adventures in science—instead of producing human progress—will continue to produce greater peril.

We can compete with a Sputnik and probably create bigger and better Sputniks of our own. But when are we going to muster an intelligence equal to that applied against the Sputnik and dedicate it to the preservation of this Satellite on which we live?

How long can we put off salvation? When does humanity run out?

If enough of us believe strongly enough in the ability of intelligent human beings to get together on some basis of a just accord, we might somehow, somewhere, in some way, make a start on it.

We can't sit about waiting for some felicitous accident of history that may somehow make the world all right. Time is running against us.

If we're going to save ourselves from the instruments of our own intellect, we had better soon get ourselves under control and make the world safe for living.

ALBERT S. BIGELOW

Albert S. Bigelow (1906–1993) was just the sort of pacifist that pacifists like to present to skeptics. Born into a prominent Boston family, he went to Harvard, studied architecture at MIT, and then joined the Navy, commanding first a submarine chaser and then a destroyer escort during World War II. After the war he was for a time housing commissioner of Massachusetts; he volunteered as a Massachusetts precinct captain for Eisenhower.

He was on the bridge of the destroyer escort sailing into Pearl Harbor when he learned of the dropping of the atomic bomb; "it was then," he later wrote, "that I realized for the first time that morally war is impossible." The consequences of that moment shaped the rest of his life. He resigned his commission in the Naval Reserve in 1952, two months before he would have become eligible for a pension. His wife Sylvia Weld had become a Quaker in 1948, and Bigelow himself later did the same. Through their Quaker connections the couple housed two of the "Hiroshima Maidens," young Japanese women disfigured by the bomb who were brought to the United States in 1955 for reconstructive surgery. They made a strong impression on Bigelow, partly because of the injuries they had sustained, partly because they were so free of resentment toward him and toward Americans generally. By 1957 Bigelow was working to protest the proliferation of nuclear weapons by any means necessary. He attempted to deliver a petition against nuclear testing to Maxwell Rabb, the secretary to the Cabinet; Rabb refused to meet with him. He was arrested trying to enter the Nevada Test Site shortly before a nuclear detonation.

The Navy man and the antiwar activist came together in the action Bigelow is most often remembered for, his attempt in 1958 to sail the *Golden Rule* into the Eniwetok Proving Ground, the Atomic Energy Commission's atmospheric test site in the Marshall Islands. The ketch was intercepted twice by the Coast Guard, and Bigelow and his crew spent sixty days in jail, but their example inspired Earle and Barbara Reynolds to sail their yacht, the *Phoenix of Hiroshima*, into the test zone at Bikini Atoll, and indirectly inspired the subsequent work of Greenpeace. (His account of the protest appeared in *Liberation* in February 1958.)

Bigelow remained active in antiwar work after the *Golden Rule* expedition. He was also a champion of African American civil rights, sitting with John Lewis on a Greyhound bus to New Orleans during the 1961 Freedom Rides. (The two were severely beaten attempting to enter a whites-only waiting room in Rock Hill, South Carolina.) Bigelow's legacy lives on in one quite wonderful way: the *Golden Rule* was raised from the bottom of Humboldt Bay in 2010, and the group Veterans for Peace undertook to restore and sail it as a symbol and floating classroom. It was relaunched on June 20, 2015.

Why I Am Sailing into the Pacific Bomb-Test Area

My friend Bill Huntington and I are planning to sail a small vessel westward into the Pacific H-bomb test area. By April we expect to reach nuclear testing grounds at Eniwetok. We will remain there as long as the tests of H-bombs continue. With us will be two other volunteers.

Why? Because it is the way I can say to my government, to the British government, and to the Kremlin: "Stop! Stop this madness before it is too late. For God's sake, turn back!"

How have I come to this conviction? Why do I feel under compulsion, under moral orders, as it were, to do this?

The answer to such questions, at least in part, has to do with my experience as a Naval officer during World War II. The day after Pearl Harbor was attacked, I was at the Navy recruiting offices. I had had a lot of experience in navigating vessels. Life in the Navy would be a glamorous change from the dull mechanism of daily civilian living. My experience assured me of success. All this adventure ahead and the prospect of becoming a hero into the bargain.

I suppose, too, that I had an enormous latent desire to conform, to go along with the rest of my fellows. I was swayed by the age-old psychology of meeting force with force. It did not really occur to me to resist the drag of the institution of war, the pattern of organized violence, which had existed for so many centuries. This psychology prevailed even though I had already reflected on the fantastic wastefulness of war—the German *Bismarck* hunting the British *Hood* and sending it to the bottom of the sea, and the British Navy hunting the *Bismarck* and scuttling it.

I volunteered, but instead of being sent to sea, I was assigned to 90 Church Street in New York and worked in project "plot" establishing the whereabouts of all combat ships in the Atlantic. In a couple of months I escaped from this assignment and was transferred to the Naval Training Station at Northwestern University.

I had not been at Northwestern very long when I sensed that because of my past experience I would be made an instructor there and still not get to sea. So I deliberately flunked an examination in navigation and before long was assigned to a submarine chaser in the Atlantic.

From March to October of 1943 I was in command of a submarine chaser in the Solomon Islands, during the fighting. It was during this period that more than 100 Japanese planes were shot down in one day. This was called "the Turkey Shoot." The insensitivity which decent men must develop in such situations is appalling. I remember that the corpse of a Japanese airman who had been shot down was floating bolt upright in one of the coves, a position resulting from the structure of the Japanese life belts, which were different from our Mae Wests. Each day as we passed the cove we saw this figure, his face growing blacker under the terrific sun. We laughingly called him Smiling Jack. As a matter of fact, I think I gave him that name myself and felt rather proud of my wit.

Later in World War II, I was Captain of the destroyer escort *Dale W. Peterson*—DE 337—and I was on her bridge as we came into Pearl Harbor from San Francisco when the first news arrived of the explosion of an atomic bomb over Hiroshima. Although I had no way of understanding what an atom bomb was I was absolutely awestruck, as I suppose all men were for a moment. Intuitively it was then that I realized for the first time that morally war is impossible.

I don't suppose I had the same absolute realization with my whole being, so to speak, of the immorality and "impossibility" of nuclear war until the morning of August 7, 1957. On that day, I sat with a score of friends, before dawn, in the Nevada desert just outside the entrance to the Camp Mercury testing grounds. The day before, eleven of us, in protest against the summer-long tests, had tried to enter the restricted area. We had been arrested as we stepped one after another over the boundary line, and had been carried off to a ghost town which stands at the entrance to Death Valley. There we had been given a speedy trial under the charge of trespassing under the Nevada laws. Sentencing had been suspended for a year, and later in the afternoon we had returned to Camp Mercury to continue the Prayer and Conscience Vigil along with others who had remained there during our civil disobedience action.

In the early morning of August 7 an experimental bomb was exploded. We sat with our backs to the explosion site. But when the flash came I felt again the utterly impossible horror of this whole business, the same complete realization that nuclear war must go, that I had felt twelve years before on the bridge of U. S. S. *Dale W. Peterson*, off Pearl Harbor.

I think also that deep down somewhere in me, and in all men at all times, there is a realization that the pattern of violence meeting violence makes no sense, and that war violates something central in the human heart—"that of God," as we Quakers sometimes say. For example, when each of us at the trial the afternoon before had told why we were committing civil disobedience against nuclear tests, our attorney, Francis Heisler, said: "There isn't one of us in this court room who doesn't wish that he had walked into the testing grounds with these people this morning." Everybody, including the police and court officers, nodded assent.

However, I am ahead of my story. At the close of the War, in spite of what I had felt on the bridge of that destroyer, I did not break away from my old life. For a time I was Housing Commissioner of Massachusetts. Like many other people who had been through the War, I was seeking some sort of unified life-philosophy or religion. I did a good deal of religious "window-shopping." I became impressed by the fact that in one way or another the saints, the wise men, those who seemed to me truly experienced, all pointed in one direction—toward nonviolence, truth, love, toward a way and a goal that could not be reconciled with war. For quite a while, to use a phrase of Alan Watts', I "sucked the finger instead of going where it pointed." But finally I realized that I did have to move in that direction, and in 1952 I resigned my commission in the Naval Reserve. It was promptly and courteously accepted. I felt a bit proud of doing it a month before I would have come into a pension. Such little things we pride ourselves on!

I came into contact with the Quakers, the Society of Friends. My wife, Sylvia, had already joined the Society in 1948. As late as 1955 I was still fighting off joining the Society, which seemed to me to involve a great, awesome commitment. I suppose I was like the man in one of Shaw's plays who wanted to be a Christian—but not yet.

Then came the experience of having in our home for some months two of the Hiroshima maidens who had been injured and disfigured in the bombing of August 6, 1945. Norman Cousins and other wonderful people brought them to this country for plastic surgery. There were two things about these girls that hit me very hard and forced me to see that I had no choice but to make the commitment to live, as best I could, a life of nonviolence and reconciliation. One was the fact that when they were bombed in 1945 the two girls in our home were nine and thirteen years old. What earthly thing could they have done to give some semblance of what we call justice to the ordeal inflicted upon them and hundreds like them? What possible good could come out of human action—war—which bore such fruits? Is it not utter blasphemy to think that there is anything moral or Christian about such behavior?

The other thing that struck me was that these young women found it difficult to believe that *we*, who were not members of their families, could love *them*. But *they* loved *us*; they harbored no resentment against us or other Americans. How are you going to respond to that kind of attitude? The newly-elected president of the National Council of Churches, Edwin T. Dahlberg, said in his inaugural talk that instead of "massive retaliation" the business of Christians is to practice "massive reconciliation." Well, these Hiroshima girls practiced "massive reconciliation" on us, on me, who had laughed derisively at "Smiling Jack." What response can one make to this other than to give oneself utterly to destroying the evil, war, that dealt so shamefully with them and try to live in the spirit of sensitivity and reconciliation which they displayed?

As I have said, I think there is that in all men that abhors and rejects war and knows that force and violence can bring no good thing to pass. Yet men are bound by old patterns of feeling, thought and action. The organs of public opinion are almost completely shut against us. It seems practically impossible, moreover, for the ordinary person by ordinary means to speak to, and affect the action of, his government. I have had a recent experience of this which has strengthened my conviction that it is only by such acts as sailing a boat to Eniwetok and thus "speaking" to the government right in the testing area that we can expect to be heard.

I was asked by the New England office of the American Friends Service Committee to take to the White House 17,411 signatures to a petition to cancel the Pacific tests. Ten thousand signatures had previously been sent in. I realize that even a President in good health cannot see personally everyone who has a message for him. Yet the right of petition exists—in theory—and is held to be a key factor in democratic process. And the President presumably has assistants to see to it that all serious petitions are somehow brought to his attention. For matters of this kind, there is Maxwell Rabb, secretary to the cabinet.

Twenty-seven thousand is quite a few people to have signed a somewhat unusual petition. The A. F. S. C. is widely known and recognized as a highly useful agency. I am known to Maxwell Rabb with whom I worked in Republican politics in Massachusetts. I was a precinct captain for Eisenhower in the 1952 primaries. Yet a couple of days' work on the part of the staff of the Friends Committee on National Legislation failed to secure even an assurance that some time on Tuesday, December 31, the day I would be in Washington, Max Rabb would see me to receive the petitions. On that day I made five calls and talked with his secretary. Each time I was assured that she would call me back within ten minutes. Each time the return call failed to come and I tried again. The last time, early in the afternoon, I held on to the telephone for ten minutes, only to be told finally that the office was about to close for the day.

Each time I telephoned, including the last, I was told I could, of course, leave the petitions with the policeman at the gate. This I refused to do. It seems terrible to me that Americans can no longer speak to or be seen by their government. Has it become their master, not their servant? Can it not listen to their humble and reasonable pleas? This experience may in one sense be a small matter but I am sure it is symptomatic—among other things—of a sort of fear on the part of officials to listen to what in their hearts they feel is right but on which they cannot act without breaking with old patterns of thought. At any rate, the experience has strengthened in me the conviction that we must, at whatever cost, find ways to make our witness and protest heard.

I am going because, as Shakespeare said, "Action is eloquence." Without some such direct action, ordinary citizens lack the power any longer to be seen or heard by their government.

I am going because it is time to *do something* about peace, not just *talk* about peace.

I am going because, like all men, in my heart I know that *all* nuclear explosions are monstrous, evil, unworthy of human beings.

I am going because war is no longer a feudal jousting match; it is an unthinkable catastrophe for all men.

I am going because it is now the little children, and, most of all, the as yet unborn who are the front line troops. It is my duty to stand between them and this horrible danger.

I am going because it is cowardly and degrading for me to stand by any longer, to consent, and thus to collaborate in atrocities.

I am going because I cannot say that the end justifies the means. A Quaker, William Penn, said "A good end cannot sanctify evil means; nor must we ever do evil that good may come of it." A Communist, Milovan Djilas, says, "As soon as means which would ensure an end are shown to be evil, the end will show itself as unrealizable."

I am going because, as Gandhi said, "God sits in the man opposite me; therefore to injure him is to injure God himself."

I am going to witness to the deep inward truth we all know, "Force can subdue, but love gains."

I am going because however mistaken, unrighteous, and unrepentant governments may seem, I still believe all men are really good at heart, and that my act will speak to them.

I am going in the hope of helping change the hearts and minds of men in government. If necessary I am willing to give my life to help change a policy of fear, force and destruction to one of trust, kindness, and help.

I am going in order to say, "Quit this waste, this arms race. Turn instead to a disarmament race. Stop competing for evil, compete for good."

I am going because I have to—if I am to call myself a human being.

When you see something horrible happening, your instinct is to do something about it. You can freeze in fearful apathy or you can even talk yourself into saying that it isn't horrible. I can't do that. I have to act. This is too horrible. We know it. Let's all act.

JEANNETTE RANKIN

Jeannette Rankin (1880–1973), the first woman to be elected to Congress, was one of only fifty members of the House of Representatives to vote against America's entry into World War I, and the only vote against declaring war on Japan twenty-four years later. Connecting these distinctive accomplishments does not mean that women are inevitably peacemakers; it does suggest that exploring the connection between gender and war resistance may be meaningful, and in fact Rankin's life and work centered on these two causes.

She started out her professional life as a social worker but disliked the tasks she was assigned; later, in 1910, she became an activist for women's suffrage. She was elected to Congress as a Republican from Montana in 1916 (the state had extended the vote to women two years before), campaigning on, among other things, the slogan "preparedness for peace." Her vote against the war in 1917 alienated some suffragists, who claimed it had set the movement back by years.

She was not reelected, at least partly in consequence of her antiwar vote, and like Jane Addams and Emily Greene Balch, worked with the Women's International League for Peace and Freedom, and with other peace and justice organizations. She was elected to Congress a second time in 1940, campaigning for American neutrality and American military preparedness. But after Pearl Harbor, when again a declaration of war came before her, she again voted no. Her explanation was as follows: "As a woman I can't go to war, and I refuse to send anyone else." Angry war supporters threatened her and reporters swarmed; at one point she had to take refuge in a telephone booth in the Capitol. But the journalist William Allen White wrote of her that "when in one hundred years from now, courage, sheer courage based on moral indignation, is celebrated in this country, the name of Jeannette Rankin, who stood firm in folly for her faith, will be written in monumental bronze not for what she did but for the way she did it." (Her own account of these votes, included below, was first published in March 1958.)

In 1968, she led the Jeannette Rankin Brigade in a protest against the Vietnam War, joining with Coretta Scott King to present a petition on behalf of Women Strike for Peace.

Two Votes Against War: 1917, 1941

As the first woman to sit in the legislature of any sovereign nation, I cast my first vote in April, 1917 against the entry of the United States into World War I. As I said at the time, I wanted to stand by my country, but I could not vote for war. I look back with satisfaction to that momentous occasion.

I had been deeply involved in the preceding years in the struggle for woman suffrage. That struggle and the struggle against war were integrally related in my youthful thoughts and activities. After the World War had broken out and it had become increasingly clear that the United States was going to be drawn in, I was the angriest person you ever saw. I was in a rage because no one had ever seriously taught us about the nature of war itself or given us any inkling of the causes of this specific war. I was not so naive as to think that war just started in a minute. Behind the scenes preparation had to be made and was made for it. But nobody in school or later had talked to us about such things. Now we seemed, in 1914, suddenly and inexplicably to be on the eve of war.

Deep down, I guess I had always felt strongly about war. I remember that in college, when I was assigned to read publicly a poem glorifying war and soldiers, I told the professor: "But this is hideous. I can't read it."

As we went about in Montana in 1914 campaigning for the vote, we would see long lines of people before the newspaper bulletin boards in every town and city. A large proportion of these people were foreign born, eagerly scanning the notices for war news that would give them some notion as to what was happening to relatives in their native countries. War was on everybody's mind. So we talked about suffrage in relation to war. I argued that women should get the vote because they would help keep the country out of war. It was a persuasive argument at that stage.

I do not want to give the impression that anti-war talk was universally popular. In a speech in Butte, Montana, I happened to suggest that, instead of sending youth into war, the old men ought to fight the wars. The papers picked up this suggestion and made a big thing of it. Then speeches began to be made and letters written to the papers on how presumptuous and shocking it was for an unmarried woman to consider herself competent to discuss such matters.

I recall one curious incident that made a great impression on me during a suffrage campaign. It illustrates how we never know what will evoke our deepest feelings. Minnie J. Reynolds of New Jersey, a prominent suffrage campaigner, and I were walking down a street in Seattle. We passed a window full of baby chicks. Minnie stopped, pointed to them and talked passionately for some minutes about the loveliness and helplessness of those little chicks and how everyone would be outraged if someone were to start wantonly to torture them. She then went on to talk about men, women, old people, children all over the world, and men in war going out to kill them.

In the Fall of 1916, I was elected Congresswoman-at-large from Montana. The women's vote helped. It was an additional advantage that the state was not divided into Congressional districts, because candidates who stand for something are likely to have a better chance under this set-up, especially women. Everyone could vote for both a man and a woman. It is harder to manipulate and control the voters of a whole state than those of a single district. Also people were not subjected to a radio and TV barrage and we could go from town to town, speaking on the street corners and in the homes.

Several women ran for Congress in various states that year, but I was the only one who really had a chance, and I was elected. Under the procedures in effect at that time, the outgoing Congress carried over until the first Tuesday in March of the following year and the newly-elected Congress would not convene in session until autumn. I had plans made for an extensive and, I hoped, remunerative lecture tour on woman suffrage and peace, capitalizing on the curiosity about a "female" Representative. But Woodrow Wilson, who had been elected on the slogan that he would keep us out of war, had decided that it was the duty of all, and especially of good liberals and idealists, to support intervention. He called a special session of Congress early in April, read his famous war message, and appealed to the newly-elected Congress to declare war.

That time it took a week of tense debate to bring the matter to a vote, and in the House I was not the only one to vote "No." Forty-nine men in the House voted against entry.

Among them were all the veterans of the Civil War who were in Congress. Claude Kitchin, the floor leader of the Democratic majority, voted "No" and wept unashamedly as he cried out: "It takes neither moral nor physical courage to declare a war for others to fight." It is one token of how the situation has deteriorated since that time that Kitchin was retained in the leadership in spite of this vote and the fact that he remained unenthusiastic about war measures. Champ Clark, the Speaker of the House, refrained from voting on this crucial measure. In the Senate, the elder Robert M. LaFollette made his brilliant and courageous speech and cast his negative vote, as did five other Senators.

I am sorry to have to say that the attitude of most of the leaders of the woman suffrage movement was far from sympathetic to my stand. They thought that the "cause" would have been much better off if I had taken what they considered a patriotic stand. They brought a good deal of pressure to bear on me. As a matter of fact, the war advanced the movement to give women the vote and undermined opposition to it, and there is no reason to suppose that my vote on the war declaration had any appreciable effect on this issue.

It did have an effect on my own career. Running for re-election to the House of Representatives in 1918 was out of the question. In the period between the two world wars, I devoted a great deal of time to the effort to achieve the object for which the war had ostensibly been fought—the permanent abolition of war. During part of that time I was on the staff of the National Council for Prevention of War, of which Frederick J. Libby was for many years the director. Some of my experiences in this work and reflections on them may be of use.

If any results in Congress are to be accomplished at all, it is necessary to get to the people—the grass roots, as the saying goes—and to do a lot of personal work with individuals and small groups. In dealing with Congress itself, you have to think largely in terms of the individual Congressman who is in a key position. In 1936 when the great struggle for the Neutrality Act was on, as part of our strategy to keep the United States from becoming embroiled for a second time in European conflicts, Roosevelt was confident he could defeat us. But at the very hour when he was assuring a House delegation in his office that the Senate would defeat the measure, the Senate passed it. Then the administration's struggle to defeat the measure was intensified. The key man in the House was Democratic Representative McReynolds from Chattanooga, Tennessee, who was chairman of the Committee that was handling the bill. We took ten of his twelve counties in Tennessee and with the cooperation of women, clergy, and school superintendents held dozens of meetings, large and small. This was shortly before Christmas. McReynolds was abroad. We carefully refrained from attacking him, and simply urged people "to let Mr. McReynolds know what you think." When McReynolds returned from his trip and learned what his constituents were thinking, he changed his mind and voted for the Neutrality Act.

People often ask what they can do in Washington. My answer is that, almost always, the only really effective thing people can do is to work with their own representatives. If they are going to write, they should write to their own Senators or Representatives. A Congressman seldom pays attention to anybody who is not a constituent. Don't write him what you think or start out by telling him what to do. Ask him a question. When he answers, as he is almost certain to do, write again, thank him, and ask him another question. He is not likely to think that a constituent is really interested and will work in the district unless he has written half a dozen times.

On the other hand, in order to give a balanced picture, I ought to emphasize that just about everything possible is done to enable a Congressman to keep his constituents from knowing what he really thinks and even how he votes, and that in Congress itself free speech does not really obtain. In my earlier days, there was a lot of stir about the then czar of the House, Speaker "Uncle Joe" Cannon of Illinois. He decided who could or could not speak, for how long, and so on. There was a liberal revolt. With what result? That there is now a Rules Committee, which decides who can or cannot speak, and for how long. In a sense, the only place where uninhibited free speech still exists in the United States is—paradoxically—in the Senate when a filibuster is on. Procedures in Congress, let me add, are so arranged that with a little agility a Representative, if allowed to speak and in good standing with the powers that be, can make speeches on one side of an issue, and then vote on the other side. He can vote one way in a voice vote and the other way when the tellers are called—and can tell various types of constituents the part of the story that makes them feel good.

But let me resume the account of my own Congressional experience. In 1939, I began to think of running for Congress again the following year. The first move I made was to write a letter to all the high school principals in Montana, informing each that I would be at his school on such and such a date and available to address the students. I did not give a return address, lest some should reply that it would be inconvenient to have me. So I addressed virtually all the high school assemblies in the state on the subject of war. I explained the futility of the war method as a means of settling disputes between nations. I never directly attacked the Army or Navy; I just made fun of some of their doings. Thus, in discussing the talk about the Japanese coming to attack San Francisco, I would remark that the distance from San Francisco to Tokyo was exactly the same as from Tokyo to San Francisco. I told the children to write President Roosevelt letters about their ideas on war, but not to write the letters until they had talked it over with their parents. In this way, I made sure that a lot of voters in Montana heard my name and heard something about my ideas on war. I also told the children not to say how old they were—that I never did.

In this context, I told the students a story from my own high school days. We had in my class a boy who, as a baby, had been carried in a covered wagon across territory in which hostile Indians still roamed. Early one morning, the caravan heard Indians coming. There was a considerable number of them, women as well as men. The white men in the caravan ran for their guns. But the mother of the boy who was to become my classmate took her baby in her arms and walked ahead alone. When she reached the Indians, who had halted when they saw her approaching, she handed her baby to one of them; quite possibly, it was the first white baby they had ever seen. The Indians took this as a sign of trust and friendship. They handed the baby back to the mother, and went on their way. I would say to the children when I had finished the story, "You will not be able to hand your Senator a baby when he comes to your town, but you can do something to make him understand that you really care about abolishing strife and hatred among men." The following year, when my candidacy had been announced and I was again going from town to town campaigning, I would meet these high school students, their parents and friends. That round of high school visits was undoubtedly an important element in the victory which sent me back to Congress for a second time, after the lapse of twenty-three years.

Once again, the nation was moving toward war. In November, 1941, and early December, many people assumed that we would go in any day. As late as Saturday evening, December 6, I still felt that the country was not ready and that therefore entry would be put off. I was scheduled to speak in Detroit at an important meeting on Monday. On Sunday, though the attack on Pearl Harbor had occurred, I left Washington for Pittsburgh, *en route* to Detroit. I took it for granted that Congress would debate the declaration of war for a week, as it had in 1917, or at any rate for several days. But on arrival in Pittsburgh, I learned that we were living in another time and that Congress was going to vote on Monday. I hurried back to Washington. I secluded myself. I did not want to talk with anyone. I was much more upset than I had been in 1917. Then I had been sad. But this time I was grieved at seeing the men who were as opposed to going into the war as I was slipping away from their position at the critical moment. There were some important Republicans who wished to have all the Republicans vote against entry, partly from conviction, partly, I suppose, to embarrass Roosevelt. Nothing came of it.

This time I stood alone. It was a good deal more difficult than it had been the time before. Yet I think the men in Congress all sensed that I would vote "No" again. If I had done otherwise, I do not think I could have faced the remaining days in Congress. Even the men who were most convinced that we had to get into the war would have lost respect for me if I had betrayed my convictions.

When the first anniversary of that vote came around, on December 8, 1942, I extended remarks in the record in which I brought out some points which may well be recalled at the present critical moment. I referred, for one thing, to a book by an English author, Sidney Rogerson, entitled *Propaganda in the Next War.* It had been published in London in 1938 but banned from export to the United States by the British censorship in 1939. Rogerson had stated in his book that it would be much more difficult to bring the United States into the war than it had been in World War I. "The position," said Rogerson, "will naturally be considerably improved if Japan were to be involved . . . At any rate, it would be a natural and obvious object of our propaganda to achieve this, just as during the Great War they succeeded in embroiling the United States with Germany."

I next reminded the Congress of Henry Luce's historic reference in *Life* magazine for July 20, 1942 to "the Chinese for whom *the U. S. had delivered the ultimatum that brought on Pearl Harbor.*" I introduced evidence that at the Atlantic Conference, August 12, 1941, Winston Churchill had sought, and Roosevelt had given, assurances that the United States would bring economic pressure to bear on Japan. I cited the State Department Bulletin of December 20, 1941, which revealed that on September 3 a communication had been sent to Japan demanding that it accept the principle of "non-disturbance of the status quo in the Pacific," which amounted to demanding guarantees of the inviolateness of the white empires in the Orient.

On the subject of economic pressure on Japan, I had sought data from both the State and Commerce Departments. I had received from both an identical response: "Because of a special Executive Order, statistics on trade with Japan beginning with April 1941 are not being given out." There was, however, plenty of material from other sources to show that, in line with Roosevelt's assurances to Churchill, the Economic Defense Board, under Henry Wallace's chairmanship, had gotten economic sanctions under way less than a week after the Atlantic Conference. On December 2, 1941, the New York *Times* reported that Japan had been "cut off from about 75% of her normal trade by the Allied blockade."

In this connection, I recalled a statement made on April 4, 1942 by a member of Roosevelt's own party, Hatton W. Summers of Texas, chairman of the House Judiciary Committee: "This blaming the Pearl Harbor tragedy on the treachery of the Japs is like the fellow who had been tickling the hind leg of a mule trying to explain his bungled-up condition by blaming the mule for having violated his confidence."

There was one other development preceding Pearl Harbor, of which I reminded the House, namely the statement of Lieutenant Clarence E. Dickinson, U. S. N., in a *Saturday Evening Post* article, October 10, 1942, to the effect that, on November 28, 1941, Vice Admiral William F. Halsey, Jr. had given instructions to him and others to "shoot down anything we saw in the sky and to bomb anything we saw on the sea. In that way there could be no leak to the Japs." Such orders could hardly have been issued without Presidential sanction. I raise now, as I did on that first anniversary of Pearl Harbor, the question whether Roosevelt had not, at least nine days before the Japanese attacked Pearl Harbor without a declaration of war, authorized an identical attack upon the Japanese—also without a declaration of war.

And how much do the people and even the members of Congress know about the moves now being made by our government or other governments which may lead to another war? Our being kept in ignorance arouses my apprehensions today as it did more than forty years ago when World War I burst upon my world.

PAUL REPS

Paul Reps (1895–1990) introduced generations of American readers to East Asian philosophy and religion with his beautifully illustrated collections of Buddhist stories, haiku-influenced poetry, and writings on Buddhism like *Zen Flesh, Zen Bones* (1957), *Zen Telegrams* (1959), and *Square Sun, Square Moon* (1967). He personally practiced what he called "Reps Zen," freely adapting various traditions.

Several accounts have circulated about the origins of his poem "drinking a bowl of green tea"—first published in *Zen Telegrams*—all of them possibly apocryphal. According to one, he hoped to travel to Kyoto to visit with a particular Zen master, but was denied a visa: nonmilitary travel to Japan, then the main staging area for UN troops heading to Korea, was routinely discouraged. Disappointed, he poured himself a cup of tea, savored it, and made another appeal to the visa clerk, who finally granted his request.

What "war" it was that Reps stopped, drinking his cup of tea, is open to question—his conflict with a visa clerk, his inner turmoil, or even, wishfully or prayerfully, the larger war out in the world. The relation between such "inner" and "outer" wars is important in antiwar writing—it is what is at stake in Gandhi's injunction to "be the change you seek in the world"—and Reps's poem raises it powerfully and without fuss.

In a recent course I taught on the writing in this anthology, Reps's poem split the class down the middle; half the students loved the association it made between inner and outer war, half of them ardently rejected it. None were indifferent.

drinking
a bowl of green tea
I stopped the war

PETE SEEGER AND JOE
HICKERSON

I heard Pete Seeger (1919–2014) give a concert when I was twelve or so, in the auditorium of my grammar school, almost the only concert I can remember at which it felt utterly, irresistibly natural and joyous to sing along. Seeger had that effect on a good many people; he was perhaps the greatest American song leader of the two American centuries he lived in.

He grew up in an intensely musical family; his father Charles was a distinguished musicologist, his mother Constance de Clyver a concert violinist and Juilliard violin teacher. Also in the Seeger family atmosphere was the intertwining of music and politics; his father was forced to resign from the music department at Berkeley in 1918 because of his pacifism. Charles and Constance divorced when Seeger was seven and Charles married Ruth Crawford, who would become one of the most important American composers of the twentieth century; all four of Charles and Ruth's children became folksingers.

Seeger gravitated as a boy to the ukulele, then heard the banjo for the first time in 1936 while traveling with Charles and Ruth in North Carolina. He enrolled in Harvard but dropped out in 1938, and without quite intending it was increasingly drawn into the world of folk music and left-wing politics. He joined the Young Communist League as a teenager and then the Communist Party itself from 1942 to 1949. A job with Alan Lomax gave him access to authentic folk music; working with Woody Guthrie showed him how music can change hearts and minds. Following the party line, his lyrics during the period of the Hitler-Stalin pact opposed the draft and American rearmament; after Hitler invaded the Soviet Union, he sang prowar songs like "Round and Round Hitler's Grave" and "Dear Mr. President." He enlisted in the Army and served in the Pacific, mostly, as he said, "strumming his banjo" for the troops.

Seeger wrote the first three verses of "Where Have All the Flowers Gone" in 1955, on his way to a concert at Oberlin College, one of the few organizations willing to hire him during the McCarthy era, looking at some notes he had taken on a Cossack folk song. Later the folksinger Joe Hickerson (b. 1935), longtime director of the Archive of Folk Song for the Library of Congress, added the fourth and fifth verses and, by a wonderful inspiration, a repetition of the first verse as the final verse. Like Ed McCurdy's "Strangest Dream," "Where Have All the Flowers Gone?" has been recorded by numerous artists and translated into many languages; like "Strangest Dream," its antiwar force is indirect, hinted at only in the relation between the orderly account of flowers, young women, young men, young soldiers, new graves, and the recurring question "When will they"—and in the last verse "When will *we*"—"ever learn?"

Seeger lived a long life, was the most beloved American folksinger of his time, attended to an astonishing variety of causes and repertories, opposed the arms race and the Vietnam War and the pollution of the Hudson River, supported Solidarity, and kept singing and holding to his socialist principles right till the end. (In 2011 he marched with Occupy Wall Street; in 2012 he sang at a concert for Leonard Peltier.) When he died in 2014, President Obama aptly noted that he had been called "America's tuning fork."

Where Have All the Flowers Gone?

Where have all the flowers gone, long time passing?
Where have all the flowers gone, long time ago?
Where have all the flowers gone?
Girls have picked them, every one!
When will they ever learn?
When will they ever learn?

Where have all the young girls gone, long time passing?
Where have all the young girls gone, long time ago?
Where have all the young girls gone?
Taken husbands, every one!
When will they ever learn?
When will they ever learn?

Where have all the young men gone, long time passing?
Where have all the young men gone, long time ago?
Where have all the young men gone?
Gone for soldiers, every one!
When will they ever learn?
When will they ever learn?

Where have all the soldiers gone, long time passing?
Where have all the soldiers gone, long time ago?
Where have all the soldiers gone?

Gone to graveyards, every one!
When will they ever learn?
When will they ever learn?

Where have all the graveyards gone, long time passing?
Where have all the graveyards gone, long time ago?
Where have all the graveyards gone?
Covered with flowers, every one!
When will we ever learn?
When will we ever learn?

JUANITA NELSON

It is impossible for me to write about Juanita Nelson (1923–2015) without memories of her surfacing in my mind. She was sixty-six when I got to know her, in connection with the IRS seizure of houses owned by war tax resisters Bob Bady, Betsy Corner, and Randy Kehler. She was already an eminence in the war tax resistance movement, but not a laurels-sitting eminence; she was gracious and fierce and courtly and funny. (She was implacable on the question of lending money at interest, which she opposed.) Her home on Woolman Hill, near Deerfield, Massachusetts, was a place of hospitality and radical simplicity (no electricity, no running water, an outhouse), with neither getting in the way of the other. Over the years she became still more eminent, almost legendary, but never stopped having those other traits as well.

She was born in Cleveland, enrolled in Howard University in 1941, was the secretary to that university's NAACP chapter, and was first arrested in 1943 for a protest against lunch counter segregation. (For her as for many, opposing war and opposing segregation were not separate issues.) She was working as a journalist when she met Wally Nelson in 1943; they got married and stayed married till Wally's death in 2002. In 1948 they helped found Peacemakers, an organization devoted to war tax and draft resistance; she recounts an episode in her fight against war taxation in her essay "A Matter of Freedom," first published in 1960.

Along with their antiwar work, the Nelsons were farmers, seeking to live a simple life, in the line of war resistance that leads from Woolman to the Nelsons by way of Thoreau and Scott Nearing; they heated and cooked with wood, preserved food, and made soap. When they moved to Woolman Hill in 1974, they found, animated, and were animated by a remarkable community of like-minded people for the rest of both of their lives, as farmers, citizens, and pacifists.

A Matter of Freedom

IN March 1959, I hunted through the Sears-Roebuck sales catalogue for something to throw around my nakedness when I emerged from the bath or lounged around the house, an economical garment to double as a beach robe. I finally ordered J934: white terrycloth, full back, worn with or without a belt, three-quarter length sleeves, shipping weight 1 lb. 12 oz. Over the left breast was a green, yellow, red and blue emblem, a garish enough flower for a rebel coat of arms.

I give the preceding account in all its triviality because three months later, on June 16, the versatile robe became something more than either Sears or I had intended; it became a provocative "kimona" around which revolved considerable consternation on the part of certain public officials and a great deal of reassessment on my part.

The first link between the robe and my intellectual processes was my declination to pay income taxes because most of the money goes for H-bombs and other combustibles capable of setting off conflagrations which cannot be extinguished by the average hook-and-ladder company. I balk at the notion of contributing so directly to making atomic hash of others and perhaps of my own wonderful self. The final bond was forged by the early hours kept by those who execute the orders of the United States government. They, apparently, do not require as much sleep as I do. Perhaps if I had business as important to attend to—bringing in the Body—I would not need so much sleep, either, or I would forego it for the important job I had to perform. Justice, I suppose, never slumbers, and she must demand the same insomnia of her bondmen. But I, not being affiliated in any way with justice or the Department of Justice, was sleeping soundly and in my accustomed nudity when the doorbell rang at 6:30 A.M. I slipped into the bargain bathrobe and stumbled to the door.

Two somber men stood there. As if they were in some way hooked to the hinges, they flipped open their identification wallets as soon as the door began to swing open. I did not bother to examine their credentials, accepting their word that they were U.S. marshals. I invited them in. They were all brusqueness and business as they sat on the edge of the sofa to which I waved them.

"We have an order for your arrest," said one, and thrust toward me a blue-covered legal looking document.

I was startled. For eleven years, my husband, Wally, and I had neither paid withholding taxes nor filed any forms, fully aware that we were operating on a brink-of-imprisonment policy. Wally managed to find work that did not come under withholding tax provisions. I was, therefore, able to claim him as my dependent and could earn up to about twenty-five dollars on any one job with no tax withheld. I usually held a couple of such jobs and so earned a taxable income. Then, several years ago, the revenuers tardily checked on two part-time jobs I had held simultaneously from 1952 to 1955 and began billing me for a sum which finally mounted to $959.83, including penalties for interest and fraud. And in March I had been served with a summons to appear at the Internal Revenue office in Philadelphia with my records. Our procedure all along had been not to cooperate with the collection of information, and we felt we would probably not cooperate with an arrest. Protest through individual income-tax refusal appears to most folks about as effective as scooping out the Pacific Ocean with a spoon; it seemed even more hopeless to dump each spoonful of water into a tunnel which led back to the ocean. I had refused even to accept the summons and had heard no more from that quarter. In spite of Wally's warnings that "you can never tell what those guys will do," I think that way down I had come to disbelieve that I could ever be considered enough of a threat or an affront to the government to stir up anything more than this kind of bureaucratic feinting. But even with the best intentions in the world of going to jail, I would have been startled to be awakened at 6:30 A.M. to be told that I was under arrest.

When the marshals offered me the order I said, "I am not interested in that," keeping my hands tightly clasped in my lap. I tried, in words which sounded hackneyed to my ears, to explain my position briefly.

"*We* are not interested in *that*," they said. "You can tell it to the judge."

"I would be glad to tell it to the judge," I said, "if he will come to see me. But I do not wish to go to jail to tell him these things. I am not paying taxes because the overwhelming percentage of the budget goes for war purposes. I do not wish to participate in any phase of the collection of such taxes. I do not even want to act as if I think that anyone, including the government, has a right to punish me for an act which I consider honorable. I cannot come with you."

There was less fuss than I had thought there might be. Clearly, these men had studied my dossier and were undoubtedly informed of my friendship with Maurice McCrackin, tax-refusing minister, who had just completed a six months sentence for the same offense. Mac had not been at all clerical—they'd had to carry him into court each time. And Wally they knew about too—his 33 months in prison after walking out of Civilian Public Service camp during World War II, the 108-day fast (with force-feeding by tube) which had preceded his release.

At any rate, they seemed not inclined to philosophize. After a few appeals to my common sense, the sterner of the two marshals said mildly, "Well, if you won't come with us we'll have to carry you in." He left to summon a red car.

I realized that I was actually going to jail. And, at that point, I became acutely conscious of the robe. Should I quietly excuse myself, get dressed, then return to take up my recalcitrant position? It would have been simpler, of course, if they had left and made their entrance again, with me fully aware that they meant business. Debating the question, I went to the bathroom, brushed my teeth, ran a comb through my hair. These simple acts of grooming brought me back to reality sufficiently to realize that I might be spirited away. Wally was off on a sales trip, and I had no way of reaching him. I put the cap back on the toothpaste and went to the telephone, which is on a wall between the dining room and the kitchen, a considerable distance down a long, high-ceilinged hallway from the living room where I'd left the deputy. I was still on the phone when I heard the click of the door announcing reinforcements. There was a tentative, "Mrs. Nelson," as though there was some fear I might be in too delicate a position to be barged in on. As I raced to get information to a friend, the deputies and two policemen converged on me. Other policemen trooped in. I remember saying as I hung up, "I'm surrounded."

Seven law enforcement officers had stalked in. I sat on the stool beneath the telephone, my back literally to the wall, the seven hemming me about in a semicircle. All of them appeared over six feet tall, and all of them were annoyed.

"Look," said one, "you're gonna go anyway. You might as well come peaceful."

There they stood, ready and able to take me at any moment.
But no move was made. The reason was obvious.

"Why don't you put your clothes on, Mrs. Nelson?" This
was a soft spoken plea from the more benign deputy. "You're
not hurting anybody but yourself." His pained expression
belied the assertion.

One policeman snorted when I attempted to say that they
needn't take me at all.

The benign deputy made a last try. "Do you believe in God,
Mrs. Nelson?" Irrationally, stalling for time, I asked, "Are you
asking me as an individual or as an official?"

The marshal answered as if the question were not at all out
of the ordinary, at least no more than the whole situation.

"I'm asking you as an individual."

"No," I said.

Taken aback, he did not go on to explain the connection
he had evidently been going to establish between God and
dressing for arrest.

When the affairs of men have reached a stalemate, there
seems always some man of action to come forward. There was
such a one among the seven. He was not a member of a debating society. These questions had nothing to do with him. I
cannot describe his physical appearance, for he was not a face or
a personality; he was a no-nonsense voice and a pair of strong
arms.

"Listen, we don't have to beg her to do anything. We'll
just take her the way she is, if that's the way she wants it."
He snapped a pair of handcuffs around my wrists and, with
another pair of brawny arms, half carried, half dragged me
down the hall, the other five trooping after. In the street, the
no-nonsense transporter delighted in maneuvering me into a
position to expose the nakedness under the robe. One of the
unencumbered tried desperately to arrange my limbs so that
the robe would fall circumspectly and unrevealingly about
my ankles. On my part there was a fleeting anxiety about the
exhibition, but I was too engrossed in anticipating next steps
to worry overmuch, especially as, at that early hour, there were
few around to gawk. I thought fleetingly of Corbett Bishop,
World War II C. O. who practiced such consistent noncooperation that he suffered a roach to go down with the mush he

was being tube fed. I did not shift from the spot where I was dumped on the floor of the paddy wagon as we drove down Market Street to the Federal Court Building.

When the doors opened, I continued to sit. My thoughts were like buckshot, so scattered they didn't hit anything or, when they did, made little dent. The robe was a huge question mark placed starkly after some vexing problems.

Why am I going to jail? Why am I going to jail in a bathrobe? What does it matter in the scheme of things whether or not you put on your clothes? Are you not making, at best, a futile gesture, at worst, flinging yourself against something which does not exist? Is freedom more important than justice? Of what does freedom of the human spirit consist, that quality on which I place so much stress? How important is the exercise of that freedom if it conflicts or seems to conflict with the maintenance of the dignity of other individuals or of institutions? Was it enough, in any case, to have made the gesture of refusing to pay for weapons of destruction? What was the purpose of extending that gesture to such complete noncooperation with legally constituted authority? Was it only a gesture? How much is one demeaning himself when he kowtows either to authority or to custom, in short, to myths? When one does not yield is he simply being rigid, humorless, arrogant, or is he defending that innermost place, the last sanctuary of selfness?

And all these questions turned around a basic question: Who am I? If I could know who I was, at least who I conceived myself to be, then I would be able to approach those other questions.

The same two stalwarts yanked me from the van, hardly giving me time to alight under my own power had I wished to do so. They divined my attitude correctly. I was becoming increasingly rigid as the situation became more ridiculous and I less certain of myself. They carried me by the elbows down a long corridor and up a flight of stairs to an elevator. One patiently endured while the other impatiently endured. I really did relate to the two men at one point. I realized how heavy an almost inert body can be as I saw the perspiration run down their faces. But did they have any conception of how difficult it was for me to be carried? They let me slide to the floor in the elevator, from where, fortunately, it was only a few steps to the cell. They sat me on the bench and left, vastly relieved to have finished their part in the business.

I did not know the time. I did not know precisely what charges had been lodged against me. I did not know when I was to be tried. I had the beginnings of a nagging headache. I had been plopped onto a wooden bench which ran along two sides of the tiny barred cell. There was a toilet and a washstand with a drinking fountain attachment. This was the first time I had been in such a cage, having been confined in ordinary rooms in previous jail experiences. A narrow corridor ran between the cell row and the outside wall. I contemplated dappled bits of sunlight scurrying through the venetian blinds covering the window opposite the cell. I could not see anyone, but I heard the murmur of voices around one end of the hall where, I supposed, were the administrative offices.

I was just soaking things in. I was feeling more sensitive about the robe, not being quite able to determine its role in the affair. I did come to one conclusion. Until I made up my mind about what I was doing and why, I would continue in the most extreme position. I would not do anything, only suffer what was done to me. Almost as if I had divined what was coming, I resolved not to leave the cell under my own power for any reason whatsoever except to go home. I remembered almost excruciatingly an experience in the Cincinnati County jail on a charge of disorderly conduct for trying to gain admission to an amusement park which barred Negroes. I did not eat during the nine days. I would not wear the prison uniform. But, thinking I was exercising what degree of freedom I had, I wandered about the floor at will and bounced downstairs to see visitors. But there was always the agony of afterwards. I could not endure being dragged upstairs each time, and returning voluntarily was degrading.

So, when the deputy interrupted my reverie to announce visitors, whom I could see in the waiting room, I told him I would leave only to be released. He shrugged his shoulders and left. Well, I thought, they're not going to get themselves into a stew about this.

In a few minutes I heard a hearty, "Well, good morning." Two fellow pacifists, one of them also a tax refuser, had been permitted to come to me, since I would not go to them. I asked them what was uppermost in my mind, what they'd do about getting properly dressed. They said that this was something I would have to settle for myself. I sensed that they thought it the better part of wisdom and modesty for me to be dressed for my appearance in court. They were more concerned about the public relations aspect of getting across the witness than I was. They were also genuinely concerned, I knew, about making their actions truly nonviolent, cognizant of the other person's feelings, attitudes and readiness. I was shaken enough to concede that I would like to have my clothes at hand, in case I decided I would feel more at ease in them. The older visitor, a dignified man with white hair, agreed to go for the clothes in a taxicab.

They left, and on their heels came another visitor. She had been told that in permitting her to come up, the officials were treating me with more courtesy than I was according them. It was her assessment that the chief deputy was hopeful that someone would be able to hammer some sense into me, and was willing to make concessions in that hope. But he had misjudged the reliance he might place in her—she was not as critical as the men. She did not know what she would do, but she thought she might wish to have the strength and the audacity to carry through in the vein in which I had started.

And she said, "You know, you look like a female Gandhi in that robe. You look, well, dignified."

That was my first encouragement. Everyone else had tended to make me feel like a fool of the first order, had confirmed fears I already had on that score. My respect and admiration for Gandhi, though not uncritical, was deep. And if I in any way resembled him in appearance I was prepared to try to emulate a more becoming state of mind. I reminded myself, too, that I had on considerably more than the loincloth in which Gandhi was able to greet kings and statesmen with ease. I need not be unduly perturbed about wearing a robe into the presence of a His Honor.

I had, I think, been immobilized partly by a sense of my own failures as a human being. Here was I, still struggling with the meaning of my own life and standing, it seemed sometimes, on dead center. How, then, did I have the effrontery to question a whole way of life that had been evolved slowly and painfully through the ages by the accumulated wisdom of mankind? How could I presume to have so much of the truth that I would defy constituted authority? What made me so certain of myself in this regard? I was not certain. But it seemed to me that if I could see only one thing clearly, it was not necessary to see all things clearly in order to act on that one thing.

One pinpoint of clarity was that it was time for man to grow out of the short pants of barbarism, of settling things by violence, and at least to get into the knee breeches of honestly seeking and trying ways more fitted to his state as a human. To take life, especially in cold-blooded, organized fashion, seems to me to be the province of no man and of no government. In the end, no government can do it—it is only men who fire guns, drop atom bombs, pierce with bayonets. If an entity called government could slay another such entity, no great harm would be done and maybe even good would come of it—at least the destruction of files of papers. My repudiation of violence is not based on any conventionally or conveniently religious motivation. I cannot say that it is against God's will, since I do not know that there is a god, nor would I be able in any case to assume that I was conversant with his will. But I do not consider, either, that men are gods, that they should determine when another man should die. I do not consider that I am capable of such judgments, either of my own volition or at the command of others. Such behavior in others I abhor, but may not be able to affect. I *can* control my own behavior. And I do not think that my participation in stupid or immoral acts can add to my stature as an individual—I think, rather, that it might detract, take me even further afield from the discovery of myself.

It may be that most people think it necessary, if wicked and perhaps self-defeating, to build atom bombs to drop on such races of devils as inhabit Hiroshimas. We must save our skin, protect our way of life. Let me first excise the horns from my own head, since it was made, I think, for something besides butting. Besides, I cannot accept any package labeled "way of life," only those particular values which seem to me worth protecting, and I must protect them in a way which seems fitting to those values.

Suppose, though, that most citizens eagerly pay their money into the government's war chest before the tax deadline, and some sacrificially give more than their share. I have decided that this is not the best depository for the fruits of my labor. But believing as I do, I must, it seems, comply in order to uphold the system of law and to act in concert with my fellows. Holding that law can be an aid but never a substitute for individual integrity, responsibility, and perception, I want immediately to know: In concert for what? If it seems that the purpose of the united action is to create misery, cannot, in fact, have any other effect, then I must decline my part in the performance. In order for men to live together, it seems efficient for them to work out bodies of regulations. But efficiency can in no way supplant morality. Is the height of man's being obedience to the common will? I think it a higher purpose to live in a creatively oriented relationship than to adopt a slavish attitude toward rules and regulations. I think it the worst part of folly to be so enamored of acting in unison that I am herded into acting inhumanly.

If those with opposing beliefs hold them so strongly, they have at least the same choice of throwing their whole weight into bringing about that state of affairs which they espouse. Not by bringing me to heel, but by giving all they have to their own visions. I cannot think that the measure of one's belief is the extent to which he tries to coerce others into believing it or acting upon it, but the extent to which he is willing to sacrifice for it himself. If, for instance, I am, because of my well-intentioned but mistaken notions, depriving the Department of Defense of ten dollars per year for making a guided missile, why does not someone convinced of the necessity of the weapon come forward and voluntarily make up that ten dollars? Is it not mere pettiness to insist that I would stand to be "protected" by this sacrifice? (I would also stand to be annihilated by it.) The money spent trying to make me comply could be squandered, instead, on the purposes for which my tax money would be used.

But, no, this non-compliance constitutes an affront which cannot be ignored. It is no doubt the fear that even one insignificant defiance will produce a rent in the whole fabric, and that the cloth may some day be beyond repair. Perhaps we do not need the garment at all and should throw it into the rag bag before it is completely in tatters. If the idea I champion is worthless, not many will be impressed to follow suit and my intransigence can be regretted, deplored and suffered. If, on the other hand, only the law keeps most people from acting with me, then this must be the worst kind of despotism—it must be the minority who are keeping the majority in line with the whip of the law. Or perhaps everyone is being kept in line with the whip, and no one dares look the thing in the face for what it is.

Most people who take any notice of my position are appalled by my lawbreaking and not at all about the reasons for my not paying taxes. Instead of trying to make me justify my civil disobedience, why do they not question themselves and the government about a course of action which makes billions available for weapons, but cannot provide decent housing and education for a large segment of the population? Actually, many people seem envious that I have for so long been able to "get away with it," with not paying taxes. I wonder what would happen if the income tax laws were repealed tomorrow. Let everyone be sent a statement of what his fair share would be, to be paid on a voluntary basis. How many of the people who bark at me, "Do you think you should use the highways if you won't pay taxes?" would send in their assessments?

Anyway, because I believe that it is more important to do what is right than what is lawful or expedient, I have declined to pay the tax. All right, then, having determined this course of action for yourself, should you not be willing to accept punishment for your defiance? Why should I? I have stated that 1) I believe this particular measure to be so intolerable that I cannot abide by it; 2) I believe that I have every right, nay, every responsibility, to act according to my best judgment, not waiting for one-hundred and fifty million others to concur. This one act may not lead inevitably to a good end, but I do not see that it can lead to a bad one. Why should I expect or accept punishment for exercising my best judgment? I was not a whit more contrite when the marshals came to arrest me than when I first declined to pay the tax. Would I go peaceably in order to show my compatriots that I do not utterly despise them and their institutions? If I must go to jail in order to demonstrate my respect, then they will have to believe as they believe; if I should go to jail willingly for that, I should undoubtedly end up despising myself at least. And how can one have respect for others without self-respect?

I think that what I was saying with my robe was that I was doing what I thought right. I was convinced enough to feel that it would be good if others were moved to do likewise. But I some time ago gave up the notion that it was my province to reform the world. But I think that if I have helped to start a fire, the first thing I must do is stop adding fuel to it. I could not very well help going to jail when seven strong men were determined I should go, but I did not wish them to think for a moment that I was on their side. You will do what you think you should, what you have been ordered to do, but I shall not help you do it, no, not even to the extent of getting dressed so that you may feel more comfortable in your mission. If a law is bad or unjust, is not every phase of its enforcement simply an extension of the law and to be as greatly resisted?

I wanted passionately, perhaps grimly, to be myself. Somewhere that self existed, independent of, though cognizant of, all other selves, a being and a striving to be in inevitable loneliness. I wanted to strip to the skeleton and clothe it with my own humanity, my own meaning. Some parts of that self could be satisfied only in the context of other selves, but that participation would have to be voluntary, whether bound to other selves in marriage, social club, or government. There is no collective conscience. I think it is too bad that anyone should suppose that holding me within their bounds, forcing me to do what they think is good, is within their prerogatives. It is no palliative that they do it impersonally, without having thought through anything, but only because notions have become automatic through codification. I saw a movie about a woman who was put to death by the state in a gas chamber. Not the man who dissolved the crystals, nor the man who pulled the switch, nor the woman who sat guard to keep the prisoner from killing herself, nor the priest who heard her last confession, nor the governor who might have commuted the sentence, not one was anxious to have any part in that degrading performance. And yet each swallowed his revulsion like vomit and, when he could not be saved by some decree, played out his part.

It is, as far as I can see, an unpleasant fact that we cannot avoid decision-making. We are not absolved by following the dictates of a mentor or of a majority. For we then have made the decision to do that—have concluded because of belief or of fear or of apathy that this is the thing which we should do or cannot avoid doing. And we then share in the consequences of any such action. Are we doing more than trying to hide our nakedness with a fig leaf when we take the view expressed by a friend who belonged to a fundamental religious sect? At the time he wore the uniform of the United States Marines. "I'm not helping to murder," he said. "I'm carrying out the orders of my government, and the sin is not mine." I could never tell whether there was a bitter smile playing around his lips or if he was quite earnest. It is a rationalization commonly held and defended. It is a comforting presumption, but it still appears to me that, while the seat of government is in Washington, the seat of conscience is in me. It cannot be voted out of office by one or a million others.

I had not answered all the questions when I was wheeled into the courtroom in an office chair mounted on casters. I had not even asked all the questions.

But I had asked and answered enough to be able to leave behind me the brown paper bag holding my clothes. The commissioner received me in my robe. A friend who was in the courtroom noted that I was "brave but halting." Even so, it was necessary for me to suppress a smile or two. The consequences for me might be grave, but it *was* a comical situation.

The commissioner cited the law which empowered him to imprison me for a year and fine me a thousand dollars, or both. But he did not wish, he said, to be the first to commit a person to jail for flouting the law. He gave me until the following Friday, this was Tuesday, to comply with the court order.

At 2 P.M. Friday I was at the ironing board, rather nostalgic that this might be the last time I would perform that humble task for some time. In baggy blue jeans, I was disreputably but more respectably dressed than I had been three days before. But they did not come for me. Some weeks later I learned from a news release that charges had been dropped, since it could not be proven that I owed anything. (I was not, as a matter of fact, arrested for not paying the tax, but for contempt arising from refusal to show records.) Still, in my Christmas mail there was a bill from the Internal Revenue Service for $950.01.

If this was the prelude to another abduction, I can only hope that those attached to the court will have achieved that degree of nonchalance which I think I have attained regarding proper court attire. Or that they will at least first send out their intelligence agents to scout for more favorable circumstances for taking me into custody.

BARBARA DEMING

The early career of Barbara Deming (1917–1984) gives little hint of what she was to become. Her mother's association with artists seems at first to be shaping the daughter, who goes to Bennington, majors in literature then in drama, gets an M.A. in drama from Western Reserve, moves to New York, publishes poems and stories and film criticism. But in 1959 Deming and her partner Mary Meigs traveled to India; there Deming found herself interested in Gandhi's work, and realized she was "in the deepest part of [her]self a pacifist." She came back, interviewed Fidel Castro, got connected with the Committee for Nonviolent Action and the Peacemakers, and was an activist against war and racism for the rest of her life.

For a good many of the writers represented here, opposition to war was inextricable from opposition to other things: sin, poverty, racism, sexism, capitalism. Few, however, consider as explicitly as Deming does in "Southern Peace Walk"—published in *Liberation* in July–August 1962—whether those causes are separable or linked. In 1962 she had urged Martin Luther King Jr. to join civil rights action to peace action; King responded at the time that civil rights needed to come first. Later, and notably in his prophetic speech against the Vietnam War, he too came to see the unity of the two struggles. What leads Deming in the essay to judge that the two struggles are one struggle is not an analysis but a set of experiences, a sense that trying to separate the two struggles cannot for her be made to seem anything but evasive.

Later in her life, much of Deming's political energy went to feminist and lesbian causes and ideas; her last major action was at the Women's Encampment for a Future of Peace and Justice demonstration in New York, her last essay an account of that action. Martin Duberman tells an extraordinary story about her death in 1984. She was in her home in Sugarloaf Key, Florida, and asked the women gathered there to sing "Leaning on the Everlasting Arms." Then, Duberman writes, "Barbara lifted her long body off the couch and with 'enormous dignity and grace' danced to the gentle rhythms." A few days later she died.

Southern Peace Walk: Two Issues or One?

THE man took a leaflet and read a few lines. "This is the Nashville, Tennessee to Washington, D. C. Walk for Peace," it

348

began; "'Since 650 B. C. there have been 1,656 arms races, only sixteen of which have not ended in war. The remainder have ended in economic collapse.'" He looked up. "Are you walking with that nigger?" he asked.

This kind of discussion of our message had been anticipated by the Committee for Nonviolent Action, when it decided that the walk should be integrated. "Token integrated," somebody later commented. Of thirteen young men and women committed to walk the whole distance, Robert Gore was the only Negro, though we hoped others might join before Washington. Whether they did or not, it was assumed that in the many talks about war and peace we would attempt to provoke along the way, we were sure to be asked a good many times whether we would be happy to see Robert married to our sisters. Before we headed south, we discussed the question of just how distracting our obvious attitude to race relations might be, and the proper way to cope with the problem. Events then proved our tentative conclusions to have been utterly inadequate.

Most of those advising us felt that battle on the two issues simply could not be combined. Of course we ought never to deny our belief in racial brotherhood; but Robert's presence was enough to confirm it. We should try to avoid talking about it; we were there to talk about *peace*. And it would be folly to seek to associate ourselves too closely with the people down there who were struggling for integration. Many people would then shy away from us. And they, the Negroes, could be harmed by it even more than we. They had enough of a burden to bear, already, without our giving their opponents added ammunition—the charge of their being "unpatriotic."

I supposed that the advice was practical, but it depressed me. I think we all left the meeting feeling unsatisfied—wondering a little why, then the walk *was* to be integrated. We'd talked about the fact that this could lead us into danger. The South was unpredictable, it was stressed: we might not run into any trouble at all; on the other hand, we just might all get killed. In a cause we were not to appear to be battling for?

I had felt for a long time that the two struggles—for disarmament and for Negro rights—were properly parts of the one struggle. The same nonviolent tactic joined us, but more than this: our struggles were fundamentally one—to commit our country in act as well as in word to the extraordinary faith announced in our Declaration of Independence: that all men are endowed with certain rights that must not be denied them. *All* men, including those of darker skin, whom it has been convenient to exploit; including those in other countries, with whose policies we quarrel; among those rights which are not to be questioned, the right to be free to pursue happiness, and among them the right not to be deprived of life. In short, the Christian faith, still revolutionary, that men are brothers and that—no matter what—our actions must respect the fact. The only mode of battle that does, implicitly, respect this fact is that of nonviolence, and I had heard that for more and more of those in the civil rights as well as in the peace movement, the very attempt to practice it had implanted a corresponding faith, however tentative. But of course it is possible to hold a faith and yet not recognize all its implications, to be struggling side by side with others and yet be unaware of them. Perhaps it wasn't realistic to think of joining ranks.

We started out, in Nashville, with only a wistful look in the direction of the integration movement. We marched past a sit-in demonstration at a "Simple Simon's" and "smiled in." We didn't even picket for a few minutes; didn't pause in our marching. "There they are"—we turned our heads. We caught a glimpse of a row of young people at a counter—a glimpse, as in a flash photograph, of young heads held in a certain proud and patient fashion; and then we had marched past. A few steps away, in front of a movie theatre, several adolescent toughs loitered—faces furtive, vacant. Did they plan trouble? In a minute, we were out of sight. It felt unnatural, I think, to all of us.

That afternoon we held a small open meeting at Scarritt College for Christian Workers. Two Negro leaders were among those present—James Lawson and Metz Rollins. Members of the group staging the sit-in—the Student Nonviolent Coordinating Committee—had been invited; but none came. Was this because they *were* shy of association with us? Or was it perhaps because, as one walker suggested, they felt that we should have done more to demonstrate solidarity with them? Rollins inclined his head, smiled. "It may well be."

Lawson spoke that afternoon. In the course of his talk, he remarked, "There is a clearcut relation between the peace walk and what some of us are seeking to do in the emerging nonviolent movement in the South. Some people have tried to classify our effort here as one that is of and for and by the Negro. They have tried to define the struggle for integration as a struggle to gain the Negro more power. I maintain that it is not the case. Go among the common ordinary people . . . for the 'leading Negroes' are not the leaders of this movement. . . . Listen to their prayers and to their speech. They are constantly thinking not in terms of civil rights but in terms of the kingdom of God on earth, the brotherhood of all men. . . . What is behind it is an effort to build a community for all of us . . . 'the beloved community.' I say that this work is related to the work for peace. . . . It might be a prototype to speak to the whole world. . . . And the peace walk is related to the task of building community here. . . . The movements are related to each other, in a sense are one and the same enterprise."

I took down the words he spoke, in my notebook, nodding, "Yes"; and at the same time, disregarding them—perhaps because I was tired from the long drive south, and the process of breaking myself in again to group life, to sleeping on the floor, to packing up and moving each day; or perhaps because the meeting room was very nearly empty: the peace movement and the civil rights movement were certainly not visibly related here.

On Easter afternoon, we walked out of Nashville, heading out along Route 70N toward Knoxville. Two Fisk students, members of S.N.C.C., did appear just before starting time, to walk with us for a little while. Their presence was well noted. The signs we carried were unconventional: "If your conscience demands it, refuse to serve in the armed forces," ". . . refuse to pay taxes for war," "Defend freedom with nonviolence"; but more conspicuous than our signs, quite obviously, were the Negro students—while they remained with us—and after a while the single figure of Robert Gore. Robert carried the "lollipop" sign that simply labelled the walk: NASHVILLE TO WASHINGTON; but he was in himself our most provocative, most instantly legible sign—walking along very quietly;

dressed, carefully, not in hiking clothes but sober sports jacket and slacks; head held high, a quiet tension in his bearing.

We encountered a certain amount of Southern courtesy—"Well, have a nice walk!"; and now and then expression of active sympathy—"God go with you!" "You mean you agree with us?" "I sure do!" But less friendly messages were of course more common—"Boo!", "Get out of here!" As we held out our leaflets, car windows were rolled up swiftly; some cars actually backed off from us in a rush; citizens on foot stepped quickly behind shop doors. Approaching a leaflet victim, one tried, by remaining very calm oneself, and looking him quietly in the eye, to prevent his flight, and infect him with corresponding calm; but the exercise was difficult. Soon the "hot rod gang" began to face us in the field. Parking their cars by the roadside, they would line up, leaning against them, awaiting our approach, assuming looks that were meant to kill—expressions glowering and at the same time pathetically vacant. We would offer leaflets, walk past; they would hop into their cars, speed past us, line up again by the roadside. And now the first warnings began to be delivered to us. I handed a leaflet to the manager of a garage, and to the Negro employee who stood beside him. "I hear they're going to shoot you a little farther down the line," the white man told me softly. "They don't like niggers there, you see." He turned and smiled fixedly into the eyes of the black man by his side—"That's what I hear." The Negro made no answer, returning the stare but allowing nothing to come to the surface of his look—his shining eyes fathomless. The white man turned back to me. "I just hope you'll be all right," he said—not pretending not to pretend. I told him, as brightly as I could, "Keep hoping."

That first night we slept on the floors of a white church near Old Hickory; the next night our "advance worker" had arranged for us to stay in a Negro church in Lebanon. Lebanon was a small town which had lately seen much violence. Fifteen months before, a young Negro minister, Reverend Cordell Sloan, had been assigned to the town to try to build a Negro Presbyterian church. He had felt called, as well, to try to build a sit-in movement. This was the first small town in the South in which the struggle had been taken up; and it involved not college but high school students. Retaliation had been vigorous. Just recently the headquarters of the group had been demolished with rocks, while the Negroes themselves stood pressed against the walls inside, and the police looked on. This day, as we filed along the highway, a car slowed down in passing, a young man leaned his head out: "You walking into Lebanon?" "That's right." "Good place for you to be walking. We're going to hang you all there." It was a bright beautiful day. Fruit trees were coming into bloom; the purple redbud was out. Horses and goats and litters of many-colored pigs ran in mixed company through the long Tennessee fields. The fields were vivid with flowering mustard. We marched along, trying not to straggle out, but to keep fairly close together. Just before mid-day a car approaching us suddenly whizzed into a side-road and stopped; the doors flew open, and several men leaped out. Well here it is, I thought; may we all behave well. Then I saw that their faces were dark. They were students from Lebanon, two of them come to walk into town with us. More planned to join us later. They held out their hands for signs to carry.

We stopped by the side of the road and shared a picnic lunch. We bought a carton of milk at a nearby store, and in a shy ritual gesture passed it from hand to hand, each drinking from the spout. On the road again, we walked past an all-Negro primary school, set high on a hill. The entire school stood out in the yard, waving to us. I ran up the hill with leaflets. A sweet-faced teacher asked me—so softly that I could hardly catch the words: "How many colored are with you?" I told her that two of the young men she saw were from Lebanon. "I thought I recognized J. T.," she said; and in her voice, in her face, was a contained, tremulous pride and excitement. A few miles further on, more students waited by the road to join us; a little further on, more; and at the town's edge, still more. As we stepped onto the sidewalks of the town, more of us were black than white.

A car sped by, an arm jerked out of the window and slung an empty coke bottle. The youngest of the team, Henry Wershaw, gave a little cry: he had been hit in the ankle. He was able soon to limp on. We kept close ranks, to be ready for worse than that; but everyone was stepping lightly; the mood among us was almost gay. One small boy, Sam, strode with us, eyes sparkling. A pretty young woman named Avis, in a light-colored summer dress, almost skipped along the street. The citizens of the town, as usual, stepped back from us in dread; withdrew behind their doors and peered out, through the glass panes, in amazement and dread, as the unarmed troop of us passed. There were several among us who bore the marks of violence at the hands of townspeople. The skull of one of the young Negroes showed, beneath his close-cropped hair, an intricate tracery of scars: he had been hit with a wrench during one of the sit-ins. There were others walking, too, who had suffered such blows; and none had ever struck back. They walked along the street now, lighthearted, as if secure, faces extraordinarily bright, while those who had, in one way or another, condoned the blows struck, drew back, in the reflex of fear. Before we headed south, the women had been cautioned against walking in public next to a Negro man; it might make things dangerous for him. At any rate, we were told, best to take our cue from the man himself. I had carefully made no move to walk next to any of these students. But now one after another, as we moved through the town, stepped alongside me, to introduce himself, to exchange a few words—free of caution. They had made their choice, had entered a fight, and if one was in it, then one was in it—ready to take what might come. At lunch one of them talked about this a little: "When you see those hoodlums arriving, you just divorce yourself from your body—prepare your body for anything: spit, fists, sticks, anything—"

Police cars had begun to drive past us at frequent intervals; but our friends remarked that we mustn't assume that they were there for our protection. During recent trouble, one woman had asked an officer whether the police intended to protect them from the mob. "We're hired to protect the city, not individuals," had been his reply. We headed for the town square now, preparing ourselves for "anything." We walked through uneventfully. Within our hearing, an officer in a squad car pulled up next to a car full of young toughs and told the driver, "Not today, Hank, not today." We turned the corner and limped the final block to Picketts Chapel Methodist Church.

In the white churches where we had stayed so far, we had had the use of the church kitchen in which to fix our meals, from supplies we carried about with us; once the pastor's wife had kindly fixed us sandwiches and lemonade; and evenings, after supper, as many as five members of the congregation had sometimes dropped in to ask questions. This day, as we sat in the churchyard easing our feet, women began to appear from the four points of the compass, carrying bowls and platters; all who had walked were soon summoned into the room behind the church to a feast: fried chicken, garden peas, turnip greens, two kinds of potato salad, three kinds of pie. After we had sat down together to eat, we were invited into the church itself; word of a meeting had been spread through the community; the door kept opening, and soon the church had filled up.

The shape this meeting took swiftly dissolved any remaining anxieties about the harm we might do to the integrationists and to ourselves if we sought association with them. Reverend Sloan spoke first—a thin handsome man with gentle but stubborn demeanor, and the luminous wide eyes of a man who is almost blind but who sees what it is that he wants to do. "I hope the town never gets over what it saw today," he began. What the town had seen of course, as we walked through its streets together, was the first integrated gathering that had ever occurred in Lebanon. The white community had seen, and the Negro community had seen, too, the brotherhood of which Sloan preached made visible—turned fact. "I hope it gets into its system, I hope it gets to the bone," said Sloan. It was clear that he meant both white community and Negro. We learned, at the end of the meeting, that this was the largest audience he had ever had there. He had made great headway with students, but adults had been largely apathetic. Because of the drama of our arrival, many adults were present tonight, gazing about them in quiet astonishment, and he was addressing them particularly.

He spoke of the struggles in which he and his followers had been involved; he spoke of the opposition they had encountered—sprayed with insecticides, hit with ketchup bottles, threatened with pistols, run down with lawn mowers, "Name it, we've had it." "The proficient, efficient, sufficient police" had been on the scene. He smiled wryly. "We like to get killed." Many had been arrested. He asked those who had been to jail to stand. A large number stood. The leader of the peace

walk, Bradford Lyttle, here interrupted to ask those among
the peace walkers who had been to jail to stand, too; and an
equal number rose. "Let no one be afraid of going to jail,"
the minister urged; "It has become an honor. . . . It's easy to
say, isn't it? But come and try it." They shouldn't be afraid,
he repeated; they should be afraid of being slaves any longer.
"The only thing I'm afraid of is going back into the old way
of living again. We've gone too far." He reminded those in the
audience who had not been fighting that when freedom came,
they too would enjoy it—unless perhaps they'd feel too guilty
to enjoy it. They had better begin to get the feeling of it right
now. Then he got very specific about the ways in which they
could help, and the ways in which they had been doing the
movement harm.

After he had spoken, Bradford Lyttle spoke about the work
of the C.N.V.A. He spoke at ease, his words briefer than they
often were—so much obviously could be assumed to be understood by this audience. He felt very strongly, he told them, that
America was in a desperate situation today. Here were the most
prosperous and happily situated people who had ever lived,
on the verge of giving up their souls—for we were professing
ourselves quite willing to murder hundreds of millions of other
human beings to try to preserve our own standards of life.
Many Americans were beginning to demonstrate in protest—to
name themselves *un*willing. He urged them to join the protest.
C.N.V.A. believed in disarming unilaterally, and in training
for defense through nonviolent resistance. Heads nodded. No
one stood up to hurl the familiar challenge: Are we supposed
to lie down and let the Russians walk right over us? Of all the
signs we carry, the sign that usually remains the most abstract
for those who read it is "Defend freedom through nonviolent
resistance"; but when the students of Lebanon walked through
their town carrying that banner, the message could not remain
abstract. If our walking beside them had made visible for the
community the substance of what Reverend Sloan had been
preaching, their walking beside us had made visible the substance of what Bradford Lyttle preached. Forty-five people in
that audience came forward to put their names on C.N.V.A.'s
mailing list.

Reverend Sloan called for a collection to be taken up for both causes. Many who had little enough to spare opened their purses. Some who had never given before gave this night. We stood and clasped hands and sang the hymn that has become the theme song of the movement in the South: "We shall overcome some day! . . . Black and white together. . . . We shall live in peace!" The words seemed to belong to both our causes.

The next day we were scheduled to walk to the small town of Carthage, set on the bluffs of the Cumberland River. A number of the people who had walked into town with us the day before turned up to see us on our way. Reverend Sloan was among them, and a leader among the students, Bobby, and Sloan's right-hand-man, a tall very homely newspaper reporter, Finley, a man of wit and feeling; and quite a few others. We expected to be escorted to the town's edge and I rather think they had expected to walk only this far, themselves; but most of them ended by walking with us all the way to Carthage. Passing motorists again leaned out of their cars to shout threatening or vile remarks. "Let not your hearts be troubled," Reverend Sloan advised, in his soft rather lilting voice. He and Finley left for a while to ride up ahead with Bradford and find a place for us to stay that night. They found it at Braden Methodist Church, where Sloan knew the assistant minister, Beulah Allen. "How could we turn you out?" she said to Bradford; "You can never tell when the stranger will be the Lord."

After we had entered Carthage with our banners, Sloan and Finley and Bobby took a little stroll about its streets. The walk had now linked them dramatically with *that* town; and who knows when their battle may not be taken up there?

Again, this evening, women of the community appeared, arms laden; a feast was spread for us in the church basement. Again, after dinner together, we moved into the "sanctuary"; and again the church filled up. It was the first integrated meeting that had ever taken place here, too. That night, the women in our group slept in the house of Beulah Allen's sister, Dona. As we tiptoed through her room, Dona's old mother woke, and Dona introduced us. "Honey, they look white," Dona's mother whispered to her. "Mama, they are," said Dona. "Lord bless us!" said the old lady.

Braden's Methodist Church was set up on a little rise just above the large town square, and as we gathered noisily first in the basement and then in the church proper, a good many of the white people of the town and of the country round the town gathered in the square and stood glaring up. A few of them had thrown some rotten fruit and vegetables, as we sat outside before dinner; a few had walked past, holding empty coke bottles—but not quite bringing themselves to throw those. During the meeting, the door would open and shut, open and shut, as more and more of the Negro community kept arriving; and one was never quite sure that some of the crowd below might not be arriving at last. But again there were a lot of cops around, and again they had decided to keep order. The crowd just stood, until past midnight, glaring up at the small frame building which resounded with our talk and laughter and singing and prayer. Dona reported to us afterward that she had gone outside once and found several white boys loitering and had asked them in. "They don't understand," she explained to us; "They've never even been outside the county." If the resistance movement had not yet taken root among the Negroes of Carthage, they hardly needed to be introduced to the idea of nonviolence. They had found it long ago in the New Testament.

This meeting was above all an old-fashioned prayer meeting. Bradford Lyttle talked again briefly—drawing a picture of the world-wide nonviolent movement. And he issued a rather shy invitation to them to walk with us the next day. Reverend Sloan then rose and declared that he would be less shy about it: he would simply tell them that they *should* walk with us. Robert Gore asked Beulah Allen if he could say a few words from the pulpit, and he spoke of how the message of Jesus—to love one's enemies—was a strange message, a revolutionary one. "That's right," came from the audience—"Amen!" But it was Beulah Allen who led the meeting, and who spoke the prayers. I think few of us had ever before this evening felt that we were being prayed for. The days we were now approaching on the walk promised to be the most trying. We were about to enter Cumberland County, where—we had been told by both friends and antagonists—no Negro was supposed to remain after nightfall. The last Negro family that had tried to build had been burned out; the last Negro who had tried to walk through the county had been found dead by the side of the road. Beulah Allen had heard these stories too. She stood solidly before the altar rail, spread out her arms, raised up her voice—half in a piercing shout, half in a song—and addressing God as though He were indeed there just above us, just beyond the roof—"Heavenly FATHER! . . . Heavenly FATHER!"—she asked Him to give us courage, and also a good night's sleep that night, asked Him to teach all of us, including the people out there in the square, and the people along the road we were going to walk, how best to behave. The words themselves vanish now in my memory, having entered too deeply that evening into my flesh. I looked about me, and the other walkers, too, were sitting up, stock still. We had all of us heard, before, theatrical versions of such prayer—intended sometimes to be funny or sometimes to be endearing; and Beulah's prayer retained for us of course something of the extravagance of theatre; but now we were in the play; we were at the heart of it, amazed.

Again we sang together. Dona, accompanying us at the upright piano, hit the keys with a heavily-pouncing, laboring but joyful, heart-felt emphasis of her own. The rhythm was always almost jazz, and as we nodded our heads, tapped our feet, our weariness and the nudging fears we'd kept down all the past days dissolved. Again, at Reverend Sloan's prompting, we sang the integration hymn—reaching out and taking hands: "We shall overcome some day!" "Now this is difficult," Reverend Sloan said, with a flickering smile, and prompted, "Black and white together some day." He prompted, "We are not afraid *today*." At the end of the meeting, Beulah Allen gave us a blessing, and exclaimed, "It's been so sweet!" At that moment, I recalled the words of James Lawson about "the beloved community." It seemed that we had been living in that community this past hour.

The next morning I learned to my astonishment that our evening's meeting had not caused the breach between us and the white community that might have been supposed. I entered one of the shops on the square to buy some things, expecting to be served with glum hostility. The young woman behind the counter—who clearly knew who I was—was full of both curiosity and warmth. She chattered eagerly about the peculiar weather they had been having this past year, and "It's the times, I think," she ventured. I asked whether she felt that atomic tests were disrupting the weather, and she nodded: "There's One who is more powerful; we forget that." As I left, "I hope you come back and see us again," she said.

In the course of the next few days, we walked into mythical Cumberland County and walked out of it, unharmed. Two Quaker couples who bravely put us up received middle-of-the-night telephone calls, threatening "roast nigger for breakfast"; one night the fire department arrived in the yard, summoned by false alarm; one night local high school students swarmed up to the house—but when invited in, sat and talked until late, quietly enough, their curiosity about us obviously deeper than their hostility. (As they left, they were arrested by the police—as eager to protect them from us as to protect us from them.) It was actually at the edge of the county, the first night after we left Carthage, that we had our nearest brush with violence. Reverend Sloan and Finley and Bobby and others had walked with us again this third day, but had taken their final leave of us at a little one-room Negro church by the side of the road, way out "nowhere," between towns. No one was in the church, but we had been told that we could spend the night there. We had crawled into our sleeping bags, scattered out on the floor between the pews, and were listening sleepily to the small country noises in the air, when abruptly the ruder sound of rocks hitting the building brought us full awake. Two of the men stepped outside and called into the dark, inviting the besiegers to come and talk to us about it. The hail of rocks stopped and the people rustled off into the dark. We could hear the crickets again for a while and then the barrage began again; a rock came crashing through one of the windows. Another two stepped outside, this time carrying flashlights aimed at themselves, to show the strangers where they were and that they were unarmed. We could hear their voices and we could hear the stones still flying and suddenly we heard a small gasping cry. Eric Weinberger had been hit on the side of the head and knocked off his feet. He staggered up, and called to them again, "It's all right. You hit me in the head, but it's all right. But now why don't you come and talk with us?"—and seven or eight young men finally emerged out of the dark and consented to talk. They were young workingmen from around there. They talked for a good while, and finally they said that well, they might perhaps agree with some of the things we said about war and peace, but they couldn't understand our walking around with a nigger, and all sleeping in the same building with him. And then one of them asked the time-worn question: "Would you let a nigger marry your sister?" The question was posed to Sam Savage, who is a Southerner himself. When he answered that yes, he would; the decision would, after all, be hers to make—they exclaimed in sudden anger and disgust: well he was no real Southerner then, and there was no use talking about anything further; and they stamped off into the dark. At which point, one might have said that the advice we had been given before starting out on the walk had now been proved to be correct: the two issues of race relations and of war and peace could not be discussed together. However, there is a final chapter to this story. After a short time, the young men returned, wanting to talk further. The talk this time went on until the one who had done the most arguing remarked that they must be up early to work and had better get some sleep. But would we be there the next evening? he wanted to know. (We had of course, unfortunately, to move on.) As they left, he shook hands with Sam, who had said that yes, he'd let his sister marry a black man. It is my own conviction that these men listened to us as they did, on the subject of peace, just *because* Robert Gore was travelling with us. It made it more difficult for them to listen, of course; it made the talk more painful; but it also snatched it from the realm of the merely abstract. For the issue of war and peace remains fundamentally the issue of whether or not one is going to be willing to respect one's fellow man.

EDMUND WILSON

Edmund Wilson (1895–1972) thought of himself as a journalist, but he is more often described as a man of letters because his work is so wide-ranging: *Axel's Castle* (1931) introduced a generation of readers to Joyce, Proust, Yeats, and other modernists; *To the Finland Station* (1940) is a masterpiece of history; *The Shock of Recognition* (1943) perhaps the best and most personal anthology of American literature; *Patriotic Gore* (1962) surely the best literary history of American Civil War writing.

What Wilson was not, for most of his life, was a politically engaged writer, and certainly not an antiwar one. He served in World War I in an army medical unit and in the intelligence service, but he came back without a strong antiwar impulse, feeling chiefly that the war had freed him from the constraints of genteel society, as indeed it had. *The Cold War and the Income Tax* (1963) is the one book of his that shows him in opposition to war, but we feel as we read it that he's being led to that opposition against his own inclination. He neglected, he tells us, to pay his income tax for several years, was found and penalized by the IRS, and got angry: at the IRS, at the nature of the tax system, and eventually at what the tax system was being used to fund, i.e., wars. He studied and got acquainted with those who refused to pay their taxes on principle, like Maurice McCrackin, whom the book portrays with great sympathy; and though Wilson was never going to take the risks that intentional war tax resisters were taking, he concludes the book, in the excerpt below, with a denunciation of the war system fiercer and more contemptuous than anything the gentle McCrackin ever wrote.

FROM

The Strategy of Tax Refusal

To one who was born in the nineteenth century, and so still retains some remnants of the belief in human progress of a moral as well as a mechanical kind, it is especially repugnant to be forced to accept preparations for the demise of our society or of a damage to it so appalling that it is impossible to see beyond it. The confident reformer of the past always saw himself confronted by an enemy, the defeat of whom would represent for him a release of the forces of life, the "dawn of a new day," the beginning of "a better world." But who today is the reformer's adversary? Not the trusts, the "malefactors of great wealth." Not "capitalism," not "communism." Simply human limitations so general as sometimes to seem insurmountable, an impulse to internecine destruction which one comes more and more to feel irrepressible. These elements, plus our runaway technology, have produced our Defense Department, with its host of secret agents and diligent bureaucrats of the Pentagon and the CIA, who have got themselves into a position where they have not merely been able to formulate policy without the approval of Congress but even to carry it out; with its pressure on Congress itself which enables it to get its vast appropriations granted; with its blackmail through bugaboo by which it makes the country live in constant terror of an invasion by Soviet Commissars; with its stimulus to the gigantic war industries, which give employment to so much labor, and its equipping of so many laboratories that give employment to technicians and scientists; with its discouragement of young men's ambitions by imposing on them two stultifying disruptive years of obligatory military service.

How to get rid of this huge growth, which is no longer a private organization, like one of Theodore Roosevelt's old trusts that could be busted, that is not even a thriving corporation protected by a business administration but an excrescence of the government itself which officially drains our resources and which stupidly and insolently threatens our lives? In our day, the possibilities for human self-knowledge and for knowledge of the universe of which we are part, for the extension, both physical and mental, of human capabilities, have been opened up in all directions. We can not only fly and dive but are learning to live in space and beneath the sea; we are beginning to understand our relation to the other animals and our development as a genus among them; we have burrowed into the ruins of cities seven thousand years old and have had glimpses of the lives of men that existed many millennia earlier; we are coming to comprehend something about the processes by which we reproduce and by which our memories work; we have mastered techniques of the fine arts and other exploits of imaginative thought that lift us as far above our squalors as our space rockets do above the earth—and yet, skilled in and inspired by all this, we are now dominated by the great lethal mushroom that expands from the splitting of atoms and poisons the atmosphere of the earth and by the great human fungus behind it, which multiplies the cells of offices, of laboratories and training camps and which poisons the atmosphere of society. I should not make the mistake I have mentioned above of isolating a human institution and regarding it as the enemy of humanity. It is admitted that, in the phenomenon of hypnotism, the victim must have the will to be hypnotized; and we have now been hypnotizing ourselves. We have created the war branches of our government in one of our own images. But now that things have gone so far, is there any chance, short of catastrophe, of dismembering and disassembling this image and constructing a nobler one that answers better to what we pretend to?

All such images, to be sure, are myths, national idealizations. But there has been enough good will behind ours to make the rest of the world put some faith in it. The present image of the United States—homicidal and menacing—is having the contrary effect. And for all our boasts of wealth and freedom we are submitting to deprivation and coercion in order to feed and increase it.

DAVID DELLINGER

If you type the term *nonviolence* into Google's Ngram Viewer, charting the relative frequency of its use over time, the data tell an interesting story. From next-to-nothing before 1920, the word slowly becomes more common; then suddenly, in the early 1950s, it shoots up at an incredible clip, peaking in 1970 and dropping off thereafter almost as fast. Surely the adoption by many in the civil rights movement of this "weapon unique in history, which cuts without wounding and ennobles the man who wields it" (as Martin Luther King Jr. described nonviolence in his 1964 Nobel lecture), largely explains the change in the language. Writing on "The Future of Nonviolence" in *Gandhi Marg* in July 1965, David Dellinger (1915–2004) assesses both the limits and huge potential of this unique "weapon" at a moment when it had begun to be wielded to great effect in America, as it had been in India a generation before.

Dellinger was no belated or secondhand observer of these phenomena, however. In 1946, along with other COs who had spent time in prison or in Civilian Public Service camps during World War II, he founded the Committee for Nonviolent Revolution, a group that aspired to take more radical action against injustice than existing pacifist organizations. (*Pacifist*, says Google, peaked in 1940, but *antiwar* is as widespread as ever.) Born to wealthy and politically conservative parents, Dellinger went "from Yale to jail," to borrow his phrase, spending time in between at the Union Theological Seminary and as an ambulance-driving volunteer in the Spanish Civil War. He founded *Liberation* with A. J. Muste in 1956, traveled to Vietnam in 1966 and was a leader of the March on the Pentagon the next year, and in 1968 was charged with inciting a riot for his role in antiwar protests at the Democratic National Convention in Chicago.

The Future of Nonviolence

THE theory and practice of active nonviolence are roughly at the stage of development today as those of electricity in the early days of Marconi and Edison. A new source of power has been discovered and crudely utilized in certain specialized situations, but our experience is so limited and our knowledge so primitive that there is legitimate dispute about its applicability to a wide range of complicated and critical tasks. One often hears it said that nonviolent resistance was powerful enough to drive the British out of India but would have been suicidal against the Nazis. Or that Negroes can desegregate a restaurant or bus by nonviolence but can hardly solve the problem of jobs or getting rid of the Northern ghettos, since both of these attempts require major assaults on the very structure of society and run head-on into the opposition of entrenched interests in the fields of business, finance, and public information. Finally, most of those who urge nonviolent methods on the Negro hesitate to claim that the United States should do away with its entire military force and prepare to defend itself in the jungle of international politics by nonviolent methods.

There is no doubt in my mind that nonviolence is currently incapable of resolving some of the problems that must be solved if the human race is to survive—let alone create a society in which all persons have a realistic opportunity to achieve material fulfillment and personal dignity. Those who are convinced that nonviolence can be used in *all* conflict situations have a responsibility to devise concrete methods by which it can be made effective. For example, can we urge the Negroes of Harlem or the *obreros* and *campesinos* (workers and peasants) of Latin America to refrain from violence if we offer them no positive method of breaking out of the slums, poverty, and cultural privation that blight their lives and condemn their children to a similar fate? It is contrary to the best tradition of nonviolence to do so. Gandhi often made the point that it is better to resist injustice by violent methods than not to resist at all. He staked his own life on his theory that nonviolent resistance was the superior method, but he never counselled appeasement or passive nonresistance.

The major advances in nonviolence have not come from people who have approached nonviolence as an end in itself, but from persons who were passionately striving to free themselves from social injustice. Gandhi discovered the method almost by accident when he went to South Africa as a young, British-trained lawyer in search of a career, but was "sidetracked" by the shock of experiencing galling racial segregation. Back in India, the humiliations of foreign rule turned him again to nonviolence, not as an act of religious withdrawal and personal perfectionism, but, in line with his South African experience, as the most practical method Indians could use in fighting for their independence. During World War I, not yet convinced that the method of nonviolence could be used successfully in such a large-scale international conflict, he actually helped recruit Indians for the British Army. By contrast, during World War II, after twenty more years of experimentation with non-violence, he counselled nonviolent resistance to the Nazis and actually evolved a plan for nonviolent opposition to the Japanese should they invade and occupy India.

In 1956 the Negroes of Montgomery, Alabama, catapulted nonviolence into the limelight in the United States, not out of conversion to pacifism or love for their oppressors, but because they had reached a point where they could no longer tolerate certain racial injustices. Martin Luther King, Jr., who later became a pacifist, employed an armed defense guard to protect his home and family during one stage of the Montgomery conflict. In 1963, one of the leaders of the mass demonstrations in Birmingham said to me: "You might as well say that we never heard of Gandhi or nonviolence, but we were determined to get our freedom, and in the course of struggling for it we came upon nonviolence like gold in the ground."

There is not much point in preaching the virtues of nonvio-lence to a Negro in Harlem or Mississippi except as a method for winning his freedom. For one thing, the built-in institu-tional violence imposed on him every day of his life looms too large. He can rightly say that he wants no part of a nonviolence that condemns his spasmodic rock-throwing or desperate and often knowingly unrealistic talk of armed self-defense, but mounts no alternative campaign. It is all too easy for those with jobs, adequate educational opportunities, and decent hous-ing to insist that Negroes remain nonviolent—to rally to the defense of "law and order." "Law and order is the Negro's best friend," Mayor Robert Wagner announced in the midst of the 1964 riots in Harlem. But nonviolence and a repressive law and order have nothing in common. The most destructive violence in Harlem is not the bottle-throwing, looting, or muggings of frustrated and demoralized Negroes. Nor is it the frequent shootings of juvenile delinquents and suspected criminals by white policemen, who often reflect both the racial prejudices of society and the personal propensity to violence that led them to choose a job whose tools are the club and the revolver. The basic violence in Harlem is the vast, impersonal violation of bodies and souls by an unemployment rate four times that of white New Yorkers, a median family income between half and two thirds that of white families, an infant mortality rate of 45.3 per thousand compared to 26.3 for New York as a whole, and inhuman crowding into subhuman housing. (It has been estimated that if the entire population of the United States were forced to live in equally congested conditions, it would fit into three of New York City's five boroughs.) Many white Americans are thrilled by the emotional catharsis of a law-abiding March on Washington (or even a fling at civil disobedience), in which they work off their guilt feelings, conscious and unconscious, by "identifying" for a day with the black victims of society. But when the project is over the whites do not return home anxious to know whether any of their children have been bitten by a rat, shot by a cop, or victimized by a pimp or dope peddler.

Commitment to nonviolence must not be based on patient acquiescence in intolerable conditions. Rather, it stems from a deeper knowledge of the self-defeating, self-corrupting effect of lapses into violence. On the one hand, Gandhi did not ally himself with those who profit from injustice and conveniently condemn others who violently fight oppression. On the other hand, he temporarily suspended several of his own nonviolent campaigns because some of his followers had succumbed to the temptations of violent reprisal. In perfecting methods of nonviolence, he gradually crystallized certain attitudes toward the nature of man (even oppressive, exploitative, foreign-invader man), which he formulated in the terminology of his native religion and which he considered indispensable for true nonviolence. These basic insights have been translated by religious Western pacifists (including Martin Luther King) from their original language to that of Christianity. Similarly, they can be retranslated into the secular humanist terminology which is more natural to large numbers of Northern Negroes and white civil-rights activists.

The key attitudes stem from a feeling for the solidarity of all human beings, even those who find themselves in deep conflict. George Meredith once said that a truly cultivated man is one who realizes that the things which seem to separate him from his fellows are as nothing compared with those which unite him with all humanity. Nonviolence may start, as it did with the young Gandhi and has with many an American Negro, as a technique for wresting gains from an unloved and unlovely oppressor. But somewhere along the line, if a nonviolent movement is to cope with deep-seated fears and privileges, its strategy must flow from a sense of the underlying unity of all human beings. So must the crucial, semi-spontaneous, inventive actions that emerge (for good or ill) in the midst of crisis.

This does not mean that Negroes, for example, must "love" in a sentimental or emotional way those who are imprisoning, shooting, beating, or impoverishing them. Nor need they feel personal affection for complacent white liberals. But it is not enough to abandon the use of fists, clubs, Molotov cocktails, and guns. Real nonviolence requires an awareness that white oppressors and black victims are mutually entrapped in a set of relationships that violate the submerged better instincts of everyone. A way has to be found to open the trap and free both sets of victims. Appeals to reason or decency have little effect (except in isolated instances) unless they are accompanied by tangible pressures—on the pocketbook, for example—or the inconveniences associated with sit-ins, move-ins, strikes, boycotts, or nonviolent obstructionism. But for any lasting gain to take place the struggle must appeal to the whole man, including his encrusted sense of decency and solidarity, his yearnings to recapture the lost innocence when human beings were persons to be loved, not objects to rule, obey, or exploit.

This reaching out to the oppressor has nothing to do with tokenism, which tends to creep into any movement, including a nonviolent one. In fact, tokenism is a double violation of the attitude of solidarity, because it permits the oppressor to make, and the oppressed to accept, a gesture which leaves intact the institutional barriers that separate them. One can gain a token victory or make a political deal without needing to have any invigorating personal contact with the "enemy," certainly without bothering to imagine oneself in his place so as to understand his needs, fears and aspirations. But the more revolutionary a movement's demands, the more imperative it is to understand what is necessary for the legitimate fulfillment of the persons who make up the opposition.

"We're going to win our freedom," a Negro leader said at a mass meeting in Birmingham last year, "and as we do it we're going to set our white brothers free." A short while later, when the Negroes faced a barricade of police dogs, clubs and fire hoses, they "became spiritually intoxicated," as another leader described it. "This was sensed by the police and firemen and it began to have an effect on them. . . . I don't know what happened to me. I got up from my knees and said to the cops: 'We're not turning back. We haven't done anything wrong. All we want is our freedom. How do you feel doing these things?'" The Negroes started advancing and Bull Connor shouted: "Turn on the water!" But the firemen did not respond. Again he gave the order and nothing happened. Some observers claim they saw firemen crying. Whatever happened, the Negroes went through the lines. The next day, Bull Connor was reported by the press to have said: "I didn't want to mess their Sunday clothes, all those people from church." Until now this mood of outgoing empathetic nonviolence has been rarely achieved in this country. It was only part of the story in Birmingham, where in the end a more cautious tokenism gripped the top leaders. But it is the clue to the potential power of nonviolence.

Vinoba Bhave indicates something of the same interaction on the level of international conflict when he says: "Russia says America has dangerous ideas so she has to increase her armaments. America says exactly the same thing about Russia. . . . The image in the mirror is your own image; the sword in its hand is your own sword. And when we grasp our own sword in fear of what we see, the image in the mirror does the same. What we see in front of us is nothing but a reflection of ourselves. If India could find courage to reduce her army to the minimum, it would demonstrate to the world her moral strength. But we are cowards and cowards have no imagination."

The potential uses of nonviolent power are tremendous and as yet virtually unrealized. But it is important to understand that nonviolence can never be "developed" in such a way as to

carry out some of the tasks assigned to it by its more naïve converts—any more than God (or the greatest scientist) could draw
a square circle. It would be impossible, for instance, to defend
the United States of America, as we know it, nonviolently. This
is not because of any inherent defect in the nonviolent method
but because of a very important strength: nonviolence cannot
be used successfully to protect special privileges that have been
won by violence. The British could not have continued to rule
India by taking a leaf out of Gandhi's book and becoming
"nonviolent." Nor would the United States be able to maintain
its dominant position in Latin America if it got rid of its armies,
navies, "special forces," C.I.A.-guerrillas, etc. Does anyone
think that a majority of the natives work for a few cents a day,
live in rural or urban slums, and allow forty-four percent of
their children to die before the age of five because they love us?
Or that they are content to have American business drain away
$500 million a year in interest and dividends, on the theory
that the shareholders of United Fruit Company or the Chase
Manhattan Bank are more needy or deserving than themselves?

It follows that advocates of nonviolence are overly optimistic
when they argue from the unthinkability of nuclear war and
the partially proven power of nonviolence (in India and the
civil rights struggle) to the position that simple common sense
will lead the United States (the richest, most powerful nation
in the world, on whose business investments and armed forces
the sun never sets) to substitute nonviolent for violent national
defense. In recent years a number of well-intentioned peace
groups have tried to convince the government and members
of the power elite that the Pentagon should sponsor studies
with this end in view. But nonviolent defense requires not only
willingness to risk one's life (as any good soldier, rich or poor,
will do). It requires renunciation of all claims to special privileges and power at the expense of other people. In our society
most people find it more difficult to face economic loss while
alive than death itself. Surrender of special privilege is certainly
foreign to the psychology of those who supply, command, and
rely on the military. Nonviolence is supremely the weapon of
the dispossessed, the underprivileged, and the egalitarian, not
of those who are still addicted to private profit, commercial
values, and great wealth.

Nonviolence simply cannot defend property rights over human rights. The primacy of human rights would have to be established within the United States and in all of its dealings with other peoples before nonviolence could defend this country successfully. Nonviolence could defend what is worth defending in the United States, but a badly needed social revolution would have to take place in the process. Guerrilla warfare cannot be carried on successfully without the active support and cooperation of the surrounding population, which must identify justice (or at least its own welfare) with the triumph of the guerrillas. Nonviolence must rely even more heavily than guerrilla warfare on the justice of its cause. It has no chance of succeeding unless it can win supporters from previously hostile or neutral sections of the populace. It must do this by the fairness of its goals. Its objectives and methods are intimately interrelated and must be equally nonviolent.

The followers of Gandhi were imprisoned, beaten and, on more than one occasion, shot by the British during the Indian independence campaign. Today, some Americans consider the death of a nonviolent campaigner as conclusive evidence that "nonviolence won't work" and call for substitution of a violent campaign—in which people will also be killed and the original aims tend to be lost in an orgy of violence. But instead of allowing the British in effect to arm them, thereby giving the British the choice of weapons, the Gandhians kept right on fighting nonviolently and in the end succeeded in "disarming" the British. In the case of a number of nonviolent marches, the first row of advancing Indians was shot, but a second and a third row kept moving forward until the British soldiers became psychologically incapable of killing any more, even risking death at the hands of their superiors by disobeying orders to keep on firing. Eventually it became politically impossible for the commanders and the Prime Ministers to issue such orders. Need I add that if the Indians had been shot while trying to invade England and carry off its wealth, it would not have mattered how courageously nonviolent they had been; they could not have aroused this response.

If a practitioner of nonviolence is killed fighting for a cause that is considered unjust, he is quickly dismissed as a fanatic.

Indeed, at this stage of the struggle that is exactly what many white Southerners have tried to do in the cases of Medgar Evers, James Chaney, Michael Schwerner, and Andrew Goodman. But if the nonviolent warriors freely risk death in devotion to a cause that people recognize, even against their wills, as legitimate, the act has a tremendous effect. Willingness to sacrifice by undergoing imprisonment, physical punishment or, if need be, death itself, without retaliation, will not always dislodge deeply engrained prejudice or fear, but its general effect is always to work in that direction. By contrast, infliction of such penalties at best intimidates the opposition and at worst strengthens resistance, but in any case does not encourage psychological openness to a creative resolution of the underlying conflict of views or values.

Perhaps we can paraphrase Karl von Clausewitz's well-known observation that war is but the continuation of the politics of peace by other means, and say that the social attitudes of nonviolent defense must be a continuation of the social attitudes of the society it is defending. A little thought should convince us of the impossibility of keeping Negroes and colonial peoples in their present positions of inferiority once privileged white America is unable to rely on overt or covert violence. Secondly, it is ludicrous to expect such persons to join their oppressors in the uncoerced defense of the society that has treated them so poorly. (Even with the power of the draft at its disposal—backed by the threat of imprisonment and ultimately the firing squad—the United States found it necessary to make unprecedented concessions and promises to Negroes during World War II in order to keep up black morale.) Finally, there is the crucial question of how we can expect to treat our enemies nonviolently if we do not treat our friends and allies so.

On the crudest level, as long as we are willing to condemn two out of five children in Latin America to early death, in order to increase our material comforts and prosperity, by what newly found awareness of human brotherhood will we be able to resist the temptation to wipe out two out of five, three out of five, or even five out of five of the children of China in overt warfare if it is dinned into us that this is necessary to preserve our freedom, or the lives of ourselves and our own children?

If we cannot respect our neighbors more than to keep large numbers of them penned up in rat-infested slum ghettos, how will we develop the sense of human solidarity with our opponents without which nonviolence becomes an empty technicality and loses its power to undermine and sap enemy hostility and aggressiveness? How will we reach across the propaganda-induced barriers of hate, fear, and self-righteousness (belief in the superiority of one's country, race or system) to disarm ourselves and our enemies?

CLINTON HOPSON
AND JOE MARTIN

On July 7, 1965, a young Mississippi veteran of the civil rights movement, John Shaw, was killed in action in South Vietnam at the age of twenty-three. Back home, their grief turning to anger, his friends Joe Martin (1943–2009) and Clinton Hopson (1935–1978) circulated a leaflet in McComb, Mississippi, in which the struggle for civil rights and the struggle against the war were suddenly one struggle. The Mississippi Freedom Democratic Party reprinted their words, without officially endorsing them, in its *Newsletter* on July 28—the same day President Johnson ordered an additional 50,000 troops to head to Vietnam.

The heart of their argument is their testimony: "we don't know anything about Communism, Socialism, and all that, but we do know that Negroes have caught hell right here under this American Democracy." Hopson, a law student from New Jersey, had indeed "caught hell" in Mississippi, suffering arrest and the bombing of the house in which he was staying. He later became a Muslim and opened a Black Liberation Center in Newark. Martin, a Mississippi native, had also been jailed and lost his job; he became a prominent citizen of McComb, working to bring legal and health services to the city's African American community and helping high school students register to vote.

The War on Vietnam

HERE are five reasons why Negroes should not be in any war fighting for America:

1. No Mississippi Negroes should be fighting in Vietnam for the White Man's freedom, until all the Negro People are free in Mississippi.

2. Negro boys should not honor the draft here in Mississippi. Mothers should encourage their sons not to go.

3. We will gain respect and dignity as a race only by forcing the U.S. Government and the Mississippi Government to come with guns, dogs and trucks to take our sons away to fight and be killed protecting Miss., Alabama, Georgia, and Louisiana.

4. No one has a right to ask us to risk our lives and kill other Colored People in Santo Domingo and Vietnam, so that the White American can get richer. We will be looked upon as traitors by all the Colored People of the world if the Negro people continue to fight and die without a cause.

5. Last week a white soldier from New Jersey was discharged from the Army because he refused to fight in Vietnam; he went on a hunger strike. Negro boys can do the same thing. We can write and ask our sons if they know what they are fighting for. If he answers Freedom, tell him that's what we are fighting for here in Mississippi. And if he says Democracy, tell him the truth—we don't know anything about Communism, Socialism, and all that, but we do know that Negroes have caught hell right here under this American Democracy.

COUNTRY JOE McDONALD

The best-known performance of Country Joe McDonald's "I-Feel-Like-I'm-Fixin'-To-Die Rag" is the captivating one recorded in *Woodstock* (1970), the brilliant documentary account of the pattern-breaking 1969 music festival of the same name. The festival had an antiwar feel to it—many of the artists performing had often appeared at antiwar rallies—and McDonald's performance in particular gave the audience a chance to affirm their solidarity. "I don't know how you expect to stop the war if you can't sing any better than that," he exhorted the 300,000 listeners assembled there; singing itself became antiwar action, and the particular character of the song, its adroit way of opposing war by impersonating, exaggerating, and caricaturing the views of war supporters, perhaps mattered less than the fact that so many sang together.

McDonald (b. 1942) grew up in Los Angeles, a "red diaper baby" in a town with a great concert hall, and went to hear everyone who performed there. He enlisted in the Army at seventeen, and was stationed in Japan. In the early sixties he moved to Berkeley, spending his time playing music with several ensembles, mostly ones he put together. Country Joe and the Fish came into being when McDonald was producing a recording of talk-songs and needed the help of friends, including Barry "The Fish" Melton, who borrowed his nickname from Chairman Mao. ("Guerillas are fish, and the people are the water in which they swim.") The "Fixin'-To-Die Rag," written in 1965, was on that first, privately produced recording, but was kept off the band's first Vanguard recording by label president Maynard Solomon, who felt it would become "a thorn in their side and prevent the band from getting any single play on the radio." In subsequent performances it usually began with the added "Fish Cheer."

After Woodstock, McDonald turned to a solo career, often in Europe. He worked on a score for the 1970 film of Henry Miller's *Quiet Days in Clichy* and for a film about the election of Salvador Allende. He continued singing and opposing war at venues large and small, earning himself a spot on President Nixon's enemies list. His degree of political engagement has not decreased over time; he has been involved in protests against then–California governor Arnold Schwarzenegger's budget cuts and, with Cindy Sheehan, against the Iraq War, and has been compared by right-wing political commentator Bill O'Reilly to Fidel Castro.

The I-Feel-Like-I'm-Fixin'-To-Die Rag

Come on all of you big strong men;
Uncle Sam needs your help again.
He's got himself in a terrible jam;
Way down yonder in Vietnam.
So put down your books and pick up a gun;
We're gonna have a whole lot a fun.

CHORUS: Cause, it's a one, two, three, "What are we fightin'
                    for?"
                "Don't ask me. I don't give a damn!" Next stop is
                    Vietnam.
                It's a five, six, seven, open up the Pearly Gates.
                There ain't no time to wonder why. "Whoopie,
                    we're all gonna die!"

Come on wall street don't be slow.
Why, Man, this is war a-Go-Go.
There's plenty good money to be made
By supplyin' the Army with the tools of its trade.
But just hope and pray that if they drop the bomb,
They drop it on the Viet Cong.

Come on Generals, let's move fast;
Your big chance has come at last.
Now you can go out and get those Reds—
Cause the only good Commie is one that's dead.
And you know that peace can only be won,
When we've blown 'em all to kingdom come.

Come on Mothers throughout the land,
Pack your boys off to Vietnam.
Come on Fathers, don't hesitate,
Send your sons off before it's too late.
And you can be the first ones in your block
To have your boy come home in a box.

A. J. MUSTE

Little in the early life of Abraham Johannes Muste (1885–1967) enables one to predict what he became later. He was born in the Netherlands and educated in the Dutch Reformed Church, married, fathered three children, and became a minister in New York with a comfortable salary. Further study at the Union Theological Seminary—a place of leftist transformation for several of the writers in this volume, as also for the noted French Huguenot preacher and anti-Nazi activist André Trocmé—radically upended his worldview, and everything came unglued. He rejected Calvinist theology, resigned from his ministry, and took a position in a Congregational church in Massachusetts. Then, after reading Tolstoy and Thoreau, he announced that he had become a pacifist, just as America was moving toward its entry into World War I; he resigned yet again. He became active in the labor movement and in the Fellowship of Reconciliation, and was chair of the faculty at Brookwood Labor College in New York from 1921 until 1933, when his principled commitment to activism over scholarship led him to a third resignation. He held in suspension two ideas often understood as contradictory, namely a commitment to revolution and a commitment to nonviolent action; and he was quicker than many of his contemporaries (these being, one should remind oneself, E. E. Cummings and Jeannette Rankin and Edmund Wilson, not the younger activists he was actually working with) to sense that these two commitments entailed a third: to the civil rights movement. Martin Luther King Jr., born some forty-five years after Muste, acknowledged the latter's large influence on him; a young Bayard Rustin was lucky enough to find him as a mentor.

After World War II Muste's activity only increased, not only as an organizer but also as a demonstrator; a famous photograph shows him in 1959, well into his seventies, climbing over a gate to enter the Mead missile base in Nebraska, for which he was arrested and spent eight days in jail. He was a characteristically early opponent of the Vietnam War, and would likely have been a principal organizer of the 1967 March on the Pentagon had he not died in February of that year.

Muste was, as his latest and best biographer Leilah Danielson calls him, an "American Gandhi," and his contributions to peace and justice work are astonishing. (Norman Mailer once described him as "the austere impeccable dean of American anarchists . . . so pure in motive that in comparison to him, Norman Thomas was as Sadie Thompson.") It is less clear how lasting his writings on peace and justice will turn out to be; most of the essays have the feel of the conservative sermons he began his career by delivering, learned and scrupulously organized, patiently elaborating arguments and considering objections, but not alive on the page in the way King's sermons are, or Abraham Joshua Heschel's. Hence the choice to represent Muste here not by a treatise but by a compressed, urgent statement of personal witness, made to a federal grand jury in 1965, at the age of eighty.

Statement Made on 12/21/65 to the Federal Grand Jury

It is impossible for me to cooperate with the Grand Jury in its present investigation of draft card burning by certain individuals and my own activity in that event.

This is not because I have any desire to hide what I have done, nor do I think any others involved in this action have any such desire.

So far from wishing to hold back anything from my fellow-citizens and fellow-religionists, I freely state that on November 6, 1965, I was present at a meeting in Union Square, New York City, where five young men burned their draft cards. I addressed that meeting expressing full support of their action and calling on others to dissociate themselves from support of United States military action in Vietnam and the foreign policy of this nation which led to this war, to military intervention in the Dominican Republic and to similar actions.

I now hold the same views that I did then. I continue to advocate them. I plan to do my utmost to bring home to my fellow-Americans the truth about war as I see it, and about the war in Vietnam and current American foreign policy, and to call upon them to face the question whether reason and conscience do not require them to withdraw all support from these policies and in particular to call for an immediate halt in American military action in Southeast Asia.

I am unable to cooperate in the Grand Jury inquisition into my belief and actions because it is an element, though perhaps a minor one, in the prosecution of the Vietnamese war and in the militarization of this country. It relates to a law about burning draft cards which is clearly intended to induce conformity in wartime, to discourage dissent, and to intimidate those who cannot in conscience support the war, from expressing and acting upon their convictions.

Demanding conformity and penalizing dissent is a pattern on which all governments tend to operate in wartime. Totalitarian governments seek not only to impose complete outward conformity but to obtain unequivocal inner conformity from their subjects.

But it is precisely in wartime and in relation to participation in war that freedom of thought, expression and association is most needed and most precious. In war, vast material resources are drawn upon and destroyed. Incalculable suffering is imposed upon vast numbers of human beings. The youth of the nation are called upon not only to sacrifice their own lives but to engage in the slaughter of the youth of another nation and even of the babies, the mothers, the children, the aged, of the national adversary.

The idea of the freedom and dignity of the human being, of his responsibility to God or his fellows or to history, is an empty mockery if precisely in such matters each individual is not free to think and to decide for himself, and free to obey or disobey orders of so-called superiors. In the presence of these ultimate issues, no man is superior to another.

Few Americans have any question that this was the case with the Germans under Hitler. At the Nuremberg trial we formally took the position as a nation that it was the responsibility of Germans to disobey orders to do evil deeds, not to obey them because a government demanded it or because the nation was at war. Shall we deprive ourselves of the privilege and the responsibility of being autonomous human beings?

To have dissent and opposition in wartime may create a problem for a democratic government, but if it does not have citizens who refuse to be coerced and regimented, it is no longer democratic.

The conclusion may well be that war itself, certainly in the nuclear age, is inhuman, undemocratic and irrational and that we should lead the way in rejecting it. As it is, we lead the world today in piling up the weapons of mass annihilation, and this nation daily dishonors itself by a war in Vietnam which has not been constitutionally declared, which violates our international obligation and in which we slaughter a people on behalf of a dictatorial puppet government which could not exist but for our support and which proclaims its refusal to negotiate.

To reverse this course would be, perhaps, something of a miracle. It would surely be to our honor to pioneer a new future for mankind by performing that miracle. As one of our foremost philosophers and writers has said: "Man has the faculty of interrupting and beginning something new, an ever present reminder that men, though they must die, were not born to die but to begin."

STUDENT NONVIOLENT COORDINATING COMMITTEE

In July 1965, when Clinton Hopson and Joe Martin urged the African American mothers of McComb, Mississippi, to keep their sons from going to Vietnam, their words reflected private grief and anger rather than the official position of any Mississippi civil rights group. Within six months—in a press release dated January 6, 1966—the national Student Nonviolent Coordinating Committee would adopt opposition to the war in Vietnam as part of its public agenda. In rhetoric much loftier than Hopson and Martin's, SNCC asked "all Americans" to fight for democracy at home, and to protest the war in Southeast Asia.

Julian Bond, SNCC's twenty-five-year-old communications director at the time, denied writing the press release but immediately endorsed it: "I like to think of myself as a pacifist and one who opposes that war and any other war," he told reporters the same day. The Georgia state legislature, to which Bond had recently been elected, attempted to refuse to seat him, calling his comments treasonous. Soon Martin Luther King Jr. would praise the young activist from the pulpit at Ebenezer Baptist. "If you're going to be a Christian, take the gospel of Jesus Christ seriously," he told his audience on January 16, "you must be a dissenter, you must be a nonconformist." By degrees, the movement was overcoming its reluctance to see its struggle as linked to that of the peace movement, just as peace activists before and since have found common cause with activists on other fronts.

Statement on American Policy in Vietnam

THE Student Nonviolent Coordinating Committee has a right and a responsibility to dissent with United States foreign policy on an issue when it sees fit. The Student Nonviolent Coordinating Committee now states its opposition to United States' involvement in Viet Nam on these grounds:

We believe the United States government has been deceptive in its claims of concern for freedom of the Vietnamese people, just as the government has been deceptive in claiming concern for the freedom of colored people in such other countries as the Dominican Republic, the Congo, South Africa, Rhodesia and in the United States itself.

383

We, the Student Nonviolent Coordinating Committee, have been involved in the black people's struggle for liberation and self-determination in this country for the past five years. Our work, particularly in the South, has taught us that the United States government has never guaranteed the freedom of oppressed citizens, and is not yet truly determined to end the rule of terror and oppression within its own borders.

We ourselves have often been victims of violence and confinement executed by United States government officials. We recall the numerous persons who have been murdered in the South because of their efforts to secure their civil and human rights, and whose murderers have been allowed to escape penalty for their crimes.

The murder of Samuel Young in Tuskegee, Ala., is no different than the murder of peasants in Viet Nam, for both Young and the Vietnamese sought, and are seeking, to secure the rights guaranteed them by law. In each case the United States government bears a great part of the responsibility for these deaths.

Samuel Young was murdered because United States law is not being enforced. Vietnamese are murdered because the United States is pursuing an aggressive policy in violation of international law. The United States is no respecter of persons or law when such persons or laws run counter to its needs and desires.

We recall the indifference, suspicion and outright hostility with which our reports of violence have been met in the past by government officials.

We know that for the most part, elections in this country, in the North as well as the South, are not free. We have seen that the 1965 Voting Rights Act and the 1964 Civil Rights Act have not yet been implemented with full federal power and sincerity.

We question, then, the ability and even the desire of the United States government to guarantee free elections abroad. We maintain that our country's cry of "preserve freedom in the world" is a hypocritical mask behind which it squashes liberation movements which are not bound, and refuse to be bound, by the expediencies of United States cold war policies.

We are in sympathy with, and support, the men in this country who are unwilling to respond to a military draft which would compel them to contribute their lives to United States aggression in Viet Nam in the name of the "freedom" we find so false in this country.

We recoil with horror at the inconsistency of a supposedly "free" society where responsibility to freedom is equated with the responsibility to lend oneself to military aggression. We take note of the fact that 16 per cent of the draftees from this country are Negroes called on to stifle the liberation of Viet Nam, to preserve a "democracy" which does not exist for them at home.

We ask, where is the draft for the freedom fight in the United States?

We therefore encourage those Americans who prefer to use their energy in building democratic forms within this country. We believe that work in the civil rights movement and with other human relations organizations is a valid alternative to the draft. We urge all Americans to seek this alternative, knowing full well that it may cost their lives—as painfully as in Viet Nam.

TULI KUPFERBERG
AND ROBERT BASHLOW

During the 1967 March on the Pentagon and its intense, earnest confrontations between marchers and soldiers, over at a different Pentagon wall The Fugs were attempting to exorcise the building itself—"out demons out," they chanted, which Norman Mailer found attractive and Robert Lowell distracting. That moment suggests something about the relation between The Fugs and the mainstream antiwar movement; The Fugs were outrageous, visionary, playful, and impudent. Most of those characteristics are on display in *1001 Ways to Beat the Draft* (1966), which is the wittiest and most obscene text included here in opposition to the Vietnam War, lacking formal discipline, argument, and logical sequence but full of Rabelaisian energy and Whitmanian capaciousness.

1001 Ways was the work of many hands and no doubt fun in the making (the book's copyright page acknowledges the contributions of twenty-five collaborators, with their initials). Robert Bashlow (1939–1979), one of its two nominal authors, was reportedly a musical prodigy in his youth but was never a band member; he published the short-lived *International Journal of Greek Love* and earned his living as a coin dealer. Tuli Kupferberg (1923–2010), the other, grew up on the Lower East Side of New York, graduated from Brooklyn College in 1944, became a medical librarian, and intended "to be a doctor at one point, like any good Jewish boy." But he turned to poems and satires, attempted suicide in 1945 by jumping off the Manhattan Bridge (an incident referred to in Allen Ginsberg's "Howl"), survived, became a beatnik celebrity and anthologized poet, and with Ed Sanders founded The Fugs in 1963 in Sanders's Peace Eye Bookstore.

FROM
1001 Ways to Beat the Draft

1   Grope J. Edgar Hoover in the silent halls of Congress.
2   Get thee to a nunnery.
3   Fly to the moon and refuse to come home.
4   Die.
5   Become Secretary of Defense.
6   Become Secretary of State.

7 Become Secretary of Health, Education and Welfare.
8 Show a li'l tit.
9 Castrate yourself.
10 Invent a time machine and go back to the 19th century.

11 Start to menstruate. (Better red than dead.)
12 Attempt to overthrow the Government of the United States by force and violence.
13 Advocate sexual freedom for children.
14 Shoot up for a day.
15 Refuse to speak to them at all.
16 Enroll at the Jefferson School of Social Science.
17 Replace your feet with wheels.
18 Rent a motel room with a ewe.
19 Rent a motel room with a ram.
20 Say you're crazy.
21 Say they're crazy.
22 Get muscular dystrophy when you're a kid.
23 Marry J. Edgar Hoover.
24 Take up residence in Albania.
25 Stretch yourself on a rack so that you become over 6½ feet tall.
26 Marry your mother.
27 Marry your father.
28 Blow up the Statue of Liberty.
29 Marry your sister.
30 Marry your brother.
31 Marry your daughter.
32 Join the Abraham Lincoln Brigade.
33 Marry your son.
34 Marry Lassie.
35 Marry President Johnson.
36 Marry Mao Tse-tung.
37 Proclaim that Mao Tse-tung is the Living God.
38 Proclaim that *you* are the Living God.

39 Stamp your foot in the earth like Rumpelstiltskin and refuse to eat until our boys return from Viet Nam.

40 Get elected Pope.

41 Get elected to the Supreme Soviet.

42 Get lost.

43 Shoot A for one month.

44 Grow seven toes on your head.

45 Commit an unnatural act with Walter Jenkins.

46 Make the world go away.

47 Wear pants made of jello.

48 Say you are a wounded veteran of the *lutte des classes.*

49 Solder your eyelids shut.

50 Ride naked through the streets on a white horse.

51 Declare war on Germany.

52 Tell the draft board that you will send your mother to fight in Viet Nam in your place.

53 Study Selective Service reports on malingering and military medicine, and/or military psychiatry texts or journal articles on the same subject, and use the clever methods they describe.

54 Organize your own army and advance on Washington.

55 Tell the psychiatrist that if he doesn't let you into the Army you'll kill him.

56 Turn yellow.

57 Infiltrate your local board.

58 Don't agree to anything.

59 Contract Addison's disease.

60 Contract Parkinson's disease.

61 Contract Bright's disease.

62 Contract Hodgkin's disease.

63 Contract Cushing's disease.

64 Contract Fröhlich's syndrome.

65 Announce that you have become the bridegroom of the Virgin Mary.

66 Announce that you have become the bridegroom of Jesus Christ.

67 Get your friends to crucify you.

68 Counterfeit money and omit the motto *In God We Trust*.

69 Become a publisher of smut and filth.

70 Become the publisher of the Little Mao Tse-tung Library.

71 Prove that Brezhnev is a Trotskyite wrecker.

72 Burn down the building located at 39 Whitehall Street.

73 ... 450 Golden Gate Ave.

74 ... 536 South Clark Street.

75 ... 55 Tremont Street.

76 ... 916 G Street NW.

77 Burn down the Pentagon.

78 Burn baby burn.

79 Write a best-selling novel which portrays the CIA as incompetent.

80 Catch St. Anthony's fire.

81 Say you'd be happy to serve because it'll be easier to kill the fucken Americans who are interfering with the freedom of Viet Nam.

> **AWOL Soldier Seized**
>
> WILKES-BARRE, Pa., March 18 (UPI)—James Richmond, 20-year-old serviceman who had been absent without leave from the Army since last June, was picked up by the Federal Bureau of Investigation Friday as he hid in a tunnel in the cellar of his mother's home in nearby Hanover Township.

82 Recite the Pledge of Allegiance 2400 times a day.

83 Cut off your ears. In ancient times no animal was sacrificed unless it was a perfect specimen.

84 Cut off your left ear and send it to the draft board.

85 Grow a tail.

86 Learn to talk with your anus.

87 Become a graduate student in a subject vital to the national security, such as the epistemology of phenomenological methodology. Achieve your degree only after fifteen years of 2-S.

> FEZ, Morocco, March 3 — King Hassan II announced today the institution of compulsory military service in a speech on the 10th anniversary of Moroccan independence and the 5th anniversary of his accession to the throne.

88 Grow old fast, or

89 When you reach the age of 17 don't get any older.

90 Drink an elixir that will cause you to shrink to a height of 2 feet, 3 inches.

91 Buy a slave and send him in your place.

92 Take your girlfriend with you when you get called and insist you will not serve unless you can sleep with her at night.

93 Take your boyfriend with you when you get called and insist that you will not serve unless you can sleep with him at night.

94 Take your mother with you when you get called and insist you will not serve unless you can sleep with *her* at night.

95 Take your chihuahua with you when you get called and insist you will not serve unless you can sleep with *it* at night.

96 Wet your bed.

97 When the doctor tells you to spread your cheeks, let him see the firecracker you have planted there beforehand.

98 Handcuff yourself to Lenin's tomb.

99 Handcuff yourself to Nicholas Katzenbach and shout: "We shall not be moved!"

100 Travel to Havana.

101 Grow a long straggly black beard with maggots crawling all over it.

102 Travel to Hanoi.

103 Travel to Tirana.

104 Travel to Peking.

105 Travel to Washington and tell them you intend to travel to one or more of the above.

106 Publish a satirical pamphlet purporting to advise young men how to beat the draft.

107 Tell the psychiatrist that you are a closet queen.

108 Tell the security officer that you are a brother of Allen Ginsberg.

109 Tell the security officer that you are a brother of Ralph Ginzburg.

110 Hand out copies of this pamphlet at the induction center. When they tell you you cannot do this ask if it's all right if you sell them.

III Make sure that by one method or another you get to see the psychiatrist. Do not let them rush you through without your chance. If necessary you should faint, scream, or start crying.

II2 Give the psychiatrist your standard three-minute lecture in favor of bisexuality, being sure to mention again and again that animals do it.

II3 Tell them that you will leap into your grave laughing.

J.	*Wars:* The names of wars are capitalized and spelled out.
	War of 1812 **World War I**
	Crimean War **Korean War**

II4 Run for the House of Representatives on the platform that Red China should be invited to send its surplus population to colonize New York and Arizona.

II5 Commence psychotherapy with Dr. Robert Soblen.

II6 Ask Gus Hall to go down to the induction center for you the day you are called.

II7 Write a letter to the New York *Daily News* stating that the Viet Cong are nothing more than peace-loving agrarian reformers.

II8 Use an American flag for a breechclout.

II9 Contract tertiary syphilis.

I20 Steal a laser and fight it out with the CIA.

I21 Develop bleeding stigmata.

I22 Cop out.

I23 Conspire with a known homosexual in the Soviet embassy in Ankara.

I24 Conspire with a known heterosexual in the U.S. embassy in Ankara.

I25 Become chairman of the Committee to Legalize Marijuana.

I26 Develop an otherworldly metaphysical system and live by its precepts.

I27 Cut off your head.

JOSEPHINE MILES

Thom Gunn wrote of the poet Josephine Miles (1911–1985) that "the unavoidable first fact about [her] was physical. As a young child she contracted a form of degenerative arthritis so severe that it left her limbs deformed and crippled. As a result, she could not be left alone in a house, she could not handle a mug . . . she could not use a typewriter; and she could neither walk nor operate a wheel." Some other facts are equally pertinent: she was the first woman to receive tenure in the English department at Berkeley, she wrote a dozen books of poetry, and she mentored many younger writers, including William Stafford in the present anthology.

"Necessities (1)" is Miles's account of one of the iconic actions of the Vietnam War, namely, the self-immolations performed by Vietnamese Buddhists to protest the injustices inflicted on the Vietnamese by the war. Unlike Yusef Komunyakaa's "2527th Birthday of the Buddha"—a poem on the same subject included later in this book—Miles focuses on the embarrassed, cautious response of her interlocutor, who feels that such action is unnecessary, wasteful, a shame. Miles is more sympathetic to the need for self-sacrifice: while "voices are voiceless," the Buddhists' self-sacrificial fires have spoken as eloquently as the tongues of the Apostles in the story of Pentecost.

Necessities (1)

He says the Buddhist immolations
Are unnecessary.
He says a flambeau
Supplies no needed way for one to die.
Too bad
These wasteful people
Depart this tasteful earth so wastefully.

But while the ears
Along his worrying kindly handsome head
Along his troubled head
Are closed,
Voices are voiceless, and the visible flames
Of flesh dart out their tongues,
Voluble, necessary.

ABRAHAM JOSHUA HESCHEL

Abraham Joshua Heschel (1907–1972) said of his participation in the 1965 civil rights march at Selma, Alabama, "I felt that my legs were praying," and thereby expressed much of himself. Prayer for him was "as necessary as faith," writes Edward K. Kaplan; but prayer had for him a capacious sense, including the civil rights and antiwar work to which he devoted abundant time and intense energy. The following sections from his great antiwar sermon "The Moral Outrage of Vietnam"—first published in *Fellowship* in September 1966—show him in both capacities, the first being a Jewish prophet's denunciation of the Vietnam War, the second a mostly secular-humanist critique of it.

Heschel was born in Warsaw, his father being a Hasidic rebbe, the son soon clearly a prodigy—but one who sought, and found, a secular education as well, in Vilna and Berlin. He published Yiddish poems, Hebrew commentaries, and German monographs, and had in the European Jewish community a standing comparable to that of Martin Buber, whom in 1937 he replaced as codirector of the Frankfurt *Lehrhaus*. He was expelled from Germany in 1938, worked briefly in Warsaw, fled to London, was invited in 1940 to teach at Hebrew Union College in Cincinnati, joined the faculty of the Jewish Theological Seminary in 1945, and was naturalized in that same year; he became the leading American exponent of Jewish tradition, and unlike most of his contemporaries remained alive and inspiring for the younger Jews who in the late 1960s and early 1970s were founding the Jewish Renewal movement and writing the *Jewish Catalogues*. Reinhold Niebuhr predicted in a 1951 review, "[Heschel] will become a commanding and authoritative voice not only in the Jewish community but in the religious life of America." Correct but too limited; Heschel's influence mattered outside America as well, in particular in the 1965 Vatican II declaration *Nostra Aetate*, with its radically new willingness to accept Judaism on its own terms.

FROM
The Moral Outrage of Vietnam

On January 31, 1967, clergymen and laymen concerned about Vietnam assembled in Washington, D.C. At the worship service, I offered the following meditation on the words of the prophet Ezekiel (34:25–31):

Ours is an assembly of shock, contrition, and dismay. Who would have believed that we life-loving Americans are capable of bringing death and destruction to so many innocent people? We are startled to discover how unmerciful, how beastly we ourselves can be.

So we implore Thee, our Father in heaven, help us to banish the beast from our hearts, the beast of cruelty, the beast of callousness.

Since the beginning of history evil has been going forth from nation to nation. The lords of the flocks issue proclamations, and the sheep of all nations indulge in devastations.

But who would have believed that our own nation at the height of its career as the leader of free nations, the hope for peace in the world, whose unprecedented greatness was achieved through "liberty and justice for all," should abdicate its wisdom, suppress its compassion and permit guns to become its symbols?

America's resources, moral and material, are immense. We have the means and know the ways of dispelling prejudice and lies, of overcoming poverty and disease. We have the capacity to lead the world in seeking to overcome international hostility.

Must napalm stand in the way of our power to aid and to inspire the world?

To be sure, just as we feel deeply the citizen's dilemma, we are equally sensitive to the dilemma confronting the leaders of our government. Our government seems to recognize the tragic error and futility of the escalation of our involvement but feels that we cannot extricate ourselves without public embarrassment of such dimension as to cause damage to America's prestige.

But the mire in which we flounder threatens us with an even greater danger. It is the dilemma of either losing face or losing our soul.

At this hour Vietnam is our most urgent, our most disturbing religious problem, a challenge to the whole nation as well as a challenge to every one of us as an individual.

When a person is sick, in danger or in misery, all religious duties recede, all rituals are suspended, except one: to save life and relieve pain.

Vietnam is a personal problem. To speak about God and remain silent on Vietnam is blasphemous.

> When you spread forth your hands
> I will hide my eyes from you;
> Yea when you make many prayers,
> I will not hear—
> Your hands are not clean.

In the sight of so many thousands of civilians and soldiers slain, injured, crippled, of bodies emaciated, of forests destroyed by fire, God confronts us with this question:

Where art thou?

Is there no compassion in the world? No sense of discernment to realize that this is a war that refutes any conceivable justification of war?

The sword is the pride of man; arsenals, military bases, nuclear weapons lend supremacy to nations. War is the climax of ingenuity, the object of supreme dedication.

Men slaughtering each other, cities battered into ruins: such insanity has plunged many nations into an abyss of disgrace. Will America, the promise of peace to the world, fail to uphold its magnificent destiny?

The most basic way in which all men may be divided is between those who believe that war is unnecessary and those who believe that war is inevitable; between those to whom the sword is the symbol of honor and those to whom seeking to convert swords into plowshares is the only way to keep our civilization from disaster.

Most of us prefer to disregard the dreadful deeds we do over there. The atrocities committed in our name are too horrible to be credible. It is beyond our power to react vividly to the ongoing nightmare, day after day, night after night. So we bear graciously other people's suffering.

O Lord, we confess our sins, we are ashamed of the inadequacy of our anguish, of how faint and slight is our mercy. We are a generation that has lost the capacity for outrage.

We must continue to remind ourselves that in a free society, all are involved in what some are doing. *Some are guilty, all are responsible.*

Prayer is our greatest privilege. To pray is to stake our very existence, our right to live, on the truth and on the supreme importance of that which we pray for. Prayer, then, is radical commitment, a dangerous involvement in the life of God.

In such awareness we pray . . .

We do not stand alone. Millions of Americans, millions of people all over the world are with us.

At this moment praying for peace in Vietnam we are spiritually Vietnamese. Their agony is our affliction, their hope is our commitment.

God is present wherever men are afflicted.

Where is God present now?

We do not know how to cry, we do not know how to pray!

Our conscience is so timid, our words so faint, our mercy so feeble.

O Father, have mercy upon us.

Our God, add our cries uttered here to the cries of the bereaved, crippled, and dying over there.

Have mercy upon all of us.

Help us to overcome the arrogance of power. Guide and inspire the President of the United States in finding a speedy, generous, and peaceful end to the war in Vietnam.

The intensity of the agony is high, the hour is late, the outrage may reach a stage where repentance will be too late, repair beyond any nation's power.

We call for a covenant of peace, for reconciliation of America and all of Vietnam. To paraphrase the words of the prophet Isaiah (62:1):

For Vietnam's sake I will not keep silent,
For America's sake I will not rest,
Until the vindication of humanity goes forth as brightness,
And peace for all men is a burning torch.

Here is the experience of a child of seven who was reading in school the chapter which tells of the sacrifice of Isaac:

Isaac was on the way to Mount Moriah with his father; then he lay on the altar, bound, waiting to be sacrificed. My heart began to beat even faster; it actually sobbed with pity for Isaac. Behold, Abraham now lifted the knife. And now my heart froze within me with fright. Suddenly, the voice of the angel was heard: "Abraham, lay not thine hand upon the lad, for now I know that thou fearest God." And here I broke out in tears and wept aloud. "Why are you crying?" asked the Rabbi. "You know that Isaac was not killed."

And I said to him, still weeping, "But, Rabbi, supposing the angel had come a second too late?"

> The Rabbi comforted me and calmed me by telling me that an angel cannot come late.

An angel cannot be late, but man, made of flesh and blood, may be.

THE CRISIS OF RESPONSIBILITY

RESPONSIBILITY is the essence of being a person, the essence of being human, and many of us are agonized by a grave *crisis of responsibility*. Horrified by the atrocities of this war, we are also dismayed by the ineffectiveness of our protests, by the feebleness of our dissent. Have we done our utmost in expressing our anguish? Does our outcry match the outrage?

This is a unique hour in human history. It is within our might to decide whether this war is a prelude to doom, the beginning of the end, or whether to establish a precedent of solving a most complex crisis by abandoning slogans and clichés.

There is no alternative, we are told. Yet have we really exhausted all possibilities of negotiation? Is the state of humanity so overcome by insanity that all rationality is gone and war left as the only way? Is it really so simple? Are we Americans all innocent, righteous, full of saving grace, while our adversaries are all corrupt, wicked, insensitive to human rights?

Collision between states is not always due to a conflict of vital interests. It is often due to the tendency toward self-enhancement inherent in the monstrosity of power.

Worse than war is the belief in the inevitability of war. There is no such thing as inevitable war. And certainly the war in Vietnam was not inevitable. It came about as a failure of vision, as a result of political clichés, of thinking by analogies, of false comparisons, of blindness to the uniqueness of an extraordinary constellation. This war will not end by dropping bigger and better bombs, by an increase in ferocity, and by the merciless use of force. Vietnam is primarily a human problem, a human emergency, human anguish. There are no military solutions to human problems; violence and bloodshed are no answer to human anguish.

We feel alarmed by a policy that continues to be dogmatic, devoid of elasticity. The root of the tragedy is in the combination of global power and parochial philosophy, of most efficient weapons and pedestrian ideas. New thinking is called for; new contacts must be made. Leaders not directly involved in present operations must be consulted.

Let the American presence in Vietnam be a presence of understanding and compassion. America's war potential is great, but America's peace potential is even greater. Let there be an effort for friendship for Vietnam. Modern war is a mechanical operation. But peace is a personal effort, requiring deep commitment, hard, honest vision, wisdom and patience, facing one another as human beings, elasticity rather than dogmatism.

Would not sending a Peace Corps prove more helpful than sending more armed divisions?

We have entered an age in which military victories are tragic defeats, in which even small wars are exercises in immense disaster.

The public enemy number one is the nuclear bomb, the population explosion, starvation, and disease. It is the fear of nuclear war that unites men all over the world, East and West, North and South. It is fear that unites us today. Let us hope that the conquest of fear and the elimination of misery will unite us tomorrow.

This war, I am afraid, will not leave the nation where it found it. Its conclusion may be the beginning of a grave alienation. The speed and the spirit in which this war will end will fashion our own lives in the years that lie ahead.

On January 22, 1917, President Woodrow Wilson in his address to the Senate uttered a point of view which we pray President Lyndon Johnson would adopt as his own: "It must be a peace without victory." Let our goal be compromise, not victory.

In the name of our kinship of being human, the American people meet the Vietnamese face to face. Only few men are marble-hearted. And even marble can be pierced with patience and compassion. Let us create a climate of reconciliation. Reducing violence and tension, acts of goodwill are necessary prerequisites for negotiations. We must seek neither victory nor defeat. Our aim is to enable the South Vietnamese to find themselves as free and independent people.

The initiative for peace must come from the strong, out of a position of strength.

We will all have to strain our energies, crack our sinews, tax and exert our brains, cultivate understanding, open our hearts, and meet with all Vietnamese, North as well as South.

This is the demand of the hour: not to rest until—by excluding fallacies, stereotypes, prejudices, exaggerations which perpetual contention and the consequent hostilities breed—we succeed in reaching the people of Vietnam as brothers.

There is still time to unlearn old follies, there is still time to seek honest reconciliation. A few months from now it may be too late; a few months from now our folly may be beyond repair, sin beyond repentance.

It is not for man to decide who shall live and who shall die, who shall kill and who shall sigh. May no one win this war; may all sides win the right to live in peace.

GEORGE STARBUCK

George Starbuck (1931–1996) is known among poets as a formalist virtuoso, and in political circles as the SUNY–Buffalo lecturer who in 1963 refused to take a loyalty oath and was fired, then took his case all the way to the Supreme Court and won, the Court finding all such oaths illegal. "Of Late" draws on the virtuoso and the protester equally; appropriately, the equally talented virtuoso Anthony Hecht has argued that, "'Of Late' is not merely the best 'protest poem' about the Vietnam War that I know [but] the only one of any merit whatever." It first appeared in *Poetry* in October 1966.

Like Josephine Miles in "Necessities (1)," Starbuck in "Of Late" is concerned with extreme political speech, with extreme political action as a mode of signifying; unlike Miles, Starbuck turns his attention to a domestic version of such action, namely, the Quaker Norman Morrison's self-immolation in 1965 below the office of then–Secretary of Defense Robert McNamara.

Of Late

"Stephen Smith, University of Iowa sophomore, burned what
    he said was his draft card."
And Norman Morrison, Quaker, of Baltimore Maryland,
    burned what he said was himself.
You, Robert McNamara, burned what you said was a
    concentration
of the enemy aggressor.
No news medium troubled to put it in quotes.

And Norman Morrison, Quaker, of Baltimore Maryland,
    burned what he said was himself.
He said it with simple materials such as would be found in
    your kitchen.
In your office you were informed.
Reporters got cracking frantically on the mental disturbance
    angle.
So far nothing turns up.

Norman Morrison, Quaker, of Baltimore Maryland, burned,
    and while burning, screamed.
No tip-off. No release.
Nothing to quote, to manage to put in quotes.
Pity the unaccustomed hesitance of the newspaper
    editorialists.
Pity the press photographers, not called.

Norman Morrison, Quaker, of Baltimore Maryland, burned
    and was burned and said
all that there is to say in that language.
Twice what is said in yours.
It is a strange sect, Mr. McNamara, under advice to try
the whole of a thought in silence, and to oneself.

DENISE LEVERTOV

Denise Levertov (1923–1997) is a test case for how we judge antiwar poetry. Her friend Robert Duncan strongly criticized "Life at War"— first collected in *The Sorrow Dance* (1967)—for its sensationalism, and he was not alone. There was something coarse and unnuanced, even propagandistic, about Levertov's most characteristic antiwar poems. Her critics may of course have been right, though whether a nuanced account of the napalming of human flesh in Vietnam can do justice to the thing it's representing is a tricky question.

Levertov was the descendant of both the Hasidic master Shneur Zalman of Liadi and the Welsh mystic Angel Jones of Mold. She was educated at home in Essex, sent poems to T. S. Eliot when she was twelve (he responded encouragingly), worked as a nurse in London during the Blitz, married the American writer Mitchell Goodman in 1947, moved with him to New York the following year, became an American citizen in 1955, was encouraged and supported by the poets Kenneth Rexroth and Robert Creeley, and was clearly moving in a promising direction as a poet of the Black Mountain school. But then the Vietnam War came along, and she became a poet of a different sort in response to it, politically engaged as a writer and as an activist, visiting Hanoi in 1972. She continued writing after the war ended, returning to the religious themes important in her earlier work but not to that work's formalism.

"Making Peace" is a later poem, first collected in *Breathing the Water* (1987), one of the few attempts made by antiwar writers to turn away from opposition and imagine in positive terms the goals that antiwar activists would seek if they won; it resulted from a question asked of her by the psychologist Virginia Shatir after a reading at Stanford.

Life at War

The disasters numb within us
caught in the chest, rolling
in the brain like pebbles. The feeling
resembles lumps of raw dough

weighing down a child's stomach on baking day.
Or Rilke said it, "My heart . . .
Could I say of it, it overflows
with bitterness . . . but no, as though

its contents were simply balled into
formless lumps, thus
do I carry it about."
The same war

continues.
We have breathed the grits of it in, all our lives,
our lungs are pocked with it,
the mucous membrane of our dreams
coated with it, the imagination
filmed over with the gray filth of it:

the knowledge that humankind,

delicate Man, whose flesh
responds to a caress, whose eyes
are flowers that perceive the stars,

whose music excels the music of birds,
whose laughter matches the laughter of dogs,
whose understanding manifests designs
fairer than the spider's most intricate web,

still turns without surprise, with mere regret
to the scheduled breaking open of breasts whose milk
runs out over the entrails of still-alive babies,
transformation of witnessing eyes to pulp-fragments,
implosion of skinned penises into carcass-gulleys.

We are the humans, men who can make;
whose language imagines *mercy*,
lovingkindness; we have believed one another
mirrored forms of a God we felt as good—

who do these acts, who convince ourselves
it is necessary; these acts are done
to our own flesh; burned human flesh
is smelling in Viet Nam as I write.

Yes, this is the knowledge that jostles for space
in our bodies along with all we
go on knowing of joy, of love;

our nerve filaments twitch with its presence
day and night,
nothing we say has not the husky phlegm of it in the saying,
nothing we do has the quickness, the sureness,
the deep intelligence living at peace would have.

Making Peace

A voice from the dark called out,
         "The poets must give us
imagination of peace, to oust the intense, familiar
imagination of disaster. Peace, not only
the absence of war."
                      But peace, like a poem,
is not there ahead of itself,
can't be imagined before it is made,
can't be known except
in the words of its making,
grammar of justice,
syntax of mutual aid.
                      A feeling towards it,
dimly sensing a rhythm, is all we have
until we begin to utter its metaphors,
learning them as we speak.
                         A line of peace might appear
if we restructured the sentence our lives are making,
revoked its reaffirmation of profit and power,
questioned our needs, allowed
long pauses . . .
              A cadence of peace might balance its weight
on that different fulcrum; peace, a presence,
an energy field more intense than war,
might pulse then,

stanza by stanza into the world,
each act of living
one of its words, each word
a vibration of light—facets
of the forming crystal.

MARTIN LUTHER KING JR.

It cost Martin Luther King Jr. (1929–1968) a good deal to speak in public against the Vietnam War, as he did on April 4, 1967, in New York's Riverside Church. Most of his advisors, including the fervent pacifist Bayard Rustin, had urged him not to touch so divisive a subject, fearing the effect his words might have on the ongoing civil rights movement, and most public commentary after the speech—including editorials in the *Washington Post* and *The New York Times*—was negative. "King felt cut off even from disagreement," historian Taylor Branch has explained, "in a void worse than his accustomed fare of veneration or disfiguring hostility, and he broke down more than once into tears."

But his four thousand hearers in the church gave him a standing ovation, and they were right. The speech is magnificent; it is characterized by King's gift for fusing prophetic vision and precise analysis in the rhetoric of the black church, and by his stubborn refusal to dehumanize his antagonists, his almost constitutional aversion to malice.

King was thirty-eight when he gave the speech; he had come a long way and was to travel a long way further before he died. He was the cherished son of a dynasty, in love with the academy and the pulpit, with a bright future in front of him. But circumstances and his own latent yearnings and talents pushed him toward a leadership role in the Montgomery bus boycott. (On the way to the first meeting to discuss the boycott, King was surprised at the dense traffic around the church where the meeting was to be held. Finally he realized that the traffic was dense because so many people were coming to the meeting. "You know, this could be something big," he said to his assistant.) Once in that role, he grew in it, working out a theory as he went along, learning about nonviolent action from such advisors as Rustin and from his own intuitions, triumphing almost miraculously in Montgomery, moving to larger venues of action, failing, failing, succeeding in the end—"all strikes fail except the last one," said Dorothy Day—moving from Montgomery to Birmingham, Albany, and Selma. Along the way, in 1964, he won the Nobel Peace Prize; also along the way, he began to make the connections that others had made before him, between the two struggles that at their roots were one struggle, and having the gift of stubbornness, came to Riverside Church and made this great speech. Exactly one year later, in Memphis to help with a garbage workers' strike, he was assassinated.

Beyond Vietnam

Mr. Chairman, ladies and gentlemen, I need not pause to say how very delighted I am to be here tonight, and how very delighted I am to see you expressing your concern about the issues that will be discussed tonight by turning out in such large numbers. I also want to say that I consider it a great honor to share this program with Dr. Bennett, Dr. Commager, and Rabbi Heschel, some of the most distinguished leaders and personalities of our nation. And of course it's always good to come back to Riverside Church. Over the last eight years, I have had the privilege of preaching here almost every year in that period, and it's always a rich and rewarding experience to come to this great church and this great pulpit.

I come to this great magnificent house of worship tonight because my conscience leaves me no other choice. I join you in this meeting because I am in deepest agreement with the aims and work of the organization that brought us together, Clergy and Laymen Concerned About Vietnam. The recent statements of your executive committee are the sentiments of my own heart, and I found myself in full accord when I read its opening lines: "A time comes when silence is betrayal." That time has come for us in relation to Vietnam.

The truth of these words is beyond doubt, but the mission to which they call us is a most difficult one. Even when pressed by the demands of inner truth, men do not easily assume the task of opposing their government's policy, especially in time of war. Nor does the human spirit move without great difficulty against all the apathy of conformist thought within one's own bosom and in the surrounding world. Moreover, when the issues at hand seem as perplexing as they often do in the case of this dreadful conflict, we are always on the verge of being mesmerized by uncertainty. But we must move on.

Some of us who have already begun to break the silence of the night have found that the calling to speak is often a vocation of agony, but we must speak. We must speak with all the humility that is appropriate to our limited vision, but we must speak. And we must rejoice as well, for surely this is the first time in our nation's history that a significant number of its religious leaders have chosen to move beyond the prophesying of smooth patriotism to the high grounds of a firm dissent based upon the mandates of conscience and the reading of history. Perhaps a new spirit is rising among us. If it is, let us trace its movement, and pray that our inner being may be sensitive to its guidance. For we are deeply in need of a new way beyond the darkness that seems so close around us.

Over the past two years, as I have moved to break the betrayal of my own silences and to speak from the burnings of my own heart, as I have called for radical departures from the destruction of Vietnam, many persons have questioned me about the wisdom of my path. At the heart of their concerns, this query has often loomed large and loud: "Why are you speaking about the war, Dr. King? Why are you joining the voices of dissent?" "Peace and civil rights don't mix," they say. "Aren't you hurting the cause of your people?" they ask. And when I hear them, though I often understand the source of their concern, I am nevertheless greatly saddened, for such questions mean that the inquirers have not really known me, my commitment, or my calling. Indeed, their questions suggest that they do not know the world in which they live. In the light of such tragic misunderstanding, I deem it of signal importance to state clearly, and I trust concisely, why I believe that the path from Dexter Avenue Baptist Church—the church in Montgomery, Alabama, where I began my pastorate—leads clearly to this sanctuary tonight.

I come to this platform tonight to make a passionate plea to my beloved nation. This speech is not addressed to Hanoi or to the National Liberation Front. It is not addressed to China or to Russia. Nor is it an attempt to overlook the ambiguity of the total situation and the need for a collective solution to the tragedy of Vietnam. Neither is it an attempt to make North Vietnam or the National Liberation Front paragons of virtue, nor to overlook the role they must play in the successful resolution of the problem. While they both may have justifiable reasons to be suspicious of the good faith of the United States, life and history give eloquent testimony to the fact that conflicts are never resolved without trustful give and take on both sides. Tonight, however, I wish not to speak with Hanoi and the National Liberation Front, but rather to my fellow Americans.

Since I am a preacher by calling, I suppose it is not surprising that I have seven major reasons for bringing Vietnam into the field of my moral vision. There is at the outset a very obvious and almost facile connection between the war in Vietnam and the struggle I and others have been waging in America. A few years ago there was a shining moment in that struggle. It seemed as if there was a real promise of hope for the poor, both black and white, through the poverty program. There were experiments, hopes, new beginnings. Then came the buildup in Vietnam, and I watched this program broken and eviscerated as if it were some idle political plaything of a society gone mad on war. And I knew that America would never invest the necessary funds or energies in rehabilitation of its poor so long as adventures like Vietnam continued to draw men and skills and money like some demonic, destructive suction tube. So I was increasingly compelled to see the war as an enemy of the poor and to attack it as such.

Perhaps a more tragic recognition of reality took place when it became clear to me that the war was doing far more than devastating the hopes of the poor at home. It was sending their sons and their brothers and their husbands to fight and to die in extraordinarily high proportions relative to the rest of the population. We were taking the black young men who had been crippled by our society and sending them eight thousand miles away to guarantee liberties in Southeast Asia which they had not found in southwest Georgia and East Harlem. So we have been repeatedly faced with the cruel irony of watching Negro and white boys on TV screens as they kill and die together for a nation that has been unable to seat them together in the same schools. So we watch them in brutal solidarity burning the huts of a poor village, but we realize that they would hardly live on the same block in Chicago. I could not be silent in the face of such cruel manipulation of the poor.

My third reason moves to an even deeper level of awareness, for it grows out of my experience in the ghettos of the North over the last three years, especially the last three summers. As I have walked among the desperate, rejected, and angry young men, I have told them that Molotov cocktails and rifles would not solve their problems. I have tried to offer them my deepest compassion while maintaining my conviction that social change comes most meaningfully through nonviolent action.

But they asked, and rightly so, "What about Vietnam?" They asked if our own nation wasn't using massive doses of violence to solve its problems, to bring about the changes it wanted. Their questions hit home, and I knew that I could never again raise my voice against the violence of the oppressed in the ghettos without having first spoken clearly to the greatest purveyor of violence in the world today: my own government. For the sake of those boys, for the sake of this government, for the sake of the hundreds of thousands trembling under our violence, I cannot be silent.

For those who ask the question, "Aren't you a civil rights leader?" and thereby mean to exclude me from the movement for peace, I have this further answer. In 1957, when a group of us formed the Southern Christian Leadership Conference, we chose as our motto: "To save the soul of America." We were convinced that we could not limit our vision to certain rights for black people, but instead affirmed the conviction that America would never be free or saved from itself until the descendants of its slaves were loosed completely from the shackles they still wear. In a way we were agreeing with Langston Hughes, that black bard from Harlem, who had written earlier:

> O, yes, I say it plain,
> America never was America to me,
> And yet I swear this oath—
> America will be!

Now it should be incandescently clear that no one who has any concern for the integrity and life of America today can ignore the present war. If America's soul becomes totally poisoned, part of the autopsy must read "Vietnam." It can never be saved so long as it destroys the hopes of men the world over. So it is that those of us who are yet determined that "America will be" are led down the path of protest and dissent, working for the health of our land.

As if the weight of such a commitment to the life and health of America were not enough, another burden of responsibility was placed upon me in 1954.* And I cannot forget that the

*King says "1954," but most likely means 1964, the year he received the Nobel Peace Prize.

Nobel Peace Prize was also a commission, a commission to work harder than I had ever worked before for the brotherhood of man. This is a calling that takes me beyond national allegiances.

But even if it were not present, I would yet have to live with the meaning of my commitment to the ministry of Jesus Christ. To me, the relationship of this ministry to the making of peace is so obvious that I sometimes marvel at those who ask me why I am speaking against the war. Could it be that they do not know that the Good News was meant for all men—for communist and capitalist, for their children and ours, for black and for white, for revolutionary and conservative? Have they forgotten that my ministry is in obedience to the one who loved his enemies so fully that he died for them? What then can I say to the Vietcong or to Castro or to Mao as a faithful minister of this one? Can I threaten them with death or must I not share with them my life?

Finally, as I try to explain for you and for myself the road that leads from Montgomery to this place, I would have offered all that was most valid if I simply said that I must be true to my conviction that I share with all men the calling to be a son of the living God. Beyond the calling of race or nation or creed is this vocation of sonship and brotherhood. Because I believe that the Father is deeply concerned, especially for His suffering and helpless and outcast children, I come tonight to speak for them. This I believe to be the privilege and the burden of all of us who deem ourselves bound by allegiances and loyalties which are broader and deeper than nationalism and which go beyond our nation's self-defined goals and positions. We are called to speak for the weak, for the voiceless, for the victims of our nation, for those it calls "enemy," for no document from human hands can make these humans any less our brothers.

And as I ponder the madness of Vietnam and search within myself for ways to understand and respond in compassion, my mind goes constantly to the people of that peninsula. I speak now not of the soldiers of each side, not of the ideologies of the Liberation Front, not of the junta in Saigon, but simply of the people who have been living under the curse of war for almost three continuous decades now. I think of them, too, because it is clear to me that there will be no meaningful solution there until some attempt is made to know them and hear their broken cries.

They must see Americans as strange liberators. The Vietnamese people proclaimed their own independence in 1954—in 1945 rather—after a combined French and Japanese occupation and before the communist revolution in China. They were led by Ho Chi Minh. Even though they quoted the American Declaration of Independence in their own document of freedom, we refused to recognize them. Instead, we decided to support France in its reconquest of her former colony. Our government felt then that the Vietnamese people were not ready for independence, and we again fell victim to the deadly Western arrogance that has poisoned the international atmosphere for so long. With that tragic decision we rejected a revolutionary government seeking self-determination and a government that had been established not by China—for whom the Vietnamese have no great love—but by clearly indigenous forces that included some communists. For the peasants this new government meant real land reform, one of the most important needs in their lives.

For nine years following 1945 we denied the people of Vietnam the right of independence. For nine years we vigorously supported the French in their abortive effort to recolonize Vietnam. Before the end of the war we were meeting eighty percent of the French war costs. Even before the French were defeated at Dien Bien Phu, they began to despair of their reckless action, but we did not. We encouraged them with our huge financial and military supplies to continue the war even after they had lost the will. Soon we would be paying almost the full costs of this tragic attempt at recolonization.

After the French were defeated, it looked as if independence and land reform would come again through the Geneva Agreement. But instead there came the United States, determined that Ho should not unify the temporarily divided nation, and the peasants watched again as we supported one of the most vicious modern dictators, our chosen man, Premier Diem. The peasants watched and cringed as Diem ruthlessly rooted out all opposition, supported their extortionist landlords, and refused even to discuss reunification with the North. The peasants watched as all of this was presided over by United States influence and then by increasing numbers of United States troops who came to help quell the insurgency that Diem's methods had aroused. When Diem was overthrown they may have been happy, but the long line of military dictators seemed to offer no real change, especially in terms of their need for land and peace.

The only change came from America as we increased our troop commitments in support of governments which were singularly corrupt, inept, and without popular support. All the while the people read our leaflets and received the regular promises of peace and democracy and land reform. Now they languish under our bombs and consider us, not their fellow Vietnamese, the real enemy. They move sadly and apathetically as we herd them off the land of their fathers into concentration camps where minimal social needs are rarely met. They know they must move on or be destroyed by our bombs.

So they go, primarily women and children and the aged. They watch as we poison their water, as we kill a million acres of their crops. They must weep as the bulldozers roar through their areas preparing to destroy the precious trees. They wander into the hospitals with at least twenty casualties from American firepower for one Vietcong-inflicted injury. So far we may have killed a million of them, mostly children. They wander into the towns and see thousands of the children, homeless, without clothes, running in packs on the streets like animals. They see the children degraded by our soldiers as they beg for food. They see the children selling their sisters to our soldiers, soliciting for their mothers.

What do the peasants think as we ally ourselves with the landlords and as we refuse to put any action into our many words concerning land reform? What do they think as we test out our latest weapons on them, just as the Germans tested out new medicine and new tortures in the concentration camps of Europe? Where are the roots of the independent Vietnam we claim to be building? Is it among these voiceless ones?

We have destroyed their two most cherished institutions: the family and the village. We have destroyed their land and their crops. We have cooperated in the crushing of the nation's only noncommunist revolutionary political force, the unified Buddhist Church. We have supported the enemies of the peasants of Saigon. We have corrupted their women and children and killed their men.

Now there is little left to build on, save bitterness. Soon the only solid physical foundations remaining will be found at our military bases and in the concrete of the concentration camps we call "fortified hamlets." The peasants may well wonder if we plan to build our new Vietnam on such grounds as these. Could we blame them for such thoughts? We must speak for them and raise the questions they cannot raise. These, too, are our brothers.

Perhaps a more difficult but no less necessary task is to speak for those who have been designated as our enemies. What of the National Liberation Front, that strangely anonymous group we call "VC" or "communists"? What must they think of the United States of America when they realize that we permitted the repression and cruelty of Diem, which helped to bring them into being as a resistance group in the South? What do they think of our condoning the violence which led to their own taking up of arms? How can they believe in our integrity when now we speak of "aggression from the North" as if there was nothing more essential to the war? How can they trust us when now we charge them with violence after the murderous reign of Diem and charge them with violence while we pour every new weapon of death into their land? Surely we must understand their feelings, even if we do not condone their actions. Surely we must see that the men we supported pressed them to their violence. Surely we must see that our own computerized plans of destruction simply dwarf their greatest acts.

How do they judge us when our officials know that their membership is less than twenty-five percent communist, and yet insist on giving them the blanket name? What must they be thinking when they know that we are aware of their control of major sections of Vietnam, and yet we appear ready to allow national elections in which this highly organized political parallel government will not have a part? They ask how we can speak of free elections when the Saigon press is censored and controlled by the military junta. And they are surely right to wonder what kind of new government we plan to help form without them, the only real party in real touch with the peasants. They question our political goals and they deny the reality of a peace settlement from which they will be excluded. Their questions are frighteningly relevant. Is our nation planning to build on political myth again, and then shore it up upon the power of a new violence?

Here is the true meaning and value of compassion and non-violence, when it helps us to see the enemy's point of view, to hear his questions, to know his assessment of ourselves. For from his view we may indeed see the basic weaknesses of our own condition, and if we are mature, we may learn and grow and profit from the wisdom of the brothers who are called the opposition.

So, too, with Hanoi. In the North, where our bombs now pummel the land, and our mines endanger the waterways, we are met by a deep but understandable mistrust. To speak for them is to explain this lack of confidence in Western worlds, and especially their distrust of American intentions now. In Hanoi are the men who led this nation to independence against the Japanese and the French, the men who sought member-ship in the French Commonwealth and were betrayed by the weakness of Paris and the willfulness of the colonial armies. It was they who led a second struggle against French domination at tremendous costs, and then were persuaded to give up the land they controlled between the thirteenth and seventeenth parallel as a temporary measure at Geneva. After 1954 they watched us conspire with Diem to prevent elections which could have surely brought Ho Chi Minh to power over a uni-fied Vietnam, and they realized they had been betrayed again. When we ask why they do not leap to negotiate, these things must be considered.

Also, it must be clear that the leaders of Hanoi considered the presence of American troops in support of the Diem regime to have been the initial military breach of the Geneva Agree-ment concerning foreign troops. They remind us that they did not begin to send troops in large numbers and even supplies into the South until American forces had moved into the tens of thousands.

Hanoi remembers how our leaders refused to tell us the truth about the earlier North Vietnamese overtures for peace, how the president claimed that none existed when they had clearly been made. Ho Chi Minh has watched as America has spoken of peace and built up its forces, and now he has surely heard the increasing international rumors of American plans for an invasion of the north. He knows the bombing and shelling and mining we are doing are part of traditional pre-invasion strategy. Perhaps only his sense of humor and of irony can save him when he hears the most powerful nation of the world speaking of aggression as it drops thousands of bombs on a poor, weak nation more than eight hundred, or rather, eight thousand miles away from its shores.

At this point I should make it clear that while I have tried to give a voice to the voiceless in Vietnam and to understand the arguments of those who are called "enemy," I am as deeply concerned about our own troops there as anything else. For it occurs to me that what we are submitting them to in Vietnam is not simply the brutalizing process that goes on in any war where armies face each other and seek to destroy. We are adding cynicism to the process of death, for they must know after a short period there that none of the things we claim to be fighting for are really involved. Before long they must know that their government has sent them into a struggle among Vietnamese, and the more sophisticated surely realize that we are on the side of the wealthy, and the secure, while we create a hell for the poor.

Surely this madness must cease. We must stop now. I speak as a child of God and brother to the suffering poor of Vietnam. I speak for those whose land is being laid waste, whose homes are being destroyed, whose culture is being subverted. I speak for the poor in America who are paying the double price of smashed hopes at home, and dealt death and corruption in Vietnam. I speak as a citizen of the world, for the world as it stands aghast at the path we have taken. I speak as one who loves America, to the leaders of our own nation: The great initiative in this war is ours; the initiative to stop it must be ours.

This is the message of the great Buddhist leaders of Vietnam. Recently one of them wrote these words, and I quote:

Each day the war goes on the hatred increases in the hearts of the Vietnamese and in the hearts of those of humanitarian instinct. The Americans are forcing even their friends into becoming their enemies. It is curious that the Americans, who calculate so carefully on the possibilities of military victory, do not realize that in the process they are incurring deep psychological and political defeat. The image of America will never again be the image of revolution, freedom, and democracy, but the image of violence and militarism.

Unquote.

If we continue, there will be no doubt in my mind and in the mind of the world that we have no honorable intentions in Vietnam. If we do not stop our war against the people of Vietnam immediately, the world will be left with no other alternative than to see this as some horrible, clumsy, and deadly game we have decided to play. The world now demands a maturity of America that we may not be able to achieve. It demands that we admit we have been wrong from the beginning of our adventure in Vietnam, that we have been detrimental to the life of the Vietnamese people. The situation is one in which we must be ready to turn sharply from our present ways. In order to atone for our sins and errors in Vietnam, we should take the initiative in bringing a halt to this tragic war.

I would like to suggest five concrete things that our government should do to begin the long and difficult process of extricating ourselves from this nightmarish conflict:

Number one: End all bombing in North and South Vietnam.

Number two: Declare a unilateral cease-fire in the hope that such action will create the atmosphere for negotiation.

Three: Take immediate steps to prevent other battlegrounds in Southeast Asia by curtailing our military buildup in Thailand and our interference in Laos.

Four: Realistically accept the fact that the National Liberation Front has substantial support in South Vietnam and must thereby play a role in any meaningful negotiations and any future Vietnam government.

Five: Set a date that we will remove all foreign troops from Vietnam in accordance with the 1954 Geneva Agreement. [*sustained applause*]

Part of our ongoing [*applause continues*], part of our ongoing commitment might well express itself in an offer to grant asylum to any Vietnamese who fears for his life under a new regime which included the Liberation Front. Then we must make what reparations we can for the damage we have done. We must provide the medical aid that is badly needed, making it available in this country if necessary. Meanwhile [*applause*], meanwhile, we in the churches and synagogues have a continuing task while we urge our government to disengage itself from a disgraceful commitment. We must continue to raise our voices and our lives if our nation persists in its perverse ways in Vietnam. We must be prepared to match actions with words by seeking out every creative method of protest possible.

As we counsel young men concerning military service, we must clarify for them our nation's role in Vietnam and challenge them with the alternative of conscientious objection. [*sustained applause*] I am pleased to say that this is a path now chosen by more than seventy students at my own alma mater, Morehouse College, and I recommend it to all who find the American course in Vietnam a dishonorable and unjust one. [*applause*] Moreover, I would encourage all ministers of draft age to give up their ministerial exemptions and seek status as conscientious objectors. [*applause*] These are the times for real choices and not false ones. We are at the moment when our lives must be placed on the line if our nation is to survive its own folly. Every man of humane convictions must decide on the protest that best suits his convictions, but we must all protest.

Now there is something seductively tempting about stopping there and sending us all off on what in some circles has become a popular crusade against the war in Vietnam. I say we must enter that struggle, but I wish to go on now to say something even more disturbing.

The war in Vietnam is but a symptom of a far deeper malady within the American spirit, and if we ignore this sobering reality [*applause*], and if we ignore this sobering reality, we will find ourselves organizing "clergy and laymen concerned" committees for the next generation. They will be concerned about Guatemala and Peru. They will be concerned about Thailand and Cambodia. They will be concerned about Mozambique and South Africa. We will be marching for these and a dozen other names and attending rallies without end unless there is a significant and profound change in American life and policy. [*sustained applause*] So such thoughts take us beyond Vietnam, but not beyond our calling as sons of the living God.

In 1957 a sensitive American official overseas said that it seemed to him that our nation was on the wrong side of a world revolution. During the past ten years we have seen emerge a pattern of suppression which has now justified the presence of U.S. military advisors in Venezuela. This need to maintain social stability for our investments accounts for the counter-revolutionary action of American forces in Guatemala. It tells why American helicopters are being used against guerrillas in Cambodia and why American napalm and Green Beret forces have already been active against rebels in Peru.

It is with such activity that the words of the late John F. Kennedy come back to haunt us. Five years ago he said, "Those who make peaceful revolution impossible will make violent revolution inevitable." [*applause*] Increasingly, by choice or by accident, this is the role our nation has taken, the role of those who make peaceful revolution impossible by refusing to give up the privileges and the pleasures that come from the immense profits of overseas investments. I am convinced that if we are to get on to the right side of the world revolution, we as a nation must undergo a radical revolution of values. We must rapidly begin [*applause*], we must rapidly begin the shift from a thing-oriented society to a person-oriented society. When machines and computers, profit motives and property rights, are considered more important than people, the giant triplets of racism, extreme materialism, and militarism are incapable of being conquered.

A true revolution of values will soon cause us to question the fairness and justice of many of our past and present policies. On the one hand we are called to play the Good Samaritan on life's roadside, but that will be only an initial act. One day we must come to see that the whole Jericho Road must be transformed so that men and women will not be constantly beaten and robbed as they make their journey on life's highway. True compassion is more than flinging a coin to a beggar. It comes to see that an edifice which produces beggars needs restructuring. [*applause*]

A true revolution of values will soon look uneasily on the glaring contrast of poverty and wealth. With righteous indignation, it will look across the seas and see individual capitalists of the West investing huge sums of money in Asia, Africa, and South America, only to take the profits out with no concern for the social betterment of the countries, and say, "This is not just." It will look at our alliance with the landed gentry of South America and say, "This is not just." The Western arrogance of feeling that it has everything to teach others and nothing to learn from them is not just.

A true revolution of values will lay hand on the world order and say of war, "This way of settling differences is not just." This business of burning human beings with napalm, of filling our nation's homes with orphans and widows, of injecting poisonous drugs of hate into the veins of peoples normally humane, of sending men home from dark and bloody battlefields physically handicapped and psychologically deranged, cannot be reconciled with wisdom, justice, and love. A nation that continues year after year to spend more money on military defense than on programs of social uplift is approaching spiritual death. [*sustained applause*]

America, the richest and most powerful nation in the world, can well lead the way in this revolution of values. There is nothing except a tragic death wish to prevent us from reordering our priorities so that the pursuit of peace will take precedence over the pursuit of war. There is nothing to keep us from molding a recalcitrant status quo with bruised hands until we have fashioned it into a brotherhood.

This kind of positive revolution of values is our best defense against communism. [*applause*] War is not the answer. Communism will never be defeated by the use of atomic bombs or nuclear weapons. Let us not join those who shout war and, through their misguided passions, urge the United States to relinquish its participation in the United Nations. These are days which demand wise restraint and calm reasonableness. We must not engage in a negative anticommunism, but rather in a positive thrust for democracy [*applause*], realizing that our greatest defense against communism is to take offensive action in behalf of justice. We must with positive action seek to remove those conditions of poverty, insecurity, and injustice, which are the fertile soil in which the seed of communism grows and develops.

These are revolutionary times. All over the globe men are revolting against old systems of exploitation and oppression, and out of the wounds of a frail world, new systems of justice and equality are being born. The shirtless and barefoot people of the land are rising up as never before. The people who sat in darkness have seen a great light. We in the West must support these revolutions.

It is a sad fact that because of comfort, complacency, a morbid fear of communism, and our proneness to adjust to injustice, the Western nations that initiated so much of the revolutionary spirit of the modern world have now become the arch antirevolutionaries. This has driven many to feel that only Marxism has a revolutionary spirit. Therefore, communism is a judgment against our failure to make democracy real and follow through on the revolutions that we initiated. Our only hope today lies in our ability to recapture the revolutionary spirit and go out into a sometimes hostile world declaring eternal hostility to poverty, racism, and militarism. With this powerful commitment we shall boldly challenge the status quo and unjust mores, and thereby speed the day when "every valley shall be exalted, and every mountain and hill shall be made low [*Audience:*] (*Yes*); the crooked shall be made straight, and the rough places plain."

A genuine revolution of values means in the final analysis that our loyalties must become ecumenical rather than sectional. Every nation must now develop an overriding loyalty to mankind as a whole in order to preserve the best in their individual societies.

This call for a worldwide fellowship that lifts neighborly concern beyond one's tribe, race, class, and nation is in reality a call for an all-embracing and unconditional love for all mankind. This oft misunderstood, this oft misinterpreted concept, so readily dismissed by the Nietzsches of the world as a weak and cowardly force, has now become an absolute necessity for the survival of man. When I speak of love I am not speaking of some sentimental and weak response. I'm not speaking of that force which is just emotional bosh. I am speaking of that force which all of the great religions have seen as the supreme unifying principle of life. Love is somehow the key that unlocks the door which leads to ultimate reality. This Hindu-Muslim-Christian-Jewish-Buddhist belief about ultimate reality is beautifully summed up in the first epistle of Saint John: "Let us love one another (*Yes*), for love is God. (*Yes*) And every one that loveth is born of God and knoweth God. He that loveth not knoweth not God, for God is love. . . . If we love one another, God dwelleth in us and his love is perfected in us." Let us hope that this spirit will become the order of the day.

We can no longer afford to worship the god of hate or bow before the altar of retaliation. The oceans of history are made turbulent by the ever-rising tides of hate. History is cluttered with the wreckage of nations and individuals that pursued this self-defeating path of hate. As Arnold Toynbee says: "Love is the ultimate force that makes for the saving choice of life and good against the damning choice of death and evil. Therefore the first hope in our inventory must be the hope that love is going to have the last word." Unquote.

We are now faced with the fact, my friends, that tomorrow is today. We are confronted with the fierce urgency of now. In this unfolding conundrum of life and history, there is such a thing as being too late. Procrastination is still the thief of time. Life often leaves us standing bare, naked, and dejected with a lost opportunity. The tide in the affairs of men does not remain at flood—it ebbs. We may cry out desperately for time to pause in her passage, but time is adamant to every plea and rushes on. Over the bleached bones and jumbled residues of numerous civilizations are written the pathetic words, "Too late." There is an invisible book of life that faithfully records our vigilance or our neglect. Omar Khayyam is right: "The moving finger writes, and having writ moves on."

We still have a choice today: nonviolent coexistence or violent coannihilation. We must move past indecision to action. We must find new ways to speak for peace in Vietnam and justice throughout the developing world, a world that borders on our doors. If we do not act, we shall surely be dragged down the long, dark, and shameful corridors of time reserved for those who possess power without compassion, might without morality, and strength without sight.

Now let us begin. Now let us rededicate ourselves to the long and bitter, but beautiful, struggle for a new world. This is the calling of the sons of God, and our brothers wait eagerly for our response. Shall we say the odds are too great? Shall we tell them the struggle is too hard? Will our message be that the forces of American life militate against their arrival as full men, and we send our deepest regrets? Or will there be another message—of longing, of hope, of solidarity with their yearnings, of commitment to their cause, whatever the cost? The choice is ours, and though we might prefer it otherwise, we must choose in this crucial moment of human history.

As that noble bard of yesterday, James Russell Lowell, eloquently stated:

Once to every man and nation comes a moment to decide,
In the strife of truth and Falsehood, for the good or evil side;
Some great cause, God's new Messiah offering each the
    bloom or blight,
And the choice goes by forever 'twixt that darkness and that
    light.
Though the cause of evil prosper, yet 'tis truth alone is strong
Though her portions be the scaffold, and upon the throne be
    wrong
Yet that scaffold sways the future, and behind the dim
    unknown
Standeth God within the shadow, keeping watch above his
    own.

And if we will only make the right choice, we will be able to transform this pending cosmic elegy into a creative psalm of peace. If we will make the right choice, we will be able to transform the jangling discords of our world into a beautiful symphony of brotherhood. If we will but make the right choice, we will be able to speed up the day, all over America and all over the world, when justice will roll down like waters, and righteousness like a mighty stream. [*sustained applause*]

1. Jane Addams (*behind the "P" in "PEACE"*) and Emily Greene Balch (*behind the final "E"*) aboard the *Noordam* in April 1915, on the way to the Women's International Congress for Peace and Freedom at The Hague.

2. Dorothy Day (*center*) as a young journalist for *The Call*, urging Americans to "KEEP OUT OF WAR," February 9, 1917.

3. Jeannette Rankin addresses a New York rally in support of the
La Follette–Wheeler presidential ticket, September 6, 1924. The first
woman elected to the United States Congress, Rankin voted against
American declarations of war in 1917 and 1941.

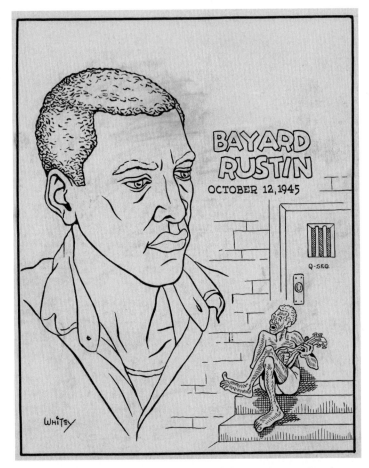

4. Bayard Rustin in the Lewisburg Federal Penitentiary on October 12, 1945, as seen by fellow conscientious objector Theo ("Whitey") Matysik.

5. Wally and Juanita Nelson, 1946.

6. Albert S. Bigelow (*right*) beside the *Golden Rule*. In May and June 1958, he and his three-man crew attempted twice to sail the vessel from Honolulu to the Eniwetok Proving Grounds to block nuclear tests. They were intercepted by the Coast Guard and spent sixty days in jail.

7. Climbing a fence around the Mead missile base near Omaha, Nebraska, on July 1, 1959, A. J. Muste launches a Committee for Nonviolent Action civil disobedience campaign against "the insane arms race."

8. Thomas Merton (*left*) and Daniel Berrigan (*center*) at a Gethsemani Abbey
Peacemakers Retreat, New Haven, Kentucky, August 1962.

9. Grace Paley (*right*) at an anti-Vietnam War demonstration, March 9, 1965.

10. Burning draft cards with homemade napalm at the Catonsville, Maryland, Selective Service office, May 17, 1968. Daniel Berrigan, who would later write *The Trial of the Catonsville Nine*, stands behind Tom Melville, adding fuel to the fire.

11. Joan Baez at an antiwar rally in London, May 29, 1965.

12. Pete Seeger at the November 13, 1969, Peace Moratorium in New York. His banjo bears the motto: "This machine surrounds hate and forces it to surrender."

13. Disabled veteran Ron Kovic protesting conditions in VA hospitals, February 28, 1974. He would later write *Born on the Fourth of July*.

14. Barbara Deming (*holding flowers*) at the Seneca Women's Encampment for a Future of Peace and Justice, summer 1983. Protesters hoped to block the suspected shipment of first-strike nuclear missiles from the Seneca Army Depot to Europe.

15. On November 12, 2002, women in Marin Country, California, spell out PEACE with their naked bodies to protest the impending invasion of Iraq.

16. Zack de la Rocha, lead singer of Rage Against the Machine, at a protest in Denver outside the Democratic National Convention led by Iraq Veterans Against the War, August 27, 2008.

ROBERT BLY

Robert Bly (b. 1926) wrote a good many poems against the Vietnam War: some vast and prophetic, like "The Teeth-Mother Naked at Last," some short and didactic, many frequently anthologized. Of the shorter poems, none is quite so fruitfully compressed as "Counting Small-Boned Bodies," a brief, ragingly sardonic fantasia on the notion of "body count," a phrase heard every night during those years on radio and television, to the point that it seemed a shorthand for war itself, though a shorthand designed to erase the means by which living beings became countable bodies. Bly's poem reanimates the phrase, extrapolates it to its absurd conclusion, and turns the phrase's logic against the war that brought it into prominence.

Bly grew up in Minnesota, enlisted in the Navy in 1944, went to Harvard; early in his career he translated and promoted the work of poets then largely unknown in the English-speaking world, including Pablo Neruda, with whom he felt a particular affinity. A prolific writer of prodigious energy, he was also a prominent poetic opponent of the Vietnam War, cofounding American Writers Against the Vietnam War, signing the Writers and Editors War Tax Protest pledge, and donating the National Book Award given him for *The Light Around the Body* (1967), in which "Counting Small-Boned Bodies" first appeared, to draft-resistance organizations. In 1975 he organized the first Great Mother Conference—still held every year—believing that an exploration of "the divine feminine" was needed as antidote to the unbalanced, pathological masculinism that had led to war. Later, in *Iron John* (1990), he became a sort of Jungian guru of American manhood; the book was a surprise bestseller, making him famous in a way that none of his poetry had.

Counting Small-Boned Bodies

Let's count the bodies over again.

If we could only make the bodies smaller,
The size of skulls,
We could make a whole plain white with skulls in the
    moonlight!

If we could only make the bodies smaller,
Maybe we could get
A whole year's kill in front of us on a desk!

If we could only make the bodies smaller,
We could fit
A body into a finger-ring, for a keepsake forever.

JAMES BALDWIN

Only once was I in the presence of James Baldwin (1924–1987): in the Cathedral of St. John the Divine in New York, where I was then a singer in the choir and to which Baldwin had been invited to give a sermon. He gave a fiery speech, though not so much a sermon as a prophetic denunciation of Richard Nixon and the Vietnam War, culminating in the vivid but indecorous exhortation, "we've got a little old motherfucker in the White House and we've got to figure out how to get him out." So though Baldwin is famous as a novelist and essayist pondering race and civil rights, for me he has always been what he is in the piece included here, a prophetic, eloquent opponent of unjust wars.

Hence his being invited by Bertrand Russell to sit on the Russell-Sartre Tribunal in 1966, brought into being to judge American conduct in Vietnam. (The tribunal was an early and nongovernmental version of the International Criminal Court, without influence but full of interesting people, among them not only Baldwin but also David Dellinger and Stokely Carmichael.) Baldwin's comments emerge from that context, and are characteristically unsparing of everyone. His judgments bear first on the tribunal itself, whose limitations and hypocrisies he begins by skewering. But then he turns to the Vietnam War, and in an argument by now familiar but still alive in the words he expresses it in, denounces the American hypocrisies the war manifests and reveals: "a racist society can't but fight a racist war" is the beautifully distilled essence of his argument (dated, appropriately enough, from Istanbul and published in *Freedomways* in the summer of 1967).

Baldwin was raised in Harlem, attended P.S. 24 and wrote its school song, attended Frederick Douglass Junior High and was taught poetry there by Countee Cullen. At fourteen he converted to Pentecostalism, drawing big crowds as a youthful Pentecostal preacher. Later he turned away from Christianity and religion generally; when asked about his religious identity by Nation of Islam founder Elijah Muhammad, he responded, "Nothing. I'm a writer. I like doing things alone."

He also liked hanging out with friends and artistic mentors in Greenwich Village, where he began to write, to become aware of his homosexuality, and to put himself in situations where American racism was especially vivid. Worn down by being the object of two modes of prejudice simultaneously, he left for Paris; he spent most of his later life in France, often in his house in Saint-Paul de Vence, which became a gathering place for his friends, painters and actors and musicians among them. He wrote abundantly: novels, extraordinary essays and long-form journalism, songs (including some for Ray Charles), plays. But he did not seek to keep above the battle, and was active in both civil rights work—he marched with King at Selma—and antiwar work, joining other writers in the Writers and Editors War Tax Protest pledge in 1968. (Other signatories represented here: Daniel Berrigan, Robert Bly, David Dellinger, Barbara Deming, Paul Goodman, Denise Levertov, Jackson Mac Low, Norman Mailer, Grace Paley, Adrienne Rich, Muriel Rukeyser, Kurt Vonnegut Jr., and Howard Zinn.)

Toni Morrison wrote an extraordinary eulogy for Baldwin, which ends: "This then is no calamity. No. This is jubilee. 'Our crown,' you said, 'has already been bought and paid for. All we have to do,' you said, 'is wear it.'"

The War Crimes Tribunal

My name is included among the members of Lord Russell's War Crimes Tribunal, and it is imperative, therefore, that I make my position clear. I do indeed have my own reservation concerning this Tribunal. There may be something suspect in the spectacle of Europeans condemning America for a war which America inherited from Europe, inherited, in fact, directly from France. In spite of my somewhat difficult reputation, I have never had any interest in attacking America from abroad. I know too much, if I may say so, concerning the complex European motives, of which envy and fury are not the least. It might be considered more logical, for example, for any European, and especially any Englishman, to bring before an international tribunal the government of South Africa, or the government of Rhodesia, which I would do, if I had the power, at nine o'clock tomorrow morning. No Englishman has suggested this. Neither did Jean-Paul Sartre suggest that France be brought before an international tribunal during the war which we have inherited from France, or during the French-Algerian war. It is possible, in short, to consider the Tribunal to be both misguided and inept, and I can see to what extent that this is so. But I can also see why. The Tribunal, ideally, wishes to make the conscience of the world aware of the crimes being committed in Southeast Asia by the American government, in the name of the American people; and wishes to do this, not only to bring the horror to an end, but to pull all of us back from the brink of total disaster. But this world can only be the Western world, this conscience can only be the Western conscience, and all the Western world is guilty. If I should make the attempt to accuse the Western powers of the crimes they are now committing in Rhodesia, Angola, South Africa—to leave it at that; or should I attempt to bring to the world's attention the actual intention, and the actual result, of those treaties the Europeans, who were not yet Americans, signed with the American Indian; to say nothing of what happened to the blacks, concerning which we know at once too much and too little; I would certainly encounter from the Western powers the very same opposition that Lord Russell's Tribunal has encountered. And for the very same reason: such an attempt not only brings into question the real morality of the Western world, it also attacks what that world considers to be its material self-interest. Such a trial should really be held in Harlem, USA. No one, then, could possibly escape the sinister implications of the moral dilemma in which the facts of Western history have placed the Western world.

I speak as an American Negro. I challenge anyone alive to tell me why any black American should go into those jungles to kill people who are not white and who have never done him any harm, in defense of a people who have made that foreign jungle, or any jungle anywhere in the world, a more desirable jungle than that in which he was born, and to which, supposing that he lives, he will inevitably return. I challenge anyone alive to convince me that a people who have not achieved anything resembling freedom in their own country are empowered, with bombs, to free another people whom they do not know at all, who rather resemble me—whom they do not know at all. I challenge any American, and especially Mr. Lyndon Johnson and Mr. Hubert Humphrey and Mr. Dean Rusk and Mr. Robert McNamara to tell me, and the black population of the United States, how, if they cannot liberate their brothers— repeat: *brothers*—and have not even learned how to live with them, they intend to liberate Southeast Asia. I challenge them to tell me by what right, and in whose interest, they presume to police the world, and I, furthermore, want to know if they would like their sisters, or their daughters to marry any one of the people they are struggling so mightily to save. And this is by no means a rhetorical challenge, and all the men I have named, and many, many more will be dishonored forever if they cannot rise to it. I want an answer: If I am to die, I have the right to know why. And the non-white population of the world, who are most of the world, would also like to know. The American idea of freedom and, still more, the way this freedom is imposed, have made America the most terrifying nation in the world. We have inherited Spain's title: the nation with the bloody foot-print.

The American war in Vietnam raises several questions. One is whether or not small nations, in this age of super-states and superpowers, will be allowed to work out their own destinies and live as they feel they should. For only the people of a country have the right, or the spiritual power, to determine that country's way of life. Another question this war raises is just how what we call the under-developed countries became under-developed in the first place. Why, for example, is Africa under-populated, and why do the resources of, say, Sierra Leone belong to Europe? Why, in short, does so much of the world eat too little and so little of the world eat too much? I am also curious to know just how a people calling itself sovereign allows itself to be fighting a war which has never been officially declared, and I am curious to know why so few people appear to be worried about the arresting precedent thus established. I am curious indeed to know how it happens that the mightiest nation in the world has been unable, in all these years, to conquer one of the smallest. I am curious to know what happens to the moral fabric, the moral sense, of the people engaged in so criminal an endeavor.

Long, long before the Americans decided to liberate the Southeast Asians, they decided to liberate me: my ancestors carried these scars to the grave, and so will I. A racist society can't but fight a racist war—this is the bitter truth. The assumptions acted on at home are also acted on abroad, and every American Negro knows this, for he, after the American Indian, was the first "Viet Cong" victim. We were bombed first. How, then, can I believe a word you say, and what gives you the right to ask me to die for you?

The American endeavor in Vietnam is totally indefensible and totally doomed, and I wish to go on record as having no part of it. When the black population of America has a future, so will America have a future—not till then. And when the black populations of the world have a future, so will the Western nations have a future—and not till then. But the terrible probability is that the Western populations, struggling to hold on to what they have stolen from their captives, and unable to look into their mirror will precipitate a chaos throughout the world which, if it does not bring life on this planet to an end, will bring about a racial war such as the world has never seen, and for which generations yet unborn will curse our names forever.

I think that mankind can do better than that, and I wish to be a witness to this small and stubborn possibility.

PAUL GOODMAN

Paul Goodman (1911–1972) was a counterculture hero when I was growing up, not for his antiwar work but for *Growing Up Absurd* (1960). That book, more than any other writing I encountered as a young man, suggested why certain modes of respectable life felt meaningless.

The two pieces included here show different aspects of Goodman. In the first, he mourns his son's death, and as a mourner draws on the part of himself that wrote novels and poems, the open-hearted, sharp-eyed, loving observer. We have no better portrait of a pacifist growing up (non-absurdly) than the one Goodman offers us here.

His son's death shattered him, his friends said, and perhaps one can feel that shatteredness in "A Causerie at the Military-Industrial," delivered less than three months after young Mathew Goodman's death; the speech feels almost self-destructively confrontational. Here was Goodman, invited to speak before the National Security Industrial Association on "Planning for the Socio-Economic Environment," and here is what he has to say to the four hundred members of that association, as if daring them to throw him out: "you are the military-industrial of the United States, the most dangerous body of men at present in the world . . . the best service that you people could perform is rather rapidly to phase yourselves out." But few antiwar speeches from the period feel more alive on the page than this one, animated by its anger.

Goodman had astonishingly numerous interests, careers, and talents. He grew up in New York, got a B.A. at City College, majoring in philosophy and studying with Morris Cohen. He began to write—poems, plays, stories. He taught drama, became a graduate student in literature, published his first novel in 1942, taught at Manumit Preparatory School, and was dismissed for "homosexual behavior" (later he was dismissed from Black Mountain College for the same reason). He published essays and novels, studied and practiced psychoanalysis, wrote about urban planning and gestalt therapy and education and sexuality. The Living Theatre staged his plays, and everyone read *Growing Up Absurd*.

A Young Pacifist

I.

My son, Mathew Ready Goodman, was killed mountain-climbing on August 8, 1967, age 20. Burton Weiss, a close friend of his at Cornell, has sent me an account of Matty's political activities there—to which I will preface some memories of his similar activities before he went to college. Matty was essentially an unpolitical person; his absorbing intellectual interest was in sciences—in which he had gifts, and he wanted to live and let live in a community of friends—at which he remarkably succeeded. Nevertheless, he was continually engaged in political actions, against war and irrational authority. This pattern is common to many hundreds, and in increasing numbers, of brave and thoughtful young people these days; it is worthwhile to describe it in a typical example. In any case, the group at Cornell—Burt, Jerry Franz, Tom Bell, Bruce Dancis, and a few others whom I did not know personally—have managed to make that unlikely school one of the most radical in the country, with a strongly characteristic style: undoctrinaire yet activist, deeply communitarian and imbued with an extraordinary honesty and good faith. In this group, Matty was an important spirit.

Emotionally, from early childhood, Matty's pacifism was certainly related to his unusual protectiveness of his many animals. He identified with their lives. I remember him and his mother medicating and sometimes saving sick little turtles, tropical fish, white rats. Yet there was nothing squeamish or sentimental in his attitude. If he needed to feed his lizards, he calmly caught flies, tore their wings off and offered them; but otherwise he would not kill a fly but adroitly catch it and let it out the door. He gave up fishing around age 10 and began to rescue the fish and return them to the river. Mostly he liked just to watch the fish and pond life, for hours, in their natural habitat.

More intellectually, he was an ardent conservationist, indignant at the spoliation, opposed to insecticides. The focus of his scientific interests (in my opinion) was ecology, the community of living things in the appropriate environment. And in method he strongly favored—so far as the distinction can be made—naturalistic observation, letting things be, rather than experimenting and imposing programs. These were also his political biases.

My first political recollection of him is when, in junior high school, he called my attention to corporation advertising being used in his class. He collected the evidence and we succeeded, temporarily, in having it expelled. This involved his being called down and rebuked by the principal.

During his first year at Bronx Science High School he wrote a report on the life of Gandhi, who impressed him deeply. For a reason known only to himself, he took to fasting one day a week—and continued this sporadically later.

He was active in the antibomb protests in 1960–62. He used to take part in the "General Strike For Peace" thought up by Julian Beck. Since people were supposed to leave off work for a day and picket for peace, Matty took off from school and picketed the Board of Education on Livingston Street. Naturally he was captured as a truant and I had to go and rescue him. This was one of the few moments of pure delight I have ever had in the peace movement.

He was at the Times Square demonstration against the bomb-testing when the police rode their horses into the crowd. Matty was in the line of fire and came home shaken, saying, "This is serious."

As a junior in high school, he refused to take part in a shelter drill and he and three others who would not recant were suspended. But there was considerable newspaper publicity and they were reinstated and allowed to stand aside during the drills, which were soon discontinued. His reasons for nonparticipation were (1) the shelters were unscientific, (2) the drill was an insult to intelligence in its form and (3) it predisposed to accepting nuclear war.

When reinstated, he was told he had a black mark on his record. I wrote to Admissions at Harvard asking if this was a disadvantage; when we received the expected reply that it would rather be judged as a sign of critical independence, Matty had the letter copied off and distributed around Bronx Science—which sorely needed the nudge.

By now he was a seasoned radical and when he was again threatened with punishment for pasting antiwar stickers in the school subway station, he faced down the administration by pointing out that the subway was not in its jurisdiction.

At age 15 he and other high-school students formed a city-wide association to protest against nuclear war. This came to nothing.

When he applied for admission to Cornell, Professor Milton Konvitz phoned me in alarm that he was likely to be rejected because he had sent a photo of himself with uncombed hair. Matty said, "If they don't want me as I really look, they can keep their lousy school." They admitted him anyway, but sometimes they may have regretted not following their routine impulse. Matty loved Cornell and therefore fought it tooth and nail.

At 18, he refused to register for the draft. I shall return to this later, but I recall that, the following summer, he distributed antiwar leaflets in front of the Army recruiting station in St. Johnsbury, Vermont, near where we have a summer home. This made me anxious, since of course he had no draft card. But he explained, "I can't live in fear every day. I must act as I ordinarily would." My guess is that he loved St. Johnsbury and wanted to redeem it for having a recruiting station.

2.

Burt Weiss writes as follows about Matty at Cornell (my own comments are in brackets):

"Students for Education, SFE, organized themselves in late February, 1965. Matty was in almost from the beginning. He was most active in the Grading Committee, whose only proposal he and I hammered out. The S-U option in it has since come to be offered in much weakened form by most of the Cornell colleges.

[In fact, insisting on another option in the proposal, Matty got his professors not to grade him at all, or to keep his grades secret from him. Later, to his annoyance, he found his name on the Dean's list, and crossed it out with a crayon and complained.]

"Astonishingly, Mathew attended all meetings and rallies of SFE and its steering committee. Such an attendance record was unique for him. He had little toleration for contentious political meetings, especially when the contention was made by those he loved. When he guessed that a meeting was likely to be angry and unfruitful, he usually stayed home. If he went despite his guess, or if the angry mood of a meeting took him by surprise, he left early. Several times, when he stuck it out, he was moved to the point of tears or actually cried. I loved him then very much, and respected his ability to mourn. He mourned that people were acting stupidly, timidly, or dishonestly. He mourned the sudden vanishing of community spirit.

"Later that spring, Matty took part in the 24-hour vigil in the Arts Quad and in the walkout while Rockefeller was speaking at the centennial celebration. Nobody got in trouble for either of these actions. But then came the Harriman lecture and the resulting fracas widely reported in the press. Before Harriman spoke, he received the enclosed letter written by Matty and Jerry Franz. [The letter complains that official spokesmen evade real questions and warns that the students will insist on real answers. Harriman's behavior did turn out to be insulting to college-level intelligence and the students sat down around him.]

"In May came the sitdown to block the ROTC review in Barton Hall. All (70) participants were prosecuted by the University, but Matty and Jerry walked out of the hearing before the Faculty Committee on Student Conduct. Here, according to the Cornell *Sun*, is what they said: 'The members of the group made a definite commitment to stand by each other if there was anything like differential punishment. Tonight they went back on their commitment. The group agreed that it was necessary to have a collective hearing so that past offenses could not be taken into account. Tonight the group agreed to let them take past offenses into account. Therefore we can no longer be associated.' They were summarily suspended, but reinstated when they appeared, just the two of them, at the next meeting of the Committee. They were placed on Disciplinary Probation.

"That was an exciting spring. We kept rushing about in no particular direction, although everything we did seemed to be of a piece. Most important things happened late at night, leaflet-writing, mimeographing, emergency meetings, passionate revelatory dialogue among friends.

"During our months in Europe—fall of '65—Matty had little to do with politics. One day in Paris—I think it was an International Day of Protest, Oct. 1965—he picketed the American Embassy. He had expected to meet others there. As it turned out, he was all alone, but picketed anyway. In Seville we went to see the American consul to register our protest against the Vietnam war. We did nothing to end the war, but did get a good idea of the sort of person who is appointed to American consulships.

"At Cornell in the spring of 1966, Matty and some friends founded the Young Anarchists. The group never did much, but it put out some neat broadsides. Nevertheless, as I later learned by accident, the very existence of a group of that name intimidated the administration and extensive files were kept, including glossy blown-up photos of every member.

[It is touching that I, a long-time anarchist, never heard of these Young Anarchists from my son.]

"In May a hundred students sat in at President Perkins' office to protest against Cornell's complicity with Selective Service. Matty was one of the first seven to get there and so was able to enter the presidential suite before the campus police locked the doors. The latecomers were kept in the corridor. Only the 'inner seven' were prosecuted by the University. The Undergraduate Judiciary Board, composed entirely of students, voted 'no action' and made us all proud. The Faculty Committee, however, changed this to 'reprimand.'

"The day after the sit-in, the University Faculty met in special session to discuss the relation between Cornell and Selective Service. As faculty members entered the meeting, they were handed 'A Plea Against Military Influence at Cornell,' written by Matty and Jerry.

"In the last year of his life, Matty was deeply involved with two groups, Young Friends and the Ithaca We Won't Go group. He was committed to the people in these groups and to the fraternal and community spirit among them. This was the only time since SFE that he was so committed.

"In the fall Matty helped organize the Five-Day Fast for Peace, explained in the enclosed leaflet that Matty helped to write. The fast was very successful in terms of the number who participated, the interest and sympathy roused on campus and in town, and the amount of money raised for medical aid [for North and South Vietnamese]. For some reason Matty gradually became the chief PR man for Young Friends. He was rather inept in that position.

[Again, I was surprised to learn of his Quaker connections. His mother and I had never been able to interest him in religion at all, even to read the Bible as literature.]

"Also that fall, Matty, Tom Bell, and I began talking about starting a local draft resistance group. The group grew slowly and beautifully, just as Tom Bell explained in *New Left Notes* last March. When Matty returned from inter-session in February, he was excited about the possibilities for mass draft-card destruction, and the desirability of starting on April 15 in New York. Everybody was interested, yet nobody seemed moved to action. Finally, Jan Flora and I were startled to realize how soon it would be April 15. We called Matty, rounded up a small meeting, and decided to go ahead. I was going to New York later that night and so I was asked to find out what people there thought. You were the first person I saw. The rest you know.

[I tried to rally help for them by a letter, to academics who had signed Vietnam ads in the *Times*, of which Matty distributed six thousand copies. On April 15, about 160 students burned their cards in the Sheep Meadow. Matty, who had no card, held up a sign—"20 Years Unregistered."

[And proud Matty would have been on October 16, that so many who were leaders of the 1500 who turned in their cards had been his fellows in the Sheep Meadow on April 15.]

"For Matty, the most painful occurrence in connection with the draft-card destruction was the breakdown of community spirit that it, and the Easter Peace Bridge demonstration, occasioned in Young Friends. SDS was soliciting pledges in the student union. The Proctor was citing those responsible to appear before the Judiciary boards and suspending those who refused to give their names. Matty and others tried to get Young Friends to solicit the same pledges at their own table, in solidarity with fellow war-resisters. At first Young Friends went along, but then began to talk about backing out. At about the same time, Matty saw the official 'instructions' for the Easter demonstration at the Peace Bridge, in which Young Friends, including Epi and himself, had planned to participate. This document had nothing to do with love, fellowship, or respect for the individuality and holy spirit in every person, what Matty conceived to be the essence of Quakerism. There were strict rules governing both the demonstration itself and the personal behavior and attire of the participation. Worse, the document advised male participants to bring along their draft cards to show at the border. The whole thing made Matty sick. Yet his feelings seemed to be shared by only a minority of Young Friends. The group was falling apart in front of his eyes. . . .

"Matty had planned to go to Brazil this summer as part of a Cornell anthropological project. His main purpose, as he explained at the first meeting, would have been to work politically with Brazilian students and thereby help to foster an international community of radical students.

[This project was abandoned when, at the disclosure of C.I.A. tampering with American students, the Brazilian students had to dis-invite the Cornellians. Matty told me that previous South American trips had been exciting and useful. He had worked hard learning Portuguese.

When Brazil was closed off, Matty at once proposed that the entire group should go to Cuba; this would be a reasonable and necessary retaliation to the C.I.A. system and was also worthwhile in itself. Dr. William Rogers, who was the director of the project, has written me as follows: "I won't detail the debate that followed Matty's proposal. It was the age-old struggle of the soul between the single act of moral purity and courage, and the prudential and tactical considerations of effectiveness. We spoke of Jesus' parable of the Pearl of Great Price. Was this act the pearl for which a man will sell all that he has, in order to possess it? Matty, with an eschatological sense akin to the New Testament, seemed to think so. Considerations of the future did not weigh heavily with him. The important thing was to be moral, thoroughly moral, now. How much longer can we wait?" Unfortunately, Matty did not persuade them.]

"Early in the spring Matty took part—as who did not?—in the riotous demonstration which defeated the DA when he came on campus to suppress the sale of the literary magazine. Matty's battle-cry was entirely his own: 'Fuck you, Thaler,' he said to that unfortunate man's face.

"Later in the spring he made it his business to operate the printing press in the We Won't Go office. He intended, next year, to spend considerable time there doing routine work."

On August 7, Matty and I drove down from Expo in Montreal, where we had attended the Hiroshima Day youth rally.

In his sleeping bag Matty had hidden some contraband, a book of short stories bought at the Cuban pavilion as a gift for his teacher in a course on Mexican revolutionary novels. However, we decided to declare it, in order that the book might be seized and burned and we could complain to Robert Kennedy. The Customs offices obligingly acted up in the face of our high literary disdain, so we had fun planning our indignant letter. Next day Matty died on the mountain, but I have sent the letter.

3.

Matty refused to register for the draft on general pacifist grounds—the subsequent worsening of the Vietnam war merely confirmed what he already knew.

His method of refusal was not to recognize the draft system at all and to continue as usual, including, of course, his overt antiwar activity—now without a draft card. In fact, he stepped up this activity, but I think this was because of Vietnam rather than to force a showdown. I never saw any sign that he courted going to jail. He did not regard himself as a Witness in any way. On the other hand, he was entirely too open to live "underground." And the "tactical approach," of trying for C.O. or accepting II-S in order to carry on revolutionary activity, was also against his disposition: he could not live on an ambiguous basis. Besides, he believed it was bad politics; his enthusiasm for the mass draft-card burning meant that he believed in open massive noncooperation and active nonviolent resistance. His eyes twinkled at the idea of "nonviolent terrorism": if one is arrested, five others burn their cards on the courthouse steps.

The F.B.I. first got in touch with him in November 1966, purportedly about a classmate applying for C.O., for whom Matty had agreed to be a reference! (This was part of his "business as usual.") They visited him as a nonregistrant in March 1967 and set the wheels of prosecution going.

Matty's approach—to "do nothing"—is appropriate, in my opinion, only to young people who are sure of their own integrity and the human use of their own developing careers, who just need to be let be. Matty had this confidence. Besides, he was a balky animal: he would have found it impossibly

humiliating, paralyzing, to try to move his feet toward anything he strongly disbelieved in, such as filling out a draft
form. He was not, in my experience, "rebellious," defiant of
authority as such. But he had learned that authority was very
often irrational, petty, dishonest and sometimes not benevolent, so he was antiauthoritarian. (The school administrations
he had dealt with were certainly not models of magnanimity,
American democracy or even simple honor; and these are the
only officials that a growing boy knows, unless he is a juvenile
delinquent or on relief.) Matty was also unusually stubborn
in general. He had to do things his own way, at his own pace,
according to his own slowly developing concern or fantasy.
This was often too slow for other people's wishes, including
mine, but there was no hurrying him. Once he cared, he acted
with energy and determination.

He refused to be a leader—at Cornell, as at Berkeley in its
best days, leadership was regarded as a poor form of social
organization. Yet it is clear in the above accounts that Matty
often did lead. But this was because he acted according to
his own inner belief, without ambition or ideology. He was
frank, loyal and consistent, and his integrity was legendary.
If, in an action, he was among the first, or seemed to be the
most intransigent and unwilling to compromise, it was not that
he was brash or doctrinaire, but because of some elementary
human principle. Naturally, then, others found security in him
and went along. So far as I can discover, he had no enemies.
Even administrators liked him personally and have sent me
touching letters of condolence. His lust for community seems
to have been equal to my own, but he had more luck with it.

After he became seriously illegal at 18 he, like others in a
similar plight, showed signs of anxiety, a certain tightness,
a certain hardness. This roused my indignation more than
anything else, that the brute mechanical power of the State
was distorting the lives of these excellent youth. For nothing. For far worse than nothing—abstract conformity, empty
power, overseas murder. Nevertheless, in Matty's case at
least, his formula of dismissing fear and acting as he ordinarily would, seemed to work spectacularly. Once he had made
the hard choice, he threw himself into all his activities with
increased enthusiasm; new energy was released and during this

period—whatever the causal relationship—he embarked on an uninterrupted and pretty happy love affair with Epi Epton, who shared his convictions; this of course must have immensely increased his security, assertiveness and courage.

As I said at the outset, Matty was not essentially political; he was politically active only by duty, on principle. Rather he was a daring swimmer, a good handball player. He ground his own telescopes. He jeopardized his nonexistent II-S deferment and took off for Europe for a semester. He had found a method of meditation that suited him. Hungry for music, he sat for hours at the piano and was in charge of selecting the records in the library. He was an Honors student in anthropology and he was, I am told by Professor Joseph Calvo and Dr. Elizabeth Keller, beginning to do original work in genetics. But his political activity also blessed him with friends and community.

My own hope was that, after he was arrested, he would—having fought through to the end—skip bail and go to Canada, since jail did not seem to be the best environment for him. He said he would make up his mind when it was necessary. He had looked into it and made connections so that it would be possible for him to work politically in Canada.

Every pacifist career is individual, a unique balance of forces, including the shared hope that other human beings will become equally autonomous. Most people want peace and freedom, but there are no pacifist or anarchist masses.

As I tearfully review my son's brief pacifist career, the following seems to have been his philosophy: He had a will to protect life in all its forms and to conserve the conditions for it. With this, he had a kind of admiring trust in the providence of natural arrangements and liked to gaze at them. He felt that human beings too could form a natural and wise community and he was daringly loyal to this possibility. He was astonished to see people act with timidity, pettiness or violence. Yet he was not naive. He knew that people in power and people bureaucratized are untrustworthy and one has to be prepared for their stupidity and dishonesty and confront them. (I don't know if he thought that people as such could be malevolent.) As for himself, he felt that there was plenty of time to brood and mull and observe and wait for the spirit; it did not delay, and there was no need for pressuring or forcing votes. What he himself could do to help was to be open to the facts, honest in speech and as consistent as possible. When a practical idea occurred to him, it was never complicated or dilatory, but always a simplification and a way of immediately coming across.

It is a beautiful soul we have lost, who behaved well and had a good influence.

A Causerie at the Military-Industrial

The National Security Industrial Association (NSIA) was founded in 1944 by James Forrestal, to maintain and enhance the beautiful wartime communication between the armament industries and the government. At present it comprises 400 members, including of course all the giant aircraft, electronics, motors, oil, and chemical corporations, but also many one would not expect: not only General Dynamics, General Motors, and General Telephone and Electronics, but General Foods and General Learning; not only Sperry Rand, RCA, and Lockheed, but Servco and Otis Elevators. It is a wealthy club. The military budget is $84 billion.

At the recent biennial symposium, held on October 18 and 19 in the State Department auditorium, the theme was "Research and Development in the 1970s." To my not unalloyed pleasure, I was invited to participate as one of the seventeen speakers and assigned the topic "Planning for the Socio-Economic Environment." Naturally I could make the usual speculations about why I was thus "co-opted." I doubt that they expected to pick my brains for any profitable ideas. But it is useful for feeders at the public trough to present an image of wide-ranging discussion. It is comfortable to be able to say, "You see? these far-outniks are impractical." And business meetings are dull and I am notoriously stimulating. But the letter of invitation from Henri Busignies of ITT, the chairman of the symposium committee, said only, "Your accomplishments throughout your distinguished career eminently qualify you to speak with authority on the subject."

What is an intellectual man to do in such a case? I agree with the Gandhian principle, always cooperate within the limits of honor, truth, and justice. But how to co-operate with the military

*industrial club! during the Vietnam war 1967! It was certainly not
the time to reason about basic premises, as is my usual approach,
so I decided simply to confront them and soberly tell them off.*

*Fortunately it was the week of the demonstration at the Pen-
tagon, when there would be thousands of my friends in Washington. So I tipped them off and thirty students from Cornell
and Harpur drove down early to picket the auditorium, with a
good leaflet about the evil environment for youth produced by the
military corporations. When they came, the white helmets sprang
up, plus the cameras and reporters. In the face of this dangerous invasion, the State Department of the United States was put
under security, the doors were bolted, and the industrialists (and
I) were not allowed to exit—on the Twenty-third Street side.
Inside, I spoke as follows:*

R & D FOR THE SOCIO-ECONOMIC
ENVIRONMENT OF THE 1970S

I am astonished that at a conference on planning for the future,
you have not invited a single speaker under the age of thirty,
the group that is going to live in that future. I am pleased that
some of the young people have come to pound on the door
anyway, but it is too bad that they aren't allowed to come in.

This is a bad forum for this topic. Your program mentions
the "emerging national goals" of urban development, continuing education, and improving the quality of man's environment. I would add another essential goal, reviving American
democracy; and at least two indispensable international goals,
to rescue the majority of mankind from deepening poverty,
and to insure the survival of mankind as a species. These goals
indeed require research and experimentation of the highest
sophistication, but not by you. You people are unfitted by your
commitments, your experience, your customary methods, your
recruitment, and your moral disposition. You are the military-
industrial of the United States, the most dangerous body of
men at the present in the world, for you not only implement
our disastrous policies but are an overwhelming lobby for them,
and you expand and rigidify the wrong use of brains, resources,
and labor so that change becomes difficult. Most likely the
trends you represent will be interrupted by a shambles of riots,

alienation, ecological catastrophes, wars, and revolutions, so that current long-range planning, including this conference, is irrelevant. But if we ask what *are* the technological needs and what ought to be researched in this coming period, in the six areas I have mentioned, the best service that you people could perform is rather rapidly to phase yourselves out, passing on your relevant knowledge to people better qualified, or reorganizing yourselves with entirely different sponsors and commitments, so that you learn to think and feel in a different way. Since you are most of the R & D that there is, we cannot do without you as people, but we cannot do with you as you are.

In aiding technically underdeveloped regions, the need in the foreseeable future is for an intermediate technology, scientifically sophisticated but tailored to their local skills, tribal or other local social organization, plentiful labor force, and available raw materials. The aim is to help them out of starvation, disease, and drudgery without involving them in an international cash nexus of an entirely different order of magnitude. Let them take off at their own pace and in their own style. For models of appropriate technical analyses, I recommend you to E. F. Schumacher, of the British Coal Board, and his associates. Instead, you people—and your counterparts in Europe and Russia—have been imposing your technology, seducing native elites mostly corrupted by Western education, arming them, indeed often using them as a dumping ground for obsolete weapons. As Dr. Busignies pointed out yesterday, your aim must be, while maintaining leadership, to allow very little technical gap, in order to do business. Thus, you have involved these people in a wildly inflationary economy, have driven them into instant urbanization, and increased the amount of disease and destitution. You have disrupted ancient social patterns, debauched their cultures, fomented tribal and other wars, and in Vietnam yourselves engaged in genocide. You have systematically entangled them in Great Power struggles. It is not in your interest, and you do not have the minds or the methods, to take these peoples seriously as people.

The survival of the human species, at least in a civilized state, demands radical disarmament, and there are several feasible political means to achieve this if we willed it. By the same

token, we must drastically de-energize the archaic system of
nation-states, e.g., by internationalizing space exploration,
expanding operations like the International Geophysical
Year, denationalizing Peace Corps and aid programs, opening scientific information and travel. Instead, you—and your
counterparts in Europe, Russia, and China—have rigidified
and aggrandized the states with a Maginot-line kind of policy
called Deterrence, which has continually escalated rather than
stabilized. As Jerome Wiesner has demonstrated, past a certain
point your operations have increased insecurity rather than
diminished it. But this has been to your interest. Even in the
present condition of national rivalry, it has been estimated, by
Marc Raskin who sat in on the National Security Council, that
the real needs of our defense should cost less than a fourth
of the budget you have pork-barreled. You tried, unsuccess-
fully, to saddle us with the scientifically ludicrous Civil Defense
program. You have sabotaged the technology of inspection for
disarmament. Now you are saddling us with the antimissile
missiles and the multi-warhead missiles (MIRV). You have
corrupted the human adventure of space with programs for
armed platforms in orbit. Although we are the most heavily
armed and the most naturally protected of the Great Powers,
you have seen to it that we spend a vastly greater amount and
perhaps a higher proportion of our wealth on armaments than
any other nation.

This brings me to your effect on the climate of the economy.
The wealth of a nation is to provide useful goods and services,
with an emphasis first on necessities and broad-spread comforts, simply as a decent background for un-economic life and
culture; an indefinitely expanding economy is a rat-race. There
ought to be an even spread regionally, and no group must be
allowed to fall outside of society. At present, thanks to the
scientific ingenuity and hard work of previous generations, we
could in America allow a modest livelihood to everyone as a
constitutional right. And on the other hand, as the young have
been saying by their style and actions, there is an imperative
need to simplify the standard of living, since the affluent standard has become frivolous, tawdry, and distracting from life
itself. But you people have distorted the structure of a rational
economy. Since 1945, half of new investment has gone into

your products, not subject to the market nor even to Congressional check. This year, 86 percent of money for research is for your arms and rockets. You push through the colossally useless Super-Sonic Transport. At least 20 percent of the economy is directly dependent on your enterprises. The profits and salaries of these enterprises are not normally distributed but go heavily to certain groups while others are excluded to the point of being out-caste. Your system is a major factor in producing the riots in Newark. [*At this remark there were indignant protests.*]

Some regions of the country are heavily favored—especially Pasadena and Dallas—and others disadvantaged. Public goods have been neglected. A disproportionate share of brains has been drained from more useful invention and development. And worst of all, you have enthusiastically supported an essentially mercantilist economics that measures economic health in terms of abstract Gross National Product and rate of growth, instead of concrete human well-being. Both domestically and internationally, you have been the bellwether of meaningless expansion, and this has sharpened poverty in our own slums and rural regions and for the majority of mankind. It has been argued that military expenditure, precisely because it is isolated and wasteful, is a stabilizer of an economy, providing employment and investment opportunities when necessary; but your unbridled expansion has been the chief factor of social instability.

Dramatically intervening in education, you have again disrupted the normal structure. Great universities have come to be financed largely for your programs. Faculties have become unbalanced; your kind of people do not fit into the community of scholars. The wandering dialogue of science with the unknown is straitjacketed for petty military projects. You have been mentioning the need for personal creativity, but this is not to listen to the Creator Spirit for ideas, but to harness it to your ideas. This is blasphemous. There has been secrecy, which is intolerable to true academics and scientists. The political, and morally dubious co-opting of science, engineering, and social science has disgusted and alienated many of the best students. Further, you have warped the method of education, beginning with the primary grades. Your need for narrowly expert personnel has led to processing the young to be test-passers, with a gross exaggeration of credits and grading. You have used the wealth of public and parents to train apprentices for yourselves. Your electronics companies have gone into the "education industries" and tried to palm off teaching machines, audiovisual aids, and programmed lessons in excess of the evidence for their utility. But the educational requirements of our society in the foreseeable future demand a very different spirit and method. Rather than processing the young, the problem is how to help the young grow up free and inventive in a highly scientific and socially complicated world. We do not need professional personnel so much as autonomous professionals who can criticize the programs handed to them and be ethically responsible. Do you encourage criticism of your programs by either the subsidized professors or the students? [*At this, Mr. Charles Herzfeld, the chairman of the session, shouted "Yes!" and there was loud applause for the interruption, yet I doubt that there is much such encouragement.*] We need fewer lessons and tests, and there ought to be much less necessity and prestige attached to mandarin requirements.

Let us turn to urbanism. *Prima facie*, there are parts of urban planning—construction, depollution, the logistics of transportation—where your talents ought to be peculiarly useful. Unfortunately, it is your companies who have oversold the planes and the cars, polluted the air and water, and balked at even trivial remedies, so that I do not see how you can be morally trusted with the job. The chief present and future problems in this field, however, are of a different kind. They are two. The long-range problem is to diminish the urbanization and suburban sprawl altogether, for they are economically unviable and socially harmful. For this, the most direct means, and the one I favor, is to cut down rural emigration and encourage rural return, by means of rural reconstruction and regional cultural development. The aim should be a 20 percent rural ratio instead of the present 5 percent. This is an aspect of using high technology for simplification, increasing real goods but probably diminishing the Gross National Product measured in cash. Such a program is not for you. Your thinking is never to simplify and retrench, but always to devise new equipment to alleviate the mess that you have helped to make with your previous equipment.

Secondly, the immediately urgent urban problem is how to diminish powerlessness, anomie, alienation, and mental disease. For this the best strategy is to decentralize urban administration, in policing, schooling, social welfare, neighborhood renewal, and real-estate and business ownership. Such community development often requires heightening conflict and risking technical inefficiency for intangible gains of initiative and solidarity. This also is obviously not your style. You want to concentrate capital and power. Your systems analyses of social problems always tend toward standardization, centralization, and bureaucratic control, although these are not necessary in the method. You do not like to feed your computers indefinite factors and unknown parameters where spirit, spite, enthusiasm, revenge, invention, etc., will make the difference. To be frank, your programs are usually grounded in puerile theories of social psychology, political science, and moral philosophy. There is a great need for research and trying out in this field, but the likely cast of characters might be small farmers, Negro matriarchs, political activists, long-haired students, and assorted sages. Not you. Let's face it. You are essentially producers of exquisite hardware and good at the logistics of moving objects around, but mostly with the crude aim of destroying things rather than reconstructing or creating anything, which is a harder task. Yet you boldly enter into fields like penology, pedagogy, hospital management, domestic architecture, and planning the next decade—wherever there is a likely budget.

I will use the last heading, improving the quality of man's environment, as a catch-all for some general remarks. In a society that is cluttered, overcentralized and overadministered, we should aim at simplification, decentralization, and decontrol. These require highly sophisticated research to determine where, how, and how much. Further, for the first time in history, the scale of the artificial and technological has dwarfed the natural landscape. In prudence, we must begin to think of a principled limitation on artifice and to cut back on some of our present gigantic impositions, if only to insure that we do not commit some terrible ecological blunder. But as Dr. Smelt of Lockheed explained to us yesterday, it is the genius of American technology to go very rapidly from R & D to application; in this context, he said, prudence is not a virtue. A particular case is automation: which human functions should be computerized or automated, which should not? This question—it is both an analytic and an empirical one—ought to be critical in the next decade, but I would not trust IBM salesmen to solve it. Another problem is how man can feel free and at home within the technological environment itself. For instance, comprehending a machine and being able to repair it is one thing; being a mere user and in bondage to service systems is another. Also, to feel free, a man must have a rather strong say in the close environment that he must deal with. But these requirements of a technology are not taken into account by you. Despite Dr. Smelt, technology *is* a branch of moral philosophy, subordinate to criteria like prudence, modesty, safety, amenity, flexibility, cheapness, easy comprehension, repairability and so forth. If such moral criteria became paramount in the work of technologists, the quality of the environment would be more livable.

Still a further problem is how to raise the scientific and technical culture of the whole people, and here your imperialistic grab of the R & D money and of the system of education has done immeasurable damage. You have seen to it that the lion's share has gone to your few giant firms and a few giant universities, although in fact very many, perhaps more than half of, important innovations still come from independents and tiny firms. I was pleased that Dr. Dessauer of Xerox pointed this out this morning. If the money were distributed more widely, there would probably be more discovery and invention, and what is more important, there would be a larger pool of scientific and competent people. You make a fanfare about the spinoff of a few socially useful items, but your whole enterprise is notoriously wasteful—for instance, five billions go down the drain when after a couple of years you change the design of a submarine, sorry about that. When you talk about spinoff, you people remind me of the TV networks who, after twenty years of nothing, boast that they did broadcast the McCarthy hearings and the Kennedy funeral. [*This remark led to free and friendly laughter; I do not know whether at the other industry or at their own hoax.*] Finally, concentrating the grants, you narrow the field of discovery and innovation, creating an illusion of technological determinism, as if we *had* to develop in a certain style. But if we had put our brains and money into electric cars, we would now have electric cars; if we had concentrated on intensive agriculture, we would now find that this is the most efficient, and so forth. And in grabbing the funds, you are not even honest; 90 percent of the R & D money goes in fact to shaping up for production, which as entrepreneurs you should pay out of your own pockets.

No doubt some of these remarks have been unfair and ignorant. [*Frantic applause.*] By and large they are undeniable, and I have not been picking nits.

These remarks have certainly been harsh and moralistic. We are none of us saints, and ordinarily I would be ashamed to use such a tone. But you are the manufacturers of napalm, fragmentation bombs, the planes that destroy rice. Your weapons have killed hundreds of thousands in Vietnam and you will kill other hundreds of thousands in other Vietnams. I am sure that most of you would concede that much of what you do is ugly and harmful, at home and abroad. But you would say that it is necessary for the American way of life, at home and abroad, and therefore you cannot do otherwise. Since we believe, however, that that way of life itself is unnecessary, ugly, and un-American [*Shouts of "Who are we?"*]—we are I and those people outside—we cannot condone your present operations; they should be wiped off the slate.

[Most of the 300 in the audience did not applaud these remarks, but there was quite strong applause from a couple of dozen. Afterward these sought me out singly and explained, "Thanks for having the courage" or more significantly, "Those kids outside are right. My son is doing the same thing in Boston—Ohio State—etc."

The chairman of the session, Charles Herzfeld of ITT, felt obliged to exclaim, "The remark about our committing genocide in Vietnam is obscene. He does not say what is really intolerable there, the Viet Cong single out college graduates for extermination."!!

*More poignantly, the director of the symposium, a courteous
and intelligent man, apologized to the gathering for having
exposed them to me, which must have been a wrench for him to
say. He had of course seen my text beforehand.*

*We went out by the exit onto the other avenue, and I was able
to rejoin the more amiable company of the young people, who were
now sitting with their backs pressed against the auditorium doors,
still among the white helmets. I answered their questions about
the proceedings and we dispersed. That night* NBC-TV *showed a
picture of the pickets, and next morning I got a story in the* Post.]

Where is it at? Unquestionably the week of Resistance demonstrations was successful and made its point, that thousands
and probably tens of thousands are now willing to go to jail or
get their heads broken to stop the Vietnam war. There were no
disappointments: Turning in the draft-cards, resistance at the
induction centers and staging areas and against the Dow and
Navy recruiters, the crowd in Washington and the melee at the
Pentagon, all proved strong enough.

We are witnessing a test of legitimacy, and in my opinion the
government position is now untenable. Despite a few exotic slogans, there is a groundswell of American populism, including
sporadic populist violence as in 1890 or 1933, but mainly solidly
secure in the belief that it is itself the democratic voice and LBJ
is a usurper. As was not reported in the press, the night vigil
on the Pentagon steps on October 22 sang "The Star-Spangled
Banner." It was probably a mistake for the President to have
exposed so many troops to the young resisters who were mostly
peaceful but obviously spunky and sometimes persuasive.

The climate is beginning to feel like the eve of the French
withdrawal from Algeria, including the same coalition of the
young, the intellectuals, and the Algerians (Negroes). The
question remains, is the American structure so rich and tech-
nologically powerful that its government can dispense with
legitimacy? I don't know. And while the NLF and the North
Vietnamese have been hanging on and continuing to counter-
attack (and their people and our people are dying), American
opinion has finally begun to veer sharply toward getting out.
The hawk spokesmen have become divided and confused.

There is a persistent rumor in Washington that the President (or the hidden government) is about to cast the die and approve the prepared invasion of North Vietnam in December. If so, a hundred thousand youth and many many others will resist non-violently or violently and there will be martial law and concentration camps. I will not speculate further along this atomic line.

But there is evidence that shrewder counsel might prevail; to write off this odious war, adopt a somewhat less adventurous foreign policy, put a little more money into the cities, divert some of the military-industrial enterprise into Outer Space and "long-range planning," and come to a solid understanding with the Russians. I think this is the meaning of the rapidly increasing dovishness in Congress and the sudden conversion of the Republicans who threaten to nominate Percy or Gavin. The strategy is similar to the New Deal: when the going gets too rough domestically, accommodate and go on to build a grander corporate structure that is, in some respects, better—temporarily. For this plan, however, Johnson would have to go, since it now seems impossible for him to sound a retreat from Vietnam without getting shot by the irate father of a young man who died in vain. Whether we would then get Robert Kennedy or a moderate Republican is probably unimportant.

Needless to say, this is not the outcome that the radical young are after. They fear, justifiedly, that if we stop the war, most of the Americans will again fall morally and politically asleep. Yet they, like the rest of us, do want to stop the Vietnam war; there are few indeed who are so fanatical for world upheaval as to want that particular evil to continue so that good may come . . . This is not the stuff of new humanism. For instance, those who objected to being processed at Berkeley will have to think seriously about Chairman Mao's little red book. And those who want to make love not war but who also want to imitate Che Guevara in American cities, must ask themselves what adequate guerrilla tactics would be in a high technology, namely to poison the water, wreck the subways, and cause power failures in New York and Chicago; is this what they intend?

But I do not think the young themselves will fall asleep. They have been through remarkable experiences and have found one another. There is the potentiality of a kind of youth international. Most important, the present power-systems of the world are indeed unfit for modern conditions, and this will become increasingly apparent. If the young continue to be in conflict, to try out innovations, and to study professionally what ought to be done with our technology and ecology, mores and authority-structure, and the fact of one world, they will gradually shape for themselves a good inheritance to come into. Considering the tremendous power and complexity of the systems they want to displace, twenty years is a short time to devise something better.

NORMAN MAILER

No account of a protest known to me is as capacious and engaging as Norman Mailer's account of the October 1967 March on the Pentagon, in *The Armies of the Night: History as a Novel, the Novel as History* (1968). Whatever prejudices and egotisms Mailer is possessed by—and he is possessed by many—he is interested in absolutely everything and tenacious in setting it all down. The excerpts included here show him at his best: as a camera-like observer of the costumes and styles of the marchers, and as a reluctant but therefore all the more convincing admirer of the most extreme pacifists participating in the march, in whose hunger strike while in prison Mailer (1923–2007) sees both heroism and redemption.

Mailer grew up in Brooklyn, went to Harvard, and was drafted for service in World War II, working chiefly as a cook but seeing enough at first hand to write *The Naked and the Dead*, published in 1948, his first novel and arguably his best; it figured on the *New York Times* bestseller list for sixty-two weeks. His subsequent novels met with mixed reactions, but he was indisputably successful as a journalist. He cofounded the *Village Voice*, made a sensation with his 1957 essay "The White Negro," and began to explore the innovative forms and approaches that became what we now call the New Journalism; *Armies of the Night* is the greatest work in that genre, and won both a National Book Award and a Pulitzer Prize.

Mailer's later career is harder to summarize; each book feels like a new beginning and a new form, from *Marilyn: A Biography* (1973), to *The Executioner's Song* (1979), an account of the murderer Gary Gilmore, to *Ancient Evenings* (1983), set during the reign of Rameses II, to the 1,300-page *Harlot's Ghost* (1991), which explores the history of the CIA. He directed films, staged plays, and acted in films. In 1969 he ran for mayor of New York, coming in fourth of five candidates in the Democratic primary.

FROM

The Armies of the Night

THE trumpet sounded again. It was calling the troops. "Come here," it called from the steps of Lincoln Memorial over the two furlongs of the long reflecting pool, out to the swell of the hill at the base of Washington Monument, "come here, come here, come here. The rally is on!" And from the north and the east,

from the direction of the White House and the Smithsonian
and the Capitol, from Union Station and the Department of
Justice the troops were coming in, the volunteers were answering the call. They came walking up in all sizes, a citizens' army
not ranked yet by height, an army of both sexes in numbers
almost equal, and of all ages, although most were young. Some
were well-dressed, some were poor, many were conventional in
appearance, as often were not. The hippies were there in great
number, perambulating down the hill, many dressed like the
legions of Sgt. Pepper's Band, some were gotten up like Arab
sheiks, or in Park Avenue doormen's greatcoats, others like
Rogers and Clark of the West, Wyatt Earp, Kit Carson, Daniel
Boone in buckskin, some had grown mustaches to look like
Have Gun, Will Travel—Paladin's surrogate was here!—and
wild Indians with feathers, a hippie gotten up like Batman,
another like Claude Rains in *The Invisible Man*—his face
wrapped in a turban of bandages and he wore a black satin top
hat. A host of these troops wore capes, beat-up khaki capes,
slept on, used as blankets, towels, improvised duffel bags; or
fine capes, orange linings, or luminous rose linings, the edges
ragged, near a tatter, the threads ready to feather, but a mus-
keteer's hat on their head. One hippie may have been dressed
like Charles Chaplin; Buster Keaton and W. C. Fields could
have come to the ball; there were Martians and Moon-men
and a knight unhorsed who stalked about in the weight of real
armor. There were to be seen a hundred soldiers in Confederate
gray, and maybe there were two or three hundred hippies in
officer's coats of Union dark-blue. They had picked up their
costumes where they could, in surplus stores, and Blow-your-
mind shops, Digger free emporiums, and psychedelic caches of
Hindu junk. There were soldiers in Foreign Legion uniforms,
and tropical bush jackets, San Quentin and Chino, California
striped shirt and pants, British copies of Eisenhower jackets,
hippies dressed like Turkish shepherds and Roman senators,
gurus, and samurai in dirty smocks. They were close to being
assembled from all the intersections between history and the
comic books, between legend and television, the Biblical arche-
types and the movies. The sight of these troops, this army with
a thousand costumes, fulfilled to the hilt our General's oldest
idea of war which is that every man should dress as he pleases

if he is going into battle, for that is his right, and variety never hurts the zest of the hardiest workers in every battalion (here today by thousands in plaid hunting jackets, corduroys or dungarees, ready for assault!) if the sight of such masquerade lost its usual unhappy connotation of masked ladies and starving children outside the ball, it was not only because of the shabbiness of the costumes (up close half of them must have been used by hippies for everyday wear) but also because the aesthetic at last was in the politics—the dress ball was going into battle. Still, there were nightmares beneath the gaiety of these middle-class runaways, these Crusaders, going out to attack the hard core of technology land with less training than armies were once offered by a medieval assembly ground. The nightmare was in the echo of those trips which had fractured their sense of past and present. If nature was a veil whose tissue had been ripped by static, screams of jet motors, the highway grid of the suburbs, smog, defoliation, pollution of streams, over-fertilization of earth, anti-fertilization of women, and the radiation of two decades of near blind atom busting, then perhaps the history of the past was another tissue, spiritual, no doubt, without physical embodiment, unless its embodiment was in the cuneiform hieroglyphics of the chromosome (so much like primitive writing!) but that tissue of past history, whether traceable in the flesh, or merely palpable in the collective underworld of the dream, was nonetheless being bombed by the use of LSD as outrageously as the atoll of Eniwetok, Hiroshima, Nagasaki, and the scorched foliage of Vietnam. The history of the past was being exploded right into the present: perhaps there were now lacunae in the firmament of the past, holes where once had been the psychic reality of an era which was gone. Mailer was haunted by the nightmare that the evils of the present not only exploited the present, but consumed the past, and gave every promise of demolishing whole territories of the future. The same villains who, promiscuously, wantonly, heedlessly, had gorged on LSD and consumed God knows what essential marrows of history, wearing indeed the history of all eras on their back as trophies of this gluttony, were now going forth (conscience-struck?) to make war on those other villains, corporation-land villains, who were destroying the promise of the present in their self-righteousness and greed and secret lust (often unknown to themselves) for some sexo-technological variety of neo-fascism.

Mailer's final allegiance, however, was with the villains who were hippies. They would never have looked to blow their minds and destroy some part of the past if the authority had not brainwashed the mood of the present until it smelled like deodorant. (To cover the odor of burning flesh in Vietnam?) So he continued to enjoy the play of costumes, but his pleasure was now edged with a hint of the sinister. Not inappropriate for battle. He and Lowell were still in the best of moods. The morning was so splendid—it spoke of a vitality in nature which no number of bombings in space nor inner-space might ever subdue; the rustle of costumes warming up for the war spoke of future redemptions as quickly as they reminded of hog-swillings from the past, and the thin air! wine of Civil War apples in the October air! edge of excitement and awe—how would this day end? No one could know. Incredible spectacle now gathering—tens of thousands traveling hundreds of miles to attend a symbolic battle. In the capital of technology land beat a primitive drum. New drum of the Left! And the Left had been until this year the secret unwitting accomplice of every increase in the power of the technicians, bureaucrats, and labor leaders who ran the governmental military-industrial complex of super-technology land.

WHEN the count was made, there proved to be one thousand arrests. It was not a small number; it was not an enormous number—it was certainly a respectable number to be arrested over thirty-two hours in protest of a war. Six hundred had charges pressed. The others were taken to the back of the Pentagon, photographed, and driven away in buses to be released on the street. Of the six hundred arrested, no felony charges for assault were brought in, indeed only a dozen were charged with assault, only two went to trial, and both were acquitted.

Yes, the end seemed to have come, and the immediate beneficiary of the March could be nobody other than the President of the United States. Lyndon Johnson made a point to have his picture taken Saturday sitting at a table on the White House lawn with Hubert Humphrey, Dean Rusk, and Orville Free-man. The caption informed that he had spent the day in work. Headlines on Monday: "LBJ Hits Peaceniks." He had sent a memorandum to Defense Secretary McNamara and Attorney General Clark. "I know that all Americans share my pride in the man in uniform and the civilian law enforcement person-nel for their outstanding performance in the nation's capital during the last two days. They performed with restraint, firm-ness and professional skill. Their actions stand in sharp contrast to the irresponsible acts of violence and lawlessness by many of the demonstrators."

The press was, in the aftermath, antagonistic to the March. Some measure of the condemnation and the abuse can be indi-cated by quoting Reston of the *Times* who was not immoderate in his reaction. Nor untypical.

> It is difficult to report publicly the ugly and vulgar provocation of many of the militants. They spat on some of the soldiers in the front line at the Pentagon and goaded them with the most vicious personal slander.
>
> Many of the signs carried by a small number of the militants, and many of the lines in the theatrical performances put on by the hippies, are too obscene to print. In view of this underside of the protest, many officials here are surprised that there was not much more violence.

The rest of the stories went about that way.

Emphasis was put on every rock thrown, and a count was made of the windows broken. (There were, however, only a few.) But there was no specific mention of The Wedge. Indeed, stories quickly disappeared. No features nor follow-up a few days later. In six weeks, when an attempt was made in New York to close down the draft induction centers, it seemed that public sentiment had turned sharply against resistance. The Negro riots had made the nation afraid of lawlessness. Lyndon Johnson stood ten percentage points higher in the popularity polls—he had ridden the wave of revulsion in America against demonstrators who spit in the face of U.S. troops—when it came to sensing new waves of public opinion, LBJ was the legendary surfboarder of them all.

It probably did not matter. Ever since he had been in office, the popularity of LBJ had kept going up on the basis of his ability to ride every favorable wave, and had kept going down on the unwillingness of the war in Vietnam to fulfill the promises his Administration was making. So his popularity would go up and down again. There would be many to hope it did not go up in the last week before election. In the demonstrations in New York in December against the draft centers, Teague was arrested for carrying a knife—to anyone who had listened to his verbal militancy in jail it seemed altogether likely that a knife was not his weapon, and he had been framed. And a month later, Dr. Spock, and Coffin, and Marcus Raskin, and Michael Ferber, and Mitch Goodman were indicted by a grand jury for advocating resistance to the draft law. Such advocacy was a felony—their sentences, if guilty, could run to five years.

Mitch Goodman called a meeting at Town Hall. Five hundred and sixty people (including Allen Ginsberg, Noam Chomsky, and Mailer) signed statements implicating themselves legally to aid and abet draft resisters. Macdonald, Lowell, and Paul Goodman had already signed such statements. They could now all receive the same sentence. So the weekend in Washington which had begun with a phone call from Mitch Goodman gave promise of ending in Harrisburg or Leavenworth.

But probably it was in Occoquan and the jail in Washington, D.C., that the March ended. In the week following, prisoners who had chosen to remain, refused in many ways to cooperate, obstructed prison work, went on strikes. Some were put in solitary. A group from the Quaker Farm in Voluntown, Connecticut, practiced noncooperation in prison. Among them were veterans of a sleep-in of twenty pacifists at the Pentagon in the spring before. Now, led by Gary Rader, Erica Enzer, Irene Johnson, and Suzanne Moore, some of them refused to eat or drink and were fed intravenously. Several men at the D.C. jail would not wear prison clothing. Stripped of their own, naked, they were thrown in the Hole. There they lived in cells so small that not all could lie down at once to sleep. For a day they lay naked on the floor, for many days naked with blankets and mattress on the floor. For many days they did not eat nor drink water. Dehydration brought them near to madness.

Here was the last of the rite of passage, "the chinook salmon . . . nosing up the impossible stone," here was the thin source of the stream—these naked Quakers on the cold floor of a dark isolation cell in D.C. jail, wandering down the hours in the fever of dehydration, the cells of the brain contracting to the crystals of their thought, essence of one thought so close to the essence of another—all separations of water gone—that madness is near, madness can now be no more than the acceleration of thought.

Did they pray, these Quakers, for forgiveness of the nation? Did they pray with tears in their eyes in those blind cells with visions of a long column of Vietnamese dead, Vietnamese walking a column of flame, eyes on fire, nose on fire, mouth speaking flame, did they pray, "O Lord, forgive our people for they do not know, O Lord, find a little forgiveness for America in the puny reaches of our small suffering, O Lord, let these hours count on the scale as some small penance for the sins of the nation, let this great nation crying in the flame of its own gangrene be absolved for one tithe of its great sins by the penance of these minutes, O Lord, bring more suffering upon me that the sins of our soldiers in Vietnam be not utterly unforgiven—they are too young to be damned forever."

The prayers are as Catholic as they are Quaker, and no one will know if they were ever made, for the men who might have made them were perhaps too far out on fever and shivering and thirst to recollect, and there are places no history can reach. But if the end of the March took place in the isolation in which these last pacifists suffered naked in freezing cells, and gave up prayers for penance, then who was to say they were not saints? And who to say that the sins of America were not by their witness a tithe remitted?

CONTRIBUTORS TO
WIN MAGAZINE

That iconic photograph of the lone protester placing a flower into the barrel of a military policeman's rifle at the March on the Pentagon? At least two photographers took images that day—October 21, 1967—that have since become famous, Bernie Boston of George Edgerly Harris III, a young actor who subsequently died of AIDS, and Marc Riboud of Jan Rose Kasmir, who later carried her celebrated picture in protests against the Gulf War. It takes many such acts and many such people to make a movement.

Recognizing that it would be "impossible to report in full" on the events of "a demonstration involving 150,000 people and a demonstration that took place in many places at once," the editors of *WIN Magazine* decided to cover the march, in un-Mailerish, collective fashion, with a collage of short sketches by multiple contributors, all of them affiliated in various ways with the New York Workshop in Nonviolence, a pacifist direct-action group associated with the War Resisters League, and the publisher of *WIN*. The writers are, in alphabetical order, Maris Cakars (1942–1992), Marty Jezer (1940–2005), Paul Johnson (1935–2006), Susan Kent (b. 1942), Dorothy Lane, Jackson Mac Low (1922–2004), and Allan Solomonow (b. 1937)—some of them notable in their subsequent activist or literary careers, others having left few clear traces of themselves in the historical record.

FROM
Mobilization! Oct. 21

"WE will enter the Pentagon and sit down in offices, in meeting rooms, and across hallways. If this seems impossible, we will block doorways and entrances. If police and armed forces make this impossible, we will clog service roads, preventing deliveries and obstructing vehicles."

This was the plan of the National Mobilization Committee's Direct Action Committee. The response of the government was to call out a total of 8,500 soldiers—military police and members of the 82nd Airborne Division who had seen action in Vietnam, the Dominican Republic and Detroit—to protect the Pentagon. It was the first time since 1932, when Herbert

Hoover called in 1,000 cavalry and infantrymen under Douglas MacArthur to put down the Bonus March, that federal troops were called to the nation's capital. But the troops were only the most dramatic aspect of the hard position that the government had taken towards the peace demonstration. In negotiations for the permit necessary to hold the march and rally, the government at first announced that no permits would be granted unless the Mobilization Committee publicly renounced plans for civil disobedience. When it became clear that the Mobilization would not do that, the government, in the person of Henry Van Cleve, General Counsel for the General Services Administration and chief government negotiator, changed its position. Nevertheless, it categorically denied the Mobilization the use of more than one bridge to get from Washington to the Pentagon, permission to picket the building in any more than one area, access to the picketing of "activity" area except during very limited hours, a march route wide enough to enable the march to reach the Pentagon in a reasonably short amount of time, and the area for a rally that the Mobilization considered most suitable.

To a certain extent the precautions on the part of the government must have been the result of the rumors of violence that circulated widely prior to the demonstration. The New York based "Revolutionary Contingent" had circulated a leaflet calling on everyone to participate in a snake dance that it would hold at the Pentagon. There were reports of groups planning to bring lead pipes for "self defense." The hippies, it was said, were planning to come with water pistols. And then there was the memory of Newark and Detroit.

Against this backdrop, some 150,000 Americans arrived in Washington on October 21 to demonstrate their repugnance for the war in Vietnam. They came to hear speeches made by Dr. Spock, Lincoln Lynch, Clive Jenkins of the British Labor Party, and many others. They came to exorcise the Pentagon and "do their thing." They came to shut down the Pentagon.

—MARIS CAKARS

*   *   *

DR. Spock named Lyndon "the real enemy," Dagmar Wilson was understood to say we won't have peace as long as Dean Rusk is alive, and John Wilson of SNCC called for silence in the memory of Che Guevara. But otherwise, it was the same old rally. Perfect weather, pleasant surroundings, nobody really listening. People were courteous—amazingly so, as newcomers to the movement often remark—and for the most part, patient throughout all delays.

We played the two most popular games at rallies: looking out for old friends, and spotting new signs. Among the original slogans I saw were "Remember the Bastille" and "Beat LBJ into a Ploughshare." Another stunner, held by a husky type I took at first for a counter-demonstrator, said "Shoot a Curl, Not a Vietnamese North Wing Surf Club for Peace."

We talked about the small numbers of both blacks and hippies present, and wondered whether this weekend would come to be looked upon as the end of the peace movement's illusions about gaining substantial support from either group. Phil Ochs and Peter, Paul and Mary were very nice, but there was a lot of disappointment when the rock groups never appeared.

—PAUL JOHNSON

*   *   *

THERE were many levels—grassy embankments and stone steps, psychological levels, symbolic levels—which lay between the happening at the reflecting pool and the happenings at the Pentagon. The gathering together was pleasant and color-ful, but impatience was greater than on the other October, March and April days, because we had someplace to go. The march, this time, was not so much for the march itself as to get where we were going, even though it seemed unclear to everyone just what we would do when we got there or what they would do when we got there. Our pace quickened as we approached and passed the mounds of freshly turned earth around new wooden poles supporting the fence with its double row of barbed wire at the top. (How frightened they must have been!) At the parking lot, when the first choice was made in response to a loudspeaker announcement, "Those who want to attend the rally, stay here; those who wish to sit in at the Pentagon, turn right," the vector led toward the right. At the first embankment, a team helped others up and urged them on over the slippery grass, over the trampled fence and into the next decision stage. There, some people were asking each other how they'd arrived in the place and why, but the area was getting crowded and we had further to go: between some other bushes and into another unknown.

It proved to be a vast lawn, filled with people and trees and people in the trees. Friends were there and the yellow submarine and the pacifist section marker "D." We looked over and saw masses of people and thought, at first, that they were the later marchers, outside and beyond, still converging on the parking lot. They were converging still, but these masses were already inside the broken fence, already trespassers. Some were leaning over the wall above. A wave on the left broke through the guards on the ramp and we rushed up to join the "storming of the gates," but the heavy guard reformed. From behind, "break through, let's go . . ." and from the front, "don't push, let's not stampede ourselves . . ." We moved over to the edge to escape the crush and found an easy path up through some shrubbery behind the troops. It led to the last level, next to the Pentagon.

—DOROTHY LANE

*   *   *

THE head of the march arrived in the Pentagon's North Parking Area about 3:30. The scheduled departure from Lincoln Memorial had been delayed in order to give the General Services Administration extra time to remove a fence separating the North Parking Area from the Mall. Only a small portion of the fence was removed so, half an hour late and equipped with ten wire cutters, the march stepped off. The marshals had their hands full. Trained by Cordell Reagan, one of the original Freedom Singers and the chief marshal of the Meredith March and other civil rights demonstrations, they struggled with the press, obstructionist Nazis, and Josef Mrotz-Mroz, the eternal counter-picket.

By 4:00, when the second rally was starting, perhaps a thousand people had already gone over to the Mall, tearing down a good deal of the fence as they went. Donald Duncan, Carl Davidson and others spoke at the rally, but all attention was focused on the steps to the Mall entrance to the Pentagon. Even as the speakers spoke, people kept streaming over to what was called in the permit the "Post–North Parking Rally Activity Area." By 4:30 the leaders—Dellinger, Spock, Robert Lowell, Dwight MacDonald, Father Rice—were ready to lead the civil disobedience. They walked in a group to the Mall and found the steps to the entrance packed with people. So, in order to encourage blocking doors on the other four sides of the building, they went up on Washington Boulevard, the highway running along the west side of the Mall and the Pentagon, and attempted to get to the heliport side. As they advanced, a line of soldiers stationed across the highway began to advance. The notables and the fifty or so people acompanying them, myself included, sat down. Only Dellinger remained standing and, bullhorn in hand he addressed the troops. Then Noam Chomsky of MIT took his turn, but as he was speaking the troops once more advanced. Robot-like they came forward, one slow step after another until they were almost on top of the seated pacifists. Then a remarkable thing happened. They advanced right over and around us. Stepping carefully to avoid hurting anyone they passed right through the crowd and went right on down the highway. Chomsky turned to follow and now the whole group was following the troops, going away from the Pentagon. After a minute or two we reversed ourselves and began marching back towards our original destination. Again we were confronted by a line of soldiers, again we sat down. The second line was not so gentle. After advancing to the point where it was stepping on people, it turned over the job of making arrests to the U.S. marshals who, with a little more force than necessary, proceeded to do their job. (U.S. marshals had been assigned the task of making arrests and made virtually all of them that week-end.) They took people off in three ways, but left Spock, MacDonald, Lowell and Rice. Even the military is sensitive.

Had anyone else been arrested at this point, it would have been an irrelevant action. As it was, the demonstrators were deprived of some of their leadership. Not that these were the only leaders, or that leadership was so badly needed; but given the size of the crowd, if leaders were to lead there had to be many of them. As it turned out, the people hardly needed leaders, but they thought they did, and their absence contributed to a general feeling of insecurity and lack of definition in the situation.

—M. C.

*   *   *

A BLAND-FACED marshal moves his club across my throat as I step directly in front of him. I point out to him that we mean no violence and we will commit no violence; perhaps I suggest that he can accomplish his purpose as easily by putting the club across my chest. Something flies out of the crowd barely missing the back troops so Val Green of FOR and I help form a line of persons directly between the marshals and the crowd. The next marshal over puts his club to my chest when I move against him: they will not arrest me and I cannot get through without being violent.

To the left, cheers are raised as a stream of protestors head to the corner entrance. Not a soldier from those in front of us runs over. There are cries as the troops pour in front of them; a Negro and a young girl climb underneath the flatbed truck separating our groups. Both are bloody. Another fellow with a camera comes out from under the truck but beyond the marshals' line; a marshal begins to club him while he is on his hands and knees; the marshal in front of me edges into this marshal, throwing him off balance and giving the kid a chance to get free; the marshal I had been facing winks and offers me a mint.

—ALLAN SOLOMONOW

SUDDENLY there were cries from the top of the stairs. We grabbed hands and ran back, hearing rumours that an MP had defected. What excitement, we left just as the most important event occurred. Everyone was shouting Join us, Join us. We could not make it up one stairway so tried the other side, and got right to the front by the press trucks. Later, there were other reports of another, then another defector.

We sat down again cold and hungry. Soon contingents from the outside were bringing food. At first, there was little, so a sandwich was passed around for everyone to have a bite. But after the sandwich came another and some pretzels, and cookies, and peanut butter, crackers, and an apple, and a clark bar. We thought it the height of luxury when a beer was passed round. But then came home-made cookies and a huge blue tin of cookies and whole balonies and loaves of bread. Someone said they wanted an egg salad sandwich, and a plastic container of egg salad came by. Soon everyone was full and rejecting the food. Earlier, joints had been passed around. The parking lot of the Pentagon, safest place in the world to turn on.

—SUSAN KENT

*   *   *

UP among the demonstrators everyone seemed to be giving orders over bullhorns. EVERYONE WHO HAS A BULL-HORN BECOMES A POLICY-MAKER. Those with better bullhorns were paid more attention. One seemed to be controlled mostly by SDS people. Theirs was much better than that of the pro-NLF committee, but these people had their flags up on the large flat truck that was parked to the left of the upper platform. Most of the night a lone anarchist stood holding a black flag directly over the line of troops beside the truck.

It was during a relatively quiescent period (as I remember it) that the MP's all put on gas masks. Only individuals had been rushing between the MP's from time to time, most of them being dragged back to the other side by the MP's, roughly but not with bloody violence. One soldier or MP was moving back & forth (after the gas masks had been put on) with a gun that looked like a contrabass bassoon. Then, without warning, one tear gas shell burst with a dull thud among the crowd in front of the MP's. Most of the crowd retreated a little way back from the line of MP's, but a scarf across my nose seemed sufficient to avoid anything except a slight burning sensation in the nasal passages—at least, this was my experience. Many around me were coughing, choking, their eyes were tearing copiously, however. I don't know whether this was because they'd been nearer to the original burst (it didn't seem much more than 10 feet away from me). Crowd surges took place several more times, but the tear gas shells seemed to be set off in the quiescent periods (at least twice more) and not when the movement of the crowd up to the MP's was strong. . . .

—JACKSON MAC LOW

*   *   *

A SORT of speakers' stand is operating now (after 2:00 A.M.) on the top of the parapet between the two levels. Greg Calvert of SDS speaks over the bullhorn: "We're boxed in again. This is all a failure? Perhaps but it's still beautiful. We've desanctified this institution." (then, addressing the government leaders:) "The troops you employ belong to us and not to you. They don't belong to the generals. They belong to a new hope for America that those generals never could participate in. The real enemy is not here (the troops) but there (the generals etc.)—not those who take orders but those who give orders"—then suddenly: "WHO IS THAT BEING BROUGHT IN ON A STRETCHER—IS HE ALIVE OR DEAD???"

Now on the right bullhorn, Sidney Peck saying that "we're the soldiers' brothers. Let's show the troops that if we have the option of accepting arrest, we'll accept it." Asks for some people in authority: I don't get the names.

A boy on the left parapet cries out that they just hit a girl. That it was horrible. Covers eyes. Someone else on another bullhorn addresses troops: "When you go home tonight, think about this. Why does a man with a gun hit someone who is doing nothing?" Orion and the moon are bright overhead. . . .

—J. M. L.

*   *   *

BY now the tension was very high. The police were inching forward crowding us back. On the speakers we were being told to link arms and crowd close together. And sit down. Behind us at the edge of the steps many were standing and throwing things at the MPs in spite of protests from all of us.

At this point some girl got on the bullhorn and said it was dangerous and everyone should leave and gather around the fire. We all shouted, "No!" Bob Greenblatt, national coordinator of the Mobilization, got on and said those in the front wanted to leave and were all being prevented by the militants standing at the rear. We all shouted, "No!" And we stayed, but all felt our "leadership" had sold us out. Instead of supporting us, it helped cause mass desertions.

Using typical military strategy, the MPs were pushing hardest in the middle to divide the group in two. There would be a noise from the middle, the press would turn their lights on the area, while we all had a good view of MPs kicking the seated and intertwined demonstrators. It was not always clear what the demonstrators were doing, because they were now on the ground, but they certainly were not given a chance to be violent if they wanted to, as feet kicked and billy clubs and rifle butts were smashed into people's heads. It was terrifying to watch people who were only sitting there being beaten badly and carried out with concussions and broken bones. Many of the people sitting got up and ran. Those standing threw things. Those of us sitting bunched closer together, and sang softly, We shall overcome, We shall live in peace, We are not afraid, Soldiers are our friends, Kumbaya, my Lord, Kumbaya. . . . We talked with the soldiers in front of us, looking at them pleadingly: "You don't want to hurt us, will you do that, will you have to, please don't hurt us, arrest us, but don't hurt us, we mean no harm to you. . . ."

In the middle people were slowly being beaten and removed from the line to paddy wagons. The scene was terrifying; many ran. Everyone was shouting, "Get the girls out of there," but we stayed, afraid but wanting to stay, to stay with and support our men, to eliminate the violence, not to run and excuse ourselves from a dangerous position, to show the soldiers we were sure they would not hurt us, to make our position clear, about the war, to fight it here.

The police wedge broke through the middle. People ran. Those we thought most committed to staying ran in the face of brutality. We were surrounded. In keeping with the pacifistic approach of our small section, we realized there was no point in keeping our arms linked, we couldn't stop the advance of the troops and would only get hurt ourselves, and cause others to have to hurt us. We let go and covered our heads. A boy behind me put his hands on my head to protect me. The marshals lifted us out of the line carefully, one by one. The violence was gone. It was over for us.

—S. K.

*   *   *

THE last few hours of the demonstration were the most agonizing, traumatic, and the most beautiful. By then the 150,000 had been reduced to a few hundred who had been through a lot together. They had faced the cold night, tear gas, beatings, indecision. And they came through it all with a new respect for themselves, a real (not just slogan-level) sympathy for the troops, and the beginnings of an understanding of what was needed in a confrontation with the American government. They found that linked arms, missiles and violent charges gained them no ground against the army, that they resulted only in bloodied heads. Many who had started out years ago as pacifists, then abandoned nonviolence for the rhetoric of Che and Giap, saw once again that a violent struggle gains nothing. Self-protection and—even more important—communicating with the troops we were facing—turned the whole group to a nonviolent stance. This was not something that the pacifists in the crowd imposed. Jerry Rubin and Stewart Albert, no pacifists in anyone's book, were the most eloquent in pleading for nonviolence. Stew even called for any of the soldiers who intended to use violence to raise their hands (one did).

The Mobilization's permit expired at midnight Sunday. In the last few minutes, as the demonstrators sang "We Shall Overcome" and "America the Beautiful," several hundred more soldiers emerged from inside the Pentagon and took up positions in front of the demonstrators. Then a voice from within the building announced over and over that the permit was about to expire, that those who remained would be arrested, that those who wished to leave could take buses supplied by the government. No more than two dozen left, most choosing to walk. About two hundred stayed and were gently arrested.

—M. C.

*   *   *

THE actions then turn into a blur of images in my mind, held in a matrix of terror and warmth and pity and confusion and something akin to a feeling of exultation. The clouds of tear gas and a choking sensation. Troops forming at the side of the Pentagon and marching down with bayonets pointed directly at us. A dialogue in fear between them and the demonstrators who instinctively sat down in their path. The twitching of the soldiers' jaws on their otherwise immobile faces when needless taunts came at them from the crowd. An impulse to turn and run away, mixed with the urge to bravely act the way the books in the theory of nonviolent power suggest. Trying to see, somewhere, that tiny nugget of humanity underneath in those guards who beat and dragged defenseless demonstrators. A girl walking from soldier to soldier at bayonet point, offering each one a flower—and then the image of that flower, lying in the dust at their feet. Of five men guarding one of the little embankments, two who had the decency not to put on their gas masks when the toxic fumes drifted over, standing with the same tears in their eyes that we had in our own. People wandering through the crowds, passing out water and apples and damp wash rags. The beautiful sight of hundreds sitting close together in front of the doors to the massive fortress. The sound of singing. The glow of bonfires in the dark. And the Sunday bright sun, shining on the tired, courageous people who had stayed throughout the night and were still sitting there, waiting their turn to be arrested—and who had won the battle of the Pentagon.

—D. L.

*   *   *

DEAR Paul & Everyone Else,

Let this letter stand as notes for me to refer to when I get out of here (Occoquan). There's a lot I want to write about the Saturday night confrontation on the Pentagon Mall; about the incredible brutality of the U. S. marshals; about all of us who refused to fight back, and those asses in the rear who wouldn't join us on the front lines, but from their safe positions tossed things at the troops, causing them to hit the beautiful kids at their feet; about 36 of us enclosed in a truck, airless, for an hour and a half—like Jews—waiting to be processed; about so much!

We spent the first day in a dorm having a ball. This morning (Oct. 23) we were down to a few kids who chose to do time rather than pay out. Then—commotion at the door. In walked Gary Rader, Abbie Hoffman, Jerry Rubin, Bob Murphy—200 more who were busted Sunday night. Now we're in small, single cells; I've got Keith Lampe on one side, Peter Bates (a frosh at Cornell) on the other. Peter's the kid who stood up to the troops for hours, stared right at them, until they pulled him out of the line. He got five days— for assault! All the kids with bandaged heads were getting charged with assault.

They've brought in Fed prison guards from all over to handle us. They've been so great, I couldn't non-cooperate— why make them work harder? We are relating to each other as individuals, as humans.

About half the kids here are into the hippie bag; there isn't a Trot in the house. Little political talk; the word is love; the unifying factor is pot.

What happened the past two days is the turning point. The Pentagon isn't rising. It's crumbling. And despite all the talk against N-V, it was nonviolence that did it. The brothers and the sisters are beautiful.

> WE SHALL OVERCOME
> LOVE, PEACE,
> MARTY JEZER

*   *   *

THE Greyhound station was jammed on Sunday with hundreds who hadn't been able to find their chartered buses. Behind me in line, there was the very model of an ivy league frat brother. I didn't ask what school, but his friend was a Bennington girl. It was the first demonstration for both, and they'd loved it. They spent the whole night on the Mall. Now they effused about how great everyone had been, sharing coats, blankets, food. His blazer still looked straight from the cleaners, but her ironed brown hair was a trifle snarled. "She burned my draft card up there," he told us proudly, as she blushed and they squeezed each other's hand.

—P. J.

HOWARD ZINN

"If you want to read a real history book," says Matt Damon's title character in the film *Good Will Hunting* (1997), "read Howard Zinn's *A People's History of the United States.* That book will knock you on your ass." A good characterization of Zinn's most celebrated and influential work, first published in 1980: it is every left-wing activist's go-to counterhistory, now in its umpteenth printing with more than two million copies sold, and available also in a children's version and as a comic book.

His life led him graciously and inexorably to writing *A People's History.* Zinn (1922–2010) grew up in Brooklyn in modest circumstances, his parents being factory workers. After high school he started out as an apprentice shipfitter, then joined the Army Air Corps in 1943, serving as a bombardier and, in the last month of the war, dropping napalm on the French town of Royan. (He later returned to France to investigate the incident, and found that the raid had had no legitimate military objective and had killed hundreds of civilians; "the history of bombing . . . is a history of endless atrocities," he wrote.)

Zinn studied at New York University and at Columbia, wrote a master's thesis on the Colorado coal strikes of 1914 and a dissertation on Fiorello LaGuardia, and became professor of history at Spelman College. During his seven years there he advised the Student Nonviolent Coordinating Committee, but was dismissed in 1963 for his support of student activists working against segregation; he then came to Boston University and stayed there until his retirement in 1988. He was an early opponent of the Vietnam War, publishing *Vietnam: The Logic of Withdrawal* in 1967, visiting Hanoi with Daniel Berrigan in 1968, and helping to edit the *Pentagon Papers*; he also protested the Gulf War and the Iraq War. The FBI file on him, released in 2010, was 423 pages long.

"Dow Shalt Not Kill," written in 1967 to defend some BU students who obstructed on-campus recruiting efforts by Dow Chemical, is a characteristically scholarly piece, commenting in rich historical detail on corporate personhood, civil liberties, and civil disobedience. It thus enriches one of the ongoing discussions this anthology documents, namely, the relation between opposition to war and opposition to those individuals and companies who make the weapons by which the war is pursued—in this case napalm, which Zinn had dropped on France during World War II, which the Catonsville Nine were later to use to destroy draft records, and nearly 400,000 tons of which were dropped by American forces on Vietnam.

Dow Shalt Not Kill

MANY faculty members and students, being passionate opponents of American violence in Vietnam and also insistent civil
libertarians, are troubled by the recent demonstrations against
Dow Chemical. No dilemma exists where the action is merely
protest—by picketing, leafleting, speaking—against Dow,
napalm, and the war. That is a plain exercise of speech, press
and assembly. But physical interposition, where Dow recruiters
are blocked from carrying on their recruiting, opens puzzling
questions. As one concerned both with civil liberties and the
war, I would like to think aloud for awhile, in print, and try to
reach some conclusions.

First, it seems to me that the "civil liberties" of Dow Chemical are not in question. "Civil liberties" encompass various
forms of freedom of expression, as well as certain procedural
guarantees against arbitrary police or judicial action, and are
fairly well covered by the first, eighth and fourteenth Amend-
ments. No one is abrogating Dow's right to express its views;
indeed, the recent demonstrators in this area invited the Dow
representative to state his case publicly, and gave him a platform
for this purpose. If Dow wanted to set up a table, or hold a
meeting, to declare its views, any interference would be a violation of civil liberties.

However, the *actions* of an individual or group, which
(unlike even the most malicious or slanderous speech) have
immediate and irremediable effects on the lives and liberties
of others, must sometimes be restricted for the health and
safety of the public. Thus we pass laws against murder, rape,
arson. Thus we regulate the sale and manufacture of harmful products. We even restrict the restaurant owner's freedom
to choose his customers by racial standards. To put it more
broadly: the whole body of criminal and social legislation is
designed to restrict some people's freedom of action (not their
civil liberties) in order to safeguard the health and happiness of
others. Therefore, a law which prevented Dow Chemical Co.
from recruiting people who might be engaged in the manufacture, sale or promotion of a substance to be dropped on men,
women and children in order to burn them to death would
be easily as justifiable as the Meat Inspection Act of 1906. It

would (unlike a law interfering with talk for or against such a substance) no more be an infringement of civil liberties than a law barring the indiscriminate sale of deadly poisons at the corner grocery.

The doctrine that the "civil liberties" of corporations are violated by regulatory laws was predominant in this country during the age of the "Robber Barons" and was constitutionally sanctioned for about fifty years, until 1938. Then, a sharply-worded opinion by Justice Black (*Connecticut General Life Insurance v. Johnson*) declared that corporations should no longer be considered "persons" to be protected by the due process clause of the 14th Amendment. It soon became established in constitutional law that the regulation of business was *not* a deprivation of a civil liberty, that what is known as "substantive due process" would apply only to cases where real persons were being deprived of their rights of free expression. Today, it is well-established constitutionally that the U. S. government could make illegal the manufacture of napalm, and charge any persons recruiting for a napalm-manufacturing company with conspiring to violate the law.

But: there is no such law. Indeed, the government itself has ordered the napalm manufactured by Dow, and is using it to burn and kill Vietnamese peasants. Should private citizens (students, faculty—in this instance) act themselves, by physical interposition, against Dow Chemical's business activities? To do so would be to "take the law into your own hands." That is exactly what civil disobedience is: the temporary taking of the law into one's own hands, in order to declare what the law *should* be. It is a declaration that there is an incongruence between the law and humane values, and that sometimes this can only be publicized by breaking the law.

Civil disobedience can take two forms: violating a law which is obnoxious; or symbolically enacting a law which is urgently needed. When Negroes sat in at lunch counters, they were engaging in both forms: they violated state laws on segregation and trespassing; they were also symbolically enacting a public accommodations law even before it was written into the civil rights act of 1964.

Most of us, I assume, would support civil disobedience under *some* circumstances: we would commend those who defied the Fugitive Slave Act by harboring a Negro slave, and those who symbolically enacted emancipation by trying to prevent soldiers in Boston from returning Anthony Burns to his master. Otherwise—to declare that the law in *all* circumstances is to be obeyed—is to suppress the very spirit of democracy, to surrender individual conscience to an omnipotent state. Thus the issue becomes: under what circumstances is civil disobedience justified and is the Dow Chemical situation one of those circumstances?

It seems to me there are two essential conditions for the right to civil disobedience. One is that the human value at stake must involve fundamental rights, like life, health, liberty. There is no real cause, for instance, to disobey a traffic light because it is inconveniently long. But human slavery, or racism, or war—they are overwhelmingly important. Thus, the argument "what if everyone disobeyed the law every time it displeased them" falls before the observable fact that those who engage in civil disobedience are almost always law-abiding citizens who on certain very important issues deliberately, openly, temporarily violate the law to communicate a vital message to their fellow citizens.

What of Dow Chemical and napalm? Four American physicians, in a report, "Medical Problems of South Vietnam," have written: "Napalm is a highly sticky inflammable jelly which clings to anything it touches and burns with such heat that all oxygen in the area is exhausted within moments. Death is either by roasting or by suffocations. Napalm wounds are often fatal (estimates are 90%). Those who survive face a living death. The victims are frequently children." Napalm is dropped daily on the villages, the forests, the people of Vietnam by American bombers; the saturation bombing of that tiny country is one of the cruelest acts perpetrated by any nation in modern history; it ranks with the destruction of Lidice by the Germans, the crushing of the Hungarian rebellion by the Russians, the recent mass slaughter in Indonesia. Dr. Richard E. Perry, an American physician, wrote in *Redbook*, in January 1967, on his return from Vietnam: "I have been an orthopedic surgeon for a good number of years, with a rather wide range of medical experience. But nothing could have prepared me for my encounters with Vietnamese women and children burned by napalm. It was shocking and sickening, even for a physician, to see and smell the blackened flesh."

We are not, then, dealing with trivialities, but with monstrous deeds. This fact somehow becomes lost in the bland reasoned talk of businessmen and university officials, who speak as if Dow were just another business firm, recruiting for some innocuous purpose, making radios or toothpaste.

The root issue, it should be clear, is not simply napalm; it is the Vietnam war as a whole, in which a far-off country is being systematically destroyed, and its population decimated, by the greatest military power on earth. The war itself is the object of the civil disobedience; the use of napalm is one particularly bestial tactic in this war.

This brings us to the second condition for civil disobedience: the inadequacy of legal channels for redressing the grievance. This is manifestly true in the case of the Vietnam war, which is being waged completely outside the American constitutional process, by the President and a handful of advisors. Congress is troubled, but follows sheep-like what the White House decrees. The Supreme Court, by tradition, leaves foreign policy questions to the "political" branches of government (the President and Congress) but recently one of its more conservative members, Justice Potter Stewart, said that perhaps the Court should review the constitutionality of the war. This, after 100,000 American casualties! Citizens have taken to the auditoriums and to the streets precisely because they have no other way to protest; yet both President and Vice-President declare with the brazenness of petty dictators that no civic outcry will change their policy. If ever there was an issue which called for civil disobedience, it is this run-away war.

Then why do we become uneasy when students interfere with Dow Chemical? Occasionally, we read of housewives blocking off a busy intersection because children have been killed there as a result of the lack of traffic lights. These housewives thereby interfere with the freedom of automobiles and of pedestrians, in order to temporarily regulate, or even disrupt, traffic on behalf of the lives of children—hoping this will lead to the permanent regulation of traffic by government. (Those are not *the* automobiles that killed the child, any more than *this* Dow Chemical representative, or the student he is recruiting, is actually dropping the napalm bomb.)

Why do we so easily sympathize with actions like that, where perhaps one child was killed, and not with actions against Dow Chemical, where countless children have been victims? Is it possible that we subconsciously distinguish between the identifiable children down the street (who move us), and the faceless children of that remote Asian land (who do not)? Is it possible also that the well-dressed, harassed representative of Dow Chemical is more human, therefore more an object of sympathy to the well-dressed, harassed officials of the University (and to us), than the burning, bleeding, blurred faces of the Vietnamese?

There is a common argument which says: but where will these student actions lead? If we justify one act of civil disobedience, must we not justify them all? Do they then have the right to disobey the Civil Rights Acts? Where does it stop? That argument withers away, however, once we recognize the distinction between free speech, where absolute toleration is a social good, and free action, where the existence of values other than free speech demands that we *choose* right over wrong—and respond accordingly. We should remember that the social utility of free speech is in giving us the informational base from which we can then make social choices in action. To limit free speech is to distort our capacity to make such choices. To refrain from making choices is to say that beyond the issue of free speech we have no substantive values which we will express in action. If we do not discriminate in the actions we support or oppose, we cannot rectify the terrible injustices of the present world.

Whether the issue of the Vietnam war is more effectively presented by protest and demonstration (that is, the exercise of speech, press, assembly) rather than by civil disobedience, is a question of tactics, and varies with each specific situation. Different student groups (at Harvard and MIT, for instance) have used one or another against Dow recruitment, and each tactic has its own advantages. I tend to favor the protest tactic as keeping the central issue of the war clearer. But if students or faculty engaged in civil disobedience, I would consider that morally defensible.

So much for student-faculty action—but what of the University administration? The University's acceptance of Dow Chemical recruiting as just another business transaction is especially disheartening, because it is the University which tells students repeatedly on ceremonial occasions that it hopes students will be more than fact-absorbing automatons, that they will choose humane values and stand up for them courageously. For the University to sponsor Dow Chemical activities as a protective civil liberty means that the University (despite its courses in constitutional law) still accepts the 19th century definition of substantive due process as defending corporations against regulation, that (despite a library with books on civil liberties) the University does not understand what civil liberties are, that (despite its entrance requirement of literacy) the University has not read in the newspaper of the terrible damage our napalm bombs have done to innocent people.

The fact that there is only an indirect connection between Dow recruiting B. U. students and napalm dropped on Vietnamese villages, does not vitiate the moral issue. It is precisely the nature of modern mass murder that it is not visibly direct like individual murder, but takes on a corporate character, where every participant has limited liability. The total effect, however, is a thousand times more pernicious, than that of the individual entrepreneur of violence. If the world is destroyed, it will be a white-collar crime, done in a business-like way, by large numbers of individuals involved in a chain of actions, each one having a touch of innocence.

Sometimes the University speaks of the "right of recruitment." There is no absolute right of recruitment, however, because (beyond the package of civil liberties connected with free expression and procedural guarantees, which are the closest we can get to "absolute" right) all rights are relative. I doubt that B. U. would open its offices to the Ku Klux Klan for recruiting, or that it would apply an absolute right of private enterprise to peddlers selling poisonous food on campus. When the University of Pennsylvania announced it would end its germ-warfare research project, it was saying that there was no absolute right to do research on *anything* for *any* purpose.

The existence of University "security" men (once known as campus police) testifies that all actions on campus are not equally tolerable. The University makes moral choices all the time. If it can regulate the movement of men into women's dormitories (in a firm stand for chastity or perhaps some other value equally dear), then why cannot it regulate the coming and going of corporations into the University, where the value is human life, and the issue is human suffering?

And if students are willing to take the risks of civil disobedience, to declare themselves for the dying people of Vietnam, cannot the University take a milder step, but one which makes the same declaration—and cancel the invitation to Dow Chemical? Why cannot the University—so much more secure—show a measure of social commitment, a bit of moral courage? Should not the University, which speaks so often about students having "values," declare some of its own? It is written on no tablets handed down from heaven that the officials of a university may not express themselves on public issues. It is time (if not now, when? asks the Old Testament) for the University to forsake the neutrality of the IBM machines, and join the human race.

W. S. MERWIN

W. S. (William Stanley) Merwin (b. 1927) has had a distinguished career as a poet, winning the Yale Younger Poets prize, the Pulitzer Prize (twice), the National Book Award, and the Tanning Prize, and becoming the poet laureate of the United States in 2010. He grew up in Scranton, attended Princeton, and has lived in Spain, London, Boston, and New York; since the 1970s he has made his home on a former pineapple plantation in Hawaii, and has gradually restored its native flora.

Merwin's stand on war is straightforward in life and complex in his poetry. When he won the Pulitzer in 1971, he donated his prize money to the draft-resistance movement and set out his objections to the Vietnam War in the *New York Review of Books.* (W. H. Auden, who had awarded him the Yale prize, took exception to what he regarded as Merwin's wrongheaded politicization of the Pulitzer.) Few of his Vietnam-era poems are transparently oppositional, however, and even "When the War Is Over"—first collected in *The Lice* (1967)—is too ambiguous on the page to support any political program. In the brilliant and explicit broadside version reproduced here, the poem is much less ambiguous; the blood dripping from the bottom line of the text provides a vivid and powerfully negative image of the war the poem refers to.

WHEN THE WAR IS OVER

by W. S. Merwin

When the war is over
We will be proud of course the air will be
Good for breathing at last
The water will have been improved the salmon
And the silence of heaven will migrate more perfectly
The dead will think the living are worth it we will know
Who we are
And we will all enlist again

THOMAS MERTON

Thomas Merton (1915–1968) was the antiwar movement's theorist, for at least some of its practitioners.

He grew up in several places, Bermuda and France and England among them, but returned to the United States in 1935, majoring in English at Columbia and becoming Catholic in 1938 (at Corpus Christi Church in New York, where the noted French antiwar activist and writer Simone Weil was to come to pray in 1942). He planned to write a dissertation on Gerard Manley Hopkins; but then he changed course, his religious impulses being even more powerful than his literary ones, and entered the Trappist Abbey of Our Lady of Gethsemani in Kentucky as a postulant in 1941, making his final vows in 1947 and being ordained to the priesthood in 1949. His autobiography, *The Seven Storey Mountain* (1948), was an unlikely bestseller.

The autobiography focused on the inward life, as Merton had been doing; in the 1950s and 1960s, however, he turned his attention outward, and wrote abundantly on questions of civil rights, nonviolence, and nuclear weapons. His writing was widely read, and exercised a significant influence on discussions of these things despite, or because of, his distance from any concrete engagement with the facts on the ground. He occupied a middle ground, one might say: resolutely committed to nonviolence, and so opposed to war and wars, weapons of mass destruction and all the phenomena of language associated with them, but uneasy on principle with some of the more confrontational, quasi-violent or violent actions of more radical Catholic war resisters like Daniel Berrigan.

Nonviolence Does Not—Cannot—Mean Passivity

THERE seems to be a general impression that nonviolence in America has been tried and found wanting. The tragic death of Martin Luther King Jr. is supposed to have marked the end of an era in which nonviolence had significance, and the Poor People's March has been described as a sort of Post Mortem on nonviolence. From now on, we hear, it's violence only. Why? Because nonviolence not only does not get results, but it is not even effective as communication.

I might as well say bluntly that I do not believe this at all. And in spite of the fact that the Montgomery Bus Boycott, for

485

instance, was a great example of the effective use of nonviolence both as tactic and as communication, in spite of the Freedom Rides, Birmingham, Selma, etc., I don't think America has yet begun to look at nonviolence or to understand it. It is not my business to tell the SNCC people how to manage their political affairs. If they feel that they can no longer make good use of nonviolence, let them look to it. There are certainly reasons for thinking that a seemingly passive resistance may not be what the black people of America can best use. Nor do I think, incidentally, that "Black Power" means nothing but mindless and anarchic violence. It is more sophisticated than that.

But we are considering the Peace Movement.

The napalming of draft records by the Baltimore nine is a special and significant case because it seems to indicate a new borderline situation: as if the Peace Movement too were standing at the very edge of violence. As if this were a sort of "last chance" at straight nonviolence and a first step toward violent resistance. Well, we live in a world of escalation in which no one seems to know how to de-escalate, and it does pose a problem. The Peace Movement may be escalating beyond peaceful protest. In which case it may also be escalating into self-contradiction. But let me make it clear that I do not think the Baltimore nine have done this.

What were the Berrigans and the others trying to do?

It seems to me this was an attempt at prophetic nonviolent provocation. It bordered on violence and was violent to the extent that it meant pushing some good ladies around and destroying some government property. The nine realized that this was a criminal act and knew that they would probably go to jail for it. They accepted this in the classic nonviolent fashion. The standard doctrine of nonviolence says that you can disobey a law you consider unjust but you have to accept the punishment. In this way you are distinguished from the mere seditious revolutionary. You protest the purity of your witness. You undergo redemptive suffering for religious—or anyway ethical—motives. You are "doing penance" for the sin and injustice against which you have protested. And in the case of the Berrigans, I imagine there is present a sort of "jail mystique," as a way of saying dumbly to the rest of the country that in our society nobody is really free anyway, that we are all prisoners of a machinery that takes us inevitably where we don't want to go. Presumably *everyone* in the country wants peace in one way or other. But most Americans have prior commitments—or attachments—to other things which make peace impossible. Most people would rather have war and profits than peace and problems. Or so it seems. In such a situation, we speak peace with our lips but the answer in the heart is war, and war only. And there is a certain indecency involved when Christians, even prelates, canonize this unpleasant fact by saying that the war in Vietnam is an act of Christian love. Small wonder that certain more sensitive and more questioning people are driven to extremities.

The evident desperation of the Baltimore nine has, however, frightened more than it has edified. The country is in a very edgy psychological state. Americans feel terribly threatened, on grounds which are partly rational, partly irrational, but in any case very real. The rites of assassination recur at more and more frequent intervals, and there is less and less of a catharsis each time. The shocking thing about the murder of another Kennedy is that we seem to have such a terrible propensity to destroy the things and people we admire, the very ones we identify with. (I say "we" insofar as we all have a real stake in the society which makes such things not only possible but easy.) There is then a real fear, a deep ambivalence, about our very existence and the order on which we think it depends. In such a case, the use of nonviolence has to be extremely careful and clear. People are not in a mood for clear thinking: their fears and premonitions have long ago run away with their minds before anyone can get to them with a cool nonviolent statement. And it has long ago become automatic to interpret nonviolence as violence merely because it is resistance.

The classic (Gandhian) doctrine of nonviolence, even in a much less tense and explosive situation, always emphasized respect for the just laws in order to highlight clearly and unambiguously the injustice of the unjust law. In this way, nonviolence did not pose a sort of free-floating psychological threat, but was clearly pinpointed, directed to what even the adversary had to admit was wrong. Ideally, that is what nonviolence is supposed to do. But if nonviolence merely says in a very loud voice "*I don't like this damn law*," it does not do much to make the adversary confess that the law is wrong. On the contrary, what he sees is an apparently arbitrary attack on law and order, dictated by emotion or caprice—or fanaticism of some sort. His reply is obviously going to be: "Well if you don't like law and order, you can go to jail where you belong." And he will send you to jail with a firm and righteous conviction that his law is just. He will not even for a moment have occasion to question its justice. He will be too busy responding to what he feels to be aggressive and indignant in your near-violent protest.

It seems to me that protest against the Selective Service Law is too much oriented to the affirmation of the rightness, the determination and the conviction of the protesters, and not enough to the injustice of the law itself. In other words, people who are protesting against the draft seem to be communicating, before everything else, their own intense conviction that the law is wrong, rather than pointing out where and how the law is wrong. It boils down to saying "We don't like this law and feel strongly that it is bad." To which the opposition is content to reply: "The real reason why you don't like the draft is that you are a coward."

What is to be done? First, on a short-term and emergency basis, the whole Vietnam problem has to be solved even if it demands a certain political compromise. It is idiotic to hold out for negotiations in which the position of the other side is completely ignored. Senator McCarthy seems to me to be the only presidential candidate who has the remotest idea of how to end the war, and he is the only one for whom I personally, in conscience, can vote. The war being ended, I think it is necessary that we realize the draft law is unjust, useless and an occasion of further interference in the affairs of small countries we cannot understand. It should be abolished. It has no relation to the real defense needs of our nation. On a long-term basis, I think the Peace Movement needs to really study, practice and use nonviolence in its classic form, with all that this implies of religious and ethical commitment. The current facile rejection of nonviolence is too pragmatic. You point to one or two cases where it does not seem to have got results and you say it has completely failed.

But nonviolence is useless if it is merely pragmatic. The whole point of nonviolence is that it rises above pragmatism and does not consider whether or not it pays off politically. *Ahimsa* is defense of and witness to *truth*, not efficacy. I admit that may sound odd. Someone once said, did he not, "What is truth?" And the one to whom he said it also mentioned, somewhere: "The truth shall make you free." It seems to me that this is what really matters. If this is so, nonviolence is not a tactic you use one time and abandon the next. It is for keeps.

FROM

War and the Crisis of Language

A CLASSIC example of the contamination of reason and speech by the inherent ambiguity of war is that of the U.S. major who, on February 7, 1968, shelled the South Vietnamese town of Bentre "regardless of civilian casualties. . . . to rout the Vietcong." As he calmly explained, "It became necessary to destroy the town in order to save it." Here we see, again, an insatiable appetite for the tautological, the definitive, the *final*. It is the same kind of language and logic that Hitler used for his notorious "final solution." The symbol of this perfect finality is the circle. An argument turns upon itself, and the beginning and end get lost: it just goes round and round its own circumference. A message comes in that someone thinks there might be some Vietcong in a certain village. Planes are sent, the village is destroyed, many of the people are killed. The destruction of the village and the killing of the people earn for them a final and official identity. The burned huts become "enemy structures"; the dead men, women, and children become "Vietcong," thus adding to a "kill ratio" that can be interpreted as "favorable." They were thought to be Vietcong and were therefore destroyed. By being destroyed they became Vietcong for keeps; they entered "history" definitively as our enemies, because we wanted to be on the "safe side," and "save American lives"—as well as Vietnam.

The logic of "Red or dead" has long since urged us to iden- tify destruction with rescue—to be "dead" is to be saved from being "Red." In the language of melodrama, our grandparents became accustomed to the idea of a "fate worse than death." A schematic morality concluded that if such and such is a fate worse than death, then to prefer it to death would surely be a heinous sin. The logic of warmakers has extended this not only to the preservation of one's own moral integrity but to the fate of others, even of people on the other side of the earth, whom we do not always bother to consult personally on the subject. We weigh the arguments that they are not able to understand (perhaps they have not even heard that arguments exist!). And we decide, in their place, that it is better for them to be dead— killed by us—than Red, living under our enemies.

The Asian whose future we are about to decide is either a bad guy or a good guy. If he is a bad guy, he obviously has to be killed. If he is a good guy, he is on our side and he ought to be ready to die for freedom. We will provide an opportunity for him to do so: we will kill him to prevent him falling under the tyranny of a demonic enemy. Thus we not only defend his interests together with our own, but we protect his virtue along with our own. Think what might happen if he fell under communist rule *and liked it*!

The advantages of this kind of logic are no exclusive possession of the United States. This is purely and simply the logic shared by all war-makers. It is the logic of *power*. Possibly American generals are naive enough to push this logic, without realizing, to absurd conclusions. But all who love power tend to think in some such way. Remember Hitler weeping over the ruins of Warsaw after it had been demolished by the Luftwaffe: "How wicked these people must have been," he sobbed, "to make me do this to them!"

Words like "pacification" and "liberation" have acquired sinister connotations as war has succeeded war. Vietnam has done much to refine and perfect these notions. A "free zone" is now one in which anything that moves is assumed to be "enemy" and can be shot. In order to create a "free zone" that can live up effectively to its name, one must level everything, buildings, vegetation, everything, so that one can clearly see anything that moves, and shoot it. This has very interesting semantic consequences.

An American Captain accounts for the levelling of a new "Free Zone" in the following terms: "We want to prevent them from moving freely in this area. . . . From now on anything that moves around here is going to be automatically considered V.C. and bombed or fired on. The whole Triangle is going to become a Free Zone. These villagers here are all considered hostile civilians."

How did the Captain solve the semantic problem of distinguishing the hostile civilian from the refugee? "In a V.C. area like this there are three categories. First there are the straight V.C. . . . Then there are the V.C. sympathizers. Then there's the . . . There's a third category . . . I can't think of the third just now but . . . there's no middle road in this war."*

"Pacification" or "winning the hearts" of the undecided is thus very much simplified. "Soon" says a news report,† "the Government will have no need to win the hearts and minds of Bensuc. There will be no Bensuc." But there are further simplifications. A "high ranking US Field commander is quoted as saying: 'If the people are to the guerrillas as oceans are to the fish . . . we are going to dry up that ocean.'"‡ Merely by existing, a civilian, in this context, becomes a "hostile civilian." But at the same time and by the same token he is our friend and our ally. What simpler way out of the dilemma than to destroy him to "save American lives"?

*See Jonathan Schell in *The New Yorker* (July 15, 1967), p. 59.
†*New York Times*, Jan. 11, 1967.
‡Quoted in the *New Statesman* (Mar. 11, 1966).

JOAN BAEZ

Pacifists love to quote Joan Baez's "What Would You Do If?" from her memoir *Daybreak* (1968): they are used to being asked such hypothetical questions. Baez does far better than most in her attempt to respond; she is playful and concrete in her answers, and charmingly unshakeable, revealing her interlocutor's "what ifs" for the tendentious and imperfect critiques they really are.

Baez (b. 1941) is a leading American folksinger and activist, the activist and singer being inextricably intertwined in her. I heard her tell a story once, during a radio interview: one right-wing admirer of her singing, unable to separate the politics he disliked from the songs he did, said to her, "you are making things very difficult!" Baez herself said that social justice "loomed larger than music" in her life.

She was born in New York to a family that became Quakers in her early years, and moved around a lot with her father Albert, one of the inventors of the x-ray microscope, her mother Joan, her elder sister Pauline, and her younger sister, the late Mimi Fariña. At thirteen she heard Pete Seeger for the first time, and began learning his repertory.

Her career began in Boston and Cambridge, the family having moved there when her father was hired at the Massachusetts Institute of Technology. Her debut was inauspicious—there were eight people in the audience at Cambridge's Club 47 in 1958, all of them friends and relatives—but she persisted and prevailed. (It was also the year of her first act of civil disobedience, her refusal to participate in a high school air-raid drill.) She was invited by Bob Gibson to perform with him at the first Newport Folk Festival in 1959, and her triumph there led to her being signed by Vanguard Records. Having been helped by such singers as Gibson, she helped other singers in her turn, including Bob Dylan, whose songs then became part of her own repertory.

She performed "We Shall Overcome" at the 1963 March on Washington and for the 1964 free speech movement demonstrations in Berkeley, California, marching in that following year from Selma to Montgomery with Martin Luther King. Also in 1963, in protest against the Vietnam War, she began refusing to pay 60 percent of her income taxes. (She and the environmental activist Julia Butterfly Hill are probably the most famous American war tax resisters; in 2006 the two spent the night in a tree together.) She traveled to North Vietnam in 1972 and was caught there in the American Christmas bombing of Hanoi, but later became quite critical of the North Vietnamese government for its human rights violations.

Her singing, songwriting, and activism have all continued, flourished, and diversified over the course of her long career. In 2009 she performed at the fiftieth Newport Folk Festival, fifty years after her debut there; in 2011 Amnesty International named its award for Outstanding Inspirational Service in the Global Fight for Human Rights after her, and Baez was unsurprisingly the award's first winner. That same year she played a set of songs for the protesters of Occupy Wall Street.

What Would You Do If?

"OK. You're a pacifist. What would you do if someone were, say, attacking your grandmother?"

"Attacking my poor old grandmother?"

"Yeah. You're in a room with your grandmother and there's this guy about to attack her and you're standing there. What would you do?"

"I'd yell, 'Three cheers for Grandma!' and leave the room."

"No, seriously. Say he had a gun and he was about to shoot her. Would you shoot him first?"

"Do I have a gun?"

"Yes."

"No. I'm a pacifist, I don't have a gun."

"Well, say you do."

"All right. Am I a good shot?"

"Yes."

"I'd shoot the gun out of his hand."

"No, then you're not a good shot."

"I'd be afraid to shoot. Might kill Grandma."

"Come on. OK, look. We'll take another example. Say you're driving a truck. You're on a narrow road with a sheer cliff on your side. There's a little girl standing in the middle of the road. You're going too fast to stop. What would you do?"

"I don't know. What would *you* do?"

"I'm asking you. You're the pacifist."

"Yes, I know. All right, am I in control of the truck?"

"Yes."

"How about if I honk my horn so she can get out of the way?"

"She's too young to walk. And the horn doesn't work."

"I swerve around to the left of her, since she's not going anywhere."

"No, there's been a landslide."

"Oh. Well, then. I would try to drive the truck over the cliff and save the little girl."

Silence.

"Well, say there's someone else in the truck with you. Then what?"

"What's my decision have to do with my being a pacifist?"

"There's two of you in the truck and only one little girl."

"Someone once said, 'If you have a choice between a real evil and a hypothetical evil, always take the hypothetical one.'"

"Huh?"

"I said why are you so anxious to kill off all the pacifists?"

"I'm not. I just want to know what you'd do if—"

"If I was with a friend in a truck driving very fast on a one-lane road approaching a dangerous impasse where a ten-month-old girl is sitting in the middle of the road with a landslide one side of her and a sheer drop-off on the other."

"That's right."

"I would probably slam on the brakes, thus sending my friend through the front windshield, skid into the landslide, run over the little girl, sail off the cliff and plunge to my own death. No doubt Grandma's house would be at the bottom of the ravine and the truck would crash through her roof and blow up in her living room where she was finally being attacked for the first, and last, time."

"You haven't answered my question. You're just trying to get out of it . . ."

"I'm really trying to say a couple of things. One is that no one knows what he'll do in a moment of crisis. And that hypothetical questions get hypothetical answers. I'm also hinting that you have made it impossible for me to come out of the situation without having killed one or more people. Then you can say 'Pacifism is a nice idea, but it won't work.' But that's not what bothers me."

"What bothers you?"

"Well, you may not like it because it's not hypothetical. It's real. And it makes the assault on Grandma look like a garden party."

"What's that?"

"I'm thinking about how we put people through a training process so they'll find out the really good, efficient ways of killing. Nothing incidental like trucks and landslides . . . Just the opposite, really. You know, how to growl and yell, kill and crawl and jump out of airplanes . . . Real organized stuff. Hell, you have to be able to run a bayonet through Grandma's middle."

"That's something entirely different."

"Sure. And don't you see that it's so much harder to look at, because it's real, and it's going on right now? Look. A general sticks a pin into a map. A week later a bunch of young boys are sweating it out in a jungle somewhere, shooting each other's arms and legs off, crying and praying and losing control of their bowels . . . Doesn't it seem stupid to you?"

"Well you're talking about war."

"Yes, I know. Doesn't it seem stupid?"

"What do you do instead, then? Turn the other cheek, I suppose."

"No. Love thine enemy but confront his evil. Love thine enemy. Thou shalt not kill."

"Yeah and look what happened to him."

"He grew up."

"They hung him on a damn cross is what happened to him. I don't want to get hung on a damn cross."

"You won't."

"Huh?"

"I said you don't get to choose how you're going to die. Or when. You can only decide how you're going to live. Now."

"Well I'm not going to go letting everybody step all over me, that's for sure."

"Jesus said, 'Resist not evil.' The pacifist says just the opposite. He says to resist evil with all your heart and with all your mind and body until it has been overcome."

"I don't get it."

"Organized nonviolent resistance. Gandhi. He organized the Indians for nonviolent resistance and waged nonviolent war against the British until he'd freed India from the British Empire. Not bad for a first try, don't you think?"

"Yeah, fine, but he was dealing with the British, a civilized people. We're not."

"Not a civilized people?"

"Not dealing with a civilized people. You just try some of that stuff on the Russians."

"You mean the Chinese, don't you?"

"Yeah, the Chinese. Try it on the Chinese."

"Oh dear. War was going on long before anybody dreamed up Communism. It's just the latest justification for self-righteousness. The problem isn't Communism. The problem is consensus. There's a consensus out that it's OK to kill when your government decides who to kill. If you kill inside the country you get in trouble. If you kill outside the country, right time, right season, latest enemy, you get a medal. There are about one hundred and thirty nation-states, and each of them thinks it's a swell idea to bump off all the rest because he is more important. The pacifist thinks there is only one tribe. Three billion members. They come first. We think killing any member of the family is a dumb idea. We think there are more decent and intelligent ways of settling differences. And man had better start investigating these other possibilities because if he doesn't, then by mistake or by design, he will probably kill off the whole damn race."

"It's human nature to kill."

"Is it?"

"It's natural. Something you can't change."

"If it's natural to kill why do men have to go into training to learn how? There's violence in human nature, but there's also decency, love, kindness. Man organizes, buys, sells, pushes violence. The nonviolenter wants to organize the opposite side. That's all nonviolence is—organized love."

"You're crazy."

"No doubt. Would you care to tell me the rest of the world is sane? Tell me that violence has been a great success for the past five thousand years, that the world is in fine shape, that wars have brought peace, understanding, brotherhood, democracy, and freedom to mankind and that killing each other has created an atmosphere of trust and hope. That it's grand for one billion people to live off of the other two billion, or that even if it hasn't been smooth going all along, we are now at last beginning to see our way through to a better world for all, as soon as we get a few minor wars out of the way."

"I'm doing OK."

"Consider it a lucky accident."

"I believe I should defend America and all that she stands for. Don't you believe in self-defense?"

"No, that's how the Mafia got started. A little band of people who got together to protect peasants. I'll take Gandhi's nonviolent resistance."

"I still don't get the point of nonviolence."

"The point of nonviolence is to build a floor, a strong new floor, beneath which we can no longer sink. A platform which stands a few feet above napalm, torture, exploitation, poison gas, A and H bombs, the works. Give man a decent place to stand. He's been wallowing around in human blood and vomit and burnt flesh screaming how it's going to bring peace to the world. He sticks his head out of the hole for a minute and sees an odd bunch of people gathering material and attempting to build a structure above ground in the fresh air. 'Nice idea but not very practical,' he shouts and slides back into the hole. It was the same kind of thing when man found out the world was round. He fought for years to have it remain flat, with every proof on hand that it was not flat at all. It had no edge to drop off or sea monsters to swallow up his little ship in their gaping jaws."

"How are you going to build this practical structure?"

"From the ground up. By studying, learning about, experimenting with every possible alternative to violence on every level. By learning how to say no to the nation-state, no to war taxes, 'NO' to the draft, 'NO' to killing in general, 'YES' to the brotherhood of man, by starting new institutions which are based on the assumption that murder in any form is ruled out, by making and keeping in touch with nonviolent contacts all over the world, by engaging ourselves at every possible chance in dialogue with people, groups, to try to begin to change the consensus that it's OK to kill."

"It sounds real nice, but I just don't think it can work."

"You are probably right. We probably don't have enough time. So far we've been a glorious flop. The only thing that's been a worse flop than the organization of nonviolence has been the organization of violence."

MURIEL RUKEYSER

Muriel Rukeyser's "Poem," published in 1968 with its simultaneously modest and ambitious title, is among the most restrained of American antiwar poems, and among the most resonant. No rage, no arguments or campaigns or names, just a portrait of a person struggling to cope in "the first century of world wars," reaching out to the like-minded, living in the moment of contact, trying to "construct peace," or more simply "to wake."

Rukeyser (1913–1980) grew up in Manhattan, went to Vassar and founded an undergraduate leftist journal there, attended the Roosevelt School of Aviation and learned to fly, wrote about that experience in "Theory of Flight" in 1935, in a volume that W. H. Auden selected to receive the Yale Younger Poets prize. Her own political life was more explicitly committed than "Poem" might suggest. At nineteen she was arrested for talking with African American reporters at the Scottsboro trials; at twenty-three she was reporting on silicosis in West Virginia miners. She worked with the Spanish Medical Bureau during the Spanish Civil War and spoke for the Loyalists when she returned to the United States. After World War II she taught at the California Labor School, then at Sarah Lawrence (Alice Walker was one of her students). Her opposition to the Vietnam War led her to protest in Hanoi and in Washington, D.C., where she was arrested.

Like Denise Levertov, and for some of the same reasons, Rukeyser was disparaged by some critics—for didacticism, for emotionalism. But she mattered to Anne Sexton and Adrienne Rich; Kenneth Rexroth called her the greatest poet of her "exact generation." She died in Greenwich Village.

Poem

I lived in the first century of world wars.
Most mornings I would be more or less insane,
The newspapers would arrive with their careless stories,
The news would pour out of various devices
Interrupted by attempts to sell products to the unseen.
I would call my friends on other devices;
They would be more or less mad for similar reasons.
Slowly I would get to pen and paper,
Make my poems for others unseen and unborn.

In the day I would be reminded of those men and women
Brave, setting up signals across vast distances,
Considering a nameless way of living, of almost unimagined
     values.
As the lights darkened, as the lights of night brightened,
We would try to imagine them, try to find each other.
To construct peace, to make love, to reconcile
Waking with sleeping, ourselves with each other,
Ourselves with ourselves. We would try by any means
To reach the limits of ourselves, to reach beyond ourselves,
To let go the means, to wake.

I lived in the first century of these wars.

SHIRLEY CHISHOLM

Shirley Chisholm (1924–2005) was the first African American congresswoman, winning her seat by defeating civil rights activist James Farmer in a hard-fought race in Brooklyn in 1968. She had come up the hard way, the traditional way: from a Brooklyn Democratic clubhouse by way of the Bedford-Stuyvesant Political League, the Unity Democratic Club, and the New York State Assembly.

Arriving in Washington, D.C., Chisholm was anything but deferential to her senior colleagues: assigned to the Agriculture Committee, and within that committee to the subcommittee on forestry, she denounced the assignment publicly ("apparently all they know here in Washington about Brooklyn is that a tree grows there"). Surprisingly, she won reassignment and a position on the committee on veterans affairs; later she gained a seat on the Education and Labor Committee and helped found the Congressional Black Caucus. In 1972 she sought the Democratic nomination for president; she continued to serve in the House until 1982, then taught at Mount Holyoke and Spelman.

The text included here was Chisholm's maiden speech in Congress, delivered on March 26, 1969. Her oratory is of the plainspoken kind, in Theodore Parker's tradition, without flourishes, proceeding directly to the goal, full or quiet authority. But her argument is an unusual one in the present context. It is not a moral argument, not an African American argument against American racial hypocrisy, but a representative's argument, a practical argument on behalf of her constituents: that the cost of fighting the war is making it impossible to tend to the needs of her constituents and of the American needy everywhere.

"The Business of America Is War and It Is Time for a Change"

Mr. Speaker, on the same day President Nixon announced he had decided the United States will not be safe unless we start to build a defense system against missiles, the Headstart program in the District of Columbia was cut back for the lack of money.

As a teacher, and as a woman, I do not think I will ever understand what kind of values can be involved in spending $9 billion—and more, I am sure—on elaborate, unnecessary, and impractical weapons when several thousand disadvantaged children in the Nation's Capital get nothing.

When the new administration took office, I was one of the many Americans who hoped it would mean that our country would benefit from the fresh perspectives, the new ideas, the different priorities of a leader who had no part in its mistakes of the past. Mr. Nixon had said things like this:

> If our cities are to be livable for the next generation, we can delay no longer in launching new approaches to the problems that beset them and to the tensions that tear them apart.

And he said:

> When you cut expenditures for education, what you are doing is short-changing the American future.

But frankly, I have never cared too much what people say. What I am interested in is what they do. We have waited to see what the new administration is going to do. The pattern now is becoming clear.

Apparently launching those new programs can be delayed for a while, after all. It seems we have to get some missiles launched first.

Recently the new Secretary of Commerce spelled it out. The Secretary, Mr. Stans, told a reporter that the new administration is "pretty well agreed it must take time out from major social objectives" until it can stop inflation.

The new Secretary of Health, Education, and Welfare, Robert Finch, came to the Hill to tell the House Education and Labor Committee that he thinks we should spend more on education, particularly in city schools. But, he said, unfortunately we cannot "afford" to, until we have reached some kind of honorable solution to the Vietnam war. I was glad to read that the distinguished Member from Oregon (Mrs. Green) asked Mr. Finch this:

> With the crisis we have in education, and the crisis in our cities, can we wait to settle the war? Shouldn't it be the other way around? Unless we can meet the crisis in education, we really can't afford the war.

Secretary of Defense Melvin Laird came to Capitol Hill, too. His mission was to sell the anti-ballistic-missile insanity to the Senate. He was asked what the new administration is doing about the war. To hear him, one would have thought it was 1968, that the former Secretary of State was defending the former policies, that nothing had ever happened—a President had never decided not to run because he knew the Nation would reject him, in despair over this tragic war we have blundered into. Mr. Laird talked of being prepared to spend at least 2 more years in Vietnam.

Two more years, 2 more years of hunger for Americans, of death for our best young men, of children here at home suffering the life-long handicap of not having a good education when they are young. Two more years of high taxes, collected to feed the cancerous growth of a Defense Department budget that now consumes two-thirds of our Federal income.

Two more years of too little being done to fight our greatest enemies, poverty, prejudice, and neglect here in our own country. Two more years of fantastic waste in the Defense Department and of penny pinching on social programs. Our country cannot survive 2 more years, or 4, of these kinds of policies. It must stop—this year—now.

Now I am not a pacifist. I am, deeply, unalterably, opposed to this war in Vietnam. Apart from all the other considerations, and they are many, the main fact is that we cannot squander there the lives, the money, the energy that we need desperately here, in our cities, in our schools.

I wonder whether we cannot reverse our whole approach to spending. For years, we have given the military, the defense industry, a blank check. New weapons systems are dreamed up, billions are spent, and many times they are found to be impractical, inefficient, unsatisfactory, even worthless. What do we do then? We spend more money on them. But with social programs, what do we do? Take the Job Corps. Its failures have been mercilessly exposed and criticized. If it had been a military research and development project, they would have been covered up or explained away, and Congress would have been ready to pour more billions after those that had been wasted on it.

The case of Pride, Inc., is interesting. This vigorous, successful black organization, here in Washington, conceived and built by young inner-city men, has been ruthlessly attacked by its enemies in the Government, in this Congress. At least six auditors from the General Accounting Office were put to work investigating Pride. They worked 7 months and spent more than $100,000. They uncovered a fraud. It was something less than $2,100. Meanwhile millions of dollars—billions of dollars, in fact—were being spent by the Department of Defense, and how many auditors and investigators were checking into their negotiated contracts? Five.

We Americans have come to feel that it is our mission to make the world free. We believe that we are the good guys, everywhere, in Vietnam, in Latin America, wherever we go. We believe we are the good guys at home, too. When the Kerner Commission told white America what black America has always known, that prejudice and hatred built the Nation's slums, maintains them, and profits by them, white America would not believe it. But it is true. Unless we start to fight, and defeat, the enemies of poverty and racism in our own country and make our talk of equality and opportunity ring true, we are exposed as hypocrites in the eyes of the world when we talk about making other people free.

I am deeply disappointed at the clear evidence that the No. 1 priority of the new administration is to buy more and more and more weapons of war, to return to the era of the cold war, to ignore the war we must fight here—the war that is not optional. There is only one way, I believe, to turn these policies around. The Congress can respond to the mandate that the American people have clearly expressed. They have said, "End this war. Stop the waste. Stop the killing. Do something for our own people first." We must find the money to "launch the new approaches," as Mr. Nixon said. We must force the administration to rethink its distorted, unreal scale of priorities. Our children, our jobless men, our deprived, rejected, and starving fellow citizens must come first.

For this reason, I intend to vote "No" on every money bill that comes to the floor of this House that provides any funds for the Department of Defense. Any bill whatsoever, until the time comes when our values and priorities have been turned right-side up again, until the monstrous waste and the shocking profits in the defense budget have been eliminated and our country starts to use its strength, its tremendous resources, for people and peace, not for profits and war.

It was Calvin Coolidge I believe who made the comment that "the Business of America is Business." We are now spending $80 billion a year on defense—that is two-thirds of every tax dollar. At this time, gentlemen, the business of America is war and it is time for a change.

ANGELA DAVIS

Like Shirley Chisholm, Angela Davis (b. 1944) is an African American woman who has run for national office (in 1980 and 1984 she was the candidate for vice president on the Communist ticket); but this important similarity aside, the two women differ sharply. Davis grew up in a Communist-leaning environment (her mother was an officer of the Communist-influenced Southern Negro Youth Congress), and at Elizabeth Irwin High School in Greenwich Village she was recruited by the Communist youth group Advance. She studied with Herbert Marcuse at Brandeis, majored in French, went to Paris. After graduation she attended the University of Frankfurt, studying philosophy and participating in actions sponsored by the German equivalent of the American Students for a Democratic Society. She might have stayed, might have led a life like that of Susan Sontag; but the formation of the Black Panther Party, and the increasing radicalism of the Student Nonviolent Coordinating Committee, drew her back to the United States. She again studied with Marcuse, now at San Diego, and after getting her master's degree there was hired by the philosophy department of UCLA.

That gets us to the moment of the text included here, a speech given at a Black Panther rally on November 12, 1969. Like Barbara Deming's essay appearing earlier, it asks whether the antiwar movement and the civil rights movement are one struggle or two, and comes to the same conclusion. But the temperature is hotter; the Vietnam War is pressing; the government's war, as Davis would put it, against the Black Panthers is also pressing; and the civil rights activists on whose behalf Davis is speaking are not nonviolent activists but fiercely confrontational militants.

In 1970 Davis was fired from her UCLA job because of her membership in the Communist Party, then rehired by court order, then fired again for "inflammatory language." That same year she became a prominent supporter of George Jackson, one of three black inmates charged with the murder of a guard at Soledad prison. In August 1970 Jackson's younger brother Jonathan took hostages in an attempt to free the "Soledad Brothers" that ended in the killing of four people. When the guns used by Jonathan Jackson were traced to Davis, she fled, was apprehended, and eventually was acquitted of murder and kidnapping charges.

The remainder of Davis's life until the present moment is that of a radical activist and scholar. She traveled to Cuba, and to the Soviet Union to accept the Lenin Peace Prize. She taught at San Francisco State University from 1980 till 1984, and at Santa Cruz, in the History of Consciousness program and the Feminist Studies Departments, from 1991 till her retirement in 2008. Much of her recent work focuses on the prison system, which she seeks to abolish; she is also active in black feminist circles and in campaigns against the death penalty.

The Liberation of Our People

YEAH, I'd just like to say that I like being called sister much more than professor, and I've continually said that if my job—if keeping my job—means that I have to make any compromises in the liberation struggle in this country, then I'll gladly leave my job. This is my position. Now, there has been a lot of debate in the left sector of the anti-war movement as to what the orientation of that movement should be. And I think there are two main issues at hand. One group of people feels that the movement, the anti-war movement, ought to be a single-issue movement: the cessation of the war in Vietnam. They do not want to relate it to the other kinds and forms of repression that are taking place here in this country. There's another group of people who say that we have to make those connections. We have to talk about what's happening in Vietnam as being a symptom of something that's happening all over the world, of something that's happening in this country. And in order for the anti-war movement to be effective, it has to link up with the struggle for black and brown liberation in this country, with the struggle of exploited white workers. Now, I think we should ask ourselves why that first group of people want the anti-war movement to be a single-issue movement. Somehow they feel that it's necessary to tone down the political content of that movement in order to attract as many people as possible. They think that mere numbers will be enough in order to affect this government's policy. But I think we have to talk about the political content. We have to talk about the necessity to raise the level of consciousness of the people who are involved in that movement. And if you analyze the war in Vietnam, first of all it ought to become obvious that if the United States government pulled its troops out of Vietnam that that repression would have to crop up somewhere else. And in fact, we're seeing that as this country is being defeated in Vietnam, more and more acts of repression are occurring here on the domestic scene. And I'd just like to point to the most dramatic one in the last couple of weeks, which is the chaining and gagging of Chairman Bobby Seale and his sentence to four years for contempt of court. I think that demonstrates that if the link-up is not made between what's happening in Vietnam and what's happening here we may very well face a period of full-blown fascism very soon.

Now, I think there's something perhaps more profound that we ought to point to. This whole economy in this country is a war economy. It's based on the fact that more and more and more weapons are being produced. What happens if the war in Vietnam ceases? How is the economy going to stand unless another Vietnam is created, and who is to determine where that Vietnam is gonna be? It can be abroad, or it can be right here at home, and I think it's becoming evident that that Vietnam is entering the streets of this country. It's becoming evident in all the brutal forms of repression, which we can see every day of our lives here. And this reminds me, because I think this is very relevant to what's happening in Vietnam—that is, the military situation in this country. I saw on television last week that the head of the National Guard in California decided that from now on their military activities are gonna be concentrated in three main areas. Now what are these areas? First of all, he says, disruption in minority communities, then he says disruption on the campus, then he says disruption in industrial areas. I think it points to the fact that they are going to begin to use that whole military apparatus in order to put down the resistance in the black and brown community, on the campuses, in the working-class communities. I think that they are really preparing for this now. It's evident that the terror is becoming not just isolated instances of police brutality here and there, but that terror is becoming an everyday instrument of the institutions of this country. The chief of the National Guard said that outright. It's happening in the courts. There is terror in the courts: that judge, whose name is Hoffman, proved that he is going to take on the terror in the society and bring it into the courts, that he is going to use what is supposed to be a court of law, justice, equality, whatever you wanna call it, in order to mete out all of these, you know, fascist acts of repression.

Now, something else has been happening in the courts, and I think this is an incident that we all ought to be aware of because it's another instance of terror entering into the courts. Down in San Jose, not too long ago, a young Chicano was on trial, and I'd like to read a quote from the transcript, a quote by Judge—I think his name is Chargin, the fascist. He said, "Mexican people, after 13 years of age, it's perfectly all right to go out and act like an animal. Maybe Hitler was right. The animals in our society probably ought to be destroyed because they have no right to live among human beings. You are lower than animals and haven't the right to exist in organized society, just miserable lousy rotten people." Now this is the direct quote from the transcript that's happened within the walls of the courtroom. How can we fail to see that there's an intricate connection between that type of thing, between what happened to Bobby Seale, between the unwarranted imprisonment of Huey Newton, and what's happening in Vietnam. We are facing a common enemy, and that enemy is Yankee imperialism, which is killing us both here and abroad. Now I think anyone who would try to separate those struggles, anyone who would say that in order to consolidate an anti-war movement, we have to leave all of these other outlying issues out of the picture, is playing right into the hands of the enemy. I mean, it's an old saying; I think it's been demonstrated over and over that it's correct that once the people are divided, the enemy will be victorious. We will face defeat. And I think the attempt to isolate what's happening on the domestic scene from the war in Vietnam is playing right into the hands of the enemy, giving him the chance to be victorious.

And I think there's a much more concrete problem. If you talk about the anti-war movement as a separate movement, what happens? What happens if suddenly the troops are pulled out of Vietnam? What happens if Nixon suddenly says we're gonna bring all of the boys home? The people, the thousands, the millions of people who had been involved in that movement would feel as if they had been victorious. I think perhaps a number of them would think that they could return home and relish in their victory and say that we have won, completely ignoring the fact that Huey Newton is still in jail, that Erica Huggins and all the other sisters and brothers in Connecticut are still in jail. This is what we are faced with if we cannot make that connection between the international scene and the domestic scene. And I don't think there's any question about it. We can't talk about protesting the genocide of the Vietnamese people without at the same time doing something to stop the genocide that is—that liberation fighters in this country are being subjected to. Now I think we can draw a parallel between what's happening right now and what's—what happened during the 1950s. As the United States government was being defeated in the Korean War, more and more repression did occur on the domestic scene. The McCarthy witch hunt started. This is the Communist Party, which was the main target of that. I think we have to ask ourselves why that period served to completely stifle revolutionary activity in this country. People were scared, they ran away, they lost their families, they lost their homes. They did not resist. This is the problem. They did not resist. Right now the Black Panther Party is the main target of the repression that's coming down in this society, and the Black Panther Party is resisting. And we all ought to talk about standing up and resisting this oppression, resisting the onslaught of fascism in this country. Otherwise, the movement is going to be doomed to failure. I think we can say that if the anti-war movement defends only itself and does not defend liberation fighters in this country, then that movement is going to be doomed to failure, just as we can say also if we in the black liberation movement and the liberation movement for all people in—all oppressed and exploited people in this country, defend only ourselves, then we too will be doomed to failure.

Within the whole liberation struggle in this country, the black liberation struggle and the brown liberation struggle, there has continually been the sentiment against the American imperialist aggressive policies throughout this world because we have been forced to see that the enemy is American imperialism. And although we feel it here at home it's being felt perhaps much more brutally in Vietnam, it's being felt in Latin America, it's being felt in Africa. We have to make these connections. [Inaudible] has to see that unless it makes that connection, it's going to become irrelevant. And what we have to talk about now is a united force, which sees the liberation of the Vietnamese people as intricately linked up with the liberation of black and brown and exploited white people in this society; and only this kind of a united front, only this kind of a united force, can be victorious.

Now, I think that there's something else that we ought to consider when we try to analyze what has happened in the anti-war movement. And the anti-war movement hasn't just depended on numbers. It hasn't just depended upon attracting more and more people into the movement regardless of their political orientation. If we remember, the debate a long time ago was whether the anti-war movement or the peace movement then should talk about demanding the cessation of bombing in Vietnam or whether it should talk about withdrawing troops. I think now it's very obvious that you have to talk about withdrawing all American troops from Vietnam. This has occurred only through the process of trying to raise the level of political consciousness of the people who were in that movement. And right now what we have to talk about is not just withdrawing American troops, but also recognizing the South Vietnamese Provisional Revolutionary Government.

Now, I think we have to go a step further. This is what's happening inside the anti-war movement, but we have to take it further. And we have to say that if they—if we demand the immediate withdrawal of American troops in Vietnam [inaudible] of the South Vietnamese Provisional Revolutionary Government, then we also have to demand the release of all political prisoners in this country, here. This is what we have to demand. And I think that the liberation struggle here sheds a lot of light on what's happening in Vietnam. It shows us that we can't just push for peace in Vietnam, that we have to talk about also recognizing a revolutionary government. There was a kind of a peace that was obtained right here in this country, in a courtroom, that was the peace which Judge Hoffman forced on Chairman Bobby Seale by coercion, by gagging him and binding him to his chair. This is not the kind of peace that we wanna talk about in Vietnam, the peace in which you have a puppet regime representing the interests of this country in which you have other means of establishing the power of this government in Vietnam.

And I think on a much more personal level, there's some parallels that we can draw. Some very profound parallels I think. And we have to say that Bobby Seale's mother, who learned that he had been chained and gagged and that he had been sentenced to four years for contempt of court, is no less grieved than an American woman who finds out that her son has been captured in Vietnam. I think we have to say that—that Erica Huggins and Yvonne Carter were no less grieved when they found that their husbands Bunchy and John [inaudible] liberation, than an American wife would feel about her husband there. But there is a different political consciousness involved, and this is what we have to show the American people today. We have to show the American people that their sons and their husbands are being victimized by American imperialism. They are being forced to go and fight a dirty war in Vietnam. They are victims too, and they have to be shown that their true loyalties ought to be with us in the liberation struggle here and with the Vietnamese people in their liberation struggle there. Now, Bobby Seale once made a statement at a peace conference in Montreal that the frontline of the battle against racism was in Vietnam. I think we have to ask ourselves what this means, because a lot of people may have thought that what this means is that we can depend on the Vietnamese to win our battle here. This is not what he was saying. He was pointing to that inherent connection between what's happening there and what's happening here. And I think we can say—and I'm talking from personal experience, I was in Cuba this summer and I met with some representatives of the South Vietnam— they told us that we were—we revolutionaries in this country—were their most important allies. And not just because we take signs and march in front of the White House saying U.S. government get out of Vietnam because—rather because we are actively involved in struggling to satisfy the needs of our people in this country, and in this way, as they point out, we are able to internally destroy that monster, which is oppressing people all over the country. I have to admit that I felt a little bit inadequate about that because what he's saying—what the representative of the South Vietnamese Provisional Revolutionary Government was saying—is that we are to escalate our struggle in this country, we ought to talk about making more and more demands for the liberation of our people here and this is going to be what they will depend on. This is going to help them in their liberation struggle. Now I think that we ought to talk in the context of this upcoming march here and in Washington about the [inaudible] to make simultaneous demands, and those demands ought to be immediate withdrawal of U.S. troops from Vietnam. There ought to be victory for the Vietnamese. There ought to be also recognition of the revolutionary government in South Vietnam, and I think this is perhaps most important, we ought to demand the release of political prisoners in this country.

Just one last thing. You know Nixon made a speech, on November 3rd I think it was, and he said something that we ought to take heed of, we ought to understand. He said, "Let us understand that the Vietnamese cannot defeat or humiliate our government. Only Americans can do that." I feel that it is our responsibility to fight on all fronts, to fight on all fronts simultaneously to defeat and to humiliate the U.S. government and all the fascist tactics by which it is repressing liberation fighters in this country.

Thank you very much.

DANIEL BERRIGAN

I wrote a tribute to Daniel Berrigan (b. 1921) when he turned eighty, for a volume of tributes edited by Askold Melnyczuk, Howard Zinn being another contributor to it, and met Berrigan at a party in his honor, though I was too shy to speak with him. My tribute reflected on a phrase of Berrigan's that Adrienne Rich had taken as the epigraph of "The Burning of Paper Instead of Children": "I was threatened with verbalizing / my moral substance out of existence." The phrase is exactly right for a poet who has also been an activist, an activist who has also been a poet; the poet wants and needs to verbalize, the activist knows the dangers of verbalizing in excess.

The phrase occurs in Berrigan's play *The Trial of the Catonsville Nine* (1970), perhaps the greatest American antiwar play, and the only play represented in this anthology. Its subject is a famous act of radical nonviolence, namely, the burning with homemade napalm of some of the files of the Catonsville, Maryland, draft board on May 17, 1968, by nine Catholic pacifists, Berrigan's brother Philip among them. *The Trial of the Catonsville Nine* distills the transcripts of the subsequent court proceedings to their essence, allowing the accused and the trial judge alike to reveal their humanity fully.

Berrigan was born in rural Minnesota, joined the Jesuits after high school, was ordained to the priesthood in 1952, began to teach theology in 1954, and won the Lamont Prize for a book of poems in 1957. A promising beginning for a mainstream clerical and intellectual career; but friendships with Dorothy Day and Thomas Merton, the promptings of his brother Philip, and above all the war in Vietnam made complacency impossible. He voiced his support for student antiwar activists, marched in Selma, founded Clergy and Laity Concerned about the War in Vietnam (with A. J. Heschel and others), and found himself increasingly out of favor with his conservative superiors. In the fall of 1965 he was "exiled" to the slums of South America, an act that had unintended consequences: his conscience galvanized and his public stature raised considerably, he was called home (after protests by liberal Catholics) ready for confrontation and civil disobedience. He marched on the Pentagon, spilled blood on draft records in Baltimore, traveled to Hanoi with Howard Zinn to receive POWs released by the North Vietnamese. Sentenced to three years for his actions at Catonsville, he went underground with Philip, making the FBI's Ten Most Wanted list and evading capture for four months before his eighteen-month stint in Danbury.

Some radicals get less radical as they grow older; Berrigan got more so. He spent time in France with Thich Nhat Hanh, then in 1980 with his brother Philip and some others founded the Plowshares Movement; members of that group walked into a nuclear weapons plant in Pennsylvania, damaged missiles, and poured blood onto files; after years of appeals he again found himself in prison. In 1989 he came to preach in Colrain, Massachusetts, in the house of Randy Kehler and Betsy Corner, seized by the IRS for its owners' principled nonpayment of war taxes; in 2012 he was to be heard speaking on behalf of the activists of Occupy Wall Street.

FROM
The Trial of the Catonsville Nine

DEFENSE
>   Could you state to the court what your intent was in
>   burning the draft files?

DANIEL BERRIGAN
>   I did not want the children
>   or the grandchildren of the jury
>   or of the judge
>   to be burned with napalm

JUDGE
>   You say your intention was to save these children, of the
>   jury, of myself, when you burned the records? That is
>   what I heard you say. I ask if you meant that.

DANIEL BERRIGAN
>   I meant that
>   of course I mean that
>   or I would not say it
>   The great sinfulness
>   of modern war is
>   that it renders concrete things abstract
>   I do not want to talk
>   about Americans in general

JUDGE
>   You cannot think up arguments now that you would
>   like to have had in your mind then.

DANIEL BERRIGAN
>   My intention on that day

was
to save the innocent
from death by fire
I was trying to save the poor
who are mainly charged with
dying in this war
I poured napalm
on behalf of the prosecutor's
and the jury's children
It seems to me quite logical
If my way of putting the facts
is inadmissible
then so be it
But I was trying to be concrete
about death   because death
is a concrete fact
as I have throughout my life
tried to be concrete
about the existence of God
Who is not an abstraction
but is someone before me
for Whom I am responsible

In Hanoi I think we were the first Americans
to undergo
an American bombing attack
When the burned draft files
were brought into court yesterday
as evidence
I could not but recall
that I had seen in Hanoi
evidence of a very different nature
I saw   not boxes of burned papers
I saw parts of human bodies   preserved in alcohol
the bodies of children   the hearts and organs and limbs
of women
teachers   workers   peasants   bombed
in fields and churches and schools and hospitals

I examined our "improved weaponry"
It was quite clear to me
during three years of air war
America had been experimenting
upon the bodies of the innocent
We had improved our weapons
on their flesh

JUDGE

He did not see this first hand. He is telling of things he
was told in Hanoi, about some things that were preserved
in alcohol.

DANIEL BERRIGAN

French   English   Swedish experts   doctors
testified
these were actually the bodies
whose pictures
accompanied the exhibits
The evidence was unassailable
The bombings
were a massive crime against man
The meaning of the air war in the North
was the deliberate systematic destruction
of a poor and developing people

JUDGE

We are not trying the air war in North Vietnam.

DANIEL BERRIGAN

I must protest the effort
to discredit me on the stand
I am speaking of what I saw
There is a consistent effort
to say that I did not see it

JUDGE

The best evidence of what some "crime commission"
found is not a summary that you give.

DANIEL BERRIGAN

So be it
In any case we brought the flyers home
I think as a result of the trip to Hanoi
I understood the limits
of what I had done before

and the next step that must come
On my return to America
another event
helped me understand
the way I must go
It was the self-immolation
of a high school student
in Syracuse New York
in the spring of 1968
This boy had come to a point of despair
about the war   He had gone
into the Catholic cathedral
drenched himself with kerosene
and immolated himself in the street
He was still living a month later
I was able to gain access to him
I smelled the odor
of burning flesh
And I understood anew
what I had seen in North Vietnam
The boy was dying in torment
his body like a piece of meat
cast upon a grille
He died shortly thereafter
I felt that my senses
had been invaded in a new way
I had understood
the power of death in the modern world
I knew I must speak and act
against death
because this boy's death
was being multiplied
a thousandfold
in the Land of Burning Children
So I went to Catonsville
and burned some papers   because
the burning of children
is inhuman and unbearable
I went to Catonsville
because I had gone to Hanoi

because my brother was a man
and I must be a man
and because
I knew at length
I could not announce the gospel
from a pedestal
I must act as a Christian
sharing the risks and burdens and anguish
of those whose lives were placed
in the breach by us
I saw suddenly   and it struck with the force of lightning
that my position was false
I was threatened with verbalizing
my moral substance out of existence
I was placing upon young shoulders
a filthy burden   the original sin of war
I was asking them to enter a ceremony of death
Although I was too old
to carry a draft card   there were other ways
of getting in trouble with a state
that seemed determined upon multiplying the dead
totally intent upon a war
the meaning of which   no sane man could tell
So I went to Hanoi
and then to Catonsville
and that is why I am here

DEFENSE

Did you not write a meditation to accompany the statement
issued by the nine defendants at Catonsville?

DANIEL BERRIGAN

Yes sir

DEFENSE

Would you read the meditation?

DANIEL BERRIGAN

Certainly
"Some ten or twelve of us (the number is still uncertain)
will if all goes well (ill?) take our religious bodies
during this week
to a draft center in or near Baltimore
There we shall   of purpose and forethought

remove the I–A files   sprinkle them in the public street
with home-made napalm   and set them afire
For which act we shall beyond doubt
be placed behind bars for some portion of our natural lives
in consequence of our inability
to live and die content in the plagued city
to say 'peace peace' when there is no peace
to keep the poor poor
the thirsty and hungry thirsty and hungry
Our apologies   good friends
for the fracture of good order   the burning of paper
instead of children   the angering of the orderlies
in the front parlor of the charnel house
We could not   so help us God   do otherwise
For we are sick at heart   our hearts
give us no rest for thinking of the Land of Burning Children
and for thinking of that other Child of whom
the poet Luke speaks   The infant was taken up
in the arms of an old man whose tongue
grew resonant and vatic at the touch of that beauty
And the old man spoke: this child is set
for the fall and rise of many in Israel
a sign that is spoken against
Small consolation   a child born to make trouble
and to die for it   the First Jew (not the last)
to be subject of a 'definitive solution'
And so we stretch out our hands
to our brothers throughout the world
We who are priests to our fellow priests
All of us who act against the law
turn to the poor of the world   to the Vietnamese
to the victims   to the soldiers who kill and die
for the wrong reasons for no reason at all
because they were so ordered by the authorities
of that public order which is in effect
a massive institutionalized disorder
We say: killing is disorder
life and gentleness and community and unselfishness
is the only order we recognize
For the sake of that order

we risk our liberty   our good name
The time is past when good men may be silent
when obedience
can segregate men from public risk
when the poor can die without defense
How many indeed must die
before our voices are heard
how many must be tortured dislocated
starved maddened?
How long must the world's resources
be raped in the service of legalized murder?
When at what point will you say no to this war?
We have chosen to say
with the gift of our liberty
if necessary our lives:
the violence stops here
the death stops here
the suppression of the truth stops here
this war stops here
Redeem the times!
The times are inexpressibly evil
Christians pay conscious   indeed religious tribute
to Caesar and Mars
by the approval of overkill tactics   by brinkmanship
by nuclear liturgies   by racism   by support of genocide
They embrace their society with all their heart
and abandon the cross
They pay lip service to Christ
and military service to the powers of death
And yet   and yet   the times are inexhaustibly good
solaced by the courage and hope of many
The truth rules   Christ is not forsaken
In a time of death some men
the resisters   those who work hardily for social change
those who preach and embrace the truth
such men overcome death
their lives are bathed in the light of the resurrection
the truth has set them free
In the jaws of death
they proclaim their love of the brethren

We think of such men
in the world   in our nation   in the churches
and the stone in our breast is dissolved
we take heart once more"
DEFENSE
Nothing further.

HENRY COSBY, JOE HINTON, AND PAM SAWYER

"I Should Be Proud," released in February 1970, was the first Motown antiwar protest song (though not the last, being followed within a year or so by the Temptations' "Ball of Confusion," Edwin Starr's "War," and Marvin Gaye's "What's Going On"). It was the only antiwar song recorded by Martha & the Vandellas—better known for their 1964 hit "Dancing in the Street"—and did only moderately well on the charts, its message too controversial for many radio stations.

That message is an unusual one. The singer's Johnny has been killed in action in Vietnam, and she is told to be proud of him. But she is not; she resents the way she has been informed of the death, and is skeptical of the rationales offered her—"he was keepin' me free," she is told, but she rejects the claim. In most of the song, she seems simply and very movingly to want him alive—one of the oldest antiwar motives, the gist of which is, the war's rationale does not justify the death of this person I loved. Rejecting the posthumous consolations of "honor and glory," military medals, and community regard, she begins to resent the "evils" of the system that has taken Johnny from her.

"I Should Be Proud" was written by Joe Hinton (not to be confused with the R&B singer of the same name) and Pam Sawyer (b. 1936) and arranged and produced by Henry Cosby (1928–2002), Hinton and Cosby native-born Motown musicians and Sawyer an east London expatriate. But it is Martha Reeves's intense performance that makes the song live. She identified with it, she later recalled, "because I had a brother who had gotten hurt and damaged in Vietnam and came home and died."

I Should Be Proud

I was under the dryer when the telegram came:
"Private John C. Miller was shot down in Vietnam."
Through my tears I read: "No more information at this time.
He's missin' in action somewhere on the Delta Line."

And they say that I should be proud; he was fightin' for me.
They say that I should be proud, those too blind to see.

But he wasn't fightin' for me, my Johnny didn't have to fight
for me,
He was fightin' for the evils of society.

Now I prayed night and day that my Johnny wouldn't die.
Love, faith, and hope was all that kept me alive.
Then six weeks later came that cold and heartless letter:
"Private Johnny was killed in action, number 54327."

And they say that I should be proud; he was keepin' me free.
They say that I should be proud, those too blind to see.
But he wasn't fightin' for me, my Johnny didn't have to die
for me,
He was fightin' for the evils of society.

(*Spoken*) They shipped him home with medals of honor and
glory.
Even our local paper ran a front-page story.
(*Sung*) But the whole town came to praise him, and said how
honored I should be.
But I don't want no silver star, just the good man they took
from me.

Yet they tell me I should be proud; he was fightin' for me.
They say that I should be proud, those too blind to see.
But he wasn't fightin' for me, my Johnny didn't have to die
for me,
He's a victim of the evils of society.

I should be proud of my Johnny,
They tell me that I should be proud; they just don't want
Johnny for me.
They tell me that I should be proud of my Johnny . . .

J. K. OSBORNE

J. K. Osborne (b. 1941) was just a few days shy of his twenty-seventh birthday when he was sentenced, in June 1968, to four years in prison for draft resistance—an unusually heavy sentence, though in the end he was released after eighteen months. His memoir of that time, *I Refuse* (1971), is unusually candid—as in the excerpt that follows, which stands out both for its account of the sexual violence Osborne was threatened with and to a still greater degree for its account of Osborne's rage at the threat being made, and his readiness, surprising even him, to reach for a weapon of destruction in self-defense.

Raised in poverty in Mandan, North Dakota, Osborne had won a scholarship to Dickinson State College and later graduated from Regis College, working by day to earn his tuition; he had taught junior high school in Seattle, met a girl he hoped to marry, and applied to join the Peace Corps. After his release he published two books of poetry—*Leaving It All Behind* (1970) and *First Things* (1976)—and coedited the Seattle literary magazine *Madrona*. He retired from high school teaching in the 1990s and now lives in Marica, Brazil.

FROM

I Refuse

For many months after I came to prison, I was confident in my ability to withstand all sorts of pressures, hardships, and conflicts; I felt that in whatever trials I was forced to endure, the strength of my convictions would see me through. I had then, and I have now, a belief—among the hierarchy of my beliefs, one of the highest—in the efficacy of nonviolence to overcome all hatred. I believed myself, at that time, to be incapable of resorting to violence as a personal measure to ensure my safety, or someone else's, or as a means to an end, however good that end might appear. This belief is put to the test often in the course of a peaceful man's life. My own is no exception.

I had been importuned, on a number of occasions, to participate in activities among other prisoners which were personally distasteful to me, although I cannot condemn the practice of such activities where it is entirely voluntary. Demands were made by a particular convict that I be used as his sexual outlet.

I had time and time again refused, but apologetically, as is my habit. The man would not be put off.

One day I was sitting alone at a table in the dining room having lunch. The fellow, whose friendship I had hoped to cultivate while not giving in to his sexual desires, approached the table, greeted me, and sat down. He put his hand on my knee. I moved away. He grabbed my wrist tightly in his hands—he was a large man while I am slightly smaller than the average—and, turning my wrist, snarled in my face: "You meet me in the library lounge tonight at third period, and this time no excuses. I'm going to get what I want from you one way or another."

An unfamiliar feeling took hold of me. My whole body tightened and my head rang as if filled with giant gongs. For a few seconds I lost sight of everything except his face; all around it everything was black, and filled with strange movements of color, as if I had been struck nearly unconscious by a blow on the head. My free hand felt for the fork beside my tray, and I clenched it tightly. Raising it up slowly to the level of my chest, I began unwillingly to rise from my chair. My ears were still ringing, louder than before. In that instant that we stood glaring at each other, our brotherhood was confirmed. He released his grip, and with a wry smile said, "Remember, third period." He turned and walked away.

I sat down at my place. I don't know how long I sat there, fork tight in my hand, my blood pounding as if to burst all its vessels and arteries and the heart itself. My full sight returned, the ringing stopped, and I gradually resumed my normal composure. But for quite a while afterward I felt a chill.

What was it that I had experienced? What had I undergone? I gave much thought to this episode for a long time after it had passed. It has left me with a little understanding of myself, and perhaps also of man. Was it fear I had experienced? Perhaps to some degree fear was present in it. Fear itself is not new to me, although it is an emotion I do not usually find myself burdened with. What it was that had caused me to grab my fork and raise up out of my chair, what had caused my head to ring and impaired my sight was, I believe, hatred. Pure and solitary hatred. At that moment, I had been seized with what man has been striving to overcome for all his turbulent centuries; I had been seized, and very nearly moved to become anti-man, by hatred.

I did not meet the fellow later nor, in fact, did I ever consequently have anything more than a nodding relationship with him. What had caused him to discontinue his advances is unknown to me, although there are those who will see in this episode a justification for violence. But since that incident in the lunchroom, I have seen the whole question of pacifism in a clearer light.

I know now that I, as a fallible human, am capable of surrendering to hatred and fear and striking out at another being. I am even ready to admit my capability to kill another man. I can see, too, where this instinct lies in every man, in man's nature. I also see that it is *because* we are all capable of murder that it is imperative to the survival of man that we purify ourselves of this unholy and satanic failing. A century ago, it may not have been as urgent as it is today.

But it must be recognized that, since we now possess the means of destroying all of mankind and of throwing nature itself off balance, the question of whether or not we must change the nature of man from an aggressive one to a peaceful one can no longer be debated, delayed, or doubted. It is quite simply a matter of deciding whether or not we want man to continue his existence on this earth.

JOHN KERRY

As I write this note, John Kerry (b. 1943) is the U.S. secretary of state, the architect of a deal with Iran that, as Kerry has presented it, will keep that nation from acquiring nuclear weapons and possibly avert a war: the kind of high-level diplomacy that is in its own way a mode of antiwar action, and one of the most important.

In 1971, though, he was working against war from outside the government. He had served in Vietnam, had been awarded a Silver Star, a Bronze Star, and three Purple Hearts, then joined Vietnam Veterans Against the War and became one of its spokespersons, a role that brought him on April 23 of that year to testify before the Senate Committee on Foreign Relations, and let him make this remarkable speech, known best for its heartbreaking question, "How do you ask a man to be the last man to die for a mistake?"

Kerry was born in Colorado, attended boarding school in New England, went to Yale, majored in political science, played on the varsity soccer team, took flying lessons, triumphed in debates. After returning from Vietnam he got a law degree from Boston College, served as an assistant district attorney and then as Michael Dukakis's lieutenant governor in Massachusetts. In 1984 he was elected to the Senate, where he distinguished himself by his tenacious investigations of the Reagan administration's funding of the Nicaraguan Contras. He was the Democratic candidate for president in 2004, lost to George W. Bush, returned to the Senate, and became secretary of state in 2013.

Statement of John Kerry, Vietnam Veterans Against the War

MR. KERRY. Thank you very much, Senator Fulbright, Senator Javits, Senator Symington, Senator Pell. I would like to say for the record, and also for the men behind me who are also wearing the uniforms and their medals, that my sitting here is really symbolic. I am not here as John Kerry. I am here as one member of the group of 1,000, which is a small representation of a very much larger group of veterans in this country, and were it possible for all of them to sit at this table they would be here and have the same kind of testimony.

I would simply like to speak in very general terms. I apologize if my statement is general because I received notification yesterday you would hear me and I am afraid because of the injunction I was up most of the night and haven't had a great deal of chance to prepare.

I would like to talk, representing all those veterans, and say that several months ago in Detroit, we had an investigation at which over 150 honorably discharged and many very highly decorated veterans testified to war crimes committed in Southeast Asia, not isolated incidents but crimes committed on a day-to-day basis with the full awareness of officers at all levels of command.

It is impossible to describe to you exactly what did happen in Detroit, the emotions in the room, the feelings of the men who were reliving their experiences in Vietnam, but they did. They relived the absolute horror of what this country, in a sense, made them do.

They told the stories at times they had personally raped, cut off ears, cut off heads, taped wires from portable telephones to human genitals and turned up the power, cut off limbs, blown up bodies, randomly shot at civilians, razed villages in fashion reminiscent of Genghis Khan, shot cattle and dogs for fun, poisoned food stocks, and generally ravaged the countryside of South Vietnam in addition to the normal ravage of war, and the normal and very particular ravaging which is done by the applied bombing power of this country.

We call this investigation the "Winter Soldier Investigation." The term "Winter Soldier" is a play on words of Thomas Paine in 1776 when he spoke of the Sunshine Patriot and summertime soldiers who deserted at Valley Forge because the going was rough.

We who have come here to Washington have come here because we feel we have to be winter soldiers now. We could come back to this country; we could be quiet; we could hold our silence; we could not tell what went on in Vietnam, but we feel because of what threatens this country, the fact that the crimes threaten it, not reds, and not redcoats but the crimes which we are committing that threaten it, that we have to speak out.

I would like to talk to you a little bit about what the result is of the feelings these men carry with them after coming back from Vietnam. The country doesn't know it yet, but it has created a monster, a monster in the form of millions of men who have been taught to deal and to trade in violence, and who are given the chance to die for the biggest nothing in history; men who have returned with a sense of anger and a sense of betrayal which no one has yet grasped.

As a veteran and one who feels this anger, I would like to talk about it. We are angry because we feel we have been used in the worst fashion by the administration of this country.

In 1970 at West Point, Vice President Agnew said "some glamorize the criminal misfits of society while our best men die in Asian rice paddies to preserve the freedom which most of those misfits abuse," and this was used as a rallying point for our effort in Vietnam.

But for us, as boys in Asia whom the country was supposed to support, his statement is a terrible distortion from which we can only draw a very deep sense of revulsion. Hence the anger of some of the men who are here in Washington today. It is a distortion because we in no way consider ourselves the best men of this country, because those he calls misfits were standing up for us in a way that nobody else in this country dared to, because so many who have died would have returned to this country to join the misfits in their efforts to ask for an immediate withdrawal from South Vietnam, because so many of those best men have returned as quadriplegics and amputees, and they lie forgotten in Veterans' Administration hospitals in this country which fly the flag which so many have chosen as their own personal symbol. And we cannot consider ourselves America's best men when we are ashamed of and hated what we were called on to do in Southeast Asia.

In our opinion, and from our experience, there is nothing in South Vietnam, nothing which could happen that realistically threatens the United States of America. And to attempt to justify the loss of one American life in Vietnam, Cambodia, or Laos by linking such loss to the preservation of freedom, which those misfits supposedly abuse, is to us the height of criminal hypocrisy, and it is that kind of hypocrisy which we feel has torn this country apart.

We are probably much more angry than that and I don't want to go into the foreign policy aspects because I am outclassed here. I know that all of you talk about every possible alternative of getting out of Vietnam. We understand that. We know you have considered the seriousness of the aspects to the utmost level and I am not going to try to dwell on that, but I want to relate to you the feeling that many of the men who have returned to this country express because we are probably angriest about all that we were told about Vietnam and about the mystical war against communism.

We found that not only was it a civil war, an effort by a people who had for years been seeking their liberation from any colonial influence whatsoever, but also we found that the Vietnamese whom we had enthusiastically molded after our own image were hard put to take up the fight against the threat we were supposedly saving them from.

We found most people didn't even know the difference between communism and democracy. They only wanted to work in rice paddies without helicopters strafing them and bombs with napalm burning their villages and tearing their country apart. They wanted everything to do with the war, particularly with this foreign presence of the United States of America, to leave them alone in peace, and they practiced the art of survival by siding with whichever military force was present at a particular time, be it Vietcong, North Vietnamese, or American.

We found also that all too often American men were dying in those rice paddies for want of support from their allies. We saw first hand how money from American taxes was used for a corrupt dictatorial regime. We saw that many people in this country had a one-sided idea of who was kept free by our flag, as blacks provided the highest percentage of casualties. We saw Vietnam ravaged equally by American bombs as well as by search and destroy missions, as well as by Vietcong terrorism, and yet we listened while this country tried to blame all of the havoc on the Vietcong.

We rationalized destroying villages in order to save them. We saw America lose her sense of morality as she accepted very coolly a My Lai and refused to give up the image of American soldiers who hand out chocolate bars and chewing gum.

We learned the meaning of free fire zones, shooting anything that moves, and we watched while America placed a cheapness on the lives of orientals.

We watched the U.S. falsification of body counts, in fact the glorification of body counts. We listened while month after month we were told the back of the enemy was about to break. We fought using weapons against "oriental human beings," with quotation marks around that. We fought using weapons against those people which I do not believe this country would dream of using were we fighting in the European theater or let us say a non-third-world people theater, and so we watched while men charged up hills because a general said that hill has to be taken, and after losing one platoon or two platoons they marched away to leave the high [*sic*; hill] for the reoccupation by the North Vietnamese because we watched pride allow the most unimportant of battles to be blown into extravaganzas, because we couldn't lose, and we couldn't retreat, and because it didn't matter how many American bodies were lost to prove that point. And so there were Hamburger Hills and Khe Sanhs and Hill 881's and Fire Base 6's and so many others.

Now we are told that the men who fought there must watch quietly while American lives are lost so that we can exercise the incredible arrogance of Vietnamizing the Vietnamese.

Each day—

[Applause.]

The CHAIRMAN. I hope you won't interrupt. He is making a very significant statement. Let him proceed.

Mr. KERRY. Each day to facilitate the process by which the United States washes her hands of Vietnam someone has to give up his life so that the United States doesn't have to admit something that the entire world already knows, so that we can't say that we have made a mistake. Someone has to die so that President Nixon won't be, and these are his words, "the first President to lose a war."

We are asking Americans to think about that because how do you ask a man to be the last man to die in Vietnam? How do you ask a man to be the last man to die for a mistake? But we are trying to do that, and we are doing it with thousands of rationalizations, and if you read carefully the President's last speech to the people of this country, you can see that he says, and says clearly:

> But the issue, gentlemen, the issue is communism, and the question is whether or not we will leave that country to the Communists or whether or not we will try to give it hope to be a free people.

But the point is they are not a free people now under us. They are not a free people, and we cannot fight communism all over the world, and I think we should have learned that lesson by now.

But the problem of veterans goes beyond this personal problem, because you think about a poster in this country with a picture of Uncle Sam and the picture says "I want you." And a young man comes out of high school and says, "That is fine. I am going to serve my country." And he goes to Vietnam and he shoots and he kills and he does his job or maybe he doesn't kill, maybe he just goes and he comes back, and when he gets back to this country he finds that he isn't really wanted, because the largest unemployment figure in the country—it varies depending on who you get it from, the VA Administration 15 percent, various other sources 22 percent. But the largest corps of unemployed in this country are veterans of this war, and of those veterans 33 percent of the unemployed are black. That means 1 out of every 10 of the Nation's unemployed is a veteran of Vietnam.

The hospitals across the country won't, or can't meet their demands. It is not a question of not trying. They don't have the appropriations. A man recently died after he had a tracheotomy in California, not because of the operation but because there weren't enough personnel to clean the mucus out of his tube and he suffocated to death.

Another young man just died in a New York VA hospital the other day. A friend of mine was lying in a bed two beds away and tried to help him, but he couldn't. He rang a bell and there was nobody there to service that man and so he died of convulsions.

I understand 57 percent of all those entering the VA hospitals talk about suicide. Some 27 percent have tried, and they try because they come back to this country and they have to face what they did in Vietnam, and then they come back and find the indifference of a country that doesn't really care, that doesn't really care.

Suddenly we are faced with a very sickening situation in this country, because there is no moral indignation and, if there is, it comes from people who are almost exhausted by their past indignations, and I know that many of them are sitting in front of me. The country seems to have lain down and shrugged off something as serious as Laos, just as we calmly shrugged off the loss of 700,000 lives in Pakistan, the so-called greatest disaster of all times.

But we are here as veterans to say we think we are in the midst of the greatest disaster of all times now because they are still dying over there, and not just Americans, Vietnamese, and we are rationalizing leaving that country so that those people can go on killing each other for years to come.

Americans seem to have accepted the idea that the war is winding down, at least for Americans, and they have also allowed the bodies which were once used by a President for statistics to prove that we were winning that war, to be used as evidence against a man who followed orders and who interpreted those orders no differently than hundreds of other men in Vietnam.

We veterans can only look with amazement on the fact that this country has been unable to see there is absolutely no difference between ground troops and a helicopter crew, and yet people have accepted a differentiation fed them by the administration.

No ground troops are in Laos, so it is all right to kill Laotians by remote control. But believe me the helicopter crews fill the same body bags and they wreak the same kind of damage on the Vietnamese and Laotian countryside as anybody else, and the President is talking about allowing that to go on for many years to come. One can only ask if we will really be satisfied only when the troops march into Hanoi.

We are asking here in Washington for some action, action from the Congress of the United States of America which has the power to raise and maintain armies, and which by the Constitution also has the power to declare war.

We have come here, not to the President, because we believe that this body can be responsive to the will of the people, and we believe that the will of the people says that we should be out of Vietnam now.

We are here in Washington also to say that the problem of this war is not just a question of war and diplomacy. It is part and parcel of everything that we are trying as human beings to communicate to people in this country, the question of racism, which is rampant in the military, and so many other questions also, the use of weapons, the hypocrisy in our taking umbrage in the Geneva Conventions and using that as justification for a continuation of this war, when we are more guilty than any other body of violations of those Geneva Conventions, in the use of free fire zones, harassment interdiction fire, search and destroy missions, the bombings, the torture of prisoners, the killing of prisoners, accepted policy by many units in South Vietnam. That is what we are trying to say. It is part and parcel of everything.

An American Indian friend of mine who lives in the Indian Nation of Alcatraz put it to me very succinctly. He told me how as a boy on an Indian reservation he had watched television and he used to cheer the cowboys when they came in and shot the Indians, and then suddenly one day he stopped in Vietnam and he said "My God, I am doing to these people the very same thing that was done to my people." And he stopped. And that is what we are trying to say, that we think this thing has to end.

We are also here to ask, and we are here to ask vehemently, where are the leaders of our country? Where is the leadership? We are here to ask where are McNamara, Rostow, Bundy, Gilpatric and so many others. Where are they now that we, the men whom they sent off to war, have returned? These are commanders who have deserted their troops, and there is no more serious crime in the law of war. The Army says they never leave their wounded.

The Marines say they never leave even their dead. These men have left all the casualties and retreated behind a pious shield of public rectitude. They have left the real stuff of their reputations bleaching behind them in the sun in this country.

Finally, this administration has done us the ultimate dishonor. They have attempted to disown us and the sacrifice we made for this country. In their blindness and fear they have tried to deny that we are veterans or that we served in Nam. We do not need their testimony. Our own scars and stumps of limbs are witnesses enough for others and for ourselves.

We wish that a merciful God could wipe away our own memories of that service as easily as this administration has wiped their memories of us. But all that they have done and all that they can do by this denial is to make more clear than ever our own determination to undertake one last mission, to search out and destroy the last vestige of this barbaric war, to pacify our own hearts, to conquer the hate and the fear that have driven this country these last 10 years and more, and so when, in 30 years from now, our brothers go down the street without a leg, without an arm, or a face, and small boys ask why, we will be able to say "Vietnam" and not mean a desert, not a filthy obscene memory but mean instead the place where America finally turned and where soldiers like us helped it in the turning.

Thank you. [Applause.]

RON KOVIC

In the fall of 1964, the eighteen-year-old Ron Kovic (b. 1946) left suburban Massapequa, New York, proudly enlisting in the Marines. Ten years later—a veteran not only of two tours of combat duty in Vietnam but of hospital wards, protest rallies, police beatings, and a hunger strike—he began the memoir that would become *Born on the Fourth of July* (1976), finishing a draft in a fevered seven weeks. "Convinced," he later wrote, "that I was destined to die young," he "struggled to leave something of meaning behind, to rise above the darkness and despair."

Indeed he has risen above despair, though his war wounds have left him paralyzed from the chest down and in ongoing pain. *Born on the Fourth of July* was made into a movie in 1989, winning two Academy Awards (he cowrote the screenplay with fellow veteran Oliver Stone). Now one of the country's most recognizable antiwar activists, Kovic has spoken out against the Gulf War and the Iraq War, fought for better care for returning soldiers, and offered himself as a living example of the human costs of war. ("There are the bedsores and the catheters, the urinary tract infections and high fevers, the lack of sexual function, spasms, and terrible insomnia that torments you in the night," he wrote President Obama in 2010, then considering a request to send more troops to Afghanistan.)

In the excerpt that follows, Kovic recounts a protest by Vietnam Veterans Against the War during the election of 1972.

FROM
Born on the Fourth of July

ONE by one the other demonstrators are breaking from the line. They sit down among the cars, banging their picket sticks and yelling, their voices hoarse—"One, two, three, four. We don't want your fucking war"—tying up the traffic for blocks. We have taken the streets. People are honking their horns now, workers and secretaries hanging out their windows, busdrivers shouting their approval. Some of the demonstrators are dancing and I grab both wheels of my chair, then let go with one hand and raise my middle finger in the air as a salute to the cops and the FBI. I spin on my two wheels in front of everyone, as the shouting goes on for the war to end, for the killing to be stopped forever. I keep doing my wheelies as the police look on with envy and utter contempt, frozen on their side of the street. They seem torn between wanting to kill us and wanting to tear off their uniforms and throw away their guns. "Come join us!" we shout to them, but they do not take us up on our invitation.

Finally a tall lieutenant announces over a bullhorn that the demonstration has ended and that everyone is to clear out immediately. "How are you doing, brother?" says a man with long red hair in back of me. "Is everything okay?" He is someone I have seen at other demonstrations, but I do not know his name. "You look like you could use some help," he says, and offers to push me for a while.

The police are moving now, closing in on us. I can hear sirens in the distance. I begin yelling and screaming directions to the people around me. "Get back on the sidewalk into the line! Come on now!" I try to wheel my chair forward, but it will not move. I try again.

Suddenly the man with the red hair is leaning over from behind me, grabbing my hands. "You're under arrest." Another man whom I recognize from the picket line runs up to help him. "Come on you bastard. You're going to jail!"

I am fighting to keep them from handcuffing me, screaming for the other demonstrators to help me.

The red-headed man lifts up the handles of my chair and dumps me into the street. I fall forward on my face, my legs twisted under me.

"Get your fucking hands behind you!" The red-headed man jabs his knee into my back.

There is a tremendous commotion all around me. Someone is kicking the dead part of my body that can't feel anymore. People are yelling and screaming and clubs are flying everywhere.

"I'm a Vietnam veteran! Don't you know what you're doing to me? Oh God, what's happening." They are holding my arms. They twist them behind my back, clamp handcuffs around my wrists.

"Don't you understand? My body's paralyzed. I can't move my body, I can't feel my body."

"Get him the fuck out of here!" yells someone.

Kicking me and hitting me with their fists, they begin dragging me along. They tear the medals I have won in the war from my chest and throw me back into the chair, my hands still cuffed behind me. I feel myself falling forward because I cannot balance and the red-headed man keeps pushing me back against the chair, yelling and cursing at me to stay put.

"I have no stomach muscles, don't you understand?"

"Shut up you sonofabitch!"

There are women standing on the sidewalk nearby crying, and all around me people are being beaten and handcuffed. The two men begin dragging me in the chair to an unmarked car on the other side of the street.

The red-headed man throws my body into the back seat, my dead limbs flopping underneath me. "Get in there you fucking traitor!"

I am feeling hurt all over and I can hardly breathe. I lie bleeding in the back seat as a discussion goes on between the two of them about whether or not they have broken any of my bones. I hear them say they are going to take me to the county jail hospital for x-rays.

Something happens to them when I take my clothes off in the admitting room. They stand there looking at me. They see my scars and the rubber catheter tube going into my penis and they begin to think they have made a mistake. I can see the fear in their faces. They have just beaten up a half-dead man, and they know it. They are very careful now, almost polite. They help me put my clothes back on when the doctor is through with me.

"I was in Vietnam too," the red-headed man says, hesitating.

"We don't want the war either," says the other cop. "No one wants war."

They help me back into the chair and take me to another part of the prison building to be booked.

"What's your name?" the officer behind the desk says.

"Ron Kovic," I say. "Occupation, Vietnam veteran against the war."

"What?" he says sarcastically, looking down at me.

"I'm a Vietnam veteran against the war," I almost shout back.

"You should have died over there," he says. He turns to his assistant. "I'd like to take this guy and throw him off the roof."

They fingerprint me and take my picture and put me in a cell. I have begun to wet my pants like a little baby. The tube has slipped out during my examination by the doctor. I try to fall asleep but even though I am exhausted, the anger is alive in me like a huge hot stone in my chest. I lean my head up against the wall and listen to the toilets flush again and again.

They lead me out of the cell the next morning around ten o'clock. I am to be moved to another part of the prison until someone comes to bail me out. They have arrested seventeen other vets at the demonstration. They take them out of the cells one by one, handcuffing and chaining them together in a long line like a chain gang. I look at their faces and wonder which one of them is like the guy with long red hair and the other cop who'd pretended to be veterans the day before. Which one is the informer now? I think to myself.

They tell me to move out of the way. They cannot fit me into the line with the others. "It's too difficult with that chair of yours," one of the cops complains.

"Don't you want to put the cuffs on me again?" I say. "Don't you think I need leg chains like the others?"

He looks at me surprised, then turns away and screams, "Let's go!"

The veterans clank their chains against the cold cement floor as they file past me out of the cellblock. Seventeen of America's veterans dragging those chains, handcuffed together—America's children. I cry because I want to be walking with them and because I want so much to trust them. But after what has happened I don't know whether I will be able to trust anyone, even my closest friends now. What are they doing to me? I think. They have taken so much from me already and still they are not satisfied. What more will they take?

GLORIA EMERSON

There weren't many female war correspondents in Vietnam, and none more intrepid than Gloria Emerson (1929–2004) of *The New York Times*. Refusing to be confined to the fashion pages where she began her career, she convinced her editors to let her travel there in 1970 and ultimately won a George Polk Award for her reporting. Though she also covered conflicts in Gaza, Nigeria, and Northern Ireland, it was Vietnam that she returned to in her book *Winners and Losers* (1978)—a wide-ranging, intensely researched, and very personal account of the war's complex aftereffects. It won a National Book Award.

In the passages that follow, Emerson offers intimate portraits of two very different antiwar activists. One, a member of the Emma Goldman Brigade, looks back on the "die-ins" and other protests she and her friends organized in and around New York City as "lots of fun": it was a time of intense friendships, creativity, risk-taking, and disruptive thrills. Opposition gave her a sense of purpose she now feels less keenly. The other, a veteran not only of combat in Vietnam but of the Mississippi civil rights movement before that, finds he has returned to a country in which people are either unable or unwilling to comprehend the horrors he has witnessed. The war has profoundly altered both of their lives, and both—like Emerson herself—are frustrated by the indifference they now encounter. This is perhaps Emerson's fundamental claim: American military technology has become "so advanced that we kill at a distance and insulate our consciences by the remoteness of the killing." One task of the antiwar writer is simply to make people care about war at all.

FROM
Winners and Losers

In New York nothing worked like a liver. Jill Seiden Mahoney found out that if you mushed the liver on bandages, it made stains that looked like seeping, untreated head wounds. It looked ghastly and the smell was repulsive, which was fine. The liver was useful for the "die-ins," the name for reenactments by the antiwar movement of Vietnamese villagers receiving brutal injuries from American weapons, chemicals, bombs.

Mrs. Mahoney, who was single then, and her friends made up what they called the Emma Goldman Brigade, in honor of the anarchist. Before they demonstrated, the Brigade went to some trouble to make their faces look as if they had been scarred in the war. Their favorite method was to use a mixture of oatmeal, ketchup and liquid make-up foundations, which they put on their faces after twisting their skin with strips of Scotch tape. The effect was exactly what they wished: shocking.

The targets of their protests were often business corporations; in the spring of 1972 it was the ITT Building on Park Avenue. The ten women in the Brigade, dressed in black pajamas, with the liver-stained bandages on their heads and their faces deformed, rushed into the lobby when it was crowded in the morning with people coming to work. The first thing they did was to put up posters of wounded Vietnamese children on the marble walls.

"Then we started dying, we started our blood bath. We threw Baggies which had red stuff in them. We were screaming, yelling, dying, very dramatically. Here's the sick part: the janitors started ripping down the posters of those fucked-up hurt little babies. After fifteen minutes the police came. They seemed sort of scared of us," she said. "We were rolling on the floor; it was all they could do to get us to stand up and shut up. Each of us had a flair for drama and we were trying to imagine what it would be like for a Vietnamese woman under bombs. We had fun. It sounds childish to say that now, but it was exhilarating. That day we felt we were in control. If you're rolling on the floor, screaming, nobody wants to get near you. When we finally limped out, some people applauded.

"I never knew if they applauded because they enjoyed the show or because we were leaving or they thought they were brave," she said. "It was meant to disrupt; everybody was talking about us. Energy that might have been used in their jobs that day was going into talking about our demonstration.

"Oh, sure, I know that it is said that doing things like that alienated people. But look, any action will alienate somebody. You have to expect it."

In the sixth grade in P.S. 104 in New York, she knew that her IQ was over 130. Her parents were not surprised. After graduating from the University of Pennsylvania in 1967, she worked for an advertising agency, Cunningham & Walsh, in the city. "I was a Jewish princess," she said.

In the streets young people were passing out pamphlets denouncing the war in Vietnam, and from them she learned about it.

"I would take time off to go to antiwar demonstrations; it shocked some people, who called me a Communist. The antiwar movement was personally and socially fulfilling and it was lots of fun. I miss it very much but I'm glad the war is over. I miss the commitment and the urgency—the commitment to selflessness. When it happened I thought we were all just the greatest, as a group certainly more generous than the people in the advertising agency."

In those days she often wore a T-shirt saying "The East Is Red, the West Is Ready," while her friend Coke, an unusually pretty blonde, wore one saying "The Vietnamese People Are Not the Enemy." Both women did not care if people stared at their ample chests; they wanted the T-shirts to be read.

Some of their exploits were daring: ten of them bought tickets, at fifteen dollars apiece, to attend and disrupt the National Women's Republican Club lunch in March 1972, which honored Patricia Nixon as the Woman of the Year. It was crucial for them to look like ladies. They obliged.

"Everybody still had one good dress," Mrs. Mahoney said, who wore a pink-and-brown suit from Saks Fifth Avenue. Coke even had a fur coat which she had stopped wearing; it was skunk. The plan of the Emma Goldman Brigade was for five of them to release the rats they were carrying with them, healthy rats that had been secured from laboratories so no one could accuse them of using animals that might spread disease. They were always careful about small things like that. It went wrong in the lobby: a man she calls John Finnigan of the New York Red Squad, who was watching radicals, stopped seven of the women from going into the ballroom. Three of the rats had to be released in the lobby. Inside, Mrs. Mahoney, who did not have a rat, rose and in a strong voice spoke against the war, saying nothing—on the advice of a lawyer—that was either treasonous or obscene. Then she left, leaving the ladies at her table, who were Republicans from Westchester County, in an unpleasant, if not agitated, state of mind. Two more rats were released in the ballroom, causing some consternation, but the lunch and ceremony continued.

"The antiwar movement made a difference in me and in everybody who participated. I think if there had not been such a movement, they might have nuked Vietnam off the face of the earth," she said. "It forced people to recognize what was going on or to become totally, unnaturally, blind."

It still puzzles her why other people do not understand very much, do not even know that GVN meant the Government of Vietnam in Saigon, that DRVN meant the north, or the Democratic Republic of Vietnam, that ARVN was the army in the south.

"They can tell you someone's batting average from 1948, or who hit the big homer in the 1932 World Series, but they don't know the difference between the NLF and the NFL."

The blindness, as she called it, always surprised her. On the day of the Emma Goldman Brigade's die-in in the lobby of the ITT Building, it was raining. The group worried that the rain might wash off some of the mess they had put on their faces. It was decided to take taxis.

"We were totally mutilated. None of us were recognizable," she said. "We got into two cabs at Fifty-third and Third. In each cab one person had to sit in front, so the drivers had to see what we looked like. We told them where we wanted to go and they didn't say a word. Remember how we looked and what we wore, and besides that, we all smelled, it was the oatmeal and the other stuff. We smelled horrible. Neither driver said a word, or even did a double-take. And in one newspaper, I think it was the *Daily News*, they described us as 'slovenly hippies.' They just thought we were dirty."

The Emma Goldman Brigade did not hold together but the women have stayed friends. Her marriage in September 1973 to Peter Paul Mahoney peeled apart. They had met in the antiwar movement, gone through the hard days before and during the Gainesville trial, endured all of it, only to find out how different they were. In those days she saw him as a valiant fellow who stood out for her among all the other veterans going to war against the war.

Even when the war ended and she needed a job, Mrs. Mahoney was not one to jump over her principles. She now works for a small trade magazine, having refused to consider better-paying jobs related to the military-industrial complex, the stock market, or the manufacture of foods or consumer items she thinks are dangerous. She does not want to ever contribute in any way to the misery of any people.

She will not eat bacon or frankfurters because they contain nitrates. She is even beginning to cut back on pastrami. She will not eat canned tuna fish because she deplores the killing of the porpoises caught in the tuna nets and she thinks the waters are filthy. She is quite specific about insect parts and rodent hairs in some American chocolate. When she has time she makes her own cosmetics, but she hardly wears any.

There are no regrets, just a tiny afterthought.

"The Brigade should have used indelible red ink for blood," she said, "instead of Rite-Dye."

FOR a while there was a name for the rage and guilt felt by Vietnam veterans who had been in combat. It was Post-Vietnam Syndrome, or PVS, a label for an incapacitating guilt and anger that the survivors experienced. But in Kansas City a large and affable fellow who still wore his GI boots with the shrapnel hole in one heel didn't think the PVS stuff was that special. He insisted on calling it Post-Vietnam Struggle, not Syndrome. His name was Randy, he had been a medic with the Wolfhounds, a unit of the 25th Infantry Division. He had gone to Vietnam—not wanting to—because prison seemed much worse.

"I was in Mississippi in 1964 working with SNCC and I had the same situation. When I came back I'd say 'Wow, wow, man, the dogs jumped on these people and the sheriff's patrol beat us and blah-blah' and pretty soon people would say 'I went to a party last night,' " he said. "You could have the Post-Black Mississippi Struggle or the Post–East Harlem Struggle or the Post-Prison Struggle. It's being put in a situation you don't understand and that nobody else you like or relate to can understand either. You say 'I saw this brain laying there in the dirt and somebody put a cigarette package inside the skull to take a picture' and people answer 'I have a date tomorrow' or 'I got laid last night . . . ' "

He was nonviolent, Randy kept saying. He had not wanted to carry a weapon in Vietnam, but that was a hassle, so he did.

"The first firefight I shot up all the ammunition I had in about three or four minutes. Somebody had to come down and tell me to quit shooting. It's pretty hard to be Gandhian unless you've had a lifetime of training. I fired all the time, I fired at anything."

He thought he had been a good medic, he always tried his best. Sometimes things went very wrong. Once when the unit called in artillery because they wanted white phosphorus to hit some enemy bunkers, the shells fell short—he said the company that made them probably saved millions of dollars by shorting the powder, an ounce to every shell—and the Willy Peter, as they called it, came in about two hundred yards from their own position.

"One guy caught a great gob of it in the chest and he fell down screaming. I ran over, but I didn't know whether to shoot him with morphine and let him die happy or try and dig it out with a knife real fast. But it was burning through his chest cavity *so fast* that with one hand I was trying to scrape it off and with the other hand I was shooting him full of morphine. He kept screaming. The morphine took effect in twenty minutes and he lived about forty minutes."

In Kansas he was able to get a job with the Head Start program working in different areas with Indians, then migrants, then on career development programs. He worked with the local antiwar groups, he gave speeches and he showed his slides from Vietnam, but there were never any of the American dying. He was always too busy to stop and take pictures when there were American casualties. Or he didn't feel like it. After a while it became so ordinary to see their own dead that the soldiers stopped seeing them at all and were even able to eat their C-rations not far from corpses, for they had to eat somewhere. One morning in the war he had been out with men minesweeping a road when they discovered some Americans who had been ambushed. The faces of these men had been deformed, although he did not know whether it was done by a machete or an entrenching tool, the military name for a shovel. It was a precaution taken by the VC, he thought. None of the living felt sick or swore revenge.

"Maybe they did it that way to save ammunition; we used to go around and do it with a rifle, making sure everyone was dead," he said. "We had no reaction. After the first two or three you didn't pay any attention, unless, of course, it was a friend."

The dead man he remembered was a Vietnamese who was beginning to stiffen a little. A GI stamped on his hand to open it and then wrapped the fingers around a beer can and raised the dead man, an arm around him, to pose for a photograph. A colonel had seen it, been furious, and said leave that body alone you sadistic son of a bitch.

"But those colonels, they were as much a cause of it as anyone else. They didn't give you a pass unless you killed so many people—then they came out and gave you hell for doing stuff like that," he said.

On a trip to Washington, D.C., he had gone to see Congressman Richard Bolling, a powerful Democrat from Kansas City, first elected to the House in 1948, a World War II veteran who for years had been active in national veterans' groups. The congressman was unmoved by the encounter. "He wasn't really curt with me, but what he was saying was that I didn't represent the large majority of veterans. He didn't want to hear me out. And as far as me having any strength to do anything about the war, I could just go back to Kansas City and forget about it. I guess he was right."

He was thirty-four years old when he told all this: none of the veterans are young men any more, although it is hard to picture them as old men with wide waists and empty eyes. There had been discouragements, Randy said, the huge changes had seemed close, then not come closer at all, but even the people in the war-against-the-war could not have forgotten all that they learned.

"Look at me, yes, look at me. There is no way I'll buy the American dream again. I've seen what we've done to people. I see what we do to people in prisons, I've seen it in Vietnam, I've seen it in the civil-rights movement. I mean you're never going to sell me that shit again. That's all there is to it. There were a lot of people clubbed in Chicago who said the system is all screwed up and who are now driving Cadillacs and working as IBM salesmen. But they had experience, they got some foresight into the system. That's never going to be purged; it has a carry-over that is never going to be taken away from them."

Others are not so sure. Again and again there is someone to say we have always been people who dropped the past and then could not remember where it had been put.

CHARLES MARTIN

During the Vietnam years, amid the angry resistance of particular antiwar campaigns and actions, writers turned away from the subject of nuclear annihilation, but the fear of such annihilation never subsided. It resurfaces in Charles Martin's "Terminal Colloquy," first published in *Room for Error* in 1978, after the war was finally over. A virtuosic villanelle, Martin's poem adroitly and implacably recognizes that in the face of "the blinding flash" there will be nothing whatsoever to say, not even for poets.

A native of New York, Martin (b. 1942) attended Fordham and SUNY–Buffalo and is a distinguished poet and translator, three times nominated for the Pulitzer Prize and the winner of many other prizes and fellowships. From 2005 until 2009 he was poet-in-residence at the Cathedral of Saint John the Divine, then as in the late 1960s hospitable to antiwar writers.

Terminal Colloquy

O where will you go when the blinding flash
Scatters the seed of a million suns?
And what will you do in the rain of ash?

I'll draw the blinds and pull down the sash,
And hide from the light of so many noons.
But how will it be when the blinding flash

Disturbs your body's close-knit mesh,
Bringing to light your lovely bones?
What will you wear in the rain of ash?

I will go bare without my flesh,
My vertebrae will click like stones.
Ah. But where will you dance when the blinding flash

Settles the city in a holy hush?
I will dance alone among the ruins.
Ah. And what will you say to the rain of ash?

I will be charming. My subtle speech
Will weave close turns and counter turns—
No. What will you say to the rain of ash?
Nothing, after the blinding flash.

GRACE PALEY

Grace Paley (1922–2007) was a gifted writer of short stories and poems and a notable activist for peace and justice; the two qualities are intertwined in her, which sometimes makes it exuberantly difficult for the reader of her work to know how to take it, whether as politics or literature or both. "Cop Tales: Devastation," first collected in her book *Long Walks and Intimate Talks* in 1991, is an example of that difficulty. Her account is surely written from the standpoint of a veteran protester, her commitments and allegiances not in question. Yet it is full of the novelist's disinterested curiosity; the police attempting to restrain her fellow protesters are allowed not only their dignity but several unanswerably good lines.

The Women's Pentagon Action Unity Statement is a second example of that difficulty, though of a different kind. Most collective documents are purged of individuality; no human voice can be heard. The Declaration of Independence is our great American exception, because we can hear Jefferson in it; but so is Paley's Pentagon Statement, a "jargon-free manifesto" as Pam McAllister called it, full of vigor. Paley, like Jefferson, was called upon to write the first draft. Then, as Ynestra King recalled, "for weeks Grace took phone calls, read the statement to women in her kitchen, on the subway, in New York, Vermont, Massachusetts. . . . We all listened to each other, everyone was heard and satisfied, and we took this statement home with us to organize."

Paley was born in New York, attended Hunter College and the New School (where she studied with W. H. Auden, here as elsewhere a mentor to activist writers). In the 1950s she worked against nuclear weapons and published her first collection of short stories, *The Little Disturbances of Man* (1959). In the sixties she was much occupied with antiwar work, joining the War Resisters League and accompanying a peace mission to Hanoi to help with the release of prisoners of war. She published a second collection of stories in 1974, *Enormous Changes at the Last Minute*, linked by recurring characters to her first book and also to the next, *Later the Same Day* (1985). She taught at Sarah Lawrence from 1966 to 1989.

Cop Tales: Devastation

AT the Wall Street Action in October 1979, the police were on one side of the sawhorses. We were on the other. We were blocking Wall Street workers. The police were blocking us. One of them was very interested in solar housing. Our solar expert explained the science and economics of it all. Another cop from Long Island worried a lot about Shoreham. "Can't do anything about it," he said. "They'll build it. I hate it. I live there. What am I going to do?"

That could be a key to the police I thought. They have no hope. Cynical. They're mad at us because we have a little hope in the midst of our informed worries.

Then he said, looking at the Bread and Puppet Theater's stilt dancers, "Look at that, what's going on here? People running around the street dancing. They're going every which way. It ain't organized." We started to tell him how important the dancers were. "No, no, that's okay" he said. "The anti-war demonstrations were like this at first, mixed up, but they got themselves together. You'll get yourself together too. In a couple of years you'll know how to do it better."

Earlier, about 6 A.M., two cops wearing blue hardhats passed. One of them looked behind him. "Here come the horses," he said. "Let's get the hell out of here!" And they moved at top casual walking speed in the opposite direction.

Also at 6 A.M., but about fifteen years ago, we would walk up and down before the Whitehall Street Induction Center wearing signs that said "I Support Draft Refusal." It wouldn't take more than a couple of hours for the system to gather up its young victims, stuff them into wagons, and start them off on their terrible journey. At 9:30 on one of those mornings, about twenty women sat down all across the street to prevent the death wagons from moving. They sat for about thirty minutes. Then a plainclothesman approached an older gray-haired woman, "Missus, you don't want to get arrested." "I have to," she said. "My grandson's in Vietnam." Gently they removed her. Then with billy clubs, a dozen uniformed men moved up and down that line of young women, dragging them away, by their arms, their hair, beating them, I remember, (and Norma Becker remembers) mostly in the breast.

Last May at the rainy Armed Forces Day Parade, attended by officers, their wives, and Us, some of Us were arrested by a couple of Cops for Christ. At the desk, as they took our names, smiling, they gave us "Cops for Christ" leaflets. We gave "Disarm for Human Life" leaflets.

Another year, one of the first really large antidraft actions— also at the Induction Center at dawn. We were to surround the building. The famous people, or *Notables* as the Vietnamese used to say, sat down to bar the front entrance. That's where the TV cameras were. Our group of regulars went around to the back of the Center and sat down. Between us and the supply entrance stood a solid line of huge horses and their solemn police riders. We sat cross-legged, speaking softly as the day brightened. Sometimes someone would joke and someone else would immediately say, "Be serious." Off to one side, a captain watched us and the cavalry. Suddenly the horses reared, charged us as we sat, smashing us with their great bodies, scattering our supporting onlookers. People were knocked down, ran this way and that, but the horses were everywhere, rearing—until at the signal from the captain, which I saw, they stopped, settled down, and trotted away. That evening the papers and TV reported that a couple of thousand had demonstrated. Hundreds had been peacefully arrested.

At Wall Street too: A gentleman with a Wall Street attache case tried to get through our line. The police who were in the middle of a discussion about Arabian oil said, "Why not try down there, mister. You can get through down there." The gentleman said he wanted to get through right here and right now and began to knee through our line. The cop on the other side of the sawhorse said, "You heard us. Down there, mister. How about it?" The gentleman said, "Dammit, what are you here for?" He began to move away, calling back in fury, "What the hell are you cops here for anyway?" "Just role playing," the cop called in reply.

There were several cheerful police at the Trident demonstration last year. One officer cheerily called out to the Trident holiday visitors to be careful as they trod the heads of the demonstrators blocking the roadway. "They're doing what they believe in." He asked us to step back, but not more than six inches. He told a joke. He said he hated war, always had. Some young state troopers arrived—more help was needed. They were tall and grouchy. A Black youngster, about twelve, anxious to see what was going on, pushed against the line. One of the state troopers leaned forward and smacked the child hard on the side of the head. "Get back, you little bastard," he said. I reached out to get the attention of the cheery cop, who wore a piece of hierarchical gold on his jacket. "Officer," I said, "you ought to get that trooper out of here, he's dangerous." He looked at me, his face went icy cold, "Lady, be careful," he said. "I just saw you try to strike that officer."

Not too long ago, I saw Finnegan, the plainclothes Red Squad boss. I hadn't seen him in a long time. "Say, Finnegan," I said, "all these years you've been working at one thing and I've been working at the opposite, but look at us. Nothing's prevented either of us from getting gray." He almost answered, but a lot of speedy computations occurred in his brain, and he couldn't. It's the business of the armed forces and the armored face to maintain distance at all times.

Women's Pentagon Action Unity Statement

FOR two years we have gathered at the Pentagon because we fear for our lives. We still fear for the life of this planet, our earth, and the life of the children who are our human future.

We are women who come in most part from the northeastern region of our United States. We are city women who know the wreckage and fear of city streets; we are country women who grieve the loss of the small farm and have lived on the poisoned earth. We are young and older, we are married, single, lesbian. We live in different kinds of households, in groups, families, alone; some are single parents.

We work at a variety of jobs. We are students–teachers–factory workers–office workers–lawyers–farmers–doctors–builders–waitresses–weavers–poets–engineers–homeworkers–electricians–artists–blacksmiths. We are all daughters and sisters.

We came to mourn and rage and defy the Pentagon because it is the workplace of the imperial power which threatens us all. Every day while we work, study, love, the colonels and generals who are planning our annihilation walk calmly in and out the doors of its five sides. They have accumulated over 30,000 nuclear bombs at the rate of three to six bombs every day.

They are determined to produce the billion-dollar MX missile. They are creating a technology called Stealth—the invisible, unperceivable arsenal. They have revived the cruel old killer, nerve gas. They have proclaimed Directive 59, which asks for "small nuclear wars, prolonged but limited." The Soviet Union works hard to keep up with United States initiatives. We can destroy each other's cities, towns, schools, children many times over. The United States has sent "advisors," money, and arms to El Salvador and Guatemala to enable those juntas to massacre their own people.

The very same men, the same legislative committees that offer trillions of dollars to the Pentagon, have brutally cut day care, children's lunches, battered-women's shelters. The same men have concocted the Family Protection Act, which will mandate the strictly patriarchal family and thrust federal authority into the lives we live in our own homes. They are preventing the passage of ERA's simple statement and supporting the Human Life Amendment, which will deprive all women of choice and many women of life itself.

In this environment of contempt and violence, racism, woman hating, and the old European habit of Jew hatred—called anti-Semitism—all find their old roots and grow.

We are in the hands of men whose power and wealth have separated them from the reality of daily life and from the imagination. We are right to be afraid.

At the same time, our cities are in ruins, bankrupt; they suffer the devastation of war. Hospitals are closed, our schools deprived of books and teachers. Our black and Latino youth are without decent work. They will be forced, drafted to become the cannon fodder for the very power that oppresses them. Whatever help the poor receive is cut or withdrawn to feed the Pentagon, which needs about $500 million a day for its murderous health. It extracted $157 billion last year from our own tax money, $1,800 from a family of four.

With this wealth our scientists have been corrupted; over 40 percent work in government and corporate laboratories that refine the methods for destroying or deforming life.

The lands of the Native American people have been turned to radioactive rubble in order to enlarge the nuclear warehouse. The uranium of South Africa, necessary to the nuclear enterprise, enriches the white minority and encourages the vicious system of racist oppression and war.

The President has just decided to produce the neutron bomb, which kills people but leaves property (buildings like this one) intact.

There is fear among the people, and that fear, created by the industrial militarists, is used as an excuse to accelerate the arms race. "We will protect you," they say, but we have never been so endangered, so close to the end of human time.

We women are gathering because life on the precipice is intolerable.

We want to know what anger in these men, what fear that can only be satisfied by destruction, what coldness of heart and ambition drives their days.

We want to know because we do not want that dominance which is exploitative and murderous in international relations, and so dangerous to women and children at home—we do not want that sickness transferred by the violent society through the fathers to the sons.

What is it that we women need for our ordinary lives, that we want for ourselves and also for our sisters in new nations and old colonies who suffer the white man's exploitation and too often the oppression of their own countrymen?

We want enough good food, decent housing, communities with clean air and water, good care for our children while we work. We want work that is useful to a sensible society. There is a modest technology to minimize drudgery and restore joy to labor. We are determined to use skills and knowledge from which we have been excluded—like plumbing or engineering or physics or composing. We intend to form women's groups or unions that will demand safe workplaces, free of sexual harassment, equal pay for work of comparable value. We respect the work women have done in caring for the young, their own and others, in maintaining a physical and spiritual shelter against the greedy and militaristic society. In our old age we expect our experience, our skills, to be honored and used.

We want health care which respects and understands our bodies. Physically challenged sisters must have access to gatherings, actions, happy events, work.

We want an education for children which tells the true story of our women's lives, which describes the earth as our home to be cherished, to be fed as well as harvested.

We want to be free from violence in our streets and in our houses. One in every three of us will be raped in her lifetime. The pervasive social power of the masculine ideal and the greed of the pornographer have come together to steal our freedom, so that whole neighborhoods and the life of the evening and night have been taken from us. For too many women, the dark country road and the city alley have concealed the rapist. We want the night returned, the light of the moon, special in the cycle of our female lives, the stars and the gaiety of the city streets.

We want the right to have or not to have children—we do not want gangs of politicians and medical men to say we must be sterilized for the country's good. We know that this technique is the racist's method for controlling populations. Nor do we want to be prevented from having an abortion when we need one. We think this freedom should be available to poor women, as it always has been to the rich. We want to be free to love whomever we choose. We will live with women or with men or we will live alone. We will not allow the oppression of lesbians. One sex or one sexual preference must not dominate another.

We do not want to be drafted into the Army. We do not want our young brothers drafted. We want *them* equal with *us*.

We want to see the pathology of racism ended in our time. It has been the imperial arrogance of white male power that has separated us from the suffering and wisdom of our sisters in Asia, Africa, South America, and in our own country.

To some women racism has offered privilege and convenience. These women often fail to see that they themselves have lived under the unnatural authority and violence of men in government, at work, at home. Privilege does not increase knowledge or spirit or understanding. There can be no peace while one race dominates another, one people, one nation, one sex despises another.

We must not forget that tens of thousands of American women live much of their lives in cages, away from family, lovers, all the growing years of their children. Most of them were born at the intersection of oppressions: people of color, female, poor. Women on the outside have been taught to fear those sisters. We refuse that separation. We need each other's knowledge and anger in our common struggle against the builders of jails and bombs.

We want the uranium left in the earth, and the earth given back to the people who tilled it. We want a system of energy which is renewable, which does not take resources out of the earth without returning them. We want those systems to belong to the people and their communities, not to the giant corporations which invariably turn knowledge into weaponry. We want the sham of Atoms for Peace ended, all nuclear plants decommissioned, and the construction of new plants stopped. That is another war against the people and the child to be born in fifty years.

We want an end to the arms race. No more bombs. No more amazing inventions for death.

We understand all is connectedness. The earth nourishes us as we with our bodies will eventually feed it. Through us, our mothers connected the human past to the human future. We know the life and work of animals and plants in seeding, reseeding, and in fact simply inhabiting this planet. Their exploitation and the organized destruction of never-to-be-seen-again species threatens and sorrows us.

With that sense, that ecological right, we oppose the financial connections between the Pentagon and the multinational corporations and banks that the Pentagon serves.

Those connections are made of gold and oil.

We are made of blood and bone, we are made of the sweet and finite resource, water.

We will not allow these violent games to continue. If we are here in our stubborn thousands today, we will certainly return in the hundreds of thousands in the months and years to come.

We know there is a healthy, sensible, loving way to live and we intend to live that way in our neighborhoods and our farms in these United States, and among our sisters and brothers in all the countries of the world.

GEORGE ZABELKA

In August 1945, George Zabelka (1915–1992) was the Catholic military chaplain stationed on Tinian Island, serving the Catholics of the 509th Composite Group, members of which were preparing to drop the first atomic bombs. Zabelka knew little about that—the power of the new weapons, then referred to among the troops as "gimmick bombs," was entirely unknown to him—so he went about his business, offered the sacraments, heard confessions, set out some Catholic teachings on just war.

After the war, in 1946, he went to Nagasaki, walked through the ruins of a cathedral there, and pondered what he had done and omitted doing, thus beginning a slow, inexorable process of change. He read the work of Martin Luther King Jr. and Mohandas Gandhi and was drawn by it some distance toward pacifism as a theological position; a series of conversations in 1972 with Charles McCarthy, founder of the Center for the Study of Nonviolence at Notre Dame, brought him most of the rest of the way. In 1975 he wrote to his friends, "I have come to the conclusion that the truth of the Gospel is that Jesus was nonviolent and taught nonviolence as His way." In 1980 he gave the interview included here, shortly before his "pilgrimage" of atonement to Hiroshima and Nagasaki.

The interview is thus a backward glance; a pacifist at the age of sixty-five looks back at his younger self of thirty, trying to understand both his own complicity and the role played in his conduct by his superiors and the age he was living in. He is an unsparing analyst of his superiors and still more of himself. He says he was brainwashed but does not regard that fact as an exculpation: "on Judgment Day," he says, "I think I am going to need to seek more mercy than justice in this matter." That sense of unending, unassuaged regret is the distinguishing trait of the interview, still more than its lacerating criticism of church doctrine and military indifference.

"I Was Told It Was Necessary"

Charles McCarthy: *Father Zabelka, what is your relationship to the atomic bombing of Hiroshima and Nagasaki in August, 1945?*

Fr. Zabelka: During the summer of 1945, July, August, and September, I was assigned as Catholic chaplain to the 509th

Composite Group on Tinian Island. The 509th was the atomic bomb group.

McCarthy: *What were your duties in relationship to these men?*

Zabelka: The usual. I said mass on Sunday and during the week. Heard confessions. Talked with the boys, etc. Nothing significantly different from what any other chaplain did during the war.

McCarthy: *Did you know that the 509th was preparing to drop an atomic bomb?*

Zabelka: No. We knew that they were preparing to drop a bomb substantially different from and more powerful than even the "blockbusters" used over Europe, but we never called it an atomic bomb and never really knew what it was before August 6, 1945. Before that time we just referred to it as the "gimmick" bomb.

McCarthy: *So since you did not know that an atomic bomb was going to be dropped you had no reason to counsel the men in private or preach in public about the morality of such a bombing?*

Zabelka: Well, that is true enough; I never did speak against it, nor could I have spoken against it since I, like practically everyone else on Tinian, was ignorant of what was being prepared. And I guess I will go to my God with that as my defense. But on Judgment Day I think I am going to need to seek more mercy than justice in this matter.

McCarthy: *Why? God certainly could not have expected you to act on ideas that had never entered your mind.*

Zabelka: As a Catholic priest my task was to keep my people, wherever they were, close to the mind and heart of Christ. As a military chaplain I was to try to see that the boys conducted themselves according to the teachings of the Catholic Church and Christ on war. When I look back I am not sure I did either of these things very well.

McCarthy: *Why do you think that?*

Zabelka: What I do not mean to say is that I feel myself to have been remiss in any duties that were expected of me as a chaplain. I saw that the mass and the sacraments were available as best I could. I even went out and earned paratroop wings in order to do my job better. Nor did I fail to teach and preach what the Church expected me to teach and preach—and I don't mean by this that I just talked to the boys about their sexual lives. I and most chaplains were quite clear and outspoken on such matters as not killing and torturing prisoners. But there were other areas where things were not said quite so clearly.

McCarthy: *For example?*

Zabelka: The destruction of civilians in war was always forbidden by the Church, and if a soldier came to me and asked if he could put a bullet through a child's head, I would have told him absolutely not. That would be mortally sinful. But in 1945 Tinian Island was the largest airfield in the world. Three planes a minute could take off from it around the clock. Many of these planes went to Japan with the express purpose of killing not one child or one civilian but of slaughtering hundreds and thousands and tens of thousands of children and civilians—and I said nothing.

McCarthy: *Why not? You certainly knew civilians were being destroyed by the thousands in these raids, didn't you?*

Zabelka: Oh, indeed I did know, and I knew with a clarity that few others could have had.

McCarthy: *What do you mean?*

Zabelka: As a chaplain I often had to enter the world of the boys who were losing their minds because of something they did in war. I remember one young man who was engaged in the bombings of the cities of Japan. He was in the hospital on Tinian Island on the verge of a complete mental collapse.

He told me that he had been on a low-level bombing mission, flying right down one of the main streets of the city when straight ahead of him appeared a little boy, in the middle of the street, looking up at the plane in childish wonder. The man knew that in a few seconds this child would be burned to death by napalm which had already been released.

Yes, I knew civilians were being destroyed and knew it perhaps in a way others didn't. Yet I never preached a single sermon against killing civilians to the men who were doing it.

McCarthy: *Again, why not?*

Zabelka: Because I was "brainwashed"! It never entered my mind to publicly protest the consequences of these massive

air raids. I was told it was necessary; told openly by the
military and told implicitly by my Church's leadership. To
the best of my knowledge no American cardinals or bishops
were opposing these mass air raids. Silence in such matters,
especially by a public body like the American bishops, is a
stamp of approval.

The whole structure of the secular, religious, and military
society told me clearly that it was all right to "let the Japs
have it." God was on the side of my country. The Japanese
were the enemy, and I was absolutely certain of my country's
and Church's teaching about enemies; no erudite theological
text was necessary to tell me. The day-in-day-out operation
of the state and the Church between 1940 and 1945 spoke
more clearly about Christian attitudes toward enemies and
war than St. Augustine or St. Thomas Aquinas ever could.

I was certain that this mass destruction was right, certain
to the point that the question of its morality never seriously
entered my mind. I was "brainwashed" not by force or torture but by my Church's silence and wholehearted cooperation in thousands of little ways with the country's war
machine. Why, after I finished chaplaincy school at Harvard
I had my military chalice officially blessed by the then Bishop
Cushing of Boston. How much more clearly could the message be given? Indeed, I was "brainwashed"!

McCarthy: *So you feel that because you did not protest the morality of the bombing of other cities with their civilian populations,
that somehow you are morally responsible for the dropping of
the atomic bomb?*

Zabelka: The facts are that seventy-five thousand people were
burned to death in one evening of fire bombing over Tokyo.
Hundreds of thousands were destroyed in Dresden, Hamburg, and Coventry by aerial bombing. The fact that forty-
five thousand human beings were killed by one bomb over
Nagasaki was new only to the extent that it was one bomb
that did it.

To fail to speak to the utter moral corruption of the mass
destruction of civilians was to fail as a Christian and a priest
as I see it. Hiroshima and Nagasaki happened in and to a
world and a Christian church that had asked for it—that

had prepared the moral consciousness of humanity to do and to justify the unthinkable. I am sure there are church documents around someplace bemoaning civilian deaths in modern war, and I am sure those in power in the church will drag them out to show that it was giving moral leadership during World War II to its membership.

Well, I was there, and I'll tell you that the operational moral atmosphere in the church in relation to mass bombing of enemy civilians was totally indifferent, silent, and corrupt at best—at worst it was religiously supportive of these activities by blessing those who did them.

I say all this not to pass judgment on others, for I do not know their souls then or now. I say all this as one who was part of the so-called Christian leadership of the time. So you see, that is why I am not going to the day of judgment looking for justice in this matter. Mercy is my salvation.

McCarthy: *You said the atomic bombing of Nagasaki happened to a church that "had asked for it." What do you mean by that?*

Zabelka: For the first three centuries, the three centuries closest to Christ, the church was a pacifist church. With Constantine the church accepted the pagan Roman ethic of a just war and slowly began to involve its membership in mass slaughter, first for the state and later for the faith.

Catholics, Orthodox, and Protestants, whatever other differences they may have had on theological esoterica, all agreed that Jesus' clear and unambiguous teaching on the rejection of violence and on love of enemies was not to be taken seriously. And so each of the major branches of Christianity by different theological methods modified our Lord's teaching in these matters until all three were able to do what Jesus rejected, that is, take an eye for an eye, slaughter, maim, torture.

It seems a "sign" to me that seventeen hundred years of Christian terror and slaughter should arrive at August 9, 1945, when Catholics dropped the A-bomb on top of the largest and first Catholic city in Japan. One would have thought that I, as a Catholic priest, would have spoken out against the atomic bombing of nuns. (Three orders of Catholic sisters were destroyed in Nagasaki that day.) One would have thought that I would have suggested that as a minimal standard of Catholic morality, Catholics shouldn't bomb Catholic children. I didn't.

I, like the Catholic pilot of the Nagasaki plane, "The Great Artiste," was heir to a Christianity that had for seventeen hundred years engaged in revenge, murder, torture, the pursuit of power, and prerogative violence, all in the name of our Lord.

I walked through the ruins of Nagasaki right after the war and visited the place where once stood the Urakami Cathedral. I picked up a piece of a censer from the rubble. When I look at it today I pray God forgives us for how we have distorted Christ's teaching and destroyed his world by the distortion of that teaching. I was the Catholic chaplain who was there when this grotesque process that began with Constantine reached its lowest point—so far.

McCarthy: *What do you mean by "so far"?*

Zabelka: Briefly, what I mean is that I do not see that the moral climate in relation to war inside or outside the church has dramatically changed much since 1945. The mainline Christian churches still teach something that Christ never taught or even hinted at, namely the just war theory, a theory that to me has been completely discredited theologically, historically, and psychologically.

So as I see it, until the various churches within Christianity repent and begin to proclaim by word and deed what Jesus proclaimed in relation to violence and enemies, there is no hope for anything other than ever-escalating violence and destruction.

Until membership in the church means that a Christian chooses not to engage in violence for any reason and instead chooses to love, pray for, help, and forgive all enemies; until membership in the church means that Christians may not be members of any military—American, Polish, Russian, English, Irish, et al.; until membership in the church means that the Christian cannot pay taxes for others to kill others and until the church says these things in a fashion which the simplest soul could understand—until that time humanity can only look forward to more dark nights of slaughter on a scale unknown in history. Unless the church unswervingly and unambiguously teaches what Jesus teaches on this matter it will not be the divine leaven in the human dough that it was meant to be.

"The choice is between nonviolence and nonexistence," as Martin Luther King Jr. said, and he was not, and I am not, speaking figuratively. It is about time for the church and its leadership in all denominations to get down on its knees and repent of this misrepresentation of Christ's words.

Communion with Christ cannot be established on disobedience to his clearest teachings. Jesus authorized none of his followers to substitute violence for love; not me, not you, not Jimmy Carter, not the pope, not a Vatican council, nor even an ecumenical council.

McCarthy: *Father Zabelka, what kinds of immediate steps do you think the church should take in order to become the "divine leaven in the human dough"?*

Zabelka: Step one should be that Christians the world over should be taught that Christ's teaching to love their enemies is not optional. I've been in many parishes in my life, and I have found none where the congregation explicitly is called upon regularly to pray for its enemies. I think this is essential.

I offer you step two at the risk of being considered hopelessly out of touch with reality. I would like to suggest that there is an immediate need to call an ecumenical council for the specific purpose of clearly declaring that war is totally incompatible with Jesus' teaching and that Christians cannot and will not engage in or pay for it from this point in history on. This would have the effect of putting all nations on this planet on notice that from now on they are going to have to conduct their mutual slaughter without Christian support—physical, financial, or spiritual.

I am sure there are other issues which Catholics or Orthodox or Protestants would like to confront in an ecumenical council instead of the facing up to the hard teachings of Christ in relationship to violence and enemies. But it seems to me that issues like the meaning of the primacy of Peter are nowhere near as pressing or as destructive of church credibility and God's world as is the problem of continued Christian participation in and justification of violence and slaughter. I think the church's continued failure to speak clearly Jesus' teachings is daily undermining its credibility and authority in all other areas.

McCarthy: *Do you think there is the slightest chance that the various branches of Christianity would come together in an ecumenical council for the purpose of declaring war and violence totally unacceptable activities for Christians under all circumstances?*

Zabelka: Remember, I prefaced my suggestion of an ecumenical council by saying that I risked being considered hopelessly out of touch with reality. On the other hand, what is impossible for men and women is quite possible for God if people will only use their freedom to cooperate a little.

Who knows what could happen if the pope, the patriarch of Constantinople, and the president of the World Council of Churches called with one voice for such a council? One thing I am sure of is that our Lord would be very happy if his church were again unequivocally teaching what he unequivocally taught on the subject of violence.

YVONNE DILLING AND
MARY JO BOWMAN

I first read the following correspondence between Yvonne Dilling (b. 1955) and Mary Jo Bowman (b. 1955) many years ago, in a 3″ × 9″ pamphlet published by the A. J. Muste Institute. I thought then, and think now, that it was the greatest American conversation on violence: the most searching and respectful and dialogic, the least pretentious and dogmatic, and in my judgment, and in the judgment of the many students I've read it with, the most productive.

At the time of writing, Yvonne Dilling was a resident of Tabor House, a "contemplative political action and Third World dialogue center for hospitality" in Washington, D.C. She attended Manchester College, majored in Peace Studies, traveled extensively in Central America. Mary Jo Bowman was director of a Church of the Brethren Peace Education and Evangelism Program. She too had attended Manchester and majored in Peace Studies. The two were friends and remain friends.

The dialogue is typical of its time; all across the peace movement, activists were grappling with the question of revolutionary violence. Fine, they felt, to oppose imperialist wars, colonialist wars, wars of geopolitical calculation, wars of oppression. But what if the wars were being conducted by the colonized against the colonizers? They all read Frantz Fanon's *The Wretched of the Earth* (1961), with its implacable denunciation of nonviolence, and they all were on the side of the colonized in their struggles for self-determination. So what should one do or think if the colonized turned, as Fanon had told them to, to violence? Barbara Deming's 1968 essay "On Revolution and Equilibrium" deals precisely with this question.

But the dialogue is also unique: a dialogue between equals, Platonic in its intensity and leisureliness. Dilling was working with the Sandinistas, supportive of their cause, and—to oversimplify—supportive also of their revolutionary violence. Bowman held more closely to the commitment to nonviolence that she and Dilling had shared. Each respected the other, was curious about the other, but not deferential or passive in relation to the other. Their shared inquiry is animated by both zeal and love.

Revolutionary Violence: A Dialogue

Dear Mary Jo,

The Peace Studies Institute has heard of our lively supper-time discussions about violence and nonviolence, and has asked us to chronicle some of our reflections over the past two tumultuous years. In retrospect, trying to synthesize my past with my personal involvement in the lives and anguish of the Nicaraguan people has been at once frightening and exciting, painful and joyful. Now a year after the Sandinista victory, I need to talk with you again about where I (we) find ourselves. What I vicariously experienced of the revolution through the Nicaraguans here in D.C. and then in Nicaragua in September '79 has deeply affected me. I found myself working in solidarity with their struggle without thoroughly understanding its implications for my pacifist position. The praxis came into my life before the reflection and analysis. Diving in without first calculating the consequences has made all the difference, for I do not think my involvement would have happened any other way.

How can I explain the process through which I've come? I grew up believing that the definition of violence could be reduced to the use of guns or other direct physical attack. I now see that the limited options for change, violent or nonviolent, for most of the peoples of the world are directly related to the unlimited options offered me as a North American—in terms of health, education, food, shelter, meaningful work, a life basically free of fear. I must come to grips with the fact that my freedoms have not been acquired without struggle. The blood and suffering of native peoples, slaves, immigrants, and people of other colors from around the world have paid for our "liberty." They continue to pay, and as a Christian I must admit that reality and work with it.

I came to the Nicaraguan liberation struggle with all the academic and theological lessons down pat: thou shalt not kill; violence always breeds more violence; the oppressed historically have overthrown evil powers only to become oppressors themselves; those who live by the sword will perish by the sword; means must be consistent with desired ends; all life is equally sacred; one single life is too great a sacrifice for any cause.

My perspective on the writings of well-known proponents on both sides of the question has been altered: Christ; Gandhi; M. L. King, Jr.; Ellul; Helder Camara; Camilo Torres. I am different from the white, middle class, concerned North American, Brethren-educated Christian who two years ago came to a new job from Manchester College. I've been moved by the life, the struggle, the spirit and vision of the poor of Central America, moved to examine my own life and attitudes critically, to examine the priorities and intentions of my government. I have to begin to live those changes within me here in the city.

I came to support the Sandinista armed struggle. I understand why the Salvadorean people have resorted to armed struggle, and I support them. It is still hard for me to write that on paper, especially to be published in the *Peace Studies Bulletin*. I cannot at this point in my life say lightly, without stumbling that I am a pacifist. But I do say more humbly and more confidently that I am seeking to be a disciple of Christ, and understand the hard choices required of me as a North American.

The classical principles of nonviolence I quoted earlier are still important to me; they still hold their truth. But there are many supplemental "truths" which have acquired great significance: peace and justice are inseparable; be wise as serpents but gentle as doves; greater love shows no one than the one who lays down her/his own life for another; real change comes from the bottom up; the rich will not listen even to one who has risen from the dead.

Even if I had not had the personal involvement with the Nicaraguan struggle, as a Christian and a believer in nonviolence it would be important to study and analyze revolutionary Nicaragua today and look for evidence of the development of new forces for constructing a changed Nicaragua. The Gospels tell us time and again to "look for the signs" that proclaim the coming of the Kingdom. We must get beyond the rhetoric of "marxist Nicaragua" fed us by the U.S. press and look for the signs in Nicaragua.

Everyone who holds high the values of social and economic justice, of people-before-profits, of basic inalienable human rights for all, should be excited about Nicaragua today.

The promise of genuine change for workers and peasants has gone far beyond rhetoric in Nicaragua. "The poor will inherit the earth" resounded in my mind as I traveled through Nicaragua seven weeks after victory. The entire country seemed a chaotic, but fervent horizon of hope. I was awed by the contrast between the beautiful, natural terrain and the destruction wrought by Somoza's bombs. But amidst that devastation I saw and came to know an empowered people full of revolutionary creativity, destitute in material things, but as their victory hymn proclaims, "owners of their own history, architects of their future."

The neighborhood block organizations, called Sandinista Defense Committees (CDS), provide a forum for individual participation in building the new society. The CDSs are offspring of the neighborhood Civilian Defense Committees formed by the people to protect themselves from Somoza. In the desperation of the struggle, they accumulated experience and developed new forces which opened the way for the people to take greater charge of their lives.

I visited a CDS that had only recently stopped organizing clandestine first aid clinics and had begun distributing emergency food. On a week day evening they discussed the health hazard of the street's stagnant water puddles, as well as what it meant to elect a committee member to represent them at a city-wide meeting. They also discussed a proposed four-year national priorities plan and sent their opinions with their representative to the city-wide meeting.

That kind of grass-roots democratic process was and is happening in factories, schools, large farms and small towns. At the national level in the Council of State, every sector is guaranteed a voice—the church, the trade and peasant unions, the women's association, the council of private enterprise, the traditional political parties. The death penalty was abolished immediately after Somoza's defeat. Peasants now have access to land, and agricultural credits are weighed according to a balance between personal need and the country's larger agricultural needs. (For example, last spring the rent per hectare for land planted in corn or beans was lower than the rent charged for land cultivated for tobacco.) In spite of the destruction of 90% of the industrial capacity and a $1.5 billion foreign debt, and other enormous problems, at the people's bidding, the Government of National Reconstruction made a literacy campaign the national priority of the first year. A year later, Nicaragua's illiteracy rate has been reduced from a historically high 53% to less than 13%.

I present all these examples because it is important to ask how such human-oriented social values and priorities surfaced from the hate and violence of an armed insurrection. Probably the single most important thing for a North American pacifist to learn from the Nicaraguan liberation struggle is to put the concept of violence into its proper perspective. Institutionalized violence is not something we North American pacifists readily comprehend. We equate the violence of a military dictatorship and the violence of a people's self-defense.

The decision to use armed struggle in Nicaragua has to be viewed within the context of the brutality of the Somoza regime. Anastasio Somoza ran the country as a private estate backed by a private army. He owned banks, the air and shipping lines, the fishing industry, construction companies, factories, and 50% of the arable land. Following the 1972 earthquake which destroyed the capital city, *his* construction companies got the bids to rebuild on *his* land, using the international aid and assistance which flowed through *his* banks. He maintained his stronghold on the life and economy of the country through military terror: torture, "pacification" maneuvers, assassination of opposition leadership, slaughter of innocent youths and children. I cannot be surprised at the aggression and violence of the Nicaraguan people's eventual outpouring of anger. It was understandable.

After months of studying and translating reports of human rights violations, of seeing the Latin American press photos, of comforting the anguished friends who lost family and friends at Somoza's hands, of discovering that the National Guard learned its torture techniques from U.S. military advisors, how could I not but re-think the assertion that all violence is the same?

It becomes clear to me why those who die of malnutrition and disease, who hunger and thirst for bread and justice speak of revolution and why those who hold the reins of wealth and power speak of "gradual and peaceful change," or "working through the system." I realized last year that anything that was legal in Nicaragua was absolutely non-threatening and meaningless to the Somoza regime. In such a situation, the passage of power to the opposite hands could come only through organized popular resistance. The holders of power forced that resistance to resort to violent means. In many parts of Latin America today, the means of the resistance are no longer determined by the common people.

I do not know that any of the popular opposition groups in Nicaragua practiced nonviolent resistance on *principle*. However, the fact that they all foresaw armed insurrection as inevitable does not negate the significant fact that for many years, their resistance was *de facto* nonviolent: the crippling national strikes carried out jointly by owners and workers, the funeral services which were often silent mass protest marches, the women who occupied the United Nations building in Managua, the hunger strikes organized by health workers or by mothers of the disappeared, the occupations of churches, the preaching of sermons against the state violations.

If Nicaraguan archbishop Obando y Bravo had preached what Salvadorean Archbishop Romero preached he would have also been slain. In a Sunday homily last May, Oscar Romero spoke directly to the Salvadorean National Guard:

> Brothers, you belong to our own people. You kill your brother peasants; and in the face of an order to kill that is given by a man, the law of God should prevail that says "do not kill." No soldier is obliged to obey an order counter to the law of God. No one has to comply with an immoral law . . . I beg you, I beseech you. I order you, stop the killing.

Archbishop Romero was assassinated the day after he preached against the guardians of the ruling class in Nicaragua. The women who staged a sit-in at the UN office were tear-gassed, jailed, beaten. Peasants who asked for decent wages were murdered alongside their families in their sleep. Students who protested because the poor could not afford a bus fare hike were assaulted, tear-gassed, imprisoned, tortured, their genitals ripped off . . . I could go on.

I shall never forget the story recounted by a North American nun of two 14-year-old boys taken by the National Guard from their home beside hers, shot in the vacant field behind her street, laid on the ground with red and black FSLN kerchiefs tied around their necks, pistols placed in their hands. Their bloody photo with the accompanying article claiming to have captured and killed "communists," appeared in Somoza's newspaper the following day.

I cannot ask why after 40 years of oppression those people did not try a massive nonviolent resistance against Somoza. Rather, I ask why they tried nonviolent tactics at all. They did try them. They began with them, and never ceased trying to use them. The people suffered with one another and—out of love for their comrades—could not but resist, even when it meant armed insurrection.

In discussing my personal background with a Sandinista woman my age, she was puzzled by both the "Historic Peace Churches," and a "Peace Studies Major." On explaining those, she commented, "We're all nonviolent, you know, but we did what we had to do." As in that young woman, there was an amazing lack of hatred or vengeance in the people following victory. The people told me out of their own experiences that hate is counter-revolutionary. They knew that hate and vengeance will not bring about a more equitable and just life for the poor.

Why does hate immediately come to our minds when revolution is mentioned? Is it possible to plan a military strategy, to take up arms out of love? (I ask that question still very much opposed to the Christian Crusade theology.) The Sandinistas were not hate-filled terrorists. They were motivated by human solidarity, by compassion for their people. The important aspect of the revolution was not the armed struggle. Granted, that was chosen as the only possible means to get rid of the dictatorship. However, the emphasis of the insurrection was always the carrying through of the revolution to its ultimate goals: constructing a society based on economic, social and political justice. That translates into democracy for all, not just the few; equitable distribution of goods and services; freedom not only to walk the streets at night, but to do so with a full belly; freedom from fear of death or torture for speaking one's mind; and the opportunity for full time, meaningful employment.

I would venture to say that those FSLN objectives grew out of the Sandinistas' knowledge of and experience in the life of the poor. The FSLN was the vanguard in the insurrection, but it was grounded in the people. How else, and why else, could the Sandinistas reject the excesses of post-victory retaliation which characterizes some revolutionary struggles, such as Iran? The first post victory slogan I heard proclaimed was, "Unyielding in war, generous in victory."

FSLN leader Tomas Borge, soon after being placed in charge of the prisons holding the National Guard after victory, came face to face with the man who had tortured him during seven long years in Somoza's dungeons. Before the entire crowd of Guardsmen and Sandinistas in that prison he said, "You will live with my forgiveness. That is my only revenge."

I must ask how Nicaragua kept from being a hate-filled individualistic nation after four decades of *somocismo* and so many years of organized armed resistance. The importance of cultural revolution is clear. The people—both leadership and at the grassroots—experienced a change of consciousness through the long period of civilian resistance. The Sandinistas came to realize that the rank and file National Guard were as much victims of U.S. imperialism as were the civilian poor. Many in the middle class learned that too. By joining with the poor, they learned that the few material benefits they had known were achieved at the expense of the poor, and that the system represented by Somoza had raped them all alike. Two months after victory, I rode through the poor *barrios* of the capital city with an upper-middle-class, 20-year-old woman. Unlike anything I had heard from her class in any part of Latin America, she said, "You see those shacks? Somoza got rich by squeezing them dry. It is precisely for those people that we made the revolution, and with them we will build the new Nicaragua." I was humbled by her passion and willingness to sacrifice. She had carried a weapon with the Sandinistas.

The experiences of Nicaragua have left me with a political realism. I have learned a great deal about U.S. imperialism. By that I mean that the ruling class in our country will support any kind of regime in order to maintain the economic and political position of power it has built in the world. The United States refused to accept the will of the Nicaraguan people expressed through their full involvement with the FSLN. The United States, in fact, refused to accept the political will of the people until the moment when it became clear that the FSLN would shortly achieve a military victory. One form of power spoke to the United States: military might. The U.S. government would not even acknowledge the existence of the FSLN until they had captured enough arms and gathered enough forces to hold power once taken. When, at that time, the FSLN announced a provisional government of five representatives of the main political opposition groups, the State Department's reaction was to attempt to divide and weaken them. Self-determination for other peoples is not a priority of U.S. foreign policy.

I have had fantasies in the past about how a massive nonviolent mobilization against Somoza might have defeated his regime. The love, determination and courage of the people in the face of the National Guard could have converted the soldiers to see the evil of Somoza and the wrong of killing their own people. As a Christian, I must allow for that kind of hope for conversion. Even if that conversion had happened, though, I don't believe even that would have been enough to stop U.S. political and economic intervention. If, through nonviolent resistance, the people could have converted Somoza, I still believe the United States would have used its economic and military might to override the will of the people, installing a new face on the same repressive system.

Coming to that realization has shed a different light on my understanding of "wise as serpents." It verifies what I believe of Brazil's Helder Camara: as a well-known believer in nonviolent resistance, he is dangerous to the powerful because his nonviolent charisma is coupled with political and economic sophistication. I believe much the same of Gandhi. It is not as true of many of the believers of nonviolence in our country today. We are ineffective nonviolent resisters. Our ineffective nonviolence in this country allows our government to carry out the policies which support military dictatorships and illegitimate governments all over the world. Our ineffective nonviolence must take part of the blame for the starvation, suffering, death in most of the rest of the world. Gandhi said that, given a choice between violence and cowardice, the violence would be preferable. I believe it was preferable in Nicaragua. It will be the only viable choice in El Salvador and Guatemala unless we change in this country.

So where am I today, Mary Jo? I tell you about Nicaragua, but my concern is me (us). How do I translate the experience of these last two years into my life and work? "Nonviolence, when preached by the rich, is treason" (Arturo Paoli). In Yahweh's purpose of bringing humanity to its fullness, where does my lifestyle place me, oppressor, or with the oppressed?

Facing hard questions,
    Yvonne

*   *   *

Dear Yvonne,

You know how I've grappled with the questions raised by your support of the Sandinistas. At times during the past year and a half it may have seemed that I was mercilessly playing devil's advocate in our frequent conversations about violence and nonviolence. But I must confess to you and to all our friends who will read this article that I, too, no longer glibly say I'm a pacifist. And I suspect I squirm just as much as you do to see that in print, especially now that I'm employed as a peace advocate for the Church of the Brethren. I have shared the day-to-day struggle with the moral ambiguities you discovered amidst the revolutionary situation in Nicaragua, and have found myself trying to gain perspective on what it means to be committed to peace *and* justice in the face of such tyranny. I have drawn some painful insights, also, from my own exposure to the sufferings of the poor in this city.

Before I launch into a response to your reflection on lessons from Nicaragua, let me remind you of some of the ways that my own pacifism has been tested.

I remember my first significant experience in a large city—Chicago, fall and winter, 1975. I lived in a cooperative student household run by the Urban Life Center on the northern edge of Hyde Park, bordering the solidly black, low-income area of Kenwood. Being on the streets was like a slap in the face—the air of racial and economic tensions, the defensive aloofness most people call "street sense" stung my rural innocence. I was humbled to realize that my zealous pacifism had never really been tested; I had come from the safe Blue

Ridge Mountains of Virginia, from a Church of the Brethren farm family, and from there to the quiet Indiana agricultural town that hosts Manchester College. Aside from tussles with siblings and cousins, and occasional threats of spankings from parents, my childhood and adolescence were relatively free of confrontation. So, ever since that shocking awakening in Chicago, I have been asking myself why I'm a pacifist. With humility and joy, I can honestly say I have come a long way in understanding what motivates me and my response to violent situations.

I have come to see that my upbringing taught me to avoid conflict. The well-internalized dictum, "Don't say anything if you can't say something nice" may explain why I'm so quiet! No, seriously, I am coming to understand more deeply how an unhealthy attitude towards conflict and power played into my precocious pacifism. Only in the past five years or so have I begun to acknowledge my capacity for anger and to learn to channel it creatively. And that's all tied into the process of deepened understanding and practice of prayer and meditation, which compels me to come to grips with my fears and angers and to heed their lessons about personal and political power. My studies in the social sciences have brought me to a more sophisticated understanding of the roots of violence and the varieties of its expression. My experience of living and working with others in situations of inevitable conflict have provided experiences that back up my academic insights.

Living in Washington, D.C. has given me ample exposure to violence. Just being a woman makes traveling the streets in many parts of this city a poignant reminder of oppression. I have not been physically attacked, but I must be always wary when I'm out alone after dark, even in our neighborhood. Verbal abuse from men, even when disguised in ostensibly affirmative language, angers me in a way that helps me appreciate why victimized people lash out in frustrated self-defense. When I remember the news that a neighbor woman was raped at 2 o'clock in the afternoon no more than four blocks from my house, I know what outrage feels like. I am infuriated both because a neighbor has been violated and because I must live with the knowledge that it could have been me.

For over a year, I spent one or two nights a month with women in D.C. who have taught me a great deal about human suffering. During the day they wander from public library to park bench to cafeteria to department store to bus station, often carrying all their possessions in shopping bags. They are the homeless women of our nation's capital—several hundred of them, we think. They are on the streets because of mental or physical illness, abandonment by family or society's institutions, a heritage of poverty, or personal misfortune. In a number of overnight shelters provided by churches and religious groups, I have met them and listened to their stories—often amidst their outbursts of anger at men, the government and themselves.

On a number of smelly cigarette-smoke and dirty-clothes nights I've been struck with how different my world is from theirs. I can *volunteer* to spend the night at the shelter and then go home to my own bed to catch up on my sleep. I don't have to eat their spongy oatmeal and drink their lukewarm tea, or go out into the chilly streets every morning. Yet, I am also reminded again as I see those women on the streets, invisible to most other people they pass, that they have taught me a great deal about sanity, about survival, and about anger. The belligerence of some of the women haunts me—slaps my white, middle-class, educated face—and makes me wonder how I would cope nonviolently with the brutality so many of those women face on the streets every day, and every night when the shelters are full. Their anger is very real, very justified, and I laud it as a sign of their relentless dignity.

Some of my friends live in a nearby neighborhood that is predominantly low-income black. Particularly during the summertime, when folks there take to the streets and front stoops to find some relief from their sweltering, crowded apartments, I have felt an air of tension, a hair's breadth away from the kind of explosion that leveled much of that neighborhood in the riots twelve years ago. Unemployment, particularly among young black men in that area, is around 70%. Families are rapidly being evicted from their homes to make way for the renovation for upper-income and for higher real-estate profits.

My glimpses into the lives of some of the children in that neighborhood—through my occasional involvement as a volunteer with a day care center and girls' Saturday recreation program—have helped me understand what poverty can do to the human spirit. Just like the youth I "policed" several summers ago (I was hired as arts and crafts director for the summer recreation program) in a tobacco-growing tenant-farming area near my Virginia home, children in the inner city seem to relate to their peers and to the larger world with cruel suspicion and self-defensive hostility.

I wasn't surprised to hear a few months ago about the shooting of a policeman in a drug-related skirmish in the riot-corridor area of D.C.; I was even less surprised by the sobering news that the man who shot and killed the policeman was lauded by many in that neighborhood and around the city as a hero of the oppressed.

All of this is to say that your bringing the Nicaraguan revolution to our supper table was not my first exposure to situations in which violence, in one form or another, is a given.

But I still find the issue of armed revolutionary violence a troubling one. It forces me to once again examine my motivations, my ethics, my faith. It brings me face to face with bloody human suffering. I find that my response consists more of questions than of answers. My only conclusive response is one of faith—not of doctrines or moralisms, nor of easy answers or clear conscience. My faith calls me more and more into a life of tension and ambiguity, with compassion being my primary discipline. My spirituality and my politics are becoming more and more deeply wed these days, particularly as I grapple with Christlike responses to injustice and power and as I call myself a peacemaker and a bearer of hope.

I am challenged by the way you allowed yourself to be drawn so fully into the Nicaraguan struggle. I am grateful for how your involvement drew me in, even though I sometimes rebelled against the questions and harsh realities you brought home to share with me. My playful threats to dress as a Sandinista for Halloween last year somehow did not seem funny to either of us. Perhaps I felt the tension most keenly when I came home from a month-long sojourn (with a Manchester College group) in India last January bringing a *khadi* (homespun, handwoven cotton) banner bearing a Mahatma Gandhi quote: "Nonviolence is the greatest force available to mankind" (sic). Could we live with that proclamation hanging beside your Sandino posters? What would Gandhi have said of our dilemma?

I suspect that he would have concurred with Helder Camara's notion that commitment to the principle of nonviolence must be coupled with sophistication about the political and economic forces being confronted. Gandhi's work with the poorest of India's poor (the *harijans* or untouchables), his denouncement of unrestrained technology, and his disdain for paternalistic Christian missionary efforts in his homeland indicated that his disciplines of *satyagraha* were firmly grounded not only in India's rich, spiritual heritage but in political realism. In other words, he knew what he was up against. And you are right: from what I can gather from his writings, when faced with a choice between cowardice and violence, Gandhi would have advocated violence. His passionate commitment to suffer death before inflicting lethal violence on another still allowed him to see that violence takes various forms and calls for various responses. His compassion and sophistication made allowances for necessary compromise to those who are either ill-equipped for nonviolent resistance or who find their adversary so tyrannical that nothing short of armed defense seems tolerable. But even though he characterized the Polish resistance to the German forces in World War II as *almost* non-violent—he still maintained that suffering love is ultimately more powerful than self-defense.

I doubt that any of the classical proponents of nonviolence on your list would condemn the use of armed confrontation in a desperate resistance to tyranny. I surely cannot condemn the campesinos in Nicaragua who took up arms against Somoza. Nor can I condemn my North American friend who, in defense of himself and his Nicaraguan co-travelers, carried a gun through the Nicaraguan mountains where National Guardsmen were hiding soon after the Sandinistas declared their victory. I can empathize with those who seized the U.S. hostages in Iran. I cannot condemn the homeless woman who hurls curses at her passersby as she wanders the streets of downtown Washington.

As I come to understand more deeply the anger that wells up in me when my freedom and dignity are violated, and as I come to share glimpses of the much greater oppression of my neighbors down the street or in the third world, I find I cannot speak of peace without demanding justice.

But the nagging questions remain: What if I had been in Nicaragua during the insurrection? Would I have taken up arms? Or perhaps, less hypothetically what if *you* had decided to join the Frente? What do I say of the Nicaraguan church leaders who laud the Sandinista victory in July '79 as God's victory, or as you suggest—that the FSLN victory is a sign of the kingdom of God? What do I say of the Trappist priest Ernesto Cardenal, who hailed the FSLN's armed struggle as one not only of justice, but of love? Is it possible to love one's enemies by killing them?

You point to the lack of vengeance in the victorious Sandinista's response to the National Guard, to military commander Tomas Borge's forgiveness of his torturer, to the abolition of the death penalty, the literacy campaign, land reform. But I want to beg caution in placing unrealistic hopes in the Government of National Reconstruction, or any government. If the kingdom of God is any closer at hand in Nicaragua, we must more realistically look for the signs in the grass roots organizations where people are working together for the common good.

Pardon me, but my Anabaptism is showing. I cannot put much hope in governments or militia, even those who show extraordinary signs of concern for the people. The realism you call for in seeing U.S. imperialism for what it is must also be applied as a critical posture towards all holders of political power. Now, I would agree with you that there is a vast difference between a regime backed by the wealth and military prowess like that of the United States and that of a fledgling government such as the Nicaraguan Government of National Reconstruction, or a host of other governments in newly decolonized third world countries. (This is why I consider cooperation with the U.S. military unthinkable, while at the same time confessing my sympathies with the Sandinistas.) But I think we would be politically and spiritually naive to glorify the Sandinista victory as a victory of pure good over pure evil.

This caution nags me most relentlessly as I recall films I have seen about Nicaragua since Somoza was ousted. My stomach rebels as I see women chatting proudly about what kinds of guns they carried during the insurrection. The excitement I feel at all the positive signs of genuine change in Nicaragua stops short as I see film footage of preschool children play-acting combat scenes against the National Guard. I cannot help but wonder how the psyche of a people, and their reverence for all human life, is indelibly colored by their use of lethal violence to declare their freedom.

The Anabaptist in me also rises in resistance to how quickly liberation theologians equate Christianity with socialism, and move from that to proclaiming a just revolution approach to liberation struggles parallel to Augustine's just war theory. We must be careful that our rejection of the ancient link between Christianity and capitalism and all the other nasty-isms in the world doesn't lead us to a doctrinaire left-wing ideological position that invokes God's name to justify our own agenda and our own time frame. We must be careful if we presume to be acting on God's side, especially when that zeal leads us to support those who are deliberately killing people. Dan Berrigan's challenge to Ernesto Cardenal is appropriate here: Is not the death of a single human too heavy a price to pay for the vindication of any principle, however sacred? Of course, if I had the choice between actively supporting Somoza or an FSLN, I would choose the FSLN. But I would do so with fear and trembling, much like that of Dietrich Bonhoeffer when he chose to contemplate Hitler's murder. He knew full well that by choosing what he saw as a necessary evil he was contradicting a basic principle of his Christian faith. He chose sin for the sake of his people.

That attitude of humility—of penance, if you will—gets at the distinction I would make between not *condemning* armed revolutionary violence, but not *justifying* it either. If I had been in Nicaragua two years ago, would I have joined the Frente? I don't know, just like I don't know what I would do if someone was about to rape my grandmother! I hope—I pray—that if I felt compelled to take up arms that I would not do it arrogantly, as if a Zealot bringing in the Kingdom of God. I pray that I would not invoke Jesus' blessings to justify actions that clearly fall short of his way of responding to evil. (Jesus understood the Zealot appeal and refused it, in the face of Roman repression of his people that was likely as harsh, in many ways, as Somoza's grip on Nicaragua.) I would hope my choice, however impassioned, would allow for the most definite possibility that I could be wrong.

Perhaps it is a luxury that I even have such a choice.

That realization of privilege is the crux of the moral ambiguity I find myself confronting. My deepest agony on the whole topic of violence and nonviolence comes as I read your reiteration of what I've heard countless times about Nicaragua: the people were forced to resort to military resistance because the U.S.-supported Somoza regime gave them no choice. In a very real sense, there is blood on my hands, my bloody pacifist hands. I am guilty of murder. Forgive me if I seem to over-dramatize, but consider this: our federal tax dollars have been used time and again to fund thousands of atrocities such as the one your nun-friend described. I have never carried a gun (I even have trouble killing mice), but my money has supported and my silence has allowed some of the most brutal violence in the history of the world. The nation of which I am part has perpetuated the slow, torturous death of malnutrition and disease that our society's policies have allowed, if not caused.

The more I allow myself to face that truth about my participation in a violent world, the more my faith and my intellect call me to humility and compassion rather than to doctrinaire ethics. I cannot hope for a clear conscience. I can only hope that my ethical choices are motivated by love rather than fear. I can only pray that my increasing passion for justice can be expressed in ways that do not betray the spirit of the Prince of Peace I profess to follow.

The crucial issue for us, then, is *not* what we would have done if we had been in Nicaragua during the insurrection. We were not there, nor are we likely ever to be in such a combat situation, unless we choose to deliberately place ourselves there. The crucial question is, rather, *what does our commitment to nonviolence mean as citizens of one of the most powerful and oppressive nations in recorded history?* What does it mean to hold up Jesus' model of resisting evil by dying rather than killing, amidst a world so permeated with violence—whether it be verbal threats on the streets, psychological violence done to minorities, institutionalized violence inflicted on the unemployed, or bombings plotted to counter Central American insurrectionists?

I confess that I don't know. The older I get and the more I learn, the more tentative my answers become. The more my faith moves me towards an acquaintance with the mystery of life and gives me an increasing awe at Jesus' irrational way of confronting evil, the more passionate I become about these questions. It is becoming increasingly clear that the best way to confront the questions is not to invoke platitudes, but to place myself in the thick of the confrontations. And to pray for mercy. I know that a pacifism untested is an affront to those who suffer. I must take sides, on behalf of the victims of the oppressive powers. I must either be willing to take on suffering or keep my mouth shut.

Humbly,
MJB

*   *   *

Dear MJ,
You're right.

Love, Yvonne

No . . . thankfully, you won't let me end with that. The issues you raise need yet another response.

Thank you for bringing the violence issue home to our own soil. That is difficult for me to do. After living a year with my heart in Nicaragua and my body in the United States, it is with reluctance that I bring my heart home to work here. I would rather go to Nicaragua. I am alienated from the dominant life-style and priorities of my country, although I love the people.

Yet as you point out so well (and my Nicaraguan friends would agree), the definitive struggle for justice in Latin America and the rest of the oppressed world needs to happen here in this country. The problems in Central America cannot be solved without dealing with their roots—buried within our own affluent lifestyles and economic structures in the United States.

For Christians in Nicaragua, plunging into political life was mandatory; it required a straight yes or no, for or against

Somoza. I wish it were that clear in the United States. I raise up your question: What does our commitment to nonviolence mean as citizens of one of the most powerful and oppressive nations in history? We have structured society in a way that allows us to focus on our personal purity and not take responsibility for the poor. Or, worse yet, we can stop at bandaid efforts which help the poor tolerate the inequities of our economic system. We can boycott Nestle's products, reduce our meat consumption, register as conscientious objectors to war, and mistakenly believe our hands are clean. We can be arm-chair pacifists. Most of us are.

You remind me of the stinging fact that I will always live in luxury by the simple fact that I have a choice. I have chosen to live simply, that is to stay below a certain income level and to limit my consumption habits. Whether out of guilt, clear choice, or martyrdom, the key word "choice" will always divide me from those who are chained in poverty. Only recently have I realized that by becoming a college graduate I joined a very tiny minority of the world's population. All this is not to lay a guilt trip on myself or my upbringing, but rather to act responsibly with all that my family, my church, my position in society have given me.

So, having thoroughly flogged myself, I agree with your conclusion: my only response to the question of violence is one of faith. But that can be dangerously simplistic. Please do not let me divorce the faith from effectiveness. We are about bringing the Kingdom of fullness which, translated into concern for ending the exploitation of others, means an effective response of faith. It means taking a breath, and stepping into the political arena. The Gospel gives us strength to work for justice. However, in deciding how and where to apply that strength, we come face to face with political choices. It is here that I must step back and evaluate our Anabaptist heritage. I am ashamed to say that our Anabaptist counterparts in Nicaragua would not choose sides. In their passive nonresistance, they supported Somoza.

The violence in Nicaragua forced most Christians to move beyond the preoccupation with not compromising themselves in the struggle. Camilo Torres (Colombian revolutionary and priest) suggests that Jesus' reminder "My Kingdom is not of this world" (often misinterpreted as "not of this present life") must be held in tension with his prayer that his followers not be separated *out of* the world, but that they be preserved from evil. Considering all of Jesus' life and teachings, Camilo questions whether we peacemakers would not better concern ourselves *less* with being preserved from evil and more with *not* separating ourselves from the world and its need of redemption.

I am not advocating an end to the long-held Anabaptist doctrine of separation of church and state. The Nicaraguan church certainly wants to retain its autonomy. I apologize for sounding as if the new Nicaraguan government ought to be hailed as bringing in the Kingdom of God. (Though if I were God, I'd certainly choose those beautiful mountains and people in which to do it!) However, I doubt I would apologize if I had lived through the last four nights of Somoza's vengeance which delivered nonstop aerial bombardment on the major cities. I heard many Christians who lived through the battle describe the triumphal entry of the FSLN into the capital city as the dawning of God's Kingdom in Nicaragua, and I was neither surprised nor offended by their metaphor.

That does not mean I disregard your caution of losing perspective on the reality that the Sandinistas are an earthly government. A government is still a government, I believe you say. You are absolutely right in pinpointing the difference between the people and the government. I got carried away. But I still cannot help but feel a surge of exhilaration when I see the desires of a people—oppressed for so long—translated into state priorities. That does not mean we cease to view the Government of National Reconstruction with a critical, objective eye.

I want to share some excerpts from a November 1979 Pastoral Letter written by the Nicaraguan bishops. It moves me deeply. We should study it together as a response to your concern for Nicaraguan Christians making dangerous connections between the coming Kingdom of God and the FSLN victory.

They express in the letter the clear-sightedness you are concerned about, acknowledging that the present reconstruction stage is at once chaotic, disorderly, vulnerable to errors and abuses, while it is also a time of profound creativity and bears signs of the Kingdom of God.

We must remember that no historical revolutionary event can exhaust the infinite possibilities for justice and absolute solidarity of the Kingdom of God. We must state that our commitment to the revolutionary process does not imply naivete, blind enthusiasm, or the creation of a new idol before which everyone must bow down unquestioningly . . .

The heart of Jesus' message is the announcement of the Kingdom of God, a kingdom founded on God's love for all humanity and in which the poor hold a special place . . . To announce the Kingdom means that we have to bring it into our lives. On that effort, the authenticity of our faith in God is staked, establishing what the Holy Scriptures call "justice and right" for the poor. It is commitment which tests our faith in Christ, who gave his life to proclaim the Kingdom . . . Jesus tells us that the Kingdom means liberation and justice (Luke 4:16–20), because it is a kingdom of life. Our need to build this kingdom is the basis for our accepting and participating in the current process, whose purpose is to ensure that all Nicaraguans truly live . . . By acting as Christians we become Christians. Without such solidarity, our announcement of the Good News is but an empty phrase.

I am remembering something a friend, a Nicaraguan Christian, said about objectivity toward state powers. He said he is ashamed to see part of the church hierarchy in Nicaragua today openly criticize the Sandinista government after having remained silent during Somoza's terrible reign; Somoza may not have taken so many lives if the church had taken the risk to oppose the dictatorship when to do so promised repression and martyrdom. It took the church hierarchy many years of direct, then tacit support for the Somozas before the suffering of the people evoked a response of faith and solidarity. Where the Catholic Bishops were concerned, it was not until June 1979—six weeks before victory, that they issued a letter acknowledging the right of the Nicaraguan people to engage in revolutionary insurrection. To do what is perceived as the "Christian duty" today and criticize the government is a relatively safe move, given the climate of pluralism. A common denunciation I hear from Nicaraguans is that one must earn the right to criticize the revolutionary process by having displayed—amidst the repression—commitment to the cause of the poor. Hence, there is some eyebrow lifting at those sectors of the population who had very little to say on behalf of the poor but now have much to say on behalf of themselves.

The Bishop's Pastoral letter reflects the type of dialogue taking place all over Nicaragua. I will not attempt to predict where Nicaraguan Christians will come out. It will largely depend on their ability to remain true to what they have learned about commitment to the poor.

I do not want to make the Nicaraguan people out to be unbelievable in their compassion and love. It would be a gross exaggeration to say that every bullet which flew from a Sandinista-held gun was propelled with love for the National Guard. The reality of the death and destruction from armed struggle cannot be denied. I reluctantly agree with Ellul at that point: all violence is of one kind. It cannot be separated into good and bad, pure and evil. The human reactions of anyone, including the Sandinistas, could only be expected. The vengeance manifests itself. It must. So there are instances where victory opened the way for some to express years of pent-up anger and hatred for Somoza supporters. That was especially true where the volatile issue of land ownership is concerned. For 20 years the peasants had been absolutely denied the power that comes with owning land, and a significantly large percentage of the urban population identifies itself as displaced peasantry. Inevitably, victory brought an excuse to take revenge for the wrongs done to the campesinos.

But the manner in which local Sandinista authorities handled these cases is what I find so hopeful. Their complete dedication to not only understanding and responding to the historical context in which the people operate, but in enabling the people to work out their own solutions, however long and arduous, impresses me. Along with that, they openly admit that they are new to this business of governing and will make mistakes.

I may be too distant to see clearly, but bear with me for one more example. In the southern town of Rivas, townspeople in a local restaurant told me that immediately after victory the people gathered in the town square to elect a provisional municipal government. They elected the same "patrons" of the town whom they had elected for years—the Latin American custom of class relations. After a few weeks in which the elected patrons proved they had learned nothing through the insurrectional process, the townspeople protested. Sandinista representatives then called the people together to talk about elections under Somoza and why certain people had always been elected. They discussed how during the struggle for self-determination, leadership rose out of personal involvement in the lives of the poor. The Sandinistas then noted that it had nothing to do with wealth, or formal education, but rather was a matter of commitment to serve the people and to be with the people. Subsequently, when new elections were held, those elected to office were ones who had already proved their commitment and leadership capability during the insurrection.

All this is to say that the new Nicaragua is a scene of rapid change. The single overwhelming impression that the people gave me last September, and continue to exude, is one of a people constructing their own history. But I sway from our theme . . .

I am not so naive as to be surprised if Nicaragua became a militant society where the power of weaponry is idolized. The first anniversary celebration included a display of weapons which will be used to fight off a U.S. intervention if necessary. Nicaragua took up arms to overthrow an unjust and repressive tyrant; they did not lay down those weapons upon achievement of their goal. Rather, they organized a standing army in the traditional sense of the modern nation state, in order to defend what they have won. I did not really expect anything different.

It becomes very difficult to know how to bring this to a close. As I said at the outset, your conclusion strikes home: my only response to violence is one of faith. I don't know what I would have done had I been in Nicaragua two years ago. I think my support of the Sandinistas would have stopped short of my carrying a gun, but I would have collaborated with them, I am sure. But that is not the real issue. The question is what am I doing in the U.S.? Are there parallels in the experience of Nicaraguan Christians which can help answer that question?

One friend in particular, a Baptist pastor who did not take up arms but who collaborated fully with the Sandinistas, shared with me the memory of the day Arlen, a young woman from his parish, left to join the Sandinistas in the mountains. She asked for a book from his library to take with her: *Fuerza de Amar* (Strength to Love) by Martin Luther King, Jr. Perhaps she reached the point which Ellul seems to say is the best we can do: acknowledge that the historical moment we are in demands of us an action which does not hold up to the ideal set for us in Christ's response to violence by turning the other cheek. Arlen must have been able to accept that tension as she pulled on her boots with King's book tucked under her arm. She was killed brutally by the National Guard, so I cannot ask her. They tell me she was the most joyful person in the mountain camps. I pray we can accept the inevitable tensions in our lives with the joy that is promised in living with faith.

Adelante!
   YK

*   *   *

Dear YK,

You have left me nearly speechless. As I review our verbose confessions, I cannot help but remember one of the most disarming moments during my travels in India last year. At a tea with several Indian religious leaders there arose considerable controversy about religion and ethics. After Muslims and Hindus and Christians and Sikhs had argued for a while about the true interpretations of their various faiths, the eldest in the crowd, a modest Gandhian whose appearance brought the Mahatma himself to mind, spoke words that brought the zealous religionists and their audience to a humorous, humble silence. He simply said, "Friends, let us remember that nonviolence is not talking too much."

And so, my dear friend, lest I further taint my conscience with acts of violence, I will be brief. It seems only fair to our readers to confess that we find ourselves hard put to pose as proponents of opposite points of view. We initially thought we would call this article a "dialogue between a Sandinista and a Gandhian." But the more we have talked, agonized, and laughed over the questions we address here, the more we have realized that we basically agree; those characterizations would deny the ambiguity we both bring to this discussion.

Our temperaments and our experiences over the past two years are perhaps the most basic differences between us.

Our conclusions are few, our questions many. Let us hold the questions before us: With concern for personal purity aside, is not the refusal to inflict harm on another the most revolutionary approach to life? And, if we say "yes" to that, what do we as North Americans have to do to clean up our bloody hands? Rightly or wrongly, the Sandinistas did what they had to do. But what of those of us North Americans who join the Nicaraguans and other struggling people in the quest for self-determination? From our side of the border, what are we to do? What can we learn—about democracy, economics, and faith—from liberation movements in the Third World? How can we direct our energies in ways that truly break the cycle of violence which the United States propels by its inflated self-image and perverse foreign policies and domestic priorities? How do we take sides and still love our enemies? (You mean I must love Reagan?) Are we, too, so blinded by our riches that we will not listen to one who has risen from the dead?

We both say that our conclusions come, in the end, from our faith. You challenge me not to be apolitical. I challenge you not to become too invested in effectiveness. I would hope that we both—and all of our friends who share these questions—will learn more and more to live creatively with the tension between patience and zeal. You have taught me a lot about responding with abandon to the urgent call for justice. I hope I have helped you to remember the part of revolution which is patience.

With affection and respect, I close with excerpts from a letter between two friends who no doubt shared aspirations and questions similar to our own. Thomas Merton, Trappist monk and prolific writer on prayer and peace-making writes the following to James Forrest, now secretary of the International Fellowship of Reconciliation:

> Do not depend on the hope of results. When you are doing the sort of work you have taken on, essentially an apostolic work, you may have to face the fact that your work will be apparently worthless and even achieve no result at all, if not perhaps results opposite to what you expect. As you get used to this idea, you

start more and more to concentrate not on the results but on the value, the rightness, the truth of the work itself. And there too a great deal has to be gone through, as gradually you struggle less and less for an idea and more and more for specific people. The range tends to narrow down, but it gets much more real. In the end, it is the reality of personal relationships that saves everything . . .

The big results are not in your hands or mine, but they suddenly happen, and we can share in them; but there is no point in building our lives on this personal satisfaction, which may be denied us and which after all is not that important.

You are probably striving to build yourself an identity in your work, out of your work and your witness. You are using it, so to speak, to protect yourself against nothingness, annihilation. That is not the right use of work. All the good that you will do will come not from you but from the fact that you have allowed yourself, in the obedience of faith, to be used by God's love. Think of this more and gradually you will be free from the need to prove yourself, and you can be more open to the power that will work through you without your knowing it.

. . . If you can get free from the domination of causes and just serve Christ's truth, you will be able to do more and will be less crushed by the inevitable disappointments. Because I see nothing whatever in sight but much disappointment, frustration, and confusion . . .

The real hope, then is not in something we think we can do, but in God who is making something good out of it in some way we cannot see. If we can do His will, we will be helping in this process. But we will not necessarily know all about it beforehand.

Yes, enough of this. We must either be willing to take on suffering or keep our pens silent and our mouths shut.

Shalom,
    MJB

DON BENEDICT

In 1982, when he published his memoir *Born Again Radical,* Don Benedict (1917–2008) was a minister in the United Church of Christ in Chicago with a thirty-five-year career behind him; William Sloane Coffin Jr. called him "Mr. Urban Ministry" for his dedication to the needs of his inner-city parishioners. In 1943, though, Benedict was a CO in the Danbury Federal Correctional Institution, where several contributors to the present volume (David Dellinger, Robert Lowell, Lowell Naeve) at one point or another did time.

Benedict has become something of a legend in the literature of World War II conscientious objection for his role in a famous softball game. A peerless pitcher, he was a player the sports-loving warden desperately needed for an upcoming championship. Declining lesser offers from the warden, he finally leveraged his athletic prowess to win the release of striking prisoners from solitary confinement—and also won the championship. Benedict is less heroic, in his own eyes especially, in the excerpt that follows. Here his courage and his pacifist convictions fail him, and he decides to give up his protest against the war. He later enlisted in the Army Air Corps and served in the Pacific.

FROM
Born Again Radical

My pacifism was not a rigid philosophy in the sense of rules, nor was it a hierarchy of options. I simply had a strong feeling against violence all my life. I had always tried to break down the case for force. But when it came to acting I thought I would be ruled by my feeling at the time.

It seemed to me now that to kill in a crisis of self-defense was to strike directly at evil. This was permitted. But no matter how evil their cause, to invoke the name of justice and strike at other people when they might be brought to reason was surely wrong. To use force against misguided persons would be only an indirect blow. And how can one avoid striking through others to get at the center of evil?

Suddenly, a thought struck me, preventing me from going on. Here I was, a deep-rooted pacifist, actually trying to figure out a way to use force justly. Nazism was at the back of my mind. Was there such a thing as a just war? Were the Jews

only absorbing aggression? This might be a just war but whom
would I have to kill? And if it was a just war, what was my attitude saying? OK, it's a just war, but I won't fight—let someone
else do it? I had to abandon that line of thinking temporarily,
but I realized I would have to give more thought to my own
pacifism. What was my stand? What was I going to do?

Coming out of quarantine as a known pacifist serving my
second term, I was approached by a man called Chick who had
been a United Mine Workers organizer. After being put in jail
for failure to register, he had tried to get out by registering as
a CO but was refused because he was not religious. He wanted
me to help in another demonstration against prison as part of
the war system. I agreed, and we recruited sixteen pacifists who
would refuse to work for the rest of our terms. One man was
to quit work each Wednesday so that the warden would have
no way of knowing how widespread the strike was. Chick and
I would be the last. We would go together, signalizing the end
of the line.

When the day came, we stopped work and were immediately
put into solitary confinement. This was my second time, but it
was not to be like the first. I had no suspicion that this time it
would break me down, that I would face a terrible crisis. At first
I was elated. I was glad I had stopped reading Niebuhr's book
and that I had joined the work strike. It was the right thing to
do. I might have held back, overindulging in self-examination.
I was glad that I hadn't wavered. I had been true to myself. And
for my belief I had now gone all the way to the wall. But by the
end of the next day I was wondering how long they would keep
me in solitary. Probably just a few days, then back to a lock-in
in the cell. I could understand why men in solitary spent their
days waiting for the only events in their lives—the rattle of the
lock, the swish of the door opening, and the sound of the food
tray in the slot.

By the seventh night I no longer felt I was in solitary because
of this last work strike. I was there because of my entire past
life, and the question that faced me was not whether I could
continue in solitary for the term of my sentence but for the
rest of my life. There was no way to follow Jesus and mitigate
the suffering. There was no way without, in the end, facing
crucifixion. I knew this and I had always been prepared for

it. I would go out from jail into a system I would resist and I would be sent back. In prison, too, I would continue to follow my convictions, and that meant solitary. There is no way to compromise when one follows the perfect One.

But was I strong enough? Always before I had thought I was, but now I was racked by doubt. From boyhood, I had believed violence was wrong. Now I faced a direct contradiction. The mere demonstration of the power of force in the Detroit streets had stopped the riots. I had to face that fact. Here was the one case that disproved my convictions. Not only could force bring order and peace; it had to be a superior force. This was hard for me to accept. Violence ought not to be stopped by violence. Where would it end? Nevertheless, my belief in pacifism as an absolute was shaken. How could I stay in solitary if I was unsure that what I was doing was right? What if I were wrong? No answer came. All day and through the night I was repeating a litany:

I have refused to fight. *Lord, hear me.*

I have tried to love everyone. *Lord, hear me.*

I have tried to be like Jesus, the perfect One, and the more I have tried the more impossible it becomes. *Lord, hear me.*

Midge Miller, shortstop. *Shot down over Germany!*

Lou Krueger, first base. *Killed at Anzio!*

The harder I struggle, the more bitter I become with others who say they are Christians. *Lord, hear me.*

Ed Breezee, Tecumseh High. *Crashed in the Himalayas!*

Maybe it makes a difference who wins the war. *Lord, hear me.*

I have never compromised. *Lord, hear me.*

I have followed my conscience. *Lord, hear me.*

I have striven for perfection and I have become only self-righteous. *Lord, hear me.*

I have given up all sources of income except the bare necessities. *Lord, hear me.*

When I lose count of the trays will I know day from night? *Lord, hear me.*

I am entirely removed from the world. *Lord, hear me.*

I am utterly alone. *Lord, hear me.*

God, God, are you hearing me? What good can I do here? Does it make a difference? How can I get out? How can I get out of here when I talked the others into striking? Is pacifism the only choice? There is nothing here. There is nothing ahead. How can I go on? There is no ground, no place to step. I don't have enough faith. Why am I thinking these things? Am I thinking these things trying to make myself guilty for staying in solitary? Selfish for going to prison? Am I thinking these things because I am losing my mind? I don't know what I believe. Only that I believe in you. You are my faith. And yet how can I go on? Into nothingness? Or have I already made the step?

I fell on the mattress, lying there, tossing from side to side. Gradually, the sense of the terrible silence changed to a feeling of quiet, then of peace. I thought it must be almost morning. I was exhausted and seemed to be falling asleep. I closed my eyes and began to drift, and then the words came, not a voice speaking, only the words, clear, in my mind: *You are my beloved.* This was the word of God to all people who have faith. For the first time I realized that word was also meant for me. I, myself, was loved by God—loved with all my guilt and imperfections; I felt surrounded and supported by love. And I slept.

I slept for an hour. When I awoke I knew I was going to get out. Not just go back on work detail and get out of solitary; I was going to get out of prison. But by the time the guard came and I asked for the razor I was shattered and shaking again. That hour of calm had left me.

I put on my shirt, and as the door opened I was thinking that when I got to the warden's office I would write a note to the other pacifists. I felt I owed them an explanation.

It was the morning of the eighth day, and I stood in the doorway, blinking. A draft of fresh air came through, and a shaft of sunlight fell across the floor. The light almost hurt my eyes. I turned to look back into that cold, dim cell and felt for a moment intense sadness. Something fine was being left behind. Also certitude. Also my youth. I knew I would never come back.

EUGENE J. McCARTHY

Those who worked on the 1968 presidential campaign of Eugene McCarthy (1916–2005) remember how frustrating and evasive he could be, how often he held back from full-throated positions and restricted himself to irony, hints, poems. But they were working for him because he had had the courage to run as an antiwar candidate for the Democratic presidential nomination, against a sitting president with great political skill and a vengefully long memory, and because somehow, against all expectations, his campaign had led Lyndon Johnson not to run for reelection.

The same irony is on display in the piece included here, a satire prompted by McCarthy's discovery of an IRS document called "A Design of an Emergency Tax System," exploring how taxes might be collected in the event of thermonuclear war. Underneath his deceptively bland prose, McCarthy ridicules those shortsighted enough to imagine thermonuclear war as an event to which rational calculation can be applied, and reminds us that such calculations make nuclear catastrophe a little less unthinkable. An "Emergency Tax System" seems to him like something out of *Dr. Strangelove* (1964)—an absurdity on the way to doomsday. McCarthy was campaigning to regain his Minnesota Senate seat when he published his satire, on August 15, 1982. What other candidate for such an office has allowed himself or herself so indirect and enigmatic a commentary on a matter of life and death? (He was not returned to office.)

McCarthy grew up Catholic in Minnesota, excelled as an athlete, taught science, got a master's in sociology at the University of Minnesota, and taught economics and education at St. John's University, where he had been an undergraduate. He thought of becoming a monk but chose not to after a nine months' novitiate. He became active in local politics, won election to the House of Representatives in 1948, and spent a decade or so in forthright opposition to Joseph McCarthy, then a senator from Wisconsin. His courage got him noticed, and he was elected to the Senate in 1958, junior senator to the Hubert Humphrey he later found himself so bitterly at odds with over the Vietnam War. McCarthy was an early and eloquent opponent of that war, and the natural choice to be the candidate of the "Dump Johnson" movement of 1968, whatever his inner reservations. Throngs of college students, I among them, got "clean for Gene"; though in the end the prowar Humphrey would win the nomination (while outside, in Grant Park, Allen Ginsberg chanted "Om" and thousands of demonstrators were beaten by police), the prowar Nixon would defeat Humphrey in the general election, and the war would go on.

The IRS' Plan for the Hereafter

An axiom of long standing is that "nothing is more certain than death and taxes." At the same time, whereas it is generally held that there is life after death, it has also been held that once an estate was settled, there would be no more taxes after death.

So taxpayers who looked forward or upward to the relief from taxes as one of the joys of the Hereafter must have been deeply disillusioned by a recent announcement from the Treasury Department.

In anticipation of a nuclear attack and the destruction, confusion, and near chaos that might follow, a senior Treasury official has prepared a plan "for collecting taxes even under those difficult conditions." Even annihilation does not bring escape from the IRS.

The plan is called "A Design of an Emergency Tax System." The "design's" first concern is to perpetuate the Individual Income Tax system by securing the records on the basis of which taxes are determined. Taxes owed by those who are annihilated will be assessed as best they can be, the report states.

It would be a convenience to the IRS if the nuclear attack could be coordinated with the April 15 deadline (no pun intended) for income tax payments. If that date is not possible, perhaps the powers that be could manage it on or soon after one of the days on which quarterly payments of estimated taxes are scheduled.

The Treasury "design" does not make public its plans for the safety and survival of IRS agents. Possibly the agents may be lost, but in the short run—for five or six months after the attack—the computers, in some safe place, will continue the essential work of the IRS.

The "design" notes that nuclear war might be so disastrous that in addition to the destruction of millions of people, major industrial installations, and major population centers, it might even destroy the tax system. This, the IRS seems to believe, would be the most serious consequence of nuclear war. There are some experts in post-nuclear war survival who hold that along with cockroaches, the income tax system is likely to be among the few survivors of such war.

Taking no chances, however, the author of the "design" proposes a stand-by tax program in the form of a general sales tax to be applied at the point of purchase.

Such a tax, the author holds, would have two advantages—it would encourage savings and "aid in rebuilding the capital stock" of the country.

The Treasury expert has even set the percentage level for the tax: 20 percent. He says this should do it. That does not quite square with the Mutual Assured Destruction concept, developed by Robert McNamara as secretary of defense, which held that deterrence would occur at the prospect of the loss of 20 percent of the population and 50 percent of industrial capacity.

The "design" does not make clear who will collect the tax or whether it will be applied to the costs of mortician services, although in the immediate post-bombing period such goods and services would make up a major part of the gross national product.

The danger with a plan of this kind, a contingency plan, is not in its being there in anticipation of the emergency for which it was drafted. It is probably as good a plan as any that could be devised for conditions which no one can anticipate.

The danger lies in the fact that Treasury and the IRS may become attached to the plan to the point that without the nuclear war for which it was prepared, they may come to believe that the plan offers a better tax system than the one currently in place. They might offer it as a substitute, with the sustaining argument that apart from the merits of their tax program, it would be a good idea to have the emergency program established in advance of the emergency.

A contingency plan can be a destabilizing force, as those who conceived it may become more and more attached to it, and eager to test it, with or without an emergency.

The attempted takeover of a military government in Greece a few years ago by another military group is a recent example. The attempt was based on a contingency plan to take over the government if it were communist controlled—which this one was not.

The lesson is to beware of bureaucrats (or generals) bearing contingency plans. Possibly, under bureaucracy, you not only cannot take it with you, but you cannot even leave it behind.

WALLY NELSON

Born in Altheimer, Arkansas, Wally Nelson (1909–2002) grew up in a family of sharecroppers, then attended Ohio Wesleyan University. He got his fierce pacifism, he tells us here, not from politics but from his father's mode of dealing with racial injustice: teaching his children that, in one of Wally's favorite phrases, "there was only one race, the human race," the implication being not only that blacks and whites belonged to the same race but that Americans and Germans and Japanese did too. ("Wally" rather than "Nelson" because I knew him—"Nelson" feels impossibly impersonal.)

Wally was already a committed antiwar activist when World War II broke out; he had participated in the national student "Strike Against War" campaign back in 1934–35. At first he registered as a conscientious objector, and spent a year in a Civilian Public Service Camp near Coshocton, Ohio (he later referred to the camps as "civilian public slavery"). But then he chose to withdraw from such cooperation with the government and walked out, receiving a five-year prison sentence and ultimately serving thirty-three months in the Cuyahoga County Jail and in federal prisons in Milan, Michigan, and Danbury, Connecticut. In the last institution he went on a 114-day hunger strike, enduring force-feeding for eighty-seven days. He also met his future wife Juanita in prison; she was then a reporter working on a story.

After his release in 1946 Wally participated in the first Freedom Rides; in 1948 he and Juanita helped found the Peacemakers; in the early 1950s he was the first national field officer for the Congress of Racial Equality. Much of Wally's life after 1948 is recounted on page 334, in the note to his wife Juanita's essay "A Matter of Freedom"; they were together from that year until his death, each supporting the other in their similarities and differences alike.

Unlike Juanita, he was not by temperament a writer, but he was a lively, engaging talker, gracious and fierce. The graciousness made the fierceness surprising; you kept thinking that someone so gracious would yield on some matter of principle, but Wally never did. What he said about Tiananmen Square is characteristic: "What happened in China last month was because you had people following orders." Or, more generally: "I never accuse presidents of doing anything—we do it." Deena Hurwitz and Craig Simpson interviewed him in his mid-seventies for their oral history *Against the Tide: Pacifist Resistance in the Second World War* (1984), and to their credit Wally spoke to them openly and with great force, focusing mostly on his upbringing and on his experiences during World War II.

"One Race, the Human Race"

I WAS quite taken with the Sermon on the Mount and trying to make Christianity something more than just going to church. This I got from my father, my one influence who believed very much that if you say you believe in a thing, you demonstrated it by doing it or attempting to do it. I got strong influences from my home not to think in terms of pacifism as such. No one knew anything about the word "pacifism" when I was a child, but the whole concept of love, of understanding that there is one family—the human race—I got that at home back in Arkansas in situations where I was being confronted in a most brutal way.

For example, as a child between the ages of eight and ten, I could be walking down the street with a playmate or two in a certain section of the city and someone would whistle. We'd look around and the street would be filled with guys on bicycles and running, and all of them teenagers. And here we were just kids. We'd start running, and they'd start chasing us, and they would catch some of us occasionally and beat us. Most of us would run home crying and hating, hating the whites and this type of thing. My father almost instinctively would be trying to give some consolation to his kids who faced this. What could he say? I think he was hard put to know what he could say. He would say words to remind us that these people were misguided, that we were all a part of the human race, and that we were required to love everybody, even those people who mistreated us. Then he would say, "even the whites, even the whites." It was that type of preaching that affected me very much as I was trying to make up what it was I believed and which way I wanted to build my life. By the time I was seriously thinking about this, I'd accepted the thesis that there's one race, the human race.

———————

By the time the war came along, I was well enough along in my thinking that when I was invited to go and kill the Germans and Japanese, I knew I was being invited to kill my brothers and sisters. It was just as real to me to say, "OK, the

Nelson family is a pretty bad lot, and we want you to take this gun and kill your family because they can't get along, so we need to have peace, take this gun and kill your siblings and your mother and father." Another thing, by that time, if I'd believed that violence solved problems and particularly that type of problem, I would have already been dead because I would have already gone out with a gun and started killing people. But it would have been people who I'd had personal contact with. But no one is going to write me from Washington or anywhere else and go "Hey, there's a woman named Deena Hurwitz we're disturbed with, and if we tell you what she's done, you'd be disturbed with her, and go over there and blow her head off!" Uh, uh! None of this stuff! I will have to know you and you will have to have demonstrated to me, I would say, "Boy that woman is evil! Now I gotta do something about it!" Nobody but nobody is gonna tell me that I got enemies 100 miles away whom I have never seen, or never met, nor will I ever meet.

They had a system in the house where they put us: you walked into a cell, the guy way up at the head of the outside would hit something and all the doors would come together and lock at the same time. They couldn't do that until every door was closed. So all the guys went in the cells, they all pulled the doors closed. I didn't do anything to the door, so the guy hollered to me, "Close the door." He didn't call me by name, as a matter of fact, he didn't know my name. Didn't make any difference. So I didn't do anything. He said, "Hey" and I still didn't say anything. Now he didn't want to walk down there, that was his position. These people like to use the least amount of energy, physical or otherwise. So he and another guy were up there, and they were about as far as that door from me, they were standing outside where they could operate this thing. But they couldn't do it when the door to the cell I was in wasn't closed.

Finally he said, "The guy that's in the cell," and he called out the number cell I was in. I stuck my head out the door and I said, "I don't close jail doors." "What'd you say?" "I said,

I don't close prison doors." They opened that door and they bounced down there, boom, boom, boom, both of them came down there. He said something to me and I answered. He drew back to hit me, and the other man caught his arm. He was just so angry because he had to come down there, and that's all he was angry about.

By the time I got to Danbury people knew I was coming. They knew I was a noncooperator, so they immediately took me to a place where they didn't try to process me. When you're a noncooperator, that's when things happen to you. They don't try to process you through all that rigamarole, they get rid of you as soon as they possibly can.

During my hunger strike, there was a change of wardens. The new warden came to see me real soon. He introduced himself, "I'm the new warden, I came to meet you and also I want to know what type of parole, what type of supervision will you accept?" I said, "The only thing I would accept, you open the door, and I'll go home, and I will not come back to haunt you. That's the only thing I would accept." "Well, I thought you would say that." He said, "I want you guys out of here. I got a beautiful program for my prison but I cannot do it with you guys sitting up here. I'm gonna see that you get out of here." So, in a couple of months or so, they did release us.

Right next to the cell in Milan, Michigan was a young Nazi. He was in the German army, he was a lieutenant and they captured him. So he was a prisoner of war out in Arizona, broke out of camp, stole a car, and they caught him in some state somewhere across the country. They brought him to federal prison on the Dyre Act, which says that driving a stolen car across the state line becomes a federal offense. So he winds up in Milan, Michigan.

He was a Nazi Youth, he grew up with all the stuff they taught. This was their education, and this was what he grew up believing. He accepted *Mein Kampf* as being true. We discussed *Mein Kampf*, we discussed all types of things. It was very interesting that he could discuss this with me without feeling that he was betraying his Nazi beliefs. You see in terms of the ladder of human scale, I was on the bottom. In terms of the ability of human beings, you see, the person of black skin just had no ability at all. They were apt to be very violent from *Mein Kampf*'s point of view.

So we carried on, and I think that our conversations were somewhat consciousness raising for him, because we went into all these things. I didn't accuse him of being a devil or anything like this, we just discussed various points. I tried to argue my point, to show him how unreasonable I thought such a policy was. This went on for days, this type of discussion. I do think that he was affected somewhat by our conversations, but we never got into any recriminations. Two people who thoroughly disagreed. There were some questions, perhaps, on his mind. This was someone who I had begun to appreciate and like as an individual because he was a very likable person even though he believed these theories.

It was a very good type of contact for me to have in that situation. He reassured me that he and anyone coming from that whole scene was every bit as human as anyone I'd known, just misled.

———

Finally I began to feel, I came to the conclusion that I was cooperating not only with my imprisonment, but by this time I was getting to know that prisons are very bad, that no one should be in prisons, I was very strongly against prisons by this time and I began to see that by feeding my body, I was helping them to keep my body there. And it came to me clearly that if they were going to continue to keep me in prison it was going to be their full responsibility to keep me there. They must keep me alive and everything, because I wasn't going to participate. I notified the authorities of my decision and said, as of such and such a date, I was through with their ball game. "If you want the body to stay alive, it is absolutely your responsibility. I'm not going to maintain my body here in this prison. When you release me I will take responsibility for my body." Now that became the most important decision I've ever made. It was the decision that really gave me insight into what freedom is. Because here I stopped being afraid of death. I wasn't afraid of dying. I was clear of what I was doing. I was clear of what could happen.

It was the most freeing decision in my life. I haven't eaten in jail since, and I've been in jail many times since that time. I haven't participated in trials or this type of thing. Whenever I'm dragged off to jail, it is the jail and court's business when I get out. I don't plan with people that I'm going to be out at a certain time. The only plan I have is that when they open the door I will leave. If they don't open the door, I am here.

I'm through with power, I'm not interested in power, I'm not interested in helping people to attain power. One of my strongest criticisms of the so-called "black movement" is that they are into power. The women's movement is into power; all these movements. But that's not where it's at. We're not going to get one place until we get off this power trip and get on the human trip, stop jockeying for power and really try to become real human beings and support each other's humanity.

THOMAS BANYACYA

Born in Moenkopi, Arizona, just outside the Hopi Reservation, Thomas Banyacya (1909–1999) was given the name Thomas Jenkins by the Bureau of Indian Affairs and sent away to school. He returned home in 1932 with a degree from Bacone College, a Baptist missionary institution, and began teaching—but he also began studying anew with tribal elders, learning the Hopi sacred traditions that his prior education had neglected.

When World War II broke out, Banyacya joined five other members of his tribe in refusing to register for selective service. Ancient Hopi prophecy had warned that "great trouble will come involving many nations," and that "the Hopi should show our bows and arrows to no one at that time"; tribal elders explained this at his 1941 trial in Phoenix, but their voices had no effect, and Banyacya spent seven years in prison. In the excerpt that follows—from an interview by Deena Hurwitz and Craig Simpson, published in their 1984 oral history *Against the Tide*—Banyacya recalls the thinking that led him to follow his people's "Spiritual Way."

After his release, and in the wake of the use of atomic weapons in Hiroshima and Nagasaki, Banyacya was appointed to "carry the Hopi message of peace" to the world, and was instrumental in the revelation of Hopi prophecy. In 1992, after many attempts, he spoke at the United Nations: "If we humans do not wake up to the warnings, the great purification will come to destroy this world just as the previous worlds were destroyed."

"Like the Elders Say"

I STARTED with the Elders back in 1931 or '32. When the Second World War started to break out, the President of the United States talked over the radio, "All of those 18 have to register to go to the Army." I was single then and was living by myself in Old Oraibi. I had just finished all the pages in the book called *Century of Dishonor* when I heard the President of the United States telling Indians, "Look, we done you all kinds of things and we help you with these things and we took care of you and now you should appreciate and go fight for your country." But I saw what happened all these years. And I can't seem to agree. All this time I listened to the Elders, all this spiritual instruction and teaching. By that time I was convinced they (the Elders) were telling the truth. By that time I was taking part in the ceremony, so I know what they are talking about. Then being forced into school and learning to read the spiritual instructions and teachings, books written by the world religious people and memorizing the many verses which include the Ten Commandments. And one of these is "Thou Shalt Not Steal and Lie" and all that. And that made sense to me. I listened to my Elders' instruction and warning. And I look at the Bible and other world religions' warning all the same, and we are all under one power of God or whatever you call him. In Hopi we call him *Massau'u*. I better leave and go the way of the Hopi belief and follow the Hopi to maintain the peaceful way, Hopi life of truth, honest and peaceful, kind. And so I want to follow that.

So I never think of violating United States law. I just firmly believe in my people and stand by them. So that night when I hear the President of the United States talk about registration, I decided to wait awhile. And then I saw in my mind that I better not register. I think it best that I follow the law of the Great Spirit. So that decision was made there in myself during the night after the message of the President and finishing that book. Then I just decided I must hold onto the Spiritual Way like the Elders say. Then I waited and I thought I was the only one that didn't register, but later I found a couple others. By that time I was helping my Elders in speaking out against certain things that they don't want and writing letters and calling meetings with the Bureau of Indian Affairs.

GENE R. LA ROCQUE

Gene R. La Rocque (b. 1918) joined the Army at seventeen and served in the Navy from 1940 until 1972; he was on the destroyer USS *Macdonough* in Pearl Harbor when the Imperial Japanese Navy attacked, saw extensive combat during World War II, then worked in the Strategic Plans Directorate of the Joint Chiefs of Staff, rising to the rank of rear admiral. After his retirement—turned from zealot to skeptic by the Vietnam War—he founded the Center for Defense Information, seeking to provide the public with skeptical, informed assessments of military budget requests.

Unlike many of the antiwar soldier-writers in this anthology— a good-sized group from Ambrose Bierce to Camilo Mejía by way of John F. Kendrick, Kurt Vonnegut, and Ron Kovic—La Rocque remains every inch the pragmatic military analyst. Vietnam disillusioned him not because it was wrong but because it was in his judgment unwinnable, and its bombing operations ineffective. The argument in the piece included here focuses specifically on nuclear weapons, but here too there is no moral argument; nuclear war is for him intrinsically unwinnable, and to be opposed on that ground. What is winnable, he argues, is the public debate; his practical exhortation is directed toward the citizens he is addressing, and to the importance of such unglamorous but useful actions as writing letters to one's representatives and calling the White House.

The Role of the Military in the Nuclear Age

I AM very pleased and very proud to accept this award as Distinguished Statesman. It's an award I will treasure, and I accept with great humility—because for just about as long as I can remember I have been exhibiting a most unstatesmanlike behavior.

For nearly 50 years my profession has been one of war, not statesmanship. When I was 17 years old, the army first put a rifle in my hands, and I've spent the rest of my life in military organizations. Next year that will be an even 50 years. I went from the infantry to the horse cavalry (yes, we had horses), to the army air corps, to the United States Navy and then chose Pearl Harbor to welcome the Japanese. My active duty spans three wars. My last active combat, actual combat, was Vietnam.

So for 50 years I've dedicated my intellect and my energies to preparing for wars, fighting in wars and analyzing wars. I'm here to tell you tonight that war is a very dumb way to settle differences between nations. And nuclear war is utterly insane.

I'm supposed to talk tonight about the role of the military in the Nuclear Age. As always, the role of the military is the same—it is to fight and win wars. That's our job. That's what you have asked us to do. Our success depends on our professionalism, and a professional military force is one that kills and destroys efficiently. An unprofessional force kills inefficiently, ineffectively.

I want to tell you, we've got one of the most professional military forces in the world. Each branch of the service—the army, the navy, the air force and the marine corps—is striving always for greater professionalism. That professionalism leads us to try to acquire better and better weapons; that is, more destructive weapons, weapons that kill and destroy more efficiently. It is for that reason that we're building more and more nuclear weapons. You see, the urge to acquire better weapons leads us to the acquisition of nuclear weapons. Why? Because nuclear weapons are the best weapons man has ever invented.

Some of my colleagues tell me nuclear weapons can never be used, but nuclear weapons are desired by every branch of the military service because they are the most efficient way to kill and destroy. You may have forgotten—many of you may not—but in World War II we killed 50 million people. We civilized human beings killed 50 million people. So, you see, it's not a great big jump to be talking about killing hundreds of millions.

So pervasive have nuclear weapons become in our military today that they are now the conventional weapons. We've nuclearized our army divisions, our air wings, and 80 percent of U.S. Navy warships routinely carry nuclear weapons. When you see a warship off your coast, if it's a U.S. Navy warship, you've got an 80 percent chance that it is floating around with nuclear weapons.

When I had command of a guided missile cruiser, the Providence, in 1964, we used to ride up and down your coast with nuclear weapons. We were one of the first to get them on surface ships, and when I had command nobody told me I couldn't use them. Nobody said I had to get a message from anybody to use them. They were my main battery. They were, in fact, the only weapons that I had to shoot down a Soviet or any other enemy missile or aircraft that were any good. As a matter of fact, while I'm mentioning that, the only way that we could destroy a Soviet submarine today is with a nuclear weapon. The only way the Soviets can destroy one of our submarines today is with a nuclear weapon. The old-fashioned depth charges are gone. We have nuclearized our military forces.

We've got them, you'll say, but we're never going to use them. Well, the United States and the Soviet Union are both planning, training, arming and practicing for nuclear war every day.

Okay, you say, but are we going to have nuclear war? Yes, we are. We are going to have a nuclear war if we stay on this course. We and the Soviet Union are on a collision course. They're trying to expand. We're trying to control them. We don't like their economic system. They're anti-God. We don't like their political system. We don't like anything about them, and we and the Soviets are on a collision course. It is a course which is going to lead to nuclear war if we stay on it.

Our Secretary of Defense has identified the Soviet Union as the enemy. Our President says the Soviet Union is an evil empire and ought to be relegated to the ash heap of history. Our Vice-President says we can fight and win a nuclear war. We're dramatically increasing the number of nuclear weapons we have. You and I are building five nuclear weapons a day. In a ten-year period, we're building 17,000 new nuclear weapons. There's eight billion dollars this year in the Department of Energy budget for the sole purpose of building nuclear weapons. If you don't want them there, do something about it. If you don't want to build those nuclear weapons, then the control you have is not to spend the $8 billion to build them this year. We are also building many new vehicles to carry those nuclear weapons to the Soviet union, as if we didn't already have more than enough.

Nuclear war can start by accident. We may very well work with the Nuclear Age Peace Foundation to try to find ways to prevent an accidental start of a nuclear war. Nuclear war can start by miscalculation, computer error, electronic malfunction, or it can start by design. Don't forget: Maggie Thatcher can start a nuclear war. So can Mitterrand. So can the Chinese. So can the Russians. So can we. Give us another 15 years to the end of this century, and there'll be a lot more countries that can start a nuclear war.

Everybody says that they don't want a nuclear war. But both sides are acting as if they did. If we stay on this course, we're going to have a nuclear war. But we don't have to, and that's where I think the Nuclear Age Peace Foundation and all of you come in. We don't have to stay on this course, but you'd better do something. Can you win a nuclear war? No. No way to win it. But our Vice-President said we could. He thought we could. When our President, Mr. Reagan, submitted his budget to the Congress of the United States for fiscal year 1983, here is what the budget report said: *"The military posture of the United States is to give us the capability to fight successfully a conventional and a nuclear war."*

That's what we're arming for: to fight successfully a nuclear war. That's why we're building the MX, the Trident II, the Pershing II, and yes, the Star Wars Space Defense Initiative. We are trying to find a way to fight and win a nuclear war, and we're building the weapons to do it. We're not satisfied with simply providing a retaliatory capability to deter an attack. We want to prevail in a nuclear war, which is what Mr. Weinberger says publicly often.

I was giving a talk at one of our major war colleges a couple of years ago to colonels, captains, generals and admirals, and I said, "Look, fellows, we're all professionals. You know, I know, there's no way to fight and win a nuclear war, right?" I finished my lecture, and a colonel gets up and says, "Admiral, you're right. We don't know how to fight and win a nuclear war. But it's our job to *find* a way to win a nuclear war!" That's what's driving the arms race. I said, "Colonel, I understand where you're coming from. Sure, you and I didn't join this outfit to fight a war to a draw. We didn't join this outfit to lose a war, but you ought to level with the American public. Tell them you don't know how to win a nuclear war, and stop trying to fool them by suggesting that if they'll give you thousands of more nuclear weapons and billions of more dollars that you can find a way to win a nuclear war." There isn't a way. That's the dangerous part of Mr. Reagan's Space Defense Initiative.

You hear a lot of people, even in the military, talk about controlling a nuclear war. "We're gonna use a few nukes, and they'll use a few nukes. We're gonna control it." That is just *crazy*. Once you start exploding nuclear weapons, the lid is off. You see, it takes only one country to start a nuclear war: the British, the French, the Chinese, the Russians, ourselves. But what does it take to stop a nuclear war once you've started one in Europe? It takes an agreement among four nations, the British, the French, the Russians, and ourselves to stop—otherwise somebody will keep exploding nuclear weapons.

If we have a nuclear war, we can't win it. Can we survive it? I don't know. Nobody knows. That's the tragedy of it—nobody knows. Anybody that tells you that this many people are going to be killed and this many are going to survive doesn't know what he's talking about. I'll tell you why. We've only exploded one nuclear weapon at a time in the history of man. We know what happened in Nagasaki—it killed 100,000 people and destroyed a city with a little peanut of a bomb. But what we don't know is what is going to happen when thousands of nuclear weapons go off in the United States, the Soviet Union, Europe, and God knows where else. We simply don't know. There *may* be some survivors. The only question is, really, whether or not the plants and animals on this planet will survive. They may well not. Carl Sagan and his colleagues don't think that they will.

We're getting closer to a war we don't want, a war we can't control, a war in which we can't defend ourselves, a war we can't win, and a war we probably can't survive. So what do we do? Mr. Reagan's idea is to build a Space Defense Initiative, and try to defend ourselves. I don't think that's going to work. It's going to waste a lot of money. It's a theft from the American public because there is no way to defend a country against nuclear weapons. There are too many ways to get around it, the defense; too many ways to deliver nuclear weapons.

How about the negotiations over in Geneva? Are we going to get a treaty? No. We're not going to get an agreement over there to reduce arms. Because there is not one weapons system

that we in the United States want to give up. Can anybody
here think of one weapon we'd like to give up? Do you think
we're going to give up the MX? The Trident II? The Pershing
II? Cruise missiles, the B-1, the stealth bomber? No. Not even
the Space Defense Initiative. We want to build them all. So
don't look for any negotiated settlement to this arms race. In
fairness, I suspect the Soviets don't have any weapons they
want to give up either.

Is the United Nations going to solve our problems? No. A
hundred and sixty countries there, and they're not going to
solve them either. I wish they could, but when we ask can the
U.N. do it, we're really saying: "Will somebody else solve our
problems?" Nobody else is going to.

Einstein said that we had to have new ways of thinking. I
think Einstein was right, but only half right. I think we must
find new ways of acting, not just new ways of thinking! We
must *act* as if there are nuclear weapons around. Yes, we may
have to think differently, but we must find some new ways of
acting in this world or we're going to blow ourselves up and
end the whole thing.

We have a tremendous responsibility. We're the most powerful country in the world. We started this whole thing! We
invented the atomic bomb. We blew up Hiroshima and Nagasaki. We're three to five years ahead of the Soviets in the development in every strategic weapon system that has been built.
We're still ahead of them, and we're determined to stay ahead
of them. We have a certain arrogance that wants us to stay
ahead when it has become meaningless. Once both sides can
destroy each other, who is ahead has lost all significance. But
we keep the arms race going. We keep building more sophisticated weapons that can arrive more quickly on target. That's
not so bad, you say, that's just technology—but it puts a hair
trigger on the response of both sides.

There is an inherent danger in this continual build-up of
better and more destructive weapons. We may be the most
powerful country in the world, but we're only 5 percent of the
world's population. We're only one of 160 countries. We don't
run the world anymore. We ran it for a while, but we don't
run it anymore. We're going to have to adjust to the fact that

we're one of 160 countries and 5 percent of the world's population; and there are some wonderful things going on in other
countries—as wonderful as ours is.

I've been to 86 countries in this business, and everywhere I
go I find nice people like all of you. They want to make love,
they want to listen to the radio, they want to play tennis, they
want to do their own thing. They are not very much concerned
about ideological, economic and political differences. They
want to live their lives very quietly.

I think that you need to do something every day if you want
to avert a nuclear war. You ought to be writing your Congressman. Oh, that's old stuff, you say. I've got a better idea that
I want to suggest to you. There is one thing in this country
that is different from other countries, and that is simply this:
You can call the White House. You can't call the Kremlin; you
can't call the Blue House in Korea; but you can call the White
House. And I want to suggest that you do that on any weekday
from 9 to 5. I call every week. When you call, they'll answer:
"White House, Executive Office," and you say, "I'd like to
speak to the Comment Section, please." Then say, "I want
to tell Mr. Reagan to please not buy more nuclear weapons."
And the lady will say, "yes, thank you, anything else?" Say
that you'll call him next week about something else. I know
about this because my wife, Lili, was a volunteer in the White
House under Mr. Carter. They do keep records. Here's the
telephone number, and you don't even have to write it down.
Just call Washington, area code 202, then 4-5-6 (everybody
can remember 4,5,6), and then the others are 76-39. You see,
I'm 76, and Lili's 39. Now give the President a call; it's a very
exciting and wonderful experience in participatory democracy
because after you've called the White House a couple of times,
you'll want to start calling everybody else, and that's good. The
more people you call, the better off we're going to be.

I say do something every week. People often say to me, what
should I do? What can I do? Well, I would say do whatever you
feel comfortable doing. If you feel like a Daniel Berrigan or
somebody else, go do that. If you feel like writing letters, do
that. But you must do something. Join a group. If you don't
belong to the Nuclear Age Peace Foundation, you ought to.
One thing you have to do is give a little money to them. My

mother sends us $3 every year, and I promise her I'm going to spend it wisely. If you do not do anything, if *we* do not do anything, we're going to spend the rest of our years in perpetual fear and tension, draining the wealth of our nation, or we're going to have a nuclear war. And neither of those options is very nice to contemplate. Perpetual fear and tension, or nuclear war. So we must do something.

We have a great deal of pride in our country, and we should have. But it's *our* country, and I sometimes wonder when we talk about "our leaders" whether or not in fact we have any leaders in a democracy. I think it's a cop-out sometimes when we talk about "our leaders." We're the leaders! Mr. Reagan is on your payroll. He's on my payroll; I've hired him to go to Washington to work for four years, and renewed his contract for another four. He works for us; he works for you and he works for me. So I end on this note: the role of the military is very much the same in peacetime in preparation for the so-called non-nuclear war as it is in the preparation for nuclear war. The military is trying to fight and win a nuclear war. That's the job we've given them. That's the job they think you pay them to perform. But I would submit to you that war, as Clemenceau said, is much too important to be left to the generals, and survival is too important to be left to anyone but us.

DONALD WETZEL

Donald Wetzel (1921–2007) had a long literary career—publishing six novels including *A Wreath and a Curse* (1950) and *The Rain and the Fire and the Will of God* (1957), the former adapted as a Broadway play—before turning to his World War II experiences in *Pacifist: Or, My War and Louis Lepke*, in 1986. These experiences may have been difficult to revisit: sent into solitary confinement on his arrival at the federal prison in Chillicothe, Ohio, where he would serve time as a conscientious objector, he suffered a nervous breakdown and ended up in the psychiatric ward, sedated and confined between wet sheets. He spent most of his jail time simply trying to make himself as inconspicuous as possible, and to survive (prison was "every rotten thing that all the books written by prisoners say it is," he wrote). Here, he describes how he and his nonviolent fellows had to respond not just to the war outside but to the assaults of "conventionally red-blooded" criminals with whom they were housed. Was it a compromise of principle, one wondered, to dodge a blow?

FROM
Pacifist: Or, My War and Louis Lepke

I'M NOT sure how long I remained at Chillicothe—a few months at most—before I was transferred to the federal prison at Ashland, Kentucky.

At Chillicothe, as at most federal prisons where conscientious objectors were being held, objectors tended to be employed, along with embezzlers and other white collar criminals, in the administrative office of the prison, so that we objectors often knew what was going on in the prison and in the prison system itself well before many of the prison civilian employees did. So it was that I knew in advance that I was to be transferred to Ashland, and transferred there as an agitator.

This last came as quite some surprise, as it had seemed prudent to me—upon entering the general prison population and after looking around and listening about—to remain as modestly inconspicuous as possible without being obviously chicken. My fellow non-pacifist inmates, whatever their other social failings, were virtuously, even violently, patriotic. They were young, conventionally red-blooded; when denied all access to the sexual or criminal outlets of their choosing, patriotism did indeed become their last refuge. They were hardly those among whom a thoughtful worker for social justice and world peace would seek to win converts. There were, of course, a few pacifists who tried, but I, fresh from the psycho ward or not, was not among them.

(I would guess, as a matter of fact, that a more patriotic group cannot be found in any nation during wartime than in its prisons and reformatories. And I would suggest that this tells us something at least about one of the reasons why men are willing to go to war in the first place; not so much that they are all that hot to defend what they have and what they are, as they are to escape it.)

And while that may not have been an observation first made by me—as to what can persuade a man to put down his welding torch or pocket calculator and to pick up the real or symbolic gun and go off to kill or get killed instead—it was for certain an observation brought home to me at first hand, and most forcibly, as it was to other objectors, with a fist in the mouth or a knee in the groin, as this or that imprisoned patriot would have it.

We cowards numbered, I'm sure, not more than fifty; probably less, in a population of many hundreds. With such odds, it was remarkable that although we were most of us more than once beaten, none of us, at Chillicothe, were actually beaten to death.

Friday nights, I remember, were movie nights, and the movies more often than not were war movies. And so on weekends, with nothing else for the general prison population to do, it was open season on conscientious objectors. We joked about it among ourselves; couldn't the administration at least show the bloodier movies on week nights?

Steve was a socialist, a scholar, a New Englander; precise in speech, deliberate, logical, often devastating in debate. He had that sort of detached intelligence—a respect for clear thinking in and of itself—that could not easily remain silent in the face of aggressive and otherwise unchallenged stupidity. At the time I met him, he had, as well, discovered that it lessened the impact of a blow to the head if one moved one's head with the blow. Steve asked me about it during our first meeting. Was it, he wanted to know—was moving one's head with the blow—in my opinion, a compromise of the principle of non-violent resistance?

I told him I thought not.

I also pointed out to him that by leaning forward toward a blow to the head—most of which blows your average brawler throws in a round-house fashion—the blow will wrap harmlessly around the neck, or better yet, bruise or bust some knuckles on the bastard's hand as it comes up against the harder part of one's skull. Make them, for God's sake, hit your head, not your face, I told him. At that first meeting his face was a bruised and lacerated mess.

We became friends. Steve was impressed, if somewhat taken aback, by my occasional gutter vocabulary and my familiarity with the skills involved in fighting with one's fists. He confessed that he found me a rather unconventional fellow member of the Fellowship of Reconciliation. I had told him of my meeting with Lepke. He doubted that he himself could have ever quite so hit it off with the man. Steve talked like that.

I remember him telling me one day, quite thoughtfully, that he supposed it must be extremely difficult for one of my background and so earthly an orientation just to stand there and take it.

You have no fucking idea how difficult it is, I said. But I think he did.

I ducked, went around all such confrontations, avoided all such "taking of it" as decently I could.

Steve, I'm sure, understood. But for himself, he stayed and contended, and rolled with the blows as best he could.

He was no kind of an athlete at all.

Many of the pacifists and war resisters I met in prison were from the traditional peace churches; they were brave in the strength of their traditions and their faiths. Others, like Steve, were men only of principle, without faith or illusion; they were simply brave.

BILL WATTERSON

On my desk is a framed print of the 1986 *Calvin and Hobbes* cartoon included here, and I have it there for two reasons. One is its antiwar satire, climaxing in Calvin's remark, "Kind of a stupid game, isn't it?" Not an original thought, to be sure, but a perfect distillation of a common one. (It evokes the computer's comment on thermonuclear war in the 1983 film *War Games*: "the only winning move is not to play.") The other reason is the more broadly suggestive implication of the first two panels. "How come we play war and not peace?" asks Hobbes, and Calvin answers, with a sophistication beyond his years, "Too few role models." Anyone making an anthology like this one is responding to the problem Calvin identifies, and hoping to offer a partial remedy: to help people learn how to "play peace" if they so desire.

Calvin and Hobbes ran from 1985 to 1995; it was created by Bill Watterson (b. 1958), and concerns a boy named Calvin and his stuffed tiger Hobbes. Watterson grew up in Chagrin Falls, Ohio, drew his first cartoon when he was eight, in fourth grade wrote to Charles Schulz (who wrote back), drew cartoons all through grammar and high school. He went to Kenyon, majored in political science, drew Michelangelo's *Creation of Adam* on the ceiling of his dorm room. After graduation he worked for four years in an advertising agency, then turned back to what he loved and created the comic strip. While drawing the strip he steadfastly resisted all commercialization of it and was an eloquent advocate for the medium he was working in. He stopped drawing the strip ten years later, explaining that he had done what he could do "with the constraints of daily deadlines and small panels."

BERNARD OFFEN

Bernard Offen (b. 1929) grew up in Kraków, was sent by the Nazis to several concentration camps, and survived. After the war—having lost his parents and his sister, but reunited with two brothers—he emigrated to the United Kingdom, then to the United States in 1951. He enlisted in the Army and served in the Korean War. Eventually he produced four documentary films about his concentration camp experiences and wrote a memoir, *My Hometown Concentration Camp* (2008); in 1981 he revisited Poland for the first time, later leading tours of the camps and the former Kraków ghetto.

War tax resisters write all sorts of letters to the IRS, offering all sorts of rationales and self-portraits. Offen's stands out among them for the devastating parallel he makes between his father's acquiescence in paying taxes—"For Zyklon B gas. For gas ovens. For his destruction"—and his own refusal to support "a nuclear arms race . . . that is both homicidal and suicidal."

To: Internal Revenue Service

To: Internal Revenue Service:

The guards at Auschwitz herded my father to the left and me to the right. I was a child. I never saw him again.

He was a good man. He was loyal, obedient, law-abiding. He paid his taxes. He was a Jew. He paid his taxes. He died in the concentration camp. He had paid his taxes.

My father didn't know he was paying for barbed wire. For tattoo equipment. For concrete. For whips. For dogs. For cattle cars. For Zyklon B gas. For gas ovens. For his destruction. For the destruction of 6,000,000 Jews. For the destruction, ultimately, of 50,000,000 people in World War II.

In Auschwitz I was tattoo # B-7815. In the United States I am an American citizen, taxpayer # 370-32-6858. Unlike my father, I know what I am being asked to pay for. I am paying for a nuclear arms race. A nuclear arms race that is both homicidal and suicidal. It could end life for 5,000,000,000 people, five billion Jews. For now the whole world is Jewish and nuclear devices are the gas ovens for the planet. There is no longer a selection process such as I experienced at Auschwitz.

We are now one.

I am an American. I am loyal, obedient, law-abiding. I am afraid of the IRS. Who knows what power they have to charge me penalties and interest? To seize my property? To imprison me? After soul-searching and God-wrestling for several years, I have concluded that I am more afraid of what my government may do to me, mine, and the world with the money if I pay it . . . if I pay it.

We have enough nuclear devices to destroy the world many times over. More nuclear bombs are not the answer. They do not create security; they have the opposite effect.

I do believe in taxes for health, education, and the welfare of the public. While I do not agree with all the actions of my government, to go along with the nuclear arms race is suicidal. It threatens my life. It threatens the life of my family. It threatens the world.

I remember my father. I have learned from Auschwitz. I will not willingly contribute to the production of nuclear devices. They are more lethal than the gas Zyklon B, the gas that killed my father and countless others.

I am withholding 25 percent of my tax and forwarding it to a peace tax fund.

Yours for a just world at peace,
Bernard Offen

THOMAS MCGRATH

Some writers against nuclear weapons are haunted by fears not of annihilation but of mutation, of what misshapen children might be born in an irradiated world. Among the works dramatizing those fears the most eerily zestful is Thomas McGrath's "War Resisters' Song," first collected in 1988: "Fornicating (like good machines) / We'll try the chances of our genes."

McGrath (1916–1990) grew up in a North Dakota farming community; watched as his family was foreclosed on; met Industrial Workers of the World members, "Wobblies," among the seasonal farm workers; and became a radical. He worked as a labor organizer in New York, editing a union newspaper there, then served in the Army, in the Aleutian Islands, during World War II. He taught at Colby College and at Los Angeles State College, from which latter post he was dismissed for his 1953 noncooperation with the House Committee on Un-American Activities. (He said: "a teacher who will tack and turn with every shift of the political wind cannot be a good teacher.") He found other jobs later, at North Dakota State University and Minnesota State University at Moorhead. The critic Reginald Gibbons called him "the most important American poet who can lay claim to the title 'radical'."

War Resisters' Song

Come live with me and be my love
And we will all the pleasures prove—
Or such as presidents may spare
Within the decorum of Total War.

By bosky glades, by babbling streams
(Babbling of Fission, His remains)
We discover happiness' isotope
And live the half-life of our hope.

While Geiger counters sweetly click
In concentration camps we'll fuck.
Called traitors? That's but sticks and stones
We've Strontium 90 in our bones!

And thus, adjusted to our lot,
Our kisses will be doubly hot—
Fornicating (like good machines)
We'll try the chances of our genes.

So (if Insufficient Grace
Hath not fouled thy secret place
Nor fall-out burnt my balls away)
Who knows? but we may get a boy—

Some paragon with but one head
And no more brains than is allowed;
And between his legs, where once was love,
Monsters to pack the future with.

YUSEF KOMUNYAKAA

Yusef Komunyakaa's "2527th Birthday of the Buddha" is a poem of documentation, representing one of the most famous protest actions during the Vietnam War: the self-immolation of the Buddhist monk Thích Quảng Đức on June 11, 1963. Unlike Josephine Miles, whose poem on the same subject is included earlier in this book, Komunyakaa (b. 1947) goes straight for the heart of the event itself, trying to imagine himself as a witness.

Komunyakaa grew up in Louisiana, then served in the Army in Vietnam, writing for the paper *Southern Cross*. After the war he began to write poetry, studying and earning graduate degrees at the University of Colorado and the University of California at Irvine. He has taught in the New Orleans public school system and at Indiana University, Princeton, and New York University. He won the Dark Room Poetry Prize for his 1988 collection *Dien Cai Dau*, based on his Vietnam experiences, from which the poem is taken; the title means "crazy in the head." He won the Pulitzer Prize in 1993 for *Neon Vernacular*, and his dramatic adaptation of the Tale of Gilgamesh was produced in 2013 by the Constellation Theatre Company in Washington, D.C.

2527th Birthday of the Buddha

When the motorcade rolled to a halt, Quang Duc
climbed out & sat down in the street.
He crossed his legs,
& the other monks & nuns grew around him like petals.
He challenged the morning sun,
debating with the air
he leafed through—visions brought down to earth.
Could his eyes burn the devil out of men?
A breath of peppermint oil
soothed someone's cry. Beyond terror made flesh—
he burned like a bundle of black joss sticks.
A high wind that started in California
fanned flames, turned each blue page,
leaving only his heart intact.
Waves of saffron robes bowed to the gasoline can.

TIM O'BRIEN

Tim O'Brien (b. 1946) grew up in small-town Worthington, Minnesota, and graduated from Macalester College, where he had joined in occasional protests against the Vietnam War. Then he was drafted—"even getting on the plane for boot camp, I couldn't believe any of it was happening to me"—and spent most of 1969 and early 1970 as an infantryman in Quang Ngai province, in the division that contained the unit that had committed the My Lai massacre. He returned home, received a Purple Heart for shrapnel wounds sustained during a grenade attack, went to Harvard, got an internship at the *Washington Post*. He wrote about his war experiences in books like *If I Die in a Combat Zone, Box Me Up and Ship Me Home* (1973) and *Going After Cacciato* (1978), which won the National Book Award.

"On the Rainy River," from his 1990 story collection *The Things They Carried*, describes a young draftee much like himself who imagines escaping to Canada, even travels to the border, but in the end chooses to fight. Which makes it an odd selection for an anthology of antiwar writing, surely! But O'Brien offers no praise or fanfare for this young man, this fictional version of his younger self. Instead, his decision to serve his country is presented as an act of cowardice, of failing to live up to his convictions and his conscience.

On the Rainy River

THIS is one story I've never told before. Not to anyone. Not to my parents, not to my brother or sister, not even to my wife. To go into it, I've always thought, would only cause embarrassment for all of us, a sudden need to be elsewhere, which is the natural response to a confession. Even now, I'll admit, the story makes me squirm. For more than twenty years I've had to live with it, feeling the shame, trying to push it away, and so by this act of remembrance, by putting the facts down on paper, I'm hoping to relieve at least some of the pressure on my dreams. Still, it's a hard story to tell. All of us, I suppose, like to believe that in a moral emergency we will behave like the heroes of our youth, bravely and forthrightly, without thought of personal loss or discredit. Certainly that was my conviction back in the summer of 1968. Tim O'Brien: a secret hero. The Lone Ranger. If the stakes ever became high enough—if the evil were evil enough, if the good were good enough—I would simply tap a secret reservoir of courage that had been accumulating inside me over the years. Courage, I seemed to think, comes to us in finite quantities, like an inheritance, and by being frugal and stashing it away and letting it earn interest, we steadily increase our moral capital in preparation for that day when the account must be drawn down. It was a comforting theory. It dispensed with all those bothersome little acts of daily courage; it offered hope and grace to the repetitive coward; it justified the past while amortizing the future.

In June of 1968, a month after graduating from Macalester College, I was drafted to fight a war I hated. I was twenty-one years old. Young, yes, and politically naive, but even so the American war in Vietnam seemed to me wrong. Certain blood was being shed for uncertain reasons. I saw no unity of purpose, no consensus on matters of philosophy or history or law. The very facts were shrouded in uncertainty: Was it a civil war? A war of national liberation or simple aggression? Who started it, and when, and why? What really happened to the USS *Maddox* on that dark night in the Gulf of Tonkin? Was Ho Chi Minh a Communist stooge, or a nationalist savior, or both, or neither? What about the Geneva Accords? What about SEATO and the Cold War? What about dominoes? America was divided on these and a thousand other issues, and the debate had spilled out across the floor of the United States Senate and into the streets, and smart men in pinstripes could not agree on even the most fundamental matters of public policy. The only certainty that summer was moral confusion. It was my view then, and still is, that you don't make war without knowing why. Knowledge, of course, is always imperfect, but it seemed to me that when a nation goes to war it must have reasonable confidence in the justice and imperative of its cause. You can't fix your mistakes. Once people are dead, you can't make them undead.

In any case those were my convictions, and back in college I had taken a modest stand against the war. Nothing radical, no hothead stuff, just ringing a few doorbells for Gene McCarthy, composing a few tedious, uninspired editorials for the campus newspaper. Oddly, though, it was almost entirely an intellectual activity. I brought some energy to it, of course, but it was the energy that accompanies almost any abstract endeavor; I felt no personal danger; I felt no sense of an impending crisis in my life. Stupidly, with a kind of smug removal that I can't begin to fathom, I assumed that the problems of killing and dying did not fall within my special province.

The draft notice arrived on June 17, 1968. It was a humid afternoon, I remember, cloudy and very quiet, and I'd just come in from a round of golf. My mother and father were having lunch out in the kitchen. I remember opening up the letter, scanning the first few lines, feeling the blood go thick behind my eyes. I remember a sound in my head. It wasn't thinking, just a silent howl. A million things all at once—I was too *good* for this war. Too smart, too compassionate, too everything. It couldn't happen. I was above it. I had the world dicked—Phi Beta Kappa and summa cum laude and president of the student body and a full-ride scholarship for grad studies at Harvard. A mistake, maybe—a foul-up in the paperwork. I was no soldier. I hated Boy Scouts. I hated camping out. I hated dirt and tents and mosquitoes. The sight of blood made me queasy, and I couldn't tolerate authority, and I didn't know a rifle from a slingshot. I was a *liberal*, for Christ sake: If they needed fresh bodies, why not draft some back-to-the-stone-age hawk? Or some dumb jingo in his hard hat and Bomb Hanoi button, or one of LBJ's pretty daughters, or Westmoreland's whole handsome family—nephews and nieces and baby grandson. There should be a law, I thought. If you support a war, if you think it's worth the price, that's fine, but you have to put your own precious fluids on the line. You have to head for the front and hook up with an infantry unit and help spill the blood. And you have to bring along your wife, or your kids, or your lover. A *law*, I thought.

I remember the rage in my stomach. Later it burned down to a smoldering self-pity, then to numbness. At dinner that night my father asked what my plans were. "Nothing," I said. "Wait."

I spent the summer of 1968 working in an Armour meatpacking plant in my hometown of Worthington, Minnesota. The plant specialized in pork products, and for eight hours a day I stood on a quarter-mile assembly line—more properly, a disassembly line—removing blood clots from the necks of dead

pigs. My job title, I believe, was Declotter. After slaughter, the
hogs were decapitated, split down the length of the belly, pried
open, eviscerated, and strung up by the hind hocks on a high
conveyer belt. Then gravity took over. By the time a carcass
reached my spot on the line, the fluids had mostly drained
out, everything except for dense clots of blood in the neck and
upper chest cavity. To remove the stuff, I used a kind of water
gun. The machine was heavy, maybe eighty pounds, and was
suspended from the ceiling by a thick rubber cord. There was
some bounce to it, an elastic up-and-down give, and the trick
was to maneuver the gun with your whole body, not lifting
with the arms, just letting the rubber cord do the work for you.
At one end was a trigger; at the muzzle end was a small nozzle
and a steel roller brush. As a carcass passed by, you'd lean forward and swing the gun up against the clots and squeeze the
trigger, all in one motion, and the brush would whirl and water
would come shooting out and you'd hear a quick splattering
sound as the clots dissolved into a fine red mist. It was not
pleasant work. Goggles were a necessity, and a rubber apron,
but even so it was like standing for eight hours a day under a
lukewarm blood-shower. At night I'd go home smelling of pig.
It wouldn't go away. Even after a hot bath, scrubbing hard, the
stink was always there—like old bacon, or sausage, a greasy
pig-stink that soaked deep into my skin and hair. Among other
things, I remember, it was tough getting dates that summer. I
felt isolated; I spent a lot of time alone. And there was also that
draft notice tucked away in my wallet.

In the evenings I'd sometimes borrow my father's car and
drive aimlessly around town, feeling sorry for myself, thinking
about the war and the pig factory and how my life seemed to
be collapsing toward slaughter. I felt paralyzed. All around
me the options seemed to be narrowing, as if I were hurtling
down a huge black funnel, the whole world squeezing in tight.
There was no happy way out. The government had ended most
graduate school deferments; the waiting lists for the National
Guard and Reserves were impossibly long; my health was solid;
I didn't qualify for CO status—no religious grounds, no history as a pacifist. Moreover, I could not claim to be opposed
to war as a matter of general principle. There were occasions, I
believed, when a nation was justified in using military force to

achieve its ends, to stop a Hitler or some comparable evil, and I told myself that in such circumstances I would've willingly marched off to the battle. The problem, though, was that a draft board did not let you choose your war.

Beyond all this, or at the very center, was the raw fact of terror. I did not want to die. Not ever. But certainly not then, not there, not in a wrong war. Driving up Main Street, past the courthouse and the Ben Franklin store, I sometimes felt the fear spreading inside me like weeds. I imagined myself dead. I imagined myself doing things I could not do—charging an enemy position, taking aim at another human being.

At some point in mid-July I began thinking seriously about Canada. The border lay a few hundred miles north, an eight-hour drive. Both my conscience and my instincts were telling me to make a break for it, just take off and run like hell and never stop. In the beginning the idea seemed purely abstract, the word Canada printing itself out in my head; but after a time I could see particular shapes and images, the sorry details of my own future—a hotel room in Winnipeg, a battered old suitcase, my father's eyes as I tried to explain myself over the telephone. I could almost hear his voice, and my mother's. Run, I'd think. Then I'd think, Impossible. Then a second later I'd think, *Run*.

It was a moral split. I couldn't make up my mind. I feared the war, yes, but I also feared exile. I was afraid of walking away from my own life, my friends and my family, my whole history, everything that mattered to me. I feared losing the respect of my parents. I feared the law. I feared ridicule and censure. My hometown was a conservative little spot on the prairie, a place where tradition counted, and it was easy to imagine people sitting around a table down at the old Gobbler Café on Main Street, coffee cups poised, the conversation slowly zeroing in on the young O'Brien kid, how the damned sissy had taken off for Canada. At night, when I couldn't sleep, I'd sometimes carry on fierce arguments with those people. I'd be screaming at them, telling them how much I detested their blind, thoughtless, automatic acquiescence to it all, their simpleminded patriotism, their prideful ignorance, their love-it-or-leave-it platitudes, how they were sending me off to fight a war they didn't understand and didn't want to understand. I held them responsible. By God, yes, I *did*. All of them—I held them personally and individually responsible—the polyestered Kiwanis boys, the merchants and farmers, the pious churchgoers, the chatty housewives, the PTA and the Lions club and the Veterans of Foreign Wars and the fine upstanding gentry out at the country club. They didn't know Bao Dai from the man in the moon. They didn't know history. They didn't know the first thing about Diem's tyranny, or the nature of Vietnamese nationalism, or the long colonialism of the French—this was all too damned complicated, it required some reading—but no matter, it was a war to stop the Communists, plain and simple, which was how they liked things, and you were a treasonous pussy if you had second thoughts about killing or dying for plain and simple reasons.

I was bitter, sure. But it was so much more than that. The emotions went from outrage to terror to bewilderment to guilt to sorrow and then back again to outrage. I felt a sickness inside me. Real disease.

Most of this I've told before, or at least hinted at, but what I have never told is the full truth. How I cracked. How at work one morning, standing on the pig line, I felt something break open in my chest. I don't know what it was. I'll never know. But it was real, I know that much, it was a physical rupture—a cracking-leaking-popping feeling. I remember dropping my water gun. Quickly, almost without thought, I took off my apron and walked out of the plant and drove home. It was midmorning, I remember, and the house was empty. Down in my chest there was still that leaking sensation, something very warm and precious spilling out, and I was covered with blood and hog-stink, and for a long while I just concentrated on holding myself together. I remember taking a hot shower. I remember packing a suitcase and carrying it out to the kitchen, standing very still for a few minutes, looking carefully at the familiar objects all around me. The old chrome toaster, the telephone, the pink and white Formica on the kitchen counters. The room was full of bright sunshine. Everything sparkled. My house, I thought. My life. I'm not sure how long I stood there, but later I scribbled out a short note to my parents.

What it said, exactly, I don't recall now. Something vague. Taking off, will call, love Tim.

I drove north.

It's a blur now, as it was then, and all I remember is velocity and the feel of a steering wheel in my hands. I was riding on adrenaline. A giddy feeling, in a way, except there was the dreamy edge of impossibility to it—like running a dead-end maze—no way out—it couldn't come to a happy conclusion and yet I was doing it anyway because it was all I could think of to do. It was pure flight, fast and mindless. I had no plan. Just hit the border at high speed and crash through and keep on running. Near dusk I passed through Bemidji, then turned northeast toward International Falls. I spent the night in the car behind a closed-down gas station a half mile from the border. In the morning, after gassing up, I headed straight west along the Rainy River, which separates Minnesota from Canada, and which for me separated one life from another. The land was mostly wilderness. Here and there I passed a motel or bait shop, but otherwise the country unfolded in great sweeps of pine and birch and sumac. Though it was still August, the air already had the smell of October, football season, piles of yellow-red leaves, everything crisp and clean. I remember a huge blue sky. Off to my right was the Rainy River, wide as a lake in places, and beyond the Rainy River was Canada.

For a while I just drove, not aiming at anything, then in the late morning I began looking for a place to lie low for a day or two. I was exhausted, and scared sick, and around noon I pulled into an old fishing resort called the Tip Top Lodge. Actually it was not a lodge at all, just eight or nine tiny yellow cabins clustered on a peninsula that jutted northward into the Rainy River. The place was in sorry shape. There was a dangerous wooden dock, an old minnow tank, a flimsy tar paper boathouse along the shore. The main building, which stood in a cluster of pines on high ground, seemed to lean heavily to one side, like a cripple, the roof sagging toward Canada. Briefly, I thought about turning around, just giving up, but then I got out of the car and walked up to the front porch.

The man who opened the door that day is the hero of my life. How do I say this without sounding sappy? Blurt it out—the man saved me. He offered exactly what I needed, without questions, without any words at all. He took me in. He was there at the critical time—a silent, watchful presence. Six days later, when it ended, I was unable to find a proper way to thank him, and I never have, and so, if nothing else, this story represents a small gesture of gratitude twenty years overdue.

Even after two decades I can close my eyes and return to that porch at the Tip Top Lodge. I can see the old guy staring at me. Elroy Berdahl: eighty-one years old, skinny and shrunken and mostly bald. He wore a flannel shirt and brown work pants. In one hand, I remember, he carried a green apple, a small paring knife in the other. His eyes had the bluish gray color of a razor blade, the same polished shine, and as he peered up at me I felt a strange sharpness, almost painful, a cutting sensation, as if his gaze were somehow slicing me open. In part, no doubt, it was my own sense of guilt, but even so I'm absolutely certain that the old man took one look and went right to the heart of things—a kid in trouble. When I asked for a room, Elroy made a little clicking sound with his tongue. He nodded, led me out to one of the cabins, and dropped a key in my hand. I remember smiling at him. I also remember wishing I hadn't. The old man shook his head as if to tell me it wasn't worth the bother.

"Dinner at five-thirty," he said. "You eat fish?"

"Anything," I said.

Elroy grunted and said, "I'll bet."

We spent six days together at the Tip Top Lodge. Just the two of us. Tourist season was over, and there were no boats on the river, and the wilderness seemed to withdraw into a great permanent stillness. Over those six days Elroy Berdahl and I took most of our meals together. In the mornings we sometimes went out on long hikes into the woods, and at night we played Scrabble or listened to records or sat reading in front of his big stone fireplace. At times I felt the awkwardness of an intruder, but Elroy accepted me into his quiet routine without fuss or ceremony. He took my presence for granted, the same way he might've sheltered a stray cat—no wasted sighs or pity—and there was never any talk about it. Just the opposite. What I remember more than anything is the man's willful, almost ferocious silence. In all that time together, all those hours, he never asked the obvious questions: Why was I there? Why alone? Why so preoccupied? If Elroy was curious about any of this, he was careful never to put it into words.

My hunch, though, is that he already knew. At least the basics. After all, it was 1968, and guys were burning draft cards, and Canada was just a boat ride away. Elroy Berdahl was no hick. His bedroom, I remember, was cluttered with books and newspapers. He killed me at the Scrabble board, barely concentrating, and on those occasions when speech was necessary he had a way of compressing large thoughts into small, cryptic packets of language. One evening, just at sunset, he pointed up at an owl circling over the violet-lighted forest to the west. "Hey, O'Brien," he said. "There's Jesus." The man was sharp—he didn't miss much. Those razor eyes. Now and then he'd catch me staring out at the river, at the far shore, and I could almost hear the tumblers clicking in his head. Maybe I'm wrong, but I doubt it.

One thing for certain, he knew I was in desperate trouble. And he knew I couldn't talk about it. The wrong word—or even the right word—and I would've disappeared. I was wired and jittery. My skin felt too tight. After supper one evening I vomited and went back to my cabin and lay down for a few moments and then vomited again; another time, in the middle of the afternoon, I began sweating and couldn't shut it off. I went through whole days feeling dizzy with sorrow. I couldn't sleep; I couldn't lie still. At night I'd toss around in bed, half awake, half dreaming, imagining how I'd sneak down to the beach and quietly push one of the old man's boats out into the river and start paddling my way toward Canada. There were times when I thought I'd gone off the psychic edge. I couldn't tell up from down, I was just falling, and late in the night I'd lie there watching bizarre pictures spin through my head. Getting chased by the Border Patrol—helicopters and searchlights and barking dogs—I'd be crashing through the woods, I'd be down on my hands and knees—people shouting out my name—the law closing in on all sides—my hometown draft board and the FBI and the Royal Canadian Mounted Police. It all seemed crazy and impossible. Twenty-one years old, an ordinary kid with all the ordinary dreams and ambitions, and all I wanted was to live the life I was born to—a mainstream life—I loved baseball and hamburgers and cherry Cokes—and now I was off on the margins of exile, leaving my country forever, and it seemed so grotesque and terrible and sad.

I'm not sure how I made it through those six days. Most of it I can't remember. On two or three afternoons, to pass some time, I helped Elroy get the place ready for winter, sweeping down the cabins and hauling in the boats, little chores that kept my body moving. The days were cool and bright. The nights were very dark. One morning the old man showed me how to split and stack firewood, and for several hours we just worked in silence out behind his house. At one point, I remember, Elroy put down his maul and looked at me for a long time, his lips drawn as if framing a difficult question, but then he shook his head and went back to work. The man's self-control was amazing. He never pried. He never put me in a position that required lies or denials. To an extent, I suppose, his reticence was typical of that part of Minnesota, where privacy still held value, and even if I'd been walking around with some horrible deformity—four arms and three heads—I'm sure the old man would've talked about everything except those extra arms and heads. Simple politeness was part of it. But even more than that, I think, the man understood that words were insufficient. The problem had gone beyond discussion. During that long summer I'd been over and over the various arguments, all the pros and cons, and it was no longer a question that could be decided by an act of pure reason. Intellect had come up against emotion. My conscience told me to run, but some irrational and powerful force was resisting, like a weight pushing me toward the war. What it came down to, stupidly, was a sense of shame. Hot, stupid shame. I did not want people to think badly of me. Not my parents, not my brother and sister, not even the folks down at the Gobbler Café. I was ashamed to be there at the Tip Top Lodge. I was ashamed of my conscience, ashamed to be doing the right thing.

Some of this Elroy must've understood. Not the details, of course, but the plain fact of crisis.

Although the old man never confronted me about it, there was one occasion when he came close to forcing the whole thing out into the open. It was early evening, and we'd just finished supper, and over coffee and dessert I asked him about my bill, how much I owed so far. For a long while the old man squinted down at the tablecloth.

"Well, the basic rate," he said, "is fifty bucks a night. Not counting meals. This makes four nights, right?"

I nodded. I had three hundred and twelve dollars in my wallet.

Elroy kept his eyes on the tablecloth. "Now that's an on-season price. To be fair, I suppose we should knock it down a peg or two." He leaned back in his chair. "What's a reasonable number, you figure?"

"I don't know," I said. "Forty?"

"Forty's good. Forty a night. Then we tack on food—say another hundred? Two hundred sixty total?"

"I guess."

He raised his eyebrows. "Too much?"

"No, that's fair. It's fine. Tomorrow, though . . . I think I'd better take off tomorrow."

Elroy shrugged and began clearing the table. For a time he fussed with the dishes, whistling to himself as if the subject had been settled. After a second he slapped his hands together.

"You know what we forgot?" he said. "We forgot wages. Those odd jobs you done. What we have to do, we have to figure out what your time's worth. Your last job—how much did you pull in an hour?"

"Not enough," I said.

"A bad one?"

"Yes. Pretty bad."

Slowly then, without intending any long sermon, I told him about my days at the pig plant. It began as a straight recitation of the facts, but before I could stop myself I was talking about the blood clots and the water gun and how the smell had soaked into my skin and how I couldn't wash it away. I went on for a long time. I told him about wild hogs squealing in my dreams, the sounds of butchery, slaughterhouse sounds, and how I'd sometimes wake up with that greasy pig-stink in my throat.

When I was finished, Elroy nodded at me.

"Well, to be honest," he said, "when you first showed up here, I wondered about all that. The aroma, I mean. Smelled like you was awful damned fond of pork chops." The old man almost smiled. He made a snuffling sound, then sat down with a pencil and a piece of paper. "So what'd this crud job pay? Ten bucks an hour? Fifteen?"

"Less."

Elroy shook his head. "Let's make it fifteen. You put in twenty-five hours here, easy. That's three hundred seventy-five bucks total wages. We subtract the two hundred sixty for food and lodging, I still owe you a hundred and fifteen."

He took four fifties out of his shirt pocket and laid them on the table.

"Call it even," he said.

"No."

"Pick it up. Get yourself a haircut."

The money lay on the table for the rest of the evening. It was still there when I went back to my cabin. In the morning, though, I found an envelope tacked to my door. Inside were the four fifties and a two-word note that said EMERGENCY FUND.

The man knew.

Looking back after twenty years, I sometimes wonder if the events of that summer didn't happen in some other dimension, a place where your life exists before you've lived it, and where it goes afterward. None of it ever seemed real. During my time at the Tip Top Lodge I had the feeling that I'd slipped out of my own skin, hovering a few feet away while some poor yo-yo with my name and face tried to make his way toward a future he didn't understand and didn't want. Even now I can see myself as I was then. It's like watching an old home movie: I'm young and tan and fit. I've got hair—lots of it. I don't smoke or drink. I'm wearing faded blue jeans and a white polo shirt. I can see myself sitting on Elroy Berdahl's dock near dusk one evening, the sky a bright shimmering pink, and I'm finishing up a letter to my parents that tells what I'm about to do and why I'm doing it and how sorry I am that I'd never found the courage to talk to them about it. I ask them not to be angry. I try to explain some of my feelings, but there aren't enough words, and so I just say that it's a thing that has to be done. At the end of the letter I talk about the vacations we used to take up in this north country, at a place called Whitefish Lake, and how the scenery here reminds me of those good times. I tell them I'm fine. I tell them I'll write again from Winnipeg or Montreal or wherever I end up.

On my last full day, the sixth day, the old man took me out fishing on the Rainy River. The afternoon was sunny and cold. A stiff breeze came in from the north, and I remember how the little fourteen-foot boat made sharp rocking motions as we pushed off from the dock. The current was fast. All around us, there was a vastness to the world, an unpeopled rawness, just the trees and the sky and the water reaching out toward nowhere. The air had the brittle scent of October.

For ten or fifteen minutes Elroy held a course upstream, the river choppy and silver-gray, then he turned straight north and put the engine on full throttle. I felt the bow lift beneath me. I remember the wind in my ears, the sound of the old outboard Evinrude. For a time I didn't pay attention to anything, just feeling the cold spray against my face, but then it occurred to me that at some point we must've passed into Canadian waters, across that dotted line between two different worlds, and I remember a sudden tightness in my chest as I looked up and watched the far shore come at me. This wasn't a daydream. It was tangible and real. As we came in toward land, Elroy cut the engine, letting the boat fishtail lightly about twenty yards off shore. The old man didn't look at me or speak. Bending down, he opened up his tackle box and busied himself with a bobber and a piece of wire leader, humming to himself, his eyes down.

It struck me then that he must've planned it. I'll never be certain, of course, but I think he meant to bring me up against the realities, to guide me across the river and to take me to the edge and to stand a kind of vigil as I chose a life for myself.

I remember staring at the old man, then at my hands, then at Canada. The shoreline was dense with brush and timber. I could see tiny red berries on the bushes. I could see a squirrel up in one of the birch trees, a big crow looking at me from a boulder along the river. That close—twenty yards—and I could see the delicate latticework of the leaves, the texture of the soil, the browned needles beneath the pines, the configurations of geology and human history. Twenty yards. I could've done it. I could've jumped and started swimming for my life. Inside me, in my chest, I felt a terrible squeezing pressure. Even now, as I write this, I can still feel that tightness. And I want you to feel it—the wind coming off the river, the waves, the silence, the wooded frontier. You're at the bow of a boat on the Rainy River. You're twenty-one years old, you're scared, and there's a hard squeezing pressure in your chest.

What would you do?

Would you jump? Would you feel pity for yourself? Would you think about your family and your childhood and your dreams and all you're leaving behind? Would it hurt? Would it feel like dying? Would you cry, as I did?

I tried to swallow it back. I tried to smile, except I was crying.

Now, perhaps, you can understand why I've never told this story before. It's not just the embarrassment of tears. That's part of it, no doubt, but what embarrasses me much more, and always will, is the paralysis that took my heart. A moral freeze: I couldn't decide, I couldn't act, I couldn't comport myself with even a pretense of modest human dignity.

All I could do was cry. Quietly, not bawling, just the chest-chokes.

At the rear of the boat Elroy Berdahl pretended not to notice. He held a fishing rod in his hands, his head bowed to hide his eyes. He kept humming a soft, monotonous little tune. Everywhere, it seemed, in the trees and water and sky, a great worldwide sadness came pressing down on me, a crushing sorrow, sorrow like I had never known it before. And what was so sad, I realized, was that Canada had become a pitiful fantasy. Silly and hopeless. It was no longer a possibility. Right then, with the shore so close, I understood that I would not do what I should do. I would not swim away from my hometown and my country and my life. I would not be brave. That old image of myself as a hero, as a man of conscience and courage, all that was just a threadbare pipe dream. Bobbing there on the Rainy River, looking back at the Minnesota shore, I felt a sudden swell of helplessness come over me, a drowning sensation, as if I had toppled overboard and was being swept away by the silver waves. Chunks of my own history flashed by. I saw a seven-year-old boy in a white cowboy hat and a Lone Ranger mask and a pair of bolstered six-shooters; I saw a twelve-year-old

Little League shortstop pivoting to turn a double play; I saw a sixteen-year-old kid decked out for his first prom, looking spiffy in a white tux and a black bow tie, his hair cut short and flat, his shoes freshly polished. My whole life seemed to spill out into the river, swirling away from me, everything I had ever been or ever wanted to be. I couldn't get my breath; I couldn't stay afloat; I couldn't tell which way to swim. A hallucination, I suppose, but it was as real as anything I would ever feel. I saw my parents calling to me from the far shoreline. I saw my brother and sister, all the townsfolk, the mayor and the entire Chamber of Commerce and all my old teachers and girlfriends and high school buddies. Like some outlandish sporting event: everybody screaming from the sidelines, rooting me on—a loud stadium roar. Hotdogs and popcorn—stadium smells, stadium heat. A squad of cheerleaders did cartwheels along the banks of the Rainy River; they had megaphones and pom-poms and smooth brown thighs. The crowd swayed left and right. A marching band played fight songs. All my aunts and uncles were there, and Abraham Lincoln, and Saint George, and a nine-year-old girl named Linda who had died of a brain tumor back in fifth grade, and several members of the United States Senate, and a blind poet scribbling notes, and LBJ, and Huck Finn, and Abbie Hoffman, and all the dead soldiers back from the grave, and the many thousands who were later to die—villagers with terrible burns, little kids without arms or legs—yes, and the Joint Chiefs of Staff were there, and a couple of popes, and a first lieutenant named Jimmy Cross, and the last surviving veteran of the American Civil War, and Jane Fonda dressed up as Barbarella, and an old man sprawled beside a pigpen, and my grandfather, and Gary Cooper, and a kind-faced woman carrying an umbrella and a copy of Plato's *Republic*, and a million ferocious citizens waving flags of all shapes and colors—people in hard hats, people in headbands— they were all whooping and chanting and urging me toward one shore or the other. I saw faces from my distant past and distant future. My wife was there. My unborn daughter waved at me, and my two sons hopped up and down, and a drill sergeant named Blyton sneered and shot up a finger and shook his head. There was a choir in bright purple robes. There was a cabbie from the Bronx. There was a slim young man I would one day kill with a hand grenade along a red clay trail outside the village of My Khe.

The little aluminum boat rocked softly beneath me. There was the wind and the sky.

I tried to will myself overboard.

I gripped the edge of the boat and leaned forward and thought, *Now.*

I did try. It just wasn't possible.

All those eyes on me—the town, the whole universe—and I couldn't risk the embarrassment. It was as if there were an audience to my life, that swirl of faces along the river, and in my head I could hear people screaming at me. Traitor! they yelled. Turncoat! Pussy! I felt myself blush. I couldn't tolerate it. I couldn't endure the mockery, or the disgrace, or the patriotic ridicule. Even in my imagination, the shore just twenty yards away, I couldn't make myself be brave. It had nothing to do with morality. Embarrassment, that's all it was.

And right then I submitted.

I would go to the war—I would kill and maybe die—because I was embarrassed not to.

That was the sad thing. And so I sat in the bow of the boat and cried.

It was loud now. Loud, hard crying.

Elroy Berdahl remained quiet. He kept fishing. He worked his line with the tips of his fingers, patiently, squinting out at his red and white bobber on the Rainy River. His eyes were flat and impassive. He didn't speak. He was simply there, like the river and the late-summer sun. And yet by his presence, his mute watchfulness, he made it real. He was the true audience. He was a witness, like God, or like the gods, who look on in absolute silence as we live our lives, as we make our choices or fail to make them.

"Ain't biting," he said.

Then after a time the old man pulled in his line and turned the boat back toward Minnesota.

I don't remember saying goodbye. That last night we had dinner together, and I went, to bed early, and in the morning Elroy fixed breakfast for me. When I told him I'd be leaving, the old man nodded as if he already knew. He looked down at the table and smiled.

At some point later in the morning it's possible that we shook hands—I just don't remember—but I do know that by the time I'd finished packing the old man had disappeared. Around noon, when I took my suitcase out to the car, I noticed that his old black pickup truck was no longer parked in front of the main lodge. I went inside and waited for a while, but I felt a bone certainty that he wouldn't be back. In a way, I thought, it was appropriate. I washed up the breakfast dishes, left his two hundred dollars on the kitchen counter, got into the car, and drove south toward home.

The day was cloudy. I passed through towns with familiar names, through the pine forests and down to the prairie, and then to Vietnam, where I was a soldier, and then home again. I survived, but it's not a happy ending. I was a coward. I went to the war.

ADRIENNE RICH

Adrienne Rich (1929–2012) opposed pretty much every war she had an occasion to take a position on, from Vietnam to Iraq, but as a poet she characteristically linked causes and themes rather than separating them; in relatively few of her poems is an opposition to war, in general or in particular, distinguishable from a more wide-ranging critique of society as it is. The present selection, section XI of her long poem "An Atlas of the Difficult World," first published in 1991, is more pointedly oppositional than most of her work, but even here the most distilled antiwar proclamations—"A patriot is not a weapon," "every flag that flies today is a cry of pain"—are part of a more comprehensive meditation on the nature of patriotism, of belonging and not belonging, of the relations between peace and justice.

Rich's early years are beautifully evoked in her 1972 essay "When We Dead Awaken." She grew up in Baltimore, her father a noted pathologist, her mother a former concert pianist—"my own luck was being born white and middle-class into a house full of books, with a father who encouraged me to read and write," she wrote. She went to Radcliffe, married, had three children. In 1951 she was chosen to receive the Yale Younger Poets prize by W. H. Auden, who said of her poems, "[they] are neatly and modestly dressed, speak quietly but do not mumble, respect their elders but are not cowed by them, and do not tell fibs."

But her growing sense of the political, and of the political in the personal, destabilized and energized her way of being and her way of writing. Awarded the National Book Award in 1973 for *Diving into the Wreck*, she accepted it with her fellow nominees Audre Lorde and Alice Walker on behalf of all women. She began to write wonderfully implacable essays, notably her 1980 "Compulsory Heterosexuality and Lesbian Existence," and came out as a lesbian. Her political commitments expanded, her intensity of political commitment deepened, centering more and more on feminist and lesbian issues. Her Jewishness became more central to her and her work. She turned steadily toward more open, more inclusive poetic forms.

Like some other poets, Rich refused a presidential honor; unlike them, she refused it not in relation to war but in relation to politics in general. She was awarded the 1997 National Medal of Arts, and in refusing wrote, "I could not accept such an award from President Clinton or this White House, because the very meaning of art as I understand it is incompatible with the cynical politics of this administration."

FROM
An Atlas of the Difficult World

XI

One night on Monterey Bay the death-freeze of the century:
a precise, detached calliper-grip holds the stars and the
        quarter-moon
in arrest: the hardiest plants crouch shrunken, a "killing
        frost"
on bougainvillea, Pride of Madeira, roseate black-purple
        succulents bowed
juices sucked awry in one orgy of freezing
slumped on their stems like old faces evicted from cheap
        hotels
—*into the streets of the universe, now!*

Earthquake and drought followed by freezing followed by
        war.
Flags are blossoming now where little else is blossoming
and I am bent on fathoming what it means to love my
        country.
The history of this earth and the bones within it?
Soils and cities, promises made and mocked, plowed contours
        of shame and of hope?
Loyalties, symbols, murmurs extinguished and echoing?
Grids of states stretching westward, underground waters?
Minerals, traces, rumors I am made from, morsel, minuscule
        fibre, one woman
like and unlike so many, fooled as to her destiny, the scope of
        her task?
One citizen like and unlike so many, touched and untouched
        in passing
—each of us now a driven grain, a nucleus, a city in crisis
some busy constructing enclosures, bunkers, to escape the
        common fate
some trying to revive dead statues to lead us, breathing their
        breath against marble lips

some who try to teach the moment, some who preach the
    moment
some who aggrandize, some who diminish themselves in the
    face of half-grasped events
—power and powerlessness run amuck, a tape reeling
    backward in jeering, screeching syllables—
some for whom war is new, others for whom it merely
    continues the old paroxysms of time
some marching for peace who for twenty years did not march
    for justice
some for whom peace is a white man's word and a white
    man's privilege
some who have learned to handle and contemplate the shapes
    of powerlessness and power
as the nurse learns hip and thigh and weight of the body he
    has to lift and sponge, day upon day
as she blows with her every skill on the spirit's embers still
    burning by their own laws in the bed of death.
A patriot is not a weapon. A patriot is one who wrestles for the
    soul of her country
as she wrestles for her own being, for the soul of his country
(gazing through the great circle at Window Rock into the
    sheen of the Viet Nam Wall)
as he wrestles for his own being. A patriot is a citizen trying
    to wake
from the burnt-out dream of innocence, the nightmare
of the white general and the Black general posed in their
    camouflage,
to remember her true country, remember his suffering land:
    remember
that blessing and cursing are born as twins and separated at
    birth to meet again in mourning
that the internal emigrant is the most homesick of all women
    and of all men
that every flag that flies today is a cry of pain.
    Where are we moored?
    What are the bindings?
    What behooves us?

GREGORY NEVALA CALVERT

In his book *Democracy from the Heart* (1991), published almost a quarter-century after the March on the Pentagon, Gregory Nevala Calvert (1937–2005) looks back at some of the fierce debates that were then stirring behind the scenes—debates less clearly visible in accounts by contemporary writers like Norman Mailer or the correspondents of *WIN Magazine*. As Calvert tells it, a new "mood of militancy" had gripped Students for a Democratic Society (SDS), of which he was then national secretary; nonviolent resistance had begun to many to seem insufficient, a sellout, and plans were afoot to fight with police in the streets and "trash" downtown Washington, D.C. Counseled by David Dellinger and Barbara Deming—the latter in particular helping him to articulate a "non-heterosexual perspective" on the movement's still-underacknowledged "violence-prone machismo"—he managed to hold the group together and kept it from splintering at least for a time.

Soon enough, the SDS did split—some female members forming feminist groups, the Weather Underground bombing the Capitol, the Pentagon, the State Department—and Calvert withdrew from his former role. He went on to work for the Illinois State Drug Rehabilitation program; edited and wrote for *The Rag*, an alternative newspaper; began a practice in Buddhist psychotherapy; and went back to school.

FROM
Democracy from the Heart

THE PENTAGON

UNDER the banner of "From Protest to Resistance," the Pentagon demonstration was scheduled for Saturday, October 21, 1967, the day after the end of the Oakland Stop-the-Draft-Week. I spent that week in non-stop meetings preparing for the largest, most militant demonstration against the war yet to take place. Plans for the demonstration included a rally at the Lincoln Memorial followed by a march across the Potomac to a second rally a short distance from the Pentagon and then a final march, by the most determined, right up to the Pentagon itself where civil disobedience was planned.

I was in a quandary about what to do. The new mood of militancy fed by the ghetto riots of the previous summer was creating the same dynamic on the East Coast that fueled the events in Oakland. I was approached by friends of several persuasions arguing that events in the black community demanded an equally militant response by white activists and specifically that the situation required that whites prove their ability and willingness to fight with the police in the street. The example of the Japanese Zengakuren's tactics of using bamboo poles in street confrontation with police was held up for Americans to emulate. In the Washington, D.C., office of the Mobe, Jerry Rubin, former Berkeley activist who had been brought onto the Mobe staff at the urging of Dave Dellinger to be a project coordinator for the Pentagon action, argued that after the initial rally marchers should sit down *en masse* on the Washington freeways and provoke the disruption of the entire Eastern Seaboard's transportation system. Several members of the "SDS house" in Washington, including Cathy Wilkerson and Tom Bell, wanted to organize a spray-painting spree targeting downtown buses. Students of former-Trotskyist-turned-anarchist Murray Bookchin who constituted the Up-Against-the-Wall-Motherfucker Lower Eastside of New York chapter of SDS wanted to trash downtown Washington in Zengakuren formations.

As I shuttled from New York to Washington, D.C., for Mobe meetings and negotiations with the GSA (the General Services Administration in charge of the capital's five police forces), I had long talks with Dave Dellinger about the necessity of adhering to the principles of nonviolence if the Movement was to maintain its balance and humanity and not self-destruct in adventuristic violence. Dave Dellinger had become a beloved friend and perhaps my closest ally. In addition, he was a true teacher whose vision of revolutionary nonviolence seemed increasingly to me to provide the only framework which could guide the Movement in a sane direction. Although I came to have serious differences with Dave Dellinger about strategic initiatives in the following year, he was one of the most important influences on my life and thinking and I credit him with having helped me maintain my political equilibrium at a crucial moment.

Another practitioner of nonviolence and Movement theorist, Barbara Deming of the CNVA (Committee for Non-Violent Action), also provided me with important guidance at this critical juncture. During a long conversation from New York to the GSA headquarters in Washington, Barbara Deming asked me more significant and provocative questions than I was accustomed to in a month. This brilliant and humane woman raised precisely the kinds of psychological and political issues that I was asking myself. I did not have a male friend in the Movement with whom I could freely share my convictions on psycho-sexual-political questions. As a result of her prodding, I began to conceive of the idea of a teach-in to the troops at the Pentagon. In retrospect, I have wondered if what I shared with Barbara Deming for that short period of time was a non-heterosexual perspective on the issues of masculinity and manhood-proving, which made us both question the wave of violence-prone machismo threatening to overwhelm the Movement. Barbara Deming later presented some of her insights in a brilliant article, "On Revolution and Equilibrium," which was the first major challenge in print to the politics of Black Power by a Movement radical. Her views were later elaborated in a book, *Revolution and Equilibrium*. Dismayed by the force of sexism and machismo in the Movement, Barbara Deming later became a radical separatist feminist.

Bolstered by my contacts with these advocates of radical nonviolence, I faced my comrades at the SDS House in Washington on the day before the demonstration and announced that if they were going to rampage through downtown D.C., I was going to join Dave Dellinger at the Pentagon and get arrested performing civil disobedience. They were appalled.

When I made it clear that I was absolutely serious, I became an instant outcast, but I remained firm and knew where I stood. I fully expected to be arrested the next day. If I was not able to prove to my friends that this was the only sane option, at least I wanted to make clear that in a choice between adventurism and moral protest, I had come down squarely on the side of nonviolence. At that point, I did not have a clear notion of how nonviolent action in such a situation could be infused with radical content and I was resigned to being liberal-baited out of the New Left. (The gay-baiting was already making my life quite painful in any case.)

That evening (Friday, October 20) while Berkeley radicals were celebrating the "victory" of mobile tactics and street fighting, I sat down for dinner with Dave Dellinger to discuss the morrow's action. Also present was a man I had not known before, Arthur Kinoy, one of the brightest and most dynamic lawyers I ever met, who worked as legal counsel for the Mobe. For two hours the three of us pondered the situation with agonized concern over the splits that were happening in the Movement and might get dramatically worse the following day. I explained the painful dilemma I was in and my decision to stand with Dave Dellinger on the question of nonviolence even if it meant the end of my career in SDS. Kinoy painted a picture that dispelled my gloom. He presented two interrelated and compelling arguments for the correctness of our decision to go to the Pentagon and demonstrate nonviolently. First, he justified the target by arguing that the U.S. government had itself drawn the line at the Pentagon by stationing troops inside and also by putting all U.S. military on alert from the East Coast to Colorado. Secondly, he argued that nonviolence was appropriate because it was the only way to maintain the "unity of the Movement." By the end of dinner, the three of us were elated. Arthur Kinoy and I went off to the SDS House where for two hours we argued the necessity of maintaining the unity of the Movement through nonviolence and the necessity of confronting the state at the Pentagon where it had chosen to demonstrate its military power.

We slowly won over the audience. Those who were not absolutely convinced by one or the other argument had been forced to think twice about the other alternatives. At no point did the argument degenerate into the false dichotomy between ineffective nonviolent moral protest and trashing (or other forms of violence or adventurism). Militant, radical nonviolence seemed to have won out over the impulse toward tactical adventurism and fighting with the police. There were, however, rumblings of discontent. My female companion of the preceding six months, Karen Ashley (later of the Weather Underground), would not speak to me because, she said, I had betrayed the

Movement. I sensed that what I had really betrayed was her dream of being the partner of a revolutionary hero.

THE PENTAGON PARADOX

On Saturday, October 21, perhaps 50,000 people gathered in front of the Lincoln Memorial to rally against the war. The crowd was restive. Just what did it mean to move "from protest to resistance"? For many it meant at least doing something more than easing their consciences by listening to speeches at rallies. The need "to put their bodies on the line," that act of determination in the New Left which had always expressed its sense of ultimate existential commitment, was a driving force for many as they filed out from the first rally and marched across the Potomac to a second site where yet more speeches were to be heard. The official plan of the Mobe was to make the second rally an opportunity for those who wanted to do civil disobedience at the Pentagon to participate one last time with the bulk of the demonstrators before separating and continuing on.

As soon as we had crossed the Potomac and long before reaching the second rally site, Tom Bell grabbed me by the arm and yelled: "Let's Go!" Almost before I knew it, I had become part of the new line of march which was half running towards the Pentagon. After about half a mile, we discovered that the GSA had carried out its threat to build a chain-link fence between the second rally site and the Pentagon in order to prevent demonstrators from reaching the building itself. The first canisters of tear gas were already being thrown by police. It was both exciting and somewhat frightening. When we reached the fence, Tom Bell, whose years as a full-back on the football team in high school and college had conditioned him well for physical confrontations, started to overwhelm the fence with sheer force. My many years as a farm boy had taught me much about both building and tearing down fences and I threw myself into the task.

With the fence now partially flattened, we ran straight for the Pentagon steps, avoiding the clouds of tear gas as best we could. Ahead of us was a group of adventuristic crazies, the

"Revolutionary Contingent" from New York armed with long bamboo poles held upright and flying Viet Cong flags. We started up the Pentagon steps with hundreds of demonstrators now following behind us. The rank of marchers we now were part of included Marilyn Buck and Cathy Wilkerson.

When we emerged onto the great terrace between the top of the stairs and the actual doors of the Pentagon perhaps fifty yards away, we were facing a long line of federal marshals standing shoulder to shoulder with their billy clubs drawn. In front of us the Revolutionary Contingent was using its flag-topped bamboo poles to try to provoke a violent confrontation with the marshals. I was very afraid that the marshals would be provoked into firing tear gas into the crowd which, had it panicked and attempted to flee back down the steps, would almost certainly have trampled people in the surging mass that now poured up the stairs.

My instinctive reactions, formed by a childhood fraught with physical violence, were fear and the compelling need to get the situation under control in order to prevent bloodshed and violence. Tom Bell's reactions, conditioned by years on the football team, were to rally the team and urge them to head for the doors of the Pentagon. Some far-sighted SDSers had commandeered a set of bullhorns and Tom Bell grabbed one of them. Now standing on a balustrade, waving and yelling through the bullhorn for the crowd to charge ahead to the doors, he was suddenly faced with a federal marshal, baton in the air and ready to strike. With the grace and strength of a true athlete, he grasped the baton in mid-air and slowly twisted it out of the marshal's hand. The frightened cop slowly backed away and Tom Bell again began to urge the crowd to press ahead and break through the line. At the same time, the Revolutionary Contingent was still trying to provoke violence and a lone determined pacifist was trusting his throat against a cross-held billy club, taunting a marshal and trying to get arrested.

It was one of the tensest moments of my life. I was scared and I hated football, and Tom Bell appeared to me totally possessed by the heroic gridiron role he had played out for years. With fear in my guts and a certain sadness in my heart, I jumped up beside him, looked straight in his eyes, and told him with all the force I could summon to stop before someone got killed and to get down off the balustrade. "This is *not* a fucking football game," I yelled. He faltered, began to deflate, and slowly got down. I took the bullhorn and began urging the crowd to sit down. Paul Millman, another SDSer with a bullhorn, did the same from another balustrade a hundred feet away. Slowly what could have been a violent confrontation became a mass nonviolent sit-in and teach-in to the hundreds of troops who had suddenly appeared from the doors of the Pentagon and replaced the federal marshals with three ranks of young soldiers. The forces of the state had indeed been called to act by using the Army to defend the Citadel of American Imperialism. It was a serious error on their part.

Suddenly the anti-war movement was faced with the same young men it had been urging to resist the draft and not to fight in Vietnam. We were nose-to-nose with the very soldiers to whom we wanted to talk. Instead of provoking them to bloodshed we were able to exercise the most powerful tool a radical nonviolent movement has—the appeal to the human heart—and we communicated a very clear and compelling message: "You don't belong to the generals up there in their offices. You belong with us. This is their war, not yours or ours." And then with a tremendous shout that rang over and over through the afternoon and evening air we chanted the most beautiful mantra I have ever heard: "Join Us! Join Us! Join Us!"

A few did—throw down their arms and join us.

Later that night, after being forced to change its wavering contingents of youthful soldiers several times, the generals in the Pentagon ordered a squad of fresh troops to drive a wedge into the seated crowd and to beat and arrest all who resisted. Some speakers took the bullhorn and begged for mercy, asking that they be allowed to be arrested peacefully. That seemed to me a psychological disaster, which threatened to turn a radical victory into a liberal defeat. It seemed to me that a radical nonviolent movement needed to be able to claim its victory and then call for a retreat. It did not need to deliver itself into the hands of the state.

I climbed up on the balustrade once again and gave a speech claiming a victory in which I sincerely believed. I addressed myself to the troops with the same message of solidarity that had been embodied in the appeal to "Join Us!" Then I said we should retreat—until we returned one day as part of a larger movement of the majority of the American people who would come to dismantle the Pentagon together with the structures of power and empire for which it stood. Most of the crowd responded with relief and simply walked away. A small minority, largely pacifists, stayed and got arrested. Later that night Jerry Rubin denounced the "SDS sell-out" of the demonstration. Later still he met with a man named Abbie Hoffman and together they made plans to join forces in the Youth International Party (a media-oriented radical group).

I left the Pentagon that night absolutely convinced radical nonviolence had worked and was the salvation of the Movement. Furthermore I was convinced that we had demonstrated that it was possible to confront the state nonviolently and effectively without falling into adventuristic tactics of street-fighting with police or trashing property. The event changed my life. It was another step in the completion of a new political gestalt that has guided me ever since. Others experienced the event in very different ways and drew very different conclusions than I did. There is no doubt in my mind that this moment in the history of the New Left, not just at the Pentagon but in the weeks preceding and following it across the country, marked the Great Divide in the Movement of the 1960s. I have recounted the story in personal, experiential terms because I believe no account of abstract ideas can explain the fate of the New Left. Only the lived experience of its participants holds the key to understanding its power and its self-destruction.

Part of what happened to me at the Pentagon was the deepening of an understanding that I found most clearly expressed years later when I read an interview with Jean-Paul Sartre, who said quite simply: "The real revolution will happen when we can all tell the truth about ourselves."

WILLIAM HEYEN

William Heyen's book-length poem *Ribbons: The Gulf War* (1991) documents Operation Desert Storm and its aftermath from the relative tranquility of Brockport, New York, where Heyen (b. 1940) was then an English professor. Like most Americans, he experienced the war mainly from his "television chair"; and while he was against the war from the start, writing "a newspaper column . . . a complex of againsts" to oppose it, there is nothing strident or rallying in his poems (as there is, for a counterexample, in June Jordan's "The Bombing of Baghdad," on page 677). Indeed Heyen is often concerned about the limits of poetry in the face of war and his own complicity in it, as a taxpayer and sometimes too eager watcher of CNN, "waiting for [his] money's worth."

"The Truth"—the poem's thirty-eighth section, of forty-one—is a mild exception. Frustrated by the yellow ribbons that had begun to appear in Brockport as elsewhere across the country, Heyen climbed his roof and tied "a large black configuration of bow & ribbons" to his TV antenna. It was an enigmatic protest to be sure, and one that he never fully owned—but still an act of public dissent, at a time and in a place where there were few.

Heyen retired from teaching in 2000 but continues to live in Brockport. Since then, he has edited *September 11, 2001: American Writers Respond* (2002) and has written several books of poetry including *Shoah Train* (2003), *A Poetics of Hiroshima* (2008), and most recently *Crazy Horse & the Custers* (2015).

The Truth

Across Brockport Village, a blight of orange & yellow ribbons
meant to remember our half-million participants
in "Operation Desert Storm," those who put their lives on line
to protect our country, as our president says.
Darkening ribbons encircle trees, telephone poles,
mailboxes, porch rails—so I was understandably half bored
& half nuts with war & ugliness, so climbed to my roof
& tied a large black configuration of bow & ribbons
to my aerial. Up there, I saw how it divides the winter sky
with its alphabet of one emotional letter, a vowel. . . .

At first, no one noticed, but then a car turned around.
Later, a police cruiser slowed down, & then another.
A reporter stopped for that infamous photo that appeared in
      Time
& the first of a hundred interviews I declined,
& neighbors gathered. My phone kept ringing off the wall,
people yelling "bastard," & "traitor," & "get it the hell down,
or else." . . . Eventually, my best friend came to my door
& asked me why. I explained, "I can't explain." Others
      followed,
& insisted. "No comment," I said. "I don't want trouble,"
I said. "Read Hawthorne's 'The Minister's Black Veil.'"

I still like the way the black bow & ribbons flutter,
stark but suggestive of comic dark, serious, direct,
my own American allegiance & patriotic light.
Parson Hooper had his reasons, & half understood them,
but when he slept or spoke, his breath trembled the veil,
& even holy scripture seemed filtered by the terrible
transformation of black crepe into symbol. In the end,
not even his creator could commend the visionary parson
who espied the truth that separates & condemns.
Above my village, this beauty of black bow & ribbons.

S. BRIAN WILLSON

A fair amount of antiwar writing offers graphic depictions of war, the goal being by such depictions to lead readers to oppose the horrors they are reading about. Such texts can be hard to read, the depiction of horrors nearly unbearable. None of them, though, in this anthology or anywhere else, is harder for me to bear than Brian Willson's direct, devastating account of having his legs crushed beneath an oncoming military train, on September 1, 1987, outside the Naval Weapons Station in Concord, California. Willson and other Veterans for Peace were on the tracks to protest U.S. military intervention in El Salvador and Nicaragua. They had notified all relevant personnel of their intention, and presumed that the train would stop. It did not; Willson ultimately lost both legs below the knees and suffered severe damage to his right frontal lobe. He sued the government and train crew; in a settlement, he was awarded $920,000. He later said the incident had given him "third world legs," deepening his sense of solidarity with those he had been attempting to defend; his account of it, *On Third World Legs*, appeared in 1992.

Willson (b. 1941) served in Vietnam, left the Air Force as a captain, became a member of Veterans for Peace, attended law school at American University. He held a variety of positions, among them some promising political ones, including one on Senator John Kerry's veterans' advisory committee. But he was also studying, and reacting with great intensity to, American policies in Latin America and elsewhere; he was thus moving gradually but inexorably toward a more radical opposition to American foreign policy, which led him to the Veterans Fast for Life action in 1986 and to the Concord train tracks that day in 1987. Since his injury he has been no less active, writing two memoirs and undertaking a documentary about the Korean War, working on permaculture projects and with numerous local organizations in Portland, Oregon, where he lives.

The Tracks

NUREMBURG ACTIONS

A RELATIVE of mine had been a young military officer who served with the United States prosecution team at Nuremburg. The chief United States prosecutor there, Justice Robert H. Jackson, grew up in the Jamestown, New York area, a few miles from Ashville. Upon signing the London Agreement of 1945 creating the International Military Tribunal, Jackson stated: "For the first time, four of the most powerful nations have agreed not only upon the principle of liability for war crimes of persecution, but also upon the principle of individual responsibility for the crime of attacking international peace."

When I returned from Nicaragua in the late spring of 1987, a number of friends and I decided to try to interdict the flow of arms from the United States to Central America. Charlie Liteky and I put out a leaflet in which we called for "thousands of people to participate in sustained strategic actions in the United States to block the flow of arms to Nicaragua." Later a group of us organized Nuremburg Actions at the Concord Naval Weapons Station in California.

The Concord Naval Weapons Station (CNWS), at Port Chicago about thirty five miles northeast of San Francisco, is the largest munitions depot on the West Coast. Its bunkers store a variety of bombs and munitions, including nuclear weapons. Many of these means of war are transported by train and truck from storage areas to the pier, for shipment by boat to their destinations. The train, consisting of a locomotive pulling box cars, has to pass through an area open to public use on its way from one piece of government property to the other.

During the Vietnam War, anti-war activists blocked both trains and trucks in the Bay Area. Members of the Berkeley Vietnam Day Committee sat down on the tracks in front of trains carrying soldiers bound for Vietnam. There were four such blockades in August 1965 alone. In May 1966, four women in San Jose blocked trucks loaded with napalm bombs for seven hours outside a trucking company. When they returned to the same location the next day, a truck driver told them that the company had decided to stop bringing napalm through that point. The women then moved on to an enormous bomb storage facility in nearby Alviso. There they had some success in delaying the loading of bombs onto barges for transit to Port Chicago. Marches, lengthy vigils, and frequent blocking of trains and trucks also occurred throughout the Vietnam War at CNWS itself.*

*The facts in this paragraph about blocking of trains and trucks during the Vietnam War are drawn from an unpublished manuscript by Tom Wells,

We decided to revive the historic Bay Area focus on the Concord Naval Weapons Station. We had a copy of a contract with the government of El Salvador (procured through the Freedom of Information Act) disclosing that a number of bombs, white phosphorus rockets, and other munitions had been shipped to El Salvador from CNWS in June 1985. I had learned of substantial bombings of villages in El Salvador during my trips to Nicaragua and El Salvador. An item in the July 1987 *Harper's* indicated that 230 Salvadoran villages had been bombed or strafed by the Salvadoran Air Force in 1986. This behavior is a grotesque violation of international law. Furthermore, I had spent time with Eugene Hasenfus, both on a visit to the crash site and while he was imprisoned in Nicaragua in November 1986, and learned of the air drop routes used to transport United States military supplies from bases in El Salvador to the contras in Nicaragua. (Hasenfus, a Wisconsin native and ex-Marine in Vietnam, had previously participated in secret missions over Southeast Asia for the CIA-owned airline, Air America. He was caught red-handed in October 1986 dropping supplies from the United States to contra terrorists in the interior of Nicaragua when the secret plane he was on was shot down by the Nicaraguan Army. He parachuted to safety before being captured.) We had plenty of reason to ask that CNWS refrain from any further illegal shipment of munitions to kill civilians in Central America.

On June 2, 1987, Chris Ballin and I wrote to the CNWS. "We are planning a nonviolent action beginning June 10th. We are writing you because we wish to maintain open contact with all law enforcement agencies and military personnel. . . . We welcome the opportunity to discuss in person why we feel so strongly about this matter and the plans for the on-going resistance."

CNWS personnel cabled to their superiors in Washington as follows:

BRIAN WILLSON, COORDINATOR OF A PACIFIST ORGANIZATION KNOWN AS QUOTE VETERANS FAST FOR LIFE AND VETERANS PEACE ACTION TEAMS

"The War over the War: Protestors and the White House During the Vietnam Era."

UNQUOTE INFORMED PUBLIC AFFAIRS OFFICER
THIS COMMAND THAT ON 10 JUNE HIS ORGANI-
ZATION WILL BEGIN A PERPETUAL ATTEMPT TO
BLOCK WEAPONS STATION CONCORD EXPLOSIVE
RAIL AND TRUCK MOVEMENT BETWEEN THE
STATION'S INLAND AND TIDAL AREAS BY PERMA-
NENTLY STATIONING PERSONNEL ON RAIL TRACK
AND IN ROADWAY. HE FURTHER STATED THAT
WHEN ONE PERSON IS ARRESTED, ANOTHER WILL
TAKE HIS OR HER PLACE FOR AS LONG AS THEY
HAVE PEOPLE REMAINING, WITH THOSE ARRESTED
RETURNING TO THE SCENE AFTER RELEASE FROM
CUSTODY TO REPEAT ACTION. WILLSON IS SAME
PERSON WHO FASTED IN WASHINGTON, DC, EAR-
LIER THIS YEAR PROTESTING U.S. CENTRAL AMERI-
CAN POLICY WITH RESULTING HIGH VISIBILITY
NATIONAL MEDIA ATTENTION. MEMBERS OF GROUP
HAVE BEEN SEEKING TO BUY OR RENT RESIDENCE
IN AREA TO HOUSE MARATHON PROTESTERS.
WILLSON SAYS THEY HOPE TO KEEP EFFORT GOING
FOR AT LEAST SEVERAL MONTHS. SINCE TRACK
AND ROADWAY INVOLVED EASILY ACCESSIBLE
TO PUBLIC AND UNDER JURISDICTION OF CIVIL
AUTHORITIES, THIS SITUATION COULD REQUIRE
PERMANENT POLICE PRESENCE AND HAS SERIOUS
SAFETY AND SECURITY IMPLICATIONS.

The sustained vigil began on June 10. I was not emotionally
or spiritually prepared at first to bodily block vehicles, risking likely arrest. The very first day we watched a locomotive
hauling two dozen or so box cars loaded with lethal weapons
move slowly by our solemn vigil at the train speed limit of
five miles per hour. All of a sudden I burst into tears. In my
mind I saw each box car stacked ceiling-high with bodies of
Nicaraguans and Salvadorans. It was as if I were a German
standing alongside a Nazi train loaded with Jews on their way
to the death camps.

Truck blocking went on throughout June with regular arrests and erratic jailings by the police. I was a support
person from the sidelines. Train blocking was part of the plans
of Nuremburg Actions but had not happened by early July.
A local insurance salesman, who had been present on several

occasions to support the vigil but who had not taken the prescribed nonviolence training, stepped out on the tracks on his own, without giving notice, when few vigilers were present as a munitions train slowly moved toward him. The locomotive came to within several feet of this man and stopped. The spotters standing on front of the locomotive grabbed the sign from his arms and removed his body from the tracks.

Our presence continued throughout the summer, always at the same location on the Port Chicago side of the public highway at the place where the munitions trains cross the highway. There were nearly always more than one, and sometimes a couple of dozen, persons present during daylight hours from June 10 to September 1.

Sometime in early or mid July I made plans to escalate my own participation in Nuremburg Actions beginning September 1, 1987. On that day, the first anniversary of the beginning of the Veterans' Fast For Life, I and others would start a forty day water-only fast and begin blocking munitions trains. We would attempt to block movement of the trains for every day during that period. We would fast on the tracks adjacent to the location where we had regularly vigiled since June 10.

Others were invited to join and several persons agreed to participate. Duncan Murphy, a participant in the 1986 fast, also agreed to be part of the forty day fast on the tracks.

We had examined the history of people blocking trains and had concluded that the train would certainly stop. The base would be notified in advance of our action. I still have some of the photographs we collected: for example, *Life* magazine pictures in the October 8, 1956 and May 19, 1972 issues showing locomotives stopping for protesters.

A doctor was planning to monitor my condition throughout the fast. I expected to spend some or most of the forty days in jail and had briefed the doctor on my need for potassium supplements during the fast to protect nutrition of the heart, and asked that he talk to jailers about the importance of my receiving these supplements.

On August 21, 1987, I sent a letter to CNWS Commander Lonnie Cagle explaining in detail the nature and philosophy of the September 1 plans. The letter asked for a personal meeting at least four times.

This letter . . . requests a personal meeting with you. . . . I want you to know in advance of this plan. . . . Because of the seriousness of these matters I ask that we have a personal meeting to discuss them. This action is not intended to harass you or any military or civilian personnel. . . . I would like to discuss with you your views and response to our concerns. . . . I hope that you will respond so that we can set up a mutually convenient time to meet.

Copies of the letter were sent to the Contra Costa County Sheriff, the Concord Police Department, the California Highway Patrol, and a number of elected officials, including U.S. Senators Cranston and Wilson of California, U.S. Representatives Boxer, Miller, and Edwards of California, and U.S. Senators Kerry, Kennedy, Leahy, and Jeffords of Massachusetts and Vermont, where I had lived most of my life since 1980. I had received no replies as of September 1.

On August 23, Holley Rauen and I were married. We committed ourselves "to be prepared for the risks and prices required, individually and collectively, to live and promote a radical transformation in our North American society."

Another cable from CNWS to Washington was sent on August 31. It revealed no confusion about our intentions and showed that the Navy was quite clear about our expressed plans.

RECEIVED LETTER FROM GROUP IDENTIFIED AS VETERANS FAST FOR LIFE AND VETERANS PEACE ACTION TEAMS ADVISING THAT PROTESTERS PLAN TO FAST FOR 40 DAYS ON RAILROAD TRACK USED TO TRANSPORT MATERIAL BETWEEN STATION INLAND AND TIDAL AREAS. LETTER AND NEWS ARTICLE QUOTING PROTEST PRINCIPAL, MR. S. BRIAN WILLSON, STATES FAST TO BEGIN 1 SEPT AND THAT FASTERS WILL NOT MOVE FOR APPROACHING RAIL TRAFFIC. LOCAL SHERIFF AND POLICE OFFICERS AWARE OF THREAT. SHOULD POTENTIAL INTERRUPTION OF RAIL SERVICE OCCUR, THEY WILL BE REQUESTED TO REMOVE PROTESTOR(S). COMMANDING OFFICER'S ASSESSMENT: INTERRUPTION OF NORMAL STATION OPERATIONS NOT ANTICIPATED. . . .

The morning of September 1 arrived. We planned a worship service on the tracks after a press conference announcing the formal launching of the fast and the train blockade. Having never been arrested or jailed before, I was a bit anxious. I was most concerned about the prospect that as the fast progressed and I grew weaker, I might be hurt in the arresting process by officers repeatedly removing me from the tracks. Fasting on the Capitol steps appeared easy in comparison to fasting on train tracks at the same time I was attempting to block munitions trains, and subjecting myself to continual arrests.

Besides Duncan Murphy and myself, David Duncombe, a World War II and Korean veteran and a chaplain at the University of California Medical School in San Francisco, would be fasting for forty days on the tracks. Others might join us for different periods.

My wife Holley and stepson Gabriel accompanied me as I drove to CNWS, along with fellow faster Duncan Murphy and another friend. Two photographer friends and a friend with a video camera were present to record the press conference, worship service, blocking action, and anticipated arrests.

There were only a few media representatives present for the press conference. We conducted a worship and meditation service with the thirty or forty fasters and supporters. I said the following:

> My hope is that today will begin a new era of sustained resistance like the salt march in India and like the civil rights movement in the 1950s and 1960s where people, every day, realize that we, the people, are the ones that are going to make peace. Peacemaking is full-time. Warmaking is full-time. And so my hope is that we will establish or create a kind of action here that revives the imagery of the sustained resistance of the past such as in the salt march and the civil rights movement where people are committed every day to say, "As long as the trains move munitions on these tracks we will be here to stop the trains." Because each train that goes by here with munitions, that gets by us, is going to kill people, people like you and me.
>
> And the question that I have to ask on these tracks is: Am I any more valuable than those people? And if I say No then I have to say, You can't move these munitions without moving my body

or destroying my body. So today, from the spirit of a year ago on the steps and then for five months in Central America and coming back, the Nuremburg Actions and today, I begin this fast for atonement for all the blood that we have on our hands and that I have on my hands.

And I begin this fast to envision a kind of resistance, an empowering kind of spirit, that we hope to participate in with many people, saying, These munitions will not be exploded in our names and they will not be moved any longer in our names and we must put our bodies in front of them to say, stronger than ever, that this will not continue in our name. The killing must stop and I have to do everything in my power to stop it.

And I hope that when people ask us what they can do to support us: what they can do is they can come to the tracks and stand with us on the tracks to stop the trains. That's all we want. We want more people to join hands and say, This will not continue. And only we the people can stop it. Thank you.

At about 11:40 A.M. the three of us took our positions on the tracks. Two others held a large banner across the tracks just behind us that stated in bold letters: "NUREMBURG ACTIONS: Complicity in the Commission of a Crime Against Peace, a War Crime, or a Crime Against Humanity, Is a Crime Under International Law."

I experience what the doctors call regional amnesia. Though I'm told that I was conscious the entire time prior to and after being struck by the train, except for the time in the hospital under anesthesia during surgery, I have no memory over a several-day period. So I will finish my account of what happened on September 1 with this transcript of a cassette recording made by a friend.

VOICE: Okay. Here comes the train.

MALE VOICE: We're not leaving the tracks, right?

MALE VOICE: We're not leaving.

MALE VOICE: It's planning, preparation, initiation, waging a war of aggression or a war in violation of international

[INAUDIBLE DUE TO TRAIN WHISTLE]

[TRAIN WHISTLE IS HEARD FOR NINETEEN SECONDS BEFORE IMPACT]

[TRAIN WHISTLE CEASES]

MALE VOICE: No.

FEMALE VOICE: Oh, my God! Oh, my God! Oh, my God! Stop the train! Stop the—Oh, my God!

MALE VOICE: Help.

FEMALE VOICE: Come help me!

FEMALE VOICE: Ambulance is here.

MALE VOICE: Look what you did, you're the murderers.

GABRIEL: You murderers! You killed my father! You killed my father!

MALE VOICE: Where's the fucking ambulance?

MALE VOICE: Get an ambulance.

FEMALE VOICE: My God!

[SIRENS]

[MULTIPLE VOICES—INDISCERNIBLE]

GABRIEL: You killed my father! Killed my father! You did that, by God!

MALE VOICE: Stay right there.

MALE VOICE: We love you, Brian.

HOLLEY: I'm holding the bleeding.

MALE VOICE: You want me to hold that [INDIS-CERNIBLE]

HOLLEY: Yes. You have to press very hard so that no more blood comes out.

MALE VOICE: Relax. Real, real hard.

HOLLEY: Right here.

[MULTIPLE VOICES—INDISCERNIBLE]

MAN OPERATING TAPE RECORDER: The train—there's total confusion. There's a fire truck that came. There's still no ambulance. It's been five minutes since the train came barrelling down the tracks, blowing its horn. The three men who were on the tracks had panic in their eyes and two of them jumped aside. One of them who was kneeling fell back under the train, had his foot rolled over and cut off. Was dragged and bumped and dragged again. His head split open. His other foot cut off. And finally bumped into the inside of the track where the train then pulled on and stopped 400, 500 feet down the road.

The—I never saw the eyes of the guys in the caboose. There were two guys on the cowcatcher, sort of screaming and yahooing and "Here we come." The Marine guards who are around with their M-16s look panic-stricken. Now there are several veterans who are enraged and yelling and screaming at the soldiers who are starting to surround the crowd and keep people off the tracks. There is still no ambulance. There's been a County Sheriff and a fire truck and a military vehicle of some kind with an official person with a radio coming around calling for things.

Holley, Brian's wife, is holding his leg trying to keep it from bleeding. His skull is open, you can see his brain inside. It's probably a four or five inch gaping hole in his skull. He's stunned. Stunned—fuck! Grief, all around.

The man from the fire department is attempting to suture and bandage what he can but he—the military keeps telling people to step across the fucking yellow line. I can't believe it.

Why don't you guys do something constructive? Jesus Christ!

MALE VOICE: The train was going full bore.

FEMALE VOICE: We heard the screaming. I [INAUDIBLE]

MALE VOICE: Didn't touch the throttle. Didn't even touch the throttle.

MALE VOICE: Fucking unbelievable.

MAN OPERATING TAPE RECORDER: They've attached something to his nostril. I just picked up a huge chunk of bone. Duncan Murphy is leaning over Brian, trying to hold on to life. Brian's eyes are closed. I'm not sure at this point.

Gabriel, Brian's stepson, is still distraught and screaming. As you look around, some of the responses are changing from shock and grief to anger.

Here comes the ambulance. Five, six, seven minutes later.

This was not a surprise. This had been a well-publicized protest. Brian had sent letters to some fifteen or twenty people, the base commander amongst others, last week. Everyone knew full well that this was going to be a day where the train was going to be stopped and the train did not stop.

Looks like military nursing personnel have arrived. He's still blinking, still holding on. Brian is such a strong character.

FEMALE VOICE: Let's get a small no-pressure dressing—bandage, a Kurlex.

MALE VOICE: I've got [INAUDIBLE]. I've got everything under control.

MALE VOICE: Okay.

MALE VOICE: John, is that the only way you can stop it, is with that?

MALE VOICE: —have a tourniquet.

MALE VOICE: Hold on, man.

VOICE: Let's make a hole.

MALE VOICE: Need anything, buddy?

MALE VOICE: No. Looking good. Looking good.

FEMALE VOICE: How you doing, guy?

MALE VOICE: Pretty good.

FEMALE VOICE: I'm Petty Officer McGee. I'm a Navy Corpsman, okay? Let us help you.

MALE VOICE: I couldn't tell you, myself.

FEMALE VOICE: Don't hold pressure. Just hold it there.

FEMALE VOICE: 110 over 80 bp, Bob.

HOLLEY: You're doing good. Your blood pressure is good, honey. You're hanging in there.

FEMALE VOICE: You're doing great, guy. You're doing great.

FEMALE VOICE: How're you doing? You doing all right?

FEMALE VOICE: Yeah.

MALE VOICE: Okay. Keep your hands [INAUDIBLE].

HOLLEY: I love you, Brian.

MALE VOICE: We all love you, Brian.

FEMALE VOICE: Brian. Brian.

MALE VOICE: How many victims do you have?

MALE VOICE: What?

MALE VOICE: How many victims do you have?

FEMALE VOICE: Two that I—there's one minor victim down there.

MALE VOICE: Where's the other one?

FEMALE VOICE: Everybody's making a circle around you for healing, Brian.

HOLLEY: Honey, you've gotta be brave, okay?

GABRIEL: Why didn't you dodge it? I wanted you to dodge. Why didn't you dodge it? Dodge it. You should have dodge—My God, that's a piece of him! That's a piece of him!

HOLLEY: Tell him you love him, Gabe. Just tell him you love him.

GABRIEL: My God, that's a piece of Dad.

MALE VOICE: It's all right.

HOLLEY: Just tell him you love him.

GABRIEL: That's a piece of my Dad!

HOLLEY: Tell him you love him. Bring him up here.

MALE VOICE: It's all right.

FEMALE VOICE: Dan, tell him you love him.

HOLLEY: Hey, Gabe, listen, I'm going to go to the hospital with Brian and—

VOICE: I want to go with you.

FEMALE VOICE: I'll take you there.

HOLLEY: Okay, they'll take you and you meet us at the hospital, okay?

FEMALE VOICE: I'll take you there, Gabe. I promise you.

FEMALE VOICE: Okay? Okay? Okay?

VOICE: God.

HOLLEY: He's going to be okay, honey.

GABRIEL: No, it's not going to be all right, that's my Dad.

HOLLEY: Yeah, we know. You know? I know, honey, I saw the whole thing.

FEMALE VOICE: Right now we need to get out of the way so they can [INAUDIBLE].

GABRIEL: God, you have blood all over you!

HOLLEY: I was stopping the bleeding on his legs, honey.

MAN OPERATING TAPE RECORDER: They brought a stretcher now. They're placing Brian's torso, that's what it is. His legs are gone below the knees. His head is wide open. He's still hanging on. His blood pressure is pretty good. People have formed a semi-circle around him, holding hands, trying to help pump life.

It's still a pretty confusing situation. Duncan Murphy is still hanging on as is Holley. And the Corps is working to strap him to a piece of plywood now to lift him up into the ambulance.

Now there are police vehicles everywhere. Highway Patrol, Concord Police, County Sheriff; as well as all the military police. Lots of little radios calling someone somewhere.

The train is still stopped, ironically, down the track some 500 feet, meters, I don't know: some distance down the road with this little triangle of explosive or dangerous cargo highlighting the back of it.

The engineer is still standing on the cab looking back. The two guys on the cowcatcher, I don't know where they are. They are behind the fence and the sentries so we can't approach them. It's on military property and they're making it very clear that we don't cross the yellow line.

The young Marine guards whose responsibility that is, initially came out here trying to look serious but sort of with a chuckle. This was another day, another job. And all of a sudden it's a different day.

People are yelling. Some of the veterans are angry and yelling at the—I don't know—at the air, at the fates, at the gods.

This whole thing had been orchestrated and planned and the train didn't stop. [*End of transcript*]

WHY DID THE UNITED STATES GOVERNMENT CONSIDER ME A TERRORIST?

When I became conscious, I saw Holley Rauen sitting next to my bed. I saw many green plants throughout the room. I thought this was a very unusual jail cell. It seemed more like a greenhouse. Holley explained to me that I was in John Muir Hospital, Walnut Creek, California. The train (on September 1 a locomotive hauling two boxcars) had crashed into me and continued moving over my body until the last of the two box cars was inside the fenced base area guarded by United States Marines.

I asked what happened to Duncan Murphy and David Duncombe who were part of the blockade. I learned that David, who was crouching (not sitting like me), jumped out of the way just before the train would have hit him. Duncan, also crouching, made a mighty leap straight up—quite a feat for a sixty-seven-year-old veteran—and grabbed the cowcatcher railing, cutting his knee but otherwise escaping injury.

It took several days for this reality to sink in. I began to watch television news reports on the wall-mounted hospital TV, which continued to carry stories about the assault, including selected cuts from the amateur video footage provided the media by my friend Bob Spitzer. For several days I saw the speeding train with two human spotters standing on the platform above the cowcatcher barrelling down on the three of us on the tracks.

I began to comprehend the life-altering nature of my injuries. The most serious of my injuries were a severely fractured skull, missing a golf-ball-size piece from the right forehead area; a seriously cut and damaged right frontal brain lobe; a severed but sewn-back-on left ear; and two legs missing below my knees. That I was alive at all seemed the more remarkable when I learned that a United States Navy ambulance arrived on the bloody scene within the first few minutes after I was hurt but refused to provide medical assistance or transportation to a hospital, apparently because my body was not lying on government property.

People who were present told me that I was conscious throughout and talked with those attending to my very vulnerable body. Holley directed a series of emergency medical procedures with the aid of several horrified supporters, stopping the bleeding from my right leg stump, from my mangled and twisted left leg, from my almost severed ear, and from the hole in the right forehead portion of my skull. These procedures, in addition to the nourishing love of those present, kept my fragile being alive until the county ambulance arrived some twenty minutes later.

Why hadn't the train stopped, I asked? They knew we were there. Visibility was excellent. The speed limit was a slow five miles per hour.

Holley was as shocked as I was, as every one was. She said that as she was standing off to the side, carrying a political sign as part of the support demonstration of thirty to forty people, she saw the two human spotters standing on the front of the locomotive distinctly shaking their heads from side to side as if to say, "We are not stopping, no way!"

From the beginning a lot of people came up to me and said, "You know this couldn't have happened without it being designed and intended to happen that way." I'm not a very conspiratorial-thinking person, nor a particularly paranoid person. I'm kind of naive.

I started thinking differently after the Congressional hearing held on November 18, 1987. Navy officials admitted that they knew a lot about me. Navy Captain S. J. Pryzby told the Congressional committee that the Navy knew about me, about the fasts, the trips to Nicaragua, and my being at the tracks since June 10, and he seemed to be describing me as a man of my word. I sat there thinking, "They knew that I wouldn't get off the tracks."

Then I found the notes of the unsanitized Navy report that had not been made public lying on the table in the room next to the hearing room. I started reading them and thought, "My God, this is in the original report that they didn't release to the public." I put the notes in my briefcase.

Later I got a copy of the sheriff's report, which was not included in the Navy report. It contained interviews with the train engineer, who said he was under orders not to stop the train.

Finally, I learned that at the time of the assault I was being investigated by the government as a terrorist. I was in the ABC-TV studio in Washington, D.C. in November 1987. They showed me the FBI documents and said, "We want your face on camera looking at these documents." I hadn't known anything about them until then.

Let's restate what happened on September 1 according to what we now know. The protesters, including myself, began the blockade after elaborate prior notice at about 11:40 A.M. A few minutes later the munitions train came into view. Upon seeing three men blockading the tracks, the train stopped near the main gate to await further instructions. CNWS personnel notified the county sheriff. The sheriff told them it would take his forces thirty minutes to reach the scene.

Up to this point every one's actions were consistent with the expectation, which I confidently shared, that the locomotive would not move until the sheriff's men arrived and arrested us.

Just after 11:55 A.M. the train began to move forward again. The FBI concluded after examining Bob Spitzer's videotape that the train was speeding at about 17 miles per hour, over three times its legal speed limit of five miles per hour. It was a bright sunny day. There was clear visibility for at least 650 feet according to the Navy's report. Yet the locomotive not only did not stop, but seems to have accelerated after striking me, as evidenced in a photograph revealing a fresh burst of smoke issuing from its smoke stack at the time of impact and after, as I lay mangled under the train.

The train did not stop because the train crew had been instructed not to stop. Ed Hubbard, railroad supervisor at CNWS, says "he told the crew, if the protesters started climbing on the train, to continue until the train was inside the gates and the marines could take over." David Humiston, the engineer, and Ralph Dawson, one of the two spotters, said they received orders not to stop if the protesters started "boarding the locomotive or the cars it was pulling." The statements of the crew members are quoted in "Weapons train that maimed pacifist was under Navy orders not to stop," *National Catholic Reporter*, Jan. 29, 1988.

Now, of course, we who were on the tracks had no intention of boarding the train or climbing on the locomotive and box cars, and we never did anything of the kind. But it seems that the Navy expected us to do so. And because of this expectation, the crew was instructed not to stop until it reached base property, or perhaps, not to stop if we did anything causing them to think we might be about to board the train.

From what source did the Navy derive its apparent belief that those who sat down on the tracks on September 1 would also try to board the train? We had written to the CNWS commander, distributed leaflets throughout the area, and talked extensively with the media. In none of these many statements did we state or suggest that we might seek to do anything but sit quietly on the tracks. I believe the source for the Navy's mistaken anticipation may have been the FBI. On October 10, 1986, while the Veterans' Fast For Life was in progress, U.S. Senator Warren Rudman of New Hampshire released a letter stating in part: "In my opinion, their actions are hardly different than those of the terrorists who are holding our hostages in Beirut." See "Rudman Likens Fasting Veterans To Terrorists," *Boston Globe*, Oct. 11, 1986. In that same month the FBI directed its agents to begin an inquiry into the alleged terrorism of those conducting the Veterans' Fast For Life. FBI agent John C. Ryan told his superiors in a memorandum of December 4, 1986 that he refused to take part in the investigation of a group that had a "totally non-violent posture." He was fired after nearly twenty-two years of service. See "The cost of a fired FBI agent's journey to Catholic nonviolence," *National Catholic Reporter*,

Nov. 27, 1987; "FBI Probe of Willson Reported," *San Francisco Chronicle*, Dec. 12, 1987.

These facts support the conclusion that the United States government expected "terrorists" like Brian Willson to try to seize the locomotive and its boxcars, just as terrorists hijack airplanes; and therefore, at some level higher than the CNWS train crew and its supervisor, decided not to stop the train.

I continue to believe that the decision to move and accelerate the train on September 1, 1987, cannot be fully understood outside the context of the government's demonstrated interest in my activities before September 1. The precise relationship of this prior interest to the decision intentionally and recklessly to move the train has yet to be unravelled. At a minimum it created a milieu of lack of concern, contempt, and wanton disregard. At a maximum, it was attempted murder.

I have a lot of empathy for the train crew. First of all, they're all living the way I used to live; I believe they're brainwashed just as I was. Second, they probably do have traumatic stress (which is what they sued me for) because I think they were caught in a conflict between following their orders and following their consciences. They were on the lower end of a chain of command that's involved in a diabolical, criminal national policy. They're the grunt men, just as we were in Vietnam.

The solution to their stress is to endure a transformational process within themselves, not to sue me. But if they were going to sue, they should have sued the Navy, which gave the order and possesses money.

I condemn their action. I just plead with them to be open to transformation, which is the only way to heal their stress, and to tell the truth about who gave the order and as to their state of mind.

POSTSCRIPT. As of the date of this writing (June 1, 1992), Nuremburg Actions has steadfastly resisted movement of munitions trucks and trains at CNWS for 1,817 consecutive days, temporarily blocking well over a thousand such trucks and trains, weathering cold, rain, 1,700 arrests, a number of jail terms, and hostile and violent responses from local residents. Rev. David Duncombe, himself having narrowly escaped injury or death on September 1, 1987, has continued his participation in Nuremburg Actions, being present *every* Thursday since that date when not in jail. He has been arrested numerous times for blocking the movement of munitions trucks and trains, while continuing to maintain his position as Chaplain and Professor at the University of California at San Francisco Medical School. He has been convicted twice in jury trials, serving a number of weeks in jail on each sentence. In both trials the judge excluded from jury consideration the violations of international (and therefore United States Constitutional) law by the United States government, and its agent, the United States Navy, in committing war crimes, crimes against peace, and crimes against humanity in the murdering and maiming of innocent civilians in Latin America.

NAOMI SHIHAB NYE

"Jerusalem" is in some senses not an antiwar poem: there is no particular war it is opposing, being set rather in the context of the intractable conflict in Israel-Palestine. Opposition to war in the strict sense is stated only by a character in the poem: the child who writes, "I don't like wars, they end up with monuments."

"Jerusalem" is, though, a peace poem, imagining reconciliation: "I'm interested in people getting over it." It is filled with images of almost fantastic peace and joy—the child's "bird with wings / wide enough to cover two roofs at once," for example. It is an indirect exploration of the place in the poet's brain "where hate won't grow."

Naomi Shihab Nye (b. 1952) was born in St. Louis, then moved to the West Bank with her family (her father was Palestinian), spent considerable time there with her Palestinian grandmother, and moved back to the United States a year later, settling in San Antonio. She began writing poems at the age of seven, and now writes poems and children's stories (she won the 2013 NSK Neustadt Prize for Children's Literature). She calls herself "the wandering poet," traveling often and around the world to direct workshops in writing.

Jerusalem

"Let's be the same wound if we must bleed.
Let's fight side by side, even if the enemy
is ourselves: I am yours, you are mine."

—TOMMY OLOFSSON, Sweden

I'm not interested in
who suffered the most.
I'm interested in
people getting over it.

Once when my father was a boy
a stone hit him on the head.
Hair would never grow there.
Our fingers found the tender spot
and its riddle: the boy who has fallen
stands up. A bucket of pears

in his mother's doorway welcomes him home.
The pears are not crying.
Later his friend who threw the stone
says he was aiming at a bird.
And my father starts growing wings.

Each carries a tender spot:
something our lives forgot to give us.
A man builds a house and says,
"I am native now."
A woman speaks to a tree in place
of her son. And olives come.
A child's poem says,
"I don't like wars,
they end up with monuments."
He's painting a bird with wings
wide enough to cover two roofs at once.

Why are we so monumentally slow?
Soldiers stalk a pharmacy:
big guns, little pills.

If you tilt your head just slightly
it's ridiculous.

There's a place in my brain
where hate won't grow.
I touch its riddle: wind, and seeds.
Something pokes us as we sleep.

It's late but everything comes next.

JUNE JORDAN

June Jordan (1936–2002), the only child of Jamaican immigrants, grew up in Harlem and Bedford-Stuyvesant; she attended Northfield Mount Hermon School and Barnard College, forming her consciousness in relation and opposition to these elite, largely white institutions. (At Barnard, she wrote, "no one ever presented me with a single Black author.") She published her first book of poems in 1969, and more than twenty-five more—poems, memoirs, essays, columns, novels, biographies, and a libretto—over the course of her prolific but too short life. She taught at numerous colleges and universities, among them the State University of New York at Stony Brook from 1978 until 1989 and the University of California at Berkeley (where she founded the "Poetry for the People" program) from 1989 until her death.

"The Bombing of Baghdad"—first collected in *Kissing God Goodbye* (1997)—has a sharp anger to it, and the rhythms of enraged, repetitive, almost incantatory speech. One can easily imagine it as a spoken word piece, galvanizing hearers to cheers and outrage. But Jordan's poem also has an implicit argument; she links the bombing of Baghdad during the Gulf War to Custer's war against the Lakota, seeing in the two events two white attacks on non-white peoples, and she positions herself unambiguously with the latter: "And I am cheering for the arrows and the braves."

The Bombing of Baghdad

I

began and did not terminate for 42 days
and 42 nights relentless minute after minute
more than 110,000 times
we bombed Iraq we bombed Baghdad
we bombed Basra/we bombed military
installations we bombed the National Museum
we bombed schools we bombed air raid
shelters we bombed water we bombed
electricity we bombed hospitals we
bombed streets we bombed highways
we bombed everything that moved/we
bombed everything that did not move we
bombed Baghdad

a city of 5.5 million human beings
we bombed radio towers we bombed
telephone poles we bombed mosques
we bombed runways we bombed tanks
we bombed trucks we bombed cars we bombed bridges
we bombed the darkness we bombed
the sunlight we bombed them and we
bombed them and we cluster bombed the citizens
of Iraq and we sulfur bombed the citizens of Iraq
and we napalm bombed the citizens of Iraq and we
complemented these bombings/these "sorties" with
Tomahawk cruise missiles which we shot
repeatedly by the thousands upon thousands
into Iraq
(you understand an Iraqi Scud missile
is *quote* militarily insignificant *unquote* and we
do not mess around with insignificant)
so we used cruise missiles repeatedly
we fired them into Iraq
And I am not pleased
I am not very pleased
None of this fits into my notion of "things going very well"

                                II

The bombing of Baghdad
did not obliterate the distance or the time
between my body and the breath
of my beloved

                                III

This was Custer's Next-To-Last Stand
I hear Crazy Horse singing as he dies
I dedicate myself to learn that song
I hear that music in the moaning of the Arab world

                                IV

Custer got accustomed to just doing his job
Pushing westward into glory

Making promises
Searching for the savages/their fragile
temporary settlements
for raising children/dancing down the rain/and praying
for the mercy of a herd of buffalo
Custer/he pursued these savages
He attacked at dawn
He murdered the men/murdered the boys
He captured the women and converted
them (I'm sure)
to his religion
Oh, how gently did he bid his darling fiancee
farewell!
How sweet the gaze her eyes bestowed upon her warrior!
Loaded with guns and gunpowder he embraced
the guts and gore of manifest white destiny
He pushed westward
to annihilate the savages
("Attack at dawn!")
and seize their territories
  seize their women
  seize their natural wealth

V

And I am cheering for the arrows
and the braves

VI

And all who believed some must die
they were already dead
And all who believe only they possess
human being and therefore human rights
they no longer stood among the possibly humane
And all who believed that retaliation/revenge/defense
derive from God-given prerogatives of white men
And all who believed that waging war is anything
  besides terrorist activity in the first
  place and in the last

And all who believed that F-15's/F-16's/"Apache"
    helicopters/
B-52 bombers/smart bombs/dumb bombs/napalm/artillery/
battleships/nuclear warheads amount to anything other
than terrorist tools of a terrorist undertaking
And all who believed that holocaust means something
    that happens only to white people
And all who believed that Desert Storm
    signified anything besides the delivery of an American
    holocaust against the peoples of the Middle East
All who believed these things
they were already dead
They no longer stood among the possibly humane

And this is for Crazy Horse singing as he dies
because I live inside his grave
And this is for the victims of the bombing of Baghdad
because the enemy traveled from my house
            to blast your homeland
            into pieces of children
            and pieces of sand

And in the aftermath of carnage
perpetrated in my name
how should I dare to offer you my hand
how shall I negotiate the implications
    of my shame?

My heart cannot confront
this death without relief
My soul will not control
this leaking of my grief

And this is for Crazy Horse singing as he dies
And here is my song of the living
who must sing against the dying
sing to join the living
with the dead

GINA VALDÉS

Born in Los Angeles and raised on both sides of the U.S.-Mexico border, Gina Valdés (b. 1943) has taught Spanish and creative writing at Colorado College and various campuses of the University of California and is the author of two bilingual poetry collections, *Comiendo lumbre (Eating Fire)* (1986) and *Puentes y fronteras (Bridges and Borders)* (1996). Her poem "Hearts on Fire"—first published in George Mariscal's *Aztlán and Viet Nam: Chicano and Chicana Experiences of the War* (1999)—explores what she calls the "interrelatedness between all beings," the lives of its speaker, her young friend, and many beyond them, all linked in joy and in pain.

Hearts on Fire

1968,

the year you were born
in Saigon to a Vietnamese dancer
and an American soldier
you have never met, Ngoc,

some hearts broke
into chants, others
into flames.

Our voices circled your city, your birth,
students chanting to Ho Chi Minh.

Thich Nhat Hanh intoned the Heart Sutra,
Brother Martin prayed with him, was silenced,
César and Dolores recited the red earth mantra.

Cousin Popo's prayers exploded
in a mine, next to a Vietnamese boy,
a nearby rice field,

green shoots turning to ashes
and grief.

Monks and nuns
opened their lotus hearts
and caught fire.

BARBARA EHRENREICH

Barbara Ehrenreich's 1997 *Blood Rites: Origins and History of the Passions of War* is a quirky book, focused on her notion that many of these "passions of war" got rooted in us by way of our prehistoric combats with predatory beasts. But it is full of interesting passages, and its conclusion, reprinted below, is remarkable. Ehrenreich takes up William James's idea of a "war against war," and is able to amplify it because she is writing nearly a century later, cognizant of what has happened in antiwar movements over that time. She is severe in characterizing those movements, "admittedly feeble undertakings compared to that which they oppose." But she also sees the lesson that they have taught, a Jamesian lesson but stated by Ehrenreich with empirical rather than prophetic certainty: "the passions we can bring to war can be brought just as well to the struggle *against* war."

Ehrenreich (b. 1941) grew up in a union household in Butte, Montana. She majored in chemistry at Reed College and later earned a Ph.D. in immunology from Rockefeller University, but became a journalist and policy activist rather than a scientist, publishing books on the history and politics of women's health and other subjects. Her best-known work may be *Nickel and Dimed: On (Not) Getting By in America* (2001), an account of her attempt to survive as a minimum-wage worker, made into a play by Joan Holden in 2002. Most recently she has written *Living with a Wild God: A Nonbeliever's Search for the Truth About Everything* (2014).

Fighting War

WAR, at the end of the twentieth century, is a more formidable adversary than it has ever been. It can no longer be localized within a particular elite and hence overthrown in a brilliant act of revolution. Revolution, in fact, was redefined by Lenin and others as little more than a species of war, fought by disciplined "cadres" organized along the same hierarchical lines as the mass armies of the modern era. Meanwhile, war has dug itself into economic systems, where it offers a livelihood to millions, rather than to just a handful of craftsmen and professional soldiers. It has lodged in our souls as a kind of religion, a quick tonic for political malaise and a bracing antidote to the moral torpor of consumerist, market-driven cultures.

In addition, our incestuous fixation on combat with our own kind has left us ill prepared to face many of the larger perils of the situation in which we find ourselves: the possibility of drastic climatic changes, the depletion of natural resources, the relentless predations of the microbial world. The wealth that flows ceaselessly to the project of war is wealth lost, for the most part, to the battle against these threats. In the United States, military spending no longer requires a credible enemy to justify it, while funding for sanitation, nutrition, medical care, and environmental reclamation declines even as the need mounts. In the third world and much of the postcommunist world, the preparedness for war far surpasses the readiness to combat disease—witness Zaire's fumbling efforts to contain the Ebola outbreak of 1995, or the swiftly declining life expectancy of the former Soviets.

But in at least one way, we have gotten tougher and better prepared to face the enemy that is war. If the twentieth century brought the steady advance of war and war-related enterprises, it also brought the beginnings of organized human resistance to war. Anti-war movements, arising in massive force in the latter half of the century, are themselves products of the logic of modern war, with its requirements of mass participation and assent. When the practice and passions of war were largely confined to a warrior elite, popular opposition to war usually took the form of opposition to that elite. But in the situation where everyone is expected to participate in one way or another, and where anyone can become a victim whether they participate or not, opposition could at last develop to the institution of war itself.

This represents an enormous human achievement. Any anti-war movement that targets only the human agents of war—a warrior elite or, in our own time, the chieftains of the "military-industrial complex"—risks mimicking those it seeks to overcome. Anti-war activists can become macho and belligerent warriors in their own right, just as revolutionaries all too often evolve into fatigue-clad replacements for the oppressors they overthrow. So it is a giant step from hating the warriors to hating the war, and an even greater step to deciding that the "enemy" is the abstract institution of war, which maintains its grip on us even in the interludes we know as peace.

The anti-war movements of the late twentieth century are admittedly feeble undertakings compared to that which they oppose. They are reactive and ad hoc, emerging, usually tardily, in response to particular wars, then ebbing to nothing in times of peace. They are fuzzy-minded, moralistic, and often committed to cartoonish theories of the sources of war—that it is a product of capitalism, for example, or testosterone or some similar flaw.

But for all their failings, anti-war movements should already have taught us one crucial lesson: that the passions we bring to war can be brought just as well to the struggle *against* war. There is a place for courage and solidarity and self-sacrifice other than in the service of this peculiarly bloody institution, this inhuman "meme"—a place for them in the struggle to shake ourselves free of it. I myself would be unable to imagine the passions of war if I had not, at various times in my life, linked arms with the men and women around me and marched up, singing or chanting, to the waiting line of armed and uniformed men.

And we will need all the courage we can muster. What we are called to is, in fact, a kind of war. We will need "armies," or at least networks of committed activists willing to act in concert when necessary, to oppose force with numbers, and passion with forbearance and reason. We will need leaders—not a handful of generals but huge numbers of individuals able to take the initiative to educate, inspire, and rally others. We will need strategies and cunning, ways of assessing the "enemy's" strength and sketching out the way ahead. And even with all that, the struggle will be enormously costly. Those who fight war on this war-ridden planet must prepare themselves to lose battle after battle and still fight on, to lose security, comfort, position, even life.

But what have all the millennia of warfare prepared us for, if not this Armageddon fought, once more, against a predator beast?

PHYLLIS AND ORLANDO RODRÍGUEZ

On the morning of September 11, 2001, Phyllis Rodríguez (b. 1943) returned home from an early walk along the Bronx River to find a frantic message on the answering machine from her son Greg: there had been a terrible accident at the World Trade Center where he worked, he was okay, please call his wife Elizabeth to tell her. Over the next few days, as it became clear that their son was not okay, not hurt or missing, but one of thousands killed in an act of terror, she and her husband Orlando (b. 1942) found the astonishing strength, in their grief, to speak out against the "direction of violent revenge" in which the nation seemed to be heading. In the letters that follow—the first written on September 14, the second a few days later, both circulated widely by email at the time—they foresaw the wars to come, and took their first steps to urge a different course. (Years before, their son had volunteered for CISPES, the Committee in Solidarity with the People of El Salvador, hoping to end the war there.)

The Rodríguez family has been working for peace ever since. Together, they helped to found September 11th Families for Peaceful Tomorrows, a group that seeks "to break the cycles of violence engendered by war and terrorism." Orlando, a professor of sociology and criminology at Fordham, has taught courses on "Global Conflict: War and Religion" and "Terrorism and Society." Phyllis has formed an unlikely friendship with Aïcha el-Wafi, mother of convicted Al Qaeda terrorist Zacarias Moussaoui, pleading at his trial that he be spared the death penalty. *In Our Son's Name*, a documentary about their journey, premiered in February 2015.

Not in Our Son's Name

TO THE NEW YORK TIMES

Our son Greg is among the many missing from the World Trade Center attack. Since we first heard the news, we have shared moments of grief, comfort, hope, despair, fond memories with his wife, the two families, our friends and neighbors, his loving colleagues at Cantor Fitzgerald / ESpeed, and all the grieving families that daily meet at the Pierre Hotel.

We see our hurt and anger reflected among everybody we meet. We cannot pay attention to the daily flow of news about this disaster. But we read enough of the news to sense that our government is heading in the direction of violent revenge, with the prospect of sons, daughters, parents, friends in distant lands dying, suffering, and nursing further grievances against us. It is not the way to go. It will not avenge our son's death. Not in our son's name.

Our son died a victim of an inhuman ideology. Our actions should not serve the same purpose. Let us grieve. Let us reflect and pray. Let us think about a rational response that brings real peace and justice to our world. But let us not as a nation add to the inhumanity of our times.

TO PRESIDENT GEORGE W. BUSH

Dear President Bush:

Our son is one of the victims of Tuesday's attack on the World Trade Center. We read about your response in the last few days and about the resolutions from both Houses, giving you undefined power to respond to the terror attacks.

Your response to this attack does not make us feel better about our son's death. It makes us feel worse. It makes us feel that our government is using our son's memory as a justification to cause suffering for other sons and parents in other lands.

It is not the first time that a person in your position has been given unlimited power and came to regret it. This is not the time for empty gestures to make us feel better. It is not the time to act like bullies. We urge you to think about how our government can develop peaceful, rational solutions to terrorism, solutions that do not sink us to the inhuman level of terrorists.

Sincerely,

Phyllis and Orlando Rodríguez

BARBARA LEE

Like Jeannette Rankin in 1941, Barbara Lee (b. 1946) in 2001 cast a lone vote in Congress against a popular war. (It cannot be coincidence that both votes were cast by women.) It was three days after the attacks of September 11, 2001, and Lee was opposing what was to become the war in Afghanistan, which despite its backers' confident expectations of quick success has become the longest war in American history. She was no rabble-rouser, but spoke on behalf of restraint and deliberation, explicitly recalling Wayne Morse's prophetic vote against the Tonkin Gulf Resolution in 1964. "I fear the consequences," she said, and like Morse she was justified. Like Rankin, she was called a traitor, and received enough death threats to be given police protection. Unlike Rankin she was not voted out of office, and remains the representative for California's thirteenth district.

Lee was born in Texas to a military family, moved to California, went as a single mother of two to Mills College, and then to Berkeley. Her entrance into politics was by way of the Black Panther Party; she volunteered at its Community Learning Center and worked on Bobby Seale's Oakland mayoral campaign in 1973. Later she served on Ron Dellums's staff and as a state legislator in California before entering the House in 1998, the first woman to represent what was then California's ninth district.

Speech on House Joint Resolution 64

Mr. Speaker, I rise today with a heavy heart, one that is filled with sorrow for the families and loved ones who were killed and injured in New York, Virginia, and Pennsylvania. Only the most foolish or the most callous would not understand the grief that has gripped the American people and millions across the world.

This unspeakable attack on the United States has forced me to rely on my moral compass, my conscience, and my God for direction.

September 11 changed the world. Our deepest fears now haunt us. Yet I am convinced that military action will not prevent further acts of international terrorism against the United States.

I know that this use-of-force resolution will pass although we all know that the President can wage a war even without this resolution. However difficult this vote may be, some of us must urge the use of restraint. There must be some of us who say, let's step back for a moment and think through the implications of our actions today—let us more fully understand its consequences.

We are not dealing with a conventional war. We cannot respond in a conventional manner. I do not want to see this spiral out of control. This crisis involves issues of national security, foreign policy, public safety, intelligence gathering, economics, and murder. Our response must be equally multi-faceted.

We must not rush to judgment. Far too many innocent people have already died. Our country is in mourning. If we rush to launch a counter-attack, we run too great a risk that women, children, and other non-combatants will be caught in the crossfire.

Nor can we let our justified anger over these outrageous acts by vicious murderers inflame prejudice against all Arab Americans, Muslims, Southeast Asians, or any other people because of their race, religion, or ethnicity.

Finally, we must be careful not to embark on an open-ended war with neither an exit strategy nor a focused target. We cannot repeat past mistakes.

In 1964, Congress gave President Lyndon Johnson the power to "take all necessary measures" to repel attacks and prevent further aggression. In so doing, this House abandoned its own constitutional responsibilities and launched our country into years of undeclared war in Vietnam.

At that time, Senator Wayne Morse, one of two lonely votes against the Tonkin Gulf Resolution, declared, "I believe that history will record that we have made a grave mistake in subverting and circumventing the Constitution of the United States. . . . I believe that within the next century, future generations will look with dismay and great disappointment upon a Congress which is now about to make such a historic mistake."

Senator Morse was correct, and I fear we make the same mistake today. And I fear the consequences.

I have agonized over this vote. But I came to grips with it in the very painful yet beautiful memorial service today at the National Cathedral. As a member of the clergy so eloquently said, "As we act, let us not become the evil that we deplore."

BARBARA KINGSOLVER

It has often been said that after the attacks of September 11, 2001, every American was in a state of post-traumatic stress. The attack on Pearl Harbor set a larger war in motion, and unlike the more recent attacks was launched by a state one could go to war with; but it took place far away from the centers of American power and vitality, and it took a year before newsreels presented an uncensored view of what had happened. The September 11 attacks, on the other hand, were played and replayed to the point that the images of the falling towers began to seem more real than the attacks that created them, and more devastating. The attacks were hard events to respond to, being in multiple ways unprecedented.

Barbara Kingsolver (b. 1955) stands out for her ability to find words for responding. In "A Pure, High Note of Anguish," published in the *Los Angeles Times* on September 23, she brings to bear a novelist's sense of mortality, a historian's sense of perspective, and a mother's desire to give direct answers to her child's questions. Like Barbara Lee, she was denounced as a traitor.

Kingsolver grew up in rural Kentucky, lived briefly in Congo, studied biology at DePauw (she was there on a music scholarship, as a pianist), and took part in antiwar protests there. Later she went to the University of Arizona and received an M.A. in ecology and evolutionary biology. She began her career as a science writer at that university, branched out to journalism, won a short story contest in a local newspaper, and was launched. Her first novel, *The Bean Trees*, was published in 1988, and her most famous one, *The Poisonwood Bible*, in 1998. She has also published poems and essays and a 2007 memoir of eating locally called *Animal, Vegetable, Miracle*; each book of hers published since 1993 has been on the *Times* best seller list.

A Pure, High Note of Anguish

Tucson—I want to do something to help right now. But I can't give blood (my hematocrit always runs too low), and I'm too far away to give anybody shelter or a drink of water. I can only give words. My verbal hemoglobin never seems to wane, so words are what I'll offer up in this time that asks of us the best citizenship we've ever mustered. I don't mean to say I have a cure. Answers to the main questions of the day—Where was that fourth plane headed? How did they get knives through security?—I don't know any of that. I have some answers, but only to the questions nobody is asking right now but my 5-year-old. Why did all those people die when they didn't do anything wrong? Will it happen to me? Is this the worst thing that's ever happened? Who were those children cheering that they showed for just a minute, and why were they glad? Please, will this ever, ever happen to me?

There are so many answers, and none: It is desperately painful to see people die without having done anything to deserve it, and yet this is how lives end nearly always. We get old or we don't, we get cancer, we starve, we are battered, we get on a plane thinking we're going home but never make it. There are blessings and wonders and horrific bad luck and no guarantees. We like to pretend life is different from that, more like a game we can actually win with the right strategy, but it isn't.

And, yes, it's the worst thing that's happened, but only this week. Two years ago, an earthquake in Turkey killed 17,000 people in a day, babies and mothers and businessmen, and not one of them did a thing to cause it. The November before that, a hurricane hit Honduras and Nicaragua and killed even more, buried whole villages and erased family lines and even now, people wake up there empty-handed. Which end of the world shall we talk about? Sixty years ago, Japanese airplanes bombed Navy boys who were sleeping on ships in gentle Pacific waters. Three and a half years later, American planes bombed a plaza in Japan where men and women were going to work, where schoolchildren were playing, and more humans died at once than anyone thought possible. Seventy thousand in a minute. Imagine. Then twice that many more, slowly, from the inside.

There are no worst days, it seems. Ten years ago, early on a January morning, bombs rained down from the sky and caused great buildings in the city of Baghdad to fall down—hotels, hospitals, palaces, buildings with mothers and soldiers inside—and here in the place I want to love best, I had to watch people cheering about it. In Baghdad, survivors shook their fists at the sky and said the word "evil." When many lives are lost all at once, people gather together and say words like "heinous" and "honor" and "revenge," presuming to make this awful moment stand apart somehow from the ways people die a little each day from sickness or hunger. They raise up their compatriots'

lives to a sacred place—we do this, all of us who are human—
thinking our own citizens to be more worthy of grief and less
willingly risked than lives on other soil. But broken hearts are
not mended in this ceremony, because, really, every life that
ends is utterly its own event—and also in some way it's the
same as all others, a light going out that ached to burn longer.
Even if you never had the chance to love the light that's gone,
you miss·it. You should. You bear this world and everything
that's wrong with it by holding life still precious, each time,
and starting over.

And those children dancing in the street? That is the hardest
question. We would rather discuss trails of evidence and whom
to stamp out, even the size and shape of the cage we might
put ourselves in to stay safe, than to mention the fact that our
nation is not universally beloved; we are also despised. And
not just by "The Terrorist," that lone, deranged non-man in
a bad photograph whose opinion we can clearly dismiss, but
by ordinary people in many lands. Even by little boys—whole
towns full of them it looked like—jumping for joy in school
shoes and pilled woolen sweaters.

There are a hundred ways to be a good citizen, and one of
them is to look finally at the things we don't want to see. In
a week of terrifying events, here is one awful, true thing that
hasn't much been mentioned: Some people believe our country
needed to learn how to hurt in this new way. This is such a
large lesson, so hatefully, wrongfully taught, but many people
before us have learned honest truths from wrongful deaths.
It still may be within our capacity of mercy to say this much
is true: We didn't really understand how it felt when citizens
were buried alive in Turkey or Nicaragua or Hiroshima. Or
that night in Baghdad. And we haven't cared enough for the
particular brothers and mothers taken down a limb or a life at
a time, for such a span of years that those little, briefly jubilant
boys have grown up with twisted hearts. How could we keep
raining down bombs and selling weapons, if we had? How
can our president still use that word "attack" so casually, like
a move in a checker game, now that we have awakened to see
that word in our own newspapers, used like this: Attack on
America.

Surely, the whole world grieves for us right now. And surely it also hopes we might have learned, from the taste of our own blood, that every war is both won and lost, and that loss is a pure, high note of anguish like a mother singing to any empty bed. The mortal citizens of a planet are praying right now that we will bear in mind, better than ever before, that no kind of bomb ever built will extinguish hatred.

"Will this happen to me?" is the wrong question, I'm sad to say. It always was.

BARACK OBAMA

As I write, Barack Obama (b. 1961) is nearing the end of his second term as president of the United States, and is among the most famous people on earth. In October 2002, though, when he delivered the speech against the Iraq War included here, he was just an Illinois state senator with a gift for oratory. Not a small gift, though. In a speech full of complex sentences and careful concessions (to the idea of just wars, to the fact of Saddam Hussein's brutality), his use of repetition is particularly effective; again and again, insistently, he returns to his fundamental argument against "dumb wars" and their unintended consequences.

Obama was born in Honolulu, spent part of his childhood in Indonesia (and Indonesian-language schools), went to Occidental College (where he made his first public speech, advocating that Occidental divest from South Africa) and Columbia. He worked for a while as a community organizer in Chicago, then went to Harvard Law School, where he became the first African American president of the *Harvard Law Review.* He taught at the University of Chicago Law School for twelve years and might have stayed in the academy, but he was also working on voter registration and civil rights litigation and in 1996 turned to elective politics. He spoke out against the Iraq War at a moment when he had no power except that of oratory to stop it; the local *Hyde Park Herald* was the only place his words appeared in print. Two years later he was elected United States senator from Illinois, and became a player on the national stage. He was awarded the Nobel Peace Prize in 2009.

Weighing the Costs of Waging War in Iraq

GOOD afternoon. Let me begin by saying that although this has been billed as an anti-war rally, I stand before you as someone who is not opposed to war in all circumstances.

The Civil War was one of the bloodiest in history, and yet it was only through the crucible of the sword, the sacrifice of multitudes, that we could begin to perfect this union, and drive the scourge of slavery from our soil.

I don't oppose all wars.

My grandfather signed up for a war the day after Pearl Harbor was bombed, fought in Patton's army. He saw the dead and dying across the fields of Europe; he heard the stories of fellow troops who first entered Auschwitz and Treblinka. He fought in the name of a larger freedom, part of that arsenal of democracy that triumphed over evil, and he did not fight in vain.

I don't oppose all wars.

After September 11th, after witnessing the carnage and destruction, the dust and the tears, I supported this Administration's pledge to hunt down and root out those who would slaughter innocents in the name of intolerance, and I would willingly take up arms myself to prevent such tragedy from happening again.

I don't oppose all wars. And I know that in this crowd today, there is no shortage of patriots or of patriotism.

What I am opposed to is a dumb war. What I am opposed to is a rash war. What I am opposed to is the cynical attempt by Richard Perle and Paul Wolfowitz and other armchair, weekend warriors in this Administration to shove their own ideological agendas down our throats, irrespective of the costs in lives lost and in hardships borne.

What I am opposed to is the attempt by political hacks like Karl Rove to distract us from a rise in the uninsured, a rise in the poverty rate, a drop in the median income—to distract us from corporate scandals and a stock market that has just gone through the worst month since the Great Depression.

That's what I'm opposed to. A dumb war. A rash war. A war based not on reason but on passion, not on principle but on politics.

Now let me be clear—I suffer no illusions about Saddam Hussein. He is a brutal man. A ruthless man. A man who butchers his own people to secure his own power. He has repeatedly defied UN resolutions, thwarted UN inspection teams, developed chemical and biological weapons and coveted nuclear capacity.

He's a bad guy. The world, and the Iraqi people, would be better off without him.

But I also know that Saddam poses no imminent and direct threat to the United States, or to his neighbors, that the Iraqi economy is in shambles, that the Iraqi military is a fraction of its former strength, and that in concert with the international community he can be contained until, in the way of all petty dictators, he falls away into the dustbin of history.

I know that even a successful war against Iraq will require a US occupation of undetermined length, at undetermined cost, with undetermined consequences.

I know that an invasion of Iraq without a clear rationale and without strong international support will only fan the flames of the Middle East, and encourage the worst, rather than best, impulses of the Arab world, and strengthen the recruitment arm of Al Qaeda.

I am not opposed to all wars. I'm opposed to dumb wars.

So for those of us who seek a more just and secure world for our children, let us send a clear message to the president today.

You want a fight, President Bush? Let's finish the fight with Bin Laden and Al Qaeda, through effective, coordinated intelligence and a shutting down of the financial networks that support terrorism, and a homeland security program that involves more than color-coded warnings.

You want a fight, President Bush? Let's fight to make sure that the UN inspectors can do their work, and that we vigorously enforce a non-proliferation treaty, and that former enemies and current allies like Russia safeguard and ultimately eliminate their stores of nuclear material, and that nations like Pakistan and India never use the terrible weapons already in their possession, and that the arms merchants in our own country stop feeding the countless wars that rage across the globe.

You want a fight, President Bush? Let's fight to make sure our so-called allies in the Middle East, the Saudis and the Egyptians, stop oppressing their own people, and suppressing dissent and tolerating corruption and inequality and mismanaging their economies so that their youth grow up without education, without prospects, without hope, the ready recruits of terrorist cells.

You want a fight, President Bush? Let's fight to wean ourselves off Middle East oil, through an energy policy that doesn't simply serve the interests of Exxon and Mobil.

Those are the battles that we need to fight. Those are the battles that we willingly join. The battles against ignorance and intolerance. Corruption and greed. Poverty and despair.

The consequences of war are dire, the sacrifices immeasurable. We may have occasion in our lifetime to once again rise up in defense of our freedom and pay the wages of war. But we ought not—we will not—travel down that hellish path blindly. Nor should we allow those who would march off and pay the ultimate sacrifice, who would prove the full measure of devotion with their blood, to make such an awful sacrifice in vain.

MAXINE HONG KINGSTON

In the summer of 1993, Maxine Hong Kingston (b. 1940) began a modest experiment that has become what she has called her "life's work." The widely lauded author of *The Woman Warrior* (1976), *China Men* (1980), and many other books—the first a winner of the National Book Critics Circle Award, the second of the National Book Award—Kingston was still haunted by "the problem of war" in her own family and in the world. (Her mother had survived the Japanese bombing of Canton [Guangzhou], and two of her brothers had served in Vietnam, one returning with severe PTSD.) So she invited local veterans to a workshop in Berkeley—"Reflective Writing, Mindfulness, and the War: A Day for Veterans & Their Families"—hoping to find community, heal wounds, and quite literally "write peace." The workshops continued and grew; other writers joined (including Grace Paley, represented in the present anthology); former enemies were invited (as Kingston describes here, in an excerpt from *The Fifth Book of Peace* [2003]); some of the results were published (in *Veterans of War, Veterans of Peace* in 2006). Kingston has opposed war in other ways—in 2003, for example, she was arrested with fellow writers Alice Walker and Terry Tempest Williams in a protest against the invasion of Iraq. But with these workshops, she has shown how writing can be more than for, against, or "about" war and peace: it can be a way of finding and making peace in itself.

FROM
The Fifth Book of Peace

THE writer veterans continued to meet season after season, year after year.

We had a gathering to which I invited Vietnamese veterans, from the North, Hanoi, to join us. It happened in October, near my birthday, fire season, fire weather. In the Tenth Month in Viet Nam, the dead come to the market place; you can visit them in the banyan tree. Vietnamese have Días de los Muertos too.

Earll, Lee Swenson, and I were parking our car under the eucalyptus trees at Mills College when another car, carrying Ho Anh Thai and Nguyen Qui Duc, pulled in next to us. All of us piled out of our cars, and effused friendliness, shaking hands, looking into faces, smiling. Ho Anh Thai, North Vietnamese, a slight man in a dark suit with a buttoned-up dark shirt, no tie, said quietly in English, "It is an honor to meet you, Mrs. Hong." Nguyen Qui Duc—or "Duc Nguyen, which Americans can remember better"—identified himself as translator, journalist, editor, writer, and Asian American. Thai and Duc could be from two different Asian races, Duc Nguyen a stolid young Chinese, and Ho Anh Thai Filipino. They're both very alert, listening hard. Lee and Earll walked with Thai between them to our plain classroom, where the tea and coffee and breakfast pastries were set up. I offered tea, the most polite thing to do in China. Maybe same-same Viet Nam. I made the tea for Ho Anh Thai, and served it to him with both hands. Some vets had gotten there even earlier than we had; they went up to each of the Vietnamese and introduced themselves. They must have felt relieved to speak American English fast with Duc, and to hear American naturally flow from his large square mouth.

George Evans and the writer and editor Wayne Karlin came in, escorting Le Minh Khue. She looked too young to have been in the U.S.–Viet Nam War. She does not speak English; she and I took each other's hands and held on. She smiled a slow, sweet smile but a sad smile, sad downturned eyes. I tried to say a lot with my eyes. I got her some tea.

I lined George's bus posters along the chalk trays—Dorothea Lange's photos, and poems by Wallace Stevens, Langston Hughes, Carl Sandburg, William Carlos Williams, Lorine Niedecker, Charles Reznikoff. More veterans entered, saw the Vietnamese—Khue easily seen, large features, long curly brown hair—and went over to meet them. Ann Marks, a peace activist who had gone alone to Viet Nam during the war, rushed for and grabbed Khue's attention, which annoyed some of the vets, that the FNG was taking over. I mobilized the organizing of the school chairs in a circle. It was long past the starting time that I'd scheduled. I kept walking to my place to sit down, but nobody followed my lead. I got up, tried again. I gestured with my hands and my whole body: welcome, sit. Wayne and George were unpacking and arranging books on the table. Most of our vets seated themselves, and still the guests were standing outside the circle. I wondered whether the Vietnamese felt as shy as they appeared. It must be scary to get into a ring of American veterans, the enemy who'd warred on them. I kept standing up, walking over to them and inviting them, gesturing, nodding, heading for the chairs; they nodded Yes-yes and smiled, and stayed standing there. Forgot all about the bell.

At last, they walked with George and Wayne into the circle and took their seats. They sat all in a row, not interspersed, as I would've liked.

Ellen Peskin invited the bell. Its peals faded into silence. Everyone composed himself or herself in attitudes of meditation or prayer. They landed. They folded their wings. Silence settled upon us, gathered us, held us. Worries, unexpressed, stilled. It did not matter that we did not speak the same language. We are not arguing. We are not shooting, bombing, booby-trapping one another. We are alive, breathing together. Nothing else needs to be done. This is it. This is peace. *Now* the war is over.

JONATHAN SCHELL

Jonathan Schell's book *The Unconquerable World: Power, Nonviolence, and the Will of the People* (2003), a vivid history of nonviolent civil resistance, attempts to understand how so many apparently impossible revolutions in the twentieth century, overthrowing and transforming apparently unshakeable dictatorships, took place largely without bloodshed. The explanation for him lies in the power of nonviolent civil resistance, a power so strong that he calls it, as his book's title indicates, "unconquerable." He sees in popular resistance what William James called "the moral equivalent of war . . . It was the equivalent of a third world war except in one particular—it was not a war." The book is represented here with an excerpt from a two-part summary of it that appeared in *Harper's* in 2003, under the title "No More unto the Breach."

Schell (1943–2014) grew up in New York, went to the Putney School and Harvard, then traveled to Vietnam as a war correspondent. He was twenty-four when he wrote *The Village of Ben Suc*—an extraordinary account, based on direct observation, of the American destruction of a "prosperous village of some thirty-five hundred people." (*The New Yorker* devoted an entire issue to it.) Other works on the Vietnam War followed, of broader scope, and were in their turn followed by still vaster and more ambitious works, notably *The Fate of the Earth* (1982), his exploration of our capacity to destroy the planet by nuclear weapons, and our unwillingness to relinquish it. That book was his most devastating indictment; *The Unconquerable World* was his most inspiring celebration.

FROM
No More unto the Breach

LIVING IN TRUTH

THE forms of political power that appeared in people's war had a further development. For most of history, military victory has been the royal road to political rule over a rival country, a sequence crystallized in the single word "conquest." It was the genius of the inventors of people's war to challenge this deceptively self-evident proposition by discovering, in the very midst of battle, the power of what they called politics. What if, the inventors of people's war had asked, those on the losing side declined to obey the invader even after conventional battlefield defeats? They showed that victory by this means was possible. In people's war, politics did not stand on its own; it was inter-woven with the military struggle into what Mao Zedong called a "seamless fabric." Yet Mao and others placed political orga-nization first in the order of importance and military action only second, and this ranking at least suggested the question of whether, if the fabric were unraveled, political action alone might thwart an occupying power. Did revolutions have to be violent? Could nonviolent revolution—that is, purely nonvio-lent revolution—succeed?

That was the utterly unexpected accomplishment of the activ-ists in Eastern Europe and the Soviet Union who pushed the Soviet empire into its grave. They in fact had an anti-imperial predecessor of whom, it appears, they were only dimly aware: Mohandas Karamchand Gandhi, leader of India's successful, nonviolent movement for independence from British rule. At the beginning of the century, when Gandhi was fighting for the rights of the Indian community in South Africa, he had thought deeply about the nature of political power and arrived at a conclusion. All government, he steadily believed, depends for its existence on the cooperation of the governed. If that cooperation were withdrawn, the government would be help-less. Government was composed of civil servants, soldiers, and citizens. Each of these people had a will. If enough of them refused to carry out its commands, it would fall. This idea had admittedly occurred to political thinkers in the past. The phi-losopher of the English Enlightenment David Hume likewise believed that all government, even tyranny, rested on a kind of support. "The soldan of Egypt, or the emperor of Rome," he wrote, "might drive his harmless subjects, like brute beasts, against their sentiments and inclination: but he must, at least, have led his *mamalukes*, or *praetorian bands*, like men, by their opinion." And James Madison once wrote, "All governments rest on opinion."

Gandhi, however, was the first to found upon this belief a thoroughgoing program of action and a new understanding of the relationship between violence and politics. The central role of consent in all government meant that noncooperation—the withdrawal of consent—was something more than a morally satisfying activity; it was a powerful weapon in the real world. He stated and restated the belief in many ways throughout his life:

> I believe, and everybody must grant that no Government can exist for a single moment without the cooperation of the people, willing or forced, and if people suddenly withdraw their cooperation in every detail, the Government will come to a standstill.

Gandhi's politics was not a politics of the moral gesture. It rested on an interpretation of political power and was an exercise of power—power that played a decisive role in ending British rule in India and, indeed, the British Empire in its entirety. From his surprising premises Gandhi drew a conclusion more surprising still:

> The causes that gave [the English] India enable them to retain it. Some Englishmen state that they took and they hold India by the sword. Both these statements are wrong. The sword is entirely useless for holding India. We alone keep them.

Gandhi does not merely say that English rule is made possible by Indian acquiescence; he goes a step further and charges that Indians "keep" the English, almost as if the English were struggling to get away and the Indians were pulling them back. His claim flew in the face of the one conviction on which everyone else in the imperial scheme, whether ruler or ruled, agreed—that, in the words of the London *Times*, it was "by the sword that we conquered India, and it is by the sword that we hold it." Some enthusiastically approved of this supremacy of the sword, some bowed to it, and some despised it, but only Gandhi denied that it was a fact. Not only, in Gandhi's thinking, was force not the final arbiter; it was no arbiter at all. What arbitrated was consent, and the cooperation and support that flowed from it, and these were the foundation of dictatorship as well as democratic government.

Many observers later claimed that Gandhi's movement could thrive only because in Britain he faced an imperial overlord that, although repressive in India, based its rule on consent and law at home. Faced with a totalitarian foe, they believed, nonviolent resistance would have been powerless. Certainly, if you believed that force was the final arbiter in political affairs, then no state had ever looked more thoroughly immune to challenge from within than the Soviet Union. The nuclear stalemate only seemed to add its pressure to the already crushing weight of totalitarian repression. As Václav Havel, the leader of Czech resistance to Soviet rule and until recently the president of the Czech Republic, wrote in his analysis of the Soviet empire, the "stalemated world of nuclear parity, of course . . . endows the system with an unprecedented degree of external stability." After Stalin's death, the Soviet ruling class congealed into the privilege- and status-hungry nomenklatura, the "new class," or "Red bourgeoisie." The historian Adam Ulam has aptly called their philosophy *immobilisme* and the state they ran a bureaucrats' paradise. A conviction, unknown perhaps since the days of the Roman Empire or certain dynasties of ancient China, took root that the current shape of things was likely to remain unchanged more or less forever.

And yet the universal conviction that Soviet rule could not be challenged from within proved wrong—stupendously wrong. The Cold War, frozen solid at the upper reaches of the world order, was in the lower reaches moving toward its denouement along unnoticed, circuitous pathways. Change, blocked in the time-tested arteries of military action, was forced into the world's unremarked-on capillary system, where, disregarded, it quietly advanced. And then it burst forth in mass resistance by entire societies. A politics so novel that one of its pioneers, the writer Gyorgy Konrád of Hungary, called it "Anti-politics," was about to initiate the downfall of an immense empire. The actors were, among others, workers on factory floors, rebellious students, intellectuals talking to one another over kitchen tables or "writing for the drawer," dissidents who were promptly dispatched to concentration camps, disaffected technocrats, and even bureaucrats in the state apparatus. Every step they took was ventured without a chart or a clear destination. Yet the revolution they made was peaceful, democratic, and thorough.

Until very late in the day, the Eastern European activists who initiated the process of the Soviet collapse did not envision even the downfall of their local, satellite governments, much less the downfall of the whole Soviet system. On the contrary, one of their greatest achievements in the late 1970s was to discover a way to fight for more modest, immediate goals without challenging the main structures of totalitarian power. Their ambition—itself widely condemned as utopian by Western observers—was merely to create zones of freedom, including free trade unions, within the Soviet framework. Activism, Havel said, should be directed at achieving immediate changes in daily life. He proposed what he called "living in truth," which consisted of an unshakable commitment to achieving modest, concrete goals in one's life and locality. "Defending the aims of life, defending humanity," he asserted, "is not only a more realistic approach, since it can begin right now and is potentially more popular because it concerns people's everyday lives; at the same time (and perhaps precisely because of this) it is also an incomparably more consistent approach because it aims at the very essence of things." In Poland in 1976 meanwhile, the activist Adam Michnik was explaining, "I believe that what sets today's opposition apart from the proponents of those ideas [of reform in the past] is the belief that a program for evolution ought to be addressed to an independent public, not to totalitarian power. Such a program should give directives to the people on how to behave, not to the powers on how to reform themselves."

Michnik's words fell on fertile ground. They anticipated (and helped to produce) a blossoming of civic and cultural activity in Poland. An early example was the Workers' Defense Committee. Its purpose was to give concrete assistance to workers in trouble with the authorities—assistance that the organization referred to as "social work." Aid was given to the families of workers jailed by the government. Independent, underground publications multiplied. A "flying university," which offered uncensored courses in people's apartments and other informal locations, was founded. Organizations devoted to social aims of all kinds—environmental, educational, artistic, legal— sprouted. In both form and content, these groups were precursors to the 10-million-strong Solidarity movement that arose in 1980. Of such was the stuff of revolution without violence.

For once the disintegration of totalitarian rule had begun in society, it turned out, to the surprise of its creators, to spread unstoppably to the satellite regimes, and from there, in new variations, to the heart of the empire, the Soviet Union. The contagion, which at every stage combined a longing for national self-determination with a longing for freedom, proceeded, in an unbroken progression from the Eastern European satellites to the peripheral republics of the union (in particular, Lithuania), and then to Moscow itself, where, under the leadership of its newly elected president, Boris Yeltsin, great Russia joined the company of rebels against the Soviet Union, which, lacking now any territory to call its own, melted into thin air. Seeking modest, limited change, the anti-Soviet activists found, to their own astonishment and everyone else's, that they had opened a new era in world history.

A NEW KIND OF POWER

That the nonviolence of the Soviet collapse was no historical fluke is indicated by the fact that both before and after that event dozens of other repressive regimes of every ideological coloration were ushered out of power by nonviolent processes. Nations in which this occurred include Greece, Portugal, Spain, the Philippines, South Korea, Argentina, Chile, Brazil, South Africa, Indonesia, and Serbia. Of equal importance, almost all of the governments founded by mainly nonviolent means were democratic. The liberal democratic revival of the late twentieth century, which has been celebrated and even over-celebrated by many writers, was at the same time a flowering of nonviolent action. By that unexpected means, the threads of liberal development that had been snapped by the global descent into violence in 1914 were picked up again in the century's final years.

No less striking is the historical inclination, which has also been commented on recently by many writers, of liberal democracies to refrain from war among themselves. The liberal democratic revival, however, must have a central place in any discussion of peacemaking for a reason that is deeper and more integral to the nature of this form of government. The goal of taming the violence endemic in human affairs has always been at the very core of the liberal program. To the degree that the ideal is realized, a country's constitution and its laws become a hugely ramified road map for the peaceful settlement of disputes, large and small. The liberal democratic state systematizes nonviolence. For if it is true, as the Romans said, that when arms speak the laws fall silent, it is equally true that when the laws speak arms fall silent. Otherwise, who would bother with laws? Every peaceable transfer of power in accord with the decision of an electorate is a coup d'état avoided. Every court case—however acrimonious the lawyers—is a possible vendetta or bloodbath averted. And so the spread of democracy, if it rests on a solid foundation, is an expansion of the zone in which the business of politics is conducted along mainly nonviolent lines. In this basic respect, the long march of liberal democracy is a "peace movement"—possibly the most important and successful of them all.

Thus in some parts of the world, at least, a beneficent cycle—a sort of cycle of nonviolence—had made a dramatic appearance. Peaceful revolution tended to produce peaceful rule (liberal democracy), which in turn has contributed to international peace. Even as, thanks to nuclear arms, the structures of war—the immemorial final arbiter—were being paralyzed, a new arbiter, a new kind of political power, was making its debut. It was the political power of people to resist oppressors and achieve self-rule, and it didn't flow from the barrel of a gun. Nor was the appearance of this force—let us call it cooperative power, as distinct from the coercive power of warfare and other violence—a marginal historical phenomenon. Political power is a capacity to decide something and make the decision stick in the realm of human affairs. In conventional wisdom, power has been equated with force. If you didn't use force you would lose, and therefore to shun force was to abdicate: to let the foe into your country, perhaps to destroy your town and kill your family; to dictate your faith; to rule over you; to determine the shape of the future. But in our era the bearers of superior force have, in an ever-widening sphere, failed to make their decisions stick. If force remained the essence of power and the final arbiter in politics, then the British today would rule India, the United States would preside over South Vietnam, the apartheid regime would survive in South Africa, the Communist Party would rule over the Soviet Union, and the Soviet Union would rule over Eastern Europe. That none of these things is the case testifies to the capacity of cooperative power to defeat superior force. The popular resistance that brought down the Berlin Wall was as historically consequential—as final an arbiter—as either of the two world wars. Has what William James called the "moral equivalent of war" ever been more clearly demonstrated? It ended Soviet Communism and with it the famous "specter" of "international communism." It finished off a great empire whose origins in fact predated the Communists by hundreds of years. It set in motion the creation of more than a dozen new countries. It was the equivalent of a third world war except in one particular—it was not a war.

ROBERT BYRD

Senator Robert Byrd (1917–2010) was eighty-five when he made the speech that follows, standing up on the floor of the Senate to oppose the Iraq War. He is the last of the political orators represented in this anthology, in a line running from William Lloyd Garrison to Byrd by way of Theodore Parker, Eugene Debs, and Barbara Lee; and in that group he is the courtliest, the most exquisitely formal, his evident distress at the impending war modulated by his patriotism and his senatorial code of courtesy. His argument is both patriotic—"today I weep for my country"—and practical—"this war will last many years and surely cost hundreds of billions of dollars." On the latter points he was not wrong.

Byrd grew up in coal-mining West Virginia and had all his schooling there; it was in West Virginia also, in the early 1940s, that Byrd founded a chapter of the Ku Klux Klan. Later he would filibuster the Civil Rights Act of 1964 and oppose the Voting Rights Act of 1965; still later he would repent these actions and dispositions of mind. It was a long distance he had traveled when he got up to make his great antiwar speech.

He was a shipyard welder during World War II, afterwards turning to politics, first local then national. He was elected to the House of Representatives, took night classes at American University to earn his J.D., and finally entered the Senate in 1958, serving there until his death and earning particular respect for his exquisite command of parliamentary procedure. He was also an accomplished country fiddler; mourners at his funeral paid tribute with a performance of the song "Take Me Home, Country Roads."

America's Image in the World

MADAM PRESIDENT, I believe in this great and beautiful country. I have studied its roots and gloried in the wisdom of its magnificent Constitution and its inimitable history. I have marveled at the wisdom of its Founders and Framers. Generation after generation of Americans has understood the lofty ideals that underlie our great Republic. I have been inspired by the story of their sacrifice and their strength.

But today I weep for my country. I have watched the events of recent months with a heavy, heavy heart.

No more is the image of America one of strong, yet benevolent peacekeeper. The image of America has changed. Around the globe, our friends mistrust us, our word is disputed, our intentions are questioned.

Instead of reasoning with those with whom we disagree, we demand obedience or threaten recrimination. Instead of isolating Saddam Hussein, we seem to have succeeded in isolating ourselves. We proclaim a new doctrine of preemption which is understood by few but feared by many. We say that the United States has the right to turn its firepower on any corner of the globe which might be suspect in the war on terrorism. We assert that right without the sanction of any international body. As a result, the world has become a much more dangerous place.

We flaunt our superpower status with arrogance. We treat U.N. Security Council members like ingrates who offend our princely dignity by lifting their heads from the carpet. Valuable alliances are split. After war has ended, the United States will have to rebuild much more than the country of Iraq. We will have to rebuild America's image around the globe.

The case this administration tries to make to justify its fixation with war is tainted by charges of falsified documents and circumstantial evidence. We cannot convince the world of the necessity of this war for one simple reason: This is not a war of necessity, but a war of choice.

There is no credible information to connect Saddam Hussein to 9/11, at least up to this point. The twin towers fell because a world-wide terrorist group, al Qaida, with cells in over 60 nations, struck at our wealth and our influence by turning our own planes into missiles, one of which would likely have slammed into the dome of this beautiful Capitol except for the brave sacrifice of some of the passengers who were on board that plane.

The brutality seen on September 11th and in other terrorist attacks we have witnessed around the globe is the violent and is desperate efforts by extremists to stop the daily encroachment of Western values upon their cultures. That is what we fight. It is a force not confined to territorial borders. It is a shadowy entity with many faces, many names, and many addresses.

But, this administration has directed all of the anger, fear, and grief which emerged from the ashes of the Twin Towers and the twisted metal of the Pentagon towards a tangible villain, one we can see and hate and attack. And villain he is. But he is the wrong villain. And this is the wrong war. If we attack Saddam Hussein, we will probably drive him from power. But the zeal of our friends to assist our global war on terrorism may have already taken flight.

The general unease surrounding this war is not just due to "orange alert." There is a pervasive sense of rush and risk and too many questions unanswered. How long will we be in Iraq? What will be the cost? What is the ultimate mission? How great is the danger at home?

A pall has fallen over the Senate Chamber. We avoid our solemn duty to debate the one topic on the minds of all Americans, even while scores of thousands of our sons and daughters faithfully do their duty in Iraq.

What is happening to this country—my country, your country, our country? When did we become a nation which ignores and berates our friends and calls them irrelevant? When did we decide to risk undermining international order by adopting a radical and doctrinaire approach to using our awesome military might? How can we abandon diplomatic efforts when the turmoil in the world cries out for diplomacy?

Why can this President not seem to see that America's true power lies not in its will to intimidate, but in its ability to inspire?

War appears inevitable. But I continue to hope that the cloud will lift. Perhaps Saddam will yet turn tail and run. Perhaps reason will somehow still prevail. I along with millions, scores of millions of Americans will pray for the safety of our troops, for the innocent civilians—women, children, babies, old and young, crippled, deformed, sick—in Iraq, and for the security of our homeland.

May God continue to bless the United States of America in the troubled days ahead, and may we somehow recapture the vision which for the present eludes us.

ZACK DE LA ROCHA

People my age, who were college students in the 1960s, often think that all the best protest songs were written back then. A false idea; more recent musicians are writing in different modes, but with no less energy or power to move people. As witness the songs of the Beastie Boys or John Mellencamp, and as witness in particular the collaboration between Zacharias Manuel de la Rocha (b. 1970), lead singer of Rage Against the Machine, and DJ Shadow (Joshua Paul Davis, b. 1972) to produce the angry, virtuosically rhymed, hard-driving rap song "March of Death," released on March 21, 2003, in protest—vain protest, as it turned out—against the imminent Iraq War. Anyone who wanted to hear the song could download it for free ("I'm releasing this song for anyone who is willing to listen," said de la Rocha in a statement accompanying it, a gesture of protest in itself against the economic rules of the music industry). Like a good many other antiwar songs of the period—Eminem's 2004 "Mosh" is another example—it is motivated both by opposition to the war and by a visceral dislike of then-President George W. Bush.

De la Rocha grew up in California, his father being a muralist and a member of the art collective Los Four. He was a performer even in elementary school, made his first reputation with Inside Out around 1988, turned to hip-hop in the early 1990s, and with Tom Morello formed Rage Against the Machine, one of the few politically engaged bands ever to get extensive airtime from both radio and MTV, just as de la Rocha himself is one of the few headline singers to have such fierce political commitments: against the Iraq War, on behalf of Leonard Peltier and Mumia Abu-Jamal (he made a speech about him at the UN), and above all on behalf of the Zapatistas of Mexico, whose flag has served as a backdrop for Rage concerts since their 2007 reunion.

DJ Shadow found his medium as quickly as de la Rocha found his, experimenting with a four-track recorder while still in high school; while a student at University of California–Davis he was working as a disc jockey, beginning to work out the innovative, "trip hop" sounds associated with the mixmaster he was to become.

March of Death

I was born with the voice of a riot, a storm
lightening the function, the form, far from the norm

I won't follow like cattle, I'm more like the catalyst
calm in the mix of battle
who let the cowboy on the saddle? He don't know a
missile from a gavel!
para terror troopin flippin loops of death upon innocent flesh
but i'm back in the cipher my foes and friends, with a verse
    and a pen
against a line I won't tow or defend, instead I curse at
    murderous men
in suits of professionals who act like animals
man child, ruthless and wild
who gonna chain this beast back on the leash?
this Texas fuhrer, for sure a, compassionless con who serve a
lethal needle to the poor, the cure for crime is murder?

on the left, left, right, left
but it's just a march of death

I read the news today, oh boy, a snap shot of a midnight ploy
vexed and powerless, devoured my hours I'm motionless with
    no rest
'cause a scream now holds the sky, under another high-tech
    driveby
a lie is a lie this God is an eagle or a condor for war nothing
    more
Islam peace, Islam stare into my eye brother please off our
    knees
to beef now we feed their disease, interlocked our hands
    across seas
what is a flag but a shroud out loud, and outside my window
    is a faceless crowd
'cause a cowering child just took her last breath, one snare in
    the march of death

on the left, left, right, left
but it's just a march of death

here it comes the sound of terror from above
he flex his Texas twisted tongue

the poor lined up to kill in desert slums
for oil that boil beneath the desert sun
now we spit flame to flip this game
we are his targets taking aim
we're the targets are taking aim
all his targets are taking aim

MINNIE BRUCE PRATT

"Driving the Bus: After the Anti-War March," first published in 2003, is only indirectly about the war; its focus is a loving portrait of the bus driver taking the protesters home. The protest they are returning from is in the background, getting three lines of the poem, and those being less vivid than the lines showing us the driver, her ordinary compassion and inevitable involvement in the consequences of war, when soldiers come home "cocked like guns, sometimes they blasted and / blew their own heads off, sometimes a woman's face," like the face of the driver's best friend.

Minnie Bruce Pratt (b. 1946) was born in Selma, graduated from a segregated high school, and entered the University of Alabama in Tuscaloosa a year after segregationist governor George Wallace had "stood in the schoolhouse door." She got her doctorate at Chapel Hill, worked as a grassroots organizer, taught at historically black universities, collaborated on lesbian-feminist projects with Barbara Smith and Audre Lorde and others, has published six books of poetry, and teaches at Syracuse University. She is the widow of the writer and activist Leslie Feinberg.

Driving the Bus: After the Anti-War March

We had a different driver on the way home. I sat
on the seat behind her, folded, feet up like a baby,
curled like a silent tongue in the dark jaw of the bus
until she flung us through a sharp curve and I fell.
Then we talked, looking straight ahead, the road
like a blackboard, one chalk line down the middle.
She said, nah, she didn't need a break, she was good
to the end. Eighteen hours back to home when
she was done, though. Fayetteville, North Carolina,
a long ways from here. The math of a mileage marker
glowed green. Was Niagara Falls near Buffalo? She'd
like to take her little girl some day, too little now, won't
remember. The driver speaks her daughter's name,
and the syllables ring like bells. I say I lived in her town
once, after another war. The boys we knew came home
men cocked like guns, sometimes they blasted and
blew their own heads off, sometimes a woman's face.

715

Like last summer in Fort Bragg, all those women dead.
She says, *One was my best friend*. Husband shot her
front of the children, boy and girl, six and eight. She calls
them every day, no matter where she is. They get very
upset if she doesn't call. Her voice breaks, her hands
correct the wheel, the bus pushes forward, erasing nothing.
There was a blue peace banner from her town today,
and we said stop the war, jobs instead, no more rich
men's factories, refineries, futures built on our broke bodies.
She said she couldn't go to the grave for a long time,
but she had some things to get right between them so
she stood there and spoke what was on her mind. Now
she takes the children to the grave, the little boy
he wants to go every week. She lightly touches and
turns the big steering wheel. Her hands spin
its huge circumference a few degrees here, then
there. She whirls it all the way around when she
needs to. Later I hear the crinkle of cellophane. She
is eating some peppermint candies to stay awake.

KENT JOHNSON

Parents who have read Margaret Wise Brown and Clement Hurd's *Goodnight Moon* (1947) to their children will experience Kent Johnson's "Baghdad," a bitter parody of that wonderful book, as an almost unbearable assault; everything that is orderly, gracious, and tranquil in the book is made jarring in the hallucinatory, war-ravaged Baghdad into which Johnson transposes it. But the transposition is what gives the poem its antiwar edge; war is what turns the beauty of the children's book into something monstrous, and on that count alone is to be opposed.

Johnson (b. 1955) has spent much of his life in Latin America; he taught in rural Nicaragua during the Sandinista revolution. He now lives in Freeport, Illinois, where he has been an instructor in English and Spanish at Highland Community College for the past twenty-five years. He has been a prolific and celebrated poet, editor, and translator, and a figure of some controversy in both literary and political circles; he published a book suggesting that Frank O'Hara's "A True Account of Talking to the Sun at Fire Island" had in fact been written by Kenneth Koch, and his *Lyric Poetry After Auschwitz: Eleven Submissions to the War* (2005) was among the first books of American poetry to confront the Afghanistan and Iraq Wars. "Baghdad" was first published in Sam Hamill's anthology *Poets Against the War* in 2003.

Baghdad

Oh, little crown of iron forged to likeness of imam's face,
what are you doing in this circle of flaming inspectors and
    bakers?

And little burnt dinner all set to be eaten
(and crispy girl all dressed with scarf for school),
what are you doing near this shovel for dung-digging,
hissing like ice-cubes in ruins of little museum?

And little shell of bank on which flakes of assets fall,
can't I still withdraw my bonds for baby?

Good night moon.
Good night socks and good night cuckoo clocks.

717

Good night little bedpans and a trough where once there was
    an inn
(urn of dashed pride),
what are you doing beside little wheelbarrow
beside some fried chickens?

And you, ridiculous wheels spinning on mailman's truck,
truck with ashes of letter from crispy girl all dressed with
    scarf for school,
why do you seem like American experimental poets going
    nowhere
on little exercise bikes?

Good night barbells and ballet dancer's shoes
under plastered ceilings of Saddam Music Hall.

Good night bladder of Helen Vendler and a jar from Tennessee.
(though what are these doing here in Baghdad?)

Good night blackened ibis and some keys.
Good night, good night.

(And little mosque popped open like a can, which same
    as factory of flypaper has blown outward, covering
    the shape of man with it (with mosque): He stumbles
    up Martyr's Promenade. What does it matter who is
    speaking, he murmurs and mutters, head a little bit on
    fire. Good night to you too.)

Good night moon.
Good night poor people who shall inherit the moon.

Good night first editions of Das Kapital, Novum Organum,
The Symbolic Affinities between Poetry Blogs and Oil Wells,
and the Koran.

Good night nobody.

Good night Mr. Kent, good night, for now you must
soon wake up and rub your eyes and know that you are dead.

BRIAN TURNER

Brian Turner (b. 1967) grew up and was educated in California and Oregon. He served in the Army, being deployed in 1999 and 2000 to Bosnia and Herzegovina and in 2003 to Iraq. *Here, Bullet* (2005), from which "Sadiq" comes, is based on his Iraq experiences, and won him the Beatrice Hawley Award.

"Sadiq" is a soldier's poem, knowing about the energies that animate and have animated soldiers in war, not asking the soldier to renounce those energies, to refuse to let them animate his or her destructive work, whether by the guns Turner used or the bows and arrows evoked in the Persian poet Sa'di's epigraph. What Turner asks is something else than not to kill, something less that is also something more: "it should break your heart to kill." A high standard to meet, and meeting it would get in the way of most wars.

Sadiq

It is a condition of wisdom in the archer to be,
patient because when the arrow leaves the bow, it
returns no more.

—SA'DI

It should make you shake and sweat,
nightmare you, strand you in a desert
of irrevocable desolation, the consequences
seared into the vein, no matter what adrenaline
feeds the muscle its courage, no matter
what god shines down on you, no matter
what crackling pain and anger
you carry in your fists, my friend,
it should break your heart to kill.

CAMILO MEJÍA

On March 15, 2004, having failed to return to his unit in Iraq, Staff Sergeant Camilo Mejía (b. 1975) publicly surrendered to military authorities and filed an application as a conscientious objector—among the first soldiers during the Iraq War to protest as he did. He would serve nine months in prison for desertion and receive a bad conduct discharge in the wake of his actions, and went on to oppose the war in every way he could, joining Veterans for Peace and Iraq Veterans Against the War and telling his story in *Road from ar Ramadi* (2007), a memoir of combat, doubt, and resistance.

Mejía had enlisted in the Army at nineteen against the wishes of his parents, his mother Maritza Castillo a recent immigrant from Nicaragua, and his father, who remained there, the famous Sandinista folk musician Carlos Mejía Godoy. At the time, the Army seemed to him to offer not only his best chance at higher education but a "place in the world." Eight years later, his contractual commitments to the National Guard extended by a wartime "stop-loss" order, he was called to active duty in Iraq. Though he had private doubts about the invasion from the beginning, he "didn't want to be labeled a coward," held his tongue, and served on the war's front lines for five months.

In the excerpt from his memoir that follows, Mejía begins to realize—in front of a roomful of angry Iraqi civilians—that he has the power to refuse his orders. He now lives in Coconut Grove, Florida, and works as a community organizer.

FROM

Road from ar Ramadi

THE friendliness of Iraqis brought me close to one man in particular, the manager of a propane station just west of our base, which the different company squads took turns guarding twenty-four hours a day. Guarding the station was a desired task for many soldiers of my unit because the employees there could help us get food, drinks, and ice from the city stores. Our squad even bought a TV set there. We could also use a satellite phone to call the States for two dollars a minute.

It was there that I became addicted to *tepsi*, an Iraqi stew made with eggplant and tomatoes, which was exquisite with rice or bread and perfect for a vegetarian like me. Other favorites among the troops were the shish kebabs and the baked chicken, eaten with flat bread and washed down with soda, or even beer—all of which could be bought from the station's employees.

But what I enjoyed most at the station was the companionship of its manager, whose name was Mohammed. A tall bearded man with light-colored skin, Mohammed had learned English at the university, where he had studied geology; we talked regularly and at length. Once we discussed the Holy Koran, a book of which I was completely ignorant. Mohammed explained to me that reading the sacred scripture was open to non-Muslims as long as they were clean when they read it.

"You really should take a shower before touching the Holy Koran," he told me. "But just wash your hands, and that should be enough for now, given the circumstances."

"Is it not *haram* for you to share the Koran with a Christian?" I asked him, using the Arabic word for sin.

"It would be *haram* if I didn't share it with you," he answered with a kind and honest smile. "You see, we as Muslims have a duty to spread the Holy Scripture. Whenever the opportunity presents itself, a good Muslim should always share the word; otherwise he is not doing his duty as a Muslim. As long as the people are willing to listen, a Muslim should always be willing to speak."

With that dialogue started a relationship I cherish to this day, although I have now lost touch with Mohammed. Many things that I learned from our conversations at the propane station have stayed with me. It was there that I discovered that Muslims have a deep respect for Jesus, not as the Messiah, but certainly as a valued prophet. The Virgin Mary is not only esteemed but also considered a good example of behavior and of devotion to God for Muslim women to emulate.

Mohammed was a Sunni Muslim who had worked for the Ba'ath party during Saddam's regime.

"I never much agreed with Saddam," he explained one day while we were drinking tea in his office. "But I didn't have much of a choice, especially as a geologist; I had to work for the government."

Although much of the food in ar Ramadi was cooked using wood, gas stoves were also commonplace. That meant many Ramadis had to go to Mohammed's station to get their propane. One day an elderly Shiite Muslim and his son showed up at the station to buy their gas. They were old friends of Mohammed, who did not miss the opportunity to introduce us.

"He wants to know why Americans treat Iraqis like dogs," asked Mohammed, translating for the old man.

"We don't mean to treat Iraqis like dogs," I responded. "But sometimes, when we're attacked, we have to respond, and that's when things happen."

I wasn't sure I believed my own words. Deep inside I probably didn't, but for some reason I felt like I had to defend the purpose of our presence there. The old man wasn't buying it, and he seemed pretty upset. His son, a man in his late thirties or early forties, stood with his arms crossed behind the couch where his father sat, staring at me with a serious look on his face. I glanced around the room and saw that everyone there was staring at me. Though I had taken off my helmet, I was still wearing all my gear, and I had a cup of tea in one hand and my rifle in the other. The grenades on my vest and belt made it hard for me to get comfortable. I felt as if I was being interrogated by a citizens' tribunal. Yet at no time during the whole conversation did I feel unsafe or threatened, only ashamed.

"He wants to tell you something that happened to him just last week," said Mohammed, as he and I both watched the old man lift up his robe to uncover a huge bruise he had on his left knee.

"What happened to him?" I asked.

"He says a group of men dropped into his property from helicopters," Mohammed translated. "They held everyone in the house at gunpoint until they left, taking him away to some U.S. Army base. He injured his knee when they threw him into the helicopter."

I noticed that there was a cane leaning up against the couch the man was sitting on. Every one else present remained silent as the old man spoke in Arabic, now and then pointing at his knee, and at his son, who still stood behind him but who let his father do all the talking.

"They interrogated him for a few days, until they finally let him go. The soldiers were from the U.S. Special Forces. They thought he was some insurgent leader," Mohammed continued. I wondered how they knew the soldiers were from the Special Forces. "They finally admitted their mistake and took him back to his home, but they never paid for any of the damage they did to the house."

The old man seemed really upset, and with reason, but part of me couldn't help thinking there must have been some justification for the soldiers' actions. And they had apologized and even taken the old man back to his family. As things looked to me then, it didn't seem unreasonable.

"Now it hurts when he walks," said Mohammed, looking at the cane.

"I'm really sorry that happened," I said, switching my attention between Mohammed and his Shiite friend. "We don't really want to be here."

"Oh, I know, I know," said Mohammed. "He is not upset with you, but he wants the American army to leave Iraq."

The conversation continued in that fashion, with complaints about U.S. brutality following rapidly, one after the next, in a way that made the argument that it was all an "unfortunate and isolated mistake" not only hard for them to accept but for me to use. These were educated men, especially the old man with the banged knee, who seemed to command respect even among the Sunnis, a majority of those present. It occurred to me that the deference shown to him stemmed not just from his wisdom and advanced years but also because he was perhaps some kind of religious eminence.

I felt as though I was present at a tribunal judging the American occupation, with me cast in the dual role of defense counsel and accused, and the elderly Shiite speaking on behalf of the entire Iraqi people. I didn't feel qualified to match my formidable opponent.

In spite of his anger about the occupation, the old Shiite did not descend to personal attacks on me, engaging instead in a dignified and elegant dialogue about Iraq's right to self-determination. Though he still seemed upset, he was very cordial to me as he left. Mohammed and I continued talking about Iraq and the U.S. occupation. At one point, pressed by

Mohammed's searching questions and having run out of other answers, I suggested to Mohammed that we were in Iraq to bring freedom to the country and its people.

"Freedom?" Mohammed looked at me, incredulous.

"Yes," I insisted with a straight face, not even believing my own words.

"But you said that you don't want to be here," pressed Mohammed, also with a straight face.

"I don't," I continued.

"And you said that your contract with the army was over," continued my friend, reminding me of something I had told him in the past.

"Yes, I said that," I admitted.

"Then why are you here?"

"Because the army can keep you in after the end of your contract," I explained, sensing where he was going with his questions. "At least if there is a war they can."

"Against your will?" he asked with his eyebrows raised.

"Yes," I said, quietly.

"So how can you bring freedom to us, when you don't have freedom for yourselves?"

I was unable to answer that question, but I remember thinking that Mohammed just didn't know how armies worked, even though I was aware he had been conscripted into the Iraqi army in his youth. Besides, neither freedom nor its absence had anything to do with my participation in a war that I had opposed from the outset. My misfortune was tied to a decision I had made at age nineteen when I signed a military contract and forfeited most of my rights. From that point on I had to push aside all other considerations—political, moral, and spiritual—in pursuit of whatever mission I was ordered to undertake. No, I kept telling myself, freedom had nothing to do with it.

But deep inside I felt differently. I knew that, in the end, no one could force me to do anything I didn't want to do. I knew I could say no to keeping prisoners on sleep deprivation, and to blocking ambulances on their way to the hospital. I could say no to senseless missions that put the lives of both soldiers and innocent civilians in unnecessary danger. I could assert my freedom and say no. The problem was that everyone else was doing what they were told, and the easiest thing was to keep my mouth shut and think that Mohammed just didn't understand. I hadn't just lost the freedom to think for myself as an individual with moral and spiritual values, independent from the military; I had also lost the freedom to accept the fact that I wasn't free.

ANDREW J. BACEVICH

"I Lost My Son to a War I Oppose," first published in *The Washington Post* on May 27, 2007, is among the saddest, angriest pieces in *War No More*. The saddest, because in it a father—the Vietnam veteran, career soldier, public intellectual, and self-described "Catholic conservative" Andrew J. Bacevich (b. 1947)—mourns the death of a son, First Lieutenant Andrew J. Bacevich Jr., killed by a suicide bomb in Iraq at twenty-seven. And angry at many: the Bush administration for capriciously launching an unwinnable war; the moneyed interests of the United States and those who support them, Republicans and Democrats alike, because the money power "maintains the Republican/Democratic duopoly of trivialized politics"; and himself, most laceratingly, because, he writes, "while [my son] was giving his all, I was doing nothing. In this way, I failed him." (In an email to me, Bacevich noted that his own title for the piece had been "A Father's Responsibility.")

I Lost My Son to a War I Oppose. We Were Both Doing Our Duty

Parents who lose children, whether through accident or illness, inevitably wonder what they could have done to prevent their loss. When my son was killed in Iraq earlier this month at age 27, I found myself pondering my responsibility for his death.

Among the hundreds of messages that my wife and I have received, two bore directly on this question. Both held me personally culpable, insisting that my public opposition to the war had provided aid and comfort to the enemy. Each said that my son's death came as a direct result of my antiwar writings.

This may seem a vile accusation to lay against a grieving father. But in fact, it has become a staple of American political discourse, repeated endlessly by those keen to allow President Bush a free hand in waging his war. By encouraging "the terrorists," opponents of the Iraq conflict increase the risk to U.S. troops. Although the First Amendment protects antiwar critics from being tried for treason, it provides no protection for the hardly less serious charge of failing to support the troops—today's civic equivalent of dereliction of duty.

What exactly is a father's duty when his son is sent into harm's way?

Among the many ways to answer that question, mine was this one: As my son was doing his utmost to be a good soldier, I strove to be a good citizen.

As a citizen, I have tried since Sept. 11, 2001, to promote a critical understanding of U.S. foreign policy. I know that even now, people of good will find much to admire in Bush's response to that awful day. They applaud his doctrine of preventive war. They endorse his crusade to spread democracy across the Muslim world and to eliminate tyranny from the face of the Earth. They insist not only that his decision to invade Iraq in 2003 was correct but that the war there can still be won. Some—the members of "the-surge-is-already-working" school of thought—even profess to see victory just over the horizon.

I believe that such notions are dead wrong and doomed to fail. In books, articles and op-ed pieces, in talks to audiences large and small, I have said as much. "The long war is an unwinnable one," I wrote in this section of *The Washington Post* in August 2005. "The United States needs to liquidate its presence in Iraq, placing the onus on Iraqis to decide their fate and creating the space for other regional powers to assist in brokering a political settlement. We've done all that we can do."

Not for a second did I expect my own efforts to make a difference. But I did nurse the hope that my voice might combine with those of others—teachers, writers, activists and ordinary folks—to educate the public about the folly of the course on which the nation has embarked. I hoped that those efforts might produce a political climate conducive to change. I genuinely believed that if the people spoke, our leaders in Washington would listen and respond.

This, I can now see, was an illusion.

The people have spoken, and nothing of substance has changed. The November 2006 midterm elections signified an unambiguous repudiation of the policies that landed us in our present predicament. But half a year later, the war continues, with no end in sight. Indeed, by sending more troops to Iraq (and by extending the tours of those, like my son, who were already there), Bush has signaled his complete disregard for what was once quaintly referred to as "the will of the people."

To be fair, responsibility for the war's continuation now rests no less with the Democrats who control Congress than with the president and his party. After my son's death, my state's senators, Edward M. Kennedy and John F. Kerry, telephoned to express their condolences. Stephen F. Lynch, our congressman, attended my son's wake. Kerry was present for the funeral Mass. My family and I greatly appreciated such gestures. But when I suggested to each of them the necessity of ending the war, I got the brushoff. More accurately, after ever so briefly pretending to listen, each treated me to a convoluted explanation that said in essence: Don't blame me.

To whom do Kennedy, Kerry and Lynch listen? We know the answer: to the same people who have the ear of George W. Bush and Karl Rove—namely, wealthy individuals and institutions.

Money buys access and influence. Money greases the process that will yield us a new president in 2008. When it comes to Iraq, money ensures that the concerns of big business, big oil, bellicose evangelicals and Middle East allies gain a hearing. By comparison, the lives of U.S. soldiers figure as an afterthought.

Memorial Day orators will say that a G.I.'s life is priceless. Don't believe it. I know what value the U.S. government assigns to a soldier's life: I've been handed the check. It's roughly what the Yankees will pay Roger Clemens per inning once he starts pitching next month.

Money maintains the Republican/Democratic duopoly of trivialized politics. It confines the debate over U.S. policy to well-hewn channels. It preserves intact the cliches of 1933–45 about isolationism, appeasement and the nation's call to "global leadership." It inhibits any serious accounting of exactly how much our misadventure in Iraq is costing. It ignores completely the question of who actually pays. It negates democracy, rendering free speech little more than a means of recording dissent.

This is not some great conspiracy. It's the way our system works.

In joining the Army, my son was following in his father's footsteps: Before he was born, I had served in Vietnam. As military officers, we shared an ironic kinship of sorts, each of us demonstrating a peculiar knack for picking the wrong war at the wrong time. Yet he was the better soldier—brave and steadfast and irrepressible.

I know that my son did his best to serve our country. Through my own opposition to a profoundly misguided war, I thought I was doing the same. In fact, while he was giving his all, I was doing nothing. In this way, I failed him.

PHILIP METRES

Philip Metres (b. 1970), currently professor of English at John Carroll University in Cleveland, has distinguished himself not only as a poet and antiwar activist but as a scholar and anthologist of antiwar poetry in books like *Behind the Lines: War Resistance Poetry on the American Homefront Since 1941* (2007) and *Come Together, Imagine Peace* (2008). "For the Fifty (Who Made PEACE with Their Bodies)," first published in his collection *To See the Earth* (2008), lyrically documents one of the more memorable peace protests of the new millennium, "Baring Witness": on November 12, 2002, in Marin County, California, a group of women spelled out PEACE, lying naked in a grassy field, to send a message about the impending invasion of Iraq.

Even in the digital age we chiefly make antiwar action with our bodies, and few antiwar poems do greater justice to the body, its expressive capacities and vulnerabilities, than does Metres's poem. "Baring Witness," conceived by seventy-two-year-old artist and environmental activist Donna Oehm Sheehan, grew into an international movement, tens of thousands spelling out similar messages in many languages across the globe—even in Antarctica, where protesters wore red parkas.

For the Fifty (Who Made PEACE with Their Bodies)

I.

In the green beginning,
    in the morning mist,
        they emerge from their chrysalis

of clothes: peel off purses & cells,
    slacks & Gap sweats, turtle-
        necks & tanks, Tommy's & Salvation

Army, platforms & clogs,
    abandoning bras & lingerie, labels
        & names, courtesies & shames,

the emperor's rhetoric of defense,
    laying it down, their child-
        stretched or still-taut flesh

giddy in sudden proximity,
    onto the cold earth: bodies fetal or supine,
        as if come-hithering

or dead, wriggle on the grass to form
    the shape of a word yet to come, almost
        embarrassing to name: a word

thicker, heavier than the rolled rags
    of their bodies seen from a cockpit:
        they touch to make

the word they want to become:
    it's difficult to get the news
        from our bodies, yet people die each day

for lack of what is found there:
    here: the fifty hold, & still
        to become a testament, a will,

embody something outside
    themselves & themselves: the body,
        the dreaming disarmed body.

2.

And if the exposed
    flesh of women spells,
        as they stretch prone, a word

they wish the world
    might wear, the tenderness
        of unbruised skin, juice

of itself unsipped? And then?
    Here, where flesh is marked
        & measured in market

scales of the ogler's eyes,
    will they fall, cast down
        to their own odd armor,

or gloat on the novel glut
    of flesh, the body commodity
        no Godiva can set free?

But what if unbuffed generals,
    grandfathers unashamed, stood
        before camera's judgment,

vulnerables genuflecting
    to the cold, their sag noses
        shying from all eyes—

unjockstrapped, uncupped,
    an offering of useless nipples
        & old maps of animal fur

tracing their chests? It's no use.
    Shoot out the lights, suture
        the lids, & trace with fingertips

the blind-dark rooms
    of what we are, houses
        of breath, sheltered & unshelled.

AUSTIN SMITH

In a letter to me, Austin Smith (b. 1982) characterized "That Particular Village" vividly and candidly: "I realized I hadn't shared my angriest antiwar poem with you. I'm not sure it's a good poem, but it sure is angry. I'll paste it below for the hell of it." I wrote back that I liked the anger and didn't think it hampered the poem—for all its anger at then–Secretary of Defense Donald Rumsfeld for his unwillingness to deal with the painful particulars of the Iraq War, it is a poem of considerable imaginative range, exploring Rumsfeld's sensibility knowingly and sometimes sympathetically. The poem has not been published elsewhere.

Asked for a short sketch of his life, Smith responded as follows: "Austin Smith grew up on a farm in northwestern Illinois. His first collection of poems, *Almanac* (2013), was chosen by Paul Muldoon for the Princeton Series of Contemporary Poets. He is currently a Jones Lecturer in fiction at Stanford University, and thinks officials in the U.S. government should read more Thomas Merton, paying particular attention to this passage: 'Do not think yourself better because you burn up friends and enemies with long-range missiles without ever seeing what you have done.'"

That Particular Village

"On October 22nd and 23rd, 2002, U.S. warplanes strafed the farming village of Chowkar-Karez, twenty-five miles north of Kandahar, killing at least ninety-three civilians. When asked about the incident at Chowkar, Secretary of Defense Donald Rumsfeld said, 'I cannot deal with that particular village . . .'"

> Look, here's the thing. I can deal with that
> particular village about as well today
> as I could deal with it yesterday, which is
> to say, I cannot deal with that particular
> village at all. Other villages I can deal with,
> have dealt with and will deal with in the future,
> but not that particular village. Look, think
> of the situation I'm in like this: I'm a tightrope
> walker in a circus tent in a prairie town in 1911.
> I perform with my wife and without a net.

Unbeknownst to me my wife, who happens
to be a very beautiful woman, has fallen
in love with the tiger tamer. On this night,
while walking the tightrope towards her
where she stands on the platform, I see
she has a big pair of golden garden shears
and she's preparing to cut the rope. Tell me,
what do I do? If I start to scream,
she'll cut the rope. If I say nothing,
she'll cut the rope. I can't deal with that
village in particular because I really
have to try and focus on sinking this
putt. I can't deal with it today because
tomorrow I'm flying to Chicago to participate
in the Associated Writing Programs Conference.
I've been invited to appear on a panel called:
"Tangled Umbilical: What We Can Learn
From Paying Attention to Syntax in Political
Discourse and How We Can Use It to Write Better
Flash Fiction." I can't deal with that particular
village because I was born in 1932. I cannot
deal with it today or yesterday because
my senior thesis at Princeton was entitled
"The Steel Seizure Case of 1952 and Its Effect
on Presidential Powers." I can't deal with it
because I have three children and six grand
children none of whom will have to go
to the holy wars. I can't deal with that village,
that particular village, right now because I live
in Mount Misery, the former plantation
house where a young Frederick Douglass
was sent to have his teen spirit broken
by the brutal slaveholder Edward Covey.
I can't because one day, after being beaten
many times by his master, Douglass fought
off Covey's cousin and then Covey himself
in the very yard where my wife grows camellias.
I can't because Douglass was never assaulted
by Covey again. I can't deal with that particular
village in this life nor shall I be made to answer for

what happened there in the next. Certain things
about my past make it impossible for me
to deal with it: when I was little I was an Eagle
Scout, I wrestled in high school, I didn't graduate
from Georgetown Law. Nixon called me
a ruthless little bastard. I sold the company
I was CEO of to Monsanto for $12 million.
I cannot deal with that particular village.
I can't deal with it because once upon a time
I delivered a few pistols, some medieval
spiked hammers, and a pair of golden cowboy
boots to Saddam Hussein on behalf of
President Reagan. I can't deal with it because
a few years ago I had to make a special trip
to Abu Graib to personally turn the volume
of a Bach symphony up to make a man's ears
bleed more profusely. I can't deal because
on the afternoon of September 11th an aide
scribbled down in shorthand what I was
saying on the phone: "Best info fast—
Judge whether good enough hit Saddam
at same time—not only Bin Laden—
Need to move swiftly—Near term target
needs—go massive—sweep it all up
—Things related and not." I can't . . . Look . . .
That particular village? That particular one.

NICHOLSON BAKER

Nicholson Baker (b. 1957) is one of the few distinguished novelists who is also a committed pacifist, and vice versa. Perhaps the small number of people inhabiting both categories is simply a consequence of how few committed pacifists there are; perhaps it suggests a tension between the two commitments, the two modes of living a life. Certainly some writers distrust fixed political positions—T. S. Eliot famously wrote of Henry James that he had a mind so fine that no idea could violate it—and certainly some engaged in political struggles have had little time for the subtleties of art. Baker is in that context one of the great, fruitful anomalies.

Baker's literary work is varied and often surprising. It includes essays denouncing libraries for destroying books and newspapers and card catalogs (in 1999 he established the American Newspaper Repository, to rescue endangered newspapers), abundant contributions to Wikipedia, novels about an escalator ride and John Updike and phone sex and attempts to assassinate President George W. Bush. It is on the whole remote from political questions, or at least seems not to bear on them directly.

But one of his gifts as a novelist, his capacity to absorb and be absorbed in particulars, is also what gives his political writing its distinctive energy. *Human Smoke* (2008), his unique history of the lead-up to, the resistance to, and the beginnings of World War II, is composed of vignettes, concrete and evocative, many of them taken from the newspapers he has worked so hard to preserve. If it is, as pacifist Kathy Kelly likes to say, the job of a pacifist to be concrete, then Baker has worked harder than most pacifists to meet that standard. ("Treat every murder in a war as a separate event," he said in an interview.) And the piece included here, Baker's response to the harsh critiques *Human Smoke* received, notably one by *The Nation*'s Katha Pollitt, is also notable for its specificity, its evocation of particular people in particular situations making particular choices. (It appeared in *Harper's* in May 2011.)

Baker was born in New York City, got drawing lessons from his Quaker art-instructor mother, studied at the Eastman School of Music (he was a bassoonist and wanted to be a composer) and Haverford College, then worked for a while on Wall Street. He had stories published by *The New Yorker* and *The Atlantic* when he was twenty-three, and just continued writing, never holding an academic job or a staff position at a magazine, just writing. Martin Amis said of him that "throughout his corpus there is barely an ordinary sentence or an ungenerous thought."

Why I'm a Pacifist: The Dangerous Myth of the Good War

Six months after the Japanese attack on Pearl Harbor, Abraham Kaufman, the executive secretary of the War Resisters League, stood up in the auditorium of the Union Methodist Church in Manhattan and said something that was difficult to say. Kaufman, a man of thirty-three who had put himself through City College at night and had worked Sundays selling magazines and candy in a subway station, insisted that we needed peace now—and that to get peace now, we needed to negotiate with Hitler. "This tremendous war can be ended by just one small spark of truth and sanity," he said.

To those who argued that you couldn't negotiate with Hitler, Kaufman replied that the Allies were already negotiating with Hitler, and with Japan too—over prisoners of war, for example, and the sending of food to Greece. It was important to confer *right away*, Kaufman believed, before either side had lost. Our aim should be what Woodrow Wilson had hoped for at the end of the First World War: a peace without victory. "We ask for peace now," Kaufman said, "while there is still a world to discuss aims, not when it is too late."

What explained Kaufman's urgency? It was simple: he didn't want any more people to suffer and die. Civilian massacres and military horrors were reported daily, and Kaufman feared that the war would prove to be, as he'd written to the *New York Times* two years earlier, "so disastrous as to make the 1917 adventure seem quite mild." He understood exactly what was at stake. In his view, a negotiated peace with Hitler was, paradoxically, the best chance the Allies had of protecting the world from Hitler's last-ditch, exterminative frenzy.

Kaufman was one of a surprisingly vocal group of World War II pacifists—absolute pacifists, who were opposed to any war service. They weren't, all of them, against personal or familial self-defense, or against law enforcement. But they did hold that war was, in the words of the British pacifist and parliamentarian Arthur Ponsonby, "a monster born of hypocrisy, fed on falsehood, fattened on humbug, kept alive by superstition, directed to the death and torture of millions, succeeding in no high purpose, degrading to humanity, endangering civilization and bringing forth in its travail a hideous brood of strife, conflict and war, more war." Along with Kaufman and Ponsonby—and thousands of conscientious objectors who spent time in jail, in rural work camps, in hospitals, or in controlled starvation studies—the ranks of wartime pacifists included Vera Brittain, Rabbi Abraham Cronbach, Dorothy Day, and Jessie Wallace Hughan.

I admire these people. They believed in acts of mercy rather than in fist-shaking vows of retribution. They kept their minds on who was actually in trouble. They suffered, some in small ways, some in large, for what they did and said. They were, I think, beautiful examples of what it means to be human. I don't expect you to agree, necessarily, that they were right in their principled opposition to that enormous war—the war that Hitler began—but I do think you will want to take their position seriously, and see for yourself whether there was some wisdom in it.

Praising pacifists—using the P-word in any positive way, but especially in connection with the Second World War—embarrasses some people, and it makes some people angry. I found this out in 2008, when I published a book about the beginnings of the war. *Human Smoke* was a mosaic of contradictory fragments and moments in time, composed largely of quotations: it made no direct arguments on behalf of any single interpretation of World War II. But in an afterword, I dedicated the book to the memory of Clarence Pickett—a Quaker relief worker—and other British and American pacifists, because I was moved by what they'd tried to do. "They tried to save Jewish refugees," I wrote, "feed Europe, reconcile the United States and Japan, and stop the war from happening. They failed, but they were right."

They were *what*? In a review in *The Nation*, Katha Pollitt said she pored over my book obsessively, for hours at a time— and she hated it. "By the time I finished," she wrote, "I felt something I had never felt before: fury at pacifists." Pollitt's displeasure hurt, as negative reviews from thoughtful readers generally do. But I still think the pacifists of World War II were right. In fact, the more I learn about the war, the more I understand that the pacifists were the only ones, during a time of catastrophic violence, who repeatedly put forward proposals that had any chance of saving a threatened people. They weren't naïve, they weren't unrealistic—they were psychologically acute realists.

Who was in trouble in Europe? Jews were, of course. Hitler had, from the very beginning of his political career, fantasized publicly about killing Jews. They must go, he said, they must be wiped out—he said so in the 1920s, he said so in the 1930s, he said so throughout the war (when they were in fact being wiped out), and in his bunker in 1945, with a cyanide pill and a pistol in front of him, his hands shaking from Parkinson's, he closed his last will and testament with a final paranoid expostulation, condemning "the universal poisoner of all peoples, international Jewry."

Throughout Hitler's tenure, then, the question for the rest of the world was how to respond to a man who was (a) violent; (b) highly irrational; (c) vehemently racist; (d) professedly suicidal; and (e) in charge of an expanding empire. One possibility was to build weapons and raise armies, make demands, and threaten sanctions, embargoes, and other punishments. If Hitler failed to comply, we could say, "This has gone too far," and declare war.

Pacifists thought this was precisely the wrong response. "The Government took the one course which I foresaw at the time would strengthen Hitler: they declared war on Germany," Arthur Ponsonby said in the House of Lords in 1940. The novelist Vera Brittain, who published a biweekly *Letter to Peace Lovers* in London, agreed. "Nazism thrives, as we see repeatedly, on every policy which provokes resistance, such as bombing, blockade, and threats of 'retribution,'" she wrote in her masterful 1942 polemic, *Humiliation with Honour.*

The Jews needed immigration visas, not Flying Fortresses. And who was doing their best to get them visas, as well as food, money, and hiding places? Pacifists were. Bertha Bracey helped arrange the *Kindertransport*, for example, which saved the lives of some 10,000 Jewish children; Runham Brown and Grace Beaton of the War Resisters International organized the release of Jews and other political prisoners from Dachau and Buchenwald; and André Trocmé and Burns Chalmers hid Jewish children among families in the South of France.

"We've got to fight Hitlerism" sounds good, because Hitler was so self-evidently horrible. But what fighting Hitlerism meant in practice was, largely, the five-year-long Churchillian experiment of undermining German "morale" by dropping magnesium firebombs and 2,000-pound blockbusters on various city centers. The firebombing killed and displaced a great many innocent people—including Jews in hiding—and obliterated entire neighborhoods. It was supposed to cause an anti-Nazi revolution, but it didn't. "The victims are stunned, exhausted, apathetic, absorbed in the immediate tasks of finding food and shelter," wrote Brittain in 1944. "But when they recover, who can doubt that there will be, among the majority at any rate, the desire for revenge and a hardening process—even if, for a time, it may be subdued by fear?" If you drop things on people's heads, they get angry and unite behind their leader. This was, after all, just what had happened during the Blitz in London.

"Even so," you may say, "I don't like the word 'pacifist.' If somebody came after me or someone I loved, I'd grab a baseball bat, or a gun, and I'd fight him off." Of course you would. I would, too. In fact, that's exactly what I said in college to my girlfriend—who's now my wife—when she announced that she was a pacifist. I also said, What about Hitler?

She made two observations: that her father had served in World War II and had come back a pacifist, and that sending off a lot of eighteen-year-old boys to kill and wound other eighteen-year-old boys wasn't the way to oppose Hitler. I said, Well, what other way was there? Nonviolent resistance, she replied. I wasn't persuaded. Still, her willingness to defend her position made a permanent notch, an opening, in my ethical sense.

Next came my brief, insufferable Young Republican phase. For a year, just out of college, I worked on Wall Street, at a company called L. F. Rothschild, Unterberg, Towbin. (They're gone now.) I became a confused but cocky neoconservative. I subscribed to *Commentary*, enthralled by its brilliant pugnacity.

I read F. A. Hayek, Irving Kristol, Jeane Kirkpatrick, Karl Popper, Robert Nozick, and Edmund Burke.

I wasn't interested in wars, because wars are sad and wasteful and miserable-making, and battleships and gold epaulettes are ridiculous. But I was excited by the notion of free markets, by the information-conveying subtlety of daily price adjustments, and I thought, Heck, if *Commentary* is right about F. A. Hayek, maybe they're right about fighting Communism too. Surely we had to have hardened missile silos and Star Wars satellites and battalions of Abrams tanks. And the winning of World War II was unquestionably a plume in our cap, was it not? We'd stepped into the fray; we'd turned the tide of battle. At that point I put aside political thought altogether. It was beyond me. Its prose was bad. I concentrated on writing about what struck me as funny and true.

Then came the Gulf War. I'd just finished writing an upbeat novel about phone sex. My wife and I watched Operation Desert Storm on TV, while it was actually happening. Peter Arnett and Bernard Shaw were up on the roof of the Hotel Al-Rasheed in Baghdad. We saw the tracer fire sprout up over that enormous complicated green city with its ancient name, and we saw the slow toppling of the communication tower, which looked like Seattle's Space Needle, and then, within hours (or so I remember it), we were shown grainy black-and-white clips of precision-guided bombs as they descended toward things that looked like blank, cast-concrete bunkers. Soundless explosions followed. Wolf Blitzer seemed unfazed by it all.

I thought: People are probably dying down there. They can't not be. There was something awful in being able to witness feats of violent urban destruction as they unfolded—to know that big things that had been unbroken were now broken, and that human beings were mutilated and moaning who had been whole—and to comprehend that I was, simply by virtue of being a compliant part of my country's tax base, paying for all this unjustifiable, night-visioned havoc.

Afterward we learned that those early "surgical" strikes had gone astray, some of them, and had killed and wounded large numbers of civilians. We also learned that there were many thousands of bombing runs, or "sorties"—such a clean-sounding word—and that only about 10 percent of the flights had employed "smart" weaponry. Most of the bombing of Iraq in those years, it turned out, was just as blind and dumb as the carpet bombings of World War II. There was, however, a new type of incendiary weapon in use: depleted-uranium shells, fired from Gatling guns and helicopter gunships, which became unstoppably heavy burning spears that vaporized metal on contact, leaving behind a wind-borne dust that some said caused birth defects and cancers. Then came the medical blockade, years of it, and punitive bombings. What President Bush began, President Clinton continued. I thought, No, I'm sorry, this makes no sense. I don't care what *Commentary* says: this is not right.

Later still, I saw a documentary on PBS called *America and the Holocaust: Deceit and Indifference*, about the State Department's despicable blockage of visas for Jewish refugees, which permanently broke my trust in Franklin Roosevelt. Then Bill Clinton's Air Force bombed Belgrade. They used the BLU-114/B "soft-bomb," which flung a fettuccine of short-circuiting filaments over power stations in order to bring on massive blackouts, and they also dropped a lot of conventional explosives from high altitudes, killing hundreds of people. And then, in 2002, we bombed Afghanistan, using 15,000-pound "daisy cutters," and killed more people; and then we bombed Iraq again and destroyed more power plants and killed more people—wedding parties, invalids sleeping in their beds. And as we debated the merits of each of these attacks, we inevitably referred back to our touchstone, our exemplar: the Second World War.

War is messy, we say. It's not pretty, but let's be real—it has to be fought sometimes. Cut to the image of a handsome unshaven G.I., somewhere in Italy or France, with a battered helmet and a cigarette hanging from his mouth. World War II, the most lethally violent eruption in history, is pacifism's great smoking counterexample. We "had to" intervene in Korea, Vietnam, and wherever else, because *look at World War II*. In 2007, in an article for *Commentary* called "The Case for Bombing Iran," Norman Podhoretz drew a parallel between negotiating with Iran's president, Mahmoud Ahmadinejad, and negotiating with Hitler: we must bomb Iran now, he suggested, because *look at World War II*.

True, the Allies killed millions of civilians and absurdly young conscripts, and they desolated much of Europe and Japan—that was genuinely sad. But what about the Holocaust? We had to push back somehow against that horror.

Yes, we did. But the way you push is everything.

The Holocaust was, among many other things, the biggest hostage crisis of all time. Hostage-taking was Hitler's preferred method from the beginning. In 1923, he led a group of ultra-nationalists into a beer hall in Munich and, waving a gun, held government officials prisoner. In 1938, after Kristallnacht, he imprisoned thousands of Jews, releasing them only after the Jewish community paid a huge ransom. In occupied France, Holland, Norway, and Yugoslavia, Jews were held hostage and often executed in reprisal for local partisan activity.

By 1941, as Congress was debating the Lend-Lease Act, which would provide military aid to Britain and other Allies, the enormity of the risk became clear, if it wasn't already, to anyone who could read a newspaper. On February 28, 1941, the *New York Times* carried a troubling dispatch from Vienna: "Many Jews here believe that Jews throughout Europe will be more or less hostages against the United States' entry into the war. Some fear that even an appreciable amount of help for Britain from the United States may precipitate whatever plan the Reichsfuehrer had in mind when, in recent speeches, he spoke of the elimination of Jews from Europe 'under certain circumstances.'"

In response to this threat, *The American Hebrew*, a venerable weekly, ran a defiant front-page editorial. "Reduced to intelligibility this message, which obviously derives from official sources, warns that unless America backs down, the Jews in Germany will be butchered," the paper said. So be it. The editorial went on:

> We shall continue, nay, we shall increase our efforts to bring about the downfall of the cutthroat regime that is tyrannizing the world, and we are not blind to the price we may have to pay for our determination. But no sacrifice can be too great, no price too dear, if we can help rid the world of the little Austrian messiah and his tribe, and all they stand for.

Other Jews, a minority, disagreed. ("In wars it is the minorities that are generally right," Ponsonby once said.) In 1941, Rabbi Cronbach, of the Hebrew Union College in Cincinnati, began talking to Rabbi Isidor B. Hoffman, a friendly, bald, hard-to-ruffle student counselor at Columbia University, and Rabbi Arthur Lelyveld of Omaha, Nebraska, about forming a Jewish Peace Fellowship. The fellowship would help support Jewish conscientious objectors who were then in alternative-service camps or prisons, and it would, according to the first issue of its newsletter, *Tidings*, "strengthen the devotion to pacifism of self-respecting, loyal Jews."

"Crony" Cronbach became the honorary chairman of the Jewish Peace Fellowship. He was a fine-boned man, always in a suit and tie, and he had a horror of vengeance as an instrument of national policy. He'd seen what happened in the Great War. "People of gentleness, refinement, and idealism became, in the war atmosphere, hyenas raging to assault and kill not merely the foreign foe but equally their own dissenting countrymen," he recalled in his 1937 book, *The Quest for Peace*. By supporting the earlier conflict, he suggested, America's Jews had "only helped prepare the way for the Nazi horror which has engulfed us."

The American middle class, still dimly recalling the trenches, the mud, the rats, the typhus, and the general obscene futility of World War I, was perhaps slightly closer to Cronbach's pacifism than to Roosevelt's interventionism—until December 7, 1941. Once Pearl Harbor's Battleship Row burned and sank, the country cried for the incineration of Tokyo.

The false-flag "peace" groups, such as America First, disbanded immediately; the absolute pacifists stuck to their principles. At the War Resisters League headquarters on Stone Street in Manhattan, the executive committee members (including Edward P. Gottlieb, a schoolteacher who had changed his middle name to "Pacifist") published a post–Pearl Harbor flyer that called for an early negotiated peace "on the basis of benefit and deliverance for all the peoples of the earth." The flyer got a good response, and won them some new enrollees; only a few angry letters came in, one written on toilet paper. The FBI visited the offices and began making a series of what Kaufman called "exhaustive inquiries."

Meanwhile, Hitler's anti-Semitism had reached a final stage of Götterdämmerungian psychosis. As boxcars of war-wounded, frostbitten German soldiers returned from the Russian front, and as it became obvious to everyone that the United States was entering the war, Hitler, his arm tremor now evident to his associates, made an unprecedented number of vitriolic threats to European Jewry in close succession—some in speeches, and some in private meetings. (The Jew, Hitler now claimed, was a *Weltbrandstifter*, a world arsonist.) A number of Holocaust historians—among them Saul Friedländer, Peter Longerich, Christian Gerlach, and Roderick Stackelberg—have used this concentration of "exterminatory statements" (the phrase is Friedländer's) to date, in the absence of any written order, Hitler's decision to radically accelerate the Final Solution.

The shift, Friedländer writes, came in late 1941, occasioned by the event that transformed a pan-European war into a world war: "the entry of the United States into the conflict." As Stackelberg puts it: "Although the 'Final Solution,' the decision to kill all the Jews under German control, was planned well in advance, its full implementation may have been delayed until the U.S. entered the war. Now the Jews under German control had lost their potential value as hostages."

In any case, on December 12, 1941, Hitler confirmed his intentions in a talk before Goebbels and other party leaders. In his diary, Goebbels later summarized the Führer's remarks: "The world war is here. The annihilation of the Jews must be the necessary consequence."

Chelmno, the first killing factory, had already commenced operation on December 8, 1941: Jews from the ghetto in the Polish town of Kolo were suffocated with exhaust gasses in sealed trucks. Beginning in March 1942, the Lublin ghetto was liquidated: Jews by the thousands were taken to a second extermination camp, Belzec, and gassed there. More Jews, including orphaned children and old people who had until then been excluded from the camps, were taken from Vienna at the beginning of June. Leonhard Friedrich, a German Quaker arrested in May for helping Jews, later wrote: "In the six months after the United States entered the war, the Gestapo felt under no restraints."

Even at this stage, word was spreading in the United States. On June 2, 1942, for example, a story ran in many American newspapers about Hitler's plan. It was written by Joseph Grigg, a United Press journalist who had been interned by the Germans for five months, then freed with other Americans as a result of negotiations. "There apparently was an effort to create a 'Jew-free' Reich by April 1, as a birthday gift for Hitler," Grigg reported, "but due to transportation and other difficulties the schedule could not be maintained." The massacres in Russia, Poland, and the Baltic states were, Grigg said, "the most terrible racial persecution in modern history."

Meanwhile, that June, the United States was "fighting Hitler" by doing—what? By battling the Japanese navy, by building big bombers, and by having big war parades. On June 13, with the Allied land assault on Europe still two years away, Mayor Fiorello LaGuardia of New York City threw an enormous one. It went on for a full day. There were tanks, planes, and picturesque international costumes, but there were also floats meant to stir emotions of enmity and fear. A float called "Death Rides" moved slowly by: it was a giant animated skeleton beating two red swastika-bearing drums. There was a huge mustachioed figure in a Prussian helmet and body armor, riding a Disney-style dinosaur that strode heedlessly through corpses—the float was called "Hitler, the Axis War Monster." There was a float called "Tokyo: We Are Coming!" in which American airplanes set fire to the city, frightening off a swarm of large yellow rats. The *New York Herald Tribune*'s reporter wrote that the only thing missing from the parade was subtlety. This is what the United States was doing during the early phase of the Holocaust: beating big red toy death drums on Fifth Avenue.

During this same midwar period, the Royal Air Force's attacks on German civilian life crossed a new threshold of intensity. The militarily insignificant city of Lübeck, on the Baltic Sea, crowded with wood-timbered architectural treasures, was the target of the first truly successful mass firebombing, on the night of March 28, 1942, which burned much of the old city and destroyed a famous, centuries-old painting cycle, *Totentanz* ("The Dance of Death"). "Blast and bomb, attack and

attack until there is nothing left," said the *Sunday Express.*
"Even if 'Lübecking' does not crack the morale of Germany, it
is certainly going to raise our spirits," said the *Daily Mail* (Vera
Brittain, reading through a pile of these clippings, exclaimed:
"We are Gadarene swine, inhabited by devils of our own
making, rushing down a steep place into the sea.")

Operation Millennium was the RAF's next large-scale fire
raid, at the end of May. Nearly 1,000 bombers flowed toward
the city of Cologne, where they dropped about 1,600 tons
of bombs—more firebombs than high explosives—in half an
hour, destroying tens of thousands of houses and apartments
and more than twenty churches. The area around the city's
main cathedral was a roasted ruin. "You have no idea of the
thrill and encouragement which the Royal Air Force bombing has given to all of us here," wrote Roosevelt's personal
aide, Harry Hopkins, to Churchill. He added: "I imagine the
Germans know all too well what they have to look forward to."

No doubt the Germans did know—in any case, they
promptly blamed the Jews for the bombings. In a radio broadcast, Goebbels said that Germans were now fighting for their
very skins. Then again came the overt threat: "In this war the
Jews are playing their most criminal game and they will have
to pay for it with the extermination of their race throughout
Europe and, maybe, even beyond."

In the Warsaw ghetto, that same June of 1942, Emanuel
Ringelblum read the reports and remembered an old story
about a profligate nobleman. Shlomo, the nobleman's mon-
eylender, auctioned the man's land in payment for debts. The
nobleman, enraged, bought a dog, named him Shlomo, and
beat him daily. The same thing, wrote Ringelblum, was happening to the Germans: "They are being defeated, their cities
are being destroyed, so they take their revenge on the Jews."
Ringelblum and his friends, although of several minds about
the need for retribution, agreed on one thing: "Only a miracle
can save us: a sudden end to the war, otherwise we are lost."

A sudden end to the war, otherwise we are lost. This, then,
was the context for Abraham Kaufman's June 16, 1942, talk at
the Union Methodist Church. First worry about the saving of
lives, his logic went—everything else is secondary. In July, the
SS began the liquidation of the Warsaw ghetto, loading 6,000

people onto freight cars every day. The head of the Jewish Council, Adam Czerniaków, committed suicide rather than comply; the Germans were holding his wife hostage. Knowing what we know now, wouldn't we all have stood and said what Kaufman said?

Confirmation of the Final Solution didn't get out widely in the Western press until November 1942, when Rabbi Stephen Wise, after inexplicable delays, called a press conference to reveal the substance of an urgent telegram he had received from Switzerland in August. The Associated Press reported: "Dr. Stephen S. Wise, chairman of the World Jewish Congress, said tonight that he had learned through sources confirmed by the State Department that about half the estimated 4,000,000 Jews in Nazi-occupied Europe have been slain in an 'extermination campaign.'"

Once Wise broke his silence, there was a surge of press coverage. President Roosevelt promised retribution, and, as Churchill had done not long before, quoted Longfellow: "The mills of God grind slowly, yet they grind exceeding small." Yiddish papers carried black bars of mourning. And in December, Anthony Eden, Churchill's foreign minister, read an Allied condemnation in Parliament. "The German authorities," Eden declared, "not content with denying to persons of Jewish race in all the territories over which their barbarous rule has been extended the most elementary human rights, are now carrying into effect Hitler's oft repeated intention to exterminate the Jewish people in Europe." Like Roosevelt, Eden promised that the culprits would "not escape retribution."

After Eden was finished, there was a moment of silence: a minute or two of grief for the Jews of Europe. "The whole crowded House—an unprecedented thing to do and not provided for by any Standing Order—rose to its feet and stood in silent homage to those who were about to die," Sydney Silverman, MP, recollected after the war. "We could not do much to help them. No one desired that our war activity should be moderated in any sort of way or that our war effort should be in any way weakened in order to bring succor to those threatened people."

The atrocity was so gargantuan, wrote *The Nation* a week later, that it would have to await the perspective of history to be understood. Again came the question—what to do? "Peace with Hitler for the sake of saving hostages is out of the question," the editors asserted. "Such a surrender would mean disaster for the world, for the Jews above all. Yet the harder we fight, the nearer the doom of the Nazis approaches, the fiercer will grow their homicidal mania. Let it be admitted in all solemnity that there is no escape from this ghastly dilemma." The only thing to do was fight on.

No, there was a better way, thought Jessie Wallace Hughan, founder of the War Resisters League. Hughan, a soft-faced, wide-smiling woman in her late sixties, was a poet and high school teacher (she had been Abraham Kaufman's English teacher at Textile High School). She sent a letter to two fellow pacifist leaders, asking them to help her mount a campaign.

> It seems that the only way to save thousands and perhaps millions of European Jews from destruction would be for our government to broadcast the promise of a speedy and favorable armistice on condition that the European minorities are not molested any further. I know how improbable it is that our U.S. government would accept this but if it is the only possibility, ought not our pacifist groups to take some action?

Hughan gave talks on the necessity of rescue, she wrote letters to the State Department and the White House, and she and Abraham Kaufman, with the help of volunteers, distributed thousands of pro-armistice flyers. A peace without delay, conditional upon the release of Jews and other political prisoners, might bring the end of Hitler's reign, she suggested: "There are many anti-Nazis in the Reich, and hope is a stronger revolutionary force than despair." She wrote a blunt letter on the subject to the *New York Times*: "We must act now, because dead men cannot be liberated." The *Times* didn't print it.

Other pacifists publicly took up this cause. "Peace Now Without Victory Will Save Jews," wrote Dorothy Day on the front page of her *Catholic Worker*, and the Jewish Peace Fellowship called for an armistice to prevent Jewish extermination and "make an end to the world-wide slaughter." Brittain said that Jewish rescue required "the termination or the interruption of the war, and not its increasingly bitter continuation."

Even lapsed or near pacifists—including Eleanor Rathbone in the House of Commons, and the publisher Victor Gollancz—urgently echoed this sentiment: If we failed to make some kind of direct offer to Hitler for the safe passage of Jews, we shared a responsibility for their fate. Gollancz sold a quarter of a million copies of an extraordinary pamphlet called "Let My People Go," in which he questioned the Churchill government's promise of postwar retribution. "This 'policy,' it must be plainly said, will not save a single Jewish life," he wrote.

> Will the death, after the war, of a Latvian or Lithuanian criminal, or of a Nazi youth who for ten years has been specially and deliberately trained to lose his humanity—will the death of these reduce by one jot or tittle the agony of a Jewish child who perhaps at this very moment at which I write, on Christmas day, three hours after the sweet childish carol, "O come, all ye faithful," was broadcast before the seven o'clock news, is going to her death in a sealed coach, her lungs poisoned with the unslaked lime with which the floor is strewn, and with the dead standing upright about her, because there is no room for them to fall?

What mattered, Gollancz held, was, and he put it in italics, *the saving of life now.* The German government had to be approached immediately and asked to allow Jews to emigrate. The Allies had nothing to lose with such a proposal. "If refused, that would strip Hitler of the excuse that he cannot afford to fill useless mouths," Gollancz wrote. "If accepted, it would not frustrate the economic blockade, because Hitler's alternative is not feeding but extermination."

Nobody in authority in Britain and the United States paid heed to these promptings. Anthony Eden, Britain's foreign secretary, who'd been tasked by Churchill with handling queries about refugees, dealt coldly with one of many importunate delegations, saying that any diplomatic effort to obtain the release of the Jews from Hitler was "fantastically impossible." On a trip to the United States, Eden candidly told Cordell Hull, the secretary of state, that the real difficulty with asking Hitler for the Jews was that "Hitler might well take us up on any such offer, and there simply are not enough ships and means of transportation in the world to handle them." Churchill agreed. "Even were we to obtain permission to withdraw all Jews," he wrote in reply to one pleading letter, "transport alone presents a problem which will be difficult of solution."

Not enough shipping and transport? Two years earlier, the British had evacuated nearly 340,000 men from the beaches of Dunkirk in just nine days. The U.S. Air Force had many thousands of new planes. During even a brief armistice, the Allies could have airlifted and transported refugees in very large numbers out of the German sphere.

In the American press, calls for a negotiated peace were all but inaudible. The only significant publicity that any U.S. peace advocacy group got after 1942 was negative—witheringly negative in one instance, and rightly so. It came in connection with the formation of something called the Peace Now Movement, which set up an office on Manhattan's East 40th Street in July 1943. Abraham Kaufman, while admiring the antiwar writings of the new group's chairman, George Hartmann, remained wary of its methods, and not just because its name appropriated his own group's most stirring and useful phrase. What disturbed him was that the Peace Now Movement was willing, as the War Resisters League was not, to accept support from pro-fascists and anti-Semites, or even from "the devil himself," according to Hartmann, in order to bring the war to an end.

Kaufman also had doubts about the past of one of the group's organizers, John Collett, who'd been institutionalized for a mental disorder, and whose Norwegian visa imparted a fascist taint. In any case, Collett, out on a speaking tour, self-destructed: he was arrested in Cincinnati for peeping into a sorority shower and fined a hundred dollars.

After Collett resigned, another Peace Now staffer, Bessie Simon, carried on her friendly overtures to prominent isolationists and Nazi apologists, including Charles Lindbergh. Simon also hired a pretty blonde secretary, who turned out to be a plant working under an assumed name ("Virginia Long"), and whose stolen haul of damning correspondence soon found its way to the *New York Post*: PEACE NOW ENLISTS BUNDISTS! was one front-page headline in a weeklong exposé. *Life* called the

Peace Now Movement "not only dangerous but subversive"; the House Un-American Activities Committee condemned one of the group's mailings, which encouraged churchmen to ask their congregations to follow Christ and lay down their arms. It was, the Dies Committee determined, "a plan for mass treason which was truly colossal in its conception."

As Kaufman had foreseen, the scandal of Hartmann's Peace Now Movement eclipsed much of the work he and his colleagues had done. Now if you were willing to say publicly that the killing should stop, you weren't just a harmless simpleton but a fascist fellow traveler. According to David Lawrence, a widely syndicated conservative columnist and editor of *U.S. News*, peace talk diminished Allied soldiers' fighting zeal. "It is a weapon which is worth more to the enemy than any other," he insisted. "That's why it is vital to squelch any 'peace now' activities at their very inception."

And yet Kaufman and Hughan and the others carried on. In March 1944, with thousands of Jews still living who were not destined to survive, the War Resisters League published an updated demand that the Allies call a peace conference, stipulating Jewish deliverance. "The fortunes of war have turned, and with them the responsibility for war," Hughan wrote. "The guilt is upon our heads until we offer our enemies an honorable alternative to bitter-end slaughter. Are we fighting for mere victory or, as enlightened adults, for humanity and civilization?"

We were fighting, it seems, for mere victory. It was inconceivable that we could stop, even though an end to the fighting was the solvent that would have dissolved quicker than anything the thick glue of fear that held Hitler and Germany together. By 1944, Hitler's health was failing. He was evil, but he wasn't immortal. Whether or not the German opposition, in the sudden stillness of a conditional armistice, would have been able to remove him from power, he would eventually be dead and gone. And some of his millions of victims—if such an armistice had been secured—would have lived.

Peace and quiet was what the world needed so desperately then. Time to think, and mourn. Time to sleep without fear. Time to crawl out of the wreckage of wherever you were and look around, and remember what being human was all about. Instead, what did we do? Bomb, burn, blast, and starve, waiting for the unconditional surrender that didn't come until the Red Army was in Berlin. We came up with a new kind of "sticky flaming goo," as the *New York Times* called what would later be known as napalm. Allied airplanes burned the Rouen cathedral, so that the stones crumbled to pieces when touched, destroyed Monte Cassino, and killed 200 schoolchildren during a single raid in Milan. A conservative MP, Reginald Purbrick, who had wanted the Royal Air Force to drop a big bomb into the crater of Mount Vesuvius ("to make a practical test as to whether the disturbances created thereby will give rise to severe earthquakes and eruptions"), began asking the prime minister whether the Royal Air Force might bomb Dresden and other cities in eastern Germany. Churchill eventually obliged him. Remorse works well, but it works only in peacetime.

When Vera Brittain argued against the Allied program of urban obliteration in her pamphlet *Massacre by Bombing*, the Writers' War Board, a government-funded American propaganda agency, pulled out all the stops in attacking her. MacKinlay Kantor (who later cowrote Curtis LeMay's memoir, the one that talked about bombing Vietnam "back into the Stone Age") published a letter in the *Times* dismissing Brittain's "anguished ramblings." The Japanese and Germans well understood the "language of bombs," Kantor said. "May we continue to speak it until all necessity for such cruel oratory has passed."

Some historians, still believing that bombing has a magical power to communicate, conclude from this dismal stretch of history that the Allied air forces should have bombed the railroad tracks that led to the death camps, or bombed the camps themselves. But bombing would have done absolutely nothing except kill more Jews (and Jews were already dying when Allied fighter planes routinely strafed boxcars in transit.) A cease-fire—"a pause in the fury of hostilities," as Vera Brittain called it in one of her newsletters—was the one chance the Allies had to save Jewish lives, and the pacifists proposed it repeatedly, using every means available to them.

So the Holocaust continued, and the firebombing continued: two parallel, incommensurable, war-born leviathans of pointless malice that fed each other and could each have been stopped long before they were. The mills of God ground the cities of Europe to powder—very slowly—and then the top Nazis chewed their cyanide pills or were executed at Nuremberg. Sixty million people died all over the world so that Hitler, Himmler, and Goering could commit suicide? How utterly ridiculous and tragic.

Pacifism at its best, said Arthur Ponsonby, is "intensely practical." Its primary object is the saving of life. To that overriding end, pacifists opposed the counterproductive barbarity of the Allied bombing campaign, and they offered positive proposals to save the Jews: create safe havens, call an armistice, negotiate a peace that would guarantee the passage of refugees. We should have tried. If the armistice plan failed, then it failed. We could always have resumed the battle. Not trying leaves us culpable.

At a Jewish Peace Fellowship meeting in Cincinnati some years after the war, Rabbi Cronbach was asked how any pacifist could justify opposition to World War II. "War was the sustenance of Hitler," Cronbach answered. "When the Allies began killing Germans, Hitler threatened that, for every German slain, ten Jews would be slain, and that threat was carried out. We in America are not without some responsibility for that Jewish catastrophe."

If we don't take seriously pacifists like Cronbach, Hughan, Kaufman, Day, and Brittain—these people who thought as earnestly about wars and their consequences as did politicians or generals or think-tankers—we'll be forever suspended in a kind of immobilizing sticky goo of euphemism and self-deception. We'll talk about intervention and preemption and no-fly zones, and we'll steer drones around distant countries on murder sorties. We'll arm the world with weaponry, and every so often we'll feel justified in taxiing out a few of our stealth airplanes from their air-conditioned hangars and dropping some expensive bombs. Iran? Pakistan? North Korea? What if we "crater the airports," as Senator Kerry suggested, to slow down Qaddafi? As I write, the United States has begun a new war against Libya, dropping more things on people's heads in the name of humanitarian intervention.

When are we going to grasp the essential truth? War never works. It never has worked. It makes everything worse. Wars must be, as Jessie Hughan wrote in 1944, renounced, rejected, declared against, over and over, "as an ineffective and inhuman means to any end, however just." That, I would suggest, is the lesson that the pacifists of the Second World War have to teach us.

ANNE MONTGOMERY

Rosalie G. Riegle's book *Doing Time for Peace: Resistance, Family, and Community* (2012) gathers the oral histories of over seventy-five radical peacemakers—activists who, from World War II to the present moment, have engaged in civil disobedience and spent time in jail for it, most of them moved by faith. Sister Anne Montgomery is one such, her gifts as a speaker and storyteller brought out wonderfully by Riegle's questions. The interview is practical, concrete, unpretentious—in the tradition of American self-help books, really. It is also eloquent. What stimulates her eloquence is not, perhaps surprisingly, the reasons for her radical pacifism, most notably her having entered a General Electric plant in 1980 to hammer on two missile nose cones and pour blood, her own blood, on documents stored there. It is rather the task of forming a community within which an individual can act.

Montgomery (1926–2012) was born in San Diego to a military family, became a Religious of the Sacred Heart, taught high school, and began doing civil resistance at the United Nations in 1978. In 1980 she became a member of the Plowshares Eight, the other members of which included both Philip and Daniel Berrigan and also Molly Rush, and entered the GE plant in King of Prussia, Pennsylvania. She remained active in radical pacifism till the end; in 2009 she helped cut through a fence at a naval base in Washington to take action against the Trident missiles stored there, at the age of eighty-three.

An Interview with Sister Anne Montgomery, RSCJ

Montgomery: My first experience with civil resistance was at the UN in 1978, its first session on disarmament. Through that, I came in contact with Jonah House and began to come to their summer sessions. That experience of community and action within a little group impressed me very much, so I kept coming back.

In the early spring of 1980, I was invited by John Schuchardt to be part of an action which would raise the level. It would be actually reaching some component of a nuclear weapon, disarming it, and possibly serving a long jail time. I went away to discern that and wrote down my pros and cons. Finally I just tore them all up and said, "In the end, this is an act of faith." So I decided to go ahead.

I wrote my provincial. "I'm going to do a more serious action and it might involve more jail time." She really didn't connect on how serious. Because you don't give people information that might get them a conspiracy charge, bring them up before a grand jury. We have to be very careful about that.

So we did it. We called ourselves the Plowshares Eight, and it was sort of a shocker to many people, both outside the peace movement and in, because it was the first time we'd actually taken hammers to something. Some people considered destruction of so-called property "violent." I think Dan Berrigan gave the best one-sentence definition of property: "Property is what enhances human life." If it kills human life, it's not true property, because it's not what's proper to human life.

When we were sentenced, our superior general in Rome, a woman from Spain, sent me a telegram of support. Both the international community and my local communities have been very supportive, which is wonderful, because I know other sisters who've done even simple acts of civil resistance and not had that support.

Riegle: You were really a pioneer.

Montgomery: In that respect, yes. I mean, there have been plenty of sisters involved in demonstrations or in crossing the line onto a military base, but I don't know of any before us who received felony charges. In this country.

We went to jail right after our arrest, awaiting trial. The six men were together in Norristown. Molly [Rush] and I were the only women. We were put in another county jail because the women's jail in Norristown had been condemned as unhealthy for human life, I guess. Then everybody was separated and shipped around to five different county jails. We had a very difficult time communicating, even with the lawyers. The men could plan things, but then they'd have to write us through a lawyer.

At first we were going to just let them do whatever they wanted with us, but our supporters said people needed to understand and that we needed to speak up in court, so when the bond came down, my congregation paid my bond and part of Dean Hammer's so we got out. Then the other men were put out of jail because they were organizing too much in there and weren't welcome anymore. So, in the end, we could all make decisions together.

[The Plowshares Eight were convicted of burglary, conspiracy, and criminal mischief and given sentences of five to ten years. After a complicated ten-year appeal process, their terms were reduced to time served. In the final sentencing, Judge James Buchanan "listened attentively to statements by the defendants, attorney Ramsey Clark, Dr. Robert J. Lifton, and Professors Richard Falk and Howard Zinn, placing the 'crime' in the contest of the common plight of humanity, international law, America's long tradition of dissent, and the primacy of individual conscience over entrenched political systems." Such judicial consideration rarely happens in Plowshares trials today.]

Montgomery: Actually, by the time our sentence was changed to "time served," Carl and I and Elmer were in prison for other Plowshares actions. I've been in six or six and a half actions altogether. See, there were two Kairos Plowshares, because we didn't make it to the Trident [in Groton, Connecticut] in the first one, so Kathy Maire, a Franciscan sister, and I decided to finish that one, and went back to Quonset Point and hammered on parts of the Trident submarine.

Riegle: How do people plan Plowshares actions?

Montgomery: It's a long process. I've helped with several Plowshares preparations, during the eighties especially, and we've learned that many things should be worked out before an action, because the action is more than one moment. There's a before and especially an after, when people are often separated in prisons and often can't communicate very well. Maybe you've made an agreement that you won't put up bond or sign things. But what about family emergencies? People have to be able to support people who decide to bond out, for instance, and all that stuff has to be worked out ahead of time so there are no bad feelings and people don't feel betrayed. You don't want a breakup of community. So now the process is—or should be—that there are very serious times for retreat.

First, a community forms, but they don't pick a site right away. They do research and get input on different weapons systems. They learn about biblical resistance and learn about building community and praying together, so the preparation is both spiritual and political. Also, they get to know each other—life-sharing and feelings.

Then there's a whole list of questions about how much legal stuff you want to participate in. Do you represent yourself or have a lawyer? What about bond resistance? Cooperating in prison? These things need to be talked out ahead of time and you make agreements, but you also allow for trusting each other if an emergency arises.

Most of us like to speak for ourselves in the trials. Often, generous lawyers will offer their time free of charge, to advise us and help people write briefs. You have to know all these legal technicalities, and decide if you want an opening statement and who's going to make it. And whether you'll take the stand or not, because that means you'll be questioned by the prosecutor. Are we going to question jurors or are we just going to let the first twelve be selected?

And then there's always a planning discussion on fear. What if somebody gets hurt or killed? You don't act in such a way that some young soldier or policeman is going to shoot because they're afraid, because that puts a burden on them as well as on you.

Now, this preparation has sometimes gone on for a year. People come and go. There is a point, somewhere about two-thirds of the way into the planning, where the community decides who's in and who isn't. You don't want people just deciding at the last minute. Although at the last minute, everyone is still free to say, "I'm sorry, I can't do this."

Somewhere in the process, people choose the kind of weapon they want to target. Is it depleted uranium, is it nuclear weapons, is it nuclear weapons in space? Then we scout the places where these things [are housed]. Sometimes the actual actors will go and sometimes someone who's supporting us and willing to take the risk. You get information about security and so forth. Toward the end, when the site has been decided on, a few people will offer to be support, to drive us to the site and so forth. They're willing to risk the conspiracy charge—because it *is* a risk. But not many, you know, just a couple.

Riegle: Have there in fact been conspiracy charges?

Montgomery: Prosecutors have tried, over and over again. People just refuse to speak, even though they're threatened with contempt. Usually, the actors get a conspiracy charge for each felony, because it ups the ante. Prosecutors try to force plea bargaining and all that stuff. They've learned that Plowshares people will talk to international law and to justification and refer to spiritual matters, so they present pretrial motions saying these things shall not be allowed, and the judge always goes along with it. It really limits our court witnesses.

More and more, we try to argue from our heart instead of bothering with all the legal briefs. You know, you don't want to play lawyer. You have to be human about it. The courts always insist that you need a lawyer because you don't understand, you're not expert enough, or not bright enough, or something.

That's not right. Because how can you keep a law if you can't talk about it? If you can't express it in your own language? So to change the language rather than play lawyer, which we can't do, we put it in our own words, and talk about life.

Riegle: If you're thinking of guiding—or shining a light, I guess—on people who might be coming along on this kind of thing, what would you say to them?

Montgomery: I think if they don't have a community already, they need to find others of like mind and begin talking with them, praying with them, forming a little community. We have Kairos in New York City which meets twice a month. People are free to come who've never been there before. There are no papers to sign. You pray together, you discuss what you're doing. You see, there's a principle: if we want the world to be in community, we'd better be able to act in a community ourselves and to *be* a community.

So find a community of support—others who think alike—and work with those who've had some experience. And maybe before thinking about serious action, watch people in action, so you're not so afraid anymore of the police. Then get involved in less risky things first. As Americans, to break the law—even in a little way—is a big deal. So I don't look down my nose at anybody who finds it difficult. Sometimes the hardest work is being part of a support community, because they have to keep going with their own work and do all the support work, too. And then, you know, somebody may not be called to this kind of resistance at all. They may not feel they can handle prison.

Riegle: How do you know whether you can handle it?

Montgomery: Well, I think that's part of doing something a little less risky at the beginning. When we did it, I said, "This is it. I may be in for years." And we might have. I wouldn't recommend that as a general plan of action, but I trusted the people I was with.

I think faith is important to us. When I think of the French Resistance and Camus, whose love of human beings was so great that he could do the things without the sense of support from a faith, I really admire him. It doesn't really matter what faith tradition a person comes from; if a person has that, it's a great support. Otherwise, it takes great heroism.

MIKE KIRBY

Like many preceding him in this anthology, Mike Kirby (b. 1937) began his path to war resistance while still in the military—in his case, as a young sailor, he was so alarmed by a security flaw in the design of a nuclear missile warhead, and failures to correct it, that he began to imagine doomsday. Punished for his whistleblowing, Kirby drifted into the antiwar movement, donning his civilian clothes at first to join the "raggedy-ass kids" then opposing nuclear testing. Finally he sat in, spit-shined and correct in his dress whites, at the Atomic Energy Commission in Oakland—the uniform an especially resonant detail in his account, reminding us to try to imagine, in every peace action depicted here, what people wore and what they looked like; "the dress ball was going into battle," writes Norman Mailer in *Armies of the Night* (1968), and suddenly we see the diversity of appearance among those united in their opposition to war.

Kirby's early life is set out in the piece included here, published in the *London Review of Books* on July 31, 2014; his later life he described vividly to me in a letter. He has driven cabs, worked in factories and as a home health aide, been involved in local politics, written books on local history, a novel, and a novella called *The Technician* (1981), which more fully depicts his time with the bomb. Now retired, he lives in Northampton, Massachusetts, and is working on another novel.

FROM
An Honorable Discharge

In the winter of 1961–62, things were slow in the electrical bay, and I was transferred to the mechanical bay, where I worked doing retrofits and supervised the library, checking weapon manuals in and out. I inevitably did quite a bit of reading in the process of updating manuals, and it was there, sitting at my desk, that I started to do a little research that might have made me very dangerous to everyone on the planet. But it didn't. I went to the local community college and took a couple of evening classes, and avoided talking about what I was thinking and learning to Lt. Commander Karlsven, the base commander. Karlsven was a taciturn Swede who always looked splendid in his uniform. He came to work in a green

Department of Defense sedan; we came to work on a little grey school bus. There was gold on his collar buttons, gold in the braid on his hat that hung on the three-legged hat-stand, silver in his thinning hair that he wore combed straight back. When I left, Karlsven encouraged me to read the Bible. In the college library I found all these books and magazines I never knew existed: the *New Republic*, the *Progressive*, *Partisan Review* and *Dissent*. I went to see *On the Beach*, which portrayed the final days of life on Earth after a nuclear war. I started subscribing to the magazines and soon the base security officer wanted to talk to me.

Some time in the spring, a new warhead for the Polaris arrived, the first of many that were to be shipped to the submarine fleet. I went through the warhead manual and found a number of things that disturbed me. This particular warhead was designed for use against cities. It was very compact, a weapon with a small bang and a small cross-section, but its ablative shield was an alloy of uranium, and it produced very heavy alpha fallout downwind. I thought about the world laid waste by these warheads. I wondered if you could be a good soldier and have an imagination.

There was also this. When installed on the rocket, the main warhead connection was safety-wired in place and hidden. But in our bay and out in the storage depots these warheads were stored with an unlocked weapons connector. Unzip the weather cover, and it was right there. The safety mechanisms were in the fusing assembly, not in the warhead. Bang the right pins with the right voltage, and the warhead would blow. I wrote a technical change memo, suggesting a locked cover for the warhead connector while it was in storage.

I alerted the system, but the system wasn't listening. This memo went into a drawer in my boss's desk. I remember him looking at me quizzically. Never a word, but no trouble either. I think it made me angry, not being listened to. Anyone who has tried to buck the system understands how difficult it is for an enlisted man to tell an officer what to do. All I wanted was for them to put a lockable cap on the main warhead connection. I wanted them to protect these devices from me and my madness. Stop me from doing something foolish. And thinking of something foolish became an obsession. I saw myself holding the president and the programme hostage, single-handedly bringing about disarmament. People would finally understand how dangerous these weapons were.

I walked out in the desert nights dreaming of doomsday scenarios. I wrote my first poem about the bomb. One day I thought I was about to laugh and cried instead. I found my symptoms in one of my college books on psychology. World War One veterans exhibited it. Reversal of emotions. And so I wrote another memo, the memo that is probably buried in classified files in the Department of Defense, the memo that was hot enough for my boss to look at me with a startled expression and send it on to Karlsven, who sent it to the security officer. "I want out," I said. "Or else." And this "or else" got through to them. "I will not be responsible for my actions if you keep me here in this programme."

You write a good memo and there's no taking it back; no stopping the bullet once it leaves the barrel. I lost my top secret clearance and was eventually transferred to Treasure Island near San Francisco. I cleaned urinals, swept the parade ground, and did guard duty at the brig. Every morning thousands of men were marshalled in the parade ground. Many of us were awaiting orders to ship out. My number was 3039, and every morning I was there waiting for it to be called. As the months went by, and all my shipmates came and went to other assignments, I began to understand that this was punishment duty, that I was going nowhere until my enlistment was up. San Francisco at that time was a hotbed of the peace movement. They couldn't have thought of a worse place to put me in cold storage. There were demonstrations all the time against atomic testing in the Pacific Ocean. The Soviet Union had violated an informal test ban earlier that year, and the Department of Defense's desire to test its modernised missile warheads resulted in the US conducting a series of dramatically stupid hydrogen bomb tests in the spring of 1962 near Johnston Island in the mid-Pacific.

Perhaps some of the guys I trained with in Albuquerque were on Johnston Island. Early-model Thor rockets, returned from years of deployment in England, were used to test out the feasibility of anti-ICBM defence by being detonated at high altitude. The range-safety officers had to abort four of them. The fallout came down. It wasn't like other tests where the military were held back a decent distance from ground zero. One of the Thors blew up on the pad, making practically the whole island radioactive. There were barracks on that island, and probably a detachment of my fellow GMTs to install the W49 bombs on the Thors. Naval aviators flew seaplanes in and out of the fallout. They brought in an army detachment with bulldozers who pushed many acres of radioactive coral into the lagoon. After Vietnam the island was used to store thousands of barrels of Agent Orange, and then it became a disposal site for chemical munitions. Today it's not used for anything and no one can visit without special permission.

I started going to the demonstrations against testing in civilian clothes, but I had my navy buzz-cut. These were my people. They were raggedy-ass kids like I used to be, and they were staging sit-ins and getting themselves arrested. I wanted to hold a sign and join them.

And then one day me and the master at arms had it out. I handed in my fifth or sixth chit asking for an early discharge and he told me that I was here for keeps. They weren't going to discharge me until my four years was up. "You're going to serve every goddamn day you enlisted for." So that was it.

"Well, if you won't let me out early, can I have this afternoon off?" I said.

I got the afternoon off. I went to my locker and got out my dress whites. I never had the occasion to wear them because we were always in dungarees. I spit-shined my shoes. There was a sit-in that day at the Atomic Energy Commission building in Oakland. There were five or six people sitting on the front steps when I arrived, and a small crowd milling about. They looked at me with some puzzlement. I think one of them got up and moved out of the way, thinking I wanted to go inside. "No," I said. "Gimme a sign." There was one I really liked: "Why repeat Khrushchev's crime?"

I sat down. The crowd got bigger, there were people at the windows looking down at me. The *San Francisco Chronicle* interviewed me. Twenty minutes later, the shore patrol arrived. My leave was cancelled; I was placed in custody for conduct unbecoming. There was cheering from up above when I was picked up and tossed into the paddy wagon. And for the first time in my life I felt I was where I ought to be, in full rebellion against the existing order. I was told on numerous occasions that I was going to face a general court martial on six or seven charges. Then word came down from Washington to discharge me quietly. An honourable discharge. Maybe the thinking was that the peace movement didn't need a martyr. On 16 June 1962 I was escorted to the administration building. The admiral's office on the third floor looked over the great expanse of parade ground where we were marched and stood for inspection, and where the morning meat market was held. I stood braced at attention for twenty minutes while this two-star admiral told me what he would have done to me if he had his way. Shot as a goddamn traitor, keelhauled, condemned to life in a marine brig. And as he roared and belched fire and pounded his desk my orders were tucked safely in my pocket. I touched them every now and then to make sure they were still there, and stole a glimpse out of his window from time to time at the distant chequerboard where until three days ago I had stood in square number 3039. Maybe a small smile showed itself on my face and made him that much madder. I was young and a little arrogant then.

JANE HIRSHFIELD

Jane Hirshfield (b. 1953) was born in New York, went to Princeton, has published seven books of poetry as well as essays and translations and anthologies, aiming in these last to help recover the history of women's writing. She received lay ordination in Soto Zen in 1979, and has taught at numerous academic institutions. "A profound empathy for the suffering of all living beings," wrote Czeslaw Milosz; ". . . it is precisely this I praise in the poetry of Jane Hirshfield."

Every anthology has a final piece, which in being its final piece contributes something to its overall shape. This one ends with Hirshfield's "I Cast My Hook, I Decide to Make Peace," from her book *The Beauty*, published in 2015. It is among the anthology's least dogmatic works, with little to say, even indirectly, about ongoing wars in Afghanistan, or Syria, or the Ukraine, or weapons of mass destruction (ours or theirs), or defense budgets, or the substantial legacies of the American antiwar tradition. Indeed the peace the speaker decides to make, abandoning such certainties to cast her hook, may occur entirely as a matter of individual mood. (In this, it is like the war Paul Reps stops, "drinking a cup of tea" in his poem on page 330.)

Yet from an unresponsive world—with little more than some imagination, patience, and "a little ink"—the poet makes something joyous, dramatizing the immense consequences of a simple change of heart. It may be, as W. H. Auden once said, that "poetry makes nothing happen"; but for Hirshfield as for the other antiwar and peace writers gathered here, the blank page has seemed like a place to try.

I Cast My Hook, I Decide to Make Peace

The bee does not speak to me.
The whale does not speak to me.
The horse is silent.

History does not speak to me.
Arachne is only a spider.

Nothing says "you" if I offer "I,"
"I" if I proffer "you."

I would go
to the Counter of Complaining—

there was one,
a hut of new pine wood
at the base of the Yellow Mountains in China,
the door was open, a woman sat in the chair—

but nothing says "counter,"
nothing says "yellow" or "mountain."

Erased dust of the chalkboard, barnacle,
less *sleep* than *bed*—
what can I do, faceless, with no one to kiss or shout at?

I cast my hook, my vote against it,
I decide to make peace.

I declare this intention but nothing answers.
And so I put peace in a warm place, towel-covered, to proof,
then into an oven. I wait.
Peace is patient and undemanding, it *surpasseth*.

And the bulldozers move
from the palace of breaking to the places of building.
And the students return to their classes.
Tuna swim freely.
The sky hoists the flag of the sky.

All this in the space of a half-page, a little ink,
a small bite of hubris
sweetened with raisins and honey.

I begin to consider what I will make of tomorrow's speechless.

CHRONOLOGY

SOURCES AND ACKNOWLEDGMENTS

INDEX

Chronology

c. 1450–   Warring Iroquois tribes unite in a confederacy symbol-
1600   ized by a "Tree of Great Peace."

1681   The English Quaker William Penn, having recently
            become owner and ruler of a large tract of land in North
            America, writes to the Indians there on October 18:
            "God hath written his law in our hearts; by which we
            are taught and commanded to love and help and do good
            to one another, and not to do harme and mischeif."

1755   On December 16, during the French and Indian War,
            John Woolman and others send an "Epistle of Tender
            Love and Caution" to their fellow Pennsylvania Quak-
            ers, urging nonpayment of taxes "intended for purposes
            inconsistent with our peaceable testimony."

1759   Quaker Anthony Benezet delivers a Thanksgiving
            sermon in Philadelphia on November 29, published as
            "Thoughts on the Nature of War, and Its Repugnancy
            to the Christian Life."

1777   On October 3, Delaware Quakers appoint Warner Mifflin
            and others to visit William Howe and George Washing-
            ton, generals of the British and American armies, hoping
            to persuade them to declare an armistice that might
            "lead to a good understanding and eventually to peace."

1782   Benjamin Franklin writes to an English friend, Jonathan
            Shipley, on June 10: "After much Occasion to consider
            the Folly and Mischiefs of a State of Warfare, and the
            little or no Advantage obtained even by those Nations
            who have conducted it with the most Success, I have
            been apt to think that there has never been or ever will
            be any such Thing as a good War or a bad Peace."

1785   In a letter to his former military aide David Humphreys
            on July 25, George Washington writes of war: "My first
            wish is to see this plague to Mankind banished from the
            Earth; & the Sons & daughters of this World employed
            in more pleasing & innocent amusements than in prepar-
            ing implements, & exercising them for the destruction of
            the human race."

1792   Benjamin Rush publishes "A Plan of a Peace-Office for the United States."

1794   Thomas Jefferson writes Tench Coxe on May 1: "As to myself, I love peace, and I am anxious that we should give the world still another useful lesson, by shewing to them other modes of punishing injuries than by war, which is as much a punishment to the punisher as to the sufferer."

1795   Among his "Political Observations," James Madison writes on April 20: "Of all the enemies to public liberty war is, perhaps, the most to be dreaded, because it comprises and develops the germ of every other. War is the parent of armies; from these proceed debts and taxes; and armies, and debts, and taxes are the known instruments for bringing the many under the dominion of the few."

1812   Delegates from fifty-three towns in western Massachusetts convene in Northampton on July 14, and call on President Madison to seek peace with Great Britain instead of pursuing "an offensive war, which we believe to be neither just, necessary nor expedient."

1815   The New York Peace Society, organized by David Low Dodge, is established on August 16; the first such group known to exist anywhere in the world, it aims "to discourage war, and promote peace, by circulating Tracts and other publications tending to show that war is inconsistent with Christianity, and the true interests of mankind," and counts about thirty members. Dodge publishes *War Inconsistent with the Religion of Jesus Christ*. The Massachusetts Peace Society follows soon afterward, on December 28; it is led by Noah Worcester and William Ellery Channing, and produces the quarterly journal *Friend of Peace*.

1820   More than thirty peace societies are operating in the United States.

1823   The Massachusetts Peace Society reports a membership of approximately one thousand; unlike most early peace societies, it accepts women in its ranks.

1828   On May 8, the American Peace Society is founded in New York, merging the Maine, New Hampshire, Massachusetts, New York, and Pennsylvania peace societies;

it publishes the journal *Harbinger of Peace* and later *Advocate of Peace*. William Ladd, a Maine farmer and sea captain, proposes the merger and donates his fortune to the new organization.

1838 Ralph Waldo Emerson gives one of a series of lectures sponsored by the American Peace Society in Boston on March 12. (Billed as "The Peace Principle," it is later published as "War.") The New England Non-Resistance Society is established in September at a Boston peace convention organized by William Lloyd Garrison.

1840 William Ladd publishes *An Essay on a Congress of Nations, for the Adjustment of International Disputes without Resort to Arms.*

1843 Adin Ballou is chosen as president of the New England Non-Resistance Society.

1845 George C. Beckwith edits *The Book of Peace: A Collection of Essays on War and Peace.*

1846 Elihu Burritt (the "learned blacksmith") founds the League of Universal Brotherhood, which seeks "to employ all legitimate and moral means for the abolition of all war, and all the spirit, and all the manifestations of war, throughout the world"; it claims a U.S. membership of 25,000. Theodore Parker preaches a "Sermon of War" in Boston on June 7; he will speak out against the Mexican-American War on many occasions. In July, Henry David Thoreau is arrested and spends a night in jail for refusing to pay poll taxes because of his opposition to slavery and the Mexican-American War; he later writes "Resistance to Civil Government" (also titled "Civil Disobedience") in explanation of his actions. Adin Ballou publishes *Christian Non-Resistance in All Its Important Bearings.*

1848 Abraham Lincoln (Whig–IL) describes the Mexican-American War as "unnecessarily and unconstitutionally commenced" in a speech in Congress on January 12. Elihu Burritt organizes an International Peace Congress, held in Brussels in September; he also supports congresses in Paris in 1849 and Frankfurt in 1850.

1849 Charles Sumner speaks on "The War System of the Commonwealth of Nations" before the American Peace Society on May 28.

1856   Hoping to avoid civil war, Elihu Burritt lectures widely
            to promote "compensated emancipation," and publishes
            *A Plan of Brotherly Co-Partnership of the North and South
            for the Peaceful Extinction of Slavery.*

1859   William Lloyd Garrison and others praise militant
            abolitionist John Brown at a Boston mass meeting on
            December 2, the day of Brown's hanging: "Give me,
            as a non-resistant, Bunker Hill, and Lexington, and
            Concord, rather than the cowardice and servility of a
            Southern slave plantation." Adin Ballou criticizes such
            "bellicose John Brown Non-resistants" in his journal
            Practical Christian, claiming they have abandoned their
            principles.

1861   Gerrit Smith, secretary of the American Peace Society,
            writes in a public letter on May 18: "when Slavery is
            gone from the whole world, the whole world will then
            be freed not only from a source of war, but from the
            most cruel and horrid form of war. For Slavery is war as
            well as the source of war. Thus has the Peace Society,
            as well as the Abolition Society, much to hope for from
            this grand uprising of the North." On July 20, the *New
            York Tribune* pejoratively describes conservative antiwar
            Democrats as "Copperheads."

1862   Alfred Henry Love publishes *An Appeal in Vindication
            of Peace Principles*; unlike fellow members of the Ameri-
            can Peace Society, he opposes the Union war effort.

1863   Ezra H. Heywood reaffirms pacifist principles in a Boston
            address, "The War Method of Peace," on June 14: "war is
            wrong—wrong yesterday, wrong today, wrong forever."
            Cyrus Pringle and two other conscientious objectors are
            granted parole from military service at the "urgent wish"
            of President Lincoln on November 7.

1864   Congress exempts members of "religious denominations,
            who shall by oath and affirmation declare that they are
            conscientiously opposed to the bearing of arms" from
            military service; such objectors would be assigned non-
            combatant roles in hospitals or overseeing freed slaves.

1866   The Universal Peace Union is established in Providence,
            Rhode Island, by Adin Ballou, Joshua Blanchard, Alfred
            Henry Love, Lucretia Mott, and others; they call for

immediate disarmament, publish the journal *Bond of Peace*, and begin meeting regularly each summer in "peace encampments" in Mystic, Connecticut.

1870   Julia Ward Howe, author of the "Battle Hymn of the Republic," issues an "Appeal to Womanhood throughout the World" in September, during the Franco-Prussian War, calling for an international women's peace congress "to promote the alliance of the different nationalities, the amicable settlement of international questions, the great and general interests of peace."

1871   The American Peace Society permits women to hold official positions in the organization.

1888   At Swarthmore College, William Penn Holcomb teaches "Elements of International Law, with special attention to the important subjects of peace and arbitration," the earliest known "Peace Studies" course.

1893   Chicago hosts the Fifth Universal Peace Congress in August, in association with the World's Columbian Exposition.

1895   The first Lake Mohonk Conference on International Arbitration is held at Lake Mohonk, New York; it continues annually until World War I.

1898   The American Anti-Imperialist League, established on June 15 during the Spanish-American War, opposes the annexation of Spanish territory.

1902   Textbook publisher Edwin Ginn issues the first in a series of inexpensive books and pamphlets, later named the International Library of Peace.

1903   Andrew Carnegie donates $1,500,000 for the construction of a "Temple of Peace" at The Hague, to house sessions of the Permanent Court of Arbitration.

1904   The Thirteenth Universal Peace Congress, held in Boston, is attended by three thousand.

1906   The American Society of International Law is established; it promotes the resolution of international disputes by legal means and arbitration rather than war. In a lecture titled "The Psychology of the War Spirit," later revised and published as "The Moral Equivalent of

War," William James argues that martial virtues should
be harnessed and redirected to peaceful ends. Theodore
Roosevelt is awarded the Nobel Peace Prize for his role
in negotiating treaty ending the Russo-Japanese War.

1907   Andrew Carnegie and the New York Peace Society sponsor a National Peace Congress in New York.

1910   The International School of Peace is founded by Edwin
Ginn on July 12. Later renamed the World Peace Foundation, it has as its stated purpose "educating the people
of all nations to a full knowledge of the waste and
destructiveness of war and of preparation for war, its evil
effect on present social conditions and on the well-being
of future generations, and to promote international
justice and the brotherhood of man, and generally by
every practical means to promote peace and good will
among mankind." On November 25, Andrew Carnegie
donates $10 million to a fund to "hasten the abolition of
international war, the foulest blot upon our civilization";
it is subsequently named the Carnegie Endowment for
International Peace.

1914   Carnegie donates an additional $2 million in February to
help establish the interfaith Church Peace Union.

1915   In January, the Woman's Peace Party is founded in Washington, D.C., after a meeting organized by Jane Addams
and Carrie Chapman Catt; it later becomes the American
branch of the Women's International League for Peace
and Freedom (WILPF). In May, Jessie Wallace Hughan,
Tracy Mygatt, and John Haynes Holmes form the Anti-
Enlistment League, which urges "categorical, individual
refusal to participate" in war. A group led by former
president William Howard Taft establishes the League
to Enforce Peace in July, at a meeting in Philadelphia;
they propose a postwar League of Nations. The U.S.
branch of the Fellowship of Reconciliation is founded in
November. The Henry Ford Peace Expedition, including
Ford and over one hundred delegates and reporters, sails
for Europe aboard the *Oscar II* on December 4, hoping
to establish a conference of neutral nations to implement
peace proposals.

1916   Helen Keller gives speech at Carnegie Hall against
American involvement in World War I.

1917   Woodrow Wilson gives "Peace Without Victory" speech in the Senate in January, urging support for a League of Nations and collective security agreements. Fifty members of the House (including Jeannette Rankin, the first woman elected to that body) and six senators oppose a declaration of war on Germany, on April 6. The American Peace Society declares American entry into World War I unavoidable. Quakers form the American Friends Service Committee, which provides conscientious objectors with opportunities to perform "service of love in wartime," including reconstruction and relief work in France. "It has been a bitter experience," Randolph Bourne writes in June, "to see the unanimity with which the American intellectuals have thrown their support to the use of war-technique in the crisis in which America has found herself." At Columbia University, President Nicholas Murray Butler (author of the 1913 book *The International Mind: An Argument for Judicial Settlement of International Disputes*) dismisses three antiwar faculty members; other colleges and universities fire professors for alleged disloyalty.

1918   Socialist Party leader Eugene V. Debs is convicted of sedition in September for a speech given in Canton, Ohio, on June 16, in which he had argued that "the people," not "the ruling class," should "decide the momentous issue of war or peace."

1920   Woodrow Wilson is awarded the Nobel Peace Prize for his efforts to establish the League of Nations.

1921   John Dewey, Samuel Levinson, and others found the American Committee for the Outlawry of War. Frederick J. Libby organizes the National Council for the Prevention of War, which works for armaments reductions.

1923   Jessie Wallace Hughan organizes the secular-pacifist War Resisters League (WRL), a successor to the Anti-Enlistment League.

1927   Members of the Fellowship of Reconciliation and the American Friends Service Committee travel to Nicaragua to attempt to mediate a peace agreement between Nicaraguan rebels and U.S. occupation forces.

1930   The movie *All Quiet on the Western Front*, released in
        August, depicts the brutal realities of trench warfare.
        Frank B. Kellogg is awarded the Nobel Peace Prize for
        his work on the 1928 Briand-Kellogg Pact, an agreement
        to outlaw war.

1931   The Nobel Peace Prize is awarded to Jane Addams, presi-
        dent of the Women's International League for Peace and
        Freedom, and Nicholas Murray Butler, president of the
        Carnegie Endowment for International Peace.

1933   The National Peace Conference unites thirty-seven peace
        organizations in a loose federation. Dorothy Day and
        Peter Maurin found the Catholic Worker movement,
        establishing houses of hospitality for the needy and the
        Catholic Worker newspaper, which advocates for pacifist
        causes.

1934   Approximately 25,000 students join a National Student
        Strike Against War on April 13; a year later even more
        students participate. Richard B. Gregg's *The Power of
        Non-Violence*, an explanation of Gandhian method and
        theory, is published.

1935   Jane Addams dies on May 21; in her honor, the Swarth-
        more College Peace Collection is established, gathering
        correspondence she had begun to donate some years
        before and the papers of other antiwar campaigners.
        Retired Marine Corps major general Smedley D. Butler
        publishes *War Is a Racket* in the wake of a national
        lecture tour on the same subject; the book is excerpted
        in *Reader's Digest*. Various antiwar organizations join
        together in the Emergency Peace Campaign, which over
        the next two years organizes thousands of meetings,
        conferences, talks, and educational programs.

1936   Author Munro Leaf and illustrator Robert Lawson pub-
        lish *The Story of Ferdinand*, a children's book about a bull
        who doesn't like bullfighting; it is widely received as a
        pacifist allegory. Merle Curti's *Peace or War: The Ameri-
        can Struggle, 1636–1936* appears; it is the first scholarly
        account of the history of American peace movements.

1937   The Emergency Peace Campaign sponsors the No-
        Foreign-War Crusade, helping to pass the Neutrality

Act, restricting American arms shipments to foreign belligerents, in May.

1939   James Thurber publishes an illustrated antiwar parable, *The Last Flower*.

1940   The America First Committee is established on September 4 to oppose intervention on the Allied side in World War 2; aviator Charles Lindbergh becomes its most prominent public speaker. President Franklin Delano Roosevelt signs the Selective Training and Service Act on September 16, requiring men aged 21–35 to register with local draft boards. The act allows those who object to war "by reason of religious training and belief" to perform "work of national importance under civilian direction." Approximately 12,000 men accepted such nonmilitary service requirements in Civilian Public Service camps during World War II; over 6,000 objectors, refusing these terms, served prison time.

1941   Jeannette Rankin casts the only congressional vote against a declaration of war upon Japan, on December 8; "as a woman I can't go to war," she explains, "and I refuse to send anyone else." The America First Committee urges support for the war; Jessie Wallace Hughan of the WRL writes, "the general public, in the opinion of our veteran pacifists, is much more nearly unanimous in support of the war than in 1917." WILPF loses half of its membership; readership of the antiwar *Catholic Worker* plummets.

1942   The Fellowship of Reconciliation hosts an interracial study group in its Chicago offices that becomes the Congress of Racial Equality. Lew Ayres, star of the 1930 antiwar film *All Quiet on the Western Front*, claims conscientious objector status.

1943   Conscientious objectors in the Federal Correctional Institution at Danbury, Connecticut, begin a work strike to protest racial segregation in the prison dining hall, and are placed in solitary confinement; similar strikes are held in other institutions. The People's Peace Now Committee, organized by David Dellinger, pickets in Washington, D.C., with about forty members.

1945   The National Council Against Conscription holds its
        first meeting on December 13, in Philadelphia. Cordell
        Hull, a "father of the United Nations," is awarded the
        Nobel Peace Prize.

1946   Albert Einstein and a small group of scientists form the
        Emergency Committee of Atomic Scientists, hoping to
        educate the public about the dangers of nuclear weapons.
        The Committee for Nonviolent Revolution is founded
        in February, mainly by wartime conscientious objectors,
        and plans a campaign of civil disobedience to oppose
        war and injustice. Emily Greene Balch and John Raleigh
        Mott are awarded the Nobel Peace Prize, the former for
        her leadership of the Women's International League for
        Peace and Freedom, the latter for promoting Christian
        student peace organizations.

1947   On February 12, "Break with Conscription" demonstra-
        tors burn their draft cards in New York, Washington,
        D.C., and elsewhere in protests against plans to intro-
        duce a peacetime draft. The June issue of the *Bulletin of
        the Atomic Scientists* introduces the "Doomsday Clock,"
        representing "the level of continuous danger in which
        mankind lives in the nuclear age"; members of the *Bul-
        letin*'s Science and Security Board set the clock at seven
        minutes to midnight. The Nobel Peace Prize, awarded
        to the Religious Society of Friends, is accepted by the
        American Friends Service Committee and the Friends
        Service Council.

1948   After a conference in Chicago in July on "More Disci-
        plined and Revolutionary Pacifist Activity," the group
        Peacemakers is founded; its members include former
        members of the Committee for Nonviolent Revolution.
        Peacemakers campaigns against the imposition of a
        peacetime military draft. The first undergraduate peace
        studies program begins at Manchester College in North
        Manchester, Indiana, an institution associated with the
        Church of the Brethren.

1949   The General Advisory Committee of the Atomic Energy
        Commission, a panel of leading nuclear scientists, votes
        unanimously against a program to produce the H-bomb.

1950   Peacemakers, the Catholic Worker, the War Resisters
        League, and other groups organize a "Fast for Peace"

during Easter. W.E.B. Du Bois founds the Peace Information Center in April; its newsletter the *Peace-Gram* promotes the abolition of nuclear weapons. Under pressure from the Justice Department, the group dissolves in October. Ralph Bunche is awarded the Nobel Peace Prize for negotiating armistice agreements, in 1949, between Israel and Egypt, Lebanon, Jordan, and Syria.

1955   On June 15, Dorothy Day leads a protest against New York City's first annual air raid drill; she and fellow demonstrators refuse to take shelter and instead sit on park benches.

1956   David Dellinger, A. J. Muste, and Bayard Rustin edit *Liberation* magazine, the first issue of which is published in March.

1957   In June, the "Provisional Committee to Stop Nuclear Tests" is formed; later renamed the National Committee for a Sane Nuclear Policy (SANE), it grows to over 25,000 members and more than 100 local chapters by the following summer. The group Non-Violent Action Against Nuclear Weapons demonstrates at the Nevada Test Site on August 6, and holds a "Prayer and Conscience Vigil" in Washington, D.C., in November. Stanley Kubrick's antiwar film *Paths of Glory* premieres.

1958   On January 15, Linus Pauling, a Nobel laureate in chemistry, presents the United Nations with a petition, signed by 9,235 scientists, opposing nuclear weapons testing; he publishes *No More War!* In May and June, Albert S. Bigelow and crew sail the *Golden Rule* from Honolulu in attempts to block nuclear testing in the Marshall Islands; they are arrested and towed back to port. Inspired by the *Golden Rule*, Earle Reynolds and his family then sail the *Phoenix of Hiroshima* well into the test zone before they too are arrested.

1959   Faculty at the University of Michigan, including economist Kenneth Boulding, establish the Center for Research on Conflict Resolution. The Committee for Non-Violent Action (CNVA) holds vigils and protests (the "Omaha Action") outside Mead missile base in Nebraska to protest a new ICBM system; over a dozen are arrested for acts of civil disobedience, including A. J. Muste, who is imprisoned after he attempts to enter the base.

1960   In May, SANE holds an antinuclear rally at Madison
        Square Garden in New York. Beginning in the summer,
        the CNVA stages the Polaris Action, hoping to board
        nuclear submarines near New London, Connecticut;
        swimmers reach three submarines and are arrested. On
        December 1, ten protesters affiliated with the CNVA
        begin a San Francisco to Moscow Peace Walk to pro-
        mote disarmament. Joined by others and met with both
        counterprotests and supportive rallies along their route,
        they reach Moscow on October 3 of the following year.

1961   In his farewell address to the nation on January 17,
        President Dwight D. Eisenhower warns: "we must guard
        against the acquisition of unwarranted influence . . . by
        the military-industrial complex." A small group of Boston
        physicians, concerned about the recent discovery of
        strontium-90 in children's teeth (a result of atmospheric
        nuclear testing), begins meeting in March, and later orga-
        nizes as Physicians for Social Responsibility; they publish
        "The Medical Consequences of Thermonuclear War"
        in *The New England Journal of Medicine* the following
        May, and in 1985 are awarded the Nobel Peace Prize. On
        November 1, the group Women Strike for Peace draws
        approximately 50,000 to protests across the country
        opposing atmospheric nuclear testing—protests credited
        with helping to bring about the Limited Test Ban Treaty,
        signed by President Kennedy in October 1963.

1962   CNVA organizes an interracial peace march from Nash-
        ville to Washington, D.C.; it begins in April.

1963   An interracial Quebec-Washington-Guantánamo Walk
        for Peace leaves Quebec in May. In October, Linus Pau-
        ling is awarded the Nobel Peace Prize for his contribution
        to arms control and disarmament. Arriving in Albany,
        Georgia, Quebec-Washington-Guantánamo marchers
        are arrested and imprisoned and begin a hunger strike.
        Gene Keyes of the CNVA burns his draft card outside
        the Champaign, Illinois, draft board on December 24,
        and is later sentenced to three years in prison for refusing
        induction.

1964   The Stanley Kubrick film *Dr. Strangelove or: How I
        Learned to Stop Worrying and Love the Bomb*, released on
        January 29, satirizes the absurdities of nuclear weapons

and the Cold War arms race. The Catholic Peace Fellowship is established in the spring. On May 2, the first major student protests against the Vietnam War are held in cities across the country. The Quebec-Washington-Guantánamo peace march is ended on October 27, after the Coast Guard impounds the motorboat carrying the remaining participants from Miami to Havana. Martin Luther King Jr. is awarded the Nobel Peace Prize.

1965   A "teach-in" against the Vietnam War, the first of many, is held at the University of Michigan on March 24–25. On April 17, an antiwar march in Washington, D.C. draws approximately 25,000; some 30,000 participate in a Berkeley teach-in in May. In August, *Life* magazine includes a photograph of Catholic Worker Chris Kearns burning his draft card; Congress rapidly makes the burning or mutilation of draft cards a criminal offense. David Miller of the Catholic Worker is the first to be arrested under the new law, during a demonstration in New York on October 15. Quaker pacifist Norman Morrison burns himself to death outside the Pentagon to protest the war on November 2. A March on Washington for Peace in Vietnam on November 27 attracts 15,000–25,000 participants.

1966   The Student Nonviolent Coordinating Committee issues a statement opposing U.S. involvement in Vietnam on January 6. Three Army privates—the Fort Hood Three—refuse to go to Vietnam, calling the war "illegal and immoral," and in September they are court-martialed. The Congress of Racial Equality calls for a withdrawal of U.S. troops from Vietnam. Protests against Dow Chemical, manufacturer of napalm, are held in Berkeley and Detroit in October and spread to other cities over the succeeding year.

1967   Martin Luther King Jr. leads an antiwar march in Chicago on March 25; on April 4, in a speech at Riverside Church in New York City, he announces and explains his opposition to the war. On April 15, approximately 400,000 march in New York as part of the Spring Mobilization to End the War, and 100,000 in San Francisco. In June, a group of six Vietnam veterans founds Vietnam Veterans Against the War. Muhammad Ali refuses induction into the armed services and is stripped of his heavyweight title; "I ain't got no quarrel with those Vietcong," he explains. Thousands burn draft cards during "Stop the Draft Week" in October. The March on the Pentagon, on October 21, draws nearly 100,000 to Washington, D.C., to oppose the war. Over 500 sign the Writers and Editors War Tax Protest, pledging to withhold that share of their taxes being used to finance the war in Vietnam. Senator Eugene McCarthy announces his candidacy for the Democratic presidential nomination, on an antiwar platform, on November 30.

1968   On January 15, some 5,000 women led by Jeannette Rankin march on Washington as the Jeannette Rankin Brigade, and present a peace petition to the Speaker of the House. Three days later, singer Eartha Kitt confronts Lady Bird Johnson over the war at a White House women's luncheon on crime issues: "You send the best of this country off to be shot and maimed . . . [t]hey don't want to go to school because they're going to be snatched from their mothers to be shot in Vietnam." On May 17, nine Catholic activists burn registration forms at the Catonsville, Maryland, draft board.

1969   The October 15 Vietnam Moratorium draws millions of protesters throughout the world; a March on Washington, on November 15, is attended by 500,000. On December 20, the National Chicano Moratorium Committee stages its first demonstration against the Vietnam War, in East Los Angeles.

1970   During protests against the invasion of Cambodia at Kent State University on May 4, four students are killed and nine wounded by members of the Ohio National Guard. A Chicano Moratorium demonstration against the Vietnam War on August 29, in East Los Angeles, draws approximately 20,000–30,000 marchers.

1971   In late January and early February, Vietnam Veterans Against the War gathers testimony about alleged U.S. war crimes in the Winter Soldier Investigation. Veteran John Kerry testifies before the Senate on April 22. The film *Johnny Got His Gun*, based on Dalton Trumbo's 1939 novel, is released in May. Twenty-eight activists destroy draft records in a Camden, New Jersey, draft office on August 21; all of the "Camden 28" are later acquitted. Activists based in Ann Arbor, Michigan, begin a campaign for a Peace Tax Fund, which would enable conscientious objectors to war to pay taxes into a fund used only for nonmilitary spending. The Center for Defense Information is founded by former military officers, including Rear Admiral Gene La Rocque.

1972 Ron Kovic and two other paraplegic veterans disrupt Richard Nixon's acceptance speech at the Republican National Convention in Miami on August 23, and are ejected from the hall.

1976 The Continental Walk for Disarmament and Social Justice begins in Ukiah, California, on January 23; some seven hundred participants arrive at the Pentagon on October 18.

1977 On his first day in office, President Carter grants unconditional pardons to those who had evaded the draft during the Vietnam War.

1980 In April, disarmament researcher Randall Forsberg issues "A Call to Halt the Nuclear Arms Race," providing a rallying point for the nuclear freeze movement. On September 9, the "Ploughshares 8" break into a General Electric plant in King of Prussia, Pennsylvania; they hammer the nose cones of two warheads, pour blood on documents, and pray for peace. Nearly two thousand gather in Washington for the Women's Pentagon Action on November 16–17.

1982 On June 12, between 750,000 and 1,000,000 people march from the United Nations to Central Park in New York in support of nuclear disarmament.

1983 Richard P. Turco coins the phrase "nuclear winter" to describe the environmental consequences of nuclear war, and along with Owen Toon, Thomas P. Ackerman, James B. Pollack, and Carl Sagan (the TTAPS group), publishes papers on the subject in *Science* and other journals. *The Day After*, a television film dramatizing a U.S.-Soviet nuclear war and its aftereffects, airs on November 20 and is viewed by over 100 million people.

1984   Dr. Seuss (Theodore Geisel) publishes an antiwar children's book, *The Butter Battle Book*, in January. The United States Institute of Peace is established in October by act of Congress; it seeks "to prevent, mitigate, and resolve violent conflict around the world."

1986   Approximately 1,200 people leave Los Angeles on March 1 as part of the Great Peace March for Global Nuclear Disarmament; marchers arrive in Washington, D.C., on November 14.

1987   A three-day Mobilization for Peace and Justice in Central America and Southern Africa in Washington, D.C., blocks entrances to the headquarters of the CIA in McLean; 600 are arrested.

1988   During a weeklong protest outside the Nevada Nuclear Test Site coordinated by Freeze/SANE, 1,200 are arrested on March 12, and hundreds more on subsequent days.

1989   In March, the IRS seizes the Colrain, Massachusetts, home of war tax resisters Randy Kehler and Betsy Corner; supporters from across the country subsequently occupy the property after Kehler and Corner are arrested.

1991   The Coalition Against a Vietnam War in the Middle East and the National Campaign Against the War in the Middle East organize demonstrations against the Gulf War in San Francisco and Washington, D.C., on January 19 and 26. The National Student and Youth Campaign for Peace in the Middle East coordinates an International Day of Student Action, on February 21.

1997   Jody Williams, founding coordinator of the International Campaign to Ban Landmines, receives the Nobel Peace Prize.

2001   On September 14, Barbara Lee, a Democratic congresswoman from California, is the only member in either the House or Senate to vote against a post-9/11 resolution authorizing the use of force: "I am convinced that military action will not prevent further acts of international terrorism against the United States." A peace demonstration in New York on October 7 draws 10,000.

2002   Antiwar survivors of the 9/11 attacks and families of the victims form the group September Eleventh Families for Peaceful Tomorrows on February 14. A march on Washington on April 20, organized by the National Youth and Student Peace Coalition, sees a turnout of nearly 100,000. Thousands gather in New York's Central Park on October 7 to oppose a U.S. invasion of Iraq. One hundred and thirty-three members of the House and twenty-three senators vote against the Authorization for the Use of Military Force Against Iraq Resolution of 2002, on October 10–11. Jimmy Carter is awarded the Nobel Peace Prize "for his decades of untiring effort to find peaceful solutions to international conflicts, to advance democracy and human rights, and to promote economic and social development." Hundreds of thousands march in Washington, D.C., and San Francisco on October 26. A group of about one hundred women organizes as Code Pink, and begins a four-month antiwar vigil in front of the White House on November 17.

2003   First Lady Laura Bush cancels a White House poetry symposium after invitees plan to read protest poems; Sam Hamill organizes a February 12 "Day of Poetry Against the War." Rallies across the country on February 15, coordinated with hundreds of others across the globe, oppose the invasion of Iraq (the event is claimed as the largest mass demonstration in human history). Over 1,000 are arrested in San Francisco on March 20 after the bombing of Baghdad.

2004   The group Iraq Veterans Against the War is founded in July.

2005   Cindy Sheehan, mother of Casey Sheehan, a soldier killed in Iraq, stages protests in August at "Camp Casey," near the Crawford, Texas, ranch of President George W. Bush. Hundreds of thousands march in Washington, D.C., on September 24, calling for an end to the war.

2006   Protesters in Port Olympia, Washington, attempt to block a shipment of combat vehicles bound for Iraq on May 24.

2007   Iraq Veterans Against the War set up "Camp Resistance" in support of resister Ehren Wahada on January 4.

Approximately 150 people are arrested on September 15 during antiwar protests near the Capitol.

2009   Barack Obama wins the Nobel Peace Prize "for his extraordinary efforts to strengthen international diplomacy and cooperation between peoples."

2010   Beginning in January, Specialist Bradley Manning, an intelligence analyst stationed near Baghdad, downloads classified and sensitive documents about the wars in Iraq and Afghanistan; hoping to reveal "the true nature of 21st century asymmetric warfare" and "the true cost of war," he releases the documents through WikiLeaks. Now Chelsea Manning, she is serving a thirty-five-year sentence for espionage.

Sources and Acknowledgments

The list below gives the source of each text included in this volume; these texts have been arranged in approximate chronological order of composition and have been reprinted without change, except for the correction of typographical errors. A thin rule-line indicates that a part of the text has been omitted; ellipses, spaces, asterisks, and brackets are the authors' own. A list of the sources of the illustrations included in this volume follows the list of texts.

Great care has been taken to locate and acknowledge all owners of copyrighted material included in this book. If any such owner has inadvertently been omitted, acknowledgment will gladly be made in future printings.

Iroquois Tradition, "The Tree of the Great Peace": Arthur C. Parker, "The Constitution of the Five Nations, or The Iroquois Book of the Great Law," *New York State Museum Bulletin* 184 (April 1, 1916): 8–9.

John Woolman, from *The Journal of John Woolman*; from "A Plea for the Poor": *The Journal and Major Essays of John Woolman*, ed. Phillips P. Moulton (New York: Oxford University Press, 1971), 75–77, 83–86; 254–55. Reprinted by permission of Friends United Press.

Warner Mifflin, "I Counted None My Enemy": *The Defence of Warner Mifflin Against Aspersions Cast on Him on Account of His Endeavours to Promote Righteousness, Mercy, and Peace among Mankind* (Philadelphia: Samuel Sansom, 1796), 11–13, 15–16.

David L. Dodge, "An Odd and Singular Man": *Memorial of Mr. David L. Dodge, Consisting of an Autobiography, Prepared at the Request of and for the Use of His Children* (Boston: S. K. Whipple & Co., 1854), 25–27.

Benjamin Rush, A Plan of a Peace-Office for the United States: *Essays, Literary, Moral and Philosophical* (Philadelphia: Thomas & Samuel F. Bradford, 1798), 183–88.

Joseph Smith Jr., from *The Book of Mormon* (Alma, Chapter 24): *The Book of Mormon: The Earliest Text*, ed. Royal Skousen (New Haven, CT: Yale University Press, 2009), 365–69. Reprinted by permission of Yale University Press.

Ralph Waldo Emerson, from "War": *Miscellanies* (Boston: Houghton, Mifflin and Company, 1884), 187–201.

William Lloyd Garrison, Declaration of Sentiments Adopted by the Peace Convention, Held in Boston, September 18, 19, & 20, 1838: *The Liberator* 8.39 (September 28, 1838): 154.

Henry Wadsworth Longfellow, The Arsenal at Springfield: *The Belfry of Bruges and Other Poems* (Cambridge, MA: John Owen, 1846), 23–26.

Adin Ballou, The Term Non-Resistance: *Christian Non-Resistance, in All Its Important Bearings, Illustrated and Defended* (Philadelphia: J. Miller M'Kim, 1846), 10–13.

Theodore Parker, Speech Delivered at the Anti-War Meeting, in Faneuil Hall, February 4, 1847: *Speeches, Addresses, and Occasional Sermons* (Boston: Wm. Crosby & H. P. Nichols, 1852), vol. 1, 81–90.

Thomas Corwin, from Speech of Mr. Corwin, of Ohio, on the Mexican War: *Speech of Mr. Corwin, of Ohio, on the Mexican War* (Washington, DC: Towers, 1847), 20–24.

Henry David Thoreau, Civil Disobedience: *A Yankee in Canada, with Anti-Slavery and Reform Papers* (Boston: Ticknor & Fields, 1866), 123–51.

Obadiah Ethelbert Baker, Nov. 30th To an absent Wife: *"Words for the Hour": A New Anthology of American Civil War Poetry*, ed. Faith Barrett & Christanne Miller (Amherst: University of Massachusetts Press, 2005), 365. Reprinted by permission of The Huntington Library, San Marino, CA.

Cyrus Pringle, from *The Record of a Quaker Conscience: Cyrus Pringle's Diary*: *The Record of a Quaker Conscience: Cyrus Pringle's Diary* (New York: Macmillan, 1918), 72–79.

Herman Melville, Shiloh: A Requiem: *Battle-Pieces, and Aspects of the War* (New York: Harper & Brothers, 1866), 63.

Walt Whitman, Reconciliation: *Leaves of Grass* (Philadelphia: David McKay, 1891), 250–51.

Alexander Gardner & Timothy O'Sullivan, A Harvest of Death: *Gardner's Photographic Sketch Book of the War* (Washington, DC: Philp & Solomons, [1866]), plate 36 and caption.

Julia Ward Howe, Appeal to Womanhood Throughout the World: "Appeal to Womanhood throughout the World," Broadside (Boston: [Julia Ward Howe], September 1870). Library of Congress. Printed Ephemera Collection, Portfolio 74, Folder 3.

Ambrose Bierce, Chickamauga: *The Collected Works of Ambrose Bierce*, vol. 2 (*In the Midst of Life [Tales of Soldiers and Civilians]*) (New York & Washington, DC: Neale Publishing, 1909), 46–57.

Stephen Crane, War Is Kind: *War Is Kind* (New York: Frederick A. Stokes, 1899), 9–10.

Mark Twain, Battle Hymn of the Republic (Brought Down to Date): *Mark Twain's Civil War*, ed. David Rachels (Lexington: The University Press of Kentucky, 2007), 214. Reprinted by permission of the Mark Twain

Foundation. The War Prayer: *The Complete Works of Mark Twain. Volume 20: Europe and Elsewhere* (New York: Harper & Brothers, 1923), 394–98. Reprinted by permission of the Mark Twain Foundation.

William James, The Moral Equivalent of War: *Association for International Conciliation: Leaflet No. 27*, (February 1910): 3–20.

John F. Kendrick, Christians at War: *Solidarity*, December 4, 1915.

Emma Goldman, from "Preparedness, the Road to Universal Slaughter": *Mother Earth* 10.10 (December 1915): 331–35.

Ellen N. La Motte, Heroes: *The Backwash of War: The Human Wreckage of the Battlefield as Witnessed by an American Hospital Nurse* (New York: G. P. Putnam's Sons, 1916), 3–13.

Randolph Bourne, The War and the Intellectuals: *The Seven Arts* 2 (June 1917): 133–46. Below the Battle: *The Seven Arts* 2 (July 1917): 270–77.

Traditional (Gospel), Down by the River-Side: *Rodeheaver's Plantation Melodies* (Chicago: The Rodeheaver Company, 1918), 6.

Emily Greene Balch, To The President of Wellesley College: *Beyond Nationalism: The Social Thought of Emily Greene Balch*, ed. Mercedes M. Randall (New York: Twayne Publishers, 1972), 105–6. Reprinted by permission of the Emily Greene Balch Papers, Swarthmore College Peace Collection. From "Toward Human Unity or Beyond Nationalism": *Toward Human Unity, or Beyond Nationalism: Nobel Lecture, Delivered at Oslo, April 7, 1948* (Washington, DC: Women's International League for Peace and Freedom, 1952), n.p.; reprinted from *Les Prix Nobel en 1947*. Reprinted by permission of the Emily Greene Balch Papers, Swarthmore College Peace Collection.

Eugene Debs, Address to the Jury: David Karsner, *Debs: His Authorized Life and Letters* (New York: Boni & Liveright, 1919), 23–44.

M. C. Otto, An Experiment in Conscience: *Socialist Review* 8.1 (December 1919): 50–55.

Walter Guest Kellogg, The Stierheim Case: *The Conscientious Objector* (New York: Boni & Liveright, 1919), 108–10.

Arturo Giovannitti, Scott Nearing Reprieves Democracy: *The Liberator* 2.4 (April 1919): 5–7.

Sara Teasdale, "There Will Come Soft Rains": *Flame and Shadow* (New York: Macmillan, 1920), 89–90.

Jane Addams, Personal Reactions During War: *Peace and Bread in Time of War* (New York: Macmillan, 1922), 132–51.

Reinhold Niebuhr, 1923: In Europe: *Leaves from the Notebook of a Tamed Cynic* (Chicago & New York: Willett, Clark & Colby, 1929), 46–48. Reprinted by permission of the Estate of Reinhold Niebuhr.

Oliver Wendell Holmes Jr., Dissent in *United States* v. *Schwimmer*: *United States* v. *Schwimmer*, 279 U.S. 644 (1929).

E. E. Cummings, "i sing of Olaf glad and big": *Complete Poems: 1904–1962*, ed. George James Firmage (New York: Liveright, 1991), 340. Copyright © 1931, 1959, 1991 by the Trustees for the E. E. Cummings Trust. Copyright © 1979 by George James Firmage. Reprinted by permission of Liveright Publishing Corporation.

Floyd Dell, On Trial: *Homecoming: An Autobiography* (New York: Farrar & Rinehart, 1933), 313–19. Copyright © 1933, 1961 by Floyd Dell. Reprinted by permission of Henry Holt and Company, LLC. All rights reserved.

Edna St. Vincent Millay, Conscientious Objector: *Wine from These Grapes* (New York: Harper & Brothers, 1934), 47–48. Copyright © 1934, 1962 by Edna St. Vincent Millay and Norma Millay Ellis. Reprinted by permission of The Permissions Company, Inc., on behalf of Holly Peppe, Literary Executor, The Millay Society, www.millay.org.

Dalton Trumbo, from *Johnny Got His Gun*: *Johnny Got His Gun* (New York: J. B. Lippincott, 1939), 142–55. Copyright © 1939, 1959, 1991 by Dalton Trumbo. Reprinted by permission of Kensington Publishing. All rights reserved.

William Everson, War Elegy X: *Ten War Elegies* (Camp Angel, Waldport, OR: Untide Press, 1943), n.p. Copyright © 1943 by William Everson. Reprinted by permission of Jude Everson.

Lowell Naeve, from *A Field of Broken Stones*: *A Field of Broken Stones* (Glen Gardner, NJ: Libertarian Press, 1950), 22–25.

Robert Lowell, Letter to President Roosevelt: *The Collected Prose*, ed. Robert Giroux (New York: Farrar, Straus and Giroux, 1987), 367–70. Copyright © 1987 by Caroline Lowell, Harriet Lowell, and Sheridan Lowell. Reprinted by permission of Farrar, Straus and Giroux, LLC.

Bayard Rustin, To Local Board No. 63: *I Must Resist: Bayard Rustin's Life in Letters*, ed. Michael G. Long (San Francisco: City Lights, 2012), 10–12. Reprinted by permission of City Lights Books.

Leo Szilard, A Petition to the President of the United States: U.S. National Archives, Record Group 77, Records of the Chief of Engineers, Manhattan Engineer District, Harrison-Bundy File, folder 76.

Dorothy Day, We Go on Record—: *The Catholic Worker* 12.7 (September 1945): 1.

Kurt Vonnegut, Wailing Shall Be in All Streets: *Armageddon in Retrospect, and Other New and Unpublished Writings on War and Peace* (New York: G. P. Putnam's Sons, 2008), 33–45. Originally written c. 1945–47. Copyright © 2008 by the Kurt Vonnegut Jr. Trust. Reprinted by permission of G. P.

Putnam's Sons, an imprint of Penguin Publishing Group, a division of Penguin Random House LLC.

Edgar L. Jones, from "One War Is Enough": *The Atlantic Monthly* 177.2 (February 1946): 48–50. Copyright © 1946 by Edgar L. Jones. Reprinted by permission of the Estate of Edgar L. Jones.

Naomi Replansky, Epitaph: 1945: *Collected Poems* (Jaffrey, NH: David R. Godine, 2012), 19. Copyright © 2012 by Naomi Replansky. Reprinted by permission of David R. Godine, Inc.

Karl Shapiro, The Conscientious Objector: *The Trial of a Poet, and Other Poems* (New York: Reynal & Hitchcock, 1947), 30–31. Copyright © 1946, 1973 by Karl Shapiro. Reprinted by permission of Harold Ober Associates, Inc.

William Stafford, To Meet a Friend: *Down in My Heart* (Elgin, IL: Brethren Publishing House, 1947), 85–94. Copyright © 1985. Reprinted by permission of Oregon State University Press.

Howard Schoenfeld, from "The Danbury Story": *Prison Etiquette: The Convict's Compendium of Useful Information* (Bearsville, NY: Retort Press, 1950), 24–26.

General Advisory Committee to the U.S. Atomic Energy Commission, Annexes to the General Advisory Committee Report of October 30, 1949: Herbert F. York, *The Advisors: Oppenheimer, Teller, and the Superbomb* (San Francisco: W. H. Freeman and Company, 1976), 156–59.

Ed McCurdy, Last Night I Had the Strangest Dream: *Sing Out!*, July 1951. Copyright © 1950, renewed 1951, 1955 by Folkways Music Publishers, Inc., New York, NY. International copyright secured. All rights reserved including public performance for profit. Reprinted by permission.

Ray Bradbury, August 2026: There Will Come Soft Rains: *The Martian Chronicles* (New York: Doubleday, 1950), 205–11. Copyright © 1950 by Crowell Collier Publishing Company, renewed 1977 by Ray Bradbury. Reprinted by permission of Don Congdon Associates, Inc.

Omar N. Bradley, A Decent Respect for Human Intelligence: *Bulletin of the Atomic Scientists* 14.2 (February 1958): 66. Reprinted by permission of the *Bulletin of the Atomic Scientists*, Chicago, IL.

Albert S. Bigelow, Why I Am Sailing into the Pacific Bomb-Test Area: *Liberation* 2.11 (February 1958): 4–6. Reprinted by permission of the Albert S. Bigelow Papers, Swarthmore College Peace Collection.

Jeannette Rankin, Two Votes Against War: 1917, 1941: *Liberation* 3.1 (March 1958): 4–7.

Paul Reps, from *Zen Telegrams*: *Zen Telegrams: 81 Picture Poems* (Rutland, VT: Charles E. Tuttle, 1959), 54. Reprinted by permission of Tuttle Publishing.

Pete Seeger and Joe Hickerson, Where Have All the Flowers Gone?: Folkways Records FTS–31026 (1968). Copyright © Figs. D Music (BMI) on behalf of itself and Sanga Music, Inc. (BMI) c/o The Bicycle Music Company. All rights reserved. Used by permission.

Juanita Nelson, A Matter of Freedom: *Liberation* 5.5 (September 1960): 12–16. Reprinted by permission of the Estate of Juanita Nelson.

Barbara Deming, Southern Peace Walk: Two Issues or One?: *Liberation* 7.4 (July–August 1962): 5–10. Reprinted by permission of the Barbara Deming Literary Estate.

Edmund Wilson, from "The Strategy of Tax Refusal": *The Cold War and the Income Tax: A Protest* (New York: Farrar, Straus and Giroux, 1963), 115–18. Copyright © 1963 by Edmund Wilson, renewed 1991 by Helen Miranda Wilson. Reprinted by permission of Farrar, Straus and Giroux, LLC.

David Dellinger, The Future of Nonviolence: *Revolutionary Nonviolence* (Indianapolis: Bobbs-Merrill, 1970), 293–301. Copyright © 1970 by David Dellinger. Reprinted by permission of the Elaine Markson Literary Agency.

Clinton Hopkinson and Joe Martin, The War on Vietnam: "McComb Soldier's Death in Vietnam Sparks Protest," *Newsletter* (Mississippi Freedom Democratic Party), July 28, 1965.

Country Joe McDonald, The I-Feel-Like-I'm-Fixin'-To-Die Rag: *Rag Baby*, October 1965. Words and music by Joe McDonald. Copyright © 1965, renewed 1993 by Alkatraz Corner Music. Reprinted by permission.

A. J. Muste, Statement Made on 12/21/65 to the Federal Grand Jury: *The Essays of A. J. Muste*, ed. Nat Hentoff (Indianapolis: Bobbs-Merrill, 1967), 462–64.

Student Nonviolent Coordinating Committee, Statement on American Policy in Vietnam: *Bond v. Floyd*, 251 F. Supp. 336–37 (N.D. Ga. 1966).

Tuli Kupferberg and Robert Bashlow, from *1001 Ways To Beat the Draft*: *1001 Ways To Beat the Draft* (New York: Oliver Layton Press, 1966), 3–8. Copyright © 1966 by Oliver Layton Press, copyright © 1967 by Grove Press. Reprinted by permission of Grove/Atlantic, Inc. Any third party use of this material, outside of this publication, is prohibited.

Josephine Miles, Necessities (1): *Civil Poems* (n.p.: Oyez, 1966), [9]. Copyright © 1966 by Josephine Miles. Reprinted by permission of the Estate of Josephine Miles.

Abraham Joshua Heschel, from "The Moral Outrage of Vietnam": *Vietnam: Crisis of Conscience*, Robert McAfee Brown, Abraham J. Heschel, & Michael Novak, eds. (New York: Association Press, Behrman House, & Herder and Herder, 1967), 48–52, 59–61. Copyright © 1976 by Abraham Joshua Heschel. Reprinted by permission of Susannah Heschel, Executor.

George Starbuck, Of Late: *Poetry* 109.1 (October 1966): 39. Copyright © 1966 by George Starbuck. Reprinted by permission of The University of Alabama Press.

Denise Levertov, Life at War: *The Sorrow Dance* (New York: New Directions, 1967), 79–80. Copyright © 1967 by Denise Levertov. Reprinted by permission of New Directions Publishing Corp.; reprinted in the United Kingdom by permission of Bloodaxe Books, www.bloodaxebooks.com. Making Peace: *Breathing the Water* (New York: New Directions, 1987), 40. Copyright © 1987 by Denise Levertov. Reprinted by permission of New Directions Publishing Corp.

Martin Luther King Jr., Beyond Vietnam: The Martin Luther King, Jr. Research and Education Institute, Stanford University (kinginstitute .stanford.edu/king-papers/documents/beyond-vietnam, accessed February 9, 2015). Copyright © 1967 by Dr. Martin Luther King Jr., renewed © 1995 by Coretta Scott King. Reprinted by permission of The Heirs to the Estate of Martin Luther King Jr., c/o Writers House as agent for the proprietor, New York, NY.

Robert Bly, Counting Small-Boned Bodies: *The Light Around the Body* (New York: Harper & Row, 1967), 32. Copyright © 1967 by Robert Bly. Reprinted by permission of Georges Borchardt, Inc. for Robert Bly.

James Baldwin, The War Crimes Tribunal: *Freedomways* 7.3 (Summer 1967): 242–44. Copyright © 1967 by James Baldwin. Originally published in *Freedomways*; copyright renewed; collected in *The Cross of Redemption*, published by Pantheon/Vintage Books. Reprinted by permission of the James Baldwin Estate.

Paul Goodman, A Young Pacifist: *Liberation* 12 (September–October 1967): 75–79. Copyright © 1967 by Paul Goodman. Reprinted by permission of the Estate of Paul Goodman. A Causerie at the Military-Industrial: *The New York Review of Books* 9.9 (November 23, 1967): 14–18. Copyright © 1967 by Paul Goodman. Reprinted by permission of the New York Review of Books.

Norman Mailer, from *The Armies of the Night*: *The Armies of the Night: History as a Novel, the Novel as History* (New York: New American Library, 1968), 105–8, 312–16. Copyright © 1968 by Norman Mailer. Reprinted by permission of New American Library, an imprint of Penguin Publishing Group, a division of Penguin Random House LLC; reprinted in the United Kingdom by permission of The Wylie Agency, LLC.

Contributors to *WIN Magazine*, from "Mobilization! Oct. 21": *WIN Magazine: Peace & Freedom through Nonviolent Action* 3.18 (October 30, 1967): 5–9.

Howard Zinn, Dow Shalt Not Kill: *The Idler* 37 (December 1967): 7–12. (Originally written for *BU News* and syndicated through the Liberation News

Ron Kovic, from *Born on the Fourth of July*: *Born on the Fourth of July* (New York: McGraw-Hill, 1976), 139–43; subsequently published on pages 153–57 of the 2005 Akashic Books edition. Copyright © 1976, 2005 by Ron Kovic. Reprinted by permission of Akashic Books, www.akashicbooks.com.

Gloria Emerson, from *Winners and Losers*: *Winners and Losers: Battles, Retreats, Gains, Losses and Ruins from a Long War* (New York: Random House, 1976), 205–8; 372–74. Copyright © 1972, 1973, 1974, 1975, 1976, 1985 by Gloria Emerson. Reprinted by permission of W. W. Norton & Company, Inc.

Charles Martin, Terminal Colloquy: *Room for Error* (Athens: University of Georgia Press, 1978), 14. Copyright © 1978 by Charles Martin. Reprinted by permission of the author.

Grace Paley, Cop Tales: Devastation: *Long Walks and Intimate Talks* (New York: The Feminist Press at the City University of New York, 1991), 30–32. Copyright © 1991 by Grace Paley. Reprinted by permission of The Permissions Group, Inc., on behalf of The Feminist Press at the City University of New York, www.feministpress.org. Women's Pentagon Action Unity Statement: *Just As I Thought* (New York: Farrar, Straus and Giroux, 1998), 142–47. Copyright © 1998 by Grace Paley. Reprinted by permission of Farrar, Straus and Giroux, LLC.

George Zabelka, interviewed by Charles McCarthy, "I Was Told It Was Necessary": *Sojourners* 9.8 (August 1980): 12–15. Reprinted by permission of *Sojourners*, www.sojo.net.

Yvonne Dilling and Mary Jo Bowman, Revolutionary Violence: A Dialogue: *Bulletin of the Peace Studies Institute* (Manchester College) 11.1 (June 1981): 1–13. Reprinted by permission of the authors.

Don Benedict, from *Born Again Radical*: *Born Again Radical* (New York: The Pilgrim Press, 1982), 45–48. Reprinted by permission of The Pilgrim Press via Copyright Clearance Center.

Eugene J. McCarthy, The IRS' Plan for the Hereafter: *The Washington Post*, August 15, 1982. Reprinted by permission of the Washington Post Company via Copyright Clearance Center.

Wally Nelson, "One Race, the Human Race": *Against the Tide: Pacifist Resistance in the Second World War (An Oral History)*, ed. Deena Hurwitz and Craig Simpson (New York: War Resisters League, 1984), n.p.

Thomas Banyacya, "Like the Elders Say": *Against the Tide: Pacifist Resistance in the Second World War (An Oral History)*, ed. Deena Hurwitz and Craig Simpson (New York: War Resisters League, 1984), n.p.

Gene R. La Rocque, The Role of the Military in the Nuclear Age: *The Role of the Military in the Nuclear Age* (Santa Barbara: Nuclear Age Peace

Foundation, 1985), 1–8. Reprinted by permission of the Nuclear Age Peace Foundation, www.wagingpeace.org.

Donald Wetzel, from *Pacifist: Or, My War and Louis Lepke*: *Pacifist: Or, My War and Louis Lepke* (Sag Harbor, NY: The Permanent Press, 1986), 139–42. Reprinted by permission of The Permanent Press.

Bill Watterson, Calvin and Hobbes: "How Come We Play War and Not Peace?": *The Essential Calvin and Hobbes: A Calvin and Hobbes Treasury* (Kansas City: Andrews & McMeel, 1988), 72. Copyright © 1986 by Bill Watterson. Reprinted by permission of Universal Uclick. All rights reserved.

Bernard Offen, To: Internal Revenue Service: Joel C. Taunton, "A Taxpayer Learns from Auschwitz," *Christianity and Crisis* 47.5 (April 6, 1987): 26–27.

Thomas McGrath, War Resisters' Song: *Selected Poems, 1938–1988* (Port Townsend, WA: Copper Canyon, 1988), 167. Copyright © 1988 by Thomas McGrath. Used by permission of The Permissions Company, Inc., on behalf of Copper Canyon Press, www.coppercanyonpress.org.

Yusef Komunyakaa, 2527th Birthday of the Buddha: *Dien Cai Dau* (Middletown, CT: Wesleyan University Press, 1988), 18. Copyright © 1988 by Yusef Komunyakaa. Reprinted by permission of Wesleyan University Press.

Tim O'Brien, On the Rainy River: *The Things They Carried* (New York: Houghton Mifflin, 1990), 37–58. Copyright © 1990 by Tim O'Brien. Reprinted by permission of Houghton Mifflin Harcourt Publishing Company. All rights reserved.

Adrienne Rich, from "An Atlas of the Difficult World": *An Atlas of the Difficult World: Poems 1988–1991* (New York: W. W. Norton, 1991), 22–23. Copyright © 1991, 2002 by Adrienne Rich. Reprinted by permission of W. W. Norton & Company, Inc.

Gregory Nevala Calvert, from *Democracy from the Heart*: *Democracy from the Heart: Spiritual Values, Decentralism, and Democratic Idealism in the Movement of the 1960s* (Eugene, OR: Communitas Press, 1991), 244–51. Reprinted by permission of the Estate of Gregory Nevala Calvert.

William Heyen, The Truth: *Ribbons: The Gulf War (A Poem)* (St. Louis: Time Being Books, 1991), 52. Reprinted by permission of the author.

S. Brian Willson, The Tracks: *On Third World Legs* (Chicago: Charles H. Kerr, 1992), 67–82. Reprinted by permission of Charles H. Kerr Publishing Company and the author.

Naomi Shihab Nye, Jerusalem: *Red Suitcase* (Rochester, NY: BOA Editions, 1994), 21–22. Copyright © 1994 by Naomi Shihab Nye. Reprinted by permission of The Permissions Company, Inc. on behalf of BOA Editions, Ltd., www.boaeditions.org.

ILLUSTRATIONS

1. Jane Addams and Emily Greene Balch aboard the *Noordam*. Courtesy of the Library of Congress Prints and Photographs Division, Washington, DC.

2. Dorothy Day as a young journalist for *The Call*. Courtesy of © Bettmann/CORBIS.

3. Jeannette Rankin addresses a Union Square rally. Courtesy of FPG/Getty Images.

4. Bayard Rustin in the Lewisburg Federal Penitentiary. Courtesy of the Swarthmore College Peace Collection.

5. Juanita and Wally Nelson in 1946.

6. Albert S. Bigelow beside the *Golden Rule*. Courtesy of the Swarthmore College Peace Collection.

7. A. J. Muste launches a Committee for Nonviolent Action civil disobedience campaign. Courtesy of the Swarthmore College Peace Collection.

8. Thomas Merton and Daniel Berrigan at a Gethsemani Abbey Peacemakers Retreat. Courtesy of the Merton Legacy Trust and the Thomas Merton Center at Bellarmine University.

9. Grace Paley at an anti-Vietnam War demonstration. Courtesy of Fred W. McDarrah/Getty Images.

10. Burning draft cards with homemade napalm at Catonsville, Maryland. Courtesy of The Baltimore Sun Media Group. All rights reserved.

11. Joan Baez at an antiwar rally in London. Courtesy of © Bettmann/CORBIS.

12. Pete Seeger at the Peace Moratorium in New York. Courtesy of © Bettmann/CORBIS.

13. Disabled veteran Ron Kovic protesting conditions in VA hospitals. Courtesy of © Bettmann/CORBIS.

14. Barbara Deming at the Seneca Women's Encampment for a Future of Peace and Justice. Courtesy of the Swarthmore College Peace Collection.

15. Women spelling out PEACE. Courtesy of © 2002 Art Rogers Photography, www.artrogers.com.

16. Zack de la Rocha at a protest outside the Democratic National Convention. Courtesy of Doug Pensinger/Getty Images.

Index

THE LIBRARY OF AMERICA SERIES

The Library of America fosters appreciation and pride in America's literary heritage by publishing, and keeping permanently in print, authoritative editions of America's best and most significant writing. An independent nonprofit organization, it was founded in 1979 with seed funding from the National Endowment for the Humanities and the Ford Foundation.

To subscribe to the series or to order individual copies, please visit www.loa.org or call (800) 964-5778.

*This book is set in 10 point ITC Galliard, a
face designed for digital composition by Matthew Carter
and based on the sixteenth-century face Granjon. The paper
is acid-free lightweight opaque and meets the requirements for
permanence of the American National Standards Institute.
The binding material is Brillianta, a woven rayon cloth
made by Van Heek–Scholco Textielfabrieken, Holland.
Composition by Publishers' Design and Production Services, Inc.
Printing and binding by Edwards Brothers Malloy, Ann Arbor.
Designed by Bruce Campbell.*